T0317118

# Beyond the Institution

## Transforming the Learning Environment in Architectural Education

## Reviews

## Faculty News

# Editorial

Architektur(ausbildung) stellt den Anspruch, eine formende oder treibende Kraft in gesellschaftlichen und räumlichen Veränderungsprozessen zu sein, erfolgt aber in Räumen und innerhalb einer Institution, die diesen Ansprüchen selbst meist nicht gerecht werden. Fragen zur Architekturausbildung stellen sich oft anhand der Anpassung des Curriculums: Soll es nun eher zu einer generalistischen und humanistischen Bildung führen? Oder einer Ausbildung zu einer bauenden Fachkraft? Oder gilt es, Architektur als Kunst zu vermitteln? Während diese Fragen an den Architekturfakultäten immer wieder in mehr oder weniger lang wiederkehrenden Abständen und Intensitäten diskutiert werden, werden die dafür notwendigen Räumlichkeiten und ihre grundsätzliche Ausgestaltung eher als gegeben hingenommen. In Hörsälen und Seminarräumen wird unterrichtet, in Studios gezeichnet und produziert, in Büros verwaltet, organisiert und geforscht. Die Möglichkeit, sich mit dem Thema ausführlicher auseinanderzusetzen, beispielsweise anhand der eher seltenen Gelegenheit, eine neue Architekturschule zu bauen, ist oft auch dann durch schon vorgegebene Raumprogramme begrenzt. Das Wesen der vorgegebenen Räume im Verhältnis zu Funktion, Größe oder Form bleibt ähnlich den bereits erprobten, nicht nur in Architekturfakultäten auch in allen anderen universitären Disziplinen.

Universität ist Institution und um ihre Räume zu betrachten, muss man gleichzeitig auch die dahinterliegenden Strukturen erkennen. Dieser Zusammenhang lässt sich im Kontext der Architekturausbildung besonders gut erkennbar machen, denn, so Lesley Lokko, Gründerin des kürzlich in Accra, Ghana geschaffenen African Futures Institute, „in den Architekturschulen machen wir nichts anderes, als Studierenden beizubringen über Strukturen nachzudenken."[1] Es ist dabei äußerst hilfreich, wie Lokko weiter argumentiert, „ein tieferes Verständnis dafür, was wir mit ‚strukturell' meinen", zu entwickeln, „[s]eien es strukturelle Psychologien, strukturelle Traumata, struktureller Rassismus, strukturelle Benachteiligungen. […] Mithilfe dieses spezifisch architektonischen Begriffs war ich nun in der Lage, den Studierenden das Problem anschaulich zu machen, […] sollten sie sich mit theoretischen, technischen und gesellschaftlichen Strukturen auseinandersetzen. Denn letzten Endes wäre bei-

spielsweise auch die Apartheit ohne die Komplizenschaft der Architektur nicht möglich gewesen, die Rassentrennung in Südafrika wurde in *räumlicher* Form umgesetzt."[2]

Wir wollen uns im Kontext dieser *GAM*-Ausgabe mit der Transformation universitärer Strukturen und anderen Lernräumen aus mehreren Perspektiven nähern und bewegen uns dazu über die Grenzen der Institution hinaus: nicht bloß ins bereits erprobte Homeoffice oder in die virtuellen Räume des Distance Learning, sondern in die Stadt, in die Natur, ins Museum und in die Ausstellung. Zu diesem Prozess der Grenzüberschreitung gehören auch Ideen und Konzepte, wie sie im Laufe der Zeit immer wieder an verschiedenen Orten auftauchten und verfolgt wurden. Es ist der Institution zu eigen, eine komplexe Einrichtung zu sein, in der sich Veränderungen nur schwerfällig und langsam umsetzen lassen. Dennoch spiegelt sich gesellschaftlicher Wandel auch in den Universitäten wider.

In dieser Ausgabe wird die Frage nach der Architekturausbildung über die universitären Räume auf die (städtische) Umwelt ausgeweitet und die Lernerfahrung auf unterschiedlichen Ebenen in den Fokus gerückt. Ausgehend vom räumlichen und institutionellen Status quo in Österreich stellt Petra Petersson zu Beginn Überlegungen zu sozialen und strukturellen Grenzen und Durchlässigkeiten von Architekturausbildung an. Im Anschluss wirft Charlotte Malterre-Barthes in ihren „Notizen zur pandemischen Lehre" einen Blick in den virtuellen Raum und durchleuchtet den Moment der Krise, den die Pandemie weltweit ausgelöst hat durch die Linse der Architekturschulen. In der Verlagerung der Lehre in den virtuellen Raum, respektive in die Welt der heute als Homeoffices genutzten, privaten Schlaf-und Wohnräume, offenbart Malterre-Barthes wie durch unhinterfragte Nutzung von Technologie Privilegien und soziale Ungleichheit mittransferiert werden und sich durch diesen Standortwechsel noch stärker herauskristallisieren. Christina

---

1  Lesley Lokko und Tom Emerson im Gespräch mit Tonderai Koschke und Sarah Maafi in *ARCH+* 246 – Zeitgenössische feministische Raumpraxis (2022): 168–173, hier 172.

2  Ebd.

Architecture (and architectural education) aspire to be a formative or driving force in processes of societal and spatial change, yet it takes place in spaces and within institutions that often do not live up to these aspirations themselves. Questions about architectural education often arise from adapting the curriculum. Should it lead to a more generalist and humanistic education? Should it be a training for building specialists? Or should architecture be taught as an art? These questions are repeatedly discussed in architecture faculties at varying intervals and levels of intensity, but the spaces that architectural education requires and their basic design are taken for granted. Lecture halls and seminar rooms are used for teaching, studios for drawing and production, offices for administration, organization, and research. The chance to deal with the subject in greater depth—even when, for example, the rather rare opportunity arises of building a new school of architecture—is often limited by predetermined spatial programs. The essence of the relationships between predetermined spaces and their function, size, or form remains close to the already tried and tested, not just in architecture departments but in all other university disciplines too.

Universities are institutions, and, when considering their architectural spaces, one must also take into account the societal and organizational structures that underlie them. Lesley Lokko, founder of the recently created African Futures Institute in Accra, Ghana, feels that this linkage is particularly identifiable in architectural education because, "in architecture schools, we do nothing more than simply teach students to think about structures."[1] She goes on to argue that it is extremely helpful at this stage to develop "a fuller understanding of what we mean by 'structural,' … be it structural psychologies, structural traumas, structural racism, structural discrimination. … With the help of this specifically architectural concept, I was now able to bring the problem alive for the students, … they needed to deal with theoretical, technical, and social structures. After all, even apartheid, for example, would not have been possible

without the complicit involvement of architecture; South Africa's racial segregation was implemented in *spatial* form."[2]

In the context of this issue of *GAM*, we are seeking to approach the transformation of university structures and other learning spaces from various perspectives, and to do so we move beyond the boundaries of the institution: not just into the already tried and tested home office or into the virtual spaces of distance learning, but into cities, nature, museums, and exhibitions. This process of crossing borders also includes ideas and concepts that over time have appeared repeatedly and been pursued in various different places. The university institution is inherently a complex one in which change is slow and hard to implement. Nevertheless, social change is reflected in universities too.

In this current issue, the question of architectural education is extended beyond university spaces to the (urban) environment, focusing on the learning experience at different levels. Starting with the spatial and institutional status quo in Austria, Petra Petersson's opening article reflects on the social and structural boundaries and permeabilities of architectural education. Next, Charlotte Malterre-Barthes, in her "Notes on Pandemic Teaching," takes a look at virtual space and, through the lens of architecture schools, illuminates the moment of crisis that the pandemic has triggered worldwide. She reveals how the unquestioned use of technology to shift teaching into virtual space—or, rather, into the world of private bedrooms and living rooms now used as home offices—has also transferred, and reinforced, privilege and social inequality in the process. In her article "Off Campus," Christina Linortner considers the recent history of architectural education and how far different attempts to for-

1   Lesley Lokko, Tom Emerson, Tonderai Koschke, and Sarah Maafi, "Dekarbonisieren, dekolonisieren, deinstitutionalisieren," *ARCH+* 246, Zeitgenössische feministische Raumpraxis (2022): 168–173, esp. 172.

2   Ibid.

Linortner betrachtet in ihrem Beitrag „Off Campus" wie weit in der jüngeren Geschichte der Architekturausbildung verschiedene Versuche, ebendiese Räumlichkeiten zu verlassen, überhaupt eine Überwindung ihres institutionellen Kontextes ermöglichen können.

Architekturausbildung aus dem rein universitären Kontext zu lösen und nicht nur hin zum urbanen Umfeld zu öffnen, sondern teilweise gänzlich zu vergesellschaften und zu „entschulen", versuchten in etwa zeitgleichen Vorstößen Shadrach Woods, Giancarlo De Carlo und Colin Ward. Diesem heute als radikale Pädagogik bezeichneten Unterfangen nähern sich Federica Doglio, Nicolas Moucheront, Sol Perez-Martinez und Adam Wood in einem Gespräch an. Mit einer aktuellen Form der Lehre, genauer mit der Entstehung und (dekolonialen) Kritik eines zeitgenössischen transkontinentalen Lehrformats zwischen Südafrika und Österreich, nämlich *Design Build*, setzt sich Marlene Wagner in ihrem Beitrag auseinander und ruft zu einer Kultur des kritischen Verlernens, aber auch zum Entwurf alternativer Modelle auf. „The Casa", ein hybrides und partizipatives Studio-Projekt der London Metropolitan University im italienischen Belmonte Calabro zeigt, welche Potenziale sich durch längerfristige Kollaborationen außerhalb der Universität für strukturschwache Regionen im europäischen Kontext und deren unterschiedlichen AkteurInnen eröffnen.

Der Aufgabe, neoliberalen Tendenzen der Flexibilisierung zu trotzen und Alternativen zu entwickeln, stellt sich Hélène Frichot, indem sie anhand der im Feminismus begründeten „Care-Ethik" über den Umzug der Architekturfakultät an der KTH Stockholm in ein neues Gebäude im Jahr 2015 reflektiert. Darauf folgt eine Zusammenstellung mehrerer Bildpaare, die im Rahmen einer Ausstellung, kuratiert von Björn Ehrlemark, zu Ehren des von Frichot zuvor thematisierten, 2014 aufgelassenen Fakultätsgebäudes aus den 1970er-Jahren gezeigt wurden. In genau demselben Zeitraum, in dem die Architekturschule in Schweden gebaut und bezogen wurde, besiedelte die Architekturfakultät der ETH Zürich temporär das Globus-Provisorium – ein ehemaliges, für den temporären Lehrbetrieb adaptiertes Warenhaus, das, wie Lucia Pennati in ihrem Beitrag

verdeutlicht, als Raum für pädagogische Experimente, Debatten und kulturelle Ereignisse eine maßgebliche Rolle in der Entwicklung eines neuen Currriculums an der ETH Zürich einnahm.

Eine radikale Alternative zur herkömmlichen Architekturausbildung identifiziert Simran Singh, indem sie kritisch auf die aktuellen Revitalisierungsmaßnahmen der „heiligen Stadt" Varanasi blickt und für eine Weiterentwicklung eines *mat urbanism* plädiert, wie er sich bereits historisch entlang des Gangesufers in Form einer engmaschigen urbanen Textur aus Hofhäusern entwickelt hat. Singh interpretiert die Höfe, in denen sich das Arbeits- und Privatleben der Weberfamilien abspielt, als alternierende Räumlichkeiten, die ihren NutzerInnen eine Freiheit gewähren, welche die in der Architektur üblichen planerischen Festlegungen von Funktionen in so einer Form nicht zulassen. Im Gespräch mit Karine Dana erklären Anne Lacaton und Jean-Philippe Vassal anhand ihres Entwurf für die ENSA Nantes, welche Bedeutung Programmüberschreitung und die Einbindung des angrenzenden städtischen Umfeld für Universitäten – im konkreten Fall für eine Architekturschule – haben. Der Soziologe Jean-Louis Violeau ergänzt diese Darstellung aus NutzerInnenperspektive und zeigt die vielfältigen urbanen Qualitäten und Nutzungen innerhalb des Gebäudes auf. Abschließend bespricht Petra Eckhard in einem Interview mit Jeannette Kuo von Karamuk Kuo Architects die Anforderungen an zukünftige Ausbildungsstätten am Beispiel ihrer noch im Bau befindlichen Erweiterung der Rice University School of Architecture in Houston, Texas.

Diese Ausgabe soll als Impuls dienen, aus dem eigenen Kontext hinauszutreten und einen anderen Blickwinkel auf die Institution einzunehmen, um die notwendigen räumlichen wie strukturellen Veränderungen voranzutreiben. ▪

*Petra Petersson/Christina Linortner*

sake university premises may make it generally possible to overcome their institutional context.

Shadrach Woods, Giancarlo De Carlo, and Colin Ward, in roughly synchronized forays, have attempted to detach architectural education from the purely university context, not only opening it up to the urban environment, but also, to some degree, completely socializing and "de-schooling" it. This endeavor, now called radical pedagogy, is touched on in a conversation between Federica Doglio, Nicolas Moucheront, Sol Perez-Martinez, and Adam Wood. In her contribution, Marlene Wagner deals with a current form of teaching, and specifically with the emergence and (decolonial) critique of a contemporary transcontinental teaching format between South Africa and Austria, namely *Design Build*; she calls for a culture of critical unlearning, but also for the design of alternative models. "The Casa," a hybrid and participatory studio project by London Metropolitan University in Belmonte Calabro, Italy, demonstrates the potential that longer-term collaborations outside the university open up for structurally weak regions in Europe and their various protagonists.

Hélène Frichot takes up the task of defying neoliberal flexibilization tendencies and of developing alternatives by reflecting on the architecture faculty at KTH Stockholm and its 2015 move to a new building on the basis of a "care ethic" founded in feminism. This is followed by a compilation of several paired images from an exhibition, curated by Björn Ehrlemark, in honor of the 1970s faculty building, just discussed by Frichot, which was abandoned in 2014. In the very same period that the School of Architecture in Sweden was built and occupied, the Faculty of Architecture at ETH Zurich temporarily occupied the Globus Provisorium. As Lucia Pennati's contribution makes clear, this former department store adapted for temporary teaching played a role—as a space for pedagogical experimentation, debate, and cultural events—that was crucial in developing a new ETH Zurich curriculum.

A radical alternative to conventional architecture education is identified by Simran Singh, who takes a critical look at the current revitalization of the "holy city" of Varanasi. She advocates the further development of "mat urbanism" as evolved historically along the riverbank of the Ganges, taking the form of a closely meshed urban texture of courtyard houses. Singh interprets the courtyards, which is where the working and private lives of families of weavers take place, as spaces with alternating uses that give their occupants freedom that the usual designation of room functions in architectural planning does not allow for. Anne Lacaton and Jean-Philippe Vassal explain in a conversation with Karine Dana, citing their design of ENSA Nantes, what meaning going beyond the program and the integration of the neighboring urban environment holds for universities and in this particular case, for an architecture school. The sociologist Jean-Louis Violeau supplements this account with a user-based perspective and highlights the diverse urban qualities and uses within the building. In conclusion, Petra Eckhard discusses with Jeannette Kuo of Karamuk Kuo Architects the challenges faced by future educational institutions, using as an example their extension of the Rice University School of Architecture in Houston, Texas, which is still under construction.

This issue of *GAM* is intended as an incentive to step outside our own context and explore a different perspective beyond the institution, in order to drive forward the necessary spatial changes and changes to institutional structures. ∎

*Petra Petersson/Christina Linortner*
*(Translation: John Wheelwright/Dawn Michelle d'Atri)*

Petra Petersson

# Das Schwierige einfach darstellen

## Einige Beobachtungen zur Architekturlehre und viele Fragen

# Presenting difficult things with simplicity

## Some observations on teaching architecture, and many questions

1   Hörsaal | Lecture Hall, Kronesgasse, TU Graz © KOEN, TU Graz

Es ist dunkel und sehr leise in der Halle. Keine der ca. 150 Personen, die hier sitzen, scheint auffallen zu wollen. Es ist die erste Vorlesung. Jedes Jahr, immer aufs Neue, stehe ich da vorne und versuche zu erklären, worauf die sich alle eingelassen haben.

Es sind nicht nur die Erwartungen, sondern natürlich auch die sozialen Faktoren, die dieses Schweigen hervorrufen. Wenige kennen sich und viele kommen aus immer noch stark hierarchisch aufgebauten Schulsystemen. Manche sind weit gereist und sind sich erstmal unsicher, was hier kulturell akzeptabel ist. Andere wissen tatsächlich überhaupt nicht, was ArchitektInnen so machen und sind sich noch nicht ganz sicher, warum sie dieses Studium gewählt haben. Alle EU-BürgerInnen, die einen Schulabschluss haben, der für ein Universitätsstudium qualifiziert, und alle anderen, die eine entsprechende Qualifikation vorweisen können und zusätzlich die deutsche Sprache auf einem gewissen Niveau beherrschen, dürfen bei uns anfangen. Lediglich eine Voranmeldung und ein Motivationsschreiben öffnen die Türen zur Universität.

Also Bildung für alle oder beziehungsweise fast alle?

Letzten Endes darf nicht außer Acht gelassen werden, dass die Segregation bereits in der Schule anfängt. Obwohl gerade im deutschsprachigen Raum seit vielen Jahren eine Diskussion darüber läuft und der Mehrwert einer gemeinsamen Ganztagsschule bereits mehrfach wissenschaftlich nachgewiesen ist, besteht man immer noch auf einem System, bei dem die Halbtagsschule dazu führt, dass zum großen Teil zu Hause gelernt wird und damit automatisch eine stärkere akademische Ungleichheit entsteht.

Man kann sich ja fragen, ob gute Noten in der Schule oder alternativ schöne Mappen aus dem Kunstunterricht, die an vielen anderen Standorten Europas die Voraussetzung für das Architekturstudium sind, tatsächlich bessere ArchitektInnen hervorbringen.

Wir bezeichnen unsere Studierenden als heterogen, divers wäre zu weit hergeholt.

Die Vorbildung unterscheidet sich sehr. Zu uns kommen Studierende, die bereits an einer HTL waren, einer höheren berufsbildenden Schule in Österreich, wo sie im Hochbau, Möbelbau oder anderen technischen Fächern vorgebildet wurden. Andere, insbesondere aus den östlichen Teilen von Europa, haben bereits ein entsprechendes Studium angefangen, das nur zum Teil angerechnet wird, oder in Bezug auf Darstellung

einen Vorsprung. Andere wiederum haben Architektur nicht einmal im Kunst- oder Geschichtsunterricht in der Schule behandelt.

So ist das Institut für Grundlagen der Konstruktion und des Entwerfens, das ich leite, an der TU Graz 2013 dazu neu geschaffen worden, um im ersten Jahr das Wissen und die Fähigkeiten der Studierenden so gut es geht einander anzugleichen. Salopp gesagt geht es bei den ehemaligen HTL-SchülerInnen teilweise um „unlearning" und bei anderen darum, grundsätzliche „Tools" und ein Grundwissen zu vermitteln.

Zurück in die abgedunkelte Halle.

Jetzt muss man sich entscheiden, unterschiedliche Wege gehen.

Entweder gleich damit anfangen, die Komplexität der Architektur zu beschreiben, den Entwurf, den Kontext, die Konstruktion, das dreidimensionale Denken, die ganzen Anforderungen, die gesellschaftliche Verantwortung usw. Wieviel man können muss, bevor man überhaupt etwas Sinnvolles entwerfen kann. Und darüber reden, wie lange es dauert, bevor man endlich etwas bauen darf, weil es ja so schwierig ist. Oder das Schwierige einfach darstellen und schrittweise den Studierenden die Mittel dazu geben, die komplexen Zusammenhänge selbst zu erforschen.

Der Vorwurf gegenüber der Einfachheit ist, dass sie banal ist.

Oder anders ausgedrückt, wenn die Lösung nicht kompliziert ist, kann die Frage nicht schwer genug sein. Vielleicht werden aber die Antworten in komplizierten Beschreibungen verschleiert, da es diese Antworten entweder nicht gibt oder sie von den Vortragenden selber nicht ganz verstanden wurden? Oder ist das Verkomplizieren ein Bestandteil der Institution und dient dem Erhalt einer hierarchischen Struktur? Wir sind hier an der Universität, weil wir als Lehrende denken, dass wir so ungefähr wissen, wie es gehen könnte, und wenn ich es selber verstanden habe, müsste ich es auch vermitteln können. In Folge könnte man auch annehmen: „Wenn wir es können, warum sollten es die Studierenden dann nicht lernen können?"

In unserem Leitbild zur Fakultät steht, wie an so vielen anderen Fakultäten auch, unter anderem, dass Entwerfen komplex (schwierig) sei. Eine andere These wäre: „Wenn man weiß, wie es geht, ist es eigentlich einfach." Es ist immer noch schwer, Architektur als Wissenschaft, Kunst oder als Berufsausbildung

It is dark and very quiet in the lecture hall. A hundred and fifty students are sitting here, but nobody seems to want to attract attention to themselves. This is the first lecture. Each year I stand in front of them and try to explain what they have signed up for.

It is not only expectation that causes this silence. There are social factors too. Few of them know each other, and many come from school systems that are still strongly hierarchical. Some have come from far away and are still unsure of what is culturally acceptable here. Others actually know nothing at all about what architects do, and are still not quite sure why they chose this course. All EU citizens with a school-leaving certificate that qualifies them for university studies, and all others with an appropriate qualification plus a certain level of proficiency in the German language, may start studying here with us. Pre-registration and a motivation letter are all it takes to gain entry to the university.

Education for everybody or rather almost everybody?

One should not forget that segregation already starts in school. This has been under discussion for many years, especially in German-speaking countries, and the benefits of collective all-day schooling have been repeatedly scientifically proven. But a half-day schooling system persists in which much learning is done at home, resulting in greater academic inequality.

One might ask whether good school grades or, alternatively, nice portfolios from art classes, which are an entry requirement for studying architecture in many other European countries, actually produce better architects.

The student body is varied—diverse would be too far-fetched.

Their previous education differs widely. Students come to us who have already been to an HTL (a higher vocational secondary school in Austria), where they received initial training in building construction, furniture making or other technical subjects. Others, especially from the eastern parts of Europe, have already started a similar course of study that is only partly recognized, or may already have a head start in their drawing and presentation skills. Some have not even covered the topic of architecture in art or history classes at school.

The Institute for Construction and Design Principles, of which I am the head, was founded at the TU Graz in 2013 to bring the students' knowledge and skills into alignment during the first year. To put it bluntly, with regard to the former HTL pupils it is partly a matter of "unlearning," and with regard to other students it is about teaching them basic "tools" and fundamental knowledge.

Back to the dimly lit lecture hall.

Now one has to decide. There are different ways to proceed.

One could start by describing the complexity of architecture—the design, the context, the construction, the three-dimensional thinking, all the requirements and standards, the social responsibility, etc. One could explain how much you have to be able to do before you can even design anything meaningful. One could talk about how long it takes before you're finally allowed to build something, because it's so difficult. Alternatively, one could present the difficulties in simplified terms and, step by step, give the students the means to explore the complex connections for themselves.

The argument against simplification is that it is banal.

To put it another way, if the solution is not complicated, then the question cannot have been difficult enough. But perhaps the answers are obscured by complicated descriptions, either because the answers do not exist or because they have not been fully understood by the lecturers themselves. Or is making things complicated a characteristic of institutions, to sustain a hierarchical structure? We are here at the university because we lecturers think we know roughly how it could work. If I have understood it myself, I should also be able to convey it to others. And, one might go on to presume, "If we can do it, why shouldn't students be able to learn it?"

Our faculty mission statement, like that of many other faculties, says, among other things, that designing is complex (difficult). But another way of seeing it could be, "Once you know how to do it, it's actually easy."

2   Neue Nationalgalerie, Mies van der Rohe, Berlin 2015 © KOEN, TU Graz

einzuordnen. Daher gibt es auch die drei unterschiedlichen Bildungswege: Fachhochschule, Technische Universität oder Kunstakademie. Alle drei wollen sich voneinander absetzen und gleichzeitig berechtigen alle drei Bildungswege zur Berufsbezeichnung Architektin, Architekt. In den Gesprächen an unserer Fakultät der Technischen Universität Graz über den Inhalt und die pädagogischen Konzepte der Architekturlehre ist die Diskussion von einer Gratwanderung zwischen Berufsausbildung und Theorie oder künstlerischer Gestaltung und technisch-architektonischer Gestaltung geprägt. Bei dem Argument, dass das Studium keine Berufsausbildung ist, wird oft darauf hingewiesen, dass nicht alle AbsolventInnen später ArchitektInnen werden. Genaue Zahlen haben wir hier dazu leider nicht.

Was wird aus unseren Studierenden, wenn sie fertig sind? Was soll ich ihnen sagen, worauf sie sich bei diesem Studium eingelassen haben?

Soweit ich es überblicken kann, fangen die meisten das Studium ganz profan mit dem Ziel an, ArchitektInnen zu werden, ansonsten würden sie wahrscheinlich etwas Anderes studieren. Könnte es so sein, dass die Alternativen in den Vordergrund gerückt werden, weil eine Vielzahl der Lehrenden logischerweise selber keine praktizierenden ArchitektInnen sind, sondern sich auf den theoretischen und wissenschaftlichen Teil der Architektur spezialisiert haben? Oder ist das Analysieren und die Infragestellung des eigenen Tuns eine Voraussetzung für das Entwerfen?

Seit dem Bologna-Prozess sind die Curricula angepasst worden und so wie an vielen anderen Universitäten ist auch hier in Graz eine Mischung aus Pflicht- und Wahlfächern entstanden. Bei der Diskussion über das Curriculum fällt oft der Begriff der Freiheit, des freien Studiums – im Gegensatz zur Verschulung. Aber was heißt das?

Mich hat am meisten gewundert, dass „verschult" überhaupt ein Wort ist und dass es negativ besetzt ist. Ein System, das eine undurchsichtige Wahlfreiheit zulässt, muss sich auch der Kritik stellen, dass es nur von denjenigen, die sowieso die entsprechende Vorbildung, Vorerfahrung oder Kontakte haben, sinnvoll genutzt werden kann. Also ein System, wo die Massen zugelassen werden, aber in dem vor allem die Privilegierten schaffen, sich durchzusetzen.

Ist es nicht demokratischer, allen Bildung zu ermöglichen, indem die dafür notwendigen Voraussetzungen in einem sogenannten „verschulten" System für alle zugänglich gemacht werden? Ein System mit einem Curriculum mit festen Bestandteilen, die chronologisch aufeinander folgen und mit einer Abschlussarbeit beendet werden, im Unterschied zu einzelnen Lehrveranstaltungen, die frei gewählt werden können und in ihrer Summe zu einem Abschluss führen? Schließt ein verschultes System ein Hinterfragen des Faches und der Institution aus oder schafft die Bildung die Voraussetzung für das Hinterfragen?

Bei den ca. 150 Personen, die hier sitzen, gibt es Studierende, die nicht wollen oder vielleicht sogar nicht können, dann gibt es die Vielen, und die wenigen besonders Ambitionierten. An wen richtet sich das Studium?

Für die Wenigen die ultimative Herausforderung und Inspiration zu schaffen oder die Vielen aufzuklären, um dadurch im Allgemeinen die Qualität der Baukultur zu erhöhen?

Am besten möchte man gerne beides erreichen. Letzten Endes werden nicht alle ihr eigenes Büro führen, es werden auch nicht alle als ArchitektInnen arbeiten. Es könnte das Ziel sein, den Studierenden Werkzeuge zu vermitteln, die sie benötigen, um sich auszudrücken und sich das Wissen selbst anzueignen. Anders als bei der traditionellen Meisterschule, wo vor allem gelehrt wird, wie man selbst zum eigenen Werk gekommen ist.

It is still not clear whether Architecture as a subject can be classified as a science or an art, or whether studying architecture is a professional training . That's why there are three different education paths: technical college, technical university, or art school. All three seek to distinguish themselves from each other, yet all three education paths lead towards the professional title of architect. At our faculty, at the Graz University of Technology, the discussions about the content and pedagogical concepts of teaching architecture are dominated by the questions of whether the education should focus on professional training or theoretical studies, or on artistic design or technical design. The argument that the course should not be about professional training is based on the observation that not all graduates go on to become architects. Unfortunately we do not have exact figures on this.

What will become of our students after graduation? What should I tell them about what they have signed up for?

As far as I can see, most of them start the course simply with the intention of becoming architects—otherwise they would probably study something else. Could it be that other specialisations are being highlighted because a large number of the tutors are not practicing architects, but have specialized in the theoretical and scientific aspect of architecture? Or is analyzing and questioning one's own actions a precondition for design?

Since the Bologna Process, curricula have been re-aligned, and here in Graz, as at many other universities, a mixture of compulsory and elective subjects has emerged. When discussing the curriculum, the concept of freedom, of free study (in contrast to schooling), often crops up. But what does that mean?

What surprises me most is that "verschult" is a word at all and that it has negative connotations. A system that has a freedom of choice must also face the criticism that it can only be used meaningfully by those who already have relevant previous education, experience or contacts. In other words, it is a system where the masses are admitted, but it is mainly the privileged who manage to succeed.

Is it not more democratic to make education possible for everybody by providing the students with the necessary fundamentals through a so-called "school-based" system? A system with a curriculum of fixed components that follow each other chronologically and end with a final project, as opposed to individual courses which add up to a degree? Does a school-based system rule out a questioning of the subject and the institution, or does education create the preconditions for questioning?

Among the 150 or so students sitting here, there are students who are unmotivated or are experiencing difficulties. Then there are the many and then the particularly ambitious few. Who is the course aimed at?

Should it seek to create the ultimate challenge and inspiration for the few, or to educate the many and raise the general quality of architecture ?

Preferably one wants to achieve both. After all, not everyone will head their own office, nor will everyone work as an architect. The goal could be to give students the tools they need to express themselves and to acquire knowledge by themselves, unlike the traditional "master school," where the emphasis is on teaching how the masters developed their own body of work.

At the end of the course, the final thesis is personally supervised by professors. This work is often presented as a measure for evaluating the quality of the course and of our graduates. Since I get to know the students at the start of the course and see them again at the very end of their studies, I have noticed that in the (many) years in between, some students have developed a needless awe of designing, and an associated inhibition about it. I wonder if this could be due to an over-complication of the assignments they are set, or due to the architectural refences they are given.

Over 50 percent of those sitting in the lecture hall are women—and it has been that way for many years. After graduation, though, the situation is different: less than ten percent of architects running their own practices are women, and they are usually in partnership with one or more men. This is of course a problem in society as a whole, but especially in architecture there is a big gap between the numbers of female students and the numbers of practicing female architects.

3 Exkursion „Gestalten und Entwerfen" Stockholm | Excursion "Form and Design" Stockholm 2018 © KOEN, TU Graz

Am Ende des Studiums wird bei uns die Masterarbeit durch ProfessorInnen persönlich betreut. Diese Arbeiten werden immer wieder als Beispiel oder als Messlatte vorgeführt, um die Qualität des Studiums und unserer AbsolventInnen zu bewerten. Was mir in diesem Zusammenhang auffällt, da ich ja die Studierenden am Anfang kennenlerne und dann erst ganz am Ende ihres Studiums wiedersehe, ist, dass in den (vielen) Jahren dazwischen sich bei manchen der Studierenden eine unnötige Ehrfurcht und damit verbundene Hemmung vor dem Entwerfen aufgebaut hat. So stelle ich mir die Frage, ob es vielleicht an dem Verkomplizieren der Aufgabenstellungen oder auch an den Referenzen, die immer wieder gezeigt werden, liegen kann?

In der Halle sitzen über fünfzig Prozent Frauen – und das seit vielen Jahren. Nach dem Studium sieht es anders aus, weniger als zehn Prozent der BüroinhaberInnen sind Frauen und diese sind meistens in Partnerschaft mit einem oder mehreren Männern. Das ist natürlich ein gesamtgesellschaftliches Problem, aber gerade in der Architektur gehen die Zahlen von weiblichen Studierenden und weiblichen praktizierenden Architektinnen weit auseinander.

2008 wurde ich in den Bund Deutscher Architekten gewählt, und seitdem lag alle zwei Monate die neue Ausgabe des Architekturmagazins *Der Architekt* auf meinem Schreibtisch.

Es hat ein bisschen gedauert, bevor mir klar wurde, wie beleidigend das ist. Erstens, weil ich Architektin bin, und zusätzlich, weil der Fokus auf die eine Person gelegt wird. Gemeinsam mit dem Magazin *Baumeister* sollten sich die Architekten in Deutschland vielleicht überlegen, was sie damit aussagen wollen. Und dass es vor kurzem zu *Die Architekt* umbenannt wurde, hilft nicht wirklich weiter. Es kann nicht alleine die Aufgabe der Frauen sein, zum Beispiel für jemand wie mich als eine der wenigen praktizierenden Architektinnen an unserer Universität, ein Gleichgewicht herzustellen. Auch wir Frauen sind von unserer eigenen Ausbildung vorbelastet und müssen uns aktiv darum bemühen, umzudenken.

Die AutorInnenschaft des architektonischen Werkes wird meistens mit einer bestimmten Person verknüpft und selten wird der Kontext, in dem die Architektur entsteht, erläutert. Stattdessen werden uns Werke vorgehalten, von privilegierten, weißen alten

Since I was elected to the Association of German Architects in 2008, the latest issue of its magazine *Der Architekt* lands on my desk every two months. It took me a little while to realize how offensive that is, as the male gendered title excludes me as a female architect, and also the focus is on a single person. The same goes for the magazine *Baumeister*, which also has a male gendered title. Architects in Germany should perhaps think about the image they want to project here. And that the title has recently been changed to *Die Architekt* (a linguistically incorrect mix) doesn't really help the issue. It cannot be the exclusive task of women—for example, someone like me, one of the few practicing female architects in our university—to create a balance. Moreover, we women are also hampered by our own education and must also make an active effort to rethink.

The authorship of architectural work is usually linked to a specific person, and the context in which the architecture is created is rarely mentioned. What is presented to us are works by privileged, old white men which have been awarded prizes, published and exhibited by predominantly male journalists and juries. It is suggested that it is only about being good, talented, and creative enough: our very own "American Dream." And although we know how few of us manage to build these special works, and how privileged those are who do, these works are celebrated as architectural references.

How does one change that? After all, one does want to show the students the best. So that raises the question of what is the best? How does one find the relevant examples, and how can one free oneself from the old architectural references? I can follow the argument that, for example, the works of Sverre Fehn are not worse because he is a man (and he, personally, can't help that). Somehow, though, we have to ask ourselves these

4   Sozialer Wohnungsbau | Social housing, Hägersten, Realarchitektur Petra Petersson, Stockholm 2018 © KOEN, TU Graz

Männern stammen und von vorherrschend männlich besetzten Jurys und Journalisten prämiert, publiziert und ausgestellt wurden. Es wird suggeriert, dass es nur darum geht, gut genug, talentiert und kreativ zu sein.

Unser ganz eigener „American Dream". Und obwohl wir wissen, wie wenige von uns es schaffen, diese besonderen Werke zu realisieren und wie privilegiert diese Personen wiederum sind, werden diese Werke als Referenzen gefeiert.

Wie soll man das ändern? Man will doch den Studierenden das Beste zeigen. So müsste man sich die Frage stellen, was dann das Beste ist. Wie findet man die Beispiele und wie kann man sich von den alten Referenzen befreien? Ich kann dem Argument folgen, dass zum Beispiel die Werke von Sverre Fehn nicht schlechter sind, weil er ein Mann ist (und er persönlich kann ja auch nichts dafür). Aber irgendwie müssen wir uns doch diese schwierigen Fragen stellen und das nicht nur in Bezug auf Gender oder Privilegien.

Ein Vorteil des Architekturstudiums ist, dass Architektur ohne großen Aufwand erlebt, betrachtet und untersucht werden kann. Wir müssen keine aufwendigen Experimente durchführen oder durch Mikroskope schauen, sondern nur lernen, das zu sehen, was da ist.

Das Betrachten und das Analysieren von bereits gebautem Raum sind daher schon immer zentrale Bestandteile der Ausbildung. Wenn ich singen lernen will, werde ich mir wahrscheinlich als Inspiration die Musik von den berühmtesten SängerInnen anhören und nicht nur die des lokalen Gesangsvereins. Es ist unausweichlich, gute Beispiele zu finden und diese zu zeigen. Vielleicht muss man sich nur mehr Gedanken dazu machen, was eigentlich gut ist, und das nicht nur in Bezug auf das Werk selbst, sondern auch in welchem Kontext es entstanden ist.

In ihre ewige Selbstfindung verstrickt, tut sich die Architektur schwer. So stellen sich die Studierenden in unserer Halle die Frage, ob alles, was gebaut wird, Architektur ist?

Grob gesagt, vom Gefühl her müssen die Bauten in Österreich etwas Schräges haben oder mit besonderen Auskragungen geschmückt sein, in der Schweiz mit Sichtbeton oder edlen Details und Materialien gebaut sein oder in Schweden zum Beispiel eine besondere Fassadengestaltung haben, gerne bunt, um als Architekturprojekt klassifiziert zu werden. Beim Städtebau muss man sich wiederum den komplexen sozialen Komponenten stellen, partizipativ agieren und Mobilitätskonzepte entwickeln, um

einen ernstzunehmenden städtebaulichen Entwurf zu präsentieren. Wir als ArchitektInnen sollen uns zusätzlich in der Gesetzgebung, in der Normung, in der Politik und in der Projektentwicklung engagieren. Immer größere Bestandteile der Planung werden von Generalunternehmen, IngenieurInnen und spezialisierten GutachterInnen übernommen und ArchitektInnen suchen nach neuen Aufgaben. Und natürlich muss alles nachhaltig sein. Das ist schon ein Problem für die Architektur, da es wahrscheinlich am nachhaltigsten wäre, wenn man einfach nicht mehr so viel baut, sondern sich mit dem zufrieden gibt, was da ist.

Aber das alles kann ich doch nicht sagen, am ersten Tag. Von Ehrfurcht und Angst gesteuert, ist selten etwas Neues entstanden. Was für mich selber bleibt, ist das Einfache, die Vernunft: wenn ich verstehe, wie es geht, kann ich etwas Gutes machen und etwas verändern.

So fängt das Jahr voller Engagement mit einem dreitägigen Workshop an, wo mit einfachen Modellen in Gruppen bis hin zum Eins-zu-eins-Objekt entworfen wird. Es wird die Übersetzung von Dreidimensionalität ins Zweidimensionale geübt, erste Anforderungen an Funktion, Konstruktion und Ausdruck gestellt. Es wird erprobt, in der Gruppe zu arbeiten, soziale Verbindungen herzustellen, voneinander zu lernen und Hierarchien abzubauen. Nach außen wild und kreativ, im Hintergrund allerdings genau geplant und inszeniert.

Im besten Falle werde ich nach diesen drei Tagen, bei der nächsten Vorlesung, die Studierenden um Aufmerksamkeit bitten und regelmäßig durch ihre Fragen und kritischen Kommentare unterbrochen werden. ∎

difficult questions, and not just those concerning gender or privilege.

One advantage of studying architecture is that it can be experienced, viewed, and examined without much effort. There is no need for elaborate experiments or looking through microscopes. We only have to learn to see what is there.

That is why looking at and analyzing existing built spaces has always been a central part of architectural education. If I were to learn to sing, I would probably seek inspiration by listening to the music by the most famous singers, not just that of the local choir. It is essential to find good examples and show them off. Maybe one should just think more about what is actually good, not just in terms of the work itself, but also in terms of the context in which it was created.

Entangled in its constant self-discovery, architecture is struggling. So the students in our lecture hall ask themselves whether everything that is built is architecture.

To oversimplify grossly, it feels as if, in order to be classified as an architectural project, buildings in Austria must have something at a slant or be decorated with cantilevers; in Switzerland they must be built with exposed concrete or fine details and materials; or in Sweden, for example, they must have a special façade design, preferably colorful. In urban planning, on the other hand, one must deal with complex social issues, use participatory methods and develop mobility concepts in order to be able to present a serious urban design. We as architects are also expected to get involved in legislation, standardization, policy, and project development. Ever larger components of planning are being taken over by general contractors, engineers and specialized consultants, and architects are looking for new tasks. And, of course, everything has to be sustainable. This is a problem for architecture, as the most sustainable thing to do would probably be to not build so much and to be content with what is already there.

But I can't tell them all that on the first day. Awe and anxiety rarely inspire anything new. So I am left with simplicity and common sense. If I understand how it's done, I can do something good and change things.

5   Beginners Workshop, Graz 2021 © KOEN, TU Graz

So the year begins, full of enthusiasm, with a three-day workshop, in which full scale designs are produced by groups working with simple models. They practice translating three-dimensionality into two-dimensionality and are confronted with basic requirements on function, construction and expression. They are trying out working in groups, making social connections, learning from each other, and breaking down hierarchies. On the outside wild and creative, on the inside precisely planned and presented.

In the best case, after these three days, at the next lecture, I will ask the students if I may have their attention, and will be interrupted regularly by their questions and critical comments. ∎

*Translation from German: John Wheelwright*

17

Charlotte Malterre-Barthes

# Updated Notes on Online Teaching
## A Post-Pandemic Online Future?

# Aktualisierte Anmerkungen zum Online-Unterricht
## Eine postpandemische Online-Zukunft?

1   "Windows of Isolation" | „Fenster der Isolation", 2020 © gta/TRANS

"**work, work, work, work, work, work.**"[1] In March 2020, the world stopped. Or did it? The architecture schools, like most universities across the world kept operating, albeit online. As physical premises and campuses were shutting down one after the other, educational institutions, while acknowledging the disruption brought to working routines and to personal lives in an avalanche of remorseful emails, precipitated the move to remote teaching. Teaching a discipline grounded in spatiality in a virtual arena did not appear incongruous to the decision-makers preoccupied by the continuity of architectural education. The salvific pause offered by the lockdown to privileged institutions to address possible changes in our modus operandi was not embraced. The shift to digital space was cloaked in technological triumphalism. The unprecedented adjustments regarding teaching and research activities focused on continuance at all costs. Critical questions about the profession remained largely unaddressed, while an immense effort was and still is poured into maintaining the status quo of curricula: studios should be completed, lectures attended, exams taken. This was mirrored in the building industry: amidst the pandemic, construction sites never closed.

In academia, the emerging and current discourse touted the opportunities such a crisis presented for exploring new ways of working—but never whether to build or not to build, nor structural issues in education, injustice and inequalities, or the very fact that our profession is a key agent to climate change. Moving teaching online was treated as a disruptive yet facile spatial relocation, while many faced issues of fair access to technology, bandwidth inequality, and online discrimination. Now we must interrogate the haste with which flexibility and accommodations made in 2020 is done away with as schools move to teaching again in person. While there are both impediments and benefits in remote education, we must face these struggles to take seriously the question of what a post-pandemic online future will look like.

**Everyone Can See Your Bedroom.** Clothes racks, home plants, messy shelves, posters, hanging guitars, kitchen wares, make-up tables, sometimes strolling cats and curious children, or intrusive roommates: the backgrounds of students and colleagues during design studio critiques from March 2020

onward displayed the intimacy of domestic lives in an unprecedented and crude way. These indiscrete windows revealed as much as they hid, for under the name of each participant, not all interiors were visible. Zoom, the previously unheard-of program for virtual communication that became an overnight hit, offers the option to display a fictitious background—a forest, a bookshelf, a city skyline, a Venetian painting, anything you see fit. I, for instance, chose an interior shot of the spatial station MIR. It served several agendas: it exposed the work of its designer, the little-known Soviet architect Galina Balashova; possibly signaling a left-inclined political sensibility, but also depicted an allegory of isolation within disordered technology; as well as a metaphor for existential anguish—deorbited, MIR is a defunct space station, its last remains plunged into the waters of the South Pacific Ocean in Spring 2001. But mostly it removed from view my own domestic interior, a feeble attempt to resist the school's intrusion into my private sphere. Some of the other participants in Zoom calls saw no need in hiding what seemed to be an office within a home, Virginia Woolf's legendary and feminist "room of one's own."[2] Going beyond gender to address social class, the disparity between those with a space dedicated to their individual work removed from the domestic realm, and those with a bedroom as a space for everything else became blatant: Both privacy and undisrupted thinking are privileges. While on-campus premises offer roughly the same material working conditions for every student, and a collective office for professors and assistants, the university@home cannot recreate this equalizing process—at least not spatially. Here for all to see, a fundamental flaw emerges: we are not equally equipped to face remote education.

**I'll Be On WhatsApp If You Need Me.** In the name of efficiency, continuity, and productivity, digital communication technology took over architecture education in full force during the pandemic. Virtual studio pedagogy, remote master classes, distant

---

1    Rihanna, "Work," *Anti*, 2016 © Sony/ATV Music Publishing LLC, Warner Chappell Music, Inc, Universal Music Publishing Group.

2    See Virginia Woolf, *A Room of One's Own* (London, 2020).

„work, work, work, work, work, work"[1]. Im März 2020 blieb die Welt stehen. Oder doch nicht? Die Architekturfakultäten liefen – wie die meisten Universitäten auf der Welt – weiter, wenn auch online. Als die physischen Räumlichkeiten nach und nach die Tore schlossen, stellten sich die Bildungseinrichtungen, wiewohl in einer E-Mail-Lawine wortreich die Störung ihrer Arbeitsroutinen und des persönlichen Lebens beklagend, an die Spitze des Online-Unterrichts. Einzig um die Kontinuität der Architekturausbildung besorgt, sahen die Verantwortlichen keinen Widerspruch darin, ein Fach, das durch und durch im Räumlichen verankert ist, in einer virtuellen Umgebung zu unterrichten. Die heilsame Pause, die der Lockdown privilegierten Institutionen bot, um über mögliche Änderungen ihres Modus Operandi nachzudenken, blieb ungenutzt. Das Ausweichen in den digitalen Raum wurde mit technologischem Triumphgeheul bemäntelt. Die nie zuvor dagewesenen Änderungen in Lehre und Forschung dienten der Fortsetzung um jeden Preis. Kritische Fragen zum Berufsbild wurden nicht gestellt. Stattdessen wurden ungeheure Anstrengungen zur Beibehaltung des curricularen Status Quo unternommen: Entwurfsübungen sollten beendet, Vorlesungen besucht, Prüfungen abgelegt werden. Dies spiegelte sich auch im Baugewerbe wider: Inmitten der Pandemie blieben die Baustellen in Betrieb.

Der in der akademischen Welt entstehende und weiter gepflogene Diskurs verkündete lautstark die Möglichkeiten, die eine solche Krise zur Erkundung neuer Arbeitsweisen bot, sprach aber nie über Bauen oder Nichtbauen, über strukturelle Bildungsprobleme, Ungerechtigkeit und Ungleichheit oder über unseren Beruf als wesentlichem Aktanten des Klimawandels. Die Verlegung des Unterrichts ins Netz wurde als eine disruptive, aber leicht bewältigbare räumliche Standortänderung behandelt, während viele Probleme mit fairem Technologiezugang, Bandbreitenungleichheit und Online-Diskriminierung hatten. Nun müssen wir die Eile hinterfragen, mit der die Flexibilität und die Anpassungen, die wir 2020 auf uns genommen haben, mit der Rückkehr zum Präsenzunterricht wieder vom Tisch gewischt werden. Zwar ist der Fernunterricht sowohl mit Einschränkungen als auch mit Vorteilen verbunden, aber wir müssen uns ihnen stellen, wenn wir uns ernsthaft der Frage widmen wollen, wie eine postpandemische Zukunft aussehen soll.

**Jeder sieht dein Schlafzimmer.** Kleiderständer, Zimmerpflanzen, unaufgeräumte Regale, Plakate, an der Wand hängende Gitarren, Küchenutensilien, Schminktische, herumschleichende Katzen und neugierige Kinder oder aufdringliche MitbewohnerInnen: Die Hintergründe von Studierenden und KollegInnen in Entwurfsklassenkritiken ab März 2020 gaben auf beispiellose und schonungslose Weise Einblick in deren Privatleben. Die indiskreten Fenster unserer Computer enthüllten aber nicht nur, sondern verbargen auch, denn nicht jede TeilnehmerIn gewährte über ihrem Namen Einblick in den persönlichen Wohnraum. Zoom, das zuvor unbekannte Programm für virtuelle Kommunikation, das über Nacht zum Hit geworden war, bietet nämlich die Möglichkeit, einen fiktiven Hintergrund einzublenden – einen Wald, ein Bücherregal, die Skyline einer Stadt, ein venezianisches Gemälde, was immer einem passend erscheint. Ich entschied mich zum Beispiel für eine Innenaufnahme der Raumstation MIR. Sie erfüllte mehrere Zwecke: Sie zeigte die Arbeit ihrer Gestalterin, der wenig bekannten sowjetischen Architektin Galina Balaschowa, und signalisierte damit vielleicht linke politische Neigungen, bildete aber auch eine Allegorie der Isolation in einer außer Betrieb genommenen Technik sowie eine Metapher existenzieller Angst – die MIR ist eine aufgelassene, zum Absturz gebrachte Raumstation, deren letzte Überreste im Frühjahr 2001 in den Südpazifik fielen. Vor allem aber blendete sie meine eigene Wohnung aus – ein schwacher Versuch, mich dem Eindringen der Uni in meine Privatsphäre zu widersetzen. Einige andere TeilnehmerInnen fühlten sich nicht bemüßigt, ihr Büro innerhalb der Wohnung – Virginia Woolfs legendär feministisches „Zimmer für sich allein"[2] – zu verbergen. Geschlechtsübergreifend, auf der Ebene der Klassenzugehörigkeit, wurde der Unterschied zwischen denen mit einem vom Wohnbereich abgegrenzten eigenen Arbeitsraum und denen mit einem multifunktionalen Schlafzimmer noch deutlicher: Privatheit und ungestörtes Denken sind Privilegien. Bieten die Universitätsräumlichkeiten annähernd die gleichen materiellen Arbeitsbedingungen für alle Studierenden und ein gemeinsames Büro für ProfessorInnen und AssistentInnen, kann die university@home diese Egalisierung – jedenfalls räumlich – nicht leisten. Hier tritt ein grundlegender Mangel deutlich zutage: Wir sind nicht alle gleich für den Fernunterricht gerüstet.

**Bin auf WhatsApp, falls du mich brauchst.** Im Namen von Effizienz, Kontinuität und Produktivität drang die digitale Kommunikationstechnik im Lauf der Pandemie mit Volldampf in den Architekturunterricht ein. In virtuellen Entwurfs- und Projektübungen, Online-Leseseminaren und Online-Teammeetings freundeten wir uns im Handumdrehen mit den elektronischen Medien und den Systemen der modernen materiellen Kultur an. Schließlich existierten sie bereits, nur darauf wartend,

---

1 Rihanna, „Work", *Anti*, 2016 © Sony/ATV Music Publishing LLC, Warner Chappell Music, Inc, Universal Music Publishing Group.

2 Vgl. Woolf, Virginia: *Ein Zimmer für sich allein*, Übers. Renate Gerhardt, Frankfurt am Main 1986.

reading seminars and team meetings saw us embracing electronic media and systems of modern material culture in a split second. After all, these were already there, waiting for us to fully surrender. From video conferencing and chat applications (WhatsApp, Skype, Zoom, Facetime), to team meeting programs (Microsoft Teams, Google Hangouts, Whereby, Remo) to the design exchanges interfaces (Miro, OneNote), the discussion over exchange of drawings, images as PDF or JPG files coming from Rhino, Illustrator, Photoshop, etc., replaced the pedagogical social interaction schools relied on to educate the designers of tomorrow. In many studios, a conversation on the brief, the form, and the outputs of the semester took place, with changes made to adjust to the situation. Often, these adjustments led to an increased workload for both teachers and students as new expectations (i.e., videos, virtual models, texts, websites) replaced previous ones—rather than leading to a discussion on a possible evolution of teaching structures. Some progress was made toward collaborative processes instead of one-directional format, and many embraced the potential of synchronous/asynchronous approaches. When seeking inspiring practices, many lessons can be learned from disabled people using online infrastructures for decades. Entire communities have engaged in defining methods and protocols "for remote access to protests, classrooms, doctors' offices, public meetings, and other events"[3] in the most collegial and democratic way possible. There is a bitter irony in that disabled people have demanded and been denied forms of remote teaching all these years, being told of its unfeasibility, only to see it implemented within days when urgency hit. Yet, "it is crip techno-science and disabled ingenuity that has made remote participation possible,"[4] a fact able bodies with good Wi-Fi connections must recognize, as what seemed a distant reality a few months ago has now become fact. Of course, there is a flip side: online teaching has been found guilty of perpetuating inequalities and discriminatory practices. Gender and racial bias is exacerbated by remote technology. A study conducted in the United States by the Stanford Institute for Economic Policy Research found that online, "professors … are 94% more likely to respond to a … White male than by any other race-gender combination."[5] This is possibly related to a structural issue: if faculty is white and male, because of implicit bias, like-minded individuals are mentored and rewarded. Thus online teaching simply replicates the disadvantages and discriminations suffered by racial minorities and womxn in other settings.

**My Internet crashed.** He was in the middle of his final studio presentation and suddenly disappeared from the screen. When he came back, the student apologized: "My Internet crashed, I'm now using my phone connection" as his assistant mumbled "technological incompetence." Another unsurprising trait of our times is laid bare by the rushed transfer to remote teaching: our absolute—and perhaps misplaced faith in technology. In *Staying with the Trouble*, Donna Haraway argues that we suffer from "a comic faith in technofixes, whether secular or religious: technology will somehow come to the rescue of its naughty but very clever children."[6] An explanation to the technocratic belief of schools of architecture may be found in a disciplinary and literal proximity. In Europe, many architecture departments are rooted in technological universities (TU Delft, TU Vienna, TU Berlin, ETH Zurich, EPFL). Even if at odds with their main institution, these schools are embedded in a system of ideological governance where scientific and technical knowledge rules. However, digital literacy is not a given within architecture schools, and this lack of expertise emerges now: a belief without real competence, or the insufficient teaching of these competences. The assumption that all students and faculty are properly equipped with the necessary skills to operate the myriad of online teaching tools existing as well as a home computer and a sound internet connection might be incorrect. Schools fuel the nefarious faith that technology can save us from losing our old selves, ignoring the inevitable technical, personal, and infrastructural obstacles that come along. Truth is, the pseudo-smoothness of the change keeps us from entering the era of intense questioning that we should be undertaking. "We are being enlisted into normalizing the crisis. … There is no fucking academic continuity. The most we can do is teach

3   Aimi Hamraie, "Accessible Teaching in the Time of Covid-19," *Mapping Access* (2020), available online at: https://www.mapping-access.com/blog-1/2020/3/10/accessible-teaching-in-the-time-of-covid-19 (accessed July 7, 2020).

4   Ibid.

5   Rachel Baker, Thomas Dee, Brent Evans, and June John, "Bias in Online Classes: Evidence from a Field Experiment," *Stanford Center for Education Policy Analysis* (2018), available online at: https://cepa.stanford.edu/content/bias-online-classes-evidence-field-experiment (accessed November 16, 2021).

6   Donna Haraway, *Staying with the Trouble* (Durham, 2016), 3.

dass wir uns ihnen vollständig ausliefern. Von Videokonferenzen und Chatapplikationen (WhatsApp, Skype, Zoom, Facetime) über Teammeeting-Programme (Microsoft Teams, Google Hangouts, Whereby, Remo) bis zu Interfaces für gemeinsames Entwerfen (Miro, OneNote) ersetzte die Diskussion über den Austausch von Zeichnungen, Bildern in Form von PDF- oder JPG-Dateien produziert mit Rhino, Illustrator, Photoshop usw., die pädagogische soziale Interaktion, auf die sich Universitäten bisher bei der Ausbildung der ArchitektInnen von morgen stützten. In vielen Entwurfsklassen wurden Aufgabenstellung, Form und Ergebnisse diskutiert und daraufhin Anpassungen an die Situation vorgenommen. Oft führten diese Anpassungen – wenn z.B. neue Ansprüche (Videos, virtuelle Modelle, Texte, Websites) auftauchten – zu zusätzlicher Arbeitsbelastung für Lehrende wie Studierende statt zu einer Diskussion über die mögliche Weiterentwicklung von Unterrichtsstrukturen. Ein gewisser Fortschritt war in Richtung kollaborativer Prozesse (im Gegensatz zu unidirektionalen Formaten) zu verzeichnen, und viele nutzten das Potenzial synchroner/asynchroner Ansätze. Wer nach inspirierenden Praktiken sucht, kann einiges von Menschen mit Behinderung lernen, die Online-Infrastrukturen seit Jahrzehnten benutzen. Ganze Communities haben sich auf überaus kollegiale und demokratische Weise der Definition von Methoden und Protokollen „für den Fernzugang zu Protesten, Klassenzimmern, Ordinationen, öffentlichen Versammlungen und anderen Ereignissen"[3] gewidmet. Es liegt eine bittere Ironie darin, dass Menschen mit Behinderung, denen Formen des Fernunterrichts ganze Zeit über verwehrt wurden, weil sie angeblich nicht umsetzbar seien, nun ihre Umsetzung innerhalb weniger Tage erlebten. Dennoch war es „die Technowissenschaft und der Einfallsreichtum von behinderten Menschen, die die Online-Teilnahme möglich gemacht hat"[4], wie auch unbehinderte Menschen mit guten WLAN-Verbindungen anerkennen müssen. Seitdem ist Realität, was vor ein paar Monaten noch Zukunftsmusik zu sein schien. Natürlich gibt es auch eine Kehrseite: Es hat sich gezeigt, dass der Online-Unterricht zur Perpetuierung von Ungleichheiten und diskriminierenden Praktiken beiträgt. Geschlechts- und *race*-bedingte Voreingenommenheiten werden durch die Remote-Technologie verstärkt. Eine in den USA vom Stanford Institute for Economic Policy Research durchgeführte Studie kam zu dem Ergebnis, dass „ProfessorInnen […] mit 94% höherer Wahrscheinlichkeit […] einem weißen Mann antworten als jeder anderen Geschlechts-*race*-Kombination".[5] Das ist vermutlich einem strukturellen Problem geschuldet: Wenn der Lehrkörper aufgrund einer impliziten Tendenz weiß und männlich ist, dann werden ähnlich geartete Personen betreut und belohnt. Insofern reproduziert der Online-Unterricht lediglich die Benachteiligungen und Diskriminierungen, die ethnische Minderheiten und *womxn* in anderen Kontexten erleben.

**Mein Internet ist gecrasht.** Mitten in der Präsentation seiner Entwurfsklasse war er plötzlich vom Bildschirm verschwunden. Als er wieder erschien, entschuldigte sich der Studierende: „Mein Internet ist gecrasht, ich verwende jetzt mein Handy", während sein Tutor etwas von „technischem Unvermögen" murmelte. Durch den überstürzten Übergang zur Online-Lehre tritt ein weiteres wenig überraschendes Merkmal unserer Zeit zutage: unser absoluter – und wahrscheinlich unangebrachter – Glaube an die Technik. In *Unruhig bleiben* schreibt Donna Haraway, wir litten unter einem „geradezu lächerliche[n] Glaube[n] an technische Lösungen, ob nun säkularer oder religiöser Art: Eine Technik wird auftauchen, um ihre schlimmen, aber sehr schlauen Kinder zu retten."[6] Eine Erklärung für die Technikgläubigkeit von Architekturfakultäten ist vielleicht in der fachlichen und buchstäblichen Nähe zu suchen. In Europa befinden sich die meisten Architekturfakultäten auf technischen Universitäten (TU Delft, TU Wien, TU Berlin, ETH Zürich, EPFL). Selbst wenn sie mit ihrer Mutterinstitution nicht grün sind, sind diese Fakultäten doch eingebettet in ein von Wissenschaft und Technik dominiertes ideologisches Regime. Nichtsdestotrotz ist digitale Bildung auf Architekturfakultäten keine Selbstverständlichkeit, und dieses mangelnde Wissen kommt nun zum Vorschein: ein Glaube ohne wirkliche Kompetenz, oder eine ungenügende Vermittlung dieser Kompetenz. Die Annahme, dass alle Studierenden und Lehrkräfte über die notwendigen Fähigkeiten verfügen, um die Unmenge an Tools für den Online-Unterricht zu bedienen, und auch noch über einen eigenen Rechner und eine ordentliche Internetverbindung, ist wohl unzutreffend. Die Institute fördern den unseligen Glauben, die Technik könne uns vor dem Verlust unseres alten Selbst bewahren, indem sie die unvermeidlich auf uns zukommenden technischen, persönlichen und infrastrukturellen Hürden ignorieren. In Wahrheit hindert uns der scheinbar glatte Übergang daran, in die Ära intensiven Fragens einzutreten, die wir einleiten sollten. „Wir werden dazu vergattert, die Krise zu normalisieren. […] Es gibt keine scheiß akademische Kontinuität."

3  Hamraie, Aimi: „Accessible Teaching in the Time of Covid-19", in: *Mapping Access* (2020), online unter: https://www.mapping-access.com/blog-1/2020/3/10/accessible-teaching-in-the-time-of-covid-19 (Stand: 7. Juli 2020).

4  Ebd.

5  Baker, Rachel/Dee, Thomas/Evans, Brent/John, June: „Bias in Online Classes: Evidence from a Field Experiment", in: *Stanford Center for Education Policy Analysis* (2018), online unter: https://cepa.standford.edu/content/bias-online-classes-evidence-field-experiment (Stand: 16. November 2021).

6  Haraway, Donna: *Unruhig bleiben. Die Verwandtschaft der Arten im Chthuluzän.* Übers. Karin Harrasser, Frankfurt am Main 2018, 12.

critical analysis of what the crisis has exposed. But we'll have to do so with love and care, not redesigned grading schemes and endless zoom," wrote Ananya Roy, Professor of Inequality and Democracy at the UCLA Luskin School of Public Affairs, in a tweet on March 16, 2020. Yet, this redesign—and the endless zooms, are precisely happening.

**Online Teaching and Capitalism.** A recent article posted by Goldman Sachs asked—rhetorically—"how could the adoption of virtual classrooms, in an effort to contain the spread of coronavirus, jumpstart the long-term adoption of remote learning?"[7] That one of the largest global banking institutions so wholeheartedly embraces online academia is no good news. One cannot help but think about Isabelle Stengers' prophetic work *In Catastrophic Times: Resisting the Coming Barbarism*. Stengers spells it out for us: "the capitalist machine … is incapable of hesitating: it can't do anything other than define every situation as a source of profit."[8] Swiftly shifting the whole curriculum online, architecture schools participate in the expansion of predatory academic capitalism. Because of "edtech," verbiage coined by investors to define online teaching, social interaction in the knowledge economy is under attack. The commodification of education, via technology, or academic capitalism as identified by political economist Bob Jessop, has been underway pre-pandemic, obviously.[9] However, the crisis has accelerated the process. Business newspapers reflect the trend, announcing substantial investments in companies engaged in online tutoring.[10] It is therefore urgent to conduct a conversation on the freedom and accessibility of knowledge, and to ensure that online teaching technologies are not abandoned to private companies. Remote education tools at the hands of for-profit firms indicate that technology and the internet have simply recreated a space where capitalism can thrive.

**A Post-Pandemic Online Future?** Many architecture schools have resumed teaching in their premises in the fall of 2021, and online teaching does not seem to be going away—yet. In many places, lecture series, guest talks, and reviews are still held remotely. This flexibility is a win for students who are not able to be on the university premises—perhaps the fact that those are the ones with patchy child-care or visa issues, mobility or concentration difficulties, or a longer commute etc. shows what online learning can bring to make teaching environments more inclusive. Additionally, with limitless access to a pool of international lecturers who need not be physically present, while reaching a large and unexpected audience, there are clear benefits to online teaching for the circulation of ideas and the democratization of knowledge access. Many schools retain partially asynchronous formats—thanks to the immense amount of material recorded since March 2020 ("That lecture is asynchronous—please watch it before the class"). This growing online archive holds great potential, if generously shared.

But we must not forget: Since the tools we rely on and their accompanying technological progress are intrinsically part of a dis-equilibrating process, online teaching relentlessly demands more, newer technology, fueling self-sustaining needs, devouring more resources, from data centers to rare minerals, humans and materials alike. We must also remain wary of the fact that online intellectual life holds in itself a Sisyphean form of labor and extraction without time limits, private boundaries, nor spatial dimensions. ∎

This is an altered and actualized version of a text that was originally published in *trans 37 – Alien*, ETH Zurich, 2020.

7   Adam Nordin, "How Coronavirus Is Reshaping Classroom Learning," *BRIEFINGS Newsletter of 17 March 2020* (2020), availlable online at: https://www.goldmansachs.com/insights/pages/from_briefings_17-mar-2020.html (accessed April 2, 2020).

8   Isabelle Stengers, *In Catastrophic Times: Resisting the Coming Barbarism*, trans. Andrew Goffey (Lüneburg, 2015), 8–9.

9   See Bob Jessop, "On Academic Capitalism," *Critical Policy Studies* 12, no. 1 (2018): 1–6.

10  See Julie Zhu, Yingzhi Yang, and Sherry Jacob-Phillips, "Chinese Online Tutor Zuoyebang Raises $750 Million in Fresh Round," Reuters (2020), available online at: https://www.reuters.com/article/us-zuoyebang-fundraiisng/chinese-online-tutor-zuoyebang-raises-750-million-in-fresh-round-idUSKBN240093 (accessed June 19, 2020).

Höchstens können wir lehren, wie man das, was die Krise offenbart hat, kritisch analysiert. Aber wir müssen das mit Liebe und Sorgfalt tun, nicht mit dem Umbau von Benotungsschemata und mit endlosen Zooms", twitterte Ananya Roy, Professorin für Ungleichheit und Demokratie an der UCLA Luskin School of Public Affairs, am 16. März 2020. Doch genau dieser Umbau – und die endlosen Zooms – findet statt.

**Online-Unterricht und Kapitalismus.** In einem kürzlich geposteten Artikel von Goldman Sachs wurde die rhetorische Frage gestellt: „Wie konnte die Einrichtung virtueller Klassenzimmer im Zuge der Bemühungen zur Eindämmung des Coronavirus die langfristige Einführung des Fernunterrichts auf Touren bringen?"[7] Dass eines der größten Bankhäuser der Welt aus vollem Herzen die Online-Uni gutheißt, ist keine gute Nachricht. Man kann nicht umhin, an Isabelle Stengers' prophetisches Werk *In Catastrophic Times: Resisting the Coming Barbarism* zu denken. Stengers spricht es für uns aus: „die kapitalistische Maschine […] ist unfähig innezuhalten: Sie kann nicht anders, als jede Situation als Profitquelle zu definieren."[8] Mit der schleunigen Verlegung des gesamten Lehrplans ins Internet, nehmen Architekturfakultäten an der Expansion eines akademischen Raubtierkapitalismus teil. Aufgrund der „EdTech" – ein von Investoren geprägter Begriff für den Online-Unterricht – gerät die soziale Interaktion in der Wissensökonomie unter Beschuss. Die technisch betriebene Verwandlung von Bildung in eine Ware oder der „akademische Kapitalismus", wie ihn der politische Ökonom Bob Jessop nennt, war klarerweise bereits vor der Pandemie im Gange.[9] Aber die Krise hat den Prozess beschleunigt. Wirtschaftszeitungen widmen sich dem Trend, berichten von substanziellen Investitionen in Firmen, die im Online-Unterricht tätig sind.[10] Es ist daher dringend angezeigt, eine Debatte über Freiheit und Zugänglichkeit von Wissen zu führen und dafür zu sorgen, dass die Technologie des Online-Unterrichts nicht privaten Firmen überlassen wird. Liegen die Online-Unterrichtstools in den Händen profitorientierter Firmen, bedeutet das, dass Technologie und Internet lediglich einen neuen Raum geschaffen haben, in dem sich das Kapital entfalten kann.

**Eine postpandemische Online-Zukunft?** Viele Architekturfakultäten sind Herbst 2021 wieder zum Präsenzunterricht zurückgekehrt, aber der Online-Unterricht scheint deshalb nicht verschwunden zu sein – noch nicht. Vorlesungsreihen, Gastvorlesungen, Zwischen- oder Schlusskritiken scheinen vielerorts immer noch online abgehalten zu werden. Diese Flexibilität ist ein Gewinn für Studierende, die nicht an der Uni anwesend sein können – dass das wahrscheinlich diejenigen mit Kinderbetreuungs- und Visaproblemen, Mobilitäts- und Konzentrationsschwierigkeiten oder einem längeren Weg zur Uni sind, zeigt, was der Online-Unterricht zu einem inklusiveren Bildungswesen beizutragen vermag. Mit seinem unbegrenzten Zugang zu einem internationalen Reservoir an Vortragenden, die ein großes, unerwartetes Publikum erreichen können, ohne persönlich anwesend sein zu müssen, verfügt der Online-Unterricht zudem über eindeutige Vorteile für die Verbreitung von Ideen und die Demokratisierung des Wissenszugangs. Dank der enormen Menge des seit März 2020 aufgezeichneten Materials behalten viele Institutionen zum Teil asynchrone Formate bei („Diese Vorlesung ist asynchron – bitte sehen Sie sie sich vor dem Seminar/der Übung an"). In diesem wachsenden Online-Archiv steckt großes Potenzial, sofern es großzügig geteilt wird.

Aber vergessen wir nicht, dass die Tools, die wir verwenden, und der damit einhergehende technische Fortschritt immanent Teil eines destabilisierenden Prozesses ist: Der Online-Unterricht verlangt unablässig mehr und immer neue Technologien, speist selbsterhaltende Bedürfnisse, verschlingt weitere Ressourcen, von Rechenzentren bis zu seltenen Mineralien, menschliche wie materielle. Wir müssen auch bedenken, dass das geistige Online-Leben selbst eine Form von Sisyphus-Arbeit mit sich bringt: Ausbeutung ohne Zeitlimit, private Grenzen oder räumliche Beschränkung. ∎

*Übersetzung aus dem Englischen: Wilfried Prantner*

Dieser Beitrag ist eine modifizierte und aktualisierte Fassung eines Textes, der erstmals 2020 in Band 37 von *trans*, einer Publikationsreihe des Departement Architektur der ETH Zürich, erschien.

7  Nordin, Adam: „How Coronavirus Is Reshaping Classroom Learning", in: *BRIEFINGS newsletter of 17 March 2020* (2020), online unter: https://www.goldmansachs.com/insights/pages/from_briefings_17-mar-2020.html (Stand: 2. April 2020).

8  Stengers, Isabelle: *In Catastrophic Times: Resisting the Coming Barbarism*, Trans. Andrew Goffey, Lüneburg 2015, 8f (Übers. W.P.), online unter: http://openhumanitiespress.org/books/download/Stengers_2015_In-Catastrophic-Times.pdf (Stand: 25. Januar 2022).

9  Vgl. Jessop, Bob: „On Academic Capitalism", in: *Critical Policy Studies* 12,1 (2018).

10  Vgl. Zhu, Julie/Yang, Yingzhi/Jacob-Phillips, Sherry: „Chinese Online Tutor Zuoyebang Raises $750 Million in Fresh Round", *Reuters* (2020), online unter: https://www.reuters.com/article/us-zuoyebang-fundraiisng/chinese-online-tutor-zuoyebang-raises-750-million-in-fresh-round-idUSKBN240093 (Stand: 19. Juni 2020).

Christina Linortner

# Off Campus

## Architektur lernen
## jenseits der Institution

## Architecture Learning
## beyond the Institution

1   Driftwood Village Rebuilt Score, Experiments in Environment Workshop, Sea Ranch, CA, July 6th, 1968
© Lawrence Halprin Collection, The Architectural Archives, University of Pennsylvania

Bedeutet den Campus[1] zu verlassen, zugleich die hier verorteten Institutionen hinter sich zu lassen? Am Campus, dessen Begriff aus dem US-Amerikanischen stammt, wo er 1774 erstmals in Zusammenhang mit einem Universitätsgelände – jenem des College of New Jersey (heute Princeton University) – verwendet wurde, sollten Lehrende und Studierende sich, geografisch von der Stadt abgesondert und abseits aller Ablenkungen, voll und ganz aufeinander konzentrieren und ihren Studien widmen.[2] „Die romantische Vorstellung eines Colleges in der Natur, weit weg von den korrumpierenden Kräften der Stadt," argumentiert auch der US-amerikanische Kunsthistoriker und Architekt Paul Venable Turner, „wurde zu einem amerikanischen Ideal".[3] Waren in Europa die Universitäten traditionell in den Stadtzentren angesiedelt, wurde die Idee des Campus bei Neugründungen und Erweiterungen übernommen und die Gebäude rückten mehr und mehr an die Ränder der Städte. Heute wird der Begriff Campus aber auch für innerstädtische Bereiche verwendet, wo mehrere Gebäude – nicht nur im universitären Bereich – eine funktionale Einheit oder Zusammengehörigkeit bilden wollen und gemäß neoliberaler Logiken ein gewisser Anspruch an Distinktion und Abgeschlossenheit zum städtischen Umfeld suggeriert werden soll.[4]

Ob nun innerstädtisch oder an der Peripherie situiert, sind auch die Stätten der Architekturausbildung, deren eigentlicher Gegenstand ja die Stadt und die gebaute Umwelt darstellt, Teil dieser abgetrennten und institutionalisierten Einheiten auf ihrem jeweiligen Campus. In nur scheinbarem Widerspruch dazu bieten viele Architekturschulen Lehrformate an, die außerhalb ihrer Universitätsräumlichkeiten, bzw. des Campus veranstaltet werden. Auf diese Weise die Räumlichkeiten der Universität selber hinter sich zu lassen, hat in der Architekturausbildung einige Vorläufermodelle. Seit der Einführung von Architektur als akademischem Fach auf Universitäten war die traditionelle Studienreise, angelehnt an die Grand Tour wohl schon früh Bestandteil, man reiste im (Klassen)verband oder alleine und kehrte dann voller Eindrücke der antiken Stätten und mediterraner Renaissancearchitekturen in die gewohnten Lehrräumlichkeiten zurück. „Es gab einmal eine Zeit zwischen dem sechzehnten und neunzehnten Jahrhundert," wie Michael Meredith schreibt, „wo die Grand Tour die primäre Art war, Architektur zu studieren".[5] Waren es anfangs vor allem männliche Angehörige der englischen Aristokratie (mit der Ausnahme des Arbeiterkindes John Soane[6]), denen das Privileg der akademischen Reise vorbehalten war, setzte sich diese Lehr- und Lernmethode im Laufe der Jahrhunderte durch und wurde fixer Teil der Lehrpläne.[7] Darüber hinaus gibt es in der Architekturausbildung in einigen westeuropäischen Ländern wie der Schweiz oder Frankreich obligatorische Lehrzeit außerhalb der Universität – in Architekturbüros, wo die Studierenden für einige Monate Praktika in einem konkreten Arbeitsumfeld absolvieren. Dies steht in einer Tradition ostensiver Wissenskommunikation[8] wie etwa der früheren Meisterschule, wo die (meist männlichen) Studierenden die ihnen gestellten Aufgaben in den Ateliers und Studios ihrer (meist männlichen) Professoren erledigten und gleichzeitig zusätzliche Arbeitskräfte für die Architekturbüros der Professoren bildeten. Heute gibt es die sogenannten „Live-Projekte", die in der „realen Welt" stattfinden und sich mit „echten Aufgaben", im Austausch mit „echten AkteurInnen" beschäftigen. Die beliebtesten unter ihnen in westlichen Schulen sind wahrscheinlich Design-Build-Kurse, wo Projekte im Maßstab 1:1 umgesetzt werden, bei denen die Studierenden unter anderem auch in ein anderes Land – oft in den globalen Süden – reisen, um vor Ort sozial engagierte Projekte, wie Schulen oder Kindergärten, im Selbstbau umzusetzen.

War das physische Verlassen des Campus zu Studienzwecken also bereits früh ins Studium integriert, ging auch die Suche nach neuen Wegen in der Architektur und auch deren Ausbildung, gekoppelt mit weitreichenden sozialen Protesten und Kritik an bestehenden Institutionen, besonders in der zweiten Hälfte des 20. Jahrhunderts mit einem Anstieg an experimentellen Lehrformaten, außerhalb des Campus/der Universität einher. So fanden viele der in einem von Beatriz Colomina 2013 in einer Ausstellung in Lissabon gezeigtem Forschungsprojekt

1   Das Wort Campus („Feld") ist lateinischen Ursprungs und wurde erstmals für die Bezeichnung der unbebauten Fläche verwendet, die einst an die Nassau Hall des College of New Jersey (heute Princeton University) angrenzte und die die Universität vom Nachbarort trennte. Vgl. Turner, Paul Venable: *Campus: An American Planning Tradition*, Cambridge, MA 1987.

2   Vgl. ebd.

3   Ebd., 5 (Übers. C.L.).

4   Genannt seien hier die Hauptsitze vieler international agierender Konzerne oder Banken, wie Google oder Apple in Silicon Valley, der Erste Bank Campus oder der (vormals Bank-) Austria Campus in Wien.

5   Meredith, Michael: „Radical Inclusion! (A Survival Guide for Post-Architecture)", *Perspecta* 41 (2008), 13.

6   Vgl. Darley, Gillian: „Wonderful Thing: The Experience of the Grand Tour", *Perspecta* 41 (2008), 21.

7   So wurde beispielsweise die American Academy 1897 in Rom gegründet um dort US-amerikanische Studierenden das Studium des alten Roms zu ermöglichen. Vgl. Stierli, Martino: „In the Academy's Garden: Robert Venturi, the Grand Tour and the Revision of Modern Architecture", *AA Files* 56 (2007), 43.

8   Vgl. Schnier, Jörg: „Entwurfsziele und Unterrichtsziele von Vitruv bis zum Bauhaus", in: Ralph, Johannes (Hg.): *Entwerfen. Architektenausbildung in Europa von Vitruv bis Mitte des 20. Jahrhunderts*, Hamburg 2009, 87.

Does being off campus[1] always mean leaving behind the institutions localized here? On campus—a term originating in the United States, where it was first used in 1774 in the context of university grounds, at the College of New Jersey (today Princeton University)—teachers and students are meant to be able to fully concentrate on each other and their studies, geographically separated from the city and away from any distractions.[2] "The romantic notion of a college in nature, removed from the corrupting forces of the city," as the US art historian and architect Paul Venable Turner has argued, "became an American ideal."[3] Whereas in Europe universities were traditionally spread across the center of cities, the idea of the campus has now been adopted for newly established or expanded institutions, with the buildings moving more and more to the urban periphery. However, today the word campus is also used to denote centrally located areas where several buildings—not only university-related—are meant to form a functional unit or shared identity, with a suggestion of a claim to distinction and seclusiveness from the urban environment in accordance with logics of neoliberalism.[4]

Whether located in the city center or at the periphery, the sites of architectural education—its very object of course being the city and the built environment—are also a part of such separate and institutionalized units on their respective campus. In an approach that may seem contradictory, many architecture schools offer teaching formats that are carried out off the university premises or campus. The idea of leaving the spaces of the university behind in the context of architecture education is not entirely new. One such model likely in existence since architecture was first introduced as an academic subject at universities is the traditional study trip, modeled after the "grand tour"; students traveled in (class) groups or alone and then returned to the familiar university spaces full of impressions of ancient sites and Mediterranean Renaissance architecture. "Once upon a time, between the sixteenth and nineteenth centuries," writes Michael Meredith, "the Grand Tour was the primary model of studying architecture."[5] While in the beginning the privilege of academic travel was mainly reserved for men belonging to the aristocracy in England (though John Soane, a worker's son, proved to be an exception[6]), in recent centuries this method of teaching and learning has frequently become engrained in the curriculum.[7] What is more, architecture schools in several western European countries, such as Switzerland or France, have made it mandatory for students to spend time learning outside of the university setting—such as in architectural firms, where they do internships for several months in a specific working environment. This follows the tradition of ostensive communication of knowledge,[8] such as seen in early *Meisterschulen*, with the (usually male) students completing tasks given to them in the workshops and studios of their (usually male) professors, while simultaneously serving as extra labor for the professors' architectural firms. Today there are so-called "live projects" that take place in the "real world" and deal with "real tasks" in collaboration with "real protagonists." The most of such popular programs at schools in the West are probably the design-build courses, where projects are implemented at a 1:1 scale. In many cases, students travel to another country—often in the Global South—to carry out socially committed projects on site, such as schools or kindergardens.

While physically leaving the campus to learn elsewhere was an early part of university study, the search for new paths in architecture and related training—coupled with far-reaching social protests and criticism of existing institutions, especially in the second half of the twentieth century—also went hand in hand

1  The word campus (meaning "field") is of Latin origin and was first used to describe the undeveloped area once bordering Nassau Hall at the College of New Jersey (today Princeton University), separating the university from the neighboring town. See Paul Venable Turner, *Campus: An American Planning Tradition* (Cambridge, MA, 1987).

2  See ibid.

3  Ibid., 5.

4  Examples include the headquarters of many globally active corporations and banks, such as Google and Apple in Silicon Valley or the Erste Bank Campus and the (formerly Bank-) Austria Campus in Vienna.

5  Michael Meredith, "Radical Inclusion! (A Survival Guide for Post-Architecture)," *Perspecta* 41 (2008), 13.

6  See Gillian Darley, "Wonderful Thing: The Experience of the Grand Tour," *Perspecta* 41 (2008), 21.

7  For example, the American Academy was founded in 1897 in Rome in order to give US students the opportunity to study old Rome. See Martino Stierli, "In the Academy's Garden: Robert Venturi, the Grand Tour and the Revision of Modern Architecture," *AA Files* 56 (2007), 43.

8  See Jörg Schnier, "Entwurfsziele und Unterrichtsziele von Vitruv bis zum Bauhaus," in *Entwerfen: Architektenausbildung in Europa von Vitruv bis Mitte des 20. Jahrhunderts*, ed. Johannes Ralph (Hamburg, 2009), 87.

ausgewiesenen „radikalen Pädagogiken"[9] im Architekturbereich ebenso außerhalb konventioneller Lehrräumlichkeiten in Form unterschiedlicher Lehrformate statt, darunter beispielsweise die wegweisenden Seminare von Robert Venturi, Denise Scott Brown und Steven Izenour in Las Vegas (1968) und Levittown (1970) oder die Polyark Bus Tour (1973) von Cedric Price und Peter Murray.[10]

In Italien wurden „freie Schulen" gegründet, im Feld der Architektur beispielsweise „Global Tools" (1973), in Großbritannien entwickelte Colin Ward Anfang der 1970er-Jahre ein dezentralisiertes und informelles Modell der „explodierten Schule" von (Architektur)bildung im städtischen Kontext, das aus seiner anarchistischen Weltanschauung rührte. Ebendort schlug Cedric Price 1968 vor, „Einrichtungen des Lernens kontinuierlich verfügbar zu machen", sodass „Design nicht nur im Klassenraum, oder in der Bibliothek, sondern auch daheim, im Auto, Supermarkt oder in der Fabrik Berücksichtigung finde[t]".[11] So schlug Prices Nachfolgeprojekt seines „Fun Palace", einem als „university of the streets" angelegten Gebäude, nämlich das „Potteries Thinkbelt" Projekt (1964–1966) vor, einen Universitätscampus über einen ganzen Landstrich, genauer gesagt über ein ehemaliges Industriegelände in Staffordshire zu legen, damit Industrie und Bildungswesen voneinander profitieren könnten. Unterkünfte für Studierende sollten dabei in das lokale Wohnungsprogramm integriert und entlang eines bestehenden Bahn- und Straßensystems verteilt werden.[12] Die Idee, die Universität zu vergesellschaften und mit der lokalen Wirtschaft und soziopolitischen Struktur so zu verweben, dass aus dem Nebeneinander eine Einheit würde, subsummiert Price unter dem Begriff des „Civic Design": „Erst wenn das alles geklärt ist, stellt sich die Frage nach Civic Design. Das Thinkbelt-Wohnprogramm wird nicht nur etwas Externes sein, das erfolglos auf die Potteries aufgepfropft wird. Es wird ein Katalysator sein, etwas, das in seinen Maßnahmen von der Bildungsseite des Thinkbelt gestärkt wird. Die Menschen werden beginnen, eine noch größere Verbesserung ihres sozio-zivilen Umfelds zu fordern; und der unternehmerische Instinkt wird durch die Nachfrage geweckt. Die Wohnungen werden der umliegenden Gemeinde vielleicht schneller zugutekommen als selbst die Bildungsindustrie des Thinkbelt. Aber im Laufe der Zeit werden die gesamten Potteries revolutioniert werden. Brachliegendes Land wird wieder genutzt werden und die alten Schandflecke werden verschwinden. Es wird auch eine große nationale Industrie geben, um das zu ersetzen, was sie unweigerlich verlieren werden. Andere Bereiche könnten schließlich vom Beispiel dieses riesigen Experi-

ments lernen – was dem Land gleichzeitig Geld sparen und den Gewinn von Intellekt einbringen würde. Aus diesen Versuchen, StudentInnen und Gemeinschaft zu vereinen, statt sie zu trennen, folgt, dass Studentenstipendien im Thinkbelt keine Darlehen, sondern gleich Gehälter werden sollten. Wenn Menschen Jobs machen, die die Gesellschaft von ihnen verlangt, müssen sie dafür bezahlt werden."[13]

Während Prices Vorschlag auf dem Papier blieb, und sein radikaler Vorstoß, die Studierenden zu bezahlen, statt bezahlen zu lassen, als Kritik an den bestehenden Universitätsstrukturen zu verstehen ist, bildete sich 1973 in Italien durch den Zusammenschluss unterschiedlicher Gruppen und Einzelpersonen aus dem Umfeld der italienischen radikalen Architektur das heterogene Netzwerk „Global Tools", das seine Design-Laboratorien über das ganze Land verstreute. „Global Tools" entstand aus der Enttäuschung des Verhaltens der Studierendenbewegung der 1960er-Jahre zugunsten einer „Rückkehr zu einer konservativen Haltung"[14] aber auch aus einer Kritik an der „technisch-destruktiven Komponente der historischen Rolle von Avant-gardes",[15] die die sonst sehr heterogenen ProponentInnen der italienischen radikalen Architektur einte. Obwohl Bildung, bzw. Schule der gewählte Modus Operandi war, verwehrte man sich gegen herkömmliche pädagogische Modelle und schlug stattdessen einen Katalog für Möglichkeiten des Selbstlernens vor.[16] Der Austausch mit Mitgliedern der Arte Povera-Bewegung und aus der Konzeptkunst sollte „eine Bewegung vom Objekt hin zu Verhaltensweise und vice versa" forcieren, die „zu einem Beispiel einer neuen Art der Lehre

9 „Radical Pedagogies" im Rahmen der Architektur-Triennale in Lissabon, „Closer Closer", 12. September–15. Dezember, 2013. Vgl. dazu https://radical-pedagogies.com/search-cases/

10 Die Polyark Bus Tour war eine Zusammenarbeit zwischen dem *AD Journal* und Cedric Price. Ein konvertierter Doppeldeckerbus tourte von Architekturschule zu Architekturschule, um den Austausch zwischen britischen Architekturschulen zu forcieren und auch mit lokalen Gruppen in Kontakt zu kommen. Vgl. dazu https://radical-pedagogies.com/search-cases/e12-ad-aa-polyark/ (Stand: 20. Januar 2022).

11 Price, Cedric: „Lernen", in: Holert, Tom, et al. (Hg.): *Bildungsschock. Lernen, Politik Und Architektur in den 1960er und 1970er Jahren*, Berlin 2020, 213.

12 Vgl. Price, Cedric: „Potteries Thinkbelt", *New Society* 192 (1966), online unter: http://archive.discoversociety.org/wp-content/uploads/2014/06/Thinkbelt.pdf (Stand: 20. Jänner 2022).

13 Ebd. (Übers. C.L.)

14 Borgonuovo, Valerio/Franceschini, Silvia (Hg.): *Global Tools. When Education Coincides with Life, 1973–1975*, Rom 2018, 10.

15 Branzi, Andrea zitiert in Borgonuovo/Franceschini: *Global Tools* (wie Anm. 14).

16 Vgl. ebd., 15.

with an increase in experimental teaching formats taking place off campus or outside of the university. Many of the "radical pedagogies" in architecture, for instance those identified in a research project led by Beatriz Colomina and presented at a 2013 exhibition in Lisbon,[9] likewise took place outside of conventional educational settings, instead taking various teaching formats. Examples of this include the groundbreaking seminars by Robert Venturi, Denise Scott Brown, and Steven Izenour in Las Vegas (1968) and in Levittown (1970) and the Polyark Bus Tour (1973) by Cedric Price and Peter Murray.[10]

Italy saw the establishment of "free schools," for example Global Tools (1973) in the field of architecture, whereas in Great Britain Colin Ward developed a decentralized and informal "exploding school" model in the early 1970s focused on (architecture) education in an urban context, which stemmed from his anarchistic worldview. Also in the UK, Cedric Price suggested in 1968 that "the continuous availability of learning facilities requires design recognition not merely in the classroom or library, but in the home, the car, the supermarket and the factory."[11] Price's follow-up of the Fun Palace project thus conceived a building designed as a "university of the streets," namely, the Potteries Thinkbelt project (1964–66), a university campus across an entire swathe of land, that is, across a former industrial zone in Staffordshire, enabling industry and education to benefit from each other. Student housing was to be integrated into the local housing program and spread across an existing railway and road system.[12] Price uses the term "Civic Design" to sum up the idea of socializing universities and interweaving them with the local economy and sociopolitical structure so as to turn this state of coexistence into a whole: "It is only after all this has been established that any question of Civic Design will emerge. The Thinkbelt housing will not just be something external that is unsuccessfully grafted on to the Potteries. It will be a catalyst, encouraged in its action by the educational side of the Thinkbelt. People will begin to demand an even bigger improvement in their socio-civic environment; and the entrepreneurial instinct will be awakened by the demand. The housing will perhaps be of quicker benefit to the surrounding community than even the Thinkbelt's educational

industry. But, over time, the whole of the Potteries will be revolutionised. Not only will derelict land be used again, and the old eyesores go: there will also be a major national industry to replace what they will inevitably lose. Other areas could eventually learn from the example of this vast experiment—which would simultaneously save the country money and gain it brains. It follows from this attempt to unite, rather than separate, student and community that student grants in the Thinkbelt should become, not loans, but straightforward salaries. If people are doing a job society wants them to do, they must be paid for it."[13]

Whereas Price's proposal never made it past paper, and his radical push to pay students rather than have them pay must be considered critical of the existing university structures, in 1973 the heterogeneous network Global Tools was established in Italy, bringing together various groups and individuals from the context of radical Italian architecture, its design laboratories scattered all over the country. Global Tools arose from disappointment about the student moment of the 1960s fading away in favor of a "return to a conservative stance,"[14] but also from criticism of the "technical-destructive component of the historical role of avant-gardes,"[15] which united the otherwise very heterogeneous proponents of radical Italian architecture. Although education, or school-based learning, was the chosen

9 "Radical Pedagogies" at the Lisbon Triennale "Closer Closer," September 12–December 15, 2013. See https://radical-pedagogies.com/search-cases/.

10 The Polyark Bus Tour was a collaborative project by the AD Journal and Cedric Price. A converted double-decker bus toured various architecture schools with the aim of fostering dialogue among British architecture schools and reaching out to local groups. On this, see https://radical-pedagogies.com/search-cases/e12-ad-aa-polyark/ (accessed February 5, 2022).

11 Cedric Price, "Learning," AD – Architectural Design (1968), 242.

12 See Cedric Price, "Potteries Thinkbelt," New Society 192 (1966), http://archive.discoversociety.org/wp-content/uploads/2014/06/Thinkbelt.pdf (accessed February 5, 2022).

13 Ibid.

14 Valerio Borgonuovo and Silvia Franceschini, ed., Global Tools, 1973–1975 (Rome, 2018), 10.

15 Andrea Branzi quoted in Borgonuovo and Franceschini, Global Tools (see note 14).

# TRUCKIN' UNIVERSITY

EDUCATIONAL DIVISION OF SOUTHCOAST, INC.   A FULLY ACCREDITED LIFESTYLE INSTITUTION

## Mr. Goodbar sez:
(HE'S NOT SHITTIN' AROUND!)

### GET A GOOD AMERICAN EDUCATION

WHILE YOU STILL GOT A CHANCE!!

BEN HOLMES

—GET SET FOR THE FUTURE!!
—STEP UP TO GOOD PAY!!

| NO. | INPUT/TOOLS | PROCESS | OUTPUT |
|---|---|---|---|
| 27 | SCHOOL BUS MODIFIED FOR MOBILE EDUCATIONAL STIMULI AND LIFE SUPPORT VEHICLE FOR THE FACILITATORS/CREW.  | SEE CAPABILITY OBJECTIVE AND KEEP READING  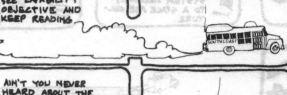 | |
| 14 | STAGE II MEDIA VAN WITH LATEST HIGH OUTPUT ACCESSORIES AND LIFE SUPPORT FACILITIES FOR CREW. | AIN'T YOU NEVER HEARD ABOUT THE SOUTHCOAST MYTH OR HOTFOOT OR ANYTHING? KEEP READING. 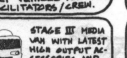 | |
| 5 | PORTABLE VIDEOTAPE CAMERA AND PORTABLE TAPE TRAP UNIT.  | SPECIAL EFFECTS DECK FOR EDITING, ALTERING, OR MONITERING VIDEO INPUT. VEHICLE 1.  | VIDEO BLOWUP PROJECTOR FOR LARGE SCALE DISPLAYS AND ENVIRONMENTAL SPECIAL EFFECTS.   |
| 10 | SUPER 8 AND 16 MM FILM CAMERAS FOR RESPONSE DOCUMENTATION.  | FACTORY FILM PROCESSING — EDITING AND SPLICING FACILITIES. VEHICLE 1.  | PROJECTORS AND VARIOUS SURFACES FOR PROJECTION... PLASTIC, PARACHUTES, BUILDINGS. 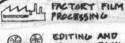  |
| 2 | 35 MM STILL CAMERA WITH COMPLETE SET OF LENS, FILTERS, AND ACCESSORIES.  | FACTORY COLOR FILM PROCESSING — MOBILE DARKROOM FACILITIES IN VEHICLE 1.    | SLIDE PROJECTORS MAY BE MODIFIED FOR HANDHELD PORTABILITY AND MAY BE PROJECTED ON A VARIETY OF SURFACES.  |
| 18 | LINEAR MEDIA MACHINES SUCH AS TYPEWRITERS AND DRAWING EQUIPMENT PLUS CREDIT CARD FOR LOCAL REPRODUCTION FACILITIES.  | ACCUMULATION AND ORGANIZATION OF MATERIAL FOR PRINTING. PUBLICATION PREPARATION FACILITIES TO BE IN VEHICLE 1.  | LINEAR MEDIA IS USEFUL AS HISTORICAL TESTIMONY OF A CHANGING REALITY. MAKES GOOD ASS WIPES TOO... TRY THIS ONE.   |
| 9 | PHONOGRAPH, AM/FM TUNER, TAPE RECORDERS, MICROPHONES, AMPLIFIER OUTPUTS FED INTO CENTRAL AUDIO CONTROL PANEL.  | CENTRAL AUDIO CONTROL PANEL SELECTS AND MODULATES OUTPUT FROM VARIOUS INPUTS.  | ASSORTMENT OF HIGH PERFORMANCE SPEAKER SYSTEMS FOR USE AS ENVIRONMENTAL MODULATORS.   |
| 35 | COMMUNICATION BETWEEN INDIVIDUALS IN DISRELATED SPECIALTY FIELDS  | ACCESS TO AND USE OF LOCALIZED, NON-MOBILE TECHNOLOGY AND RESOURCES.  | PROTOTYPICAL TECHNOLOGICAL AIDS TO ENVIRONMENTAL CONTROL, EDUCATION, CULTURE, ETC.   |

**12**

POLYETHYLENE, SILVER MYLAR, POLYTAPE, AND OTHER LARGE AREA FLEXIBLE MEMBRANES.

GROUP ENERGIES INVOLVED IN DESIGN AND EXECUTION OF PNEUMATIC ENVIRONMENTS. DISPOSABLE BUILDING SYSTEMS. CREATES A NEW INVOLVE/EVOLVE PROCESS IN STAGNANT EDUCATIONAL ENVIRONMENTS

SOUTHCOAST AIR FARCE

**76**

WOOD DOWELS, ALLOY CONDUIT, PLASTIC CONNECTIONS, RUBBER HOSE, AND OTHER COMMON INEXPENSIVE MATERIALS.

DEMONSTRATION AND EXPLANATION OF ENVIRONMENTAL STRUCTURAL SYSTEMS USING WHOLE EARTH TECHNOLOGY AND WHITE TRASH RESOURCES. GROUP INVOLVEMENT DURING ERECTION STIMULATES NEW APPLICATION OF STRUCTURAL SYSTEMS.

**6**

COMBINATION OF THE ABOVE TOOLS INTO A MOBILE THOUGHT PROCESS STIMULATION SYSTEM RELEVANT TO A SPACE AGE CULTURE.

CREATION OF ENVIRONMENTAL SENSORY OVERLOAD CONDITION WHEN PERSONAL INPUT SYSTEMS OVERLOAD PROCESSING SYSTEM (BRAIN) AND INADEQUACY OF CURRENT EDUCATIONAL/PROGRAMMING SYSTEM IS SHOWN. SEE ALSO: FREAKOUT, MIND FUCK, COSMIC TRUTH, ETC.

WOW!

**47**

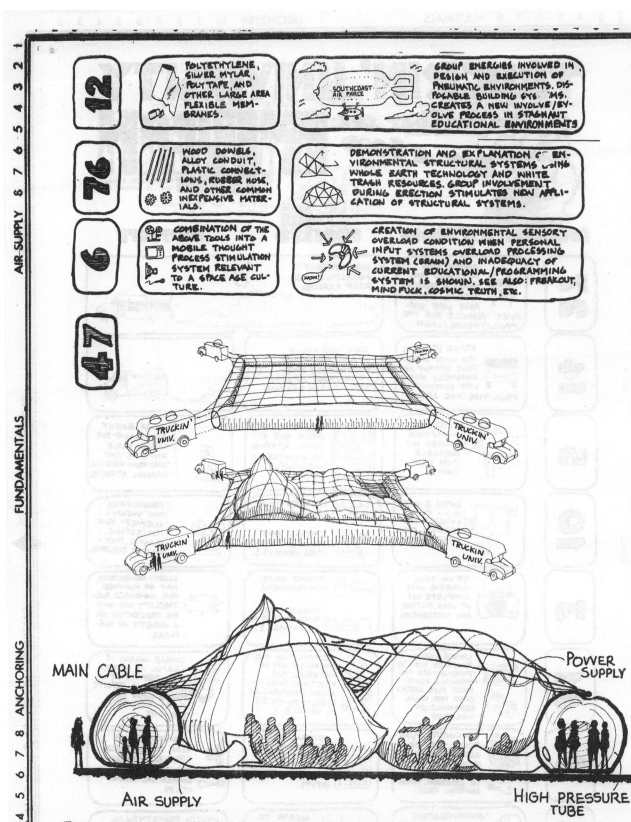

TRUCKIN' UNIV.

MAIN CABLE — POWER SUPPLY

AIR SUPPLY — HIGH PRESSURE TUBE

**Instant Site** capability, the whole paking down into four trucks. The tube provides air and access; the net when spread & tightened serves to windproof many lightweight inflatables, being built and changed according to the activities within. The main cable also provides electricity.

2 Truckin' University, Illustration aus der ersten Ausgabe von *Inflatocookbook* | Illustration from the first edition of *Inflatocookbook*, Ant Farm, 1970
© Courtesy of the University of California, Berkeley Art Museum and Pacific Film Archive

führt, in welcher die Strategien der Künste die Disziplin der Architektur um eine experimentelle, performative und konzeptuelle Dimension erweitern".[17]

In den USA schlug das Künstler- und Designerkollektiv Ant Farm die „Truckin University" (1970) vor, eine transportable, pneumatische Struktur, die sich auf vier Lastwägen von Ort zu Ort bewegen sollte, und von den jeweiligen Studierenden in einer gemeinschaftlichen Anstrengung erst errichtet werden musste (Abb. 2). Die Errichtung der Lernstruktur an unterschiedlichen Orten sollte durch verschiedene Kommunikationstechnologien und Medien dokumentiert und ergänzt werden. Kennengelernt und gegründet hatten sich Ant Farm 1968 bei einem der „Experiments in Environment"-Workshops[18], einer „alternativen Bildungsinitiative"[19] des Landschaftsarchitekten Lawrence Halprin und seiner Frau, der Tänzerin Anna Halprin, wobei interdisziplinäre und kollektive, sowie prozessorientierte Formen der Zusammenarbeit in nichtakademischen Settings in der Natur oder in Außenräumen entwickelt wurden (Abb. 1).

In Deutschland entstanden rund um die Protestbewegung von 1968 innerhalb der Universitäten eine Reihe von selbstorganisierten Initiativen, die aus politischen Motiven das damals vermittelte Berufsbild des Architekten bzw. der Architektin ablehnten und nach Verwissenschaftlichung und Interdisziplinarität verlangten.[20] Ein Beispiel dafür war die „Lehre ohne Professoren" an der Architekturfakultät Stuttgart, wo Studierende sich für eine Anpassung der Lehr- und Lernformen sowie deren Inhalte und Art der Vermittlung an zeitgemäße Ansprüche einsetzten und um mehr Autonomie, sowohl bei der Aufgabenstellung als auch bei der Gruppen- und Projektarbeit kämpften.[21]

Die Erweiterung des Architekturwissens hin zu anderen Disziplinen und die Forderung nach wissenschaftlichen Arbeitsweisen blieb ein reformistisches Unterfangen innerhalb bestehender Strukturen, dessen Umsetzung nur teilweise eingelöst wurde. Inwiefern selbst radikalere Bestrebungen wie die oben beschriebenen Gründungen eigener Initiativen es schafften, sich aus dem institutionellen Rahmen herauszubewegen, soll im Folgenden behandelt werden.

**Architekturschulen als Institution.** Die Universität gilt als „Ort der Unabhängigkeit und Freiheit, der Einheit von Forschung und Lehre und der uneingeschränkten Ausrichtung der Wissenschaft auf Wahrheit".[22] Die Universität ist aber auch eine Institution, ein Instrument zum Machtgewinn und Wahrung des Status quo, und gehört zu den von Foucault beschriebenen „Einschließungsräumen"[23], die maßgeblich für die Aufrechthaltung der disziplinierten Gesellschaft sind. Der institutionelle Rahmen manifestiert sich meistens in einer hierarchisch organisierten Struktur: Das Personal erfährt eine Unterscheidung zwischen wissenschaftlich und nicht-wissenschaftlich. Die Fächer werden nach dem Prinzip „one-to-many" von einem bzw. einer designierten Lehrenden an viele Lernende vermittelt. Ein festgelegter Lehrplan, an dessen Ende die Verleihung eines Zertifikats steht, konstituiert und verfestigt das ungleiche Verhältnis zwischen Lehrenden und Lernenden. Die Ressourcen,

17 Ebd., 11. Im Original: „A need was felt to move from object to behavior and vice versa, to preconfigure the example of a new manner of teaching in which the strategies of the arts would add an experimental, performative, and conceptual dimension to the discipline of architecture."

18 Anna Halprin gründete 1946 gemeinsam mit Welland Lathrop eine eigene Tanzschule in San Francisco, wo sie vom Bauhaus und den Ideen John Deweys inspirierte Workshops abhielt. Ab 1954 hielt sie gemeinsam mit ihrem Mann auf der Outdoor Tanzfläche in ihrem Haus in Kentfield, CA, Sommerkurse ab. Vgl. Scott, Hallie Rose: *Communicationists and Un-Artists: Pedagogical Experiments in California, 1966–1974*, Diss., The Graduate Center, City University of New York 2017, 81–85, online unter: https://academicworks.cuny.edu/gc_etds/2146 (Stand: 20. Januar 2022).

19 Ebd., 70.

20 Vgl. Gribat, Nina et al.: (Hg.): *Vergessene Schulen. Architekturlehre zwischen Reform und Revolte um 1968*, Leipzig 2017, 23.

21 Vgl. ebd., 9.

22 Horst, Johanna-Charlotte (Hg.): *Was ist Universität? Texte und Positionen zu einer Idee*, Zürich 2010, 7.

23 Dazu zählen lt. Foucault auch Institutionen wie Schule, Spital, Archiv und Gefängnis. Vgl. Foucault, Michel: *Überwachen und Strafen: Die Geburt des Gefängnisses*, Übers. Walter Seitter, Frankfurt am Main 1994.

modus operandi, they resisted conventional pedagogical models and instead proposed a catalog of self-learning opportunities.[16] Communication with members of the Arte Povera and Conceptual Art movements was meant to foster a "move from object to behavior and vice versa, to preconfigure the example of a new manner of teaching in which the strategies of the arts would add an experimental, performative, and conceptual dimension to the discipline of architecture."[17]

In the United States, the artist and design collective Ant Farm initiated the Truckin' University (1970), a transportable pneumatic structure designed to move from town to town on four trucks, and which would have to be erected by the involved students themselves in an act of mutual effort in order to be used (fig. 2). Erecting a structure for learning at different sites was meant to be documented and supplemented by various communication technologies and media. The members of Ant Farm met and established the collective in 1968 during an "Experiments in Environment" workshop,[18] an "alternative education initiative"[19] by the landscape architect Lawrence Halprin and his wife, the dancer Anna Halprin; they were developing interdisciplinary and collective forms of collaboration, as well as process-oriented ones, in nonacademic settings in nature or in outdoor spaces (fig. 1).

In Germany, around the time of the 1968 protest movement, a number of self-organized initiatives developed within universities which, for political reasons, rejected the occupational profile of the architect conveyed at the time and called for a more scientific and interdisciplinary approach.[20] An example of this was the "teaching without professors" idea at the architecture department in Stuttgart, where students wanted not only forms of teaching and learning, but also the related content and mode of delivery, to be adapted to contemporary requirements and

fought for more autonomy, both in terms of assignments and in group and project work.[21]

Expanding knowledge of architecture to include other disciplines and the call for scientific working approaches remained a reformist endeavor within existing structures, though its implementation was only realized in part. The extent to which quite radical efforts such as the self-founded projects described above succeeded in moving out of the institutional framework will be explored in the following.

**Architecture Schools as Institution.** Universities are considered to be a "place of independence and freedom, uniting research and teaching and science in its unreserved focus on truth."[22] Yet a university is also an institution, an instrument for gaining power and sustaining the status quo. It counts among the "spaces of enclosure" described by Foucault,[23] which are vital to maintaining disciplined society. The institutional framework usually manifests in a hierarchically

16  See ibid., 15.

17  Ibid., 11.

18  In 1946, Anna Halprin founded her own dance school with Welland Lathrop in San Francisco, where she held workshops inspired by the Bauhaus and the ideas of John Dewey. As of 1954, she and her husband held summer classes on an outdoor dance floor at their home in Kentfield, CA. See Hallie Rose Scott, "Communicationists and Un-Artists: Pedagogical Experiments in California, 1966–1974" (PhD diss., The Graduate Center, City University of New York, 2017), 81–85, available online at: https://academicworks.cuny.edu/gc_etds/2146 (accessed February 7, 2022).

19  Ibid., 70.

20  See Nina Gribat et al., eds., *Vergessene Schulen: Architekturlehre zwischen Reform und Revolte um 1968* (Leipzig, 2017), 23.

21  See ibid., 9.

22  Johanna-Charlotte Horst, ed., *Was ist Universität? Texte und Positionen zu einer Idee* (Zurich, 2010), 7.

23  Foucault also uses this term to describe institutions like schools, hospitals, archives, and prisons. See Michel Foucault, *Discipline and Punish: The Birth of the Prison*, trans. Alan Sheridan (1977; repr., New York, 1995).

dazu zählen Personal, Finanzen, Wissen und räumliche Gegebenheiten, sind im Besitz der Institution[24] und werden von ihr gemäß eines bestimmten Budgets verwaltet. Es kann erforderlich sein, dass Studierende vor dem Eintritt ins Studium Gebühren zahlen oder eine Zulassungsprüfung bestehen müssen. Nach Aufnahme des Studiums beginnt eine Reihe von Prüfungen; ein „pausenlos funktionierender Prüfungsapparat"[25] etabliert eine Machttechnik, die „qualifiziert, klassifiziert und bestraft".[26]

Der Unterricht findet meist in zugewiesenen Räumen innerhalb einer Universität oder Schule statt, die nach den Normen und Vorschriften gestaltet sind, die zum Zeitpunkt ihrer Erbauung am jeweiligen Ort galten und den gegebenen wirtschaftlichen Rahmenbedingungen entsprachen. Es ist davon auszugehen, dass die physischen universitären Räume – wie auch im Schulbau üblich – Teil nicht sichtbarer, aber dennoch wirksamer Kräfte sind: Es „ist ein Hidden Curriculum auch in das Schulhaus selber eingebaut, beziehungsweise ist seine Architektur Teil oder Mittel zur Durchsetzung eines nicht immer ausdrücklich artikulierten, aber trotzdem nicht minder wirksamen Lehrplans".[27] Dieser „geheime Lehrplan"[28] wurde vor allem im schulischen Bereich erforscht und bewirkt demnach, dass Kinder „akzeptiertes Verhalten, soziale Regeln und den Umgang mit Wissen lernen" und weiter, „welche Normen, Werte und Einstellungen durch alltägliche Praktiken, Rituale und Schulkulturen erworben werden".[29] Die architektonische Ordnung und Ausgestaltung der schulischen Räume, aber auch die von für Aulas, Seminarräumen oder Hörsälen mit ihrer spezifischen Anordnung der Möblierung „schafft so eine Wirklichkeit, die von den Beteiligten als natürlich empfunden wird, und stabilisiert so eine Form des Bewusstseins, die den bestehenden gesellschaftlichen Verhältnissen affirmativ gegenübersteht".[30]

Während lange Zeit das Wissen über Bauen und Wohnen von HandwerkerInnen oder Laien von Generation zu Generation weitergegeben wurde, ist Architekturausbildung heute Teil eines starren institutionalisierten Rahmens, der das durchsetzt, was Foucault als „Technologien der Gouvernementalität"[31] definierte. Während Foucault in seiner Arbeit Schulen und Universitäten als Teil eines breiteren Disziplinierungsapparates einordnete, identifizierte er den politischen Bedeutungswandel der Architektur im späten 18. Jahrhundert, wo „sich […] eine Reflexion über Architektur im Blick auf Ziele und Techniken der Regierung von Gesellschaften entwickelt".[32] Diese fundamentale Aufwertung der Bedeutung von architektonischem Entwurf und Planung besaß den institutionellen Effekt, dass zur Zeit der Französischen Revolution eine Trennung zwischen universitärer Architektur- und Ingenieursausbildung vollzogen wurde,[33] wobei die neue Struktur der Architekturlehre an der Pariser École Polytechnique ab dem Jahre 1794 auch neue Lehrmethoden etablierte, die auf den gesellschaftlichen Bedeutungszuwachs überraschenderweise mit zunehmender Formalisierung ihres Ausdrucks reagierten und in Jean-Nicolas-Louis Durand ihren wichtigsten Protagonisten fanden.

In einer Gegenbewegung zum Formalismus Durands ist das Wissen des Fachbereichs der Architektur inzwischen in Abschnitte unterteilt. Die Werkzeuge und Fähigkeiten, die dafür nötig sind, um zukünftige Design-„Probleme" zu verstehen und zu lösen, werden in verschiedenen Formaten wie zum Beispiel Entwurfsübungen, klassischen Vorlesungen oder Seminaren vermittelt. Meistens bleiben die Projekte auf einer fiktiven

24 Durch die zunehmende Neoliberalisierung des Bildungssystems in den vergangenen Jahrzehnten müssen heute viele Universitäten ihre Lehrräumlichkeiten von Holdings o.ä. dritten BesitzerInnen anmieten.

25 Foucault: Überwachen und Strafen (wie Anm. 23), 240.

26 Ebd., 238.

27 Hnilica, Sonja: Disziplinierte Körper die Schulbank als Erziehungsapparat, Wien 2003, 114.

28 Der Begriff „geheimer Lehrplan" oder „Hidden Curriculum" wurde, wie von Michael Brandmayr beschrieben, von mehreren Seiten aufgrund seiner vereinfachenden Sichtweise kritisiert. Brandmayr definierte ihn 2015 wie folgt: „Der Begriff Hidden Curriculum kann als das konkrete Ensemble von Normen, Werten und Einstellungen verstanden werden, das in der Schule durch institutionelle Arrangements, Mechanismen und Abläufe in täglicher Routine vermittelt wird. Diese Vermittlung geschieht nicht heimlich, vielmehr ‚versteckt' sich das Hidden Curriculum offen vor aller Augen in der Alltäglichkeit der schulischen Praxis, wo es SchülerInnen als ‚ganz normale' Wirklichkeit begegnet. Die Schule erzeugt so ein Passungsgefüge zwischen dem Individuum und der Gesellschaft, indem es SchülerInnen zur Anpassung an die Norm, an das Normale zwingt, integriert es sie und bewirkt die Übernahme gesellschaftlich hegemonialer Einstellungen." Brandmayr, Michael: „Die verborgenen Mechanismen politischer Bildung: Zum Verhältnis von Struktur und Inhalt am Beispiel des Basiskonzepts Macht", Momentum Quarterly. Zeitschrift für sozialen Fortschritt 4 (2015), 151.

29 Ebd., 148.

30 Ebd.

31 Foucault, Michel: „The Ethics of the Concern for Self as a Practice of Freedom", in: Lothringer, Sylvere (Hg.): Foucault Live: Collected Interviews, 1961–1984, New York 1996, 447. (Übers. C.L.)

32 Foucault, Michel/Rabinow, Paul: „Space, Knowledge, Power", in: Lothringer, Sylvere: Foucault Live. Collected Interviews, 1961–1984, New York 1996, 335.

33 Vgl. Picon, Antoine: French Architects and Engineers in the Age of Enlightenment, Cambridge, MA, 1992.

organized structure: a distinction is made between academic and nonacademic staff. Subjects are taught by a designated teacher to many learners at once according to the "one-to-many" principle. A defined curriculum that concludes with the awarding of a certificate constitutes and solidifies the unequal relationship between teachers and learners. Resources such as personnel, finances, knowledge, and spatial facilities belong to the institution[24] and are managed by it according to a certain administrative budget. Students may be required to pay fees or pass an admissions exam before entering the study program. After studies begin, a series of exams ensues; "a sort of apparatus of uninterrupted examination"[25] establishes a technology of power "to qualify, to classify and to punish."[26]

Classes are usually held in designated rooms within a university or school, designed according to the norms and specifications that were in effect at the time the buildings were erected at the respective place and to the given economic parameters. It can be assumed that the physical university spaces—as is common in school settings—are part of invisible but still certainly operative forces: there is "a hidden curriculum also built into the school building itself, that is, its architecture is a part of (or a means of) enforcing a curriculum that is not always explicitly articulated but is certainly effective all the same."[27] This "hidden curriculum"[28] has been researched primarily in the school setting and is accordingly said to cause children to "learn accepted behavior, social rules, and how to deal with knowledge" and, further, "what norms, values, and attitudes are acquired through everyday practices, rituals, and school cultures."[29] The architectural order and configuration of the school spaces, but also that of auditoriums, seminar rooms, and lecture halls, with their specific arrangement of furniture "creates a reality that is perceived as natural by those involved, thus stabilizing a form of consciousness that is affirmatively opposed to existing social conditions."[30]

Whereas knowledge about building and housing was long passed down from generation to generation by craftspeople or

laymen, architectural education today is part of a rigid institutionalized framework that enforces what Foucault defined as "technologies of government."[31] In his work, Foucault classified schools and universities as part of a broader disciplinary dispositif, yet he placed architecture's political shift in meaning in the late eighteenth century, noting that "in the 18th century one sees the development of reflection upon architecture as a function of the aims and techniques of the government of societies."[32] This fundamental revaluation of the importance of architectural design and planning had the institutional effect that, at the time of the French Revolution, a differentiation was made in university education between architecture and engineering.[33] In fact, as of 1794, the new structure of architecture education at the École Polytechnique in Paris established new teaching methods, which, surprisingly, responded to increasing importance in society by striving for a higher formalization of expression, with Jean-Nicolas-Louis Durand as its most important protagonist.

24 Due to the increasing neoliberalization of the education system in recent decades, today many universities need to rent their teaching facilities from holding companies or similar third-party owners.

25 Foucault, *Discipline and Punish* (see note 23), 186.

26 Ibid., 184.

27 Sonja Hnilica, *Disziplinierte Körper die Schulbank als Erziehungsapparat* (Vienna, 2003), 114.

28 Michael Brandmayr details how the term "hidden curriculum" has been criticized on several fronts due to its simplified viewpoint. Brandmayr defined it in 2015 as follows: "The term hidden curriculum can be seen as a specific ensemble of norms, values, and attitudes that are mediated in schools through institutional arrangements, mechanisms, and processes as part of daily routines. This mediation does not take place secretly; rather, the hidden curriculum 'hides' openly, in plain sight, in everyday school practice, where students encounter it as a 'completely normal' reality. Schools thus create a structure for fitting the individual into society, by obliging students to conform to the norm, to the normal; it integrates them and ensures that they adopt socially hegemonic attitudes." Michael Brandmayr, "Die verborgenen Mechanismen politischer Bildung: Zum Verhältnis von Struktur und Inhalt am Beispiel des Basiskonzepts Macht," *Momentum Quarterly: Zeitschrift für sozialen Fortschritt* 4 (2015), 151.

29 Ibid., 148.

30 Ibid.

31 Michel Foucault, "The Ethics of the Concern for Self as a Practice of Freedom," in *Foucault Live: Collected Interviews, 1961–1984*, ed. Sylvere Lothringer (New York, 1996), 447.

32 Michel Foucault and Paul Rabinow, "Space, Knowledge and Power," in *Foucault Live: Collected Interviews, 1961–1984*, ed. Sylvere Lothringer (New York, 1996), 335.

33 See Antoine Picon, *French Architects and Engineers in the Age of Enlightenment* (Cambridge, MA, 1992).

Ebene. Auch der Zeitaufwand von Studierenden und Lehrenden ist budgetiert und damit begrenzt. Die erworbenen Fähigkeiten reichen von künstlerischen Zeichnungen, Planerstellung, Kontext- und Materialanalysen, 3D-Modellierung bis hin zu technologischen Kenntnissen der Baukonstruktion sowie sozialer, theoretischer und historischer Beziehungen der gebauten Umwelt.

Erst seit den 1990er-Jahren werden (in Österreich) schon lange gestellte Forderungen nach Gleichstellung und Diskriminierung in den Lehrinhalten und auch in den Universitätsstrukturen hinterfragt und teilweise versucht einzulösen. Andrea Fraser bezeichnete eine durch „Selbstbefragung und Selbstreflexion" geschaffene Form der Institution als „kritische Institution".[34] Die Frage, ob es die Möglichkeit gibt, außerhalb der Institution zu stehen, verneint sie: „Institutionskritik handelt letztendlich nicht primär von den Intentionalitäten und Identitäten von Subjekten, sondern von der Politik und den Einschreibungen von Institutionen (und daher auch davon, wie Subjekte immer schon von den Fäden spezifischer und spezifizierbarer institutioneller Räume durchzogen sind)."[35]

So ließe sich auch die Frage, wie eine Bewegung der Architekturausbildung jenseits der Institution überhaupt stattfinden kann, beantworten. Verlässt die Architekturausbildung die ihr zugewiesenen Räumlichkeiten und bewegt sich in die sie umgebende gebaute Umwelt, die gleichzeitig auch Gegenstand ihrer Ausbildung ist, verlässt sie dadurch in den seltensten Fällen die Institution, es sei denn, sie ließe auch Zeitregimes, hierarchische Gefälle, oder die Unterscheidung von bezahlten und (unbezahlten bzw. zahlenden) TeilnehmerInnen hinter sich. Foucault definiert die Ausweitung der Disziplinarmechanismen wie folgt: „Während sich Dizilinarinstitutionen vervielfältigen, tendieren ihre Mechanismen dazu, sich über die Institutionen auszuweiten, sich zu ‚desinstitutionalisieren', ihre geschlossenen Festungen zu verlassen und ‚frei' zu wirken. Die massiven und kompakten Disziplinen lockern sich zu weichen, geschmeidigen, anpassungsfähigen Kontrollverfahren auf."[36] Nimmt man die kritische Selbstbefragung und Selbstreflexion von Andrea Fraser auf und führt die Frage nach dem Jenseits der Institution weiter, müsste der inzwischen in unterschiedlichsten Zusammenhängen sehr gebräuchliche Begriff der „Umwelt" (oder im Englischen „environment"[37]) in seinen Verbindungen mit Formaten in der Architekturlehre, die sich in einem so (un)definierten Raum bewegen, genauer ergründet werden. Besonders in Zeiten, wo der Ausnahmezustand der Pandemie die Räume – sei es der Campus oder sei es die Stadt – mit virtuellen Environments mehr denn je überlagert. ∎

34 Eine solche kritische Selbstreflexion stellt die Publikation *A Second Modernism*, herausgegeben von Arindam Dutta, dar. Als Aufsatzsammlung beleuchtet sie die Verschränkungen von Lehrinhalten mit industriellen AkteurInnen am Design Department des MIT in den Nachkriegsjahren und offenbart die engen Verflechtungen zwischen Regierungsprogrammen, GeldgeberInnen und Forschung sowie neuen Entwicklungen in der Architektur(ausbildung). Vgl. Dutta, Arindam (Hg.): *A Second Modernism: MIT, Architecture, and the „Techno-Social" Moment*, Cambridge, MA 2013.

35 Sheikh, Simon: „Notizen Zur Institutionskritik" (2006), online unter: https://transversal.at/transversal/0106/sheikh/de (Stand: 20. Januar 2022).

36 Foucault: *Überwachen und Strafen* (wie Anm. 23), 271.

37 Wie Florian Sprenger in seiner Ausführung zeigt, ist der Begriff des *environment* in seinem englischsprachigen Gebrauch selbstverständlich geworden und weit von seiner ursprünglichen Bedeutung aus der Evolutionsbiologie des 19. Jahrhunderts abgedriftet. Environment ist als ein offener und mehrdeutiger Begriff im allgemeinen Sprachgebrauch, der eine Vielzahl von Faktoren und deren Verhältnis zu einem Organismus, beispielsweise auch einem menschlichen Subjekt, auf einen Nenner bringt. „Als Selbstverständlichkeit bleibt der Begriff, der besonders seit den 1960er-Jahren die Grenzen der Ökologie hinter sich gelassen und bereits früh in die Bereiche der Stadtplanung, der Architektur, der Systemtheorie oder der Kunst übergegangen ist, dabei aber zumeist im Hintergrund. Er wird nicht eigens reflektiert oder auf seinen Einsatz befragt. Gerade wenn ein Begriff eine solch exkludierende Macht erlangt und zugleich selbstverständlich wird, gilt es, ihn zu hinterfragen und jene Geschichten zu schreiben, die ihn zum Maßstab für Zeitgemäßheit machen." Sprenger, Florian: „Zwischen Umwelt und Milieu. Zur Begriffsgeschichte von Environment in der Evolutionstheorie", *Forum Interdisziplinäre Begriffsgeschichte* 3, 2 (2014), 9. Vgl. dazu ausführlich: Sprenger, Florian: *Epistemologien des Umgebens. Zur Geschichte, Ökologie und Biopolitik künstlicher Environments*, Bielefeld 2019.

In a movement running counter to Durand's formalism, knowledge from the field of architecture is meanwhile subdivided into sections. The tools and skills necessary for understanding and solving future design "problems" are imparted through various formats, such as design exercises, conventional lectures, or seminars. The projects usually remain on a fictitious level. Also, the time invested by students and teachers is budgeted and thus limited. The skills acquired range from artistic drawing, development of plans, analysis of contexts and materials, and 3D modeling to technology-related knowledge of building construction, as well as social, theoretical, and historical relations to the built environment.

It has only been since the 1990s that attempts have been made (in Austria) to challenge discrimination and to respond to long-existing demands for equality in terms of teaching content and also university structures. Andrea Fraser has used the term "critical institution" to describe institutions created through self-questioning and self-reflection.[34] She responds in the negative to the question of whether it is possible to stand outside the institution: "Institutional critique is, after all, not primarily about the intentionalities and identities of subjects, but rather about the politics and inscriptions of institutions (and, thus, about how subjects are always already threaded through specific and specifiable institutional spaces)."[35]

This would also answer the question of how an architecture education movement can even take place at all beyond the institution. When architecture education leaves its assigned spaces and moves into its surrounding built environment, which is simultaneously the subject being studied, it rarely actually leaves the institution, unless it were to leave behind temporal regimes, hierarchical gradients, and the distinction between paid and (unpaid or paying) actants. Foucault defines the broadening of disciplinary mechanisms as follows: "While, on the one hand, the disciplinary establishments increase, their mechanisms have a certain tendency to become 'de-institutionalized,' to emerge from the closed fortresses in which they once functioned and to circulate in a 'free' state; the massive, compact disciplines are broken down into flexible methods of control, which may be transferred and adapted."[36] By taking up Andrea Fraser's critical self-questioning and self-reflection and applying it to the realm beyond the institution, the term "environment,"[37] which is now used in such a wide variety of contexts, would need to be explored in more detail, especially in terms of its relation to approaches to teaching architecture set in such a (un)defined space. This holds especially true in times where the pandemic state of emergency causes physical space—be it a campus or a city—to overlap more than ever with virtual environments. ∎

*Translation from German: Dawn Michelle d'Atri*

34  Such critical self-reflection is evident in the publication *A Second Modernism*, edited by Arindam Dutta. This collection of essays sheds light on the intervolving of teaching content and industrial parties at MIT's design department during the postwar years. It reveals the close interconnections between government programs, funders, and research, as well as new developments in architecture (education). See Arindam Dutta, ed., *A Second Modernism: MIT, Architecture, and the "Techno-Social" Moment* (Cambridge, MA, 2013).

35  Simon Sheikh, "Notes on Institutional Critique," *transversal texts*, January 2006, available online at: https://transversal.at/transversal/0106/sheikh/en.

36  Foucault, *Discipline and Punish* (see note 23), 211.

37  As Florian Sprenger shows in his explanation, the concept of environment has come to be taken for granted in its English-language usage, having drifted far from its original meaning derived from nineteenth-century evolutionary biology. "Environment" has come into common use as an open-ended and equivocal term denoting a multitude of factors and their relationship to an organism, including, for example, a human subject. "It is a given that the concept [of environment], which, especially since the 1960s, left the confines ecology behind in favor of, quite early on, the fields of urban planning, architecture, systems theory, or art, remains mostly in the background. It is not specifically examined or its use questioned. It is precisely when a term acquires such exclusionary power, while at the same time becoming self-evident, that it is important to call it into question and tell the stories of what made it the yardstick of contemporary relevance." Florian Sprenger, "Zwischen Umwelt und Milieu: Zur Begriffsgeschichte von Environment in der Evolutionstheorie," *Forum Interdisziplinäre Begriffsgeschichte* 3, no. 2 (2014), 9. For a more extensive analysis, see: Florian Sprenger, *Epistemologien des Umgebens: Zur Geschichte, Ökologie und Biopolitik künstlicher Environments* (Bielefeld, 2019).

Federica Doglio | Sol Perez-Martinez |
Nicolas Moucheront | Adam Wood

# Challenging Institutional Boundaries in the Works of Giancarlo De Carlo, Colin Ward, Shadrach Woods

## A Conversation

# Die Ausweitung institutioneller Grenzen im Werk von Giancarlo De Carlo, Colin Ward, Shadrach Woods

## Ein Gespräch

1 Giancarlo De Carlo and Shadrach Woods were among the contributors of *Harvard Educational Review* "Architecture and Education" |
Giancarlo De Carlo und Shadrach Woods verfassten Beiträge für die „Architecture and Education" Ausgabe des *Harvard Educational Review*, 1969
© Canadian Centre for Architecture

The following conversation was recorded on June 17, 2021 between four researchers whose archive and site-based work on the architects Giancarlo De Carlo (Italy, 1919–2005), Shadrach Woods (US/France, 1923–1973) and Colin Ward (UK, 1924–2010) investigates previous attempts at moving architecture and education beyond institutional boundaries. Adam Wood (AW), chairing the discussion, is an independent education researcher who explores how physical space is used to shape schooling. Federica Doglio (FD) is an architect based in Milan who in her PhD investigated Shadrach Wood's urban design theory in relation to his experiments in architectural education. Sol Perez-Martinez (SPM) is an architect and researcher who studied Colin Ward's environment-based pedagogical approach as part of her PhD. Finally, Nicolas Moucheront's (NM) interest for Giancarlo De Carlo's 1970s ILAUD initiative which brought together students, architects, and academics from different international universities to investigate real sites in Italy, brought him to Venice where he is currently finishing a PhD in History of Architecture.

AW: Federica, in your PhD you investigated Shadrach Woods' work and his role not only as a theoretician, but also proposing an interdisciplinary model of university education. What do you find exciting about his work?

FD: Shadrach Woods literally knocked at the door of 35 Rue de Sèvres in Paris, Le Corbusier's atelier, because he was committed to rebuild Europe from the ashes of World War II. Then, in 1948, he was sent to an experimental construction site in Marseille with Georges Candilis: the Unité d'Habitation. This inclination towards experimentation with different disciplines was fundamental in his approach; a very well-known example is The Free University in Berlin, his masterpiece, built in 1963 with the German architect Manfred Schiedhelm. Later defined as a "mat-building"[1] or a "groundscraper,"[2] and described by historian Stanley Abercrombie as one of the most radical "architectures" of the last century,[3] The Free University of Berlin might be read as Woods' manifesto, an architecture that reflects the oneness of the school, the process of integration within the city, the flexibility of spaces and ideas.

During the last decade of his life, Woods developed what he called "the architecture of education," through which he sought to reformulate ideas on how universities should function and how they should be designed.[4] He was also a core member of Team 10, an international group of architects developing from CIAMs, and partner in the firm Candilis-Josic-Woods based in Paris.[5] During the period in which Woods was active in Paris, the student revolts of the late 1960s and early 1970s profoundly altered society's political and cultural attitudes, and Woods' experimentation was important in this context too: in 1966, together with the Fluxus artist Robert Filliou, he theorized the so-called "Non-École (Non-School) de Villefranche," an experiment in the field of education, a situation for learning, but one outside traditional ideas of institutions. So, this conversation is certainly exciting for me.

AW: There is a sense of movement and how moving is important for both experimentation and architectural education, perhaps to counter some of the static, solidifying aspects of (overly) organized education. Sol, could you tell us a little about Colin Ward and his importance for architecture and education?

SPM: Colin Ward was a writer, educator, architectural draughtsman and a fully-fledged anarchist, most commonly known for his 1978 book *The Child in the City*.[6] Ward was interested in the relation between people and the places where they live. He published extensively about housing and schools, but also researched about transport, water provision, and green politics. I consider Ward an intriguing figure in British architecture because although he was regularly involved in architectural events and architecture schools, he is rarely mentioned in architectural

1   Alison Smithson, "How to Read and Recognize Mat-Building. Mainstream Architecture as It Has Developed towards a Mat-Building," *Architectural Design* 9 (1974): 573–590.

2   Manfred Schiedhelm, "Berlin Free University," *Architectural Design* 1 (1974): 14–17.

3   See Stanley Abercrombie, "Berlin Free University," *Architecture Plus* 1 (1974): 32–45.

4   See Shadrach Woods, "The Education Bazaar," *Harvard Educational Review, Architecture and Education* 4 (1969): 116–125.

5   Candilis-Josic-Woods was a successful partnership of architects (the Greek Georges Candilis, the Yugoslavian Alexis Josic, the American Shadrach Woods), founded in Paris in 1955, and mainly active until 1969 in the European scene of the reconstruction after the Second World War.

6   Colin Ward, *The Child in the City* (London, 1978).

Das folgende am 17. Juni 2021 aufgezeichnete Gespräch fand zwischen vier ForscherInnen statt, die sich in ihrer Archivforschung und ihren ortsbezogenen Studien zu den Architekten Giancarlo De Carlo (Italien, 1919–2005), Shadrach Woods (US/Frankreich, 1923–1973) und Colin Ward (UK, 1924–2010) mit früheren Versuchen auseinandersetzen, die institutionellen Grenzen von Architektur und Bildung auszuweiten. Adam Wood (AW), der die Diskussion leitete, ist ein unabhängiger Bildungswissenschaftler, der erforscht, wie physischer Raum zur Gestaltung schulischer Prozesse herangezogen wird. Federica Doglio (FD) ist eine in Mailand lebende Architektin, die sich in ihrer Dissertation mit dem Verhältnis zwischen Shadrach Woods Städtebautheorie und seinen Experimenten zur Architekturausbildung beschäftigte. Sol Perez-Martinez (SPM) ist Architektin und Wissenschaftlerin, die im Rahmen ihrer Dissertation Studien zu Colin Wards umweltbasierten pädagogischen Ansatz durchgeführt hat. Und Nicolas Moucheront (NM) führte sein Interesse für das von Giancarlo De Carlos in den 1970er-Jahren gegründete ILAUD, bei dem Studierende, ArchitektInnen und AkademikerInnen von verschiedenen internationalen Universitäten in Italien zu realen Räumen forschten, nach Venedig, wo er gegenwärtig seine Dissertation in Architekturgeschichte fertig schreibt.

**AW:** Federica, in deiner Dissertation hast du nicht nur Shadrach Woods' Werk und seine Rolle als Theoretiker untersucht, sondern auch seine Vorschläge zu einem interdisziplinären universitären Bildungsmodell. Was fasziniert dich an Woods' Werk?

**FD:** Shadrach Woods klopfte buchstäblich an die Tür von Le Corbusiers Atelier in der Rue de Sèvres in Paris, weil er sich der Aufgabe verpflichtet sah, Europa aus den Trümmern des Zweiten Weltkriegs neu aufzubauen. Damals, 1948, wurde er zusammen mit Georges Candilis an eine experimentelle Baustelle in Marseille geschickt: die Unité d'Habitation. Diese Neigung zum Experimentieren mit verschiedenen Disziplinen war für seinen Ansatz von grundlegender Bedeutung; ein sehr bekanntes Beispiel dafür ist die Freie Universität Berlin, sein 1963 zusammen mit dem deutschen Architekten Manfred Schiedhelm erbautes Meisterwerk. Die später als „mat-building" (Mattenbau)[1] oder „groundscraper" (Bodenkratzer)[2] definierte und vom Historiker Stanley Abercrombie als eine der radikalsten „Architekturen" des letzten Jahrhunderts[3] beschriebene Freie Universität Berlin könnte als Woods' Manifest betrachtet werden, ein Bauwerk, das die Einheit der Schule, den Integrationsprozess mit der Stadt und die Flexibilität von Räumen und Ideen widerspiegelt.

In seinem letzten Lebensjahrzehnt arbeitete Woods an einer „architecture of education" (Architektur der Bildung), wie er sie nannte, dem Versuch einer Neuformulierung seiner Ideen zur Funktion und Gestaltung von Universitäten.[4] Er gehörte auch zum Kern des Team 10, einer aus den CIAMs hervorgegangenen internationalen Architektengruppe und war Partner des in Paris ansässigen Büros Candilis-Josic-Woods.[5] Während der Zeit seiner Tätigkeit in Paris veränderten die Studierendenrevolten der späten 1960er- und frühen 1970er-Jahre von Grund auf die politischen und kulturellen Einstellungen der Gesellschaft, und auch daran nahm Woods' experimentierend Anteil: 1966 ersann er zusammen mit dem Fluxus-Künstler Robert Filliou die sogenannte „Non-École (Nicht-Schule) de Villefranche", ein jenseits traditioneller Institutionsvorstellungen angesiedeltes Bildungsexperiment, eine Lernsituation. Dieses Gespräch ist also sehr spannend für mich.

**AW:** Es gibt dabei auch einen Sinn für Beweglichkeit und deren Bedeutung für Experimente und die Architekturausbildung, wohl um den statischen, verfestigenden Aspekten von (übermäßig) organisierter Bildung entgegenzuwirken. Sol, könntest du uns etwas über Colin Ward und seine Bedeutung für das Thema Architektur und Bildung erzählen?

**SPM:** Colin Ward war Schriftsteller, Lehrer, Architekturzeichner und deklarierter Anarchist; am bekanntesten ist er vermutlich für sein 1978 erschienenes Buch *Das Kind in der Stadt*.[6] Ward interessierte sich für das Verhältnis von Menschen zu dem Ort, an dem sie leben. Er veröffentlichte viel zum Thema Wohnen und Schule, forschte aber auch zu Transportwesen,

1 Smithson, Alison: „How to Read and Recognize Mat-Building. Mainstream Architecture as It Has Developed Towards a Mat-Building", *Architectural Design* 9 (1974), 573–590.

2 Schiedhelm, Manfred: „Berlin Free University", *Architectural Design* 1 (1974), 14–17.

3 Vgl. Abercrombie, Stanley: „Berlin Free University", *Architecture Plus* 1 (1974), 32–45.

4 Vgl. Woods, Shadrach: „The Education Bazaar", in: *Harvard Educational Review, Architecture and Education* 4 (1969), 116–125.

5 Candilis-Josic-Woods war eine erfolgreiche Architektenpartnerschaft (bestehend aus dem Griechen Georges Candilis, dem Jugoslawen Alexis Josic und dem Amerikaner Shadrach Woods). Gegründet 1955 in Paris, war sie hauptsächlich bis 1969 in der europäischen Wiederaufbauszene nach dem zweiten Weltkrieg aktiv.

6 Ward, Colin: *Das Kind in der Stadt*, Übers. Ursula von Wiese, Frankfurt am Main 1978.

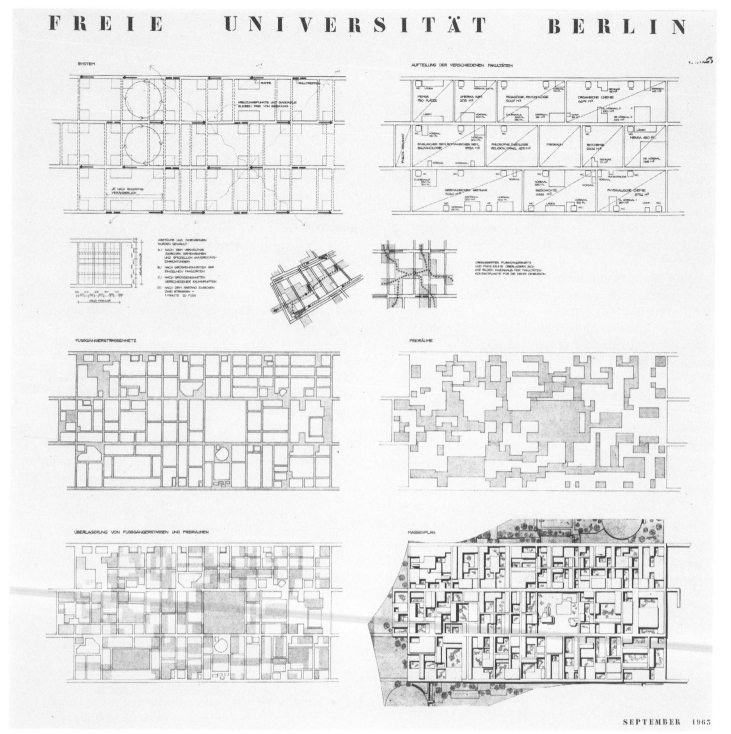

FREIE UNIVERSITÄT BERLIN

SEPTEMBER 1963

2   Shadrach Woods, Manfred Schiedhelm, 1963–1973 © Shadrach Woods architectural records and papers, 1923–2008, Avery Architectural & Fine Arts Library, Columbia University

histories. Between the 1960s and the 1990s, Ward gave lectures at the Bartlett, the RIBA, the AA and the Manchester School of Architecture and publicly informed architectural debates through radio, exhibitions, TV and printed media.[7] Although Ward worked in two well-known architecture offices of the time—Shepheard and Epstein architects (1952–1961) and

Chamberlin, Powell & Bon (1962–1964) and the Architects' Cooperative Partnership—he didn't train as an architect.[8] In

7   See Colin Ward, "Colin Ward Papers," *International Institute of Social History*, Collection ID: ARCH03180, https://search.iisg.amsterdam/Record/ARCH03180.

8   See Colin Ward and David Goodway, *Talking Anarchy* (Oakland, 2013), 3.

Wasserversorgung und grüner Politik. Ward fasziniert mich als Figur der britischen Architektur, weil er, obwohl immer wieder am Architekturgeschehen und an der Architekturausbildung beteiligt, in der Architekturgeschichte kaum Erwähnung findet. Von den 1960ern bis in die 1990er hielt Ward Vorträge an der Bartlett, am RIBA, an der AA und an der Manchester School of Architecture und brachte sich öffentlich über Radio, Ausstellungen, Fernsehen und Printmedien in Architekturdebatten ein.[7] Ward arbeitete zwar in zwei bekannten Architekturbüros seiner Zeit – Shepheard and Epstein architects (1952–1961) und Chamberlin, Powell & Bon (1962–1964) – sowie in der Architects' Co-operative Partnership, war aber kein ausgebildeter Architekt.[8] In Großbritannien, wo der Titel ArchitektIn gesetzlich geschützt ist, ist das für die Berufsbezeichnung nicht unerheblich. Auch Ward selbst bezeichnete sich nicht als Architekt, sondern als „Mann des Zeichenbretts".[9] Ich glaube, die fehlende Berufsqualifikation spielte auch eine Rolle für sein Verschwinden aus der Architektur. Shadrach Woods, vermute ich, verstand sich als Architekt, oder, Federica?

**FD:** Das ist eine Frage, die ich mir selbst stelle. Im inneren Kreis des Team 10 wurde er immer als Freund geführt, seine MitarbeiterInnen bezeichneten ihn als Architekten und Theoretiker.

**SPM:** Ich finde es interessant, sich im Zusammenhang mit Ward und Woods mit der Selbstdefinition als ArchitektIn auseinanderzusetzen. Ward war dem Beruf gegenüber kritisch eingestellt. Er wollte, dass sich jede/r in die gebaute Umwelt einbringen kann, und deshalb war es ihm auch so wichtig, über die Institution hinauszugehen. Aber die Vorstellung, die Kontrolle aufzugeben, ist für ArchitektInnen eine Herausforderung. Ich fragte mich also, wie ich mich selbst als Architektin definiere. Wenn jemand fragt: „Wer bist du?", sage ich: „Ich bin Architektin". Was bedeutet es, diese Definition abzulehnen? Oder den Titel zu teilen?

**AW:** Ja, wirklich interessant. Mir gefällt auch, was du in den Notizen geschrieben hast, die wir vor unserem heutigen Gespräch ausgetauscht haben: „Es ging nie um Colin Ward; er war nie ein Leader oder Manager, sondern überließ es anderen, die gemeinsamen Initiativen in Besitz zu nehmen." Macht abzugeben, die Kontrolle anderen zu überlassen … das ist eine persönliche Frage, wie man die eigene Rolle und ihren Wandel begreift, und sie ist eng mit Bildungsfragen verknüpft. Die Frage beweglicher Rollen ist nicht nur im Fach Architektur, sondern auch sozial und pädagogisch relevant. Nicolas, ist Beweglichkeit auch ein sinnvoller Begriff, um den italienischen Planer, Architekten und Theoretiker Giancarlo De Carlo und seine Rolle beim International Laboratory of Architecture and Urban Design (ILAUD) zu fassen?

**NM:** Die Bewegungsmetapher ist tatsächlich relevant. Eine kürzlich von Paolo Ceccarelli herausgegebene Publikation über die vergangenen und künftigen Aktivitäten des ILAUD trägt den Untertitel: „A Movable Frontier".[10] Der Titel verweist auf den ursprünglichen Status des ILAUD, das 1976 von De Carlo gegründet wurde, um Bildungsaktivitäten in Verbindung mit einem privaten Büro für Stadtforschung und Stadtplanung durchzuführen. De Carlo war davor bereits rund 30 Jahre praktisch und lehrend tätig gewesen und war Mitglied des von Federica erwähnten Team 10. Mit dem ILAUD versuchte er etwas Neues: eine Zusammenarbeit im Bereich Architektur und Bildung zwischen seinem Büro, internationalen Universitäten und italienischen Gastgeber-Städten.

Dank der Unterstützung von Carlo Bo, dem Rektor der Privatuniversität Urbino, fand die Sommerakademie des ILAUD während der ersten sechs Jahre in Urbino statt. Die Teilnahmegebühr war ziemlich hoch – 5.000 Dollar –, und die Partneruniversitäten mussten zusätzlich jeweils die Reisekosten und das Gehalt einer Vollzeit-AssistentIn tragen sowie Veranstaltungen ihres Lehrkörpers beisteuern. Sechs Studierende aus jedem Teilnehmerland (im ersten Jahr die USA, Norwegen, die Schweiz, Belgien und Spanien) wurden für die Kurse ausgewählt. Bis 1981 blieb das ILAUD in Urbino, dann zog es weiter nach Siena, San Miniato, Venedig, noch einmal Urbino, San Marino und, während der letzten Lebensjahre De Carlos, wieder nach Venedig. Die Bildungsaktivitäten des ILAUD waren stets ortsspezifisch angelegt.

**SPM:** Das Thema ortsspezifisches Lernen passt gut zu Colin Wards Zugang zur Bildung. Colin Ward und Giancarlo De Carlo waren befreundet. Sie besuchten einander und lagen politisch auf einer ähnlichen Linie. Colin Ward arbeitete auch beim ILAUD mit. Ich würde Wards Bildungsansatz als umweltbezogen beschreiben – in einer Zeit, den 1970er-Jahren, in der sich die Umwelterziehung gerade entwickelte, allerdings

7   Vgl. Ward, Colin: „Colin Ward Papers", *International Institute of Social History*, Collection ID: ARCH03180, online unter: https://search.iisg. amsterdam/Record/ARCH03180.

8   Ward, Colin/Goodway, David: *Talking Anarchy*, Oakland, CA 2014, 3.

9   Bradshaw, Ross/Ward, Harriet/Worpole, Ken: *Remembering Colin Ward*, Nottingham 2013, 22.

10  Ceccarelli, Paolo (Hg.): *Giancarlo De Carlo and ILAUD. A Movable Frontier*, Mailand 2019.

Britain, being an architect is protected by law, so professional and legal determination matters. Ward didn't call himself an architect but a "drawing-board man."[9] I believe Ward's lack of architectural qualifications played a role in his disappearance from the architectural scene. I imagine that Shadrach Woods defined himself as an architect. Is that the case, Federica?

**FD**: This is a question that I ask myself as well. In the inner circle of Team 10, he was always defined as a friend, his collaborators addressed him as an architect and a theoretician.

**SPM**: I think it is interesting to look at the idea of self-determination as an architect in relation to Ward and Woods. Ward was critical of the profession. He wanted everyone to have the opportunity to get involved in the built environment and that's why he was so strong in his proposition of going beyond the institution. But the idea of renouncing control is challenging for architects. It made me think about how I self-determine as an architect. When people ask me "Who are you?", I say "I am an architect." What does it mean to renounce to that denomination? Or to share that title?

**AW**: Yes, really interesting. I also like what you wrote in the notes we exchanged before our conversation today: "It was never Colin Ward; he was never a leader or a manager but made space for others to take ownership of their initiatives." Ceding power, giving away control to others … this is a personal question about roles, how you think of and change your role, and it's closely related to education. The question of moving roles is not only one relevant in the discipline of architecture but also socially and educationally. Nicolas, is the notion of movement a useful frame for thinking about the Italian planner, architect and theorist Giancarlo De Carlo and his role within the "International Laboratory of Architecture and Urban Design" (ILAUD)?

**NM**: The metaphor of movement is indeed relevant. A recent publication on the past and future activities of ILAUD, edited by Paolo Ceccarelli is, for instance, entitled "A Movable Frontier."[10] This title refers to the really original status of ILAUD, a platform founded in 1976 by De Carlo, to undertake educational activities and work as a private studio producing both urban survey and design. De Carlo had already been active in practice and education for nearly 30 years and was a member of Team 10 mentioned by Federica. With ILAUD, however, he's trying something new—an architectural and educational collaboration between his professional studio, international universities and hosting Italian cities.

ILAUD's summer schools were taking place in Urbino for the first six years thanks to the assistance of Carlo Bo, the rector of this free university. The rate of participation was rather expensive—5.000 dollars—and each partner university also had to cover the travel and salary of a full-time teaching assistant as well as contributions from senior faculty too. Six students were selected to attend the summer school from each participating country (United States, Norway, Switzerland, Belgium and Spain in the first year). ILAUD stayed in Urbino between 1976 and 1981, then moved to Siena, San Miniato, Venice, Urbino again, San Marino and, during the last years of De Carlo's life, came back to Venice. Teaching activities have always been planned by ILAUD in a site-specific way.

**SPM**: The issue of site-specific learning connects well with Colin Ward's approach to education. Colin Ward and Giancarlo De Carlo were friends. They visited each other and shared a political orientation. Colin Ward was a collaborator in ILAUD too. I describe Ward's approach as environment-based education at a time when environmental education was developing in the 1970s, but always biased towards the natural environment. Ward wanted to redirect that attention to the urban environment, where most people live. And in order to do that, he argued for issue-based learning, which is site-specific and connected to the local environment. I think that's relevant to De Carlo's site-specific education techniques you talked about, Nicolas.

**NM**: Indeed, it is probably a topic Giancarlo De Carlo and Colin Ward discussed together. This was another key point of ILAUD—the discussions and lectures across traditional boundaries. Sometimes the invited speakers were close friends of De Carlo, such as the urban theoretician Carlo Doglio or, as mentioned, Colin Ward who was in contact with De Carlo from the anarchist congresses of 1945 and 1946 and who came

9  Ross Bradshaw, Ben Ward, Harriet Ward, and Ken Worpole, *Remembering Colin Ward* (Nottingham, 2013), 22.

10  Paolo Ceccarelli, ed., *Giancarlo De Carlo and ILAUD. A Movable Frontier* (Milano, 2019).

International Laboratory of Architecture and Urban Design
18th Residential Course, Urbino, August–September 1993

3 August. 1800 Lecture by Colin Ward
"Why the British don't talk about New Towns any more"

Evolving a civic consciousness: Carnival Day in Marlow in the 1960s (Photo TCPA)

3 Poster for Colin Ward's lecture within the 18th ILAUD workshop. | Plakat für Colin Wards Vortrag im Rahmen der 18. ILAUD Sommerakademie, 1993, Urbino. Source: International Institute of Social History © Courtesy of Harriet Ward

mit einer Tendenz zur natürlichen Umwelt. Ward wollte den Fokus wieder in Richtung städtischer Umwelt lenken, zumal da schließlich die meisten Menschen wohnen. Zu diesem Zweck plädierte er für ein themenbezogenes, ortsspezifisches, mit dem lokalen Umfeld verknüpftes Lernen. Ich glaube, das gilt auch für De Carlos ortsspezifische Bildungstechniken, von denen du, Nicolas, erzählt hast.

**NM**: Ja, das ist vermutlich ein Thema, über das sich Giancarlo De Carlo und Colin Ward ausgetauscht haben. Das war übrigens ein weiterer Schwerpunkt des ILAUD – Diskussionen und Vorlesungen, die traditionelle Grenzen überschreiten. Die geladenen RednerInnen waren enge Freunde De Carlos, wie etwa der Urbanist Carlo Doglio oder eben Colin Ward, der mit De Carlo seit den anarchistischen Kongressen von 1945 und

4   ILAUD workshop, Urbino, 1976 © Ilaud Archive – The Civic Art Library Luigi Poletti

to Urbino in 1993, as mentioned in the *Yearbook*.[11] Lecturers with contrasting political positions and different academic skills were also invited. For instance, the critic and architecture historian Francesco Dal Co delivered a lecture for ILAUD in 1979.

AW: One reason that institutions survive is that they make life easy, reliably so. They facilitate—by simplifying, systematizing, resourcing, repeating—the work and, to some extent, the people they're intended to manage. This is problematic too (especially for education, as De Carlo noted and explored.)[12] But it's a key question for us as well. If you don't exist within an institution and choose to move beyond the protective, supportive boundaries that institutions provide, then how do you organize this work of creating platforms of discussion? How do you pay for them, maintain them? Nicolas, your mention of the practicalities just now, the 5,000 dollars, and the flexible-but-awkward position of ILAUD somewhere between private architectural/urban planning research program and university outreach, makes me want to hear more about the work involved in this experiment …

NM: ILAUD was a success for the quality of the debate it stimulated between hundreds of architects who participated in the summer schools. However, it never reached its original goal. The organization of a summer school was considered by De Carlo only as a tool to launch the activity of an international research group, but this platform never became completely autonomous from his professional studio in Milan.

As Mirko Zardini argued, the human base and conceptual toolbox of ILAUD remained Team 10.[13] This platform involved

11   In 1989 De Carlo says that he had not seen Colin Ward for a while but had the impression "to have always stayed in touch." "L'architetto e il potere," *A rivista anarchica* 19, no. 161 (1989), available online at: http://www.arivista.org/?nr=161&pag=161_12.html (accessed November 15, 2021).

12   See, for example, Giancarlo De Carlo, "Why/How to Build School Buildings," *Harvard Educational Review* 39, no. 4 (1969): 12–35, available online at: http://www.hepgjournals.org/doi/abs/10.17763/haer.39.4.r1163153200753u4 (accessed November 15, 2021). However, as early as 1947, De Carlo was already interested in the problems that educational institutions create as well as solve. See De Carlo, Giancarlo, "La Scuola e l'Urbanistica," *Domus* 220 (1947): 15–17

13   See Mirko Zardini, "From Team X to Team X. International Laboratories of Architecture and Urban Design (ILAUD)," *Lotus* 95 (1997): 76–97.

1946 in Verbindung stand und laut Jahrbuch 1993 nach Urbino kam.[11] Aber es wurden auch Vortragende mit anderer politischer Orientierung und anderen akademischen Fähigkeiten eingeladen. So etwa der Kritiker und Architekturtheoretiker Francesco Dal Co, der 1979 eine Vorlesung am ILAUD hielt.

**AW:** Einer der Gründe für das Überleben von Institutionen ist, dass sie das Leben verlässlich erleichtern. Durch Vereinfachung, Systematisierung, Bereitstellung von Mitteln und Wiederholung machen sie die Arbeit und in gewissem Maße auch die Menschen, zu deren Lenkung sie erdacht wurden, erst möglich. Das ist aber auch problematisch (speziell in der Bildung, wie De Carlo festgestellt und untersucht hat).[12] Allerdings ist es auch für uns eine zentrale Frage. Wenn man nicht innerhalb einer Institution agiert und sich entscheidet, die schützenden und stützenden Grenzen, die Institutionen nun mal bieten, zu überschreiten, wie schafft und organisiert man dann solche Diskussionsplatt-

formen? Wie bezahlt man dafür, hält sie am Laufen? Aufgrund dessen, was du gerade über die praktische Umsetzung gesagt hast, Nicolas, die 5.000 Dollar und die flexible aber schwierige Position des ILAUD irgendwo zwischen privatem Forschungsprogramm für Architektur und Stadtplanung und universitärem Outreach-Unternehmen, würde ich aber gern mehr über die Arbeit in diesem Experiment hören …

**NM:** Das ILAUD war ein Erfolg, was die Qualität der Debatte anbelangt, die es zwischen Hunderten von ArchitektInnen, die

11  1989 schreibt De Carlo, er habe Colin Ward eine ganze Weile nicht gesehen, habe aber den Eindruck, „immer in Verbindung gewesen zu sein". De Carlo, Giancarlo: „L'architetto e il potere", *A rivista anarchica* 19, 161 (1989), online unter: http://www.arivista.org/?nr=161&pag= 161_12.html, (Stand: 15. November 2021).

12  Vgl. zum Beispiel De Carlo, Giancarlo: „Why/How to Build School Buildings", *Harvard Educational Review* 39, 4 (1969), 12–35, online unter: http://www.hepgjournals.org/doi/abs/10.17763/haer.39.4.r1 163153200753u4 (Stand: 15. November 2021). Bereits 1947 interessierte sich De Carlo ebenso für Probleme, die durch Bildungsinstitutionen geschaffen wie durch sie gelöst werden. Vgl. De Carlo, Giancarlo: „La Scuola e l'Urbanistica", *Domus* 220 (1947), 15–17.

5   ILAUD workshop, Urbino, 1976 © Ilaud Archive – The Civic Art Library Luigi Poletti

6 Two women in conversation with Carlo Bo, former rector of the University of Urbino, during his visit to the second ILAUD workshop. | Zwei Frauen im Gespräch mit Carlo Bo, ehem. Rektor der Privatuniversität Urbino bei seinem Besuch der zweiten ILAUD Sommerakademie, Urbino, 1976.
© Ilaud Archive – The Civic Art Library Luigi Poletti

academic partners with different backgrounds, so it was difficult to develop a common methodology. Agreements with each academic institution were renewed each year during the preparation of the summer school, as the architect didn't want any one university to become the main promoter of ILAUD. The board remained free to define independently its own objects of study, a radical choice coherent with the anarchist political ideals of De Carlo which had several consequences. It was difficult to coordinate ILAUD research activities since graduating students, junior faculty, and professors involved in the summer school were driven by other professional priorities during the year. The board meetings were the official moments of decision, but it was not possible to use Zoom as we are doing today and ILAUD couldn't assume universities would reimburse travel expenses. De Carlo practically prepared the workshop

with the staff of his professional studio in Milan and his teaching assistants in the University Iuav of Venice and always lamented in his letters the lack of participation of most of the foreign partners.[14]

**SPM**: This education you are talking about was still directed to architecture and planning students, I imagine?

**NM**: Yes.

**SPM**: Then the proposal of Colin Ward was, in a way, more radical than De Carlo's because Ward wanted to offer that education not only to architects and planners but to anyone. I think that's why Ward talked about the "exploding school," and taking education out of the school walls, which links to what Federica was pointing out about Shadrach Woods. My interpretation is that, even though Ward was talking about rethinking schooling for children, he was also suggesting to explode the walls of architecture schools. And that, for me, is the real proposal of going beyond the institution of the architectural school. By offering a similar education to the one we receive in architecture schools to all ages: from primary school children to a lifelong learning process, where the built environment can be a resource for learning for all. Ward's proposal to extend and challenge architectural education might be the reason why he remains a person on the margins of architectural culture. He was never as well-known as De Carlo or Woods, of course. I learned about them in architecture school, but I had never heard of Ward.

**NM**: De Carlo and Ward had different approaches. De Carlo imagined ILAUD as a platform of discussion for professionals, scholars, and trained architecture students who had just concluded their studies or were preparing their final thesis. The idea was to open a professional debate between different architecture faculties in order to develop tools to take to the public. In the 1970s, De Carlo was conducting a very difficult participation process with workers of the Terni steel factory. My colleague Alberto Franchini showed in his thesis that participation was mainly related to pedagogy, in order to persuade inhabi-

14 See Modena, Archivio Ilaud, Note GDC 1983–1984: The Structure of Ilaud: A Proposal for a Change.

an der Sommerakademie teilnahmen, in Gang brachte. Es erreichte jedoch nie sein ursprüngliches Ziel. Die Ausrichtung der Sommerakademie war von De Carlo lediglich als ein Vehikel für die Aktivitäten einer internationalen Forschungsgruppe gedacht, aber diese Plattform erreichte nie eine vollkommene Unabhängigkeit von seinem Büro in Mailand.

Die Personalbasis und der konzeptuelle Werkzeugkasten des ILAUD blieb, wie Mirko Zardini festgestellt hat, das Team 10.[13] An der Plattform waren akademische Partner mit unterschiedlichem Hintergrund beteiligt, sodass es schwierig war, eine gemeinsame Methodik zu entwickeln. Die Vereinbarungen mit den akademischen Institutionen wurden jedes Jahr im Lauf der Vorbereitung der Sommerakademie neu geschlossen, da De Carlo vermeiden wollte, dass eine Universität zur Hauptträgerin des ILAUD wurde. Das Leitungsteam konnte seine Studienziele unabhängig festlegen, eine radikale Entscheidung, die im Einklang mit den politischen Idealen De Carlos stand, aber gewisse Folgen hatte. Die Forschungsaktivitäten des ILAUD waren schwer zu koordinieren, da die vor ihrem Abschluss stehenden Studierenden, der akademische Mittelbau und die ProfessorInnen, die an der Sommerakademie teilnahmen, während des Jahres andere berufliche Prioritäten hatten. Die offiziellen Entscheidungen fielen bei den Treffen des Leitungsteams, aber sie konnten nicht wie heute per Zoom abgehalten werden, und das ILAUD konnte nicht mit einem Reisekostenersatz durch die Universitäten rechnen. De facto bereitete De Carlo die Workshops mit den MitarbeiterInnen seines Mailänder Büros und seinen AssistentInnen am Iuav in Venedig vor und beklagte sich in seinen Briefen dauernd über die mangelnde Mitwirkung seiner ausländischen PartnerInnen.[14]

**SPM:** Die Ausbildung, von der du sprichst, richtete sich weiter an Studierende aus dem Bereich Architektur und Städtebau, richtig?

**NM:** Ja.

**SPM:** Dann war das Konzept von Colin Ward in gewisser Weise radikaler als das von De Carlo. Denn Ward wollte diese Bildung nicht nur für ArchitektInnen und StadtplanerInnen anbieten, sondern für jedermann/-frau. Deshalb sprach Ward auch von der „explodierenden Schule", davon, die Bildung über die Schulmauern hinauszutragen. Das trifft sich mit dem, was Federica über Shadrach Woods gesagt hat. Zwar hat Ward davon in Zusammenhang mit einem Überdenken der Schulbildung gesprochen, aber nach meiner Interpretation wollte er auch die Mauern der Architekturschulen „sprengen". Und für

mich ist das der wahre Ansatz für eine Überwindung der institutionellen Architekturausbildung. Das Angebot einer ähnlichen Art von Bildung, wie sie in Architekturschulen vermittelt wird, für alle Altersstufen: von der Grundschule bis zum lebenslangen Lernen, mit der gebauten Umgebung als Lernressource für alle. Wards Konzept einer Erweiterung und Infragestellung der Architekturausbildung mag auch der Grund dafür sein, dass er im Architekturkontext auch heute noch eine Randfigur ist. Er war nie so bekannt wie De Carlo oder Woods. Von ihnen habe ich im Architekturstudium gehört, von Ward nie.

**NM:** De Carlo und Ward verfolgten unterschiedliche Ansätze. De Carlo hatte mit ILAUD vor allem eine Diskussionsplattform für praktizierende ArchitektInnen, WissenschaftlerInnen und frisch gebackene ArchitektInnen, ArchitekturabsolventInnen oder DiplomandInnen im Sinn. Die Idee war, eine professionelle Debatte zwischen verschiedenen Bereichen zu initiieren, um öffentlichkeitstaugliche Werkzeuge zu entwickeln. In den 1970ern leitete De Carlo einen sehr schwierigen Beteiligungsprozess mit ArbeiterInnen des Stahlwerks Terni. Mein Kollege Alberto Franchini hat in seiner Dissertation gezeigt, dass es dabei hauptsächlich um Pädagogik ging, um Überzeugungsarbeit für die Qualität innovativer Wohnbautypen.[15] Dabei sollte natürlich mit einem ortsspezifischen Workshop ein Dialog zwischen BewohnerInnen und Studierenden initiiert werden; die dabei auftretenden Sprachbarrieren machten es erforderlich, grafische Werkzeuge statt der üblichen soziologisch-konzipierten Fragebögen zu entwickeln, um die Aneignung der vernakularen Architektur und öffentlichen Räume durch die BewohnerInnen zu verstehen. Das markiert den konzeptuellen Schwenk der ILAUD-Workshops in Urbino vom Versuch einer „Partizipation und Wiederverwendung" im Jahr 1978 hin zur Lektüre von „Zeichen und Einsichten" im Jahr 1979.

Andererseits könnte man das ILAUD auch als Teil einer langfristigen Partizipation an den Architektur- und Stadtplanungsaufträgen betrachten, die De Carlo zwischen 1954 und 2005 in Urbino erhielt.[16] Der Workshop fand in einem ehemaligen Kloster statt, das in den 1990ern zum neuen Hauptsitz der Fakultät für Wirtschaftswissenschaften umgewandelt wurde. In einem

13 Vgl. Zardini, Mirko: „From Team X to Team X. International Laboratories of Architecture and Urban Design (ILAUD)", *Lotus* 95 (1997), 76–97.

14 Vgl. Modena, Archivio ILAUD, Note GDC 1983–1984: The Structure of ILAUD: A Proposal for a Change.

15 Vgl. Franchini, Alberto: *Il Villaggio Matteotti a Terni. Giancarlo de Carlo e l'abitare collettivo*, Rom 2019.

16 Vgl. Moucheront, Nicolas: „Giancarlo De Carlo à Urbino, avant et après 1968. L'architecture de l'université et l'enseignement de l'architecture", in: Debarre, Anne/Maniaque, Caroline/Marantz, Eléonore/Violeau, Jean-Luis (Hg.): *Architecture 68. Panorama international des renouveaux pédagogiques*, Lausanne 2020, 147–160.

tants of the qualities of innovative housing types.[15] For sure, the idea of a site-specific workshop intended to stimulate such a dialogue between locals and students, but linguistic barriers made necessary to develop graphic tools to read the inhabitants' appropriations of vernacular architecture and public spaces instead of traditional sociologist-designed questionnaires. This is the main conceptual passage of the ILAUD workshops in Urbino from an attempt to "Participation and Re-use" in 1978 to a reading of "Signs and Insights" in 1979.

However, I think it is possible to consider ILAUD as an element of a long-term participation process related to the architecture and urban plans commissions Giancarlo De Carlo got in Urbino from 1954 to 2005.[16] The workshop took place in a former convent transformed during the 1990's in the new headquarter for the faculty of economy. So, in a certain sense, the didactic activities undertaken in this space were a kind of anticipation of an urban transformation. The final exhibitions of the 1976–1981 summer schools enabled Urbino citizens to enter this abandoned building and to imagine, thanks to the surveys and drawings produced by ILAUD, a future utilization for this part of the city center.

**FD**: This is a very interesting point and it relates both to the site-specificity of schools and to the idea of extending architecture schools beyond architects. From research at the Archivio Progetti in Venice, I found a rich correspondence between Woods and De Carlo where there is recurring discussion of the university, and the school in general, as necessarily integrated into the city. That is, something not merely architectural or urban, but cultural. It starts from the conception of the building, but is also about the integration of the landscape and the people and their activities within it. I think Woods was influenced by De Carlo here but I would also like to mention Woods's least known experiment in the field of education: the "Non-École de Villefranche" (1966). Here, the basic idea was to refuse any predetermined program and to create a school that was free, fair, and, most importantly, open to all. As described in Filliou's artists' book *Teaching and Learning as Performing Arts*, the arts must have a core role in the educational process: they should enrich it and give it new perspective.[17]

Another important principle of this experiment was the idea of non-specialization, which would open students to various dis-

ciplines and help them adapt to shifting market conditions. Filliou and Woods believed excessive specialization prevented cultural adaption. Learning at the "Non-School" was not to be based on the transmission of information. Instead, students would be given endless ways to analyze problems and then be guided in the direction of their own interests and personal inclinations. Woods envisioned the administrative management of the Non-School as constantly changing, with the theoretical direction framed by persons of international standing who would be brought in on a temporary basis. Although the Non-School was never realized, and there are no sources to understand why this didn't happen, these concepts and ideas influenced the curriculum at Harvard and other architecture schools where he taught.[18]

**SPM**: The idea of "non-schooling" reminds me that Ward was attracted to "site-specific learning," which is best known through Ivan Illich's book *Deschooling Society* (1971) and the work of other radical thinkers like Paul Goodman and Everett Reimer. The "deschoolers" explored how schools and their 'hidden curriculum' educate society to perpetuate a social order, and proposed ideas to dismantle this connection.[19] Reading the concept of "deschooling" through Ward, I argue that Ward wanted to "deschool" architecture and planning to make their practices available for everyone and promote involvement in the built environment. Ward's approach was different from Shadrach Woods', as you were explaining Federica. Ward lectured all over the country and wrote prolifically, including many architecture magazines and journals. But, from what I know, he never tried to go beyond advocacy, whether through starting a school or teaching in architecture schools. That was for others, to take action if they wanted, inspired by his ideas—reported

15 See Alberto Franchini, *Il Villaggio Matteotti a Terni. Giancarlo de Carlo e l'abitare collettivo* (Roma, 2019).

16 See Nicolas Moucheront, "Giancarlo De Carlo à Urbino, avant et après 1968. L'architecture de l'université et l'enseignement de l'architecture," *Architecture 68. Panorama international des renouveaux pédagogiques* (Lausanne, 2020), 147–160.

17 See Robert Filliou, *Teaching and Learning as Performing Arts* (Köln and New York, 1970).

18 For further information see Federica Doglio, "'The School as a City and the City as a School'–Shadrach Woods and Cedric Price: Experiments to Rethink the University," *Territorio* 86 (2018): 7–16.

19 See Ivan Illich, *Deschooling Society* (London 1995), 32.

gewissen Sinn waren die hier durchgeführten didaktischen Aktivitäten also eine Art Vorwegnahme einer urbanen Transformation. Bei den Abschlussausstellungen der 1976–1981 abgehaltenen Sommerakademien erhielten die BürgerInnen von Urbino Zutritt zum verlassenen Gebäude, um sich anhand der beim ILAUD entstandenen Untersuchungen und Zeichnungen ein Bild von der künftigen Nutzung dieses Stadtteils zu machen.

**FD:** Das ist ein sehr interessanter Punkt, der sowohl die Ortsspezifik von Schulen betrifft als auch die Erweiterung von Architekturschulen über den Kreis der ArchitektInnen hinaus. Bei Forschungen im Archivio Progetti in Venedig bin ich auf eine umfangreiche Korrespondenz zwischen Woods und De Carlo gestoßen, bei der es immer wieder um die notwendige Integration der Universität – und der Schule im Allgemeinen – in die Stadt geht, also um etwas Kulturelles, nicht nur etwas Architektonisches oder Urbanistisches. Das beginnt bei der Konzeption des Gebäudes, erstreckt sich aber auch auf die Integration der Landschaft und der Menschen mit ihren Aktivitäten darin. Ich denke, Woods war diesbezüglich von De Carlo beeinflusst, möchte aber auch auf Woods' unbekanntestes Experiment im Bereich Bildung verweisen: die „Non-École de Villefranche" (1966). Die Grundidee dabei war die Absage an jedes vorgegebene Programm, die Schaffung einer Schule, die frei, fair und vor allem für jeden zugänglich sein sollte. Wie Filliou in seinem Künstlerbuch *Lehren und Lernen als Aufführungskünste* schrieb, kommt den Künsten im Bildungsprozess eine zentrale Rolle zu: sie sollten ihn bereichern und ihm eine neue Perspektive geben.[17]

Ein weiteres wichtiges Prinzip dieses Experiments war die Nichtspezialisierung, die Studierende für verschiedene Disziplinen öffnen und ihnen helfen sollte, sich auf wechselnde Marktbedingungen einzustellen. Filliou und Woods waren der Meinung, dass übermäßige Spezialisierung die kulturelle Anpassung verhindert. Das Lernen an der „Nicht-Schule" beruhte nicht auf Wissensvermittlung. Stattdessen sollten die Studierenden mit unendlich vielen Analysemöglichkeiten ausgestattet und dann in Richtung ihrer eigenen Interessen und persönlichen Neigungen gelenkt werden. Woods stellte sich die Administration der Nicht-Schule als etwas vor, das sich laufend verändert, wobei die theoretische Ausrichtung Personen mit internationalem Ruf obliegen sollte, die temporär hinzugezogen werden. Auch wenn die Nicht-Schule nie umgesetzt wurde und es auch keine Quellen gibt, aus denen hervorginge, weshalb, so flossen diese Konzepte und Ideen doch in die Curricula der Harvard Graduate School of Design und anderer Architekturschulen ein, an denen Woods lehrte.[18]

**SPM:** Die Idee der „Nicht-Schule" erinnert mich an Wards Sympathie für die „Entschulungs-Bewegung", die am ehesten durch Ivan Illichs Buch *Entschulung der Gesellschaft* (1971) und die Arbeit anderer radikaler Denker wie Paul Goodman und Everett Reimer bekannt ist. Die Proponenten der „Entschulung" untersuchten, wie Schulen und ihr „verborgenes Curriculum" die Gesellschaft dazu erziehen, eine bestimmte soziale Ordnung aufrechtzuerhalten, und suchten nach Möglichkeiten, diese Verbindung aufzulösen.[19] Bezogen auf Ward würde ich sagen, dass er die Architektur und Stadtplanung „entschulen" wollte, um ihre Praktiken jedermann/-frau zugänglich zu machen und die Anteilnahme an der gebauten Umwelt zu fördern. Wards Ansatz war anders als der von Shadrach Woods, wie du, Federica, ja bereits erklärt hast. Ward hielt im ganzen Land Vorträge und war ein überaus produktiver Schriftsteller, auch für viele Architekturzeitschriften. Aber soweit ich weiß ging er nie über die Produktion und Verbreitung von Ideen hinaus, sei es durch Gründung einer Schule oder das Unterrichten an Architekturinstituten. Er überließ es anderen, zur Aktion zu schreiten, wenn sie das wollten – inspiriert durch seine zum Teil im *Bulletin of Environmental Education* veröffentlichten Gedanken.[20] Meines Erachtens unterscheidet sich Wards didaktisch-intellektueller Ansatz sehr von dem anderer PädagogInnen in der Architektur. Ward lenkte eher als dass er führte. Er versuchte zwar, die Architekturausbildung zu verändern, aber subtil: durch Inspiration mit seinen radikalen Bildungskonzepten.

**AW:** Ich will hier kurz die wichtigsten Aspekte unserer bisherigen Diskussion rekapitulieren: Was all die verschiedenen Aktivitäten und Strategien, über die wir gesprochen haben, gemeinsam haben, ist, dass sie versuchen, Verbindungen jenseits von Institutionen zu knüpfen, Menschen, Wissen, Erfahrungen und Umgebungen zu verbinden, die sich üblicherweise nicht begegnen. Manchmal finden sie im exklusiven und ausgrenzenden Raum der Universität statt, manchmal in der beruflichen Praxis und manchmal zwischen verschiedenen Öffentlichkeiten und Räumen. Wir haben auch von gelegentlichen Versuchen gehört, über Institutionen hinauszugehen – sie ganz zu ersetzen, zu

17 Vgl. Filliou, Robert: *Lernen und Lehren als Aufführungskünste/Teaching and Learning as Performing Arts*, unter Mitw. v. John Cage u. a., Köln/New York 1970.

18 Ausführlicher dazu Doglio, Federica: „The School as a City and the City as a School'– Shadrach Woods and Cedric Price: Experiments to Rethink the University", *Territorio* 86 (2018), 7–16.

19 Vgl. Illich, Ivan: *Entschulung der Gesellschaft*, Übers. Hartmut von Henting und Helmut Lindemann, Reinbeck 1973, 45.

20 Vgl. Perez-Martinez, Sol bei der Konferenz „Urban Studies Centres 1968–1988: Mediating Architecture and the Built Environment through Education", *Architecture Connects*, Oxford 2017.

partly in the *Bulletin of Environmental Education*.[20] I find Ward's format of advocacy very different to other figures in architecture. Ward was guiding rather than leading. He was trying to change architectural education but subtly, by inspiring through his radical proposals for education.

**AW:** Let me quickly recap our main discussion at this point. What all these different activities and strategies we've been talking about have in common is that they are all attempts to build links beyond institutions and to connect people, knowledge, experiences and environments that might not traditionally come together. Sometimes they take place in the exclusive and excluding space of the university, sometimes in professional practice and sometimes across publics and public spaces. We've also heard about occasional attempts to go further—efforts to replace the institution altogether, to "explode" it and disperse its resources, personnel, ideas and power.

For example, we've heard about Colin Ward's work to connect methods across rural and urban studies, to open up architectural knowledge and spatial practices to children and other "outsiders." Efforts to bridge environmental studies and geography, to keep architecture and planning together. The city, not simply being a setting for education but a rich, complex object of study and a pedagogical tool. Learning from what is at hand, available to all, not just what has been codified in curriculums. This might sometimes be called "site-specific learning," and I suppose it brings in both political and historical questions (if they can be separated). The political dimension is about enabling access to and understanding of one's immediate surroundings with a view to building capacity for change and independence from official institutions. This is also about challenging the ownership of educational definition: Who gets to decide what are important educational questions? How they might be studied? For what ends? In Ward's case—as you explained, Sol—these challenges seem aimed at developing educational and political autonomy. But learning from what is available has an inevitably historical dimension too—especially for De Carlo and his emphasis on reading places to inform design.[21] This emphasizes understanding how and why places are as they are, how they have come to be.

We've also heard various attempts by Woods, De Carlo, and Ward to mix up age groups, professional roles, and to subvert the authoritarian structure of traditional pedagogic relationships. Questions too about credentialization and legal protection of certain ways of doing architecture—how they contribute to identity-building of architects in addition to defining and delimiting what architecture is and who it involves. In all of this, where do buildings and places stand?

**SPM:** In the 1970s, Ward advocates that people and environment are interlinked and points out the importance of looking at the built environment as a product of decision-making. He saw buildings as an expression of power, of democracy, of complex ideas, and as such, he felt that it was an important tool for learning. The focus on buildings and cities was central in Ward's writings. He wanted people to get involved. So, people became, as he says, "masters of their own environment."[22]

**FD:** I think the answer, using Woods' words, is: "The School as a City and the City as a School."[23] He thought the space was a protagonist in the learning process. It's not that architecture disappears, but without the theory you can't go anywhere. Going back to the case of the BFU: for him it was a framework, the learning, social and emotional process would take place among the people involved. Woods and Schiedhelm thought the layout and the *groundscraper* itself would encourage the students to meet, promoting exchanges, guard against isolation. So, the space and the architectures are certainly relevant, but they need to be enriched by this particular cultural framework of "deschooling."

**NM:** I won't define De Carlo as a theorist in the sense of an architect focused on producing theoretical texts alone: throughout his career, he worked intensely as a teacher. From 1978 he also directed the review *Spazio e Società* (Space and Society) which developed the topics discussed during the ILAUD workshops. The *Yearbooks* published in English are the main documentary source about ILAUD's activities and reflections, now available online.[24]

20  See Sol Perez-Martinez, "Urban Studies Centres 1968–1988," *Architecture Connects* (Oxford, 2017).

21  Giancarlo De Carlo, "Reading and Tentative Design," *Places Journal* 12, no. 3 (1999), available online at: https://placesjournal.org/assets/legacy/pdfs/reading-and-tentative-design.pdf (accessed November 15, 2021).

22  Colin Ward, *Talking Schools: Ten Lectures* (London, 1995), 38.

23  Shadrach Woods, "The Education Bazaar," *Harvard Educational Review, Architecture and Education* 4 (1969): 116–125.

24  See https://www.ilaud.org/category/about/ (accessed February 7, 2022)

„sprengen", ihre Ressourcen, ihr Personal, ihre Ideen und ihre Macht zu verteilen.

Wir haben zum Beispiel von Colin Wards Bemühungen gehört, Methoden aus dem Studium des ländlichen Raums mit denen der Urbanistik zu verbinden, Architekturwissen und Raumpraktiken für Kinder und andere „Außenstehende" zu öffnen, Brücken zwischen Umweltstudien und Geografie zu schlagen, Architektur und Stadtplanung zusammenzuhalten, die Stadt nicht bloß als Umgebung für Bildungsaktivitäten, sondern als komplexes Studienobjekt und Lehrmittel zu nutzen, von dem zu lernen, was vorhanden und allen zugänglich ist, und nicht nur vom Kodifizierten, dem, was in Curricula eingeschrieben wurde. Das kann manchmal als ortsspezifisches Lernen bezeichnet werden, und ich vermute, es wirft sowohl politische als auch historische Fragen auf (wenn die sich überhaupt trennen lassen). Die politische Dimension betrifft die Erschließung des Zugangs zur und des Verständnisses für die unmittelbare Umwelt mit dem Ziel, die Fähigkeit zur Veränderung und die Unabhängigkeit von offiziellen Institutionen zu stärken. Es geht dabei aber auch darum, das Recht auf die Definition von Bildung infrage zu stellen: Wer bestimmt, was wichtige Bildungsfragen sind? Wie sie studiert werden sollen? Zu welchem Zweck? Bei Ward scheint diese Infragestellung – wie du erklärt hast, Sol – auf pädagogische und politische Autonomie hinauszulaufen. Aber vom Vorhandenen zu lernen, hat auch eine historische Dimension – besonders für De Carlo mit seinem Augenmerk auf das Lesen von Orten,[21] das die Gestalt beeinflussen soll. Dabei geht es darum zu verstehen, wie und warum Orte zu dem geworden sind, was sie sind.

Wir haben auch von verschiedenen Versuchen von Woods, De Carlo und Ward gehört, Altersstufen und berufliche Rollen zu mischen und die autoritäre Struktur traditioneller pädagogischer Beziehungen aufzubrechen. Dazu kamen Fragen über die Beglaubigung und den gesetzlichen Schutz bestimmter Arten, Architektur zu betreiben – und wie sie zur Identitätsfindung von ArchitektInnen beitragen und definieren, was Architektur ist und wer dazu gehört. Was aber ist der Stellenwert von Gebäuden und Orten in alledem?

**SPM:** Ward betrachtete Mensch und Umwelt in den 1970ern als miteinander verflochten und setzte sich dafür ein, die gebaute Umwelt als eine Folge von Entscheidungen anzusehen. Er sah Gebäude als Ausdruck von Macht, Demokratie, komplexen Ideen und hielt sie deshalb für ein wichtiges Lehrmittel.

Gebäude und Städte bildeten den Fokus in seinen Schriften. Er wollte, dass sich die Menschen daran beteiligen, dass sie, wie er sagte, zu „Herren ihrer eigenen Umgebung"[22] werden.

**FD:** Ich denke, mit Woods gesprochen, lautet die Antwort: „Die Schule als Stadt und die Stadt als Schule."[23] Er betrachtete den Raum als einen Protagonisten des Lernprozesses. Das heißt nicht, dass die Architektur verschwindet, aber ohne die Theorie kommt man nirgendwo hin. Um auf die Freie Universität Berlin zurückzukommen: Für ihn war sie ein Rahmen; das Lernen, das soziale und emotionale Geschehen, sollte zwischen den beteiligen Personen stattfinden. Woods und Schiedhelm glaubten, schon der Grundriss und der *groundscraper* würden die Studierenden dazu bringen, sich zu treffen, würden den Austausch fördern, gegen Isolation wappnen. Insofern sind Raum und Architektur definitiv relevant; sie müssen aber bereichert werden durch diese besondere kulturelle Orientierung der „Entschulung".

**NM:** Ich will De Carlo nicht als einen Theoretiker, einen rein auf die Produktion theoretischer Texte ausgerichteten Architekten definieren: Er war während seiner gesamten Laufbahn auch intensiv als Lehrer tätig. Ab 1978 leitete er zudem die Zeitschrift *Spazio e Società*, in der die bei den ILAUD-Workshops erörterten Themen erarbeitet wurden. Die auf Englisch publizierten und mittlerweile online verfügbaren Jahrbücher sind die dokumentarische Hauptquelle für die Aktivitäten und Reflexionen des ILAUD.[24]

Die Publikation der Jahrbücher und die sogenannten permanenten Aktivitäten sollten den Forschungen des ILAUD eine gewisse Kontinuität verleihen. Eine der Schwierigkeiten war aber Jahr für Jahr, die bei der vorangegangenen Sommerakademie entstandenen Studien einzubauen. De Carlo bat seine PartnerInnen, an der Vorbereitung der Workshops und an der Publikation mitzuwirken, aber der ständige Wechsel an Lehrenden behinderte die Organisation eines stabilen Forschungsnetzwerks. Ohne institutionelle Unterstützung und ohne permanente Geldgeber war das vermutlich ein Ding der Unmöglichkeit.

21  De Carlo, Giancarlo: „Reading and Tentative Design", *Places Journal* 12, 3 (1999), online unter: https://placesjournal.org/assets/legacy/pdfs/reading-and-tentative-design.pdf (Stand: 15. November 2021).

22  Ward, Colin: *Talking Schools: Ten Lectures*, London 1995, 38.

23  Woods, Shadrach: „The Education Bazaar", *Harvard Educational Review, Architecture and Education* 4 (1969), 116–125.

24  Vgl. https://www.ilaud.org/category/about/ (Stand: 7. Februar 2022).

The publication of the *Yearbooks* and the so-called permanent activities were supposed to give a continuity to ILAUD's research. But one of the difficulties was to implement each year the studies produced during the former summer school. De Carlo asked his partners to be involved in the preparation of the workshops and in the publication, but the natural turn-over of the teachers prevented the organization of a stable research network. Without any institutional support and a permanent source of funding, it was maybe something impossible to realize?

**AW**: Buildings facilitate institutional continuity, but organization outside of the built environment matters too …

**SPM**: Ward believed in small, localized groups taking action rather than big institutions providing an overarching structure. In Ward's theory of social organization, groups respond more effectively to people's needs when they are "loosely associated, voluntarily, functional, temporary and small," which "are networks, not pyramids."[25] In Britain, during the 1970s and 1980s, almost 40 Urban Studies Centers embedded Ward's ideas in local autonomous centers. While Ward himself didn't create a center, other people took his ideas and developed them on their terms. It's interesting to see how projects like the urban studies centers expanded without the need of an institution but by local initiative.

**AW**: Perhaps "by local initiative" is where we should start to bring things to a close. As the space where institutions meet the outside, it is perhaps by local initiatives that their work carries on (or fails and does not.) Surely, if there is to be a successful beyond the institution (in terms of space but also in sustaining activity over time) then it has to be successful locally even while nourished via the exchange of ideas nationally and internationally through writing, images, and teaching. One final question to you all: I wonder if, in a sentence or two, you could tell us why research into these particular people and their progressive work is important today?

**FD**: Woods always developed an approach based on experimentation and on interdisciplinarity (from the time of the collaboration with the ATBAT—Atelier des Bâtisseurs Afrique—in North Africa in the early 1950s). Towards the end of his life

Woods seems to have grown more and more convinced that architecture does not hold itself the tools to realize his idealistic aspirations. He therefore initiated a deployment not of his architecture, but of its methods of operation, including open collaboration, non-specialization, challenges to hierarchy, and the utilization of existing urban networks. These he sought to embed in a new "architecture of education" that, more than any building, design strategy, or disciplinary movement, might produce profound, long-lasting cultural betterment.

**SPM**: Ward offered an approach to architecture and the city that focuses on equality, diversity, and inclusion. He was ahead of his time—in his 1973 book *Anarchy in Action*, he already talked about people experiencing discrimination in the city and celebrated the initiatives for and by people of color, gay people, women and especially children *as citizens*. Ward also advocated for a two-way learning where professionals and architects in charge of designing the city learn from and with others who usually are not involved in that process. His proposals for environment-based education, inclusive design processes, and accessible architectural education are still relevant today.

**NM**: In some historical moments, alternative places of discussion such as ILAUD become necessary to welcome debates that would be impossible inside cultural institutions. For security reasons first and sanitary matters then universities are nowadays gradually closing their doors to the public while teachings are more and more separated from professions. I think ILAUD is a seminal experiment to develop alternative teaching and research platforms today. Studying its history, I would like to understand the material difficulties faced by cultural activities developed beyond the institutions.

**AW**: Sol, Federica and Nicolas, thank you for showing how the work of Giancarlo De Carlo, Colin Ward, and Shadrach Woods was both studiously local and (inter)national, how it went beyond the institution and also helps us to question and challenge the necessity of that boundary today. ▪

25  Colin Ward, *Anarchy in Action* (Oakland, CA, 2017), 160.

**AW**: Gebäude ermöglichen institutionelle Kontinuität, aber die Organisation jenseits der gebauten Umwelt spielt ebenfalls eine Rolle …

**SPM**: Ward glaubte an kleine, lokale Gruppen, die aktiv tätig werden, und nicht an große Institutionen, die eine übergreifende Struktur bereitstellen. Nach Wards Theorie sozialer Organisation gehen Gruppen effektiver auf die Bedürfnisse von Menschen ein, wenn sie „lose verbunden, freiwillig, funktional, temporär und klein", also „Netzwerke und nicht Pyramiden"[25] sind. In Großbritannien fanden Wards Ideen während der 1970er- und 1980er-Jahre Eingang in 40 lokale, autonome Urban Studies Center. Auch wenn Ward selbst kein einziges Center gründete, so haben doch andere seine Ideen aufgegriffen und selbst weiterentwickelt. Es ist interessant zu sehen, dass Projekte wie die Urban Studies Center entstanden, ohne eine Institution zu benötigen, rein aufgrund lokaler Initiativen.

**AW**: Vielleicht sollten wir die „lokale Initiative" zum Anlass nehmen, um langsam zu einem Abschluss zu kommen. Als Raum, in dem Institutionen auf die Außenwelt treffen, sind es vermutlich lokale Initiativen, in denen ihre Arbeit fortlebt (oder scheitert und versackt). Wenn es ein erfolgreiches Jenseits-der-Institution (im räumlichen Sinn aber auch im Sinn der zeitlichen Fortführung einer Aktivität) geben soll, dann muss es sicherlich auf lokaler Ebene gelingen, selbst wenn es von einem nationalen oder internationalen Ideenaustausch mithilfe von Bildern, Texten und Lehrveranstaltungen gespeist wird. Eine letzte Frage an euch alle: Könntet ihr in ein, zwei Sätzen darlegen, warum die Beschäftigung mit diesen Personen und ihrer progressiven Agenda heute von Belang ist?

**FD**: Woods hat seit jeher (seit seiner Zusammenarbeit mit dem ARBAT – dem Atelier des Bâtisseurs Afrique – in Nordafrika Anfang der 1950er-Jahre) an einem Ansatz gearbeitet, der auf Experiment und Interdisziplinarität beruht. Gegen Ende seines Lebens scheint Woods immer mehr die Überzeugung gewonnen zu haben, dass die Architektur selbst nicht über die Mittel verfügt, seine idealistischen Vorstellungen umzusetzen. So setzte er nicht seine Architektur, sondern ihre Arbeitsmethoden, offene Zusammenarbeit, Nichtspezialisierung, Infragestellung von Hierarchien und Nutzung bestehender urbaner Netzwerke ins Werk. Diese versuchte er in eine neue „Architektur der Bildung" einzubetten, die, mehr als jedes Gebäude, jede Entwurfsstrategie oder architektonische Bewegung, zu einer grundlegenden, dauerhaften kulturellen Besserung führen sollte.

**SPM**: Ward stand für einen Zugang zur Architektur und zur Stadt, der auf Gleichheit, Vielfalt und Inklusion setzte. Er war seiner Zeit voraus – schon in seinem Buch *Anarchy in Action* von 1973 sprach er von denen, die Diskriminierung im urbanen Alltag erleben, und pries Initiativen von und für People of Color, Schwule, Frauen und vor allem Kinder als BürgerInnen. Ward trat auch für ein bidirektionales Lernen ein, bei dem mit der Stadtplanung befasste Fachleute und ArchitektInnen von und mit Leuten lernen, die üblicherweise nicht am Entwurfsprozess teilnehmen. Seine Konzepte für eine umweltbasierte Bildung, die Entwurfsprozesse und eine zugängliche Architekturausbildung miteinschließt, sind auch heute noch relevant.

**NM**: In bestimmten historischen Augenblicken bedarf es alternativer Diskussionsforen wie des ILAUD, um Debatten zu führen, die in den kulturellen Institutionen nicht möglich sind. Aus Sicherheits- und Hygienegründen schließen Universitäten heute zunehmend ihre Tore für die Öffentlichkeit, und die Lehre löst sich immer weiter ab von der Praxis. Ich halte das ILAUD für ein fruchtbares Experiment für die heutige Entwicklung alternativer Lehr- und Forschungsplattformen. Durch die Beschäftigung mit seiner Geschichte möchte ich die materiellen Schwierigkeiten besser verstehen, mit denen kulturelle Aktivitäten jenseits der Institutionen konfrontiert sind.

**AW**: Sol, Federica und Nicolas, vielen Dank für eure Einblicke in die Arbeit von Giancarlo De Carlo, Colin Ward und Shadrach Woods, ihre bewusst lokale und zugleich (inter)nationale Orientierung, ihr Hinausgehen über die Institutionen und ihrem Potenzial zur heutigen Infragestellung und Ausweitung dieser Grenzen. ∎

*Übersetzung aus dem Englischen: Wilfried Prantner*

25 Ward, Colin: *Anarchy in Action*, Oakland, CA 2017, 160.

# Decolonizing DesignBuild? Construction Sites of Unlearning!

# Dekolonisieren von DesignBuild? Baustellen des Verlernens!

Marlene Wagner (MW) in Conversation with |
im Gespräch mit Christina Linortner (GAM)

1  Installation by Marlene Wagner as part of the exhibition "Mapping 'Social Architecture': Between Search and Effect" | Installation von Marlene Wagner im Rahmen der Ausstellung „Mapping ‚Social Architecture': Zwischen Suchen und Wirken", MAGAZIN – Space for Contemporary Architecture, Wien 2018 © Richard Pobaschnig

Marlene Wagner (MW) is an architect, activist, and lecturer working at the intersections of design and artistic research, participatory action, postcolonial critique, and decolonial theory and practice. She is the cofounder of the buildCollective NPO for Architecture and Development—a nonprofit organization operating between Austria and South Africa. As a doctoral candidate at Vienna University of Technology, she has adopted a practice-based, autobiographical research approach so as to critically reflect on crosscultural and transdisciplinary spatial practice between continents. In the following conversation, she shares with GAM thoughts on architecture and colonization, the practice of unlearning, and the continuities of privilege taken for granted in Western architectural (knowledge) production.

**GAM**: Marlene, as a practitioner and cofounder of an NPO that operates in various global contexts, can you tell us about your journey and the importance of reflecting on it in the context of critical practice and theories of decolonization?

**MW**: I am a curious person. I like to go places. Preferably places I have not been to. Going somewhere changes perspective and helps us to reflect on the baseline condition. I carry *whiteness*, an Austrian passport, and the freedom to believe in a good life for all. I question but still rely upon the nation-state, gender roles, and, above all, a privileged position from which to think, act, and move. A discussion on decolonizing architecture and a theorizing of lived experience through global spatial practice demands the acknowledgment and communication of positionality, referring to the context and the way a question or problem is initially designed. By intentionally using brackets in (de)colonizing, I want to highlight the need for self-reflection and tolerance of ambiguity.

Participating as an architecture student in designing and building a kindergarten on the outskirts of Johannesburg in 2006 fundamentally changed my career and further understanding of architecture and the world. During the following twelve years, I have been co-initiating, co-funding, (re)designing,

(re)building, (re)using, repairing, managing, procuring, and maintaining educational and communal facilities, technical infrastructure, or housing, as well as teaching, discussing, documenting, reflecting, publishing, presenting, and exhibiting projects in different roles and in the context of diverse organizational setups. These structures, situated between global and local centers and peripheries, physically manifested in South Africa.

My work is documented in publications and exhibitions, such as Ora Joubert and Karel Bakker's *Architecture in a Democratic South Africa*, as a call to *Think Global, Build Social!* or framed by Andres Lepik as *Afritecture* and internationally discussed by Nina Gribat and Sandra Meireis as *Social Architecture* debate. buildCollective is cited as a model of practice, placed in the missing middle, and its tactics are discussed as a hacking of international aid by the architectural theorist and educator Hannah le Roux. Nina Pawlicki of the Natural Building Lab further categorized my architectural practice as a connector defined by its deep rooting in local contexts and in a network of institutions of higher education.

**GAM**: What do you hope to achieve by looking at your own practice?

**MW**: I believe it is important to encourage discourse on our continuous need to learn, unlearn, and relearn in architecture schools, but not necessarily in class or in the professional context of architecture, not necessarily while drawing lines on plans. To entangle questions on architecture and colonialism raised within practice and its representation, I am referencing my own architectural work, its representation and contingent potential. Rather than providing answers and findings, I hope to give cause for thought and provide markers for navigation and action in a world in flux. With this autoethnographic approach, which can be described as a re-reflection or rereading of one's own archive, I follow demands for postcolonial perspectives in global architectural practice. I hope to map out the

Marlene Wagner (MW) ist Architekturschaffende, Aktivistin und Dozentin an den Schnittstellen von Design und Künstlerischer Forschung, partizipativer Aktion, postkolonialer Kritik und Dekolonialer Theorie und Praxis. Sie ist Mitgründerin von buildCollective NPO for Architecture and Development, einer gemeinnützigen Organisation, die zwischen Österreich und Südafrika tätig ist. Als Doktorandin an der Technischen Universität Wien verfolgt sie einen praxisbasierten, autobiografischen Forschungsansatz, um ihre interkulturelle und transdisziplinäre Praxis zwischen Kontinenten kritisch zu reflektieren. Im folgenden Gespräch teilt sie mit GAM Gedanken über Architektur und Kolonisierung, die Praxis des Verlernens und Privilegien, die in der westlichen Architektur-(Wissens)-Produktion als etwas Selbstverständliches betrachtet werden.

**GAM:** Marlene, kannst du uns, als Fachfrau und Mitgründerin einer Non-Profit-Organisation, die in verschiedenen globalen Kontexten tätig ist, etwas über deinen Weg erzählen, und darüber, warum es wichtig ist, darüber im Kontext der kritischen Praxis und von Theorien der Dekolonisation nachzudenken?

**MW:** Ich bin ein neugieriger Mensch. Ich reise gerne an Orte. Am liebsten an Orte, wo ich noch nicht gewesen bin. Wenn man wohin geht, verändert das die Perspektive und hilft uns dabei, über die Ausgangssituation nachzudenken. Mir sind das *weiß*-sein, ein österreichischer Reisepass und die Freiheit eigen, an ein gutes Leben für alle zu glauben. Ich kann den Nationalstaat, Genderrollen und vor allem eine privilegierte Position, von der aus ich denke, handle und mich bewege, hinterfragen und mich dennoch weiterhin auf diese Kategorien verlassen. Die Diskussion einer Dekolonisierung von Architektur und die Theoretisierung gelebter Erfahrung in der globalen räumlichen Praxis erfordert das Anerkennen und Kommunizieren des persönlichen Standpunkts, eine Bezugnahme auf den Kontext und die Art, wie eine Frage oder ein Problem formuliert wird. Indem ich ganz bewusst Klammern in (de-)kolonisieren benutze, möchte ich die Notwendigkeit der Selbstreflexion und Ambiguitätstoleranz hervorheben.

Meine Beteiligung als Studentin an der Gestaltung und Errichtung eines Kindergartens am Stadtrand von Johannesburg 2006 hat meine Laufbahn und Verständnis von Architektur und der Welt fundamental verändert. In den folgenden zwölf Jahren habe ich Bildungs- und kommunale Einrichtungen, technische Infrastruktur und Wohnraum mit-initiiert, mit-finanziert, (um)gestaltet, (um)gebaut, (um)genutzt, repariert, gemanaget und gewartet. Und im Kontext verschiedener Rollen und organisatorischer Einheiten und Einrichtungen auch unterrichtet, diskutiert, dokumentiert, reflektiert, veröffentlicht, präsentiert und ausgestellt. Diese Strukturen sind zwischen globalen und lokalen Zentren und Peripherien angesiedelt und haben in Südafrika eine physische Gestalt angenommen.

Meine Arbeit ist in Publikationen und Ausstellungen wie z.B. in Ora Joubert und Karel Bakkers *Architecture in a Democratic South Africa* oder als Aufruf *Think Global, Build Social!* dokumentiert, wird von Andres Lepik als *Afritecture* charakterisiert und international von Nina Gribat und Sandra Meireis als *Social Architecture*-Debatte diskutiert. buildCollective wird von der Architekturtheoretikerin und Lehrenden Hannah Le Roux als ein Praxis-Modell zitiert, welches sich in der fehlenden Mitte befindet, und als eine Taktik des Hackens internationaler Entwicklungszusammenarbeit fungiert. Nina Pawlicki vom Natural Building Lab kategorisiert meine architektonische Praxis darüber hinaus als ein Bindeglied, das durch seine tiefe Verwurzelung in lokalen Kontexten als auch in einem Netzwerk von Hochschulen definiert ist.

**GAM:** Was erhoffst du dir davon, deine eigene Praxis zu betrachten?

**MW:** Ich halte es für wichtig, den Diskurs unseres kontinuierlichen Bedarfs des Lernens, Verlernens und Neulernens anzuregen. In den Architekturschulen aber nicht zwangsläufig im Hörsaal und im professionellen Kontext der Architektur nicht unbedingt, indem man Linien und Pläne zeichnet.

Um Fragen zu Architektur und Kolonialismus, welche sich mir in der eigenen Praxis und ihrer Repräsentation stellen, miteinander zu verschränken, beziehe ich mich auf meine eigene Architekturarbeit, ihre Darstellung und ihr kontingentes Potenzial. Statt Antworten und Ergebnisse zu liefern, hoffe ich Anlass zum Nachdenken zu geben und Markierungen für das Navigieren und Agieren in einer im Fluss befindlichen Welt zu bieten. Mit dem autoethnografischen Ansatz, der sich als eine erneute Reflexion oder als ein Wiederlesen des eigenen Archivs beschreiben lässt, versuche ich den bestehenden Forderungen nach postkolonialen Perspektiven in der globalen Architekturpraxis nachzukommen. Ich hoffe, einen möglichen Weg jenseits der bestehenden Rahmung von internationalen Design Build-Projekten als „Soziale Architektur" zu kartieren. Es geht mir

move beyond an existing framing of international design build projects as a "Social Architecture." So I am aiming for a traceable, critical, global or rather planetary, spatial practice.

Jyoti Hosagrahar describes the potential of postcolonial theory for architecture as "thinking about built form and space as cultural landscapes that are at once globally interconnected and precisely situated in space and time."[1] With reference to Donna Haraway's critique of objectivity and universal knowledge, this begs the question of how to approach and navigate these landscapes and to position its architect, designer, and builder as a partial perspective.

**GAM**: When you are talking about "design build," do you mean a teaching method, or a form of participatory architecture? What is the context of the term?

**MW**: The entangled field, or the mentioned landscapes, I set out from is defined by the tension of being both process and product, theory and practice. It centers and decenters design build between the academy and real life, pedagogy and service delivery, architecture and development. The contested field is illustrated through its varying forms of notation.

While the terms "DesignBuild" or "designbuild studio" are used in German literature for educational projects led by university programs only, in an English-speaking context, "design-build" (spelled with a hyphen) is applied to describe the procurement and commercial form of project delivery, comparable to a *Baumeister* in Austria. By removing the hyphen in "design build," I would like to refer to a possible open practice, beyond established routes of service delivery or as a teaching method.

The design build movement in Austria was introduced in 2003 by the exhibition *Just Build It: The Buildings of Rural Studio* at Architekturzentrum Wien (Az W). Here, the works of Samuel Mockbee's Rural Studio at Auburn University from the early 1990s in the US state of Alabama were shown. Rural Studio's projects have been providing heavily referenced inspiration to many Western architecture schools, organizations, and initiatives by applying full-scale or 1:1 projects situated in so-called

"marginalized communities." In Austria, key actors in establishing the movement locally—enabling my entry to the field and own practice—were the Architekturzentrum Wien, the designbuild studio at Vienna University of Technology (founded in 2000 by Peter Fattinger), and NGO s2arch – social sustainable architecture (established in 2004). By adopting Rural Studio's social engagement in regional peripheries and transferring it to South Africa via an existing post-Apartheid aid route from Vienna to Johannesburg, design build became a particular studio format in Austrian Architecture schools and beyond. The attention placed on architecture and learning, along with a transformative vision shared by the involved educational institutions and nongovernmental organizations, was crucial in its formation. However, a closer look at the guiding principles and proclaimed intentions of the mentioned key actors in Austria and South Africa suggests different areas of focus, audiences, and beneficiaries of transformation.

The initiator and director of the Az W at the time, Dietmar Steiner, characterized the movement as initiatives that develop projects for students within the context of their standard architectural instruction, and as buildings or installations that can be actually completed by these students on site. He further points at its transformative intention, noting that "such projects might appear to be essentially harmless undertakings, but, in comparison to mainstream architectural instruction today, designbuild studios are challenging the academic system in its entirety."[2]

Over the following years, stories and pictures of collective action and experiences made, as well as built artifacts and their users in a foreign land and culture, were brought along and fed back into Western architectural discourse. Such similarities to patterns of the triangular trade route and mobilities of people,

1    Jyoti Hosagrahar, "Interrogating Difference: Post-Colonial Perspectives in Architecture and Urbanism," in *The SAGE Handbook of Architectural Theory*, ed. Greig C. Crysler, Stephen Cairns, and Hilde Heynen (London, 2012), 70.

2    Dietmar Steiner, "Design Build Movement," *ARCH+ 211/212: Think Global, Build Social!*, ed. Andres Lepik (2013): 154.

dabei um eine nachvollziehbare, kritische, globale oder vielmehr planetarische, räumliche Praxis.

Jyoti Hosagrahar beschreibt das Potenzial postkolonialer Theorie für Architektur als „ein Nachdenken über gebaute Form und Raum als Kulturlandschaften, die sowohl global wechselseitig miteinander verbunden als auch präzise in Raum und Zeit verortet sind".[1] Im Hinblick auf Donna Haraways Kritik an Objektivität wirft dies die Frage auf, wie man sich in diesen Landschaften orientiert und bewegt und nach der Positionierung deren ArchitektInnen, GestalterInnen und ErbauerInnen als eine partiale Perspektive.

**GAM:** Meinst du, wenn du von „Design Build" sprichst, eine Lehrmethode oder eine Form partizipatorischer Architektur? Was ist der Kontext des Begriffs?

**MW:** Das verschränkte oder verflochtene Feld mit den erwähnten Landschaften, von dem meine Arbeit ausgeht, definiert sich durch die Spannung sowohl ein Prozess als auch ein Produkt, Theorie und Praxis zu sein. Es zentriert und dezentriert Design Build zwischen der Hochschule und dem wirklichen Leben, Pädagogik und Dienstleistung, Architektur und Entwicklung. Die Umstrittenheit des Felds wird auch durch seine unterschiedlichen Notationsformen illustriert. Während die Schreibweise „DesignBuild" oder „DesignBuild Studio" in der deutschsprachigen Literatur für universitäre Programme forciert wird, wird im englischsprachigen Kontext „design-build" (mit einem Bindestrich) zur Beschreibung kommerzieller Projektabwicklung verwendet, die in Österreich einem *Baumeister* vergleichbar ist. Mit meinem Verständnis von „design build", als Aktivität und ohne Bindestrich, möchte ich mich auf eine möglichst offene räumliche Praxis beziehen, jenseits der etablierten Pfade als reine Dienstleistung oder Lehrmethode.

Die Entstehungsgeschichte der Design Build-Bewegung in Österreich nimmt ihren Anfang 2003 mit der Ausstellung *Just Build It: The Buildings of Rural Studio* im Architekturzentrum Wien (Az W). Hier wurden die Arbeiten von Samuel Mockbees Rural Studio an der Auburn University im US-Bundesstaat Alabama aus den frühen 1990ern in Alabama gezeigt. Die Projekte von Rural Studio haben zahlreichen westlichen Architekturschulen, Organisationen und Initiativen als Inspirationsquelle gedient, indem sie Projekte im Maßstab 1:1 in sogenannten „marginalisierten Gemeinschaften" verorteten.

In Österreich waren die entscheidenden AkteurInnen, welche meinen Einstieg in dieses Architekturfeld ermöglichten, das Architekturzentrum Wien, das (im Jahr 2000 von Peter Fattinger gegründete) DesignBuild-Studio an der Technischen Universität Wien und die (2004 ins Leben gerufene) NGO s2arch – social sustainable architecture [soziale nachhaltige Architektur]. Mit Übernahme der Idee von Rural Studio, deren soziales Engagement in regionalen Randgebieten, und dessen Übersetzung von Wien nach Johannesburg, über eine bereits existierende Route der Post-Apartheid Entwicklungszusammenarbeit, wurden internationale Design Build Projekte ein spezifisches Studioformat an österreichischen Architekturschulen und darüber hinaus. Eine entscheidende Rolle spielte dabei der gerichtete Fokus auf Architektur und Bildung durch die beteiligten Bildungseinrichtungen und Nichtregierungsorganisationen (NGOs), sowie deren transformative Vision. Bei genauerer Betrachtung der Leitprinzipien und Absichtserklärungen dieser zentralen AkteurInnen in Österreich und Südafrika, werden jedoch Unterschiede hinsichtlich ihrer jeweiligen Schwerpunkte, ihres Publikums und der angestrebten ProfiteurInnen des proklamierten Wandels deutlich.

Dietmar Steiner, als Initiator und damalige Direktor des Architekturzentrum Wien, definiert die Design-Build Bewegung als Initiativen, die Projekte für Studierende im Kontext ihrer üblichen Architekturausbildung entwickeln und als konkrete Gebäude oder Installationen, die von diesen Studierenden tatsächlich vor Ort fertiggestellt werden können. Darüber hinaus charakterisiert er die transformative Absicht als „harmlos anmutendes Unterfangen, das aber angesichts des Mainstreams der heutigen Architekturausbildung nicht weniger als das bestehende System infrage stellt".[2] Die im Lauf der folgenden Jahre vermittelten Geschichten und Bilder kollektiven Handelns und Erfahrungen, gebauter Artefakte und deren NutzerInnen in fernen Ländern und fremden Kulturen, flossen wiederum in den Architekturdiskurs ein.

Die Ähnlichkeit zu Mustern der triangulären Handelsroute und der Mobilität von Menschen, Rohstoffen, Waren und Werten, die Europa, Afrika und Amerika seit dem Europäischen Kolonialismus des 16. Jahrhundert miteinander verbinden, stellt auch die mutmaßliche Harmlosigkeit infrage. Die zentralen AkteurInnen Universität, Museum und NGO ermöglichen hier eine thematische Grenzziehung von Macht und der Produktion von Wissen, Geschichte und Entwicklung.

1  Hosagrahar, Jyoti: „Interrogating Difference: Post-Colonial Perspectives in Architecture and Urbanism", in: Crysler, Greig C./Cairns, Stephen/Haynen, Hilde (Hg.): *The SAGE Handbook of Architectural Theory*, London 2012, 70.

2  Steiner, Dietmar: „Die Design-Build Bewegung", *ARCH+ 211/212: Think Global. Build Social!*, hrsg. v. Andres Lepik (2013) 152.

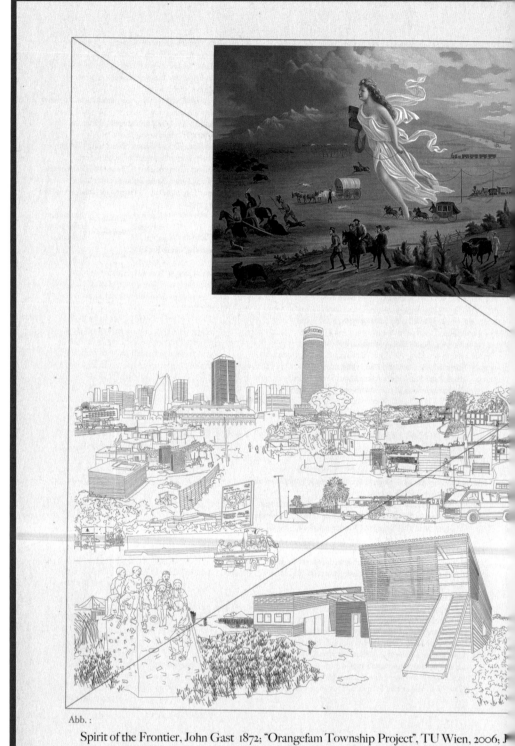

Abb.:

Spirit of the Frontier, John Gast 1872; "Orangefam Township Project", TU Wien, 2006; 

z.B.: **"discern the movements which give it historical form**

2   Montage adopting Johannes Porsch's curatorial layout of 95 frames within the exhibition *Un jardin d'hiver prese*
    *"Bottom Up: Building for a Better World"* – *9 Projects for Johannesburg* Architekturzentrum Wien (Az W), 2006.
    reference to the quote by the curator and Gayatri Spivak's suggestion of productive unease, Marlene Wagner tr
    connections between the USA, Austria, and South Africa and questions her own career path, the use of metaph
    representation and ideas of progress in architecture. | Montage, die Johannes Porschs kuratorisches Layout vor

96

[J.P].

'"Situated knowledge' or 'partial perspective' doesn't mean anymore to merely represent the view from below, to take its position or to represent it through appropriations of its 'empirical details'.
But it indicates positions and situations within invisible 'global paths', that we are pursuing (and tracing), aspects of unseen, 'infinite moving gazes', that we let circulate, where 'action' not only arises, begins, but interrupts itself: Positions and situations, where action is confronted with question of its own impossibility, This impossibility is perhaps the before mentioned gap or blank space, an [immanent] inconsistency, a trace of otherness, which as an instance of the indefinite and uncertain co-produces one's own expression and action, as a dislocation, [a rupture within] in the known, the learned." [* What to do?]

build**COLLECTIVE.**
NPO for ARCHITECTURE and DEVELOPMENT VIE AT ZVR: 9798

©Pez Hejduk

Un jardin d´hiver* presents." AzW, 2006 (2022); buildCollective NPO, 2010; Fanon 1961, Lokko 2019

nt", something that´s about to come

Rahmendisplays der Ausstellung „Un jardin d'hiver präsentiert. ‚Bottom up. Bauen für eine bessere ‚' – 9 Projekte für Johannesburg" aufgreift und weiterführt. In Referenz zu dem Zitat des Kurators und atri Spivaks Empfehlung eines produktiven Unbehagens spürt Marlene Wagner Verbindungen zwischen USA, Österreich und Südafrika nach und hinterfragt dabei ihren beruflichen Werdegang, die Verwendung Metaphern, Repräsentation und den Fortschrittsgedanken in der Architektur. © Montage: Marlene Wagner

resources, goods, and values that connected Europe, Africa, and the Americas, during the colonial era from the sixteenth century onward, put the presumed harmlessness in question. The university, the museum, and the NGO, as key actors, further allow for a thematic demarcation of power and the production of knowledge, history, and development.

GAM: How do concepts of unlearning—that is, Gayatri Spivak's idea to understand "unlearning one's privilege as one's loss"—relate to discourses on decolonization, especially in the context of the design build movement?

MW: One could argue design build as a decolonizing of architecture, through the participatory process involving students and users and the educational motivation beyond the academy or professional accreditation. But this neglects its geopolitical history, its transformative approach, and the (Western) conception of development, architecture, and the modern world.

Design build is referenced by most of its actors in terms of learning theories and is described as an alternative method of architecture teaching and practice in a number of publications. The idea of unlearning, in reference to the postcolonial scholar Gayatri Chakravorty Spivak, is a deconstructing, epistemic perspective and means to recognize inherited privileges not as guilt but rather as loss, without excusing lack of knowledge.[3] Unlearning, therefore, is a critical practice and a collective intervention at the correlation between learning, education, power, and control. With subjects being formed within social processes, every position is accompanied by a specific, situative power to act. The political scientist and educator María do Mar Castro Varela further explains Spivak's concept that privileges taken for granted and historicity ignored lead to a stabilization of existing lines of power. Therefore, it is necessary to denaturalize one's own positioning and instead understand it politically and structurally, but without victimizing or romanticizing marginalized groups. A learning of unlearning as a rather ontological and constructive perspective, which is pertinent to our role as architects, is further described by Walter D. Mignolo's decolonial border-thinking, as the "creation of another model of knowledge and understanding of the world and human

beings."[4] Hence, when we learn, we add new skills or knowledge to what we already know, but when we unlearn, we step outside the mental model or paradigm in order to create different knowledges.

As a conceptual outline of discussing (de)coloniality and design build or architecture, I like to refer to the psychiatrist, philosopher, and anti-colonialist Frantz Fanon. He points to decolonization as an incomplete historical event which "cannot be understood, it cannot become intelligible nor clear to itself except in the exact measure that we can discern the movements which give it historical form and content."[5] The architect, educator, and writer Lesley Lokko further connects to present-day questions of trans-local positions and the potential of architectural knowledge and practice when she refers in an interview on decolonizing architecture to the act of design as "an implicit faith in the idea of something that isn't yet here, something that's about to come."[6]

GAM: Can you describe how your approach and attitude toward design build has changed over time and how it has been informed by postcolonial critique?

MW: My initial contact with design build took place in the course of my studies at Vienna University of Technology, when we built a kindergarten in Orange Farm, South Africa, in 2006. The project was later on presented and contextualized in the exhibition *Un Jardin d'Hiver presents. "Bottom Up: Building for a Better World" – 9 Projects for Johannesburg*, in Vienna, Austria, the same year.

The announcement of the controversially conceived exhibition, curated by the architect, educator, and artistic researcher Johannes Porsch, framed architectural aesthetics as social and

3   See Maria do Mar Castro Varela and Nikita Dhawan, *Postkoloniale Theorie: Eine kritische Einführung*, 2nd fully revised edition, vol. 36 of *Cultural Studies*, ed. Rainer Winter (Bielefeld, 2005).

4   Madina V. Tlostanova and Walter D. Mignolo, *Learning to Unlearn: Decolonial Reflections from Eurasia and the Americas*, in the series *Transoceanic Studies* (Columbus, 2012), 15.

5   Frantz Fanon, *The Wretched of the Earth* (1961; repr., New York, 2004), 36.

6   Lesley Lokko, "Decolonising Architecture; Danielle Mileo in Conversation with Lesley Lokko," *Assemble Papers*, September 4, 2019, available online at: https://assemblepapers.com.au/2019/09/04/lesley-lokko-decolonising-architecture/ (accessed January 12, 2022).

GAM: Inwiefern betreffen Konzepte des Verlernens, d.h. Gayatri Spivaks Idee, „das Verlernen von eigenen Privilegien, die wir als Verlust begreifen sollten", den Dekolonisationsdiskurs, vor allem im Kontext der Design Build-Bewegung?

MW: Man könnte argumentieren, aufgrund des partizipativen Prozesses, dem gemeinsamen Lernen von angehenden ArchitektInnen und NutzerInnen über die Hochschule und den Berufsstand hinaus, es handele sich bei Design Build um ein Dekolonisieren von Architektur. Doch dies untergräbt die geschichtliche Dimension und geopolitischen Zusammenhänge der internationalen Projekte, ihren transformativen Ansatz sowie die (westliche) Auffassung von Entwicklung, Architektur und moderner Welt.

Für die meisten an Design Build Beteiligten stehen Theorien des Lernens im Vordergrund, und in einer Reihe von Publikationen wird Design Build als eine alternative Methode des Architekturunterrichts und der architektonischen Praxis beschrieben. Der postkolonialen Wissenschaftlerin Gayatri Chakravorty Spivak zufolge handelt es sich bei dem Konzept des Verlernens aus einer dekonstruierenden, erkenntnistheoretischen Perspektive darum, dass man ererbte Privilegien nicht als Schuld, sondern als Verlust erkennt, ohne dabei Unkenntnis als Entschuldigung gelten zu lassen.[3] Das Verlernen ist also eine kritische Praxis und eine kollektive Intervention an der Schnittstelle von Lernen, Bildung, Macht und Kontrolle. Da Menschen im Rahmen sozialer Prozesse geprägt werden, geht jede Position mit einer spezifischen, situationsbedingten Handlungsmacht einher. Die Politikwissenschaftlerin und Pädagogin María do Mar Castro Varela erklärt darüber hinaus Spivaks Konzept, dass es zu einer Stabilisierung von Machtstrukturen führt, wenn man Privilegien als etwas Selbstverständliches ansieht und Historizität ignoriert. Daher ist es erforderlich, den eigenen Standpunkt zu entnaturalisieren und ihn stattdessen politisch und strukturell zu verstehen, ohne dabei aber marginalisierte Gruppen zu viktimisieren oder zu romantisieren. Das Erlernen des Verlernens als eine eher ontologische und konstruierende Perspektive, das für unsere Rolle als ArchitektInnen relevant ist, wird darüber hinaus von Walter Mignologs dekolonialem Grenzdenken oder „border thinking" nach Gloria Anzaldúa als „Erschaffung eines anderen Modells des Wissens und des Verständnisses der Welt und der Menschen"[4] beschrieben. Wenn wir lernen, fügen wir also dem, was wir bereits wissen, neue Fertigkeiten oder Kenntnisse hinzu, doch wenn wir verlernen, verlassen wir das geistige Modell oder Paradigma, um andere Wissensformen zu erzeugen.

Im Sinne eines konzeptionellen Rahmens für die Auseinandersetzung mit (De)Kolonialität und Design Build oder Architektur beziehe ich mich einerseits auf die Position des Psychiaters, Philosophen und Anti-Kolonialisten Frantz Fanon. Er verweist auf die Dekolonisation als etwas historisch Unabgeschlossenes, „das heißt, sie kann nur in dem Maße verstanden werden, ihre Intelligibilität finden, sich selbst durchschaubar sein, in dem die geschichtsbildende Bewegung, die ihr Form und Inhalt gibt, erkannt wird".[5] Mit der Architektin, Akademikerin und Schriftstellerin Lesley Lokko verbinden sich dazu aktuelle Fragen translokaler Positionen und das Potenzial projektiven, architektonischen Wissens und Handelns. In einem Interview zum Dekolonisieren von Architektur beschreibt sie den Akt des Gestaltens als „einen impliziten Glauben an die Idee von etwas, das noch nicht da ist, etwas, das erst noch entstehen wird".[6]

GAM: Kannst du beschreiben, wie sich dein Ansatz und deine Haltung gegenüber Design Build mit der Zeit geändert hat und wie beides durch die postkoloniale Kritik geprägt wurde?

MW: Mein Erstkontakt mit Design Build fand im Rahmen meines Studiums an der Technischen Universität Wien statt, als wir 2006 unseren Entwurf eines Kindergartens in Orange Farm, Südafrika, bauten. Das Projekt wurde noch im selben Jahr in Wien in der Ausstellung „Un Jardin d'Hiver präsentiert. ‚Bottom up. Bauen für eine bessere Welt' – 9 Projekte für Johannesburg" präsentiert und kontextualisiert.

Die Ankündigung der kontrovers konzipierten Ausstellung, die von dem Architekten, Lehrenden und künstlerischen Forscher Johannes Porsch kuratiert wurde, begriff architektonische Ästhetik als soziales und gesellschaftliches Engagement.

3   Vgl. Castro Varela, María do Mar/Dhawan, Nikita: *Postkoloniale Theorie: Eine kritische Einführung*, 2. revid. Auflage, Bd. 36 von *Cultural Studies*, hrsg. v. Rainer Winter, Bielefeld 2005.

4   Tlostanova, Madina V./Mignolo, Walter D.: *Learning to Unlearn: Decolonial Reflections from Eurasia and the Americas*, in der Reihe Transoceanic Studies, Columbus 2012, 15.

5   Frantz Fanon, *Die Verdammten dieser Erde*, übers. von Traugott König, Frankfurt am Main, 1981, S. 29.

6   Lesley Lokko in einem Interview geführt von Danielle Mileo: „Decolonising Architecture", *Assemble Papers*, 4. September 2019, online unter: https://Assemblepapers.com.au/2019/09/04/lesley-lokko-decolonising-architecture/ (Stand: 12. Januar 2022).

societal engagement. The exhibition aimed to "negotiate the problem of action-oriented design and planning under postcolonial aspects" and served as a point of departure for my doctoral study. By revisiting the project's representation in Austria, in the museum where the movement originated, rather than the built structure in South Africa, I reenact the shift of attention from the architectural object to its representation and contextualization as postcolonial critique.

The first part of the show's title referred to the 1974 exhibition project *Un Jardin d'Hiver (object-subject)* by the conceptual artist Marcel Broodthaers. The curator took up Broodthaers's critique of the antagonism of nature and culture, and his link drawn between Europe's imperial history and hierarchies of taste, culture, and value, dictated by museums. The winter garden as a retreat of the nineteenth-century bourgeoisie and a symbol of appropriation alludes to an exoticized and domesticized foreignness and the desire to capture and contain presumptive originality and purity, while repressing existing power relations.

Besides the conceptual revival, Porsch adopted the original exhibition design. He inverted traditional lines of vision from architectural retrospectives and design shows and restricted the visitors' gaze. The minimal spatial setup of transparent partition walls, plastic chairs, and palm trees acting as a winter garden left just a small corridor for movement between the showcased designbuild projects. This included nine buildings realized around Johannesburg between 2004 to 2006 by architecture schools from Vienna, Graz, Innsbruck, Linz, Salzburg, Aachen, and the Vienna-based NGO s2arch. The poster of our designbuild project, including drawn plans and photographs of the realized kindergarten, were decentered from the exhibition space and pushed to the outside margins of the built-in structure. Centered and placed inside the installed winter garden were ninety-five frames of white paper with text fragments and visual depictions of architecture from the eighteenth to the twenty-first centuries. The black-and-white images set in relation to fragments of critical theory, and the writings of Spivak, Foucault, and Haraway, consisted of historical illustrations and

photographs: people designing, building, or standing in front of buildings, technical drawings, ethnographic studies, magazines, exhibitions, plans, tables, and diagrams, as artifacts of Western, male architectural history, theory, education, research, and practice. The framed and combined, supposedly conflicting texts and images are to be understood as a crafted history and relational structure opposing a universal organized canon or linear timeline.

I still remember the agitated atmosphere at the exhibition opening, but at the same time my strong resonance with the blank spot and growing discontent toward my own work, experiences made in South Africa and its reception back home. This intended rupture and welcomed "disturbance in the known, in the learned"[7] is described with the concept of catachresis, used to designate a subject or object for which no specific designation otherwise exists or which has been suppressed. The theoretical background of this spatial designation and its relationality is derived from Porsch based on methodological recommendations from Spivak's call for catachrestic approaches as "productive unease" and as a persistent critique between "the general and the narrow."[8] The curator further included text fragments by Michel Foucault wherein the philosopher describes knowledge as power and its relational matrix, not to be reduced to or determined by intentions or subjects. With Donna Haraway's "persistent vision," as part of her contribution on "situated knowledges" and "partial perspective," the curator referred to the signifying gaze and an embodied objectivity through mobile positioning as a key practice. This includes her warnings of appropriating standpoints of the subjugated.[9] The exhibition and publication *Un Jardin d'Hiver presents. Bottom Up. Building for a Better World* thereby invited one to engage in an active rereading, in a tracing of sources, references, and relations, in thinking through and ahead, time and again.

7   Johannes Porsch, "Un Jardin d'Hiver presents. 'Bottom Up: Building for a Better World – 9 Projects for Johannesburg,'" *Hintergrund* 32 (Vienna: Architekturzentrum Wien, 2006), n.p.

8   Gayatri Spivak, "More on Power/Knowledge," in *The Spivak Reader: Selected Works of Gayatri Chakravorty Spivak*, ed. Donna Landry and Gerald MacLean (New York, 1996), 141–174.

9   See Donna Haraway, "Situated Knowledges: The Science Question in Feminism and the Privilege of Partial Perspective," *Feminist Studies* 14, no. 3 (1988): 575–599.

Die Ausstellung diente „der Auseinandersetzung mit dem Problem handlungsorientierten Gestaltens und Planens unter postkolonialen Gesichtspunkten" und diente als Ausgangspunkt für meine Doktorarbeit. Indem ich mich mit der Präsentation des Projekts in Österreich befasse, in dem Museum, von dem Design Build ausgig, statt mit dem in Südafrika errichteten Bauwerk, vollziehe ich erneut die Verschiebung der Aufmerksamkeit weg vom architektonischen Objekt, hin zu seiner Repräsentation und Kontextualisierung postkolonialer Kritik.

Der erste Teil des Ausstellungstitels bezog sich auf das Ausstellungsprojekt „Un Jardin d'Hiver" (object-subject) des Konzeptkünstlers Marcel Broodthaers. Der Kurator griff Broodthaers Kritik am Gegensatz von Natur und Kultur auf und bezog sich damit auf den Zusammenhang, den der Künstler zwischen Europas Imperialismus und den von Museen diktierten Geschmacks-, Kultur- und Werthierarchien herstellte. Der Wintergarten als Rückzugsort des Bürgertums im 19. Jahrhundert sowie als Symbol der Aneignung verweist auf eine exotisierte und domestizierte Fremdartigkeit und den Wunsch, mutmaßliche Ursprünglichkeit und Reinheit zu erfassen, zu konservieren und dabei die existierenden Machtverhältnisse zu verdrängen.

Abgesehen vom konzeptionellen Revival adaptierte Porsch auch das ursprüngliche Ausstellungsdesign. Er kehrte traditionelle Blickrichtungen von Architekturretrospektiven und Designausstellungen um und schränkte die Sicht der BesucherInnen ein. Das minimale räumliche Set-up aus durchsichtigen Trennwänden, Plastikstühlen und Palmen, das als Wintergarten fungierte, bot nur einen schmalen Gang, um sich zwischen den zur Schau gestellten Design Build Projekten zu bewegen. Hierzu zählten neun Gebäude, die zwischen 2004 und 2006 von Architekturschulen aus Wien, Graz, Innsbruck, Linz, Salzburg, Aachen und der in Wien ansässigen NGO s2arch im Umland von Johannesburg realisiert wurden. Das Poster unseres Design Build Projekts, mit Plänen und Fotografien des realisierten Kindergartens, wurde aus der Mitte des Ausstellungsraums an den äußeren Rand der eingebauten Struktur gedrängt. Zentriert, im installierten Wintergarten hingen an den Plexiglaswänden stattdessen 95 Rahmen auf weißen Papierbögen, die Textfragmente und visuelle Darstellungen zu Architektur aus der Zeit des 18. bis ins 21. Jahrhundert zeigten. Die Schwarzweißbilder, die zu Fragmenten der kritischen Theorie und Schriften Spivaks, Foucaults und Haraways in Beziehung gesetzt wurden, bestanden aus historischen Illustrationen und Fotografien: Menschen, die Gebäude zeichnen, errichten oder vor ihnen stehen, technische Zeichnungen, ethnografische Studien, Magazine, Ausstellungen, Pläne, Tabellen und Diagramme als Artefakte westlicher, männlicher Architekturgeschichte, -theorie, -ausbildung, -forschung und -praxis. Die gerahmten und miteinander kombinierten, vermeintlich im Widerspruch zueinander stehenden Texte und Bilder sollten als eine gebastelte Geschichte und relationale Struktur aufgefasst werden, die sich einem universal organisierten Kanon oder einem linearen Zeitverständnis widersetzen.

Ich erinnere mich noch an die erregte Atmosphäre bei der Eröffnung der Ausstellung, aber zugleich auch an eine starke Resonanz auf den weißen Fleck und die wachsende Unzufriedenheit in Bezug zu eigener Arbeit, Erfahrungen in Südafrika und deren Rezeption zu Hause, in Österreich. Johannes Porsch benennt diesen beabsichtigten Bruch und diese mir willkommene „Störung im Gewussten, im Gelernten"[7] mit dem Begriff der Katachrese, der zur Bezeichnung eines Subjekts oder Objekts verwendet wird, für die es keine andere spezifische Bezeichnung gibt oder welche unterdrückt worden ist. Theoretischen Hintergrund dieser räumlichen Bezeichnung und ihrer Relationalität bezieht Porsch auf methodologische Empfehlungen von Spivaks Ruf nach katachrestischen Herangehensweisen als „produktives Unbehagen" und beständige Kritik zwischen „dem Allgemeinen und dem Engen".[8] Des Weiteren bezog der Kurator Textfragmente Michel Foucaults ein, in denen der Philosoph Wissen als Macht und ihre relationale Matrix beschreibt, die sich nicht auf Absichten oder Themen reduzieren oder von diesen determinieren lässt. Mit Donna Haraways „Beharrlichkeit der Vision" als Teil ihres Beitrags zu „situiertem Wissen" und „partialer Perspektive" bezog sich der Kurator auf den Bedeutung generierenden Blick und die verkörperte Objektivität durch mobile Positionierung als entscheidende Praxis. Hierzu zählt auch, dass Haraway davor warnt, sich die Standpunkte der Unterjochten zu eigen zu machen.[9] Die

7   Porsch, Johannes: „Un Jardin d'Hiver präsentiert. ‚Bottom up. Bauen für eine bessere Better Welt – 9 Projekte für Johannisburg'", *Hintergrund 32*, Wien: Architekturzentrum Wien, 2006, o.S.

8   Spivak, Gayatri: „More on Power/Knowledge", in: Landry, Donna/MacLean, Gerald: *The Spivak Reader: Selected Works of Gayatri Chakravorty Spivak*, New York 1996, 141–147.

9   Vgl. Haraway, Donna: „Situated Knowledges: The Science Question in Feminism and the Privilege of Partial Perspective", *Feminist Studies* 14, 3 (1988), 575–599.

**GAM:** How was this critical and theory-based curatorial approach received by the architecture-savy audience?

**MW:** The spatially communicated critique of international design build projects initiated rare but important discussions of a possible *neo*-colonialism in architectural discourse. Austrian newspapers tried to capture the field of tension between the benefit for students on "architecture safari," having fun while learning and earning credits, and the benefit of "shelter" for social and educational facilities, yet with a possible risk of "cultural globalization." The participants of the exhibited projects mainly reacted with disappointment and consternation, emphasizing the importance of applied learning from the "bricoleur" of the "Third World" "against a techno-narcistic academization" in the First World, as the architecture critic Otto Kapfinger had earlier described in the project's publication.[10] Representatives of design build further argued that it is the university's duty "to support students to gain their own perspective on global and local problems by stepping out of their familiar environment."[11]

Unfortunately public discourse then became fixated on formal and aesthetic questions of the built objects, and in-depth discussion on North–South relations was dismissed by the NGO, proclaiming to not have a problem with allegations of post-colonialism if that would refer to implementing an Austrian style to counter clichéd images of Africa. About ten years later, Lesley Lokko wrote the following in her introduction to the *Architectural Review* issue "Africa": "The paradigm of development-aid-charity has come to dominate African architecture to the exclusion of almost everything else."[12]

The described affect and responses triggered by the exhibition fifteen years ago question the willful blanking out of persistent colonial history in architecture discourse, teaching, and practice. These "modes of denial through repression, forgetting and disappearing" described by Donna Haraway[13] are further analyzed as "moves to innocence" by the activists and scholars of education Eve Tuck and K. Wayne Yang, within their text "Decolonization Is Not a Metaphor." Their exemplarily described "adoption fantasies" or "colonial equivocation"[14] relate to the spatial inversion by Johannes Porsch's reference to the winter garden but further ask for explicit representation, accountability, and emphasis on redistribution and action.

**GAM:** What can we learn from this for architecture in relation to colonialism? How do you see the future of design build?

**MW:** Architecture deeply entangled in practices of power is in continuous need of learning, unlearning, and relearning to understand and negotiate its relations as well as borders and limits to (de)colonization and (de)colonizing practices.

Coloniality and constitutive concepts like Race, Gender, or Class are to be understood as technologies beyond apparent physical markers—as "historic repertoires and cultural, spatial and signifying systems that stigmatize and depreciate one form [of life] for the purpose of another's health, development, safety, profit, and pleasure,"[15] as per Daniel Nemser's book *Infrastructures of Race*. Therefore, it is necessary to understand (de)colonizing not as a static state—either the past or a goal to be reached only by former colonies or colonial powers—but as a continuous trans-local process and situative practice of collective unlearning and relearning, undoing and redoing.

Architecture—and here I focus on my own practice—must move away from the notion that a universal understanding of the Western canon is appropriate for global social engagement.

10  See Otto Kapfinger, "Complex Simplicity – Reflections on the Project 'Orange Farm,'" in *Orange Farm Township Project 2006, Kindergarten Emmanuel Day Care*, ed. Peter Fattinger and Institut für Architektur und Entwerfen (Vienna: Institut für Architektur und Entwerfen, Abteilung Wohnbau und Entwerfen, 2006), 102.

11  Peter Fattinger, "Design-Build Studio: Rahmenbedingungen, Prozesse und Potentiale von Design-Build Projekten in der Architekturausbildung" (PhD diss., Vienna University of Technology, 2011), 211.

12  Lesley Lokko, "The Paradigm of Development-Aid-Charity Has Come to Dominate African Architecture to the Exclusion of Almost Everything Else," *Architectural Review* (2017), available online at: https://www.architectural-review.com/essays/the-paradigm-of-development-aid-charity-has-come-to-dominate-african-architecture-to-the-exclusion-of-almost-everything-else (accessed January 12, 2022).

13  Haraway, "Situated Knowledges" (see note 9), 584.

14  Eve Tuck and K. Wayne Yang, "Decolonization Is Not a Metaphor," *Decolonization: Indigeneity, Education & Society* 1, no. 1 (2012): 1–40.

15  Daniel Nemser, *Infrastructures of Race: Concentration and Biopolitics in Colonial Mexico*, 1st ed., from the series *Border Hispanisms* (Austin, 2017), 11.

Ausstellung und Publikation *Un Jardin d'Hiver* präsentiert. „*Bottom up. Bauen für eine bessere Better Welt – 9 Projekte für Johannisburg*" lud also dazu ein, sich immer wieder auf eine aktive Neulektüre einzulassen, Quellen, Bezügen und Beziehungen nachzuspüren sowie gründlich nach- und weiter zu denken.

GAM: Wie wurde dieser kritische und theoriebasierte kuratorische Ansatz von dem architekturversierten Publikum aufgenommen?

MW: Die räumlich kommunizierte Kritik der internationalen Design Build-Projekte führte im Architekturdiskurs zur raren, aber wichtigen öffentlichen Diskussion eines möglichen Neo-Kolonialismus. Österreichische Zeitungen versuchten das Spannungsfeld zwischen dem Nutzen für Studierende auf „Architektur-Safari", die beim Lernen und Erwerb von Scheinen auch noch Spaß hatten, und dem Nutzen eines „Dachs über dem Kopf" für soziale und Bildungseinrichtungen zu erfassen, wohl mit dem möglichen Risiko der „Kulturglobalisierung". Die TeilnehmerInnen an den ausgestellten Projekten reagierten größtenteils mit Enttäuschung und Fassungslosigkeit. Sie betonten, wie wichtig es sei, vom „Bastler" (Bricoleur) aus der „Dritten Welt" zu lernen, um sich „gegen einen techno-narzisstischen Akademismus" in der Ersten Welt zu wenden, was der Architekturkritiker Otto Kapfinger bereits in der Publikation des Projekts hinterfragt hatte.[10] RepräsentantInnen von Design Build argumentierten, dass es die Pflicht der Universität sei, „Studierende aus ihrem gewohnten Umfeld heraustreten zu lassen, um selbst eine eigene Sichtweise auf globale aber auch lokale Probleme entwickeln zu können".[11]

Die öffentliche Auseinandersetzung wurde anschließend von formalen und ästhetischen Fragen hinsichtlich der gebauten Objekte bestimmt, und eine vertiefte Diskussion der Nord-Süd-Beziehungen wurde von der NGO abgetan, indem sie erklärte, sie habe kein Problem mit dem Vorwurf eines Postkolonialismus, wenn damit das Walten einer österreichischen Ästhetik gemeint sei, um klischeehaften Bildern Afrikas entgegenzutreten. Etwa zehn Jahre später schrieb Lesley Lokko in ihrer Einleitung zur „Afrika"-Ausgabe der *Architectural Review*: „Das Paradigma Entwicklungshilfe-Wohltätigkeit bestimmt inzwischen die afrikanische Architektur und schließt alles andere fast völlig aus."[12]

Der beschriebene Affekt und die Reaktionen, die die Ausstellung vor fünfzehn Jahren hervorrief, hinterfragen ein absichtliches Ausblenden der fortdauernden Kolonialgeschichte im Architekturdiskurs, in der Architekturausbildung und -praxis.

Darüber hinaus werden die von Donna Haraway beschriebenen „Formen des Leugnens durch Verdrängen, Vergessen und Verschwinden"[13] von den AktivistInnen und kritischen PädagogInnen Eve Tuck und K. Wayne Yang in ihrem Text „Dekolonisation ist keine Metapher" außerdem als „Schritte zur Unschuld" analysiert. Die beispielhaft beschriebenen „Adoptionsfantasien" oder „koloniale Äquivokation"[14] verbinden wiederum zu Johannes Porschs räumlicher Umkehrung des Wintergartens im Museum, verlangen aber darüber hinaus nach ausdrücklicher Repräsentation, Rechenschaftspflicht, notwendiger Umverteilung und Handlung.

GAM: Können wir daraus etwas für die Architektur im Verhältnis zum Kolonialismus lernen? Wie siehst du die Zukunft von Design Build?

MW: Architektur, die tief in Machtpraktiken verstrickt ist, bedarf des ständigen Lernens, Verlernens und Neulernens, um ihre Beziehungen, ihre Grenzen und Beschränkungen zu zu (De-)Kolonisierung und (de)kolonialisierenden Praktiken zu verstehen und zu verhandeln.

Kolonialität und konstitutive Begriffe wie Rasse, Gender oder Klasse müssen dabei als Technologien begriffen werden, die über physische Kennzeichen hinausgehen – als „historische Repertoires und kulturelle, räumliche und bedeutungsgenerierende Systeme, die eine Form [von Leben] stigmatisieren und zugunsten der Gesundheit, Entwicklung, Sicherheit, des Vorteils und Vergnügens anderer abwerten",[15] wie es in Daniel Nemsers Buch *Infrastructures of Race* heißt. Daher ist es erforderlich, (de)kolonisieren eben nicht als einen statischen Zustand zu begreifen – entweder als die Vergangenheit oder als ein Ziel-

10 Vgl. Kapfinger, Otto: „Complex Simplicity – Reflections on the Project ‚Orange Farm'", in Fattinger, Peter/Institut für Architektur und Entwerfen (Hg.): *Orange Farm Township Project 2006, Kindergarten Emmanuel Day Care*, Institut für Architektur und Entwerfen, Abteilung Wohnbau und Entwerfen, Wien 2006, 102.

11 Fattinger, Peter: „Design-Build Studio: Rahmenbedingungen, Prozesse und Potentiale von Design-Build Projekten in der Architekturausbildung", PhD-Diss., Technische Universität Wien, 2011, 211.

12 Lokko, Lesley: „The Paradigm of Development-Aid-Charity Has Come to Dominate African Architecture to the Exclusion of Almost Everything Else", *Architectural Review* (2017), online unter: https://www.architectural-review.com/essays/the-paradigm-of-development-aid-charity-has-come-to-dominate-african-architecture-to-the-exclusion-of-almost-everything-else (Stand: 12. Januar 2022).

13 Haraway: „Situated Knowledge" (wie Anm. 9), 584.

14 Eve Tuck, Eve/Yang, Wayne K.: „Decolonization Is Not a Metaphor", *Decolonization: Indigeneity, Education & Society* 1, 1 (2012), 140.

15 Nemser, Daniel: *Infrastructures of Race: Concentration and Biopolitics in Colonial Mexico*, 1. Aufl., aus der Reihe *Border Hispanisms*, Austin 2017, 11.

And, moreover, disengage from the historiography of good intentions and harmless learning. Rather than enforcing functionalizing binaries of "us" and "them" "against a techno-narcistic academization,"[16] as brought forward as a reaction to the exhibition and postcolonial critique, we need to understand architectural history, knowledge, and development as Western bricolage as suggested within Porsch's exhibition. The acknowledgment of neutrality being a constructed privilege does not mean being (n)either guilty or innocent, but moving beyond oscillation around the blank spot. It enables conscious reflection on architecture's functionalizing ideologies and engagement in the highly necessary planetary discourse on architecture's practices of appropriation, extraction, absorption, formation, and situating. The in-depth study on how these structures are designed, built, and maintained through the key actors at Western universities, museums, and international aid organizations allows for further understanding of the intersectional power dynamics of architecture, its production of knowledge, history, and development.

If understood as a constant reminder and manifestation of persistent colonial entanglement, international design build projects can serve as exemplary case studies—asking how these projects fulfill or disturb existing colonial conditions and support architectures to "discern the movements which give it historical form and content,"[17] as Fanon suggests.

In relation to the statement by Lesley Lokko on the knowledge of architecture being projective, "to envision what is about to come"[18] and to move beyond existing mental models or paradigms, it is not enough to support a unilateral stepping out of familiar contexts, to question existing canon, or to invert structures of power. Rather, it is necessary to actively design and build other relations, connections, and landscapes of reference.

Instead of designing modes of denial, building "frameworks of excuses, distractions, and diversions,"[19] and retreating further within the institutionalization and formalization of international design build projects as a teaching method or universal applicable service delivery, I suggest viewing design build as a

methodological construction site of applied unlearning. As being consciously positioned within Spivak's "productive unease" and Tuck and Yang's proposed "ethic of incommensurability,"[20] between inside and outside, "the general and the narrow."[21]

Drawing on design build's situative and embodied knowledge production, its comprehensible small scale, extended process, and responsibilities, the communal experience and its affect of experimental setups beyond conventional architectural production can support the process of learning to unlearn. As the suggested "disturbance in the known, in the learned"[22] and the unsettling of innocence, a conscious negotiation of architecture's transformative vision needs to focus on designing and building other images, narratives, and values, spaces of knowledge, history, and development for other architects and architectures.

**GAM**: Thank you for the conversation. ∎

16 Otto Kapfinger referenced by Fattinger, "Design-Build Studio" (see note 11), 12; Christian Kühn, "Wie gut ist gut gemeint?," *Die Presse*, December 23, 2006.

17 Fanon, *The Wretched of the Earth* (see note 5), 36.

18 Lokko, "The Paradigm of Development-Aid-Charity" (see note 12).

19 Tuck and Yang, "Decolonization Is Not a Metaphor" (see note 14), 10.

20 Ibid., 28.

21 Spivak, "More on Power/Knowledge", (see note 8).

22 Porsch, *Un Jardin d'Hiver presents*, (note 7).

zustand, das nur ehemalige Kolonien oder Kolonialmächten zu erreichen haben, sondern als einen kontinuierlichen translokalen Prozess und eine situative Praxis des kollektiven Verlernens und Neulernens unseres Sehens und Tuns.

Architektur – und hier zentriere ich meine eigene Praxis – muss sich von der Vorstellung lösen, dass ein universelles Verständnis des westlichen Kanons für ein globales soziales Engagement angemessen ist. Und darüber hinaus die Geschichtsschreibung der guten Absichten und einer harmlosen Gelehrsamkeit unterlassen. Statt funktionalisierende Dichotomien von „wir" und „sie" „gegen eine techno-narzisstische Akademisierung"[16] zu verstärken, wie dies als Reaktion auf Ausstellung und Kritik vorgeschlagen wurde, müssen wir die Geschichte, das Wissen und die Entwicklung der Architektur als westliche Bricolage begreifen, wie dies in Porschs Ausstellung nahegelegt wurde. Anzuerkennen, dass Neutralität ein konstruiertes Privileg ist, bedeutet dabei nicht, man sei entweder nur schuldig oder unschuldig, sondern sich über die Oszillation um den weißen Fleck hinauszubewegen. Dies ermöglicht ein bewusstes Nachdenken über die funktionalisierenden Ideologien der Architektur und eine aktive Beteiligung an dem höchst notwendigen planetarischen Diskurs ihrer Praktiken der Appropriation, Extraktion, Absorbierung, Formierung und Situierung. Die Untersuchung der Art und Weise, wie diese Strukturen durch die entscheidenden AkteurInnen westlicher Universitäten, Museen und internationaler Hilfsorganisationen gestaltet, gebaut und aufrechterhalten werden, ermöglicht ein besseres Verständnis intersektionaler Machtdynamik und einhergehender Produktion von Wissen, Geschichte und Entwicklung.

Begreift man internationale Design Build Projekte als Erinnerung und Manifestation fortwährender kolonialer Verstrickungen, können sie als exemplarische Fallstudien dienen, die danach fragen, wie sie vorhandene koloniale Bedingungen erfüllen oder stören und die Architektur dabei unterstützen, die „geschichtsbildende Bewegung" zu erkennen, „die ihr Form und Inhalt gibt"[17], wie Fanon nahelegt.

In Bezug auf die Aussage Lesley Lokkos, dass das Wissen der Architektur projektiv sei, etwas zu vergegenwärtigen, „das erst noch entstehen wird"[18], und um dabei über bestehende geistige Modelle oder Paradigmen hinauszugehen, genügt es nicht, ein einseitiges Verlassen vertrauter Kontexte zu unterstützen, den existierenden Kanon zu hinterfragen oder Machtstrukturen umzukehren, sondern es ist erforderlich, aktiv andere Beziehungen, Verbindungen und Referenzlandschaften zu gestalten und bauen.

Statt Formen des Leugnens zu entwerfen, „Rahmenordnungen aus Entschuldigungen, Ablenkungen und Zerstreuungen"[19] zu schaffen und grenzüberschreitendes Gestalten und Bauen als Lehrmethode oder universell anwendbare Dienstleistung zu insitutionalisieren und zu formalisieren, schlage ich vor, Design Build als eine methodologische Baustelle angewandten Verlernens zu betrachten. Als etwas, das sich ganz bewusst in Spivaks „produktivem Unbehagen" und der von Tuck und Yang vorgeschlagenen „Ethik der Inkommensurabilität",[20] zwischen Innen und Außen, „dem Allgemeinen und dem Engen"[21] positioniert.

Die gemeinsame Erfahrung und verbindender Affekt des Gestaltens und Bauens als situative und verkörperte Wissensproduktion, als erweiterte Verantwortlichkeiten experimenteller Organisationsformen im nachvollziehbaren Maßstab, welche über die herkömmliche Architekturproduktion hinausgehen, kann den Prozess des Lernens zu Verlernen unterstützen. Als die suggerierte „Störung im Gewussten, im Gelernten"[22] und Erschütterung der Unschuld muss sich eine bewusste Verhandlung der transformativen Vision von Architektur darauf fokussieren, andere Bilder, Narrative und Werte, Räume des Wissens, der Geschichte und der Entwicklung anderer ArchitektInnen und Architekturen, zu gestalten und zu bauen.

**GAM:** Danke für das Gespräch. ∎

*Übersetzung aus dem Englischen: Nikolaus G. Schneider*

16 Otto Kapfinger zit. nach Fattinger: „Design-Build Studio" (wie Anm. 11), 12; Kühn, Christian: „Wie Gut ist Gut Gemeint?", *Die Presse*, 3. Dezember 2006.

17 Fanon: *Die Verdammten dieser Erde* (wie Anm. 5), 36.

18 Lokko: „The Paradigm of Development-Aid-Charity" (wie Anm. 12).

19 Tuck/Yang: „Decolonization Is Not a Metaphor" (wie Anm. 14), 10.

20 Ebd., 28.

21 Spivak: „More on Power/Knowledge", (wie Anm. 8).

22 Porsch: „Un Jardin d'Hiver präsentiert", (wie Anm. 7).

Jane McAllister | Sandra Denicke-Polcher

# The Casa
## Architecture Students in Residence

## Architekturstudierende in Residence

1   The Casa, located in the small mountain village of Belmonte Calabro served as the temporary residence and headquarter of students from London Metropolitan University. | Die im italienischen Bergdorf Belmonte Calabro gelegene Casa fungierte als Wohnort sowie als Projektzentrale für Architekturstudierende der London Metropolitan University © Orizzontale & Le Seppie

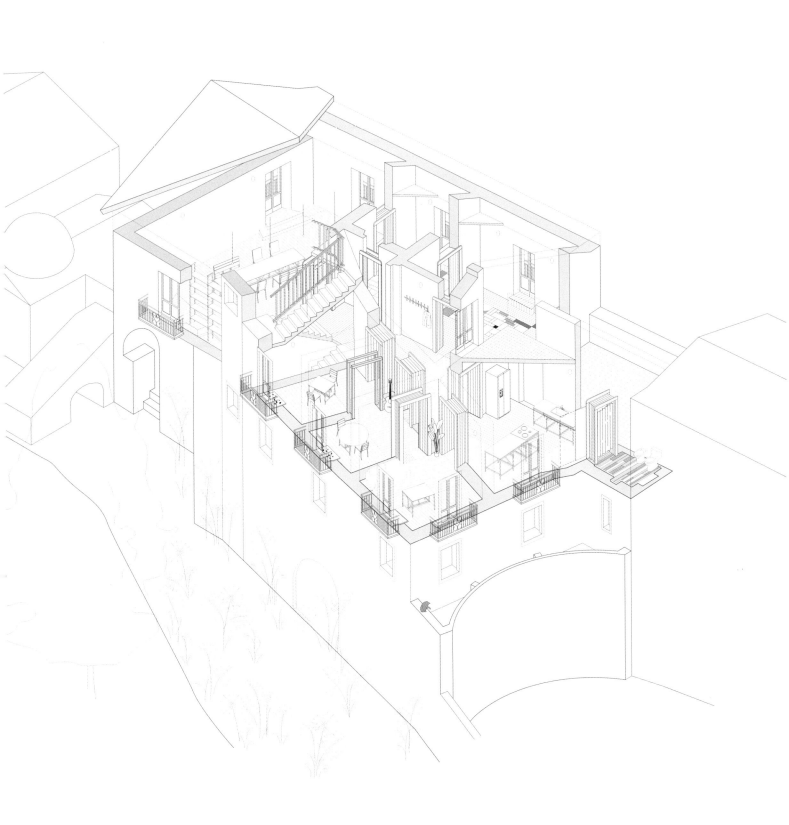

2  The Casa, Belmonte Calabro, 2021 © Photo: Armando Perna

**Site as Provocateur.** During the summer of 2020, the town and marina of Belmonte Calabro in southern Italy served as the setting for our large-scale hypothetical projects as well as for the small-scale *making projects*,[1] delivered as workshops. The partially abandoned hill-town, the post-war marina, and the attendant concerns for community sustainability have become a continuing practical and academic provocation for our students since 2016. The setting has raised questions concerning settlement, how to (re)build local communities, and what role the architect plays in the making of these communities. The region—its physical landscape, economy, and cultural heritage—which has become a fulcrum of global and local concerns, embodies the ebb and flow of migrations. People from the global South attempt to gain access to Europe, and a young indigenous population succumbs to the magnetic pull of Italy's urban centers. It is a place to slow migration and encourage people to settle.

With an already spatially fragmented university campus, enforced online teaching in autumn 2020 provided the perfect motivation to consider temporarily moving in-situ to Italy. Our hypothetical project entitled "Campus: Inhabiting, Thinking and Making" further provoked a new model for education, spatially and pedagogically. The temporary residency presented both an ideologically and physically immersive environment to test this out.

**More Outside than Inside the Institution: A Short History.** Initiated as a summer workshop in Calabria during 2016, this project brought together a mix of architecture students from London Metropolitan University as well as migrants who had recently arrived on Italy's southern shores. Both parties were alighting on Belmonte, which had its own attendant issues of diminishing population and an equally diminishing urban fabric. Neither group was local and both were overwhelmed by the richness and poverty of the unsettling socio-spatial problem, which was further challenged by their own personal histories. The disparities of backgrounds and ambitions were daunting. Working from the local up was the only way these differences could be addressed. The project has been directed by the interests of indigenous people, places and things flourishing through scales of engagement, from making to policy. Its approach has been "repair of fabric," skills and networks, and, in doing so, it has brought an assemblage of needs into one common interest for both locals and migrants.

The curation of the project has been motivated through four stages of co-dependency, developing confidence with the stakeholders and overtime allowing it to materially scale-up. The first stage started with "a shared concern" in 2016: Co-authored by elders and young people of Belmonte, the social fragility of the needs of migrants and locals was mediated through a group of architecture graduates. Practically, this was conducted through conversations in the local bar and through

1  Our working method has involved hand-made material constructions through iterative, collaborative design.

76

**Ein Ort als Provokateur.** Im Sommer 2020 waren die süditalienische Gemeinde Belmonte Calabro und ihre Marina der Schauplatz für unsere großmaßstäblichen hypothetischen Projekte, sowie sogenannte *making projects*[1], die in Form von kleineren Workshops umgesetzt wurden. Das teilweise verlassene Städtchen auf den Hügeln, die Marina aus der Nachkriegszeit und die damit einhergehenden Fragen der kommunalen Nachhaltigkeit erweisen sich für unsere StudentInnen seit 2016 als fortwährende Herausforderung in Theorie und Praxis. Dabei werden sie mit ortsimmanenten Fragen zur Besiedlung, zum (Wieder-)Aufbau lokaler Gemeinschaften und zur Rolle der ArchitektInnenschaft beim Aufbau dieser Gemeinschaften konfrontiert. Die Region – ihre physische Landschaft, ihre Wirtschaft und ihr kulturelles Erbe – ist zu einem Dreh- und Angelpunkt globaler und lokaler Belange geworden und verkörpert das Auf und Ab von Migrationsbewegungen. Menschen aus dem globalen Süden versuchen, sich Zugang zu Europa zu verschaffen, und eine junge einheimische Bevölkerung erliegt der magnetischen Anziehungskraft der urbanen Zentren Italiens. Belmonte Calabro ist ein Ort, der die Abwanderung verlangsamt und Menschen dazu ermutigt, sich in ihm niederzulassen.

Mit einem bereits räumlich stark zersplitterten Universitätscampus war die Verpflichtung zum Distance Learning im Herbst 2020 die perfekte Motivation für einen vorübergehenden Umzug nach Italien. Unser hypothetisches Projekt mit dem Titel „Campus: Wohnen, Denken und Gestalten" brachte dabei, räumlich wie pädagogisch, ein neues Bildungsmodell hervor. Erprobt wurde dieses Modell durch ein Aufenthaltsprogramm vor Ort, durch das ideologische und physische Experimente stattfinden und immersiv erfahren werden konnten.

**Vom Verlassen der Institution: Ein chronologischer Abriss.** Das Projekt wurde 2016 als Sommerworkshop in Kalabrien initiiert und versammelte ArchitekturstudentInnen der London Metropolitan University und kürzlich an der süditalienischen Küste angekommene MigrantInnen. Beide Gruppen waren auf dem Weg nach Belmonte, einer Gemeinde, in der man mit Bevölkerungsschwund und einem ebenso schwindenden Gemeindegefüge zu kämpfen hatte. Keine der beiden Gruppen war ortsansässig, und beide waren von der Reichhaltigkeit wie auch der beunruhigenden sozialräumlichen Problemstellung überwältigt, was durch ihren individuellen Erfahrungshintergrund noch verstärkt wurde. Die Disparität der Geschichten und Zielsetzungen war zunächst einschüchternd, und die Arbeit auf der lokalen Ebene die einzige Möglichkeit, sich mit diesen Unterschieden auseinanderzusetzen. Das Projekt wurde von den

Interessen der Einheimischen gesteuert, die dem Projekt, den Orten und Dingen, auf ganz unterschiedlichen Gebieten ihr Engagement schenkten, von der Gestaltung bis hin zur Politik. So war die „Reparatur von Strukturen", von Fähigkeiten und Netzwerken der zentrale Ansatz, der die unterschiedlichsten Bedürfnisse in einem übergeordneten gemeinsamen Ziel für MigrantInnen und Einheimische bündelte.

Die Kuration des Projekts war durch vier Phasen der Kodependenz motiviert, wobei das Selbstvertrauen der Beteiligten gestärkt und das Projekt im Laufe der Zeit wesentlich erweitert werden konnte. Die erste Phase begann 2016 unter dem Motto „A Shared Concern": in Zusammenarbeit mit älteren und jungen Menschen aus Belmonte vermittelte eine Gruppe von ArchitekturabsolventInnen entlang der sozialen Bruchlinien zwischen den Bedürfnissen von MigrantInnen und Einheimischen. In der Praxis erfolgte dies durch Gespräche in der ortsansässigen Bar und durch Kleinprojekte, an denen MigrantInnen und Einheimische mitarbeiteten. Die zweite Phase lief parallel zur ersten Phase von 2016 bis 2021 unter dem Motto „Stewarding the Imagination" und thematisierte unter anderem das sozialräumliche Umdenken in der Kulturlandschaft durch die Vermittlung einer Reihe von Fachkenntnissen: Wir führten hypothetische Projekte durch, in deren Rahmen die StudentInnen durch den Austausch von Fähigkeiten verschiedene Denkmodelle im Dorfkontext erkundeten. Diese wurden dann in regelmäßigen Abständen als „neu gestaltetes Porträt" an die Ortsbevölkerung und die Stadtverwaltung weitergegeben. Außerdem wurde die Universität in Reggio Calabria involviert, was weiteres Vertrauen von innen mit sich brachte. Die dritte Phase von 2017 bis 2019 stand unter dem Motto „Practicing Skills": Dazu gehörte das Erlernen von bautechnischen Fähigkeiten genauso wie der Aufbau von Vertrauen zwischen Einheimischen und MigrantInnen, zunächst in Form kleiner Handwerksprojekte wie dem Bauen von Stühlen und Tischen zur Förderung eines konvivialen Miteinanders mit dem Dorf, dann kamen größere Projekte wie die Planung und die Errichtung einer Außenküche und die Renovierung der Casa, eines ehemaligen Nonnenklosters hinzu (Abb. 1). Dies war auch der Punkt, an dem die Ortsverwaltung aktiv wurde, indem sie uns die Casa zur Entwicklung einer Projektzentrale in der Gemeinde zur Verfügung stellte. Die letzte Phase von 2019 bis 2021 war der „Policy" gewidmet. In dieser Zeit engagierte sich Vizebürgermeister Luigi Provenzano sehr für das Projekt und vermittelte Kontakte zu wichtigen GemeindevertreterInnen. Berichterstattung in den digitalen und traditionellen Medien förderte den

---

1  Unsere Arbeitsmethode beinhaltete auch handwerkliche Fertigung durch iteratives, kollaboratives Design.

small projects which engaged migrants and locals. The second stage ran concurrently with the first stage from 2016 to 2021, as "stewarding the imagination" and involved the socio-spatial re-thinking of the cultural landscape through the communication of skills sets: Our institution ran hypothetical projects as part of the students exploring different models of thinking through skills exchange in the context of the village. These were then periodically shared as a "re-imagined portrait" with the locals and municipality, as well as reaching out to the university in Reggio Calabria, which brought further confidence from inside. The third stage, from 2017 to 2019, was "practicing skills": This included building skills and confidence between locals and migrants, first, with small construction projects such as chairs and tables to facilitate conviviality with the village, then, it scaled-up to an outdoor kitchen and refurbishment of the Casa, a former nunnery (fig. 1). This was also the point where the municipality became engaged, gifting the Casa to the project to develop a headquarters in the village. The last stage, from 2019 to 2021, was "policy": During this period the vice-mayor Luigi Provenzano became very involved in the project and facilitated connections with key members of the community. Connections with local industries and international organizations were aided by digital and media coverage. This further scaled-up the project and refined the remit, participants, their actions, both closing the loop and building new networks for yet more complex iterations to come. We argue that "The Casa" is a new educational model that becomes an agora for situated practice beyond the institution.

During our satellite residency, which was hosted by the non-profit organization La Rivoluzione delle Seppie[2] the Casa became our headquarters, providing the live-work location for our Studio South students (fig. 2). Crossings, a strand of La Rivoluzione delle Seppie, grew out of a student-led summer school with our architecture students in rural Italy during summer 2016. It continues to operate with a belief in involvement, empowerment, and the flourishing of communities, which includes the need to develop skills and new ways of living within fragile socio-material cultures, new and old. It has engaged with migrants, educators, and local villagers, in which our students have become activist researchers within the village, with the intention of bringing about strategic change through collaboration and social development. In this context, our local

NGO[3] continued to act as facilitator, bridging the gap between hypothetical architecture projects, local people and the municipality. With this in mind, the residency in the Casa gave the opportunity to extend the summer school that had previously been operating.

**Situated Practices.** The coincidence of the flow of migration versus the necessity to settle has created a platform for ongoing engagement with a growing pool of stakeholders: students, graduates, tutors, local inhabitants, migrants, municipal stakeholders, local and regional government departments, agencies, community bodies and universities. The traditional contractual relationship between client and architect must, in this context, be reconstituted as a network of partnerships, drawing the stakeholders together in a way that frames the potential for a positive outcome. This social sustainability-led working method, which is based on mutual respect, allows practitioners as "spatial agents,"[4] clients, and stakeholders[5] to be integrated into Crossings as co-learners and co-creators. With this in mind, students also needed to be mindful of their role in relation to how *familiar* spatial and cultural conditions are played out in *unfamiliar* locations.[6]

The project's larger context—the politics, the effects of migration, and the lack of viable industries—significantly charged students' imaginations. These issues question their role as architects, their approach to intervention, how they observe, record, and initiate spatial practices to become effective catalysts of change and, most importantly, how they influence issues of sustainability against an imbalance of politics, economics, and social diaspora. Their task has been to reconcile the top-down delivery of their academic projects in relation

2   La Rivoluzione delle Seppie is a collective for social change. See also https://larivoluzionedelleseppie.org (accessed February 7, 2022).

3   Rita Adamo, co-founder of La Rivoluzione delle Seppie.

4   Awan Nishat, Tatjana Schneider, and Jeremy Till, *Spatial Agency: Other Ways of Doing Architecture* (London, 2011).

5   Doina Petrescu, "Relationscapes: Mapping Agencies of Relational Practice in Architecture," City, *Culture and Society* 3 (2012): 135–140.

6   See Homi K. Bhabha, "Of Mimicry and Man: The Ambivalence of Colonial Discourse," in *The Location of Culture* (Hoboken, 2012).

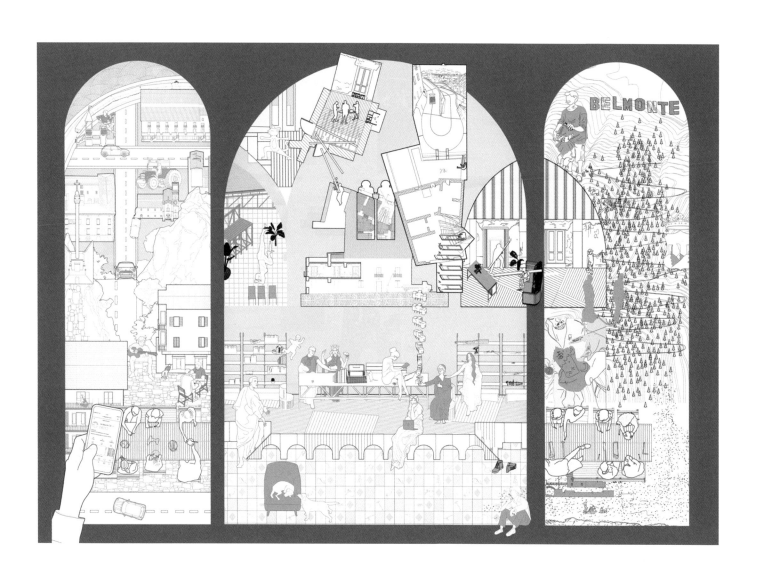

to the bottom-up experiences during the summer workshops and residency. These, we believe, are vital to the education of an architect and may only begin to be explored beyond the confines of the academic institution.

**Voices from Local Inhabitants and** *New-Makers*.[7] To test the ongoing progress of belonging, we have asked two groups of users, local inhabitants and new-makers, to name their initial hopes, the change they have already seen, and their reimagined future for the village. Vice-mayor Luigi Provenzano has supported the project since 2016, which was crucial to its communication across media networks, its value to neighboring relationships and longevity. His vision entailed enticing the small village with an over-aged population of 60 people to an international audience: "I was dreaming that an international school would settle here, which would attract young people back to the village and create a lively international environment. There are examples in the North of Italy where this has happened. After the first group of students and tutors from London visited in 2016, my personal hope was that they would come back. We know now that this has come true."[8]

The return of students bringing skills, energy, and vision has built trust through collaborative making with the villagers. He continues: "Undoubtedly, the repeated presence of the students has developed strong relationships between the students and locals. There is mutual benefit: locals have been reminded about their traditions, skills, and customs, while the students valued these and learnt new skills."[9] In addition to this, he speaks of the joy, optimism, and prosperity it had brought to the village. Every year there is either a new shop, public space development, or new event celebrating the local culture. These are signs of progress in a depopulating village with demography above the age of mid-50s, as this gradually increases the amenities and encourages a younger population to settle. Luigi's vision of the "International School" has been instrumental in transforming the Casa into a vital workplace for the young population involved in the project. It provided the main impetus for the Casa to be renovated, equipped with Wi-Fi by the

7   These come from a range of disciplines and use the Casa as a base from where they work remotely and iteratively on collaborative design.

8   Luigi Provenzano, personal conversation with the authors, October 30, 2021, Belmonte Calabro.

9   Ibid.

4   Giuseppe Grant and migrants building together | Gemeinsames Bauen: Giuseppe Grant mit MigrantInnen, Belmonte Calabro, 2021
© Photos: Domenique Guglielmo, Francesca D'Agnano

Kontakt zur lokalen Wirtschaft und internationalen Organisationen. Dies erweiterte das Projekt und entwickelte Auftrag, TeilnehmerInnen und deren Aktionen weiter, wodurch sich der Kreislauf schloss und neue Netzwerke für noch komplexere künftige Iterationen aufgebaut wurden. Wir vertreten die Auffassung, dass die Casa ein neues Bildungsmodell manifestiert und zur Agora für eine situierte Praxis jenseits der Institution geworden ist.

Während unseres von der NGO La Rivoluzione delle Seppie[2] ausgerichteten Gastaufenthalts wurde die Casa zu unserem Hauptquartier und diente den StudentInnen als ihr Wohn- und Arbeitsort namens Studio South (Abb. 2). „Crossings" eine Projektreihe von La Rivoluzione delle Seppie entstand im Sommer 2016 aus einer von StudentInnen geleiteten Sommerschule im ländlichen Raum Italiens. Sie setzt sich weiterhin für das Empowerment und das Gedeihen von Gemeinden ein, wozu auch die Notwendigkeit gehört, innerhalb fragiler – neuer und alter – sozio-materieller Kulturen neue Fachkenntnisse und Lebensweisen zu entwickeln. Sie kooperiert mit MigrantInnen, PädagogInnen und DorfbewohnerInnen, wobei unsere StudentInnen zu aktivistischen ForscherInnen im Dorf wurden, mit dem Ziel, durch Zusammenarbeit und soziale Entwicklung einen strategischen Wandel herbeizuführen. In diesem Zusammenhang fungierte unsere lokale NGO[3] weiterhin als Vermittlerin, die die Kluft zwischen den hypothetischen Architekturprojekten, den Einheimischen und der Gemeindeverwaltung überbrückte. Vor diesem Hintergrund bot der Studienaufenthalt in der Casa die Möglichkeit, die bisher durchgeführte Sommerschule zu verlängern.

**Situierte Praxen.** Das Zusammentreffen von Migrationsströmen und der Notwendigkeit, sich niederzulassen, schuf eine Plattform für die kontinuierliche Zusammenarbeit mit einer wachsenden Zahl von Projektbeteiligten: Studierenden, HochschulabsolventInnen, Lehrkräften, Einheimischen, MigrantInnen, VertreterInnen der Gemeindeverwaltung, lokalen und regionalen Regierungsstellen, Agenturen, Gemeinschaftseinrichtungen und Universitäten. Die traditionelle Vertragsbeziehung zwischen Bauherr und Architekt muss in diesem Zusammenhang neu gefasst werden – als ein Netz von Partnerschaften, das die Beteiligten in einer Weise zusammenbringt, die dem Potenzial für ein positives Resultat einen Rahmen bietet. Diese auf soziale Nachhaltigkeit ausgerichtete und auf gegenseitigem Respekt beruhende Arbeitsmethode ermöglicht es den PraktikerInnen als „räumlich wirkende Kräfte",[4] BauherrInnen und StakeholderInnen[5], als Mitlernende und Mitgestaltende in „Crossings" integriert zu werden. In diesem Sinne mussten sich die StudentInnen auch ihrer Rolle bewusst sein, wenn es darum ging, wie ihnen bekannte räumliche und kulturelle Gegebenheiten sich an ihnen unbekannten Orten entwickeln.[6]

Der breitere Kontext des Projekts – die Politik, die Auswirkungen der Migration und das Fehlen von lebensfähigen Wirtschaftszweigen – hat die Fantasie der StudentInnen angeregt. Dabei geht es um ihre Rolle als Architekturschaffende, ihre Herangehensweise an Interventionen, die Art und Weise, wie sie räumliche Praxen beobachten, aufzeichnen und initiieren, um zu wirksamen Katalysatoren des Wandels zu werden, und vor allem darum, wie sie Fragen der Nachhaltigkeit angesichts eines Ungleichgewichts von Politik, Wirtschaft und sozialer Diaspora beeinflussen. Ihre Aufgabe bestand darin, die Topdown-Ergebnisse ihrer akademischen Projekte mit den Bottom-up-Erfahrungen während der Sommerworkshops und des Studienaufenthalts in Einklang zu bringen. Wir sind der Meinung, dass diese Erfahrungen für die Architekturausbildung unerlässlich sind und derzeit nur ansatzweise über die Grenzen der akademischen Institution hinaus erforscht werden.

**Stimmen von Einheimischen und *new-makers*[7].** Um den laufenden Fortschritt der Zugehörigkeit zu überprüfen, haben wir Einheimische und *new-makers* gebeten, ihre anfänglichen Hoffnungen, die bereits eingetretenen Veränderungen und ihre neuen Zukunftsvorstellungen für den Ort zu nennen. Vizebürgermeister Luigi Provenzano unterstützt das Projekt seit 2016, was für seine Kommunikation über Mediennetzwerke, seinen Wert für Nachbarschaftsbeziehungen und seine Nachhaltigkeit von entscheidender Bedeutung gewesen ist. Luigi Provenzanos Vision bestand darin, die kleine Gemeinde mit einer überalterten Bevölkerung von 60 EinwohnerInnen für ein internationales Publikum attraktiv zu machen: „Ich träumte davon, dass sich hier eine internationale Schule ansiedeln würde, die junge Leute zurück ins Dorf locken und ein lebendiges internationales Umfeld schaffen würde. Es gibt Beispiele in Norditalien, wo dies geschehen ist. Nach dem Besuch der ersten Gruppe Studierender und Lehrender aus London im Jahr 2016 hatte ich persönlich die Hoffnung, dass sie wiederkommen würden. Wie wir jetzt wissen, ist dies in Erfüllung gegangen."[8]

2    La Rivoluzione delle Seppie ist ein Kollektiv zur Förderung gesellschaftlichen Wandels. Siehe dazu: https://larivoluzionedelleseppie.org (Stand: 12. Februar 2022).

3    Rita Adamo, Mitbegründerin.

4    Nishat, Awan/Schneider, Tatjana/Till, Jeremy: *Spatial Agency: Other Ways of Doing Architecture*, London 2011.

5    Petrescu, Doina: „Relationscapes: Mapping Agencies of Relational Practice in Architecture", in: *City, Culture and Society* 3 (2012), 135–140.

6    Vgl. Bhabha, Homi K.: „Of Mimicry and Man: The Ambivalence of Colonial Discourse", in: Bhabha, Homi K. (Hg.): *The Location of Culture*, Hoboken 2012, 121–131.

7    Sie kommen aus den unterschiedlichsten Disziplinen und nutzen das Casa als Basis, von der aus sie aus der Ferne schrittweise an der gemeinsamen Gestaltung arbeiten.

8    Gespräch mit Luigi Provenzano am 30. Oktober 2021, Belmonte Calabro.

students and activists and to be embedded within the community as an international learning space.

Luigi recognizes the richness of human interaction, participation, and conviviality. He refers to this as the "agora," suggesting that the Casa has become the microcosm of the village. In doing so, he supports the value of debate and the many voices of students, locals, and migrants, which together make the discussion valuable. He openly concedes: "The presence of the students in Belmonte has produced a very different image for our village, not only in Calabria but also nationally. I have had phone calls from other municipalities who recognized that such an experience can truly revive our villages. If this was repeated in other villages in this region, it would be a step towards revitalizing culture, study, and research in the South."[10] In recognizing this, he is arguing for a new way of reworking the social, cultural, and economic landscape, one which demands involvement and participation.

In contrast to the local voice of Luigi, the international voices of the *new-makers* are represented by three students who formed Studio South: Joe Douglas has been joining several workshops and after graduating in 2020, became a permanent resident. He now speaks Italian and has been doing both participating in projects *for* the Casa and developing London projects remotely *in* the Casa. Joe's involvement and commitment to the project has been consistent and innovative. He declares that it has nurtured "collective study" which has produced an expertise in "how to produce spaces that are comfortable and collaborative as work in progress."[11] Together with his fellow student Ian Davide he has captured this ideological way of being in a fresco drawing (fig. 3): "The fresco drawing speculates on our love for sharing an old building that facilitates work and play. 'E una città dentro una città' (A City within a City). A house without doors. Taking work as the pivotal reason for our collective gathering, we draw on the painting 'Saint Jerome in His Study' as an ideal environment to find focus. However, our energies are drawn not from isolation but from the opposite. By relocating with people who use the spaces within to their own needs, different to our own, we find ourselves more intrigued by this activity than often in our normal lives. We find

a new home away from home, more than just a getaway, but an extension to our capacities for engagement."[12]

Another student of Studio South, Madalina Podgoreanu, explains that living in the Casa during the pandemic allowed her and the other students to "understand the trials and tribulations of small communities."[13] Living themselves as a small community in the Casa and among the villagers, they came to understand the importance of joined-up thinking and the role it plays in both social and physical sustainability. This produced a way of thinking for Madalina's studio project, which started as the reforestation of the surrounding mountains and addressed the urgent need of building houses using sustainable materials. This became evident from living in the Casa, with its cheek-by-jowl close knit community, that in the marina of Belmonte was a paucity of civic spaces to be developed as her *paper* project from re-skilling and public space. She addressed this in bringing live-work, skilling, and public space into a new offer: "Exploring and testing the ideas of a mixed neighborhood, live-work and private/public through us living in the Casa developed a strong community through collectivism. It was easy to understand and transfer meaningful ways of working to my site in the marina, around the partially abandoned and disused Rivellino."[14]

Another *new-maker*, Giuseppe Grant, architect of the Rome-based architecture collective Orizzontale, works across "fields of architecture, urbanism, public art and DIY practice."[15] In 2017, he started the project by leading small-scale construction workshops. The outputs found themselves inhabiting public spaces, having the demure appearance of a family maintaining watch over the village. Giuseppe's approach has always been to

10 Ibid.

11 Joe Douglas, personal conversation with the authors, October 28, 2021, Belmonte Calabro.

12 Ian Bugarin and Joe Douglas, "The Casa: Not a Place for Quiet Contemplation," *Reimagined Living & Working Space Competition 2021*, available online at: https://www.fatrecruitment.co.uk/the-casa?fbclid=IwAR2Iwo_jIOvtQQIbF9i9PbE76bkjeo5d8NqramCI4HuQjUFOGDDN8o8UsqM (accessed October 30, 2021).

13 Madalina Podgoreanu, personal conversation with the authors, October 30, 2021, London.

14 Ibid.

15 Giuseppe Grant, personal conversation with the authors, October 31, 2021, Belmonte Calabro. See also http://www.orizzontale.org/en/ (accessed January 28, 2022).

Die Rückkehr der StudentInnen mit ihren Kenntnissen, ihrer Energie und ihren Visionen hat durch die gemeinsame Arbeit mit der Dorfbevölkerung Vertrauen geschaffen. Er ergänzt: „Die wiederholte Anwesenheit der StudenInnen hat zweifellos starke Beziehungen zwischen den StudentInnen und den Einheimischen entstehen lassen. Davon profitierten beide Seiten: Die Einheimischen wurden an ihre Traditionen, Fertigkeiten und Bräuche erinnert, während die StudentInnen diese zu schätzen lernten und neue Fähigkeiten erwerben konnten."[9] Darüber hinaus spricht er von der Freude, dem Optimismus und dem wirtschaftlichen Aufschwung, den sie dem Dorf gebracht habe. Jedes Jahr kommt entweder ein neues Geschäft, ein neues Projekt im öffentlichen Raum oder ein neuer Event hinzu, der die Lokalkultur feiert. Provenzanos Vision der Internationalen Schule hat maßgeblich dazu beigetragen, die Casa in einen lebendigen Arbeitsplatz für die am Projekt beteiligte junge Bevölkerung zu verwandeln. Sie gab den entscheidenden Anstoß für die Renovierung der Casa, deren Versorgung mit WLAN durch die StudentInnen und AktivistInnen und die Einbindung in die Gemeinde als internationaler Bildungsraum.

Provenzano weiß um den großen Wert menschlicher Interaktion, Teilnahme und Konvivialität. Er nennt dies die Agora und deutet damit an, dass die Casa zum Mikrokosmos der Gemeinde geworden ist. Damit unterstützt er den Wert der Debatte und die vielen Stimmen von StudentInnen, Einheimischen und MigrantInnen, die zusammen die Diskussion wertvoll machen. Er räumt offen ein: „Die Anwesenheit der StudentInnen in Belmonte hat unserer Gemeinde ein ganz anderes Image verliehen, nicht nur in Kalabrien, sondern auch in ganz Italien. Ich habe Anrufe aus anderen Gemeinden erhalten, die erkannt haben, dass eine solche Erfahrung unsere Gemeinden wirklich beleben kann. Wenn man dies in anderen Gemeinden dieser Region wiederholen würde, wäre das ein Schritt zur Wiederbelebung von Kultur, Studium und Forschung im Süden."[10] Indem er dies anerkennt, plädiert er für eine neue Form der Umgestaltung der sozialen, kulturellen und ökonomischen Landschaft, eine, die Engagement und Teilhabe erfordert.

Im Kontrast zu Luigi Provenzano, der Stimme der Einheimischen, repräsentieren drei Studierende, die das Studio South bildeten, die internationale Stimme der *new-makers*: Joe Douglas hat an mehreren Workshops teilgenommen und wurde nach seinem Abschluss des Architekturstudiums im Jahr 2020 zu einem ständigen Bewohner. Er spricht jetzt Italienisch und hat sowohl an Projekten *für* die Casa teilgenommen als auch Londoner Projekte aus der Ferne *in* der Casa entwickelt. Joes Beteiligung und sein Einsatz für das Projekt waren stets konsequent und innovativ. Er erklärt, dass das „kollektive Studium" Fachkenntnisse darüber hervorgebracht hat, „wie man Räume

schafft, die als *work in progress* angenehm und kollaborativ sind".[11] Zusammen mit seinem Studienkollegen Ian Davide hat er diese ideologische Seinsweise in einer Freskozeichnung festgehalten (Abb. 3): „Die Freskozeichnung ist eine Spekulation über unsere Liebe zur gemeinsamen Nutzung eines alten Gebäudes, das Arbeit und Spiel ermöglicht. ‚E una città dentro una città‘, eine Stadt in der Stadt. Ein Haus ohne Türen. Wenn wir die Arbeit als zentralen Grund für unsere kollektive Zusammenkunft betrachten, zeigt das Gemälde ‚Der heilige Hieronymus im Gehäus‘ eine ideale Umgebung, um sich zu konzentrieren. Unsere Energien ziehen wir jedoch nicht aus der Isolation, sondern aus ihrem Gegenteil. Indem wir mit Menschen zusammenziehen, die die Räume für ihre eigenen Bedürfnisse nutzen, die sich von unseren eigenen unterscheiden, ertappen wir uns dabei, wie uns dieses Tun mehr fasziniert als oft in unserem normalen Leben. Wir finden ein neues Zuhause in der Ferne, das mehr ist als nur ein Urlaubsort, nämlich eine Erweiterung unserer Möglichkeiten, uns zu engagieren."[12]

Madalina Podgoreanu, eine andere Studentin von Studio South, erklärt, dass das Leben in der Casa während der Pandemie ihr und den anderen StudentInnen half, „die Irrungen und Wirrungen kleiner Kommunen zu verstehen".[13] Indem sie selbst als kleine Kommune in der Casa und mitten unter der Dorfbevölkerung lebten, lernten sie die Bedeutung vernetzten Denkens und die Rolle kennen, die es für soziale wie physische Nachhaltigkeit spielt. Dies inspirierte Madalinas Studio-Projekt, das mit der Wiederaufforstung der umliegenden Berge begann und sich mit der dringenden Notwendigkeit befasste, Häuser mit nachhaltigen Baustoffen zu errichten. Durch das Leben in der Casa mit ihrer engmaschigen Gemeinschaft wurde deutlich, dass es in der Marina von Belmonte an zivilgesellschaftlichen Räumen mangelt, die im Rahmen ihres Projekts „Re-skilling and Public Space" ausgearbeitet werden sollten. Sie entwickelte dies, indem sie Wohnen/Arbeiten, Erwerbung neuer Fachkenntnisse und öffentlichen Raum in einem neuen Angebot zusammenbrachte: „Durch unsere Erforschung und Erprobung einer durchmischten Nachbarschaft, des Wohnens und Arbeitens sowie unseres privaten und öffentlichen Lebens in der Casa entstand durch Kollektivismus eine feste Gemeinschaft. Es war

9    Ebd.

10   Ebd.

11   Gespräch mit Joe Douglas, 28. Oktober 2021, Belmonte Calabro.

12   Bugarin, Ian/Douglas, Joe: „The Casa: Not a Place for Quiet Contemplation", in: *Reimagined Living & Working Space Competition 2021*, online unter: https://www.fatrecruitment.co.uk/the-casa?fbclid=IwAR2Iwo_jlOvtQQIbF9i9PbE76bkjeo5d8NqramCI4HuQjUFOGDDN8o8UsqM (Stand: 30. Oktober 2021).

13   Gespräch mit Madalina Podgoreanu am 30. Oktober 2021, London.

think in terms of flexibility, and this loose-fit approach sits well with collaborative projects. However, he recognizes the value of an extended stay in order to better understand the territory: "During lockdown 2020, I decided to move to Belmonte, where I shared living in the Casa with the students from London and a small community of like-minded people. This was an opportunity to slow down my previous engagement in the village, see it in a different way and strengthen communication with local craftspeople. As a result, my previous role as facilitator embedded itself within the village to become part of the community."[16] (fig. 4).

Giuseppe notes that since his longer stay, the locals have come to trust and value the group of *new-makers*. They now share similar activities such as watching football, but perhaps most importantly, are initiating innovative collaborations which view property as common ownership in the form of shared allotments. This is one of the ideological breakthroughs which stem from the ethos of "Le Seppie's" and the students' involvement, which only happened through trust.

Domenique Guglielmo is a young architect and photographer, living in the village with her family. Her mother owns the Antico Caffé Marano, which we jokingly refer to as the "ladies' bar," as it is decorated with beautiful china and personal artefacts, in contrast to the Bar dello Sport, the "men's bar," which hosts live football coverage and a table football game table for downtime. Dominique's involvement with Le Seppie has charted and archived the project from behind the camera, and she therefore has documented the changing spatial practices over time. During the 2020 lockdown, she joined the collective in the Casa as a confident communicator and was happy to engage with the *new-makers* as if part of a family. Insightful and imaginative, she noted that through the long-term engagement, the "locals have been able to travel without travelling."[17] This perception suggests that through empathy, conversation, and perhaps play, there has been a common space where the villagers have absorbed and reciprocated as much as we have from them. Domenique also felt that the locals had opened up to each other through the process. Her personal "opening-up" has been to

see architecture as a holistic process where the project facilitates "spatial agency,"[18] a collaborating "agent operating with" other stakeholders.[19]

**Conclusion.** What has been the value of working beyond the institution, who and what has it benefited and what are the restrictions? Risk, time, cost, quality? The project does not financially support those coordinating it, nor does it have investment of property. It depends on stewardship, gifting, conviviality and the need to resolve common issues of loss: migration, abandonment, lack of local industry. For these reasons, the project does not fit the traditional role of client/architect, rather it depends on working from the ground up. The resource is with the whole rather than its parts. As mentioned earlier, we have been working from both ends of the scale: small makings and large visionary projects. Simultaneously, these have developed skills and visions to develop the Casa, a place beyond the institution, which is neither small nor large, but certainly a point of departure to reimagine Belmonte.

Special thanks to Rita Adamo and Giuseppe Grant, whose constant generosity and insight have continued to make the "crossing of cultures" happen for us. ∎

16  Ibid.
17  Domenique Guglielmo, personal conversation with the authors, October 30, 2022, Belmonte Calabro.
18  Awan, Schneider and Till, *Spatial Agency* (see note 4).
19  See Doina Petrescu, "Relationscapes" (see note 5).

einfach, unsere sinnvollen Arbeitsweisen zu verstehen und auf mein Projektgrundstück in der Marina rund um das teilweise verlassene und stillgelegte Rivellino zu übertragen."[14]

Ein weiterer *new-maker*, Giuseppe Grant, ein Architekt des in Rom ansässigen Architekturkollektivs Orizzontale, arbeitet in den Bereichen Architektur, Städtebau, Kunst im öffentlichen Raum und DIY-Praxis.[15] Im Jahr 2017 beteiligte er sich an dem Projekt in Belmonte mit der Leitung kleinerer Bauworkshops. Die Ergebnisse fanden sich im öffentlichen Raum wieder und boten das nüchterne Erscheinungsbild einer über die Gemeinde wachenden Familie. Giuseppe hat schon immer flexibel gedacht, und diese lockere Herangehensweise passt gut zu Gemeinschaftsprojekten. Gleichzeitig erkennt er den Wert eines längeren Aufenthalts an, um das Umfeld besser zu verstehen: „Während des Lockdowns 2020 beschloss ich, nach Belmonte zu ziehen, wo ich mit den StudentInnen aus London und einer kleinen Gemeinschaft von Gleichgesinnten in der Casa wohnte. Dies war eine Gelegenheit, mein bisheriges Engagement in der Gemeinde zu entschleunigen, es auf eine andere Art wahrzunehmen und die Kommunikation mit den örtlichen Handwerksbetrieben zu stärken. Infolgedessen hat sich meine frühere Rolle als Vermittler in die Gemeinde eingebettet und ist Teil der Gemeinschaft geworden."[16] (Abb. 4).

Seit Giuseppes längerem Aufenthalt haben die Einheimischen mehr Vertrauen in die Gruppe der *new-maker* gefasst und sie zu schätzen gelernt. Sie schauen nun nicht nur gemeinsam Fußball, sondern initiieren auch innovative Projekte gemeinschaftlichen Eigentums, wie zum Beispiel kollektiv genutzte Kleingärten. Dies ist einer der ideologischen Durchbrüche, die sich aus dem Ethos von La Rivoluzione delle Seppie und dem Engagement der StudentInnen ergeben hat, und der nur durch Vertrauen möglich war.

Domenique Guglielmo ist eine junge Architektin und Fotografin, die mit ihrer Familie in der Gemeinde lebt. Ihrer Mutter gehört das Antico Caffé Marano, das wir als „Damenbar" bezeichnen, da es mit schönem Porzellan und persönlichen Erinnerungsstücken dekoriert ist, im Gegensatz zur Bar dello Sport, der „Herrenbar", die für eine Auszeit zwischendurch Live-Fußballübertragungen und einen Tischfußballtisch bietet. Im Rahmen ihrer Mitwirkung an La Rivoluzione delle Seppie hat Domenique das Projekt mit der Kamera begleitet, und damit die sich im Laufe der Zeit verändernden räumlichen Praktiken dokumentiert. Während des Lockdowns 2020 wurde sie als selbstbewusste Kommunikatorin Teil des Kollektivs in der Casa

und profitierte von der Zusammenarbeit in dem familienähnlichen Verbund. „Durch das langfristige Engagement", so resümiert sie, wurde es möglich, dass „die Einheimischen reisen konnten, ohne zu reisen".[17] Diese Wahrnehmung deutet darauf hin, dass durch Empathie und soziale, spielerische Interaktionen ein gemeinsamer Raum entstanden ist, in dem die Dorfbevölkerung ebenso viel von uns angenommen und gelernt hat wie wir von ihr. Zudem haben sich laut Domenique die Einheimischen durch den Prozess füreinander geöffnet. Auch sie selbst ist dadurch gewachsen, indem sich ihr Blick auf Architektur weiter geöffnet hat und diese nun als ganzheitlichen Prozess begreift. So entfaltete das Projekt eine „räumliche Wirkungskraft",[18] die von unterschiedlichen InteressensvertreterInnen gesteuert wird.[19]

**Fazit.** Welchen Wert hat die Arbeit jenseits der Institution? Wem ist sie von und was ist ihr Nutzen? Welche Einschränkungen bestehen? Risiko, Zeit, Kosten, Qualität? Das Projekt trägt weder jene, die es koordinieren finanziell, noch investiert es in Immobilien. Seine Säulen, die es tragen, sind Verantwortung, Schenkungen, Konvivialität und das Bedürfnis, sich mit dem Thema des Verlusts in seinen unterschiedlichen Ausprägungen, wie z.B. der Verlust von Heimat im Sinne der Migration oder aber der Verlust von lokalen Gewerbebetrieben in einem Dorf, zu beschäftigen. Es ist ein Projekt jenseits der traditionellen Rollenverteilung BauherrIn/ArchitektIn und beruht auf dem Bottom-up-Prinzip. Die Ressource liegt im Ganzen und weniger in seinen Teilen. Gleichzeitig haben die kleinen und großen Projekte Fachkenntnisse und Weitblick zur Entwicklung der Casa generiert, eines Ortes jenseits der Institution, der nun den Ausgangspunkt dafür bildet, um Belmonte neu zu erfinden.

Besonderer Dank gilt Rita Adamo und Giuseppe Grant, die uns durch ihre forwährende Großzügigkeit und ihr Verständnis diesen Kulturaustausch ermöglicht haben. ∎

*Übersetzung aus dem Englischen: Otmar Lichtenwörther*

14 Ebd.

15 Gespräch mit Giuseppe Grant, am 31. Oktober 2021, Belmonte Calabro. Vgl. auch http://www.orizzontale.org/en/ (Stand: 28. Januar 2022).

16 Ebd.

17 Gespräch mit Domenique Guglielmo am 30. Oktober 2021, Belmonte Calabro.

18 Awan/Schneider/Till: *Spatial Agency* (wie Anm. 4).

19 Vgl. Petrescu: „Relationscapes" (wie Anm. 5).

Hélène Frichot

# Feminist Gestures and Architectural Cares
## From Brutalist Concrete Socialism to Corten Steel Neoliberalism

# Feministische Gesten und architektonische Sorgen
## Vom brutalistischen Betonsozialismus zum Cortenstahl-Neoliberalismus

1  Anja Linna, "Urban Caring" master thesis | Diplomarbeit, 2012, Critical Studies in Architecture, KTH Stockholm, supervised by | betreut von Hélène Frichot, Meike Schalk, Katja Grillner © Anja Linna

VALUE WHAT IS HERE

L CARE

LECTIV

ACTIVISM FOR SOCIETAL

COMMONIN

MAKE USE OF WHAT IS HERE

Last night I dreamt I went to the Architecture School again. I was arriving as though for the first time, making my way from Stadion T-Bana, a Stockholm metro station, west along Östermalmsgatan toward the roundabout. I'd never been to Stockholm before, nor to any of the cold Nordic cities. I had tucked in my rucksack the old cardboard T-Bana ticket that would be rendered defunct by the plastic SL Access transport cards in a year or two. I was travelling from the other side of the world for a job interview. Turning right off the roundabout and heading north up Danderydsgatan the main campus of KTH, Stockholm's Royal Institution of Technology, could be found. I'd be there later that day to present a lecture as part of the interview process. Looking down sternly onto the roundabout with a studied lack of ornamentation, distinguishing it from its wealthy neighbors, was the Architecture School. I stood still, gazing up at the bright rainbow letters that spelled out KTH Arkitektur across its façade. I could ascend a long ramp leading in from the north, or else I could take the steep stairs. Once at the top of the stairs the glass door was locked; there was no way in unless I had a security card or unless the door was left open for a public event. Visitors would often slip in behind students. Sometimes valuables would be stolen. It is rumored that after it opened in 1970 the old Architecture School was mistaken for a prison and a women's reformatory. In fact, the site did once accommodate a prison. The building might be ungenerously described as a grey concrete bunker, or a squat fortress. It is frequently referred to as the ugliest building in Stockholm, and when smoke issued forth from its rear ateliers during the 2011 fire, the neighborhood is said to have cheered, hoping for the end of this unsightly, out of place, pile of concrete beams, columns, and blocks.

Architecturally designed environments can be ambivalent. A prison one day can become a housing development the next, a sports hall can support a basketball game as well as a grid of camp beds for refugees or for the virally infected. Space, how it is distributed, how it canalizes and disciplines the movements of peoples, how it obliges the performance of certain habits of habitation and certain gestures of an affective labor is nevertheless something that can be remarked upon and has been. Whether you read Michel Foucault on Jeremy Bentham's panopticon,[1] Robin Evans on doorways, passages and bodies in space,[2] or the more recent work of Judith Butler where she argues that urban infrastructures (such as streets and squares) produce spaces that enable or else obliterate the possibility of a body politic to gather together in peaceful protest, space, architectural space, can be recognized as doing something to us as human subjects, much as we do something to it when we mold it in one way or another and distribute its sensible materials.[3]

In what follows I tell the story of the relocation of this Architecture School from one custom built premises to another, and how, between 1970 and 2015, between the respective openings of each of these new school buildings, a reading of their spatial logics and material expression tells different stories of a politics of space in the education of architects. From one locale to the next, could it be that architecture is found to be exerting itself as an instrument of "compliance and control"[4] rather than as a spatial support system of emancipatory potential? Or else, is the socio-spatial logic of architecture always ambivalent, lending itself to the latest political cause, shuttling between ideological constraint and liberation, depending on the situation, depending on who has taken up inhabitation, and what they plan to do next?

Sweden was often in the news in the wake of the 2020 COVID-19 outbreak because of its idiosyncratic response to the virus, and subsequently because of the rising numbers of deaths in its aged care facilities. Transitioning into the twenty-first century, it has been suffering the slow retreat of an erstwhile strong social democratic welfare state, where education is, for the meantime, still free for those within the European Union, though neoliberalism has secured a hold across education, health, and housing.[5] In the story I am telling this neoliberal tendency manifests in university campus real-estate deals, including shifts in the spatial logics of teaching spaces, and a redistribution of

1   See Michel Foucault, *Discipline and Punish: The Birth of the Prison* (London, 1977).

2   See Robin Evans, *Translations from Drawings to Buildings and Other Essays* (London, 1997), 55–92.

3   See Judith Butler, "Rethinking Vulnerability and Resistance," in *Vulnerability in Resistance*, ed. Judith Butler, Zeynep Gambetti and Leticia Sabsay (Durham and London, 2016), 12–27.

4   Douglas Spencer, *The Architecture of Neoliberalism: How Contemporary Architecture Became an Instrument of Compliance and Control* (London, 2016).

5   See Eric Clark, "Making Rent Gap Theory Not True," in *Gentrification as a Global Strategy*, ed. Abel Albet and Núria Benach (London, 2017), 74–84.

Letzte Nacht träumte ich, ich ginge wieder zur Architekturfakultät. Ich lief, wie zum ersten Mal, von der T-Bana-Haltestelle „Stadion" die Östermalmsgatan Richtung Westen auf den Kreisverkehr zu. Ich war vorher noch nie in Stockholm – oder irgendeiner anderen der kalten nordischen Städte – gewesen. In meinem Rucksack steckte das alte T-Bana-Ticket aus Pappe, das ein, zwei Jahre später durch die SL Access-Card aus Plastik abgelöst werden sollte. Ich war vom anderen Ende der Welt für ein Bewerbungsgespräch angereist. Beim Kreisverkehr rechts ging es, die Danderydsgatan hoch, zum Hauptcampus der Königlichen Technischen Hochschule (KTH). Später an dem Tag würde ich dort im Rahmen meiner Bewerbung einen Vortrag halten. Den Kreisverkehr überblickte streng ein Gebäude, das sich mit geradezu ausgesuchter Kargheit von seinen schmucken Nachbarn abhob. Ich blieb stehen und starrte auf die leuchtenden regenbogenfarbenen Buchstaben, mit denen „KTH-ARKITEKTUR" quer über die Fassade geschrieben stand. Ich konnte das Gebäude entweder über die von der Nordseite zum Eingang führende Rampe oder über eine steile Treppe betreten. Oben am Treppenabsatz angekommen, fand ich die Glastür verschlossen; der Zugang war nur mit einer Security Card möglich, außer wenn die Tür für öffentliche Veranstaltungen offenblieb. BesucherInnen schlüpften meist mit Studierenden mit hinein. Manchmal kamen Wertsachen weg. Es heißt, das alte Fakultätsgebäude sei bei seiner Eröffnung für ein Gefängnis und eine Frauenbesserungsanstalt gehalten worden, wohl weil sich an dem Standort einmal ein Gefängnis befunden hatte. Tatsächlich könnte man es unschmeichelhaft als einen grauen Betonbunker oder eine plumpe Festung beschreiben. Oft wird es als das hässlichste Gebäude Stockholms bezeichnet, und als beim Brand 2011 Rauch aus den Werkstätten im Hinterhof stieg, sollen die AnwohnerInnen gejubelt haben, weil sie das Ende der unansehnlichen, deplatzierten Anhäufung von Betonträgern, -stützen und -blöcken gekommen sahen.

Architektonisch gestaltete Räume können ambivalent sein. Was am einen Tag ein Gefängnis ist, ist am nächsten vielleicht eine Wohnanlage. Eine Sporthalle kann genauso ein Basketballspiel wie im Raster angeordnete Feldbetten für Geflüchtete oder Infizierte beherbergen. Die Aufteilung des Raums, die Art, wie er die Bewegungen von Menschen kanalisiert und diszipliniert, wie er die Ausübung bestimmter Wohngewohnheiten und bestimmter Gesten affektiver Arbeit erzwingt, ist dennoch etwas, worüber man sprechen kann und worüber auch gesprochen wurde. Wenn Michel Foucault über Jeremy Benthams Panopticon schreibt,[1] Robin Evans über Eingänge, Durchgänge und Körper im Raum[2] oder Judith Butler in ihren neueren Arbeiten über durch urbane Infrastrukturen geschaffene Räume (Straßen und Plätze), die es einem Gemeinwesen ermöglichen oder verunmöglichen, sich friedlich zum Protest zu versammeln, wird der Raum, der architektonische Raum, als etwas erkennbar, das etwas mit uns als menschlichen Subjekten anstellt, so wie wir mit ihm, wenn wir ihn so oder so formen und seine empfindlichen Materialien so oder so verteilen.[3]

Im Folgenden erzähle ich die Geschichte der Umsiedlung dieser Architekturfakultät von einem eigens dafür errichteten Gebäude in ein anderes, und wie das Lesen der Raumlogik und des materiellen Ausdrucks dieser beiden 1970 bzw. 2015 eröffneten Fakultätsgebäude unterschiedliche Vorstellungen von Raumpolitik in der Ausbildung von ArchitektInnen zutage fördert. Könnte es sein, dass sich die Architektur mit dem Übergang vom einen Ort zum anderen von einem räumlichen Tragwerk für emanzipatorische Potenziale zu einem „Konformitäts- und Kontrollinstrument"[4] gewandelt hat? Oder ist die sozialräumliche Logik von Architektur immer ambivalent, unterwirft sich den aktuellsten politischen Absichten, pendelt zwischen ideologischer Beschränkung und Befreiung, je nachdem wer ihre BenutzerInnen sind und was sie als nächstes vorhaben?

Schweden war im Zuge des COVID-19-Ausbruchs 2020 zunächst wegen des eigenwilligen Umgangs mit dem Virus in den Nachrichten, und dann wegen der wachsenden Sterbezahlen in seinen Senioren- und Pflegeheimen. Mit dem Übergang ins 21. Jahrhundert hat das Land den langsamen Rückzug eines vormals starken sozialdemokratischen Wohlfahrtsstaats erlebt, in dem Bildung einstweilen zwar noch frei ist, jedenfalls für EU-Angehörige, aber der Neoliberalismus doch einen gewissen Halt im Bildungs-, Gesundheits- und Wohnungswesen gefunden hat.[5] In der Geschichte, die ich erzähle, zeigt sich diese neoliberale Tendenz im Geschäft mit Universitätsimmobilien, einschließlich einer Verschiebung in der Raumlogik von Unterrichtsräumen und einer Neuverteilung von Büroräumen in Richtung Hotdesking. Im Hintergrund finden auch andere politische Veränderungen statt. Im Gefolge der Migrationskrise

1 Vgl. Foucault, Michel: *Überwachen und Strafen: Die Geburt des Gefängnisses*, Übers. Walter Seitter, Frankfurt am Main 1977.

2 Vgl. Evans, Robin: *Translations from Drawing to Building and Other Essays*, London 1997, 55–92.

3 Vgl. Butler, Judith: „Rethinking Vulnerability and Resistance", in: dies./ Gambetti, Zeynep/Sabsay, Leticia (Hg.): *Vulnerability in Resistance*, Durham und London 2016, 12–27.

4 Spencer, Douglas: *The Architecture of Neoliberalism: How Contemporary Architecture Became an Instrument of Compliance and Control*, London 2016.

5 Vgl. Clark, Eric: „Making Rent Gap Theory Not True", in: Albet, Abel/Benach, Núria (Hg.): *Gentrification as a Global Strategy*, London 2017, 74–84.

2   Publications in the pedagogical context of the research division Critical
    Studies in Architecture | Publikationen im pädagogischen Umfeld der
    Forschungsabteilung Critical Studies in Architecture, KTH Stockholm
    © Photo: Hélène Frichot

offices tending toward a hot desking approach. In the background other political transformations have been taking place too. Following the migrant crisis of 2015, though probably bubbling away beneath the surface for far longer, a swing toward a popular Swedish nationalism could be observed with the right-wing Swedish Democrats growing in influence. I left my position in the in the School of Architecture, KTH Stockholm in late 2019, arriving in Melbourne, Australia in time for the bushfires and then the onset of the pandemic, so this minor experiment in comparative analysis of two Swedish schools of architecture works something like an afterimage. I will attempt to offer an account of an impression left behind after I have departed the scene.

In what follows I consider how the best intentions of the architect can produce aftereffects, some of which are unexpected, mixing blind spots with blind ambition, careful detailing with careless approaches to subsequent modes of occupation. I offer a brief interlude, between my account of one Architecture School and the next, about a flourishing of possibility in situating a feminist ethos in architectural studies. Folded through these reflections on the kinds of spaces in which architects come to be educated is the issue of an ethics of care, the way care can do good, and feel bad, the way it can enable, and disable, depending on how it is dispensed. Care ethics, and its feminist

genealogy, intersects here with an initiative that was taken up in the school in 2007 when a distinct turn toward architecture and gender, including the adequate representation of women in architecture and an experimental exploration of feminist and queer methodologies in architectural design, was being ventured.

**The Old Architecture School, Off Campus.** Let's begin in 1970 with the opening of a new Architecture School on Östermalmsgatan, in the wealthy neighborhood of Östermalm, just north of central Stockholm, and a couple of blocks south of the main campus of the Royal Institute of Technology (KTH). The daily paper publishes a small article about how the architecture students hosted a participatory event, a *fika* (afternoon tea) with *kanelbullar* (cinnamon buns) in order to greet the neighbors and welcome them into the newly inhabited "house."[6] Designed by the KTH inhouse architect Gunnar Henriksson, it is a formidable functionalist building with an off-form concrete structural grid filled in with concrete blockwork out of which a rhythm of windows are punched, a fortress to the street. Hence, no doubt, the efforts of the students to make friends with the neighbors and assuage them of possible concerns. At the time, the daily newspaper *Dagens Nyheter* describes the new building as egoistic and reckless in its relationship to the surrounding neighborhood; even worse, it is said to be a "mausoleum" for Swedish architecture.[7] The implicit suggestion here purportedly sounds out the death knell of local architectural culture. Within such a mausoleum how are skilled architects to be educated?

There are local controversies even before the doors open at the Architecture School. Students claim that the architecture is cold and unfeeling. The building is said to be inflexible and designed according to a pedagogical program that is outdated even before the construction is completed.[8] In one article students are rumored to threaten it with a paint job to ameliorate the drab grey façade.[9] The Architecture School has been relocated from Riddargatan 5, formally a teachers college for women, and like any experience of "moving house," the change has

6   See Sven Britton, "Motroten," *Dagens Nyheter*, December 14, 1970.
7   Ibid.
8   See "Vara trevliger städerskor tycker inte om huset," *Dagens Nyheter*, September, 14, 1971, 25.
9   See Britton, "Motroten," (see note 6).

von 2015, aber unter der Oberfläche wohl schon länger brodelnd, war eine Wendung hin zum schwedischen Nationalismus zu beobachten und die rechtspopulistischen Schwedendemokraten gewannen an Einfluss. Ich gab meine Stelle an der Architekturfakultät der KTH Stockholm Ende 2019 auf und kam pünktlich zu den Waldbränden und zum Beginn der Corona-Pandemie nach Melbourne. Dieses kleine Experiment einer vergleichenden Analyse zweier schwedischer Architekturfakultäten ist also eine Art Nachbild. Ich versuche, einen Eindruck zu schildern, den ich mit dem Verlassen des Schauplatzes hinter mir ließ.

Nachfolgend betrachte ich, wie beste Absichten von ArchitektInnen zum Teil unerwartete Nachwirkungen haben können, wenn sich blinde Flecken mit blinder Ambition, sorgfältige Detailgestaltung mit Sorglosigkeit gegenüber späteren Nutzungen mischen. Zwischen meine Darstellung der beiden Architekturfakultäten werde ich ein kurzes Zwischenspiel über die großen Potenziale einfügen, die die Einführung eines feministischen Ethos in die Architekturwissenschaft hat. Eingeflochten in diese Überlegungen über den Charakter von Räumen, in denen ArchitektInnen ausgebildet werden sollen, sind Fragen der Care-Ethik, inwiefern Achtsamkeit und Sorgfalt Gutes tun und sich schlecht anfühlen kann, inwiefern sie, je nach ihrer Verteilung, befähigen und behindern kann. In diesem Fall überschneidet sich die Care-Ethik und ihre feministische Genealogie mit einer Initiative, die in der Fakultät 2007 mit einer entschiedenen Wendung zum Thema Architektur und Gender, einschließlich der adäquaten Vertretung von Frauen in der Architektur und der experimentellen Erkundung feministischer und queerer Methoden architektonischer Gestaltung, gestartet wurde.

**Die alte Architekturfakultät außerhalb des Hochschulcampus.** Beginnen wir 1970 mit der Eröffnung der damals neuen Architekturfakultät in der Östermalmsgatan, im wohlhabenden Viertel Östermalm, unmittelbar nördlich des Stadtzentrums und ein paar Häuserblocks südlich des Hauptcampus der KTH. In einer Tageszeitung erscheint ein kleiner Artikel über eine Veranstaltung der Studierenden – ein *fika* (Kaffeekränzchen) mit *kanelbullar* (Zimtschnecken) –, um die Nachbarn zu begrüßen und ins neu bezogene „Haus" einzuladen.[6] Das vom hauseigenen Architekten der KTH Gunnar Henriksson entworfene Gebäude ist eine Respekt einflößende funktionalistische Konstruktion mit einem unförmigen Betonskelett, gefüllt mit Betonblockmauerwerk, in das ein Rhythmus aus Fenstern gestanzt ist: eine Festung hin zur Straße und zweifellos der Grund, weshalb die Studierenden versuchten, sich mit den Nachbarn anzufreunden und mögliche Bedenken zu zerstreuen. Der Artikel

in der *Dagens Nyheter* beschreibt das neue Gebäude als egoistisch und rücksichtslos gegenüber seiner Umgebung – und schlimmer noch: als ein „Mausoleum" der schwedischen Architektur.[7] Implizit wird damit die Totenglocke der lokalen Architekturkultur geläutet. Wie sollen in einem solchen Mausoleum fähige ArchitektInnen ausgebildet werden?

Es gibt interne Kontroversen, bevor die Fakultät überhaupt ihre Tore öffnet. Die Studierenden behaupten, die Architektur sei kalt und gefühllos. Das Gebäude wird als unflexibel und einem pädagogischen Programm verpflichtet beschrieben, das bereits vor der Fertigstellung des Baus überholt gewesen sei.[8] In einem Artikel wird von dem Gerücht berichtet, Studierende hätten gedroht, das Gebäude anzumalen, um der trostlosen grauen Fassade auf die Sprünge zu helfen.[9] Die Fakultät war von der Riddargattan 5, einer früheren Lehrerinnenbildungsanstalt, in das neue Gebäude umgezogen, und der Wechsel löste wie jeder Umzug Unruhe aus. Selbst die Raumpflegerinnen sollen das neue „Haus" abgelehnt haben,[10] und es sollte schließlich die Herausforderung seiner Instandhaltung, die häufig unterschätzte unsichtbare Tätigkeit der Pflege sein, die 45 Jahre später dazu führte, dass es bereitwillig aufgegeben wurde. Das akademische und operative Personal sollte genug von den kaputten Toiletten und dem schlechten Zustand der Belüftung haben und jede Hoffnung fahren lassen, dass Renovierung möglich ist.

Zwar wird das Gebäude meist als brutalistisch beschrieben, aber sein Architekt Henriksson besteht darauf, dass sein Ansatz funktionalistisch war. Er erklärt, dass er eine Lücke in der Bauordnung ausgenutzt hat, die die Größe institutioneller Unterrichtsräume festlegt. Er entwarf einen Korridor auf den Ebenen drei bis fünf, dessen Wände er später entfernte. Er erreichte damit zweierlei: größere Zeichenateliers für die Studierenden und einen direkten Zugang zu den Türen, hinter denen die Büros der ProfessorInnen lagen. Zu jeder Zeit konnte ein/e Studierende/r an die Tür klopfen und damit subtil die Machthierarchie unterlaufen. 2012, als ich anfing, lag mein Büro im vierten Stock nach Nordosten hinaus und direkt angrenzend an ein lebhaftes Zeichenatelier. Die Studierenden klopften tatsächlich an. Auf allen drei Ateliergeschossen trafen sie sich in dem Dreieck, das von den beiden Hauptflügeln entlang der Östermalmsgatan und der Rådmansgatan gebildet wird, Tag für

---

6 Vgl. Britton, Sven: „Motroten", *Dagens Nyheter*, 14. Dezember 1970.

7 Ebd.

8 Vgl. „Vara trevliger städerskor tycker inte om huset", *Dagens Nyheter*, 14. September 1971, 25.

9 Vgl. Britton, „Motroten", (wie Anm. 6).

10 Vgl. „Vara trevliger städerskor tycker inte om huset", (wie Anm. 8).

aroused unrest. Even the cleaning ladies are reported to dislike the new "house,"[10] and it will be this challenge of maintenance, too often an undervalued and invisible gesture of care, that will eventually lead to the building's willing abandonment 45 years later. The academic and professional staff will get tired of the toilets breaking down, and the generally poor condition of the ventilation, and give up on hopes of a possible renovation job.

While it is habitually described as Brutalist, its architect Henriksson insists that his approach has been that of a functionalist. He explains how he has taken advantage of a loop-hole in regulations that determine the sizes of institutional teaching spaces. He designs a corridor on floors three through to five, the wall of which he subsequently removes. This achieves two outcomes: larger studio spaces for the students, and direct access between teaching studios and the doors that open onto professors' offices. At any moment of the day a student might come knocking, thereby subtly dismantling a power hierarchy. When I arrive in 2012 my office is located on the fourth floor, facing northeast, and it opens directly into a lively studio space. Students come knocking. On each of the three studio levels, the triangle formed between the two main wings of the "house" along Östermalmsgatan and Rådmansgatan is where students gather each day for lunch, and like clockwork, at 11:55am the microwaves begin to "ding." Hidden behind the wings of the building, so unwelcoming on the street side onto which the offices face, can be found a courtyard onto which all the studios, and the dedicated architecture library look out. Here the end of year celebration is hosted, and a general sense of conviviality supported, even throughout the long cold months. In time, the concrete pile becomes a beloved object that many are reluctant to leave behind.

When it becomes clear that the building on Östermalmsgatan will be vacated, and we will be moving *en masse* back onto KTH Main Campus, our communications director, Björn Ehrlemark mounts an exhibition to celebrate the life of the building as an architecture school and writes an accompanying article.[11] Signs of change had already emerged with a new café contract. Now rather than the sometimes grim, though hearty traditional Swedish fare, a pop-up espresso bar with plastic TV dinners and throw-away cutlery has appeared as though out of

nowhere, a harbinger of things to come. Final year architecture students incorporate elements of the building into their designs. One student, Mattias Hambraeus Victorson dedicates his final design thesis to a short film telling the story of the former "Architecture House," describing the attachments students had developed to the concrete box.[12] Another student, Olga Tengvall, who I advised, embedded rooms and their spatial relations from the Architecture School into her ficto-critical project "The Moral Institute of Higher Fiction."[13] In his article Ehrlemark explains some of the original pedagogical ambitions of the "A House" as it is known today: The floor tiles originally measured 100 millimeters square to instill a sense of metric scale in students of architecture, services were explicitly revealed to demonstrate building technologies and services. Ehrlemark is convinced that the ghost of this Brutalist building persists in the new Architecture House, now located on KTH main campus at Osquars Backe 5.[14]

**Pedagogical Interlude: Feminist Gestures and Architectural Cares.** Before I offer a tour through the new "Architecture House" at Osquars Backe 5, custom built though aiming for flexibility too, I offer a brief interlude. In 2007 something wonderful erupted in the Brutalist, or if we are to listen to Henriksson, Functionalist halls of the old Architecture School: A student-led initiative to address the issue of architecture and gender head on. The simple question raised by students, perplexed by gaps and lacunae in history classes and design studio lists of recommended precedents, was: Where are the women architects? This ground swell provoked action on the part of a small crew of teachers who came to call themselves FATALE (Feminist Architecture Theory Analysis Laboratory Education).[15] Katarina Bonnevier, Brady Burroughs, Katja Grillner, Meike Schalk and the late Lena Villner together designed and delivered

10  See "Vara trevliger städerskor tycker inte om huset," (see note 8).

11  See Björn Ehrlemark, "Stockholm's Ugly Duckling: In Praise of a Concrete Campus," *Uncubed Magazine* 6 (2016), available online at: http://www.uncubemagazine.com/blog/16597791 (accessed November 26, 2021). See also the following photo essay in this *GAM* issue on page 106–125.

12  See https://arkitekturensgrannar.se/Ugly-Duckling and https://www.youtube.com/watch?v=c4BUOo6WBzI (accessed February 8, 2022).

13  See Hélène Frichot, *How to Make Yourself a Feminist Design Tool* (Baunach, 2016).

14  Conversation with Björn Ehrlemark via Zoom, June 30, 2020.

15  See Meike Schalk, Brady Burroughs, Katja Grillner and Katarina Bonnevier, "FATALE Critical Studies in Architecture," *Nordic Journal of Architecture* 2 (2012): 90–96.

Tag zum Mittagessen und pünktlich um 11:55 Uhr begannen die Mikrowellen zu piepsen. Hinter den zur Straße hin so abweisenden Gebäudeflügeln, in denen sich die Büros befanden, lag versteckt ein Hinterhof, auf den alle Zeichenateliers und die Architekturfachbibliothek hinausführten. Hier fanden die Jahresendfeiern statt und hier wurde selbst in den langen Wintermonaten ein Gemeinschaftsgefühl gefördert. So kam es, dass der unliebsame Betonklotz mit der Zeit zu einem geliebten Objekt wurde, das viele ungern zurückließen.

Als feststand, dass das Gebäude an der Östermalmsgatan aufgegeben wird und wir geschlossen auf den Hauptcampus der KTH zurückziehen werden, organisierte der Leiter unserer Öffentlichkeitsabteilung, Björn Ehrlemark, eine Ausstellung über das Leben des Gebäudes als Architekturschule und verfasste dazu einen Begleittext.[11] Erste Zeichen des Wandels hatten bereits mit einem neuen Cafeteria-Pächter Einzug gehalten. Statt der manchmal rustikalen, aber herzhaften schwedischen Kost tauchte plötzlich eine Pop-up Espressobar mit Fertiggerichten, Plastikgeschirr und Wegwerfbesteck auf, ein Vorbote kommender Verhältnisse. Architekturstudierende im letzten Jahr integrierten Elemente des Gebäudes in ihre Abschlussarbeiten. Ein Student, Mattias Hambraeus Victorson widmet seine Abschlussarbeit der Geschichte des einstigen „Architektur-Hauses", indem er in einem Kurzfilm erzählt, welche Bindungen die Studierenden an den Betonklotz entwickelten.[12] Eine weitere Studierende, die von mir betreute Olga Tengvall, baute Räume und Raumverhältnisse der Architekturfakultät in ihr fiktiv-kritisches Projekt „The Moral Institute of Higher Fiction" ein.[13] In seinem Text erklärt Ehrlemark einige der ursprünglichen pädagogischen Intentionen des „A-Gebäudes": Die 100 Millimeter im Quadrat messenden Bodenfliesen sollten den Architekturstudierenden einen Sinn für das metrische Maß vermitteln, Leitungen und Installationen lagen frei, um die Gebäudetechnik zu demonstrieren. Ehrlemark ist überzeugt, dass der Geist des brutalistischen Gebäudes in der neuen, auf dem KTH-Campus gelegenen Architekturfakultät fortlebt.[14]

**Pädagogischer Exkurs: Feministische Gesten und architektonische Achtsamkeiten.** Ehe ich eine Führung durch das neue, ebenfalls für den Zweck entworfene, aber auch auf Flexibilität bedachte Architekturgebäude am Osquars Backe 5 unternehme, möchte ich noch einen kurzen Exkurs einschieben. 2007 ereignete sich in den brutalistischen oder, wenn wir uns an Henriksson halten wollen, funktionalistischen Hallen der alten Architekturfakultät etwas Wunderbares: eine von Studierenden ausgehende Initiative, die das Thema Architektur und Gender direkt bei

den Hörnern packte. Verwundert über die Lücken in den Vorlesungen zur Architekturgeschichte und den in den Entwurfsklassen empfohlenen Beispielen, warfen sie die einfache Frage auf: Wo sind die Architektinnen? Diese Grundstimmung ließ eine kleine Gruppe von Dozentinnen, die sich später FATALE (Feminist Architecture Theory Analysis Laboratory Education) nannten, zur Aktion schreiten.[15] Katarina Bonnevier, Brady Burroughs, Katja Grillner, Meike Schalk und die mittlerweile verstorbene Lena Villner entwickelten und hielten 2008 ein einführendes Seminar zum Thema Architektur und Gender, und ab 2009 wurde eine Entwurfsklasse auf Masterniveau eingeführt, die sich aus vier Modulen zusammensetzte: feministische Entwurfswerkzeuge; dialogische Interventionen; partizipatorisches Mapping; und Verändern von Praktiken. Durchgeführt

11  Vgl. Ehrlemark, Björn: „Stockholm's Ugly Duckling: In Praise of a Concrete Campus", *Uncubed Magazine* 6 (2016), online unter: http://www.uncubemagazine.com/blog/16597791 (Stand: 26. November 2021). Vgl. auch die Fotosequenz in der vorliegenden *GAM*-Ausgabe auf den Seiten 106–125.

12  Vgl. https://arkitekturensgrannar.se/Ugly-Duckling and https://www.youtube.com/watch?v=c4BUOo6WBzl (Stand: 7. Februar 2022).

13  Vgl. Frichot, Hélène: *How to Make Yourself a Feminist Design Tool*, Baunach 2016.

14  Zoom-Gespräch mit Björn Ehrlemark, 30. Juni 2020.

15  Vgl. Schalk, Meike/Burroughs, Brady/Grillner, Katja/Bonnevier, Katarina: „FATALE Critical Studies in Architecture", *Nordic Journal of Architecture* 2 (2012), 90–96.

3  "Ghost School," KTH Stockholm © Photomontage: Hélène Frichot

an inaugural seminar dedicated to Architecture and Gender in 2008, and by 2009 a design studio was launched at Masters level composed of four modules: feminist design tools; dialogical interventions; participatory mapping; and altering practices. These were organized as a sequence of learning experiences culminating with the altering of practices, with a nod to Doina Petrescu's edited book by the same name.[16] To alter practices means to alter your approach to architecture, to speculate on its emancipatory potential and how, as a discipline and a practice, it might be inclusive, rather than exclusive. FATALE was eventually institutionalized as the teaching and research group Critical Studies in Architecture, in operation between 2008 to 2019, the year I left. It is now folded into the Architectural Theory, History and Critical Studies teaching and learning division.[17] FATALE's ambition was to imagine feminist futures that could extend beyond the academy into architectural workplaces, that could trouble oppressive power structures, that could foster critical fictions whereby alternative approaches to architecture as a discipline and a practice might be imagined.

In the introduction to *Feminist Futures of Spatial Practice*, the editors Meike Schalk, Thérèse Kristiansson, Ramia Mazé, with the graphic designer Maryam Fanni, speak of how the book project initially emerged in the pedagogical spaces of Critical Studies in Architecture, KTH Stockholm in a seminar called Feminist Futures that was delivered in 2011 and involved collaborations with *Women in the Performing Arts* and with the art project "The New Beauty Council."[18] The transdisciplinary methodologies of FATALE and its institutional formation as Critical Studies explore hands-on approaches and tools by applying theory to concrete practice examples, thereby rendering mobile the theory-practice relay. By 2016 Critical Studies in collaboration with the art and architecture collective Mycket (Katarina Bonnevier, Thérèse Kristiansson, Mariana Alves Silva)[19] was hosting the 13th International AHRA (Architectural Humanities Research Association) conference, the first to be held outside the United Kingdom where this research organization originated. By 2017, as an outcome of this conference, one edited book and two special editions of peer reviewed journals were published: *Architecture and Feminisms: Ecologies Economies Technologies*, edited by Hélène Frichot, Catharina Gabrielsson, Helen Runting;[20] a special issue of *Architecture and Culture* edited by Karin Reisinger, a postdoctoral researcher in Critical Studies and crucial co-convener of the conference,

and Meike Schalk, entitled *Styles of Queer Feminist Practices and Objects in Architecture*; and Reisinger and Schalk's co-edited special edition of *Field: A Free Journal for Architecture* dedicated to "Becoming a Feminist Architect."[21]

As a group formation FATALE emerges at much the same moment that the American sub-prime mortgage crisis is leading rapidly toward a global financial crisis, and the subject matter of real estate is coming to be reconceptualized as a fictional instrument, repackaged as toxic debt ready to explode, in the process destroying the livelihoods of vulnerable as well as ordinary home owners. A line of research emerging from Critical Studies in Architecture directs its attention to a feminist critique of architecture packaged as real estate media.[22] Here feminist critique, with an intersectional lens to acknowledge gender, class, race, and differently abled bodies, is deployed to address the biopolitical impact of architecture where it is reformatted as a spatial commodity, its interiors dressed for consumption, accessible to some, while increasingly inaccessible to so many. Housing shortages, lack of access to affordable housing, a shift from a rental approach in the Swedish context to a housing market where the value of property per square meter continues to rise, all these conditions disproportionately affect women and vulnerable minorities.

16 In reference to Doina Petrescu, ed., *Altering Practices: Feminist Politics and Poetics of Space* (London, 2007).

17 See https://www.arch.kth.se/en/forskning/architectural-theory (accessed November 3, 2021).

18 Meike Schalk, Ramia Mazé, Thérèse Kristiansson and Maryam Fanni, "Introduction: Anticipating Futures of Spatial Practice," in *Feminists Futures of Spatial Practice: Materialisms, Activisms, Dialogues, Pedagogies, Projections*, ed. Meike Schalk, Ramia Mazé, Thérèse Kristiansson, and Maryam Fanni (Baunach, 2017), 14.

19 See https://mycket.org/About-Us (accessed February 7, 2022).

20 Hélène Frichot, Catharina Gabrielsson and Helen Runting, eds., *Architecture and Feminisms: Ecologies, Economies, Technologies* (Oxon, 2017).

21 Karin Reisinger and Meike Schalk, eds., "Becoming a Feminist Architect," *Field: A Free Journal for Architecture* 7 (2017), available online at: https://field-journal.org/portfolio-items/field-7-becoming-a-feminist-architect/ (accessed November 26, 2021); Karin Reisinger and Meike Schalk, "Styles of Queer Feminist Practices and Objects in Architecture," *Architecture and Culture* 5, no. 3 (2017), 343–352.

22 A selection of this work includes: Hélène Frichot and Helen Runting, "The Promise of a Lack: Responding to (Her) Real-Estate Career," *The Avery Review: Critical Essays on Architecture* 8 (2015), available online at: http://www.averyreview.com/issues/8/the-promise-of-a-lack (accessed November 26, 2021); Hélène Frichot and Helen Runting, "In Captivity: The Real Estate of Co-Living," in *Architecture and Feminisms: Ecologies, Economies, Technologies*, ed. Hélène Frichot, Catharina Gabrielsson and Helen Runting, (Oxon, 2017); Hélène Frichot and Helen Runting, "The Illusory Autonomy of the Real Estate Interior," in *Rethinking the Social in Architecture*, ed. Roemer van Toorn, Gunnar Sandin, and Jennifer Mack (Barcelona and New York, 2018); Helen Runting and Hélène Frichot, "The Queue," *Eflux Architecture/Overgrowth*, 2019, available online at: https://www.e-flux.com/architecture/overgrowth/282654/the-queue/ (accessed November 26, 2021).

wurden sie als eine Sequenz von Lernerfahrungen, deren Höhepunkt das Verändern von Praktiken bildete.[16] Praktiken zu verändern bedeutet, den eigenen Zugang zur Architektur zu verändern, über ihr emanzipatorisches Potenzial nachzudenken und darüber, wie sie, als Disziplin und als Praxis, inklusiv statt exklusiv werden könnte. FATALE wurde schließlich in Form der Lehr- und Forschungsgruppe Critical Studies in Architecture institutionalisiert, die von 2008 bis 2019, dem Jahr meines Abgangs, aktiv war. Heute ist sie in den Unterrichtszweig Architectural Theory, History and Critical Studies integriert.[17] Ziel von FATALE war es, feministische Zukunftswelten zu ersinnen, die über die Universität hinaus in die architektonische Praxis hineinzuwirken, erdrückende Machtverhältnisse aufzubrechen und kritische Fiktionen zu begünstigen vermögen, mit denen alternative Zugänge zur Architektur als Fach und Praxis denkbar werden.

In ihrer Einleitung zu *Feminist Futures of Spatial Practice* berichten die Herausgeberinnen Meike Schalk, Thérèse Kristiansson, Ramia Mazé und die Grafikdesignerin Maryam Fanni vom Entstehen des Buches im pädagogischen Umfeld der Critical Studies in Architecture, im Rahmen eines Seminars mit dem Titel „Feminist Futures", das 2011 in Zusammenarbeit mit *Women in the Performing Arts* und dem Kunstprojekt „The New Beauty Council" durchgeführt wurde.[18] Die transdisziplinäre Methodik von FATALE und ihre institutionelle Ausprägung als Critical Studies erforschen praktische Ansätze und Tools, indem sie Theorie auf konkrete Beispiele anwenden und so den Theorie-Praxis-Nexus dynamisieren. 2016 waren die Critical Studies gemeinsam mit dem Kunst- und Architekturkollektiv Mycket (Katarina Bonnevier, Thérèse Kristiansson, Mariana Alves Silva)[19] Veranstalterinnen der 13. Internationalen Konferenz der AHRA (Architectural Humanities Research Association), der ersten, die außerhalb Großbritanniens abgehalten wurde, wo diese Forschungseinrichtung ihren Ursprung hat. 2017 erschienen als Ergebnis dieser Konferenz der Sammelband *Architecture and Feminisms*, herausgegeben von Hélène Frichot, Catharina Gabrielsson, Helen Runting,[20] sowie je ein Sonderheft der peer-reviewten Zeitschriften *Architecture and Culture* und *Field: A Free Journal for Architecture*, beide herausgegeben von Karin Reisinger, einer Postdoc in Critical Studies und wichtigen Mitorganisatorin der Konferenz, und Meike Schalk.[21]

Als Gruppe tritt FATALE mehr oder weniger zur selben Zeit in Erscheinung, in der sich die amerikanische Subprime-Krise rasch zu einer globalen Finanzkrise auswächst und das Thema Immobilienbesitz zu einem fiktionalen Instrument umgewandelt, einem toxischen Schuldtitel gebündelt wird, der jeden Moment platzen und dabei die Lebensgrundlagen gefährdeter wie auch ganz gewöhnlicher HausbesitzerInnen zerstören kann. Eine Forschungsrichtung, die aus den Critical Studies in Architecture hervorgegangen ist, widmet sich einer feministischen Kritik einer als Immobilien-Medien verpackten Architektur.[22] Dabei wird feministische Kritik – mit einem intersektionalen Blick auf Gender, Klasse, *race* und anders begabte Körper – dazu eingesetzt, die biopolitischen Wirkungen von Architektur zu thematisieren, wo sie zur räumlichen Ware umformatiert wird, die Innenausstattung auf Konsum getrimmt, der für einige erreichbar, für viele aber zunehmend unerreichbar ist. Wohnungsmangel, fehlender Zugang zu leistbarem Wohnen, die Verschiebung von Mietwohnungen hin zum Eigentum bei ständig steigenden Quadratmeterpreisen in Schweden, all das betrifft unverhältnismäßig stark Frauen und gefährdete Minderheiten.

Eine immanente Kritik ist eine Herausforderung: Wenn man mitten im Geschehen steht, gibt es keine Distanz. Die Probleme, die zur Bildung der Critical Studies in Architecture führten, sind nicht die, die sich leicht lösen lassen, sondern ständige,

16 In Anspielung auf das von Doina Petrescu herausgegebene Buch *Altering Practices: Feminist Politics and Poetics of Space*, London 2007.

17 Vgl. https://www.arch.kth.se/en/forskning/architectural-theory (Stand: 3. November 2021).

18 Schalk, Meike/Mazé, Ramia/Kristiansson, Thérèse/Fanni, Maryam: „Introduction: Anticipating Futures of Spatial Practice", in dies. (Hg.): *Feminists Futures of Spatial Practice: Materialisms, Activisms, Dialogues, Pedagogies, Projections*, Baunach 2017, 14.

19 Vgl. https://mycket.org/About-Us

20 Frichot, Hélène/Gabrielsson, Catharina/Runting, Helen (Hg.): *Architecture and Feminisms: Ecologies, Economies, Technologies*, Oxon, 2017.

21 Reisinger, Karin/Schalk, Meike (Hg.): „Becoming a Feminist Architect", *Field: A Free Journal for Architecture* 7 (2017), online unter: https://field-journal.org/portfolio-items/field-7-becoming-a-feminist-architect/ (Stand: 26. November 2021), und dies., „Styles of Queer Feminist Practices and Objects in Architecture", *Architecture and Culture* 5, 3 (2017), 343–352.

22 Zu dieser Richtung gehören u.a.: Frichot, Hélène/Runting, Helen: „The Promise of a Lack: Responding to (Her) Real-Estate Career", *The Avery Review: Critical Essays on Architecture* 8 (2015), online unter: http://www.averyreview.com/issues/8/the-promise-of-a-lack (Stand: 26. November 2021); Frichot, Hélène/Runting, Helen: „In Captivity: The Real Estate of Co-Living", in: dies.: *Architecture and Feminisms* (wie Anm. 20); Frichot, Hélène/Runting, Helen: „The Illusory Autonomy of the Real Estate Interior", in: Van Toorn, Roemer/Sandin, Gunnar/Mack, Jennifer (Hg.): *Rethinking the Social in Architecture*, Barcelona/New York 2018; Runting, Helen/Frichot, Hélène: „The Queue", *Eflux Architecture/Overgrowth*, 2019, online unter: https://www.e-flux.com/architecture/overgrowth/282654/the-queue/ (Stand: 26. November 2021).

It is challenging to undertake immanent critique, there's no distance when you are standing in the thick midst of things. The problems that led to the formation of Critical Studies in Architecture are not ones that will be easily resolved, but require persistent, tireless critique and action. It can feel like there is no outside to what Félix Guattari once called "integrated world capitalism;"[23] it can feel like neoliberalism has seeped into every pore of our existences. This is what leads me, via this feminist interlude, to a consideration of care ethics. As I have argued in opening, architectural space and the formation of subjectivities are co-constitutive, and space in all its situated specificity incorporates care as a multifaceted mode of expression. Care is fundamental to species survival, though that's not to say that its advances are always welcome. As Maria Puig de la Bellacasa argues, care is ambivalent, it can enable, and "it can oppress."[24]

It is specifically the tension between transactional interests and the moral obligation to express care and concern that we appear to be mired within today as we cope with the current pandemic, expressions of care and concern having become something of a refrain. The reassurance that we are all in this (apart) together, is beginning to ring a little hollow, as it becomes clear that inevitable acts of restructuring will leave some of us out in the cold. Such tensions as these are what Nancy Fraser describes as our contemporary crisis of care, a crisis "rooted in the structural dynamics of financialized capitalism."[25] The kind of capitalism of which Fraser speaks concerns the way in which social collectivity comes to be marketized, and how cycles of production and reproduction link up as "global care chains" filling care gaps, for instance, by inviting migrant workers from poorer countries to see to the affective labour no longer able to be fulfilled by two-earner families.[26] Architectural spatial examples might include render farms, the precarity of adjunct and sessional teaching labour, and could also be found in the purported care expressed in a participatory pop-up event that lends itself to the profit eventually gleaned by a developer keen to sell their spatial product. Such as would eventually take place in the old Architecture School.

Care ethics orientates us, placing us in relation, as care giver or as care receiver. In addition to caring about, caring for, care giving, and care receiving, there is caring *with*, what care ethicist Joan Tronto calls a fifth phase of care.[27] Described as a lifelong

affair that is part and parcel of democratic process, acts of *caring with* go along with a diligent "patterning" of care.[28] There is the time spent patterning a façade, or else there is the time spent thinking through the implications of spatial relations that might manifest within an architectural project, through it, and beyond its envelope. There is the appearance of architecture and the image-based affects it arouses and causes to circulate, and then there is the long, slow, less visible life that is supported by what architecture can do. Where the care is distributed, and by what material means, seems an important choice to be made especially when it comes to the crucial acts of caring required in spaces of architectural pedagogy.[29]

Can this tension, between a transactional emphasis and an ethics of care, be found to extend into the diagram of power relations witnessed at work in the spatial distributions of an architecture dedicated to the education of becoming architects? Too much care expressed in this detail or event might mean not enough care expressed elsewhere. If there is a relationship that can be argued to inhere between formations of subjectivity and formations of architectural space, including a consideration of care ethics, great caution needs to be taken before making any definitive pronouncements. Again, compositions of spaces and formations of subjectivities, how they express care, how they are cared for, form complex, ever dynamic assemblages.

**The New Architecture House, KTH Main Campus.** We moved into the new "Architecture House" in the summer of 2015, amidst a flurry of boxes and anxiety over whether there would be enough shelving space available in the new premises. Murmured questions rippled through the staff body wondering about what had happened to the promised office spaces. Ad hoc changes were made to level 2 where all the teaching and research staff would be relocated across an open plan. From the outside

23 Félix Guattari, *The Three Ecologies* (London, 2000), 21.

24 Maria Puig de la Bellacasa, *Matters of Care: Speculative Ethics in More than Human Worlds* (Minneapolis, 2017).

25 Nancy Fraser, "Contradictions of Capital and Care," *New Left Review* 100 (2016): 99–117.

26 Ibid., 114.

27 See Joan Tronto, *Who Cares?* (Ithaca and London, 2015).

28 See Emma Power and Kathleen Mee, "Housing: An Infrastructure of Care," *Housing Studies* 35, no. 3 (2020): 484–505.

29 I want to sincerely thank Björn Ehrlemark for his research assistance on this essay and beyond, and Anders Bergström for discussing architecture and pedagogy with me, specifically as these relate to Gunnar Henriksson's design for the former KTH School of Architecture, Stockholm.

unermüdliche Kritik und Arbeit erfordern. Es scheint, als gäbe es kein Außen dessen, was Guattari einmal als „weltweiten integrierten Kapitalismus"[23] bezeichnet hat; es scheint, als sei der Neoliberalismus in jede Pore unserer Existenz eingedrungen. Das bringt mich – über diesen feministischen Exkurs – zu einer Betrachtung der Care-Ethik oder Ethik der Achtsamkeit. Wie eingangs erwähnt konstituieren sich architektonischer Raum und Subjektivitäten gegenseitig, und in seiner situierten Spezifität beinhaltet der Raum Achtsamkeit als eine vielschichtige Ausdrucksform. Achtsamkeit ist entscheidend für das Überleben der Spezies, was aber nicht heißt, dass ihre Vorstöße immer positiv sind. Achtsamkeit ist, wie Maria Puig de la Bellacasa festgestellt hat, ambivalent; sie kann befähigen und „sie kann unterdrücken".[24]

Es ist vor allem die Spannung zwischen Transaktionsinteressen und der moralischen Verpflichtung, Achtsamkeit und Anteilnahme zu zeigen, in der wir uns heute, da wir in der Pandemie zurechtzukommen versuchen, verfangen zu haben scheinen, ist doch die Bekundung von Sorge und Anteilnahme zu einer Art Refrain geworden. Die Versicherung, dass wir alle im selben Boot sitzen (und gleichzeitig dann doch jeder in seinem eigenen), klingt allmählich ein wenig hohl, nun da sich abzeichnet, dass die unvermeidlichen Restrukturierungen einige von uns draußen im Regen stehen lassen. Die erwähnten Spannungen sind das, was Nancy Fraser als aktuelle Krise der Achtsamkeit beschreibt, eine Krise, die ihre Wurzeln „in der strukturellen Dynamik des Finanzkapitalismus"[25] hat. Der Kapitalismus, von dem Fraser spricht, meint das Marktförmig-Werden des sozialen Zusammenhalts und die Verbindung der Produktions- und Reproduktionszyklen zu „globalen Care-Ketten", die Fürsorgelücken füllen, indem sie etwa MigrantInnen aus ärmeren Ländern einladen, die affektive Arbeit zu erledigen, zu der Doppelverdienerfamilien nicht mehr imstande sind.[26] Beispiele im Bereich der Architektur könnten Renderfarmen oder prekäre Dienstverhältnisse für Lehrende sein, oder aber das angebliche Engagement für ein partizipatorisches Popup-Event, das dem Profit dient, der schließlich von einer Entwicklerfirma eingestrichen wird, die ihr Raumprodukt verkaufen will. So wie es schließlich auch bei der alten Architekturfakultät der Fall war.

Die Care-Ethik orientiert uns, setzt uns als SpenderInnen oder EmpfängerInnen von Achtsamkeit in Beziehung. Neben Wertschätzung (*caring about*) und Fürsorge (*caring for*) und dem Spenden und Empfangen von Achtsamkeit gibt es noch die Mit-Sorge (*caring with*), die die Care-Ethikerin Joan Tronto

als fünfte Phase der Achtsamkeit bezeichnet.[27] Als lebenslange Angelegenheit, die ein integraler Teil des demokratischen Prozesses ist, gehen Akte der Mit-Sorge mit einer gewissenhaften Gestaltung von Achtsamkeit einher.[28] Es ist die Zeit, die man in die Oberflächengestaltung einer Fassade steckt, oder in das Durchdenken der Auswirkungen von Raumverhältnissen, die sich in einem Architekturprojekt jenseits seiner Hülle manifestieren. Es gibt das Erscheinungsbild von Architektur, die optisch ausgelösten und in Umlauf gebrachten Affekte, und es gibt das lange, langsame, weniger sichtbare Leben, das durch die Fähigkeiten von Architektur getragen wird. Wohin und mit welchen materiellen Mitteln die Achtsamkeit verteilt werden soll, ist eine wesentliche Entscheidung, die es in Bezug auf die bedeutenden Akte der Achtsamkeit zu treffen gilt, die in den Räumen der Architekturpädagogik gefordert sind.[29]

Lässt sich die Spannung zwischen Transaktionsinteresse und einer Ethik der Achtsamkeit bis in das Diagramm der Machtverhältnisse hinein feststellen, die sich in der Raumverteilung einer der Ausbildung von ArchitektInnen gewidmeten Architektur zeigt? Zu viel Achtsamkeit für dieses Detail oder jenen Ablauf könnte bedeuten, dass etwas anderes nicht genug davon bekommen hat. Wenn behauptet werden kann, dass eine inhärente Beziehung zwischen der Formation von Subjektivität und der Formation von architektonischen Räumen besteht, auch unter Berücksichtigung der Care-Ethik, dann heißt es, sehr vorsichtig zu sein, ehe man irgendwelche endgültigen Aussagen tätigt. Die Komposition von Räumen und die Formation von Subjektivitäten und wie diese Achtsamkeit ausdrücken und was ihnen an Achtsamkeit entgegengebracht wird, bilden wiederum komplexe, unaufhörlich dynamische Gefüge.

**Das neue Architekturgebäude auf dem Hauptcampus.** Wir bezogen das neue Architekturgebäude im Sommer 2015 in

23 Guattari, Félix: *Die drei Ökologien*, Übers. Alec A. Schaerer und Gwendolin Engels, 2. Aufl., Wien 2012, 39.

24 Puig de la Bellacasa, Maria: *Matters of Care: Speculative Ethics in More than Human Worlds*, Minneapolis 2017.

25 Fraser, Nancy: „Contradictions of Capital and Care", *New Left Review* 100 (2016), 99–117.

26 Ebd., 114.

27 Vgl. Tronto, Joan: *Who Cares?*, Ithaca und London 2015.

28 Vgl. Power, Emma/Mee, Kathleen: „Housing: An Infrastructure of Care", *Housing Studies* 35, 3 (2020), 484–505.

29 Mein aufrichtiger Dank an Björn Ehrlemark für die Unterstützung bei der Recherche für diesen Artikel und anderes sowie an Anders Bergström für die Diskussionen über Architektur und Bildung, vor allem in Hinblick auf Gunnar Henrikssons Entwurf für die alte Architekturfakultät der KTH Stockholm.

though, the new school presented an impressive vision to the world, but what did it represent exactly?

What are the criteria by which an architecture can be assessed as subscribing, consciously or not, to neoliberalism? Douglas Spencer argues that the characteristics of a neoliberal architecture include some of the following: hatred for hierarchical planning; interest in spontaneous ordering and self-organization; a liberation from constraints embedded in assumptions about the inherent good of liberty and freedom (accessible to some, but not to all); a privileging of experiences of immediacy and immersion; involvement in processes of subjectification that pitch the subject as "environmentally flexible and driven

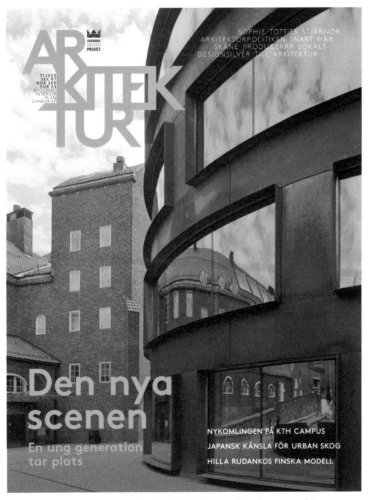

4    School of Architecture at KTH Stockholm featured on the cover of the Swedish architecture magazine *Arkitektur* | Das Gebäude der Architektur-fakultät der KTH Stockholm auf dem Cover des schwedischen Architektur-magazins *Arkitektur* 7 (2015) © Tidskriften Arkitektur

by affect"[30] and then there is the special subject that is the student on their way to becoming a "student-entrepreneur."[31] All of these characteristics defer a capacity for critical thinking, and Spencer goes so far as to argue that the forms of environmental control exerted by neoliberalism render its captivated subjects ignorant. Spencer presented some of these arguments in the largest of the entry level ateliers in the KTH new school of architecture in 2016.[32] Let's take a look inside.

The design of the new Architecture "house" on KTH main campus by celebrated Swedish architects Tham & Videgård (they even have an *El Croquis* dedicated to their work, a sure sign of architectural success in the fast lane of icons and idols)[33] was won through a competitive process. A 2007 design competition attracted entries from such world-renowned practices as SAANA and was subsequently won by the Swedish firm. Fit for a magazine cover image, the new Architecture House is something of a show pony. It is a Corten steel drum with windows punched out of the façade. In an interview with one of the support architects who worked on the design throughout its full development I was told how the greatest amount of preliminary research was dedicated to the issue of the basement, specifically how far it could be dug out so as not to jeopardize the foundations of adjoining historical buildings.[34] This was deemed crucial, as the Corten steel drum had to sit just so on the site, not too crowded, not too isolated, just so. For the money shot. The basement was to house a large amount of program to achieve this effect. The building's operative aesthetic logic works from the formal outside in, the interior layout being merely incidental.

Imagine taking the façade of the old school, laying it out orthographically as a drawing—on paper, on the screen—and then stretching it, curving it, and transmogrifying its concrete materiality into the textured surfaces of Corten steel. There persists a family resemblance between the façades of the old

30  Douglas Spencer, *The Architecture of Neoliberalism* (London, 2016), 4.

31  Ibid., 29.

32  See Douglas Spencer, "Immediate Affect," Lecture, KTH School of Architecture, April 5, 2016, available online at: https://www.youtube.com/watch?v=_2mNTy6q3i0 (accessed November 26, 2021).

33  See "Tham & Videgård," *El Croquis* 188 (2017).

34  The interview took place in 2015 soon after we moved into the new building. The anonymity of the interviewee will be maintained.

einem Gewirr aus Schachteln und der Angst, dass die Regalflächen in den neuen Räumlichkeiten nicht ausreichen würden. Unter der Mitarbeiterschaft begann die Frage zu rumoren, was aus den versprochenen Büroräumen geworden sei. Im zweiten Stock, wo das gesamte Lehr- und Forschungspersonal in einem offenen Grundriss untergebracht werden sollte, wurden ad hoc Veränderungen vorgenommen. Von außen aber bot die neue Fakultät der Welt einen imposanten Anblick. Nur was genau repräsentierte er?

Nach welchen Kriterien lässt sich ein Bauwerk als eines beurteilen, das – bewusst oder nicht – dem Neoliberalismus anhängt? Laut Douglas Spencer weist eine neoliberale Architektur einige der folgenden Züge auf: Hass auf hierarchische Pläne; Interesse an spontaner Selbst-Organisation; Befreiung von Beschränkungen, gekleidet in Annahmen über den inhärenten Nutzen der Freiheit (die manchen, aber nicht allen zugänglich ist); eine Privilegierung von Unmittelbarkeit und Immersion; Beteiligung an Subjektivierungsprozessen, die das Subjekt als „umweltflexibel und affektgetrieben"[30] darstellt und schließlich dieses besondere Subjekt des/der Studierenden auf dem Weg zum „Studierenden-Entrepreneur".[31] All diese Merkmale schieben die Fähigkeit zum kritischen Denken auf, und Spencer geht sogar so weit zu sagen, dass die vom Neoliberalismus ausgeübten Formen der Umweltkontrolle die ihm erliegenden faszinierten Subjekte verdummt. Spencer stellte einige dieser Argumente 2016 im größten Zeichenatelier für Studienanfänger an der Architekturfakultät der KTH vor.[32] Werfen wir einen Blick hinein.

Der von den gefeierten schwedischen Architekten Tham & Videgård (es gibt sogar ein *El Croquis* über ihre Arbeit, ein sicheres Zeichen dafür, dass man in der Architektur auf der Überholspur der Ikonen und Idole angekommen ist)[33] stammende Entwurf für das neue Architekturgebäude auf dem Hauptcampus der KTH ging als Siegerprojekt aus einem 2007 ausgeschrieben Wettbewerb hervor, an dem so weltbekannte Büros wie SAANA teilnahmen. In seiner Covertauglichkeit ist das neue Architekturgebäude eine Art Zirkuspferd. Es handelt sich um einen Cortenstahl-Zylinder mit ausgestanzten Fenstern. In einem Interview mit einem/einer mitarbeitenden ArchitektIn, der/die während der gesamten Entwicklung am Entwurf beteiligt war, erfuhr ich, dass der meiste Forschungsaufwand im Vorfeld in die Kellergeschosse floss, speziell in die Frage, wie tief der Grund ausgehoben werden konnte, ohne die Fundamente der benachbarten historischen Gebäude zu gefährden.[34] Die Frage wurde als entscheidend erachtet, da der Cortenstahl-Zylinder genauso dastehen sollte wie er da steht, nicht zu nah den umgebenden Gebäuden, nicht zu isoliert davon. Für den „money shot". Die Untergeschosse sollten einen erheblichen Teil des Raumprogramms aufnehmen, um diesen Effekt zu erzielen. Die ästhetische Logik des Gebäudes operiert von außen nach innen; die Anordnung im Inneren ist beliebig.

Stellen wir uns die Fassade der alten Fakultät im Aufriss vor, auf Papier oder Bildschirm gezeichnet, dann gestreckt und gekrümmt, die Betonoberfläche in die Textur von Cortenstahl umgewandelt, so zeigt sich eine Familienähnlichkeit zwischen der Fassade des alten und des neuen Gebäudes im Rhythmus der Fensteranordnung, eine gespenstische Erinnerung, die Ehrlemark aufgefallen ist. Aber weshalb Cortenstahl? Im Norden von Schweden ist Eisenerz ein großes Ding, ganze Städte wie Malmberget und Kiruna wurden umgesiedelt, nachdem man die Eisenerzstollen bis unter die früheren Werksiedlungen getrieben hatte. Bergbau hat eine lange Tradition in Schweden. Beim typisch schwedischen Haus ist die Holzverkleidung mit einem roten Pigment bemalt, das ursprünglich als Nebenprodukt im Bergbau anfiel. Tham & Videgård schlachteten Assoziationen mit dieser verbreiteten Hausform in einem anderen Projekt aus, wofür sie Datamining auf der Immobilien-Website hemnet.se betrieben. Wie Karissa Rosenfield in *ArchDaily* schreibt, ermittelte das Architekturbüro aus 200 Millionen Clicks auf hemnet.se das „statistisch meistgesuchte Haus Schwedens".[35] Der darauf basierende Entwurf ist der ästhetische Inbegriff des schwedischen Hauses. Einige Details sind übertrieben, die Fenster leicht überdimensioniert, das Giebeldach durch ein Flachdach ersetzt, was ihm insgesamt einen zeitgenössischen Anstrich verleiht, aber doch eine unheimliche Ähnlichkeit mit dem traditionellen Baustil wahrt.

30  Spencer, Douglas: *The Architecture of Neoliberalism*, London 2016, 4.

31  Ebd., 29.

32  Vgl. Spencer, Douglas: „Immediate Affect", Vortrag an der Architekturfakultät der KTH, 5. April 2016, online unter: https://www.youtube.com/ watch?v=_2mNTy6q3i0 (Stand: 26. November 2021).

33  Vgl. „Tham & Videgård", *El Croquis* 188 (2017).

34  Das Interview fand 2015 kurz nach dem Umzug in das neue Gebäude statt. Der/die InterviewparntnerIn bleibt anonym.

35  Rosenfield, Karissa: „Tham & Videgård Designs Sweden's ‚Most Sought After Home'", *ArchDaily*, 19. Mai 2015, online unter: https://www.archdaily. com/633044/tham-and-videgard-designs-sweden-s-most-sought-after-home (Stand: 1. September 2021).

and the new school in terms of the punctuated rhythm of fenestration, a ghostly reminder such as perceived by Ehrlemark. What about the use of Corten steel? To the north of Sweden iron ore is a big deal, whole towns, Malmberget and Kiruna, have been relocated as expanding iron ore mines undercut former custom-built settlements. Mining in Sweden is an old practice. The vernacular Swedish cottage is clad in timber washed in a red pigment originally derived as a by-product of the mining industry. Tham & Videgård exploit associations with this familiar house form in another project by mining Big Data sourced on the real estate product site hemnet.se. As Karissa Rosenfield explains in *ArchDaily*, the design company undertook an experiment that involved 200 million clicks on hemnet.se resulting in "Sweden's Statistically Most Sought After Home."[35] The design outcome is a celebration of the quintessential aesthetics of the Swedish home. Certain details are exaggerated, windows are slightly over-scaled, a flat roof is proposed rather than a pitched one, in all it achieves a contemporary flourish, while maintaining an uncanny similarity to the vernacular.

Tham & Videgård's new Architecture House project at KTH subsequently wins the Kasper Salin Prize for best new architecture in 2015, an award established by the Swedish Association of Architects in 1962. The jury justification focusses on the contextual fit—Corten steel is said to offer an aesthetically pleasing continuity with the red brick of the historical campus buildings by Erik Lallerstedt—the material composition, mixing concrete and pine timber lined interiors, is appreciated, the lovely large windows, and the appropriateness of relocating the architecture school back on the main campus again, back into the institutional fold, are gestures to be commended.[36] Project descriptions are to be found across such sites as *ArchDaily, Dezeen, and Designboom*. Its mediated presence circulates, but what is going on inside?

A few years prior to the opening of the new Architecture House, when asked at a lecture about the pedagogical intent of the interior organization of the building, the architects are taken aback, as though the thought had not occurred to them. In a 2015 article for the industry magazine *Arkitektur*, the architects reveal that their pedagogical ambitions are similar, after all, to Henriksson's ambitions for the former Architecture House, in that they are keen to demonstrate how things have been built.[37]

The architecture can perform as a didactic tool. At the same time, promptly contradicting themselves, they explain that the design of the building attends to no specific pedagogy, because pedagogical approaches change so rapidly these days. Remember, the situation that we are dealing with is dynamic, neoliberalism requires flexibility. They have "designed in" generality instead, and in time this generality will mean that the any-space-whatever will lend itself to generic uses: another research division will move into the second floor, for instance, displacing the School of Architecture researchers. The plan encourages flows and encounters, the architects explain. Smooth space, curved, without friction. All rooms can be used in multiple ways. Flexibility is a key term. No more raked lecture halls with fixed seating, as in the former school, but sprawling multipurpose seminar rooms on the entry level, with sinks tucked into niches off to the side, suggesting that these spaces could be used for public lectures or else for messy workshops, either way. In the rendered images submitted with the competition entry these multi-purpose rooms are called *ateljé*, that is to say, studios. Entering the new building from Osquars backe, one glides down a gently sloped concrete floor passing below the murmuring voice of a sound installation into what came to be called the "amoeba," a space that supports impromptu events, and into which the mobile student bar is regularly rolled. The inevitability of a table tennis table is to be found in a curved hollow further in.

When students ascend the drama of the two sets of internal spiral stairs, lit atmospherically from above, to occupy the three levels of open plan studio space, they are still able to discover a dedicated desk for each of the 550 or so strong student body. But the smaller seminar rooms on these levels turn out to be distorted and strange. Taking up the core of the rounded triangle that composes the building plan, crammed between the two dramatic interior stairwells, their wedge-like spaces make seminar gatherings near impossible, and in any case, they are so small that students are left gasping for air before the hour is up.

35  Karissa Rosenfield, "Tham & Videgård Designs Sweden's 'Most Sought After Home,'" *ArchDaily*, May 19, 2015, available online at: https://www.archdaily.com/633044/tham-and-videgard-designs-sweden-s-most-sought-after-home (accessed September 1, 2021).

36  See https://www.contractdesign.com/news/competitions-awards/swedish-school-of-architecture-wins-the-2015-kasper-salin-prize/; https://www.akademiskahus.se/en/news/news-room/2015/11/new-school-of-architecture-wins-2015-kasper-salin-prize/ (accessed November 26, 2021).

37  See Nina Gunne, "Nybyggaranda på anrikt campus," *Arkitekten* 9 (2015): 42–47.

Tham & Videgårds neues Architekturgebäude auf dem KTH-Campus erhält schließlich den seit 1962 von der schwedischen Architektenkammer vergebenen Kasper-Salin-Preis für das beste neue Bauwerk des Jahres 2015. Die Jurybegründung hebt den Kontextbezug hervor – der Cortenstahl stelle eine ästhetisch ansprechende Kontinuität zu den Backsteinfassaden der historischen Universitätsbauten von Erik Lallerstedt her –, würdigt die Materialwahl, die Verbindung von Beton mit den Kiefervertäfelungen in den Innenräumen, und lobt die wunderbaren großen Fenster sowie die Zurückverlegung der Architekturfakultät auf den Campus, ihre Wiedereinbettung in die Institution, als vorbildliche Gesten.[36] Auf Websites wie *ArchDaily*, *Dezeen* und *Designboom* erscheinen Projektbeschreibungen. Mediale Präsenz ist zuhauf gegeben, aber was spielt sich im Inneren ab?

Ein paar Jahre vor der Eröffnung der neuen Architekturfakultät, sind die Architekten überrascht, als sie bei einem Vortrag nach den pädagogischen Intentionen der inneren Organisation des Gebäudes gefragt werden, als hätten sie darauf nie einen Gedanken verschwendet. 2015 enthüllen die Architekten in einem Artikel für das Fachmagazin *Arkitektur*, ihre pädagogischen Absichten ähnelten letztlich denen Henrikssons für die alte Architekturfakultät, insofern auch sie zeigen wollten, wie die Dinge gebaut sind.[37] Die Architektur kann als didaktisches Werkzeug dienen. Gleichzeitig erklären sie im direkten Widerspruch dazu, der Entwurf des Gebäudes verfolge kein bestimmtes pädagogisches Programm, weil sich pädagogische Ansätze heute so rasch änderten. (Erinnern wir uns, die Situation, in der wir uns befinden, ist dynamisch, Neoliberalismus verlangt Flexibilität.) Stattdessen hätten sie Generalität mit „eingeplant", und mit der Zeit wird das bedeuten, dass sich jeder beliebige Raum generisch nutzen lässt: eine andere Forschungsabteilung könnte zum Beispiel im zweiten Stock einziehen und die der Architekturfakultät verdrängen. Der Entwurf fördere Ströme und Begegnungen, erklären die Architekten, glatte, geschwungene, reibungslose Räume, die alle multifunktional einsetzbar seien. Flexibilität ist ein Schlüsselbegriff. Keine abfallenden Vorlesungssäle mit festen Sitzreihen wie im alten Gebäude, sondern eine Ansammlung von Mehrzweck-Seminarräumen auf der Eingangsebene mit seitlich in Nischen angebrachten Waschbecken, die darauf hindeuten, dass die Räume ebenso für öffentliche Vorlesungen verwendet werden können wie für Werkstätten, in denen die Späne fliegen. In den zum Wettbewerb eingereichten gerenderten Bildern werden diese Mehrzweckräume als *atelje* – Ateliers – bezeichnet. Betritt man das Gebäude vom Osquars backe aus, gleitet man über

einen leicht geneigten Betonboden, unter dem Stimmgemurmel einer Klanginstallation hindurch, in die sogenannte „Amöbe" hinunter, einen Raum für spontane Ereignisse, in den auch häufig die mobile Studierendenbar gerollt wird. In einer runden Ausbuchtung weiter drinnen befindet sich der unvermeidliche Pingpongtisch.

Steigen Studierende über die beiden dramatischen, atmosphärisch von oben beleuchteten Wendeltreppen zu den drei offenen Atelieretagen hoch, findet dort immer noch jede/r der rund 550 Studierenden einen eigenen Schreibtisch. Die kleineren Seminarräume auf diesen Etagen erweisen sich allerdings als seltsam deformiert. Im Kern des abgerundeten Dreiecks befindlich, aus dem der Grundriss besteht, eingeklemmt zwischen den beiden dramatischen Wendeltreppen, lassen ihre keilförmigen Räume fast keine Seminarveranstaltungen zu, sind aber auf jeden Fall so klein, dass die Studierenden nach Luft schnappen, bevor die Stunde vorüber ist. Generalität heißt anscheinend eine Folge von irgendwelchen Räumen, die alle nicht zweckgemäß sind und behelfsmäßiger Eingriffe bedürfen. Studierende kleben die klimagesteuerten Jalousien an die Decke, weil sie von ihrem eigenwilligen Verhalten genug haben. In der zweiten Etage, wo die ArchitekturforscherInnen untergebracht werden sollen, wird in letzter Minute ein Teppichboden verlegt, um für Bibliotheksruhe zu sorgen, der dünstet aber stattdessen Gase aus, deretwegen manche mit Kopfschmerzen zu Hause bleiben müssen. Die große Behindertentoilette auf der zweiten Etage besitzt nicht einmal eine Dusche für die, die vielleicht gern zur Arbeit radeln oder joggen würden. Aus dem geplanten Streich, sie in eine Sauna umzuwandeln und die Kiefernvertäfelung buntgestreift zu bemalen, wird nichts. Für den Zugang zur zweiten Etage und zur Verwaltung in der obersten Etage wird eine Schlüsselkarte benötigt, wodurch die Zufallsbegegnungen zwischen Personal und Studierenden wegfallen. Die Kiefernvertäfelung der gesamten Innenräume (gerüchteweise waren astknotenarme Qualitätskiefern während der Bauzeit des Gebäudes fast nicht mehr erhältlich) vermitteln den Eindruck einer überdimensionierten Sauna. Das Zeichenatelier im obersten Stock erlebte im Lauf der ersten Jahre eine rasche Abfolge

36  Vgl. https://www.contractdesign.com/news/competitions-awards/ swedish-school-of-architecture-wins-the-2015-kasper-salin-prize/; https://www.akademiskahus.se/en/news/news-room/2015/11/ new-school-of-architecture-wins-2015-kasper-salin-prize/ (Stand: 26. November 2021).

37  Vgl. Gunne, Nina: „Nybyggaranda på anrikt campus", *Arkitekten* 9 (2015): 42–47.

Generality turns out to mean a series of any-spaces-whatever, none quite fit for purpose, all requiring ad hoc bricolage. Students tape the climate sensitive blinds to the ceiling, frustrated by their willful behavior. Carpet is added at the last minute to level 2, where the architectural researchers are to be seated, with the aim of manifesting the silence of a library, producing off-gases instead that keep some at home with headaches. The large disabled toilet on the second level does not even include a shower for those who might like to cycle or jog to work. A mischievous plot to renovate it into a sauna and to candy-stripe paint the pine timber panels goes nowhere. Entry to level 2 and to the administrative offices on the top level are by key card, which means no more incidental encounters between staff and students. The pine lining of the entire interior (rumour has it that supplies of high-quality pine with minimum knots were near exhausted during the period of the building's construction) give the general effect of an oversized sauna. The atelier on the top floor is witness to a swift series of different kinds of occupation over the opening years eventually settling on a compressed clustering of office desks and chairs, many of which are to be shared. At least the rapidly disappearing administrative staff have an office each, with windows that are openable. For the researchers on level 2, on the other hand, either someone has lost the key to the scant operable windows, or else, they are refusing to make the key available. Level 2 hits the ground at the rear where a courtyard opens up, making openable windows a security risk.

What matters, though, what counts, is that as you enter the main campus of KTH from Valhallavägen, proceeding up Osquars backe, there, with its uncompromisingly contemporary—yet historically respectful—proud curved form, a neat package of an architectural icon greets you with just the right symbolic message. Fit for the new spirit of capitalism. Every visitor pauses at approximately the same spot to catch the Instagram-ready image on their smart device. The students themselves agree that the building is designed for Instagram, and during the opening months complain of feeling like animals in a zoo, with frequent architectural tourist groups led on guided tours of the new building.[38]

What should have caused consternation, and yet which has been met with little protest, was the slow, seemingly inexorable process by which square meters of office space in the new building were incrementally lost. Originally, researchers were to claim offices and seminar rooms in an adjoining, older building, now called KTH Entré. But it became clear quite quickly, even before the big move, that this would not be financially feasible. By 2016 news columns were drawing attention to the financial straits suffered by the school as funding rules of architecture students shifted, and as the rent of the "*lokal*" proved too expensive. Then, after four years of occupation of the newly designed Architecture House, level 2 was lost, given up to the much-fêted Digital Futures research hub, the website of which sports a fun-loving cartoon image of blackboards and robotic arms.[39]

With the current "pivot" to online teaching as a result of the COVID-19 pandemic, the question of real estate, and whether expensive office spaces can be dispensed with altogether, becomes all too pressing in places of higher education as elsewhere. This slow effort toward austerity feels like a mortgage that can no longer be amortized, soon to be followed by the notices served to vacate. It feels like the dire straits in which a family home must be abruptly downscaled. The old furniture no longer fits in the new, much reduced premises. What is the *Existenzminimum* of an architectural education? What is the minimal acceptable floorspace, let alone associated services, that can yet support the becoming architect? Where these questions might once have been merely idle, with so many now working remotely, interfacing virtually, the challenge of pedagogical real estate transactions become even more threatening today.

There were a few moments of hesitation in the process that transplanted the former school of architecture from its off-campus site back on campus, and from one custom designed building into another, forcing into abrupt contrast two distinct political periods, one directed toward the welfare state, the other rushing enthusiastically toward neoliberal mores. In an opinion piece in *Dagens Nyheter*, just after the fire that destroyed the rear ateliers of the old Architecture school in 2011,

38  See Anna Björklund, "Studenterna visas upp som utställningsdjur," *Arkitekten*, March, 29, 2016, available online at: https://arkitekten.se/debatt/studenterna-visas-upp-som-utstallningsdjur/ (accessed November 26, 2021).

39  See https://www.digitalfutures.kth.se/en/om-digital-futures-1.946969 (accessed November 26, 2021).

wechselnder Nutzungen, die schließlich auf eine dichte Anhäufung an Schreibtischen und Stühlen hinauslief, wovon viele geteilt werden müssen. Wenigstens das rasch schrumpfende Verwaltungspersonal hat jeweils ein eigenes Büro mit Fenstern, die sich öffnen lassen. Bei den ForscherInnen auf Ebene 2 dagegen ging der Schlüssel für die wenigen öffenbaren Fenster entweder verloren oder er wird nicht ausgehändigt. Ebene 2 trifft nämlich im rückwärtigen Teil auf Straßenniveau und öffnet sich auf einen Hof, sodass öffenbare Fenster zum Sicherheitsrisiko werden.

Worauf es aber wirklich ankommt, ist, dass man, wenn man den Hauptcampus der KTH vom Valhallavägen über den Osquars backe betritt, von dieser kompromisslos zeitgenössischen – und doch historisch respektvollen – Rundform, dem kompakten Paket einer architektonischen Ikone mit genau der richtigen symbolischen Botschaft begrüßt wird. Reif für den neuen Geist des Kapitalismus. BesucherInnen halten durchwegs an fast derselben Stelle, um das Instagram-taugliche Bild mit ihrem Smartphone festzuhalten. Auch die Studierenden glauben, dass das Gebäude für Instagram entworfen wurde, und klagten anfangs, dass sie sich angesichts der vielen Gebäudeführungen für ArchitekturtouristInnen wie Tiere in einem Zoo fühlten.[38]

Was Bestürzung ausgelöst haben sollte und doch kaum auf Protest stieß, war der langsame, scheinbar unaufhaltsame Verlust von Quadratmeter über Quadratmeter an Bürofläche. Ursprünglich sollten die ForscherInnen Büros und Seminarräume in einem angrenzenden älteren Gebäude bekommen, das heute als KTH-Entré bezeichnet wird. Aber es wurde sehr bald, sogar schon vor dem großen Umzug, klar, dass dies finanziell nicht zu stemmen war. Bereits 2016 wiesen Zeitungskolumnen auf den finanziellen Engpass hin, dem sich die Fakultät gegenübersah, als sich die Förderbedingungen für Architekturstudierende änderten und sich die Miete für die „Location" als zu teuer erwies. Schließlich, nach vier Jahren Nutzung des neu entworfenen Architekturgebäudes, ging die Ebene 2 verloren, wurde dem viel-gepriesenen Digital Futures Forschungszentrum überlassen, dessen Website einst ein lustiger Cartoon mit Schultafeln und Roboterarmen zierte.[39]

Mit dem gegenwärtigen pandemiebedingten Fokus auf Online-Unterricht wird die Frage der Immobilienkosten und ob teure Büroflächen vielleicht ganz verzichtbar sind, in der höheren Bildung genauso virulent wie anderswo. Diese schleichende Sparpolitik fühlt sich an wie eine nicht mehr bedienbare Hypothek und der demnächst bevorstehende Räumungsbescheid. Es

fühlt sich an, wie die missliche Lage, in der eine Familie plötzlich kürzertreten muss. Die alten Möbel passen nicht mehr in die neuen, wesentlich kleineren Räumlichkeiten. Was ist das Existenzminimum einer Architekturausbildung? Was ist die kleinstmögliche Fläche, ganz zu schweigen von den dazugehörigen Dienstleistungen, die für eine werdende ArchitektIn benötigt wird? Waren das früher vielleicht müßige Fragen, so wird die Herausforderung von Immobilientransaktionen im Bildungsbereich jetzt, wo so viele von zu Hause arbeiten und sich virtuell treffen, immer bedrohlicher.

Es gab einige wenige Momente des Innehaltens in dem Prozess, der die frühere Fakultät für Architektur von ihrem Standort außerhalb des Campus auf den Campus zurück und von einem eigens dafür entworfenen Gebäude in ein anderes verpflanzte, und so einen scharfen Kontrast zwischen zwei unterschiedlichen politischen Epochen schuf – einer, die Richtung Wohlfahrtsstaat strebt, und einer, die sich begeistert in neoliberale Gewohnheiten stürzt. In einem Meinungsartikel, der 2011 kurz nach dem Brand der Werkstätten im Hinterhof der alten Architekturfakultät in der *Dagens Nyheter* erschien, wurde die Frage aufgeworfen, warum das alte Gebäude nicht renoviert werden könne.[40] Lasse sich denn nichts aus den Ambitionen des einstigen Wohlfahrtsstaats machen? Sei nicht mit dem Ausbruch des Brandes der richtige Zeitpunkt gekommen, über eine Verjüngung des Gebäudes für die es nutzenden angehenden ArchitektInnen nachzudenken? Unterschwellig lagen diesen Bemerkungen auch Befürchtungen über mögliche Immobilienspekulationen rund um Akademiska Hus zugrunde, einer vormals öffentlichen, zur schwedischen Nationalbehörde für öffentliche Bauten (KBS) gehörenden und nunmehr privatisierten Organisation, die die gesamten Universitätsgebäude verwaltet. Alle wussten um den Ruf des umgebenden Viertels mit seinen wohlhabenden BewohnerInnen, die das „hässliche Entlein" hassen. Darüber hinaus waren die Stockholmer Immobilienpreise seit Eröffnung der Fakultät im Jahr 1970 in astronomische Höhen geklettert. Doch die Entscheidung ist gefallen. Es würde mehr als die vorhandene Kraft benötigen, um das Steuer herumzureißen und vor Ort zu bleiben. Die Schachteln sind schon vor Sommer 2015 gepackt, eine Abschiedsparty wird veranstaltet

38 Vgl. Björklund, Anna: „Studenterna visas upp som utställningsdjur", *Arkitekten*, 29. März 2016, online unter: https://arkitekten.se/debatt/studenterna-visas-upp-som-utstallningsdjur/ (Stand: 26. November 2021).

39 Vgl. https://www.digitalfutures.kth.se/en/om-digital-futures-1.946969 (Stand: 26. November 2021).

40 Vgl. Hatz, Elizabeth/Hagander, Carl-Gustaf/Andersson, Ola/Bedoire, Fredrik: „Ur eld i aska. Nu kan Stockholms mest hatade hus få ett nytt ansikte", *Dagens Nyheter*, 5. Oktober 2011, https://www.dn.se/kultur-noje/kulturdebatt/ur-eld-i-aska-nu-kan-stockholms-mest-hatade-hus-fa-ett-nytt-ansikte/ (Stand: 11. Juni 2020).

questions are raised as to why the old building cannot be renovated.[40] Is there nothing to be done with former welfare state ambitions? Surely now, following the event of the fire, is the moment to consider rejuvenating the building for its population of becoming architects? Hidden in these remarks are queries as to what real estate speculation might be afoot for the privatized Akademiska Hus, a formerly public organization, once part of KBS Swedish Board of Public Buildings, that administers all university building stock. Everyone is aware of the repute of the neighborhood and the wealthy inhabitants who loathe the Ugly Duckling. Furthermore, Stockholm real estate has escalated astronomically in value in intervening years since the school was opened in 1970. But the decision has been made, and it would take a stronger will at the helm than the one we have available to turn the decision around in order to stay put. Boxes are packed in advance of the summer of 2015, a final farewell party is held, a small exhibition fondly entitled "Ugly Duckling" is mounted by Björn Ehrlemark, and then we all say goodbye.[41] As a final gesture, the large rainbow-colored sign that reads KTH Arkitektur is removed from the front façade. I'm told it is still in storage somewhere on the main campus.

At first Akademiska Hus makes clear its intention to maintain the property, transform it into a creative incubator.[42] The building voted the ugliest in Stockholm, in a radio poll no less, will be rudely maintaining its façades while simultaneously opening itself up. A chunk of its basement will become a cake shop. Plans will be realized to turn the "A Huset" (A House), as it is now called, into a meeting place supporting knowledge, creativity and entrepreneurship, with a focus on food and fashion.[43] At the same time, images from renovated sections of the building begin to appear in the local real estate pages.[44] In the end, no one really seems surprised when the building, as part of a package of building stock, is sold off to Fastighets AB Balder in a 1,3 billion SEK real estate deal. After all, in Hans Christian Andersen's fairy tale of the Ugly Duckling, the misplaced and bullied creature grows up to become an elegant swan, re-joining its finely feathered family.

Helena Mattsson and Catharina Gabrielsson, both tenured professors at KTH Stockholm, remark that neoliberal capitalism, rather than melting into the air as famously promised by Marx,

solidifies in terrifying new constellations of power and capital. They recommend, as an antidote, Isabelle Stengers's imperative to "pay attention!", which they argue begins at the level of everyday observation.[45] Care is required for attention to be paid, attention to detail, to how spaces and occupying bodies are arrayed in relation to each other, sometimes capacitated and sometimes incapacitated. There is probably no use complaining about the disorientating effects of "moving house," except to note that the affective dimensions of such a relocation should not be underestimated. The aftereffects have embedded themselves in the schools of architecture described here, and they have embedded themselves in the changing outline of the staff and student body. There are certainly more stories to be told, and additional minor histories to unearth. What has been lost? What has been gained? Much as the old architecture school eventually became an object of endearment, and its loss felt deeply, new attachments will probably be formed to the new architecture house. Staff and students will get by; they will make do. Research and student events have already claimed the new school's indeterminate spaces, such as the amoeba. The large windows facing the entry to the campus have even been occupied for the purposes of protest. At a minimum, finally, care will "get us through the day,"[46] as Puig de la Bellacasa remarks. I just hope that someone finally gets the great rainbow colored KTH Arkitektur sign out of storage and mounts it on the new façade. ∎

40  See Elizabeth Hatz, Carl-Gustaf Hagander, Ola Andersson and Fredrik Bedoire, "Ur eld i aska. Nu kan Stockholms mest hatade hus få ett nytt ansikte," *Dagens Nyheter*, October 5, 2011, https://www.dn.se/kultur-noje/kulturdebatt/ur-eld-i-aska-nu-kan-stockholms-mest-hatade-hus-fa-ett-nytt-ansikte/ (accessed June 11, 2020).

41  See https://arkitekturensgrannar.se/Ugly-Duckling (accessed November 26, 2021).

42  See "Ful' skola blir A huset," Byggvärlden, Jan 29, 2015, available online at: https://www.byggvarlden.se/ful-skola-blir-a-huset/ (accessed December 15, 2021).

43  Ibid.

44  See https://objektvision.se/Beskriv/208016294 (accessed 21 July 2020).

45  See Catharina Gabrielsson and Helena Mattsson, "Pay Attention!" *Architecture and Culture* 5, no. 2 (2017): 157–164, 158. See Isabelle Stengers, *In Catastrophic Times: The Coming Barbarism* (Ann Arbor, 2015).

46  Puig de la Bellacasa, *Matters of Care* (see note 24), 87.

und eine kleine, von Björn Ehrlemark organisierte Ausstellung mit dem liebevollen Titel „Ugly Duckling" auf die Beine gestellt, dann sagen wir alle goodbye.[41] Als letzter Akt wird die große regenbogenfarbene Aufschrift „KTH Arkitektur" von der Vorderfassade entfernt. Wie ich höre, wird sie immer noch irgendwo auf dem Hauptcampus aufbewahrt.

Zunächst gibt Akademiska Hus die Absicht bekannt, die Immobilie erhalten und in einen Kreativinkubator umwandeln zu wollen.[42] Das in einer Radioumfrage zum hässlichsten Gebäude Stockholms gewählte Objekt wird seine Fassade beibehalten und sich gleichzeitig öffnen. In einen Teil des Kellers soll eine Konditorei einziehen. Pläne werden in die Wege geleitet, das „A-Huset", wie es nunmehr heißt, in einen Treffpunkt für Wissen, Kreativität und Entrepreneurship umzuwandeln, mit Fokus auf Ernährung und Mode.[43] Zur gleichen Zeit tauchen auf den lokalen Immobilienseiten Bilder von renovierten Teilen des Gebäudes auf.[44] Am Ende ist niemand überrascht, als das Gebäude als Teil eines größeren Immobilien-Pakets um 1,3 Milliarden Schwedenkronen an Fastighets AB Balder verkauft wird. Schließlich wächst auch in Hans Christian Andersens Märchen vom hässlichen Entlein die falsch platzierte und tyrannisierte Kreatur zu einem eleganten Schwan heran und wird wieder mit ihrer feingefiederten Familie vereint.

Helena Mattsson und Catharina Gabrielsson, beide Professorinnen an der KTH Stockholm, stellen fest, dass sich der neoliberale Kapitalismus, statt sich wie von Marx versprochen in Luft aufzulösen, in erschreckenden neuen Macht- und Kapitalkonstellationen verfestigt. Als Gegenmittel empfehlen sie Isabelle Stengers' Imperativ „pay attention!", der ihrer Ansicht nach auf der Ebene alltäglicher Beobachtungen beginnt.[45] Achtsamkeit ist eine Voraussetzung für Aufmerksamkeit, das Achten auf Details, darauf, wie Räume und sich darin aufhaltende Körper zueinander ins Verhältnis gesetzt werden, manchmal ermächtigend, manchmal behindernd. Es ist wahrscheinlich sinnlos, sich über die Desorientierungseffekte von Umzügen zu beschweren, gleichwohl sollte man nicht vergessen, dass die affektiven Dimensionen so eines Umzugs nicht zu unterschätzen sind. Seine Nachwirkungen haben sich in die hier beschriebenen Architekturfakultäten und in die sich verändernde Gestalt des Lehrkörpers und der Studierendenschaft eingeschrieben. Es gäbe bestimmt noch mehr Geschichten zu erzählen und weitere kleine Erzählungen auszugraben. Was ist verloren gegangen, was wurde gewonnen? So sehr die alte Architekturfakultät schließlich zu einem geliebten Objekt wurde, dessen Verlust sehr schmerzte, genauso werden sich wahrscheinlich frische Bindungen an das neue Gebäude herausbilden. Lehrkörper und Studierende werden sich zurechtfinden, werden sich zu helfen wissen. Wissenschaftliche und studentische Veranstaltungen haben sich bereits die unbestimmten Räume des neuen Fakultätsgebäudes wie die Amöbe angeeignet. Die großen zum Campuseingang weisenden Fenster sind für Protestzwecke vereinnahmt worden. Zum Mindesten wird uns Achtsamkeit „über den Tag helfen",[46] wie Puig de la Bellacasa schreibt. Ich hoffe nur, dass jemand zu guter Letzt die große regenbogenfarbene Aufschrift „KTH Arkitektur" aus dem Lager holt und an die neue Fassade schraubt. ∎

*Übersetzung aus dem Englischen: Wilfried Prantner*

41 Vgl. https://arkitekturensgrannar.se/Ugly-Duckling (Stand: 26. November 2021). Vgl. dazu auch den nachfolgenden Beitrag in dieser *GAM* Ausgabe auf den Seiten 106–125.

42 Vgl. „Ful' skola blir A huset", *Byggvärlden*, 29. Januar 2015, online unter: https://www.byggvarlden.se/ful-skola-blir-a-huset/ (Stand: 15. Dezember 2021).

43 Ebd.

44 Vgl. https://objektvision.se/Beskriv/208016294 (Stand: 21. Juli 2020).

45 Gabrielsson, Catharina/Mattsson, Helena: „Pay Attention!", *Architecture and Culture* 5, 2 (2017): 157–164, 158. Vgl. Stengers, Isabelle: *In Catastrophic Times: The Coming Barbarism*, Trans. Andrew Goffey, Lüneburg 2015, online unter: http://openhumanitiespress.org/books/download/Stengers_2015_In-Catastrophic-Times.pdf (Stand: 8. Februar 2022).

46 Puig de la Bellacasa, *Matters of Care* (wie Anm. 23), 87 (Übers. W.P.).

# Now and Then
## The KTH School of Architecture's "A-building" in Stockholm

**Björn Ehrlemark**

At first glance, little seems to have happened in the four decades that separates the photographs on the following pages. They were taken by Sten Vilson in 1970 and by Tove Freiij in 2015 at the KTH School of Architecture's so-called "A-building" in Stockholm. It was the last to be designed by the university's in-house architecture office, a team led by architect and professor Gunnar Henriksson and architect and artist John Olsson. The pairs of photos were assembled and displayed on location in 2015 as part of the exhibition Ugly Duckling. It was the final semester before the school moved to newly built premises and the building was turned into a co-working space. A few years on, the meaning of both sets of images has shifted somewhat. The inaugural moment as recorded by Vilson's camera has been canonized further, reprinted in a recent architectural monograph and also used in advertising by the new occupants. The origin story remains pinned to the present. Meanwhile, the everydayness of student life captured by Freiij is not only something that has since vanished from these rooms. The scenes are in some sense also more relegated to the past than the more distant history which precedes it. Even if architectural education and its intense but passing activities were the very reason for constructing this architecture, it seems so much easier to remember how it started—or ended—than everything that went on in between. After all, a majority of the architects practicing in Sweden today studied here sometime between those two dates. It has left its most lasting impression through them. ▪

## Heute und damals
### Das „A-Gebäude" der Architekturfakultät an der KTH Stockholm

Auf den ersten Blick scheint sich in den vier Jahrzehnten, die zwischen den auf den folgenden Seiten gezeigten Fotografien liegen, wenig getan zu haben. Sie wurden 1970 (von Sten Vilson) und 2015 (von Tove Freiij) im sogenannten A-Gebäude der Architekturfakultät an der KTH Stockholm aufgenommen. Es war das letzte, das vom universitätseigenen Architekturbüro, geleitet vom Architekten und Professor Gunnar Henriksson und vom Architekten und Künstler John Olsson, entworfen wurde. Die Bildpaare waren 2015 Teil der Ausstellung „Ugly Duckling" („Hässliches Entlein"), die vor Ort stattfand, ehe die Fakultät in ein neu errichtetes Gebäude umzog und das alte in einen Co-Working Space umgewandelt wurde. Seither haben beide Bildreihen einen gewissen Bedeutungswandel erlebt. Der Augenblick der Eröffnung, wie er von Vilsons Kamera festgehalten wurde, ist durch den Wiederabdruck in einer kürzlich erschienen Architekturmonografie und die Verwendung in der Werbung der neuen NutzerInnen weiter kanonisiert worden. Die Ursprungsgeschichte bleibt an die Gegenwart geknüpft. Der von Freiij fotografierte Studierendenalltag ist inzwischen nicht nur aus diesen Räumen verschwunden, sondern in gewisser Weise auch weiter in die Vergangenheit gerückt als die länger zurückliegende Geschichte, die ihm vorausging. Zwar waren die Architekturausbildung und ihre intensiven, vergänglichen Aktivitäten der Grund für die Konstruktion dieses Gebäudes, doch scheint es viel leichter zu sein, sich an den Beginn und das Ende zu erinnern, als daran, was dazwischen geschah. Allerdings hat der Großteil der heute in Schweden tätigen ArchitektInnen irgendwann in dieser Zwischenzeit hier studiert. In ihren Werken hat sie ihre bleibendsten Eindrücke hinterlassen. ▪

*Übersetzung aus dem Englischen: Wilfried Prantner*

1 KTH School of Architecture studio space | Architekturfakultät KTH Stockholm, Zeichenatelier 2015 © Tove Freiij

2–3    The west-facing courtyard with atelier and workshop pavilions | Der westseitige Innenhof mit Atelier- und Workshoppavillons, 1970 © Sten Vilson;
replaced by temporary structures after the 2011 fire | nach dem Brand von 2011 durch temporäre Bauten ersetzt, 2015 © Tove Freiij

4–5    Main façade towards the street in the upscale Östermalm neighbourhood | Die straßenseitige Hauptfassade im eleganten Stadtviertel Östermalm, 1970
© Sten Vilson; the ivy intended to cover the raw concrete never really took hold | der Efeu, der den Sichtbeton überwuchern sollte, fasste nie wirklich
Fuß, 2015 © Tove Freiij

6–7 The project's young interior architect, Bror Martin Nilsson, demonstrates the stackable drawing tables of his design | Der junge Innenarchitekt des Projekts, Bror Martin Nilsson, demonstriert die von ihm entworfenen stapelbaren Zeichentische, 1970 © Sten Vilson; upon seeing the school and its furniture in 2015, Nilsson compared his emotions to that of a high school reunion | Nilsson verglich sein Gefühl beim Wiedersehen des Gebäudes und seiner Möbel mit dem eines Klassentreffens, 2015 © Tove Freiij

8–9 Steel tube and plywood chairs (something of the school's trademark) were off-the-shelf from a local manufacturer, while tables were tailor-made to go with them | Die Stühle aus Stahlrohr und Sperrholz (so etwas wie das Markenzeichen der Fakultät) waren Serienartikel eines lokalen Erzeugers, die Tische waren dazu passend maßgefertigt worden, 1970 © Sten Vilson; most of the furnishing lasted for decades, but some were replaced along the way | Das meiste Mobiliar hielt Jahrzehnte, aber einige Stücke wurden im Lauf der Zeit ersetzt, 2015 © Tove Freiij

10–11    The first generation of students moving in complained about a lack of cosiness and negotiated for communal kitchens to be added |
Die erste Studierenden-Generation, die einzog, beschwerte sich über mangelnde Gemütlichkeit und erstritt die Einrichtung von
Gemeinschaftsküchen, 1970 © Sten Vilson; microwaves instead of teapots, but more or less the same thing | Mikrowelle statt Teekannen,
aber sonst mehr oder minder wie gehabt, 2015 © Tove Freiij

12–13    Students on the staircase of the south gable entrance | Studierende auf der überdachten Treppe des Südeingangs, 1970 © Sten Vilson; by 2015 the space under the stairs is routinely used as shelter by Stockholm's homeless | 2015 wurde der Raum unter der Treppe regelmäßig von Stockholmer Obdachlosen genutzt, 2015 © Tove Freiij

14–15    The studios were designed by Christina Engdahl (later a KTH-A teacher for 20 years and head of the school for 13) | Die Ateliers wurden von Christina Engdahl (später 20 Jahre lang Dozentin an der KTH-A und 13 Jahre lang Leiterin derselben) entworfen, 1970 © Sten Vilson; including the overhead system of electrical gutters and hooks, still left exposed 45 years later | einschließlich des Kabelkanalsystems mit Haken an der Decke, das 45 Jahre später noch immer freiliegt, 2015 © Tove Freiij

16–17 Auditorium with customized steel tube folding seats | Auditorium mit eigens gefertigter Stahlrohrklappbestuhlung, 1970 © Sten Vilson; by 2015, intact but with exposed plywood after the upholstery was worn out by thousands of lecture hours | 2015 noch immer intakt, aber mit sichtbarem Sperrholz, nachdem sich die Polsterung in Tausenden Vorlesungsstunden aufgelöst hat, 2015 © Tove Freiij

Lucia Pennati

# Zürich Globus Provisorium

1   Demonstration outside of the Globus Provisorium | Demonstration vor dem Globus-Provisorium, Zürich, 1968
© ETH-Bibliothek Zürich, Bildarchiv. Photo: Comet Photo AG, Zürich

124

Between 1968 and 1976, the so-called Globus Provisorium located on Zurich's Bahnhofbrücke was a spatial example of the complex relationship established between a federal educational institution—ETH Zurich—, the city with its political will, and its students. By looking back at the 1968 student protest movement and the didactic activities at ETHZ, this paper investigates the role of the Globus Provisorium as an unconventional pedagogical facility that contributed to educational reform and interrogates the contextual entanglement among institutions, space, and learning. As a symbol of the students' claims and as a didactic platform, the Globus Provisorium generated space not only for architectural education but also for new learning values that during the 1970s found their expression in a new curriculum. In this context it is relevant to draw a parallel between the cultural shift initiated by students throughout Europe (in Paris, Prague etc.)[1] from 1968 onwards and the pandemic educational change (2020–2021) that coerced millions of university students to rethink their educational space, participation, and activity.

Located in the historic center of Zurich, the Provisorium was built in 1960 by the Swiss architect Karl Egender for the Globus department store as a temporary building to bridge the time period until the opening of Globus's new location between Bahnhofstraße and Löwenplatz. When the new Globus shop was opened in 1967, it led to the homonymous Provisorium remaining empty. Among the various interested tenants[2] was ETHZ, which in 1968 was urgently looking for new space due to the renovation of the historic Semper building[3] and the increase in enrollments[4] at the architecture department. While the planning of a completely new campus was on its way, on June 18th 1968 ETHZ signed a contract with the city of Zurich that authorized the temporary use of the so-called Globus Provisorium for the teaching activities of the architecture faculty. The decision to accommodate the second-year architecture course in the temporary infrastructure of the Globus Provisorium would become, in a general temporal trajectory, the first step towards the subsequent relocation of the entire architecture faculty—including its "rebellious students"—from the central representative building to the periphery, i.e. an isolated campus in the north of Zurich. During this process, the Globus Provisorium became a transitional learning environment and a symbolic bridge between two academic cultures: one historical, with the university located in the city center, the other modern, with the university located within a suburban campus.

In fact, the Provisorium was not only a symbolic bridge, but part of the station bridge (Bahnhofbrücke) which connects the 19th century center with the old medieval city on the other side of the Limmat river. The bridge was a strategic point for all those arriving to Zurich by train and for anyone moving within the city. It was a convenient location for ETHZ: halfway between its historic headquarters, the city, and the transport hub. Of the entire building, the federal institution rented the first and second floors. The ground and first basement floors were left to the "Lebensmittelverein Zurich, LVZ," later "COOP," with its grocery shop and a canteen, while the second underground floor accommodated a police station.[5] This configuration made the Provisorium a mixed-use building, not exclusively dedicated to education. Access to ETHZ studios on the first floor was provided by a staircase directly on Bahnhofquai opposite of today's Beatenplatz. The first and second floors were connected by an open internal staircase. The architect and ETHZ professor Werner Jaray designed the renovation of the first floor[6] and included eight rooms for studio work—so-called "Kojen"—which opened onto a large corridor that took on the identity of a multifunctional space: not only for circulation but for other events and meetings. A model workshop was placed in the center, behind which an auditorium was installed for lectures. The second floor accommodated the offices for professors and the premises for the gta history and theory of architecture institute.

1968 saw student protests in Zurich for various reasons: one of them was the demand for a new youth gathering space within the city. Instead of the semi-controlled youth center *Drahtschmidli*, the Globus Provisorium seemed the best place for an

1    The discussion about the student revolts of 1968 and the reforms in university education, especially in relation to the teaching of architecture, can be further examined in the following publications: Giancarlo De Carlo, "Why/How to Build School Buildings," *Harvard Educational Review* 39, no. 4 (1969): 12–35; Nina Gribat, Philipp Misselwitz and Matthias Görlich, *Vergessene Schule: Architekturlehre zwischen Reform und Revolte um 1968* (Leipzig, 2017); Tom Holert, ed., *Politics of Learning, Politics of Space: Architecture and the Education Shock of the 1960s and 1970s* (Berlin and Boston, 2021).

2    For example, the national carrier Swissair was also interested in using the premises of the Globus Provisorium. See "ETH Schulratsprotokolle" 1968, meeting on February 3, 1968, 15.

3    Between 1966 and 1978 the main building was renovated by the architects and professors Charles Edouard Geisendorf and Alfred Roth. In the course of the renovation two auditoriums were added in the internal courtyards.

4    See "ETH Schulratsprotokolle," 1967, meeting on September 30, 1967, 633.

5    See "ETH Schulratsprotokolle," 1968, meeting on July 6, 1968, 558.

6    See a plan dated August 8, 1968, gta archive, Zurich (Ref. 246-5-3).

Zwischen 1968 und 1976 war das sogenannte Globus-Provisorium auf der Bahnhofbrücke in Zürich ein räumliches Beispiel für die komplexe Beziehung, die zwischen einer Bildungsinstitution des Bundes, der Eidgenössischen Technischen Hochschule Zürich (ETHZ), der Stadt mit ihrem politischen Willen und den Studierenden entstanden ist. Im Rückblick auf die Studierendenunruhen von 1968 und die didaktischen Aktivitäten an der ETHZ untersucht dieser Aufsatz die Rolle des Globus-Provisoriums als einer unkonventionellen pädagogischen Einrichtung und hinterfragt die kontextuelle Verflechtung zwischen Institutionen, Raum und Bildung. Als Symbol der Forderungen der Studierenden und als didaktisches Werkzeug repräsentierte das Globus-Provisorium nicht nur einen Raum für die architektonische Ausbildung, sondern auch für neue didaktische Werte, die sich in den 1970er-Jahren in einem neuen Lehrplan niederschlugen. Relevant ist in diesem Kontext auch der Zusammenhang zwischen der kulturellen Veränderung, die seit 1968 vor sich ging und europaweit von Studierenden (in Paris, Prag usw.)[1] initiiert wurde, und den 2020–2021 pandemiebedingten Veränderungen im Bildungswesen, die Millionen von Hochschulstudierenden nötigten, ihre bildungsrelevanten Parameter Raum, Teilnahme und Aktivität zu überdenken.

Das im historischen Zentrum Zürichs angesiedelte Provisorium wurde 1960 von dem Schweizer Architekten Karl Egender für das Kaufhaus Globus als temporärer Bau errichtet, um die Zeit der Eröffnung des neuen Standortes zwischen Bahnhofstraße und Löwenplatz zu überbrücken. Nachdem das neue Globus-Warenhaus 1967 eröffnet worden war, stand das gleichnamige Provisorium zunächst leer. Unter den verschiedenen Parteien, die an der Anmietung interessiert waren,[2] stand auch die ETHZ, die 1968 aufgrund der Renovierung des historischen Semperbaues[3] und der Zunahme der Immatrikulationen[4] am Architekturdepartement, dringend neue Räumlichkeiten suchte. Obwohl bereits ein völlig neuer Campus geplant war, unterzeichnete die ETHZ am 18. Juni 1968 mit der Stadt Zürich einen Vertrag über die vorübergehende Nutzung des sogenannten Globus-Provisoriums durch die Architekturfakultät. Rückblickend betrachtet, war die Entscheidung, den Architekturkurs des zweiten Studienjahrs in der Infrastruktur des Globus-Provisoriums unterzubringen, der erste Schritt zur Loslösung der gesamten Architekturfakultät – inklusive ihrer „aufmüpfigen" Studierenden – aus dem repräsentativen Hauptgebäude und ihrer anschließenden Neuansiedlung auf einem isolierten Campus im Norden Zürichs. Im Verlauf dieses Prozesses wurde das Globus-Provisorium ein vorübergehendes Lernumfeld und

eine symbolische Brücke zwischen zwei akademischen Kulturen: einer historischen mit dem im Stadtzentrum lokalisierten Hauptgebäude und einer modernen, mit einem am Stadtrand gelegenen Campus.

In der Tat war das Provisorium nicht nur eine symbolische Brücke, sondern auch konkreter Bestandteil der Bahnhofbrücke, die das im 19. Jahrhundert entstandene Zentrum mit der alten mittelalterlichen Stadt auf der anderen Seite der Limmat verband. Als strategischer Punkt für alle, die in Zürich mit der Bahn eintrafen, und für jeden, der sich in der Stadt bewegte, wurde es auch für die ETHZ zum idealen Standort: auf halbem Weg zwischen ihrem historischen Hauptsitz, der Stadt und dem Bahnhof als Verkehrsknotenpunkt. Während die Bundeseinrichtung das erste und zweite Stockwerk des Gebäudes anmietete, überließ man das Erdgeschoss und erste Kellergeschoss dem „Lebensmittelverein Zürich, LVZ" (später „COOP") mit Lebensmittelgeschäft und Kantine. Im zweiten Kellergeschoss war eine Polizeiwache untergebracht.[5] Durch diese Konfiguration wurde das Provisorium zu einem Mehrzweckgebäude, das nicht ausschließlich dem Bildungswesen gewidmet war. Der Zugang zu den ETH-Studios im ersten Stock erfolgte über eine Treppe direkt vom Bahnhofsquai gegenüber dem heutigen Beatenplatz, während der erste und der zweite Stock im Inneren miteinander verbunden waren. Der Architekt und ETHZ-Professor Werner Jaray gestaltete die Renovierung des ersten Stockwerks,[6] das nun acht Räume, sogenannte „Kojen", für die Studioarbeit enthielt. Diese öffneten sich auf einen langen Gang hin, der als Multifunktionsraum diente, nicht nur zu Erschließungszwecken, sondern auch für Veranstaltungen und Zusammenkünfte. In der Mitte wurde eine Modellwerkstatt errichtet, dahinter ein Hörsaal für Vorlesungen angelegt. Im

1   Die Diskussion über die Studierendenrevolte von 1968 und die Reformen im universitären Bildungswesen, vor allem im Hinblick auf die Architekturausbildung, lässt sich in den folgenden Publikationen nachlesen: Giancarlo De Carlo, „Warum und wie man Schulgebäude bauen sollte", in: Holert, Tom/Haus der Kulturen der Welt (Hg.): *Bildungsschock. Lernen, Politik und Architektur in den 1960er und 1970er Jahren*, Übers. Clemens Krümmel, Berlin 2020, 220–229; Gribat, Nina/Misselwitz, Philipp/Göhrlich, Matthias (Hg.): *Vergessene Schulen. Architekturlehre zwischen Reform und Revolte um 1968*, Leipzig 2017.

2   Beispielsweise war auch das Unternehmen Swissair an den Räumlichkeiten des Globus-Provisoriums interessiert. Vgl. dazu „ETH Schulratsprotokolle" 1968, Sitzung vom 3. Februar 1968, 15.

3   Zwischen 1966 und 1978 wurde das Hauptgebäude von den Architekten und Professoren Charles-Edouard Geisendorf und Alfred Roth renoviert. Vor allem wurden dabei in den Innenhöfen zwei neue Hörsäle errichtet.

4   Vgl. „ETH Schulratsprotokolle" 1967, Sitzung vom 30. September 1967, 633.

5   Vgl. „ETH Schulratsprotokolle" 1968, Sitzung vom 6. Juli 1968, 558.

6   Vgl. dazu einen auf den 8. August 1968 datierten im *gta*-Archiv Zürich aufgefundenen Plan (Ref. 246-5-3).

2  Young protesters gather in the Globus Provisorium, demanding a self-governed youth center. | Versammlung jugendlicher DemonstrantInnen im Globus-Provisorium für ein autonomes Jugendzentrum, Zürich, 1968 © ETH-Bibliothek Zürich, Bildarchiv, Photo: Comet Photo AG, Zürich

independent space, suitable for hosting events such as concerts or assemblies.[7] Indeed, as part of the initial negotiations between Zurich and the ETHZ over the terms of the lease of the Globus Provisorium, the city tried unsuccessfully to obtain from the tenant the possibility for youth groups to meet extra-time in the Provisorium.[8] But the decision to rent the space completely to the ETHZ instead of providing the infrastructure for a youth center was the catalyst for further protests, which gathered on the Bahnhofbrücke and occupied the still empty first floor of the Provisorium. The climax of the movement—the *Globus Krawall*—occurred on June 29th 1968 with a police intervention and the arrest of around hundred young people. Ironically, those arrested spent the night on the second underground floor of the Globus Provisorium, while the other people continued the protest outside the same building.[9]

A few months later, another remarkable episode occurred linking the cultural and political protest movement, the institution with its architecture faculty and, for a short time, the Globus Provisorium: it was the opposition to the new ETHZ law, already approved by the parliament.[10] Within the Provisorium rented by ETHZ, several general assemblies were organized to discuss the changes in the university's constitution and to arrange a protest against it. Through unconventional and unexpected means, architecture students opposed the law and unexpectedly managed to convince the Swiss population to object it,

7   For further historical information about the Zurich independent youth center see: David Eugster, "Als die Schweizer Jugend ihren eigenen Staat gründete," *swissinfo.ch* (2018).

8   See "ETH Schulratsprotokolle" 1968, meeting of July 6, 1968, 559.

9   From the SRF show "50 Jahre Globus-Krawalle," on air on June 29, 2018, available online at: https://www.srf.ch/play/tv/tagesschau/video/50-jahre-globus-krawalle?urn=urn:srf:video:cb774324-9239-41c3-920f-6d23ac4d2f2a (accessed January 31, 2022).

10  In 1968, the Lausanne University of Technology (Canton Vaud) joined the ETHZ as a federal university, EPFL (École polytechnique fédérale de Lausanne). On this occasion, the ETHZ University Council made some changes to the legislation that would also apply to the newly founded EPFL.

128

zweiten Stock waren die Büros für Professoren und für das Institut für Geschichte und Theorie der Architektur (*gta*) untergebracht.

1968 fanden in Zürich Studierendenproteste statt, die verschiedene Ursachen hatten. Eine davon war die Forderung nach einem neuen Versammlungsort für Jugendliche in der Stadt. Als Alternative zum halb-kontrollierten Jugendzentrum *Drahtschmidli* ermöglichte das Globus-Provisorium einen idealen Ort für einen unabhängigen Raum, der sich auch für Veranstaltungen wie Konzerte eignete.[7] Im Rahmen der ersten Verhandlungen zwischen der Stadt Zürich und der ETHZ über die Mietbedingungen für das Globus-Provisorium ersuchte die Stadt den neuen Mieter erfolglos, die Möglichkeit einzuräumen, dass sich

Jugendgruppen auch außerhalb der Unterrichtszeiten im Provisorium treffen können.[8] Die Entscheidung, die Räume vollständig an die ETHZ zu vermieten, statt sie dem Jugendzentrum zu überlassen, löste weitere Proteste aus, die vor allem auf der Bahnhofbrücke und im damals noch leeren ersten Stock des Provisoriums stattfanden. Der Gipfel der Protestbewegung – der sogenannte Globus-Krawall – war am 29. Juni 1968 erreicht, als die

7   Weitere historische Informationen über das unabhängige Zürcher Jugendzentrum finden sich in Eugster, David: „Als die Schweizer Jugend ihren eigenen Staat gründete", *swissinfo.ch* (2018).

8   Vgl. „ETH Schulratsprotokolle" 1968, Sitzung vom 6. Juli 1968, 559.

3   Second-year course of ETH Zurichs architecture faculty staged at the Globus Provisorium | Architekturkurs des zweiten Studienjahres der ETH Zürich, abgehalten im Globus-Provisorium: Prof. Bernhard Hoesli, Peter Balla, Prof. Hans Ess, Paul Nizon, Erich Widmer (Studienberater), Zürich 1969
© ETH-Bibliothek Zürich, Bildarchiv

voting against it and eventually stopping its implementation.[11] These historically remarkable events show how the use of the Globus Provisorium by the ETHZ was, from the very beginning, deeply embedded in the political and social changes driven by the youth and student revolts.

After the ETHZ legislation came to a standstill, from 1968 to 1969 the need for educational reform was more urgent than ever.[12] However, neither the students (through various meetings, questionnaires and other media) nor the institution knew how to permanently overcome the winds of change. The main topics of discussion covered the new role of the architect, and how education should catch up and fix its methods to produce a valid response to meet these demands. In a first attempt to react to the situation, the university initiated an experimental and transitional phase in education called the "Experimental Phase," which involved new forms of teaching and learning processes in the faculty of architecture:[13] "At the end of the Sixties, … the connection to current architecture was highlighted [in lectures]; in its teaching and research activity the school was ready to contribute in a creative way to contemporary developments and not merely to chase after it. … It was a time of transition."[14] Starting in the summer semester of 1969, design teaching for second-year students took place in the Globus Provisorium. The building thus became the symbol of a transitional phase, metaphorically leading the old architecture faculty through the reformed one and finally to its new suburban location.

The "Experimental Phase" was reflected in several structural changes within the institution, such as reforms that altered both the curricula and the operational way in which education was delivered. For example, the possibility of working in groups was established, improving collaborative and discursive practice.[15] A new evaluation system was tried out, albeit with little success.[16] Within the academic body new professors were appointed, the staff was renewed and, above all, the new position of a Gastprofessor (visiting professor) was introduced: a lecturer/researcher who was less tied to the institution as her or his position was reconfirmed yearly. From the point of view of curricula, new learning strategies were introduced, which were meant to improve multidisciplinary work, reflecting the current situation in practice. One remarkable example of a product of that time was the multidisciplinary pilot studio "Lehrcanapé," which was "a real experiment, in which both teachers and assistants' teams learned like the engaged students."[17] The studio was led by the sociologist Lucius Burckhardt together with architects such as Rolf Gutmann or Rainer Senn.[18]

Compared to the historical spaces used in the main Semper building, where the proportion of the rooms, the windows and the materiality still spoke of a past with outdated hierarchical systems, in the Globus Provisorium, the flexibility of the arrangements, the fluidity of the "Koje" and the different areas provided the perfect ground for new experiments in teaching and allowed for meetings and discussions. For example, the second-year design professor Werner Jaray introduced the "Epoche Week" system, revolutionizing the classical didactical schedule in which several sessions on different topics were held each day.[19] Within the "Epoche Week" system, a new day- or week-centered program was created, in which an entire topic was explained extensively for one day or week, giving the students the opportunity to acquire a comprehensive knowledge of a topic in a shorter time and to test it through exercises. These new trials in teaching were to challenge not only education, but also the future engagement of architects in their professional environment. This was the case with Heinz Ronner, who was appointed Professor of Construction for the foundation course in 1968 and who developed a way of teaching design together with construction topics.[20] In the Globus Provisorium he conducted an innovative didactic experiment called the "Welcome Lessons."[21] The course took place as a series of seminars for newcomers during the summer of 1970. The aim was to interrogate the question "For whom do we

11  The students collected enough signatures to submit a referendum against the ETHZ law (December 1968). The referendum was approved with a [illegible] by the population (April 1969).

12  See David Gugerli et al., "Das Laboratorium der Gesellschaft: hochschulpolitische Experimente nach 1968," in *Die Zukunftmaschine. Konjunkturen der ETH Zurich 1855–2015* (Zurich, 2005).

13  The original title was "Experimentierphase." See Bernhard Hoesli, "Entwicklung und Herausforderung," in *Eidgenössische Technische Hochschule Zürich 1955–1980. Festschrift zum 125jährigen Bestehen*, ed. Jean-François Bergier and Hans Werner Tobler (Zurich, 1980), 92–104.

14  Bernhard Hoesli, *Architektur lehren (1959–1984)* (Zurich, 1989), 36.

15  See "Lehrversuche an der ETH: Eindrücke von der 'Experimentierphase,'" *Neue Zürcher Zeitung*, February 28, 1971, 35.

16  See ibid.

17  Rainer Senn in *Canape News* 1, ETHZ, 5. Semester 70/71.

18  See Silvan Blumenthal, *Das Lehrcanapé* (Basel, 2010).

19  For further information on the topic see "Lehrversuche an der ETH" (note 15).

20  See Werner Seligmann, *Heinz Ronner* (Zurich, 1991).

21  See ibid. The title of the course was "Empfangsunterricht."

Polizei einschritt und rund hundert junge Leute festnahm. Paradoxerweise wurden die Festgenommenen die Nacht über im zweiten Kellergeschoss des Globus-Provisoriums inhaftiert, sprich die Jugendlichen, die außerhalb des Gebäudes protestierten, wurden innerhalb desselben festgehalten.[9]

Einige Monate später ereignete sich eine weitere bemerkenswerte Episode, welche die kulturellen und politischen Veränderungen, das Departement Architektur der ETHZ und für kurze Zeit auch das Globus-Provisorium miteinander verband: Es war der Widerstand gegenüber dem neuen ETHZ-Gesetz, das vom Parlament bereits gebilligt worden war.[10] In dem von der ETHZ unterdessen bezogenen Provisorium wurden mehrere Vollversammlungen abgehalten, um die Veränderungen in der Verfassung der Hochschule zu diskutieren und den Protest dagegen zu organisieren. Auf unkonventionelle und unerwartete Weise widersetzten sich die Architekturstudierenden dem Gesetz und schafften es überraschenderweise, die Schweizer Bevölkerung davon zu überzeugen, es abzulehnen, indem sie mehrheitlich dagegen stimmte und die Veränderungen damit letztlich verhinderte.[11] Diese historisch bemerkenswerten Ereignisse zeigen, dass die Anmietung und die Nutzung des Globus-Provisoriums durch die ETHZ von Anfang an eng mit den politischen und sozialen Veränderungen verflochten waren, die von der Jugend- und Studierendenrevolte ausgingen.

Nachdem die ETHZ-Gesetzgebung zum Stillstand gekommen war, war das Bedürfnis nach einer Bildungsreform 1968–69 größer als je zuvor.[12] Doch weder die Studierenden (mittels verschiedener Zusammenkünfte, Fragebogen und anderer Medien) noch die Vertreter der Institution wussten, wie sie die neue Lage dauerhaft in den Griff bekommen sollten. Die wichtigsten zur Diskussion stehenden Themen betrafen das neue Berufsbild der ArchitektInnen und die Frage, wie das Bildungswesen dem gerecht werden und seine Methoden entsprechend anpassen sollte, um eine gültige Antwort auf diese Anforderungen zu finden. In einem ersten Versuch auf diese Situation zu reagieren, initiierte die Hochschule im Bildungsbereich eine als Übergang gedachte „Experimentierphase", die mit neuen Formen von Lehr- und Lernprozessen im Architekturdepartement einhergingen:[13] „Ende der sechziger Jahre [war] im Unterricht der Anschluss an die Gegenwartsarchitektur vollzogen; die Schule war bereit, in Lehre und Forschungstätigkeit an der zeitgenössischen Entwicklung gestaltend, nicht nur nachvollziehend teilzunehmen. [...] Es war eine Übergangszeit."[14] Ab dem Sommersemester 1969 fand der Unterricht im Fach Entwurf

für Studierende im zweiten Ausbildungsjahr im Globus-Provisorium statt. So wurde das Gebäude zum Symbol einer Übergangsphase und führte metaphorisch die alte Architekturfakultät durch die Reform und schließlich an ihren neuen Standort am Rand der Stadt.

Die „Experimentierphase" spiegelte sich in mehreren strukturellen Veränderungen innerhalb der Institution wider, etwa in Reformen, durch die man sowohl die Lehrpläne als auch die Art, wie die Bildungsinhalte vermittelt wurden, änderte. So führte man etwa die Möglichkeit zur Gruppenarbeit ein und verbesserte so die kooperative und diskursive Praxis.[15] Ein neues Bewertungssystem wurde ausprobiert, auch wenn ihm nur ein geringer Erfolg beschieden war.[16] Innerhalb des Lehrkörpers wurden neue Professoren ernannt, der Mitarbeiterstab erneuert und vor allem die Position einer Gastprofessur geschaffen, die weniger stark an die Institution gebunden war und deren Stelle jährlich erneut bestätigt wurde. Hinsichtlich der Studienpläne wurden neue Lernstrategien eingeführt, welche die multidisziplinäre Arbeit verbesserten und die aktuelle Situation in der Praxis widerspiegelten. Ein bemerkenswertes Beispiel für ein Produkt dieser Zeit war das multidisziplinäre Pilotstudio „Lehrcanapé", das von dem Soziologen Lucius Burckhardt und Architekten wie Rolf Gutmann und Rainer Senn geleitet wurde[17] und von dem es hieß: „Insofern handelt es sich um ein echtes Experiment, bei welchem das Dozenten- und Assistententeam ebenso lernen muss wie die beteiligten Studenten."[18]

9   Aus der SRF-Sendung „50 Jahre Globus-Krawalle", ausgestrahlt am 29. Juni 2018, online unter: https://www.srf.ch/play/tv/tagesschau/video/50-jahre-globus-krawalle?urn=urn:srf:video:cb774324-9239-41c3-920f-6d23ac4d2f2a (Stand: 28. Jänner 2022).

10  1968 wurde neben der ETHZ auch die Eidgenössische Technische Hochschule Lausanne im Kanton Waadt eine Bundesuniversität. Bei dieser Gelegenheit setzte der Hochschulrat der ETHZ einige Veränderungen an der Gesetzgebung durch, die auch für die neu gegründete EPFL (École polytechnique fédérale de Lausanne) galten.

11  Zunächst gelang es den Studierenden, genügend Unterschriften zu sammeln, um eine Volksabstimmung über das ETHZ-Gesetz durchzuführen (Dezember 1968). Bei der Abstimmung selbst wurde das Gesetz mit einer Mehrheit der Nein-Stimmen der Bevölkerung abgelehnt (April 1969).

12  Vgl. Guggerli, David/Kupper, Patrick/Speich, Daniel: Die Zukunftmaschine. Konjunkturen der ETH Zürich 1855–2015, Zürich 2005.

13  Vgl. Hoesli, Bernhard: „Entwicklung und Herausforderung", in: Bergier, Jean-François/Tobler, Hans Werner (Hg.): Eidgenössische Technische Hochschule Zürich 1955–1980. Festschrift zum 125jährigen Bestehen, Zürich 1980, 92–104.

14  Hoesli, Bernhard: Architektur lehren (1959–1984), Zürich 1989, 36.

15  Vgl. „Lehrversuche an der ETH: Eindrücke von der ‚Experimentierphase'", Neue Zürcher Zeitung, 28. Februar 1971, 35.

16  Vgl. ebd.

17  Vgl. Blumenthal, Silvan: Das Lehrcanapé, Basel 2010.

18  Senn, Rainer in den Canape News 1, ETHZ, 5. Semester 70/71.

build?" and to go beyond the traditional typological classifications of buildings according to their function.[22] An engaging, collective, and communal atmosphere characterized the study debate in the Provisorium. Usually, several guest professors and critics from different disciplines were engaged in what seemed to be a passionate and informal discussion developed from the students' projects, presented on movable panels placed in the open area. The anti-authoritarian space embraced people to use it beyond traditional and hierarchal spatial arrangements, allowing them to sit wherever they wanted.

It fostered change and a new form of anti-authoritarian educational interaction. The building's teaching environment was "a laboratory in the truest American sense,"[23] accommodating not only second-year architecture students, but also the gta institute (Institute for History and Theory of Architecture), which was established in 1967. The space became the stage for crafting important theoretical contributions, such as the German translation of Colin Rowe and Robert Slutzky's *Transparency* by Bernhard Hoesli or the monograph *Louis Kahn: Complete Work 1935–1974* by Heinz Ronner and Sharad Jhaveri.[24] These books belonged to the most relevant in the Swiss architectural discourse of the time and contributed to a specific influence. In addition, the Globus Provisorium opened its doors to the public, as it became the venue for relevant exhibitions, showing the state of research inside the institution. In 1969, for example, the exhibition *100 Years Architecture Education at ETHZ*[25] was put on display, presenting a survey of the department from 1855 to 1968. Another example would be the exhibition on the works of Aldo Rossi and John Hejduk, held in December 1973, together with a workshop with ETHZ and Cooper Union students, which also triggered a general architectural interest. Due to the coexistence of both educational and cultural activities, the Globus Provisorium was at the center of Swiss architectural debate and education and became both the arena and the catalyst of theoretical and design discourse in the late 1960s and 1970s. Moreover, the discourse on architecture and education at the ETHZ cannot be fully understood without considering the didactic role of the Globus Provisorium.

The appropriation of the spaces of the Globus Provisorium was meant to be temporary and in 1976, as a response to the continuous increase in the number of architecture students, the Faculty of Architecture moved to the Hönggerberg campus, into the building originally intended to house the Faculty of Civil Engineering.[26] In this situation, the removal of politically committed architecture students from the city's spotlight was perceived by students and some lecturers as a political act. While the Globus Provisorium provided space for new teaching and learning possibilities that were considered in the curriculum reform, it also functioned as a sounding board for the students' political opposition, which the institution did not want. Because of its temporary appropriation, the Globus Provisorium can be seen as a symbol of the transitional period that the faculty of architecture and the whole ETHZ institution were going through. It is an artefact that belongs to the 1968 debate on political agency and the role of pedagogy, university politics and society. As a built but also symbolic bridge, the Globus Provisorium encouraged contact with the outside world, the exchange of experiences and the politicization of education. It was part of the ETH institution, yet outside its spatial limits, conceived for a different use and together with other, non-educational functions. The building was open enough to allow experimental methods of teaching and to involve students in design issues. The Globus Provisorium can be considered as an activator which fostered didactic reform. Even after being cleared by the students, the Globus Provisorium remained a constant topic of discussion inside the architecture faculty. For example, various competitions have been held since the 1980s to redesign the Papierwerd Island, and in the winter semester 2018, students developed proposals for new functions and possibilities.[27] Today, the building is still subject of debate concerning the possibility of protecting it, redesigning it, demolishing it, or giving it a new function. Despite all the controversy, in 2022, the Globus Provisorium still sits on the bank of the river Limmat, still standing up against its current. ∎

22  See ibid.

23  Ibid.

24  See Colin Rowe and Robert Slutzky, *Transparenz* (Basel, 1968); Ronner Heinz and Sharad Jhaveri, *Louis Kahn: Complete work 1935–1974* (Basel, 1977).

25  The original title of the exhibition was "100 Jahre Architekturunterricht an der ETH." See ETH, *Arbeitsberichte der Architektur Abteilung ETH 1855–1915, A11* (Zurich, 1970); ETH, *Arbeitsberichte der Architektur Abteilung ETH 1916–1956, A12* (Zurich, 1970); ETH, *Arbeitsberichte der Architektur Abteilung ETH 1957–1968, A13* (Zurich, 1970).

26  ETH Zurich, Department Architektur, "Ein Laborgebäude für das D-Phys auf dem Hönggerberg," reader presented for the design studio, summer semester 2021.

27  See Jean-Claude Steinegger, "Der Wettbewerb für die Überbauung des Papierwerdeareals," *Werk, Bauen + Wohnen* 67, no. 6 (1980): 29–47; Werner Huber, "Fünf Projekte für das Papierwerd-Areal," *Hochparterre* 17, no. 15 (2004): 12-31; ETH Zurich, Department Architektur, "Kongresszentrum auf dem Papierwerd-Areal," reader presented for the design studio, fall semester 2018.

Verglichen mit den historischen Räumen, die man im Semper-Hauptgebäude nutzte, wo die Proportionen der Räume, die Fenster und die Materialität noch von den aus der Vergangenheit stammenden und überholten hierarchischen Systemen zeugten, bildeten im Globus-Provisorium die Flexibilität der Arrangements, die Fluidität der „Koje" und die unterschiedlichen Bereiche die perfekte Grundlage für neue Experimente in der Lehre, Zusammenkünfte und Diskussionen. So führte etwa der das zweite Studienjahr unterrichtende Professor für Entwurf Werner Jaray das „Epochenwoche"-System ein und revolutionierte damit den klassischen Lehrplan, bei dem an jedem Tag verschiedene Themen unterrichtet wurden.[19] Im Rahmen des „Epochenwoche"-Systems schuf man ein neues tages- oder wochenzentriertes Programm, bei dem ein Thema einen Tag oder eine Woche lang ausführlich erläutert wurde, was den Studierenden die Möglichkeit gab, in kürzerer Zeit ein umfassendes Wissen über ein Thema zu erlangen und dieses in Übungen zu überprüfen. Diese neuen didaktischen Versuche stellten nicht nur eine Herausforderung für das Bildungswesen dar, sondern auch für den zukünftigen Einsatz der ArchitektInnen in ihrem beruflichen Umfeld. Dies war etwa bei Heinz Ronner der Fall, der 1968 zum Professor für Konstruktion im Grundstudium ernannt wurde und eine Methode entwickelte, Gestaltungslehre und Themen, die das Bauwesen betreffen, miteinander zu verbinden.[20] Heinz Ronner leitete im Globus-Provisorium ein innovatives didaktisches Experiment, den sogenannten „Empfangsunterricht".[21] Der Kurs erfolgte in Gestalt einer Reihe von Seminaren für Erstsemestrige im Sommer 1970. Das Ziel derselben war es, sich mit der Frage „Für wen bauen wir?" auseinanderzusetzen und dabei über die traditionelle typologische Klassifizierung von Gebäuden nach funktionalen Gesichtspunkten hinauszugehen.[22] Die Diskussionen waren von einer angenehmen, kollektiven und gemeinschaftlichen Atmosphäre geprägt. Normalerweise beteiligten sich mehrere Gastdozenten und Kritiker aus unterschiedlichen Disziplinen an einer offenbar leidenschaftlichen und informellen Diskussion, die sich aus den Studierendenprojekten entwickelte. Diese wurden auf beweglichen Tafeln im freien Bereich präsentiert. Der antiautoritäre Raum ermöglichte es den Beteiligten, sich frei im Raum (und jenseits von Sitzordnungen) zu bewegen und sich ausschließlich von Ideen inspirieren zu lassen, und nicht durch ein bestimmtes hierarchisches System eingeengt zu werden. Er begünstigte den Wandel und eine neue antiautoritäre Interaktion im Bildungswesen. Das Umfeld, in dem hier gelehrt wurde, „war im wahrsten amerikanischen Sinne ein *work shop*[23] und nahm nicht nur Architekturstudierende im zweiten Studienjahr auf, sondern auch das 1967 gegründete Institut für Geschichte und

Theorie der Architektur (*gta*). Der Raum wurde zur Wiege bedeutender theoretischer Beiträge wie etwa der deutschen Übersetzung von Colin Rowes und Robert Slutzkys *Transparency* durch Bernhard Hoesli oder der Monografie *Louis Kahn: Complete Work 1935–1974* von Heinz Ronner und Sharad Jhaveri.[24] Diese Bücher gehörten zu jener Zeit zu den relevantesten im Schweizer Architekturdiskurs und übten einen spezifischen Einfluss aus. Darüber hinaus öffnete das Globus-Provisorium seine Türen für die Öffentlichkeit, indem es zum Schauplatz relevanter Ausstellungen wurde und den Forschungsstand innerhalb der Institution präsentierte. Hierzu zählten eine Überblicks-Ausstellung[25] 1969 über die Geschichte der Architekturabteilung von 1855 bis 1968 oder die das allgemeine Interesse an Architektur weckende Ausstellung über die Werke Aldo Rossis und John Hejduks, die im Dezember 1973 mit einem gemeinsamen Workshop von Studierenden der ETHZ und der Cooper Union stattfand. Aufgrund der Koexistenz von Bildungs- und Kulturaktivitäten stand das Globus-Provisorium im Mittelpunkt der Schweizer Architekturdebatte und -ausbildung und wurde in den späten 1960er- und 1970er-Jahren sowohl zur Arena als auch zum Katalysator des Diskurses über Theorie und Design. Darüber hinaus kann man den Diskurs über Architektur und die Ausbildung an der ETHZ ohne die Berücksichtigung der Rolle, die ein temporäres Gebäude wie das Globus-Provisorium spielte, nicht vollständig begreifen.

Die Nutzung der Räume des Globus-Provisoriums war eine Übergangslösung, und 1976 zog das Department Architektur, als Reaktion auf die stete Zunahme der Zahl der Architekturstudierenden, auf den Hönggerberg-Campus in das Gebäude, das ursprünglich für die Abteilung Bauingenieurwesen vorgesehen gewesen war.[26] In dieser Situation wurde die Entfernung

19 Weitere Informationen zu diesem Thema finden sich in „Lehrversuche an der ETH: Eindrücke von der ‚Experimentierphase'" (wie Anm. 15).

20 Vgl. Werner Seligmann, *Heinz Ronner*, Zürich 1991.

21 Vgl. ebd.

22 Vgl. ebd.

23 Ebd.

24 Vgl. Colin Rowe, Colin/Slutzky, Robert: *Transparenz*, Basel 1968; Ronner, Heinz/Jhaveri, Sharad: *Louis I. Kahn: Complete Work 1935–1974*, Basel 1977.

25 Vgl. ETH: *Arbeitsberichte der Architektur Abteilung ETH 1855–1915*, A11, Zürich 1970; ETH, *Arbeitsberichte der Architektur Abteilung ETH 1916–1956*, A12, Zürich, 1970; ETH, *Arbeitsberichte der Architektur Abteilung ETH 1957–1968*, A13, Zürich 1970.

26 ETH Zürich, Department Architektur, „Ein Laborgebäude für das D-Phys auf dem Hönggerberg", Reader Sommersemester 2021, Zürich 2021.

politisch engagierter Architekturstudierender aus dem Rampenlicht der Innenstadt von den Studierenden und einigen Dozenten als eine politische Entscheidung begriffen. Denn wenngleich das Globus-Provisorium Raum für neue Lehr- und Lernmöglichkeiten bot, die in der Lehrplanreform berücksichtigt wurden, fungierte es auch als Resonanzboden für die politische Opposition der Studierenden, eine von der Institution unerwünschte Entwicklung. Aufgrund seiner temporären Nutzung kann man das Globus-Provisorium als Symbol einer Übergangsperiode begreifen, welche die Architekturfakultät und die ETHZ als Institution insgesamt durchmachten. Es ist ein Artefakt, das zu einer Debatte gehört, die 1968 begann und sich um politische Handlungsmacht und die Rolle der Pädagogik, Hochschulpolitik und Gesellschaft drehte. Als konkrete und symbolische Brücke förderte das Globus-Provisorium den Kontakt mit der Außenwelt, den Austausch von Erfahrungen und die Politisierung des Bildungswesens. Es war Teil der Institution ETH, befand sich aber außerhalb seiner räumlichen Grenzen, war für einen anderen Gebrauch und zusammen mit anderen, nicht die Bildung betreffenden Funktionen konzipiert worden. Das Gebäude war offen genug, um experimentelle Lehrmethoden zuzulassen und Studierende in Gestaltungsfragen einzubeziehen. Das Globus-Provisorium kann daher als Aktivator begriffen werden, der die didaktische Reform der Architekturfakultät vorantrieb. Selbst nach der Freigabe durch die Studierenden blieb das Globus-Provisorium im Gespräch an der Architekturfakultät. Seit den 1980er-Jahren wurden beispielsweise verschiedene Wettbewerbe zur Neugestaltung der Papierwerd-Insel durchgeführt. Außerdem entwickelten Studierende im Rahmen des Wintersemester 2018 Vorschläge für neue Funktionen und Nutzungsmöglichkeiten.[27] Aktuell ist das Gebäude noch immer Gegenstand einer Debatte rund um Denkmalschutz, Abriss und mögliche neue Funktionen. Trotz aller Auseinandersetzungen steht das Globus-Provisorium auch 2022 noch am Ufer der Limmat und hält der Strömung stand. ∎

*Übersetzung aus dem Englischen: Nikolaus G. Schneider*

---

27 Vgl. Steinegger, Jean-Claude: „Der Wettbewerb für die Überbauung des Papierwerd-Areals", *Werk, Bauen + Wohnen* 67, 6 (1980), 29–47; Huber, Werner: „Fünf Projekte für das Papierwerd-Areal", *Hochparterre* 17, 15 (2004), 12-31; ETH Zürich, Department Architektur, „Kongresszentrum auf dem Papierwerd-Areal," Reader Herbstsemester 2018, Zürich 2018.

---

4   The Globus Provisorium on the banks of the river Limmat in the center of Zurich. | Das Globus-Provisorium am Ufer der Limmat im Zentrum Zürichs. Architekt | Architect: Karl Egender © Baugeschichtliches Archiv, Stadt Zürich, Photo: Juliet Haller, 2011

Simran Singh

# India in Anticipation, Imagination, and Alliance

# Indien in Erwartung, Vorstellung und Allianz

1   The holy city of Varanasi is undergoing a transformation in its texture from predominantly intimate parcels to an architecture of catalogued bigness. While the city is termed unmappable, it's architecture still holds qualities of domesticity and lifelong learning in its depths. | Die heilige Stadt Varanasi erlebt aktuell eine Transformation in ihrer urbanen Struktur von vorwiegend kleinen Parzellen in katalogisierte Größe. Obwohl die Stadt als unkartierbar gilt, beherbergt ihre Architektur noch immer die Qualitäten des häuslichen Lebens und lebenslangen Lernens. | Illustrations reproduced by | Bilder reproduziert von Simran Singh, 2021 © Google Earth

**From Didactics to Pedagogy.** In 2020, the Council of Architecture in India published the "Minimum Standards of Architectural Education Regulations," a revised regulatory paper enlisting mandatory directives to oversee the quality of architectural education and maintenance of its standards, 37 years after it was first structured.[1] For an organization that is burdened with the paradoxical "responsibility to regulate the education and practice of profession throughout India besides maintaining the register of architects,"[2] it is unsurprising to note that the young country witnessed a proliferating growth in institutions from 127 (in 2006/2007) to 533 (in 2018/2019), a trend that challenges its equally high rate of vacant seats.[3] Whether this was due to the latent potential of an expanding building industry that subsequently failed to deliver or a compromise after the failure to gain access to competitive engineering schools,[4] the problematization of the conditions of our built reality could benefit from analyzing the council's priorities.

At the outset, the failing framework of these regulations implores a deliberate reconstitution. The approval of a least attainable model of design instruction and its evaluation in offering a distinctive knowledge base to fulfil the official condition of attaining only the necessary qualifications, recalls the fragmentation of the colonial aftermath under the British rule. The evolution of contemporary architectural education from the Technical Schools established to supplant the traditional knowledge of the master craftsmen never gained traction to succeed beyond the didactics of producing master surveyors and draughtsmen in post-independent India.[5] The profession continued to be a subset of engineering and conform to proficiency in science as the admission criteria through the National Aptitude Test in Architecture (NATA)[6] while establishing the field as interdisciplinary, upholding the voluntary culture of self-expression onto the "candidate's innate ability which cannot be taught, learnt, or induced."[7]

Undoubtedly, the dislocation of architecture as a discipline situated in place by its commodification is a global phenomenon, triggered by the rediscovery of the architectural drawing, its consumable appeal "achieved by redefining their representational role as similar to that of early twentieth-century paintings, in the sense of being less concerned with their relation to that they represent than with their own constitution."[8] Simultaneously, there are ambiguous obstacles in architectural criticism: "The sequence of drawing before building and writing

about it afterwards limns a discursive territory inhabited by a double displacement in which the word is always needed to shape the way in which we think about the built environment: seeing after sight."[9]

In this translation from drawing to building, and building to writing, the medium to convey complex spaces and local relations that may be formal, cultural, economic, political, and technological, may not "appear to have the requisite evenness and continuity; things can get bent, broken, lost on the way."[10] This aversion towards losing all distinction between fluid categories encouraged rigorous subjects such as "ideation" and "culture of architecture" in the Model Curriculum for Bachelor of Architecture[11] by AICTE[12] and promoted a fastidiousness about the purity of vision that eventually seeped into architec-

1   See Council of Architecture, Ministry of Education, Government of India, "Standards of Architectural Education Regulations" (New Delhi, 2020), available online at: https://www.coa.gov.in/showfile.php?lang=1&level=1&sublinkid=748&lid=599 (accessed January 13, 2022).

2   Council of Architecture, Ministry of Education, Government of India, "About Us," available online at: https://www.coa.gov.in/index1.php?&lang=1&level=0&linkid=13&lid=14 (accessed February 11, 2022).

3   See Council of Architecture, Ministry of Education, Government of India, "Prospective Plan for Growth of Architectural Education," *Council of Architecture* (2020), available online at: https://www.coa.gov.in/showfile.php?layout=&lang=1&lid=605 (accessed January 13, 2022).

4   Ibid.

5   See A.G. Krishna Menon, "Architectural Education in India in the Time of Globalisation," paper presented at the symposium "FORUM II: Architectural Education for the Third Millennium," Eastern Mediterranean University, Gazimagusa, 1998, available online at: https://architexturez.net/doc/az-cf-21218 (accessed January 13, 2022).

6   "The NATA measures the aptitude of the applicant for specific field of study, i.e. architecture, through assessment of cognitive skills, visual perception, and aesthetic sensitivity tests, logical reasoning and critical thinking ability, etc., besides the learning that the candidate has acquired over the past few years and is related to the specific field of study." Council of Architecture, available online at: http://www.nata.in (accessed January 13, 2022).

7   Council of Architecture, "NATA Information Brochure," National Aptitude Test in Architecture (NATA), Council of Architecture (New Delhi, 2021), 2, available online at: http://www.nata.in/NATA_Brochure_2021_v3_FINAL.pdf (accessed January 13, 2022).

8   Robin Evans, *Translations from Drawing to Building and Other Essays* (London, 2011), 160.

9   Michael Sorkin, "Critical Mass: Why Architectural Criticism Matters," *The Architectural Review*, May 28, 2014, available online at: https://www.architectural-review.com/essays/critical-mass-why-architectural-criticism-matters (accessed February 19, 2022).

10  Evans, *Translations from Drawing* (see note 8), 154.

11  "Model Curriculum for Bachelor of Architecture," *Government of India, All India Council for Technical Education* (2019), available online at: https://www.aicte-india.org/sites/default/files/B.%20Arch%202019_compressed.pdf (accessed January 13, 2022).

12  The All India Council for Technical Education is a statutory body, and a national-level council for technical education, under the Department of Higher Education in India.

**Von der Didaktik zur Pädagogik.** 2020 veröffentlichte das Council of Architecture in Indien die „Minimum Standards of Architectural Education Regulation", ein überarbeitetes Regelwerk verbindlicher Direktiven, mit denen die Qualität der Architekturausbildung und Aufrechterhaltung ihrer Standards gewährleistet werden soll – 37 Jahre nachdem diese Regeln zum ersten Mal formuliert worden waren.[1] Bei einer Organisation, die mit der „paradoxen Verantwortung" belastet ist, „die Architekturausbildung und die Praxis des Berufs in ganz Indien zu regulieren und außerdem das Verzeichnis der ArchitektInnen zu führen",[2] überrascht es nicht, dass das junge Land ein wucherndes Wachstum von 127 (2006/2007) zu 553 (2018/2019) Institutionen erlebte, ein Trend, der durch seine ebenso hohe Anzahl freier Studienplätze herausgefordert wird.[3] Ob diese Entwicklung nun am latenten Potenzial einer expandierenden Bauindustrie lag, die in Folge verabsäumten Projekte umzusetzen, oder aber eine Reaktion auf das frühere Versäumnis war, den Zugang zu kompetitiven Architekturschulen zu gewährleisten[4] – die Problematisierung der Bedingungen unserer gebauten Wirklichkeit könnten von einer Analyse der Prioritäten des Council of Architecture profitieren.

Anfangs fordert das Council nachdrücklich eine Rekonstitution des schlecht umgesetzten Regulierungsrahmens. Die Zustimmung zu einem mindestens erreichbaren Modell der Entwurfslehre und seiner Evaluierung, um die amtliche Bedingung zur Erlangung der unerlässlichen Minimalqualifikationen zu erfüllen, erinnerte an deren Zersplitterung im Zuge der Nachwirkungen der britischen Kolonialherrschaft. Die zeitgenössische Architekturausbildung entwickelte sich aus den Technischen Schulen, die man einst gegründet hatte, um das traditionelle Wissen der Handwerksmeister zu institutionalisieren, gelangte nach der Unabhängigwerdung Indiens aber nie über die Ausbildung von Landvermessern und Bauzeichnern hinaus.[5] Der Beruf blieb weiterhin ein Teilgebiet des Ingenieurwesens und setzte eine Befähigung auf dem Gebiet der Naturwissenschaften im Einklang mit den Aufnahmekriterien des National Aptitude Test in Architecture (NATA) voraus,[6] während das Feld zugleich als interdisziplinäres etabliert wurde. Gleichzeitig hielt man an einer freiwilligen Praxis der Selbstentfaltung fest, also „angeborenen Fähigkeiten der KandidatInnen, die sich nicht unterrichten, erlernen oder herbeiführen lassen".[7]

Ohne Zweifel ist die Dislozierung der Architektur vom Status einer Disziplin, den sie durch ihre Kommodifizierung erreicht hat, ein globales Phänomen, das durch die Wiederentdeckung der Architekturzeichnung ausgelöst wurde, deren konsumierbarer Reiz „dadurch zustande kommt, dass ihre abbildhafte Rolle als derjenigen der Gemälde des frühen zwanzigsten Jahr-

hunderts ähnlich neu definiert wird, in dem Sinne, dass sie sich weniger um ihre Beziehung zu dem kümmern, was sie darstellen, als um ihre eigene Beschaffenheit".[8] Gleichzeitig gibt es mehrdeutige Hindernisse in der Architekturkritik: „Die Reihenfolge, dass man vor dem Bauen zeichnet und danach darüber schreibt, beschreibt ein diskursives Gebiet, das von einer doppelten Verschiebung bewohnt wird, in der das Wort immer benötigt wird, um die Art und Weise vorzugeben, wie wir über die gebaute Umwelt denken: Sehen nach Ansichten."[9]

Bei dieser Übersetzung vom Zeichnen zum Bauen und vom Bauen zum Schreiben besitzt das Medium zur Vermittlung komplexer Räume und örtlicher Relationen – die formaler, kultureller, wirtschaftlicher, politischer und technologischer Natur sein können – „scheinbar nicht die nötige Gleichmäßigkeit und Stetigkeit: Dinge können in diesem Prozess verbogen oder zerbrochen werden oder verloren gehen".[10] Diese Abneigung dagegen, sämtliche Unterscheidungen zwischen fluiden Kategorien einzubüßen, begünstigte strenge Unterrichtsfächer wie „Ideenbildung" und „Kultur der Architektur" im Modell-

1 Vgl. Council of Architecture, Ministry of Education, Government of India, „Standards of Architectural Education Regulation", *Council of Architecture* (2020), online unter: https://www.coa.gov.in/showfile.php?lang=1&level=1&sublinkid=748&lid=599 (Stand: 13. Januar 2022).

2 Council of Architecture, Ministry of Education, Government of India, „About Us", online unter: https://www.coa.gov.in/index1.php?&lang=1&level=0&linkid=13&lid=14 (Stand: 11. Februar 2022).

3 Vgl. Council of Architecture, Ministry of Education, Government of India, „Prospective Plan for Growth of Architectural Education", *Council of Architecture* (2020), online unter: https://www.coa.gov.in/showfile.php?layout=&lang=1&lid=605 (Stand: 13. Januar 2022).

4 Ebd.

5 Vgl. Krishna Menon, A.G.: „Architectural Education in India in the Time of Globalisation", Vortrag im Rahmen des Symposiums „FORUM II: Architectural Education for the Third Millenium", Eastern Mediterranean University, Gazimagusa 1998, online unter: https://architecturez.net/doc/az-cf-21218 (Stand: 13. Januar 2022).

6 „Der NATA (Nationale Eignungstest für Architektur) misst die Eignung der BewerberInnen für einen bestimmten Studiengang, also in diesem Fach Architektur, durch eine Beurteilung der kognitiven Fertigkeiten, visuellen Wahrnehmung und ästhetischen Sensibilität, der Fähigkeit zu logischem Schließen und kritischem Denken usw. sowie des mit dem jeweiligen Studienfach verbundenen Wissens, welches die KandidatInnen in den letzten Jahren erworben haben." Council of Architecture, online unter: http://www.nata.in (Stand: 13. Januar 2022).

7 Council of Architecture, „NATA Information Brochure", National Aptitude Test in Architecture (NATA), Council of Architecture, New Delhi 2021, 2, online unter: http://www.nata.in/NATA_Brochure_2021_v3_FINAL.pdf (Stand: 13. Januar 2022).

8 Evans, Robin: *Translations from Drawing to Building and Other Essays*, London 2011, 160.

9 Sorkin, Michael: „Critical Mass: Why Architectural Criticism Matters", *The Architectural Review*, 28. Mai 2014, online unter: https://www.architectural-review.com/essays/critical-mass-why-architectural-criticism-matters (Stand: 19. Februar 2022).

10 Evans: *Translations from Drawing* (wie Anm. 7), 154.

2　The courtyards of the *karkhanas* (manufactures). "Under the native industrial system, the child learns the hereditary craft from the father or is apprenticed to a *mistri*, or master-craftsman, who is often a relative of the pupil." "Mistri Moolchand, watchmaker and mechanic to the Maharaja of *Benares*, teaching his son in his own house." | Die Höfe der *Karkhanas* (Manufakturen). „Ursprünglich war es im industriellen Gewerbe üblich, dass das Kind das Handwerk von seinem Vater lernt oder dass es bei einem *Mistri* oder Handwerksmeister in die Lehre geht, der häufig ein Verwandter des Schülers ist." „Mistri Moolchand, Uhrmacher und Mechaniker des Maharadscha von *Benares*, der seinen Sohn in seinem eigenen Haus unterrichtet," Bromochary, Brajo Gopal, Varanasi, 1870 © The British Library Board

tural practice as well.[13] This discourse of formal procedures reorients the translation around the legacy of functionalism, through which "form is divested of its most complex derivations: type is reduced to a simple scheme of organization, a diagram of circulation routes, and architecture is seen as possessing no autonomous value."[14]

Along with the obvious classification of cities that continues to dominate the way we approach urban change in India—port city, religious city, industrial city, etc.—there are equivalent nascent but abstract aspects of design—informality, post-colonial theories, subaltern spaces, participatory urbanism—that might formulate into a neat parceling of the environment and authorship of history without the intervention of a robust and open architectural dialogue. In a similar methodology to catalyze pedagogy from the building of fields over figures, the Indian architectural discourse might benefit from a design exercise that Renee Chow developed as an exploratory form for generating disciplinary knowledge as well as problem solving in the studio. In this three-part approach, the goals "in the field" are to learn how to describe the quality of a place as a first step for collaboration and situating architecture and its scale. By "describing the field," a shared and continuous characteristic of a fabric at multiple levels is revealed. After establishing its dynamic nature, "cultivating the field" renders visible the capacity of a field to hold multiple readings or change over time.[15]

This is a counterproposal of a different architecture; translating and drawing the Indian city confronts its fascination with not just its "capacity to map, but to serve."[16] While metropolitan cities in India are extensively written off as the nodes of migration influx and "big idea" architecture, the more traditional cities with "non-city" forms of habitation are resurfacing as potential sites for large scale developments. To reassert design agency within the emerging reinvigoration of architectural ed-

13 See Evans, *Translations from Drawing* (see note 8).

14 Aldo Rossi, *The Architecture of the City* (London, 1982), 46.

15 See Renee Chow, "Field Exercises" presented at the conference "Education for an Open Architecture," Muncie, Indiana: Ball State University, 2008, available online at: http://open-building.org/conference2008/Proceedings_EOA_web.pdf (accessed January 13, 2022).

16 Sorkin, "Critical Mass" (see note 9).

Studienplan für das Bachelorstudium Architektur[11] seitens des All India Council for Technical Education (AICTE)[12] und propagierte ein Anspruchsdenken hinsichtlich der Reinheit des Blicks, das schließlich auch in die Architekturpraxis einsickerte.[13] Dieser Diskurs formaler Verfahren ordnet die Übersetzung ins Erbe des Funktionalismus ein, wodurch die „Form ihrer komplexesten Ableitungen entkleidet wird: Typus wird auf ein einfaches Organisationsschema reduziert, ein Schaubild von Verkehrsabläufen, und Architektur wird als etwas angesehen, das keinen eigenständigen Wert besitzt".[14]

Neben der offenkundigen Klassifizierung von Städten, die weiterhin die Art dominiert, wie wir uns dem städtischen Wandel in Indien nähern (Hafen, Stadt, religiöse Stadt, Industriestadt usw.), gibt es entsprechende im Werden begriffene, aber abstrakte Aspekte der Gestaltung (Formlosigkeit, postkoloniale Theorien, subalterne Räume, partizipatorischer Urbanismus), die ohne die Intervention eines widerstandsfähigen und offenen Architekturdialogs eine saubere Trennung von Umgebungsbeziehungen und historischer Autorschaft hervorbringen könnten.

In einer ähnlichen Methodologie, die ihre Pädagogik aus den Bedingungen räumlicher Felder anstelle einzelner Baukörper entfaltet, könnte der indische Architekturdiskurs von einer Entwurfsübung profitieren, die Renee Chow als eine explorative Form zur Erzeugung architektonischen Wissens sowie zur Problemlösung im Studio entwickelte. Bei diesem dreiteiligen Ansatz bestehen die Ziele „im Feld" darin, zu lernen, wie man die Beschaffenheit eines Ortes als ersten Schritt zur Zusammenarbeit und der Verortung der Architektur und ihres Maßstabs beschreibt. Durch das „Beschreiben des Feldes" wird ein gemeinsames und kontinuierliches Kennzeichen eines Geflechts auf verschiedenen Ebenen offengelegt. Nach der Etablierung seiner dynamischen Natur veranschaulicht die „Kultivierung des Feldes" seine Fähigkeit, verschiedene Lesarten zuzulassen oder sich mit der Zeit zu verändern.[15]

Dies ist ein Vorschlag für eine andere Architektur: die indische Stadt zu übersetzen und zu zeichnen, konfrontiert ihre Faszination nicht nur mit ihrer „Fähigkeit zu kartieren, sondern zu dienen".[16] Während Großstädte in Indien flächendeckend als Knotenpunkte des Migrationszuflusses und der „Big Idea"-Architektur abgeschrieben werden, treten traditionelle Städte mit „Non-City"-Wohnformen als potenzielle Standorte für umfassende Bauvorhaben wieder in Erscheinung. Um die Handlungsmacht des Designs in der sich abzeichnenden neuerlichen Stärkung der Architekturausbildung[17] wieder geltend zu machen, ist es angemessen, sich tiefergehend und jenseits der Starrheit des neoliberalen Masterplans mit Stadtgestaltung zu beschäftigen. Wie trägt die Doppeldeutigkeit der territorialen Repräsentation zur zukünftigen Destabilisierung des Banalen bei?

Welche unerwarteten Assoziationen und Gegensätze werden bei der Reklassifizierung urbaner Projekte offengelegt?

Die „heilige Stadt" Varanasi ist ein sehr gutes Beispiel einer alternativen Räumlichkeit, denn die Leichtigkeit, mit der sie ihre außergewöhnlichen und unvoreingenommenen kulturellen und raumsoziologischen Eigentümlichkeiten aufnimmt, kann als Werkzeug dafür dienen, um die Herausforderungen der zeitgenössischen Architekturpraxis und damit auch den Spielraum der pädagogischen Möglichkeiten zu skizzieren.

**Das Verorten der Typologie in Narrativen des Alltags.** Das *Moksha*[18] *Bhawan*, oder Erlösungsheim, ist eines der vielen Sterbehäuser in Varanasi, in denen diejenigen Zuflucht finden, die sterben möchten, um von dem Kreislauf von Wiedergeburt und Tod erlöst zu werden.[19] Es ist Teil der Tradition, dass die Familie nach dem Tod ihres oder ihrer Angehörigen mit Mitgliedern der *Dom*-Kaste um den Holzpreis feilscht und so den *Moksha*-Prozess einleitet. Bei der *Dom*-Kaste handelt es sich um eine Gemeinschaft von ArbeiterInnen, die seit Generationen mit Holz handeln und auch die letzten Riten für Menschen vollführen, die keine eigene Familie haben. An dem *Manikarnika Ghat*,[20] wo die Scheiterhaufen angeblich noch nie zu brennen aufgehört haben, betet der *Pandit*[21] für den friedlichen Heimgang der Seele, während der älteste Sohn das letzte Abschieds-

11 „Model Curriculum for Bachelor of Architecture", *Government of India, All India Council for Technical Education* (2019) online unter: https://www.aicte-india.org/sites/default/files/B.%20Arch%202019compressed.pdf (Stand: 16. Februar 2022).

12 Der All India Council for Technical Education ist eine Körperschaft des öffentlichen Rechts und ein auf nationaler Ebene tätiger Rat für die technische Ausbildung, der dem Department of Higher Education, der Behörde für Höhere Bildung, in Indien untersteht.

13 Vgl. Evans: *Translations from Drawing* (wie Anm. 8).

14 Rossi, Aldo: *The Architecture of the City*, London 1982.

15 Vgl. Chow, Renee: „Field Exercises", Vortrag im Rahmen der Konferenz „Education for an Open Architecture", Ball State University, Muncie, Indiana 2008, online unter: http://open-building.org/conference2008/Proceedings_EOA_web.pdf (Stand: 13. Januar 2022).

16 Sorkin: *Critical Mass* (siehe Anm. 9).

17 Die Veröffentlichung des „Prospective Plan for Growth of Architectural Education" im August 2020 initiierte Veränderungen wie frei zugängliche Vorlesungen und Zusammenarbeit durch das Portal „COA Socials". Darüber hinaus wird derzeit ein fünfteiliges Handbuch der Architekturpraktiken begutachtet.

18 Emanzipation, Befreiung

19 Shafi, Showkat: „Hotel of Death' in Indian Holy City", *Aljazeera*, 5. Dezember 2013, online unter: https://www.aljazeera.com/gallery/2013/12/5/hotels-of-death-in-indian-holy-city (Stand: 13. Januar 2022).

20 Ort der traditionellen Feuerbestattung am Ufer des Ganges.

21 Priester

ucation,[17] it becomes pertinent to elaborate on design reasoning beyond the fixity of the neo-liberal masterplan. How does the ambiguity of territorial representation assist in the future destabilization of the banal? What unexpected associations and oppositions are revealed at the reclassification of urban projects? The "holy city" of Varanasi is a strong contender in presenting an alternate spatiality, as its ease of accommodation of the unnatural and unprejudiced eccentricities can be a medium to outline the challenges of contemporary architectural practice and the scope of a pedagogue.

**Situating Typology within Everyday Narratives.** *Moksha*[18] *Bhawan*, or Salvation Home, is one of the many "hotels of death" that houses those who desire to die in Varanasi to attain salvation from the cycle of rebirth and death.[19] It is part of the tradition that after the death of their relatives, the family haggles for the price of wood with the *Dom* caste—a community of workers who has dealt with the business of wood for generations, and even provide last rites for those without family—to initiate the process of Moksha. At *Manikarnika Ghat*,[20] where pyres are said to have never stop burning, the *pandit*[21] prays for the peaceful departure of the soul as the eldest son completes the final farewell through the ritual of circumambulation. The family then turns away and does not look back as it is considered inauspicious to hinder in the soul's journey and perhaps for the better as these intimate spaces turn into sites of meditation for the *Aghori Sadhus*[22] who bathe in the ashes from the pyres to purify their souls.[23]

Contrasting its vivid celebration of death is the flourishing handloom industry of the silk saree, championed by a community of artisan and laboring class whose contribution to the economy of Varanasi can be likened to the contribution of the Indian film industry to Bombay.[24] The Benarasi saree, a six-yard silk fabric draped traditionally by women, is appreciated for its intricate embroidery of floral motifs on the handiwork warp and weft weave of the yarn, a pattern that mirrors the architecture of the city it has a stronghold over. The streets remain unchanging, a framework of scaffolding like the warp of the yarn, dotted by a weft pattern of temples, houses, and schools, until their own individual complexity of internal warp and weft continues to add on to the density of the city.

According to Nita Kumar, "the houses of all *Ansaris*[25] have a similar pattern: a dark entrance, with very likely a latrine on one side, leading to an enclosed courtyard, with tap or hand pump. The *karkhana* (loom or weaving room) is located on one side, or two, depending on prosperity, and stairs go up on the third. Above are the family rooms, all around the central opening. The kitchen is on a separate mezzanine off the stairs or on the roof itself. No furniture is kept except some string cots standing up during the day, and trunks and canisters for storage. There is a total separation of working and living areas, and the *karkhana* never doubles as sleeping or playing space for the family, though it does as a sitting room for the weavers and their guests. Even the newest, most expensive homes of *Ansari* businessmen have this basic design, which may become elaborated with the multiplication of floors, rooms, and even courtyards, and the addition of rugs, television, and refrigerator … When the pattern does not immediately seem obvious, it is always due to fraternal partitions that split the house in the center, resulting in disproportionately tall and narrow houses with only half a courtyard, rooms on only one side, and an even narrower, tunnel-like entrance."[26]

"One home-based workshop in Rasulpura is operated by some eighty-five members of an extended family. As in all the weavers' homes, the weaving, dyeing, and other tasks done by the men are all carried out in several loom rooms and open courtyards at ground level, while upstairs the women work at silk

17 The publication of the "Prospective Plan for Growth of Architectural Education" in August 2020 initiated changes such as open access lectures and collaboration with architects through the portal "COA Socials." Additionally, a five-part "Manual of Architectural Practices" is currently under review.

18 Emancipation, liberation

19 Jhunt et Shofi "'Hotels of Death' In Indian Holy City," *Aljazeera*, December 5, 2013, available online at http://www.aljazeera.com/gallery/2013/12/5/hotels-of-death-in-indian-holy-city (accessed January 13, 2022).

20 Riverfront steps

21 Priest

22 The Aghori are a small group of ascetic saints based in Uttar Pradesh, India who engage in post-mortem rituals.

23 See Diana L. Eck, *Banaras: City of Light* (New York, 1999).

24 Unlike other handicrafts, the weaving technology of Benarasi silk did not undergo major changes over the last century. It was the lack of mechanization that turned weaving into a prosperous industry through innovation and enterprise towards changing market trends of wedding seasons and international trade.

25 An Arab community, predominant in Arab and South Asian countries, the meaning of which is "supporter." The term also refers to the weaving community in India.

26 Nita Kumar, "Work and Leisure in the Formation of Identity: Muslim Weavers in a Hindu City," in *Culture and Power in Banaras: Community, Performance, and Environment 1800–1980*, ed. Sandria B. Freitag (Berkeley, 1989), 147–172, esp. 154.

ritual vollführt, indem er um den Leichnam herumgeht. Anschließend wendet sich die Familie ab und blickt auch nicht mehr zurück, da dies der Reise der Seele angeblich abträglich sein könnte. Dies ist vielleicht auch besser so, da diese privaten und heiligen Räume anschließend zu den Meditationsorten der *Aghori Sadhus*[22] werden, die in der Asche der Scheiterhaufen baden, um dadurch ihren Seelen zu reinigen.[23]

Einen deutlichen Kontrast zu dieser lebhaften Feierlichkeit des Todes bildet die florierende Handwebstuhl-Industrie, die jene grünen Saris produziert, welche von einer der ArbeiterInnen- und HandwerkerInnenklasse zugehörigen Community bevorzugt werden, und deren Beitrag zur Wirtschaftsleistung Varanasis sich mit dem Beitrag der indischen Filmindustrie zur Wirtschaft Bombays vergleichen lässt.[24] Die Wertschätzung, die der Benarasi-Sari genießt, ein 6-Zoll langer Seidenstoff, den Frauen sich auf traditionelle Weise um den Körper wickeln, verdankt sich seinen aufwendigen Stickereien mit floralen Motiven auf den handgewebten Kett- und Schussfäden, ein Muster, das die Architektur der Stadt widerspiegelt. Während die Straßen immer gleichbleiben und wie die Kettfäden beim Weben ein Gefüge von Baugerüsten bilden, fügen sich Tempel, Häuser und Schulen als Schussfaden und in Form kleiner Sprenkel in sie ein, sodass die eigene individuelle Komplexität von Kette und Schuss die Raumdichte der Stadt zusätzlich steigert.

Nita Kumar zufolge „weisen die Häuser aller *Ansaris*[25] ein ähnliches Muster auf: ein dunkler Eingang mit einer Latrine an der Seite, der zu einem umfriedeten Hof mit einem Wasserhahn oder einer Handpumpe führt. Der *Karkhana* (Webstuhl oder Webraum) befindet sich auf einer Seite oder, je nach Wohlstand, auf zwei Seiten, und an der dritten Seite führt eine Treppe in das Obergeschoss. Dort, rings um den Freiraum in der Mitte, sind die Zimmer der Familie angeordnet. Die Küche befindet sich auf einem separaten, von der Treppe aus erreichbaren Zwischengeschoss oder auf dem Dach. Außer einigen tagsüber hochgeklappten Feldbetten nebst Truhen und Kanister zur Aufbewahrung von Vorräten gibt es keine Möbel. Arbeits- und Wohnbereich sind streng voneinander getrennt, und der *Karkhana* ist niemals zugleich auch der Schlaf- oder Spielplatz der Familie, auch wenn die WeberInnen und ihre Gäste dort Platz nehmen dürfen. Selbst die neuesten, teuersten Häuser von *Ansari*-Geschäftsleuten folgen dieser Raumordnung, die lediglich durch zusätzliche Stockwerke, Zimmer, ja sogar Höfe und die Ausstattung mit Teppichen, eines Fernsehers oder Kühlschranks noch ausgefeilter sein kann. Wenn das Muster nicht unmittelbar offenkundig zu sein scheint, dann liegt dies immer daran, dass das Haus durch die Aufteilung zwischen Brüdern in der

Mitte gespalten ist, was zu unverhältnismäßig großen und engen Häusern mit nur einem Hof, Zimmern nur auf einer Seite und einem noch schmaleren, tunnelartigen Eingang führt".[26]

„Eine im Haus befindliche Werkstatt in Rasulpura wird von etwa 85 Angehörigen einer Großfamilie betrieben. Wie in allen Weberhäusern werden das Weben, Färben und andere Aufgaben, welche die Männer erledigen, in mehreren Webstuhl-Räumen und offenen Höfen im Erdgeschoss ausgeführt, während die Frauen oben als Teil ihrer täglichen Hausarbeit die Seide aufspulen und dem Stoff den letzten Schliff geben. Elf Kinder der Familie lernen derzeit das Weben und zwanzig weitere, damit zusammenhängende Tätigkeiten. Der *Karkhana* stellt auch Weber – Muslime wie Hindus – ein, die nicht zur Familie gehören, und beschäftigt manchmal einen Weber, der im Weavers' Service Centre ausgebildet wurde."[27]

In dieser nüchternen Minimalarchitektur herrscht ein sozialer Zusammenhalt, der sehr demjenigen ähnelt, der Alison Smithson bei einem horizontalen Wolkenkratzer, einem *groundscraper* oder *mat building* vorschwebte: „Man kann sagen, dass ein *mat building* das anonyme Kollektiv versinnbildlicht, in dem die Funktionen das Gefüge bereichern und das Individuum durch eine neue und gemischte Ordnung, die auf Vernetzung, engmaschigen Verbindungsmustern und Möglichkeiten des Wachsens, Schrumpfens und Wandels beruht, an Freiheit gewinnt."[28] Während der Charakter der handwerklichen Industrie in Varanasi sich nicht verändert hat und den Raum kontrolliert, ist für den Heimwerker das eigene Zuhause die Werkstatt, und er teilt sich seine Zeit selbständig ein: Im Arbeitsleben tritt seine „Freiheit" zutage.[29]

„Ein Gutteil der Arbeit wird im Freien erledigt – im Hof des Hauses des Arbeiters oder selbst auf der öffentlichen Straße

22 Die Aghori sind eine kleine Gruppe asketischer Heiliger, die in Uttar Pradesh leben und Post-Mortem-Rituale abhalten.

23 Vgl. Eck, Diana L.: *Banaras: City of Light*, New York 1999.

24 Im Gegensatz zu anderen Handwerksarten gab es in der Webtechnik der Benarasi-Seide im Verlauf des letzten Jahrhunderts keine großen Veränderungen. Die fehlende Mechanisierung machte aus der Weberei eine prosperierende Industrie, die sich durch Innovationen und Unternehmungsgeist im Hinblick auf die Hochzeitssaison und den internationalen Handel an veränderte Markttrends anpassten.

25 Eine vor allem in arabischen und südasiatischen Ländern vorherrschende arabische Gemeinschaft (wörtl. „Anhänger") und auf die Gemeinschaft der WeberInnen in Indien bezogen wird.

26 Kumar, Nita: „Work and Leisure in the Formation of Identity: Muslim Weavers in a Hindu City", in: Freitag, Sandria B. (Hg.): *Culture and Power in Banaras: Community, Performance, and Environment 1800–1980*, Berkeley 1989, 147–172, hier 154.

27 Ebd., 127.

28 Allen, Stan: „Mat Urbanism: The Thick 2-D", in: Sarkis, Hashim (Hg.): *CASE: Le Corbusier's Venice Hospital*, München 2001, 118–126, hier 122.

29 Freitag: *Culture and Power in Banaras* (wie Anm. 26).

3  *Ghats* on the holy river Ganga. A place for private rituals and communal festivities. | Ghats am heiligen Fluss Ganges. Ein Ort für private Rituale und gemeinschaftliche Festlichkeiten, Wikimedia Commons, Varanasi, 2009 © CC BY-SA 2.0

reeling and fabric finishing as part of their daily housework. There are eleven children from the family presently learning weaving as well as more than twenty related operations. The *karkhana* also hires weavers from outside the family, some Muslim and some Hindu, and sometimes employs a designer/ weaver who was trained at the Weavers' Service Centre."[27]

In this austere, bare-bones architecture thrives a pattern of social association much like the one Alison Smithson envisaged would exist in a horizontal skyscraper, the groundscraper, or mat building. "Mat building can be said to epitomize the anonymous collective: where the functions come to enrich the fabric, and the individual gains new freedom of action through a new and shuffled order, based on interconnection, close knit-patterns of association, and possibilities for growth, diminution

and change."[28] While the nature of the handicraft industry in Varanasi has remained unchanged and and controls the space, for the artisan the home is the workshop and work time is set by the artisan himself; in the work life emerges his "freedom."[29]

"A good deal of the work is done in the open—in the courtyard of the worker's house or even in the public street or lane … there is no discipline to observe. Rest and recreation are taken whenever the need is felt. Contact with the home and familiar surroundings is seldom interrupted. The usual ameni-

27  Ibid., 127.

28  Stan Allen, "Mat Urbanism: The Thick 2-D," in *CASE: Le Corbusier's Venice Hospital*, ed. Hashim Sarkis (Munich, 2001), 118–126, esp. 122.

29  Freitag, *Culture and Power in Banaras* (see note 26)

oder Gasse […] Man muss keine Regeln beachten. Ruhe- und Erholungspausen werden gemacht, wann immer man das Bedürfnis verspürt. Der Kontakt mit dem Zuhause und der vertrauten Umgebung wird selten unterbrochen. Die üblichen Annehmlichkeiten des sozialen Lebens werden nicht gestört."[30] Als Antwort auf die grundlegende urbanistische Frage bieten die Höfe der Weber Raum für die aktive Entfaltung des Alltagslebens, ohne dass die ArchitektInnen dafür verantwortlich wären, eine Form der Ordnung zu beweisen; das Versprechen besteht darin, dass Ereignisse Raum in den Leerstellen konfigurieren, außerhalb der expliziten Kontrollhülle der Architektur.[31] Obwohl die Gebäude der Handwerker in Varanasi antifigural, anti-gegenständlich und anti-monumental sind, wird die Maßstabsgröße, jenseits welcher der expansive Urbanismus von Varanasi in Erscheinung tritt, durch die Gesamtintensität von Wiederholung und Akkumulation spezifiziert (Abb. 2).[32]

**Die unkartierbare Stadt übersetzen.** Die physische Geografie Varanasis wird durch eine Serie von Hofhäusern entlang der Straßen definiert, die Nachbarschaftseinheiten ausbilden, die in sich heterogen organisiert sind, und die von der vorspringenden Biegung des Ganges umfasst werden. Ihre einzigartige Uferzone ist durch die 88 *Ghats* gekennzeichnet, stufenartige Befestigungen – umgangssprachlich auch als leuchtende Perlen am Ufer des Ganges bezeichnet – die vom Wasser hinauf zu den zahllosen Hauptstraßen führen, die jeweils nach dem *Ghat* benannt sind, auf das hin es sich öffnet. Belebte Geschäftsstraßen laufen an Kreuzungen häufig zusammen und verzweigen sich von dort aus wieder in diverse Märkte, die auf den Verkauf von Getreide, Holz-, Messing- oder Seidenarbeiten spezialisiert und repräsentativ für die traditionellen indischen Straßen sind, auf denen sich unterschiedlichste Ereignisse abspielen. Es handelt sich hier um einen lebhaften Schwellenraum, der zwischen den einzelnen *Ghats* und den ruhigeren Vierteln – dem heiligen Teil der Stadt – liegt (Abb. 3).

Dieses Stadtgefüge repräsentiert das Werk der „Götter". Der hinduistische Glaube, dass die Errichtung eines Territoriums oder Lebensraums immer gesegnet ist, hat einen kosmologischen Archetyp zur Folge: In Varanasi werden diese kosmisch-magischen Mächte[33] durch fünf heilige konzentrische Territorien von Pilgerrouten definiert und in einem kartografischen System, welches das Universum als einen Kreis versinnbildlicht, eine Reihe von Schreinen unter den 3.300 hinduistischen Heiligtümern miteinander verbindet.[34]

Dieses heilige System, das sich tief in den Stadtraum eingeschrieben hat und den saisonalen Pilgerströmen durch seine

stabile Struktur standhält, bildet auch das wirtschaftliche Rückgrat der Stadt. Während verschiedene Pilgerrouten über das eigentliche Stadtgebiet hinausführen, vollführt die innerste Route, *Antargriha*,[35] sieben Runden um den *Vishwanath*-Tempel, dem heiligsten Bereich der Hindu-Religion[36] und vorbei an den 72 Tempeln, die über die *Mohallas* verstreut sind.[37] Historisch betrachtet organisierten sich die *Mohallas* als verwaltungstechnisch autonome Wohnbezirke, die für ihren Polizeischutz, die Müllabfuhr, Abwasserentsorgung und Straßenbeleuchtung selbst verantwortlich waren.[38] Und obwohl sie mittlerweile ihre institutionelle Bedeutung eingebüßt haben, kommen die BewohnerInnen der *Mohallas* nach wie vor anlässlich lokaler Feste zusammen.[39]

Ein ähnliches interurbanes Modell wurde von van Eyck 1962 bei dem Team 10 Treffen in Abbaye Royaumont in der Absicht präsentiert, die phänomenologische Erfahrung der neuen Stadtgebiete zu verbessern.[40] Die gigantische urbane Entwurfslösung von Piet Blom, „Arche Noah", schlug Unterkünfte für eine Million Menschen vor, die dadurch zustande kommen sollten, dass man sechzig Gemeinden um Amsterdam herum miteinander verband und in siebzig „Dörfer" mit 10.000 bis 15.000 BewohnerInnen aufteilte. Jedes der 60 Hektar großen Dörfer bestand aus miteinander verzahnten Clustern, die eine breite Palette städtischer Funktionen erfüllten, d.h. Wohnungen, Büros, „Tempel", Kliniken und kulturelle und Erholungseinrichtungen vorsahen, die durch ein viergeschossiges Straßennetz miteinander verbunden waren. Das ambitionierte Projekt sollte die typischen dezentralisierenden und entropischen Prozesse der Stadtentwicklung des 20. Jahrhunderts umkehren, indem es ein

30 Ebd., 152.

31 Vgl. Allen: „Mat Urbanism" (wie Anm. 28).

32 Vgl. ebd.

33 Vgl. Singh, Rana P.B.: „Cosmic Layout of the Hindu Sacred City, Vanarasi (Benares)", *Architecture and Behaviour* 9, 2 (1993), 239–250, online unter: https://www.epfl.ch/labs/lasur/wp-content/uploads/2018/05/SINGH.pdf (Stand: 13. Januar 2022).

34 Vgl. ebd.

35 Allerheiligstes

36 Singh: „Cosmic Layout" (wie Anm. 33).

37 Laut Kiwamu Yanagisawa und Shuji Funo „besteht ein *Mohalla* aus Häusern, die zu beiden Seiten einer oder mehrerer Straßen liegen, in der ihre Identität durch die Straße gekennzeichnet ist, der es gegenüberliegt" (siehe Anm. 38), 388.

38 Vgl. Yanagisawa, Kiwamu/Funo, Shuji: „How Mohallas Were Formed: Typology of Mohallas from the Viewpoint of Spatial Formation and the Urbanization Process in Varanasi, India", *Japan Architectural Review* 1, 3 (2018): 385–395, online unter: https://onlinelibrary.wiley.com/doi/full/10.1002/2475-8876.12040 (Stand: 18. August 2020).

39 Ebd.

40 Vgl. Mumford, Eric: „The Emergence of Mat or Field Buildings", in: CASE: *Le Corbusier's Venice Hospital*, München 2001, 48–65.

ties of social life are not disturbed."[30] In response to the fundamental urbanistic question, the courtyards of the artisan weavers give space to the active unfolding of daily life without the architect's responsibility of proving a form of order; the promise is of events configuring space in the voids, outside of architecture's explicit envelope of control.[31] While the houses of the Varanasi artisans are anti-figural, antirepresentational, and anti-monumental, it is the overall intensity of repetition and accumulation that specifies the scale threshold beyond which the expansive urbanism of Varanasi emerges (fig. 2).[32]

**Translating the Unmappable City.** The recurring courtyard houses along lanes and streets form a patch of neighborhood unit with varying differences, thus constituting a physical geography of the city, contained along the jutting curve of the Ganges river. Its singular edge condition is characterized by the 88 *ghats* famed as luminous pearls lighting up the Ganga bank, from which steps lead up to the countless main streets that are named after the *ghat* it opens up to. Busy shopping lanes often converge at crossings and branch further into diverse ancient markets, each specialized in selling grain, woodwork, brass work, or silk work, and is representative of traditional Indian streets superimposed with layers of disparate events. This is a chaotic middle ground between the solitary *ghats* and the intimate neighborhoods that mirror the city's sacred region (fig. 3).

This pattern represents the work of "gods;" the Hindu belief that the creation of a territory or habitat is always consecrated results in a celestial archetype. In Varanasi these cosmos-magical powers[33] are defined by a series of five sacred concentric territories of pilgrimage routes, a mapping system symbolizing the universe as a circle connecting a number of shrines out of the 3,300 Hindu sanctuaries.[34] Deeply rooted in the local spaces, this sacred system and its spatial stability mediating with the temporal flux of annual pilgrimages is the economic backbone of the city. While various journeys extend beyond the main city's territory, the most internal route of the *Antargriha*[35] traces seven rounds around the Vishwanath temple, the holiest center of the Hindu religion,[36] and along the 72 temples scattered within the *mohallas*.[37]

Historically used as administrative tax and autonomous residential units, the *mohallas* were responsible for their own police protection, cleaning, sewage disposal, and street lighting

services.[38] While its institutional meaning has been lost, the *mohallas* continue to gather for festivals locally.[39] A similar model of an "interurban entity" was showcased by van Eyck at the 1962 Team 10 meeting at Abbaye Royaumont in an effort to improve the phenomenological experience of the new urban environments.[40]

The gigantic urban design scheme by Piet Blom, "Noah's Ark," proposed housing for a million people by linking 60 municipalities around Amsterdam and subdividing into 70 "villages" of 10,000 to 15,000 people. Each 60-hectare village was organized into interlocking-built clusters with a wide range of urban functions, including housing, offices, "temples", clinics, and cultural and recreational facilities, bound together by a four-level road network. It was one of the most ambitious efforts anywhere to invert the typical decentralizing and entropic processes of twentieth-century urban development by offering a model for future expansion of the dense urban center of Amsterdam.[41]

"The culture of particular form is approaching its end, the culture of determined relations has begun,"[42] hence the words of Piet Mondrian which also captured the spirit of the next congress of CIAM, favoring the "habitat"—understood as the entire lifeworld of the dweller—over the "dwelling" (the housing unit). Blom's project translated into a clear ideation of the

30  Ibid., 152.

31  See Allen, "Mat Urbanism" (see note 28).

32  See ibid.

33  See Rana P.B. Singh, "Cosmic Layout of The Hindu Sacred City, Varanasi (Benaras)", *Architecture and Behaviour* 9, no. 2 (1993): 239–250, available online at: https://www.epfl.ch/labs/lipid/wp-content/uploads/2018/05/SINGH.pdf (accessed January 13, 2022).

34  See ibid.

35  Inner sanctum

36  Singh, "Cosmic Layout" (see note 33).

37  According to Yanagisawa and Funo, "a mohalla consists of houses located along both sides of one or more streets, wherein its identity is characterized by the street it faces." (see note 42), 388.

38  See Kiwamu Yanagisawa and Shuji Funo, "How Mohallas Were Formed: Typology of Mohallas from the Viewpoint of Spatial Formation and the Urbanization Process in Varanasi, India," *Japan Architectural Review* 1, no. 3 (2018): 385–395, available online at: https://onlinelibrary.wiley.com/doi/full/10.1002/2475-8876.12040 (accessed August 18, 2020).

39  See ibid.

40  See Eric Mumford, "The Emergence of Mat or Field Buildings," in *CASE: Le Corbusier's Venice Hospital* (Munich, 2001), 48–65.

41  See ibid.

42  Piet Mondrian quoted in Ramsden, E.H.: *An Introduction to Modern Art* (London 1949), 17.

Modell für die zukünftige Ausdehnung des dichten Stadtzentrums von Amsterdam bot.[41]

„Die Kultur der Einzelform nähert sich ihrem Ende; die Kultur bewusster Beziehungen hat begonnen."[42] Dieser Sinnspruch Mondrians war auch das Motto des CIAM Kongresses, der das „Habitat"– also die gesamte Lebenswelt der BewohnerInnen – gegenüber der „Behausung" – also der Wohneinheit – favorisierte. Bei Bloms Projekt handelte es sich um die Umsetzung einer klaren Idee der Stadt als großes Haus, dessen einzelne Teile durch einen spielerischen Rhythmus von Einfriedung und Offenheit gekennzeichnet waren.[43] Die Absicht, die „Arche Noah" zugrunde lag, war ein möglicher Ausbau eines der Wohnviertel des Entwurfsprogramms, wurde jedoch von den Smithsons dahingehend kritisiert, dass er durch die Wiederholungshäufigkeit sämtliche Aspekte des zukünftigen städtischen Wachstums kontrollieren und eine falsche Analogie von Haus und Stadt heraufbeschwören würde.[44] Ironischerweise befanden sich Team 10 und die französischen Strukturalisten hinsichtlich der Haltung von CIAM gegenüber dem Funktionalismus in der gleich verfahrenen Lage; als Befürworter eines sozialwissenschaftlichen Entwurfsansatzes zur Festlegung der Bedeutung individueller Räume, löste die endlose Wiederholung zur Unterbringung größerer Zahlen selbst eine Krise aus.[45] „Wie konnte man das Prinzip der Wiederholung in diesem Ausmaß betonen und gleichzeitig behaupten, Lebensformen seien im Prinzip einzigartig?"[46]

Im tieferen strukturalistischen Sinne folgten Bedeutungen nicht ursächlich aus Symbolen, die eine Struktur mit einer anderen verbinden konnten. Ein solches Beharren auf der symbolischen Rolle der Architektur, der Rolle flexibler Flächenstrukturen Gestaltungsspielraum zu ermöglichen und Assoziationen zu knüpfen und damit wechselseitig zwischen Architektur und Gesellschaft zu vermitteln, war dem Wesen des Strukturalismus im Wesentlichen fremd.[47] Anders als die Smithsons, glaubte Saussure, dass der Strukturalismus nicht durch seine Inhalte konstituiert wird, sondern durch ein System reiner Unterschiede. Es geht also in diesem Sinne nicht mehr um die Identität von Architektur und Leben, sondern um den irreduziblen Unterschied zwischen ihnen und die Frage, wie BewohnerInnen damit leben können. Wenn man das Prinzip der flächigen Verdichtung von der früheren Faszination der Utopisten entkoppeln könnte und Varanasis kulturelle Identität nicht bloß auf die Religion reduzieren würde, bietet uns die Typologie des „Mat"-Urbanismus die Möglichkeit, die Architektur der Stadt von der Bildersymbolik hin zur Organisation und von einem Gebilde gebundener Formbildung hin zu einem Feld von Assemblagen neu zu lesen.[48]

**Wünsche, Diversität und Dilemmata.** Die kleinste Einheit innerhalb der *Mohalla* ist ein zwei- bis vierstöckiger Hofblock, den mindestens zwei Mauern mit dem Nachbarhaus verbinden. Charakteristisch gastfreundlich bilden seine 2 Meter breiten Gassen komplexe räumliche Streifen. Dabei tritt eine bürgerliche Häuslichkeit in Erscheinung: Offene Zugänge zum Haus laden zur Geselligkeit ein und opake Räume werden transparent, sodass die Unterscheidung zwischen „Öffentlichem" und „Privatem" auf der gesamten verdichteten Fläche des Konglomerats hinfällig wird. Mit ihrer zunehmenden Verdichtung neigt die Allmende zu exponentiell zunehmenden Variationen. Kleine Plätze an denen Theateraufführungen genauso wie Lebensmittel angeboten werden und deren Brunnen als gemeinsame Ressourcen und Orte der Häuslichkeit dienen, verknüpfen die Netze der *Mohallas* miteinander. Doch die passive Teilhabe der BesucherInnen am Alltagsleben der AnwohnerInnen ist das, was die Stadtmorphologie Varanasis von der aller anderen traditionellen Städte Indiens unterscheidet (Abb. 4).

Die Schreine und Tempel auf den Mauern, an den Eingängen und in den Höfen der Häuser sind die umstrittenste Allmende. Charakteristisch ist auch die Verbindung von mehreren Tempeln zu Verbundbauten, bei denen hinduistische Tempel durch eine spätere Erweiterung angrenzender Gebäude bedeckt, umhüllt oder eingeschlossen wurden.[49] Indem sie eine komplexe Schichtung ihrer sakralen-säkularen Urbanität offenlegen, werfen diese informellen Strukturen die Frage auf, wie sich eine partizipative Transformation und Anpassung darstellen könnte. Dem *Manu-smriti*[50] zufolge stellt die Zerstörung eines Tempels – wenn seine Errichtung mit einem spezifischen heiligen Ort verbunden war – eine Sünde dar, und seine säkulare Nutzung wird zu einem sozialen Tabu.[51] Wenn die Konvergenz der göttlichen

---

41 Vgl. ebd.

42 Piet Mondrian zitiert in Nehls, Werner: *Bauhaus und Marxismus*, München 2010, 177.

43 Vgl. Mumford: „The Emergence of Mat or Field Buildings" (wie Anm. 40).

44 Vgl. ebd.

45 Vgl. Scalbert, Irénée: „From Anthropology to Structuralism", in: *Team 10: Keeping the Language of Modern Architecture Alive*, Delft 2006, 136–144.

46 Ebd.,140.

47 Vgl. ebd.

48 Vgl. Allen: „Mat Urbanism" (wie Anm. 28).

49 Vgl. Yanagisawa, Kiwamu/Ohara, Ryosuke/Yamamoto, Shota: „Outline and Background of ‚Merged Temple': Study on Extension and Construction Surrounding Existing Hindu Temples in Varanasi Old City, India", *Japan Architectural Review* 3, 3 (2020), 359–374.

50 „Gesetzbuch des Manu" oder „Die erinnerte Tradition des Manu" gilt als der erste antike Gesetzestext und gehört als Abhandlung über angemessenes Verhalten zu den *Dharmasutras* des Hinduismus.

51 Vgl. Yanagisawa/Ohara/Yamamoto: „Outline and Background of ‚Merged Temple'" (wie Anm. 49).

city as a large house, with each part characterized by a playful rhythm between enclosure and openness.[43] The intention behind "Noah's Ark" was a possible build-out of one of the scheme's residential neighborhoods, not a detailed architectural plan, yet was subjected to criticism by the Smithsons over the plan's repetitiveness as a means to control all aspects of future urban growth and the false analogy of the house/city.[44] Ironically, Team 10 and the French structuralists were simultaneously deadlocked over CIAM's attitude towards functionalism; as advocates of applying social sciences in determining the meaning of individual spaces, the endless repetition for accommodating greater numbers itself triggered a crisis.[45] "How could one stress repetition to this degree and claim at the same time that life forms are in principle unique?"[46]

At the core of structuralism, significations were not symbols that could connect one structure with another. Such insistence upon the symbolic role of architecture, the role of flexible field structures to impart freedom and foster association as a reciprocity between architecture and society was essentially foreign to it.[47] Unlike the Smithsons' interpretation, Saussure believed that structuralism is not constituted by its contents, but by a system of pure differences. The issue is then no longer the identity between architecture and life; rather, it is the irreducible difference between them, and how inhabitants could live with it. If one could distinguish the mat from a previously engaged fascination with utopianism and Varanasi's nostalgic identity as purely religious, the typology of mat urbanism offers the opportunity to re-read the city's architecture from imagery to organization and from an entity of bounded shape making to a field of assemblages.[48]

**Desires, Diversity, and Dilemmas.** Within the *mohalla*, the smallest unit is a two to four storied courtyard block that shares at least two walls with the neighboring house. Characteristically hospitable, its two-meter-wide lanes form complex spatial striations. A civic domesticity emerges; a two-fold convivial way of life is informed at the threshold of the house by open doorways and otherwise opaque spaces are rendered transparent, discarding the trifling division of "public" and "private" across the thickened ground of the agglomeration. With its increasing densification, the commons set out to vary exponentially. Small squares offering sites of theatre and food and wells functioning as shared resource and domesticity tie

the overlapping networks of the *mohallas* together. However, it is the passive participation of visitors in the everyday life of the residents that emphasizes Varanasi's morphology as different from other traditional Indian cities (fig. 4).

The shrines and temples, superimposed on the walls, doorways, and courtyards of the homes are the most contested commons. Particular to these are merged temples, a type of composite buildings in which Hindu temples have been covered, wrapped, or enclosed by a later extension of adjacent buildings.[49] Illegal as they might be, these structures interrogate what resident-led transformation and adaptation could represent, revealing extreme layering of its sacred-secular urbanity. According to *Manu-smriti*,[50] if the establishment of temples is linked to a specific place of sacredness, its demolishment is then equivalent to a sin, while its secular use is regarded as social taboo.[51] When the convergence of the divine dwelling with the *mohalla* strengthens that ideology, who then claims ownership over the extension of their homes, when several walls threaten to engulf a common shrine?

On the other extreme is state intervention. Adjacent to the *Vishwanath* temple is the *Gyanvapi* mosque, from which streets lead to the cremation grounds of *Manikarnika ghat*. Collectively, the compound temple complex, the *mohallas* and the *ghat* form a "corridor" of religious and spiritual importance in Varanasi, enough to garner political attention for an urban transformation. This redevelopment project aims to "decongest and beautify the area" by replacing the essence of the

43 See Mumford, "The Emergence of Mat or Field Buildings" (see note 40).

44 See ibid.

45 See Irénée Scalbert, "From Anthropology to Structuralism," in *Team 10: Keeping the Language of Modern Architecture Alive*, conference proceeding (Delft University, 2006), 136–144.

46 Ibid., 140.

47 See ibid.

48 See Allen, "Mat Urbanism" (see note 28).

49 See Kiwamu Yanagisawa, Ryosuke Ohara and Shota Yamamoto, "Outline and Background of 'Merged Temple:' Study on Extension and Construction Surrounding Existing Hindu Temples in Varanasi Old City, India," *Japan Architectural Review* 3, no. 3 (2020): 359–374.

50 "Laws of Manu" or "The Remembered Tradition of Manu" is believed to be the first ancient legal text and constitution of the *dharma* (righteousness) treatise in Hinduism.

51 See Yanagisawa, Ohara and Yamamoto, "Outline and background of 'merged temple'" (see note 49).

Behausung mit der *Mohalla* diese Ideologie stärkt, wer beansprucht dann das Eigentum an der Erweiterung ihrer Häuser, wenn mehrere Wände einen gemeinschaftlichen Schrein einzuhüllen drohen?

Der staatliche Eingriff stellt das andere Extrem dar. Neben dem *Vishwanath*-Tempel befindet sich die *Gyanvapi*-Moschee, von der aus die Straßen zum Einäscherungsgelände des *Manikarnika* Ghats führen. In ihrer Gesamtheit bilden der zusammengesetzte Tempelkomplex, die *Mohallas* und das Ghat einen „Korridor" religiöser und spiritueller Bedeutung in Varanasi, der hinreichend groß ist, um die politische Aufmerksamkeit bezüglich einer städtischen Transformation auf sich zu ziehen. Das Neugestaltungsprojekt zielt darauf ab, „die Gegend verkehrsmäßig zu entlasten und zu verschönern", indem sie die Substanz der sich an der Straße orientierenden Kultur der *Mohallas* durch eine Reihe großer städtischer Plätze ersetzt.[52] Von einer „Ansammlung von Hohlräumen in weitgehend ungegliederter Masse" zu einer „Ansammlung von Massen in weitgehend unberührter Leere"[53] verleiht die Neugestaltung dem alten Glauben daran, dass „jedermann den *Vishveshvara* sehen und im *Manikarnika* baden sollte",[54] eine institutionalisierte Wende und verwandelt ehemals opake, dem Gebet dienenden Orte der Spiritualität in Orte der bürgerlichen Prunksucht (Abb. 1).[55] „Die Idee, die dem Projekt zugrunde liegt, ähnelt der ambitionierten Umgestaltung vieler historischer Städte der Welt wie Paris [im 19. Jahrhundert], wo Ghettos beseitigt wurden."[56]

Möglicherweise liegt dieser ignoranten Lesart der Mehrdeutigkeiten von Varanasis städtischem Gewebe die Furcht vor der kolossalen Aufgabe zugrunde, aus der Vielfalt der Gemeinschaftsformen Synergieeffekte zu erzielen. Durch eine Fehldeutung der eurozentrischen Planungsstrategien als naivem Funktionalismus, wurde die problematische Herausforderung der Umgestaltung erst zugänglich gemacht. Man hätte sich besser am Beispiel Barcelonas orientiert, einer Stadt, die bereits einen beträchtlichen Anteil an Umgestaltung erfahren hat. Bei der Neugestaltung des Santa-Caterina-Marktes nahm der Architekt Enric Miralles das laute Treiben und die vielfältigen Aktivitäten im Stadtzentrums Barcelonas dankend an und überschrieb die alten Spuren mit neuen. „Der Ort wird für einen Parkplatz ausgehoben, die Nutzung als Markt wird beibehalten, neue öffentliche Räume und Wohnungen werden vorgeschlagen."[57] Die bunte wellenförmige Dachkonstruktion in Leichtbauweise, welche diese miteinander konkurrierenden Spannungen vereint, ist dem horizontalen Geflecht von *Mohallas* vergleichbar, das den informellen Tempelkomplexen seine übergeordnete Macht verleiht und von der Monumentalität als einer Vorbedingung für die städtische Transformation abrückt.

Die vorbildliche Handlungsmacht der Architektur, eine lesbare städtische Ordnung herzustellen, wurde von den Smithsons bewundert, auch wenn sie die Unterscheidung zwischen Architektur und Urbanismus provozierte. Für die Architektur des *mat building* war die Gestaltung von Masse und Volumen von grundlegender Bedeutung; für den „mat-Urbanismus" von Varanasi wird die Landschaft selbst zum Vorbild für die Organisation horizontaler Oberflächen. Die performativen Effekte der Oberfläche in der Landschaft sind ein direktes Ergebnis ihrer spezifischen Materialeigenschaften – zum Beispiel der Tendenz, Wasser abzuweisen oder aufzunehmen. Da Landschaften sich nicht zur Gänze durch Kontrolle gestalten lassen, werden sie stattdessen in die Zukunft projiziert und man erlaubt es ihnen, sich im Verlauf der Zeit zu entwickeln – deshalb steht die Stadtsanierung im starken Gegensatz zu den *Mohallas*.[58]

Hier bietet sich auch ein Vergleich mit der gespaltenen Interpretation des *mat building* an: Der Gegensatz zwischen der volumetrischen Ausdehnung der spezifizierten Raumprogramme der Smithsons und dem performativen Landschaftsurbanismus von Allen steht stellvertretend für die Polarität und aktuelle Richtungslosigkeit der indischen Praktiken, die auf halbherzige Weise bestrebt sind, um der „Entwicklung" willen, spirituelle Traditionen nicht als Teil der städtebaulichen Innovationen anzuerkennen.

Einen ähnlichen Trend stellte Nita Kumar in Varanasis Grundschulen fest. Um eines effizienten Unterrichts willen muss die Bildung das Lokale unsichtbar machen.[59] „Fortschritt" und „Modernität" können nur gedeihen, wenn die Idee einer „Nation" imaginär und abstrakt ist.[60] Doch selbst „wenn das Kind nicht zur Schule geht, gibt es zwei wesentliche Möglichkeiten,

52 Vgl. Vatsa, Aditi: „Modi Wants Paris Look for Varanasi, but Residents Say City Identity ‚Under Attack from BJP'", *The Print*, 30. April 2019, online unter: https://7theprint.in/politics/modi-wants-paris-look-for-varanasi-but-residents-say-city-identity-under attack-from-bjp/229079/ (Stand: 13. Januar 2022).

53 Rowe, Colin/Koetter, Fred: *Collage City*, Übers. Bernhard Hoesli, Basel/Boston/Stuttgart 1984, 88.

54 Eck: *City of Light* (wie Anm.22).

55 Vgl. Waxman, Alan/Singh, Simran: „Harvesting the Field: Institionalizing the Spiritual in the Redevelopment of the Heart of Varanasi", AWES – Alan Waxman Ecosocial Design, 2021, online unter: https://www.awecoscial.com/varanasi (Stand: 13. Januar 2022).

56 Vatsa: „Modi Wants Paris Look for Varanasi" (wie Anm. 51).

57 Allen: „Mat Urbanism" (wie Anm. 28), 121.

58 Vgl. ebd.

59 Vgl. Nita Kumar, *The Politics of Gender, Community, and Modernity*, New Delhi 2007, 247.

60 Vgl. ebd., 247.

street-oriented culture of the *mohallas* with a series of large urban plazas.[52] From "an accumulation of voids in a largely unmanipulated solid, to the accumulation of solids in a largely unmanipulated void,"[53] the redevelopment is an institutionalized spin on the ancient belief that "everyday one should see *Vishveshvara* and bathe in *Manikarnika*"[54] and modifies the formerly opaque interiority of worship into a celebration of civic pomposity (fig. 1).[55] "The idea behind the project is similar to the ambitious redevelopment of many historical cities of the world like Paris [in the 19th century], where ghettos were removed."[56]

Perhaps underlying this baseless and ignorant reading of ambiguities in Varanasi's fabric is the fear of scale and the colossal mission to synergize the plurality of communities. By misinterpreting the Eurocentric architectural and planning strategies as naïve functionalism, the problematic challenge of redevelopment was made approachable. A better comparison would have been Barcelona, a city that has experienced its fair share of rebuilding. At the Santa Caterina Market, the architect Enric Miralles embraced the raucous mix of activities that are typical of the city center and inscribed new traces over the old. "The site is excavated for parking, the market uses are preserved, new public spaces and housing are proposed."[57] The highly figured, lightweight roof unifying these competing tensions are comparable to the web of *mohallas* that empower the act of composite temples and departs from monumentality as a prerequisite for urban transformation.

This ideal agency of architecture to bring legible urban order was admired by the Smithsons, even as they provoked the distinction between architecture and urbanism. For the architecture of the mat 'building', the design of mass and volume was foundational; for the mat urbanism of Varanasi, landscape as a model of organizing horizontal surfaces can be applicable. The performative effects of the surface in landscape are a direct result of its specific material characteristics—for example, the tendency to shed or hold water. Since landscapes cannot be designed through control in totality, they are instead projected into the future and allowed to evolve over time, which is why the redevelopment stands in stark contrast to the *mohallas*.[58]

It can be likened to the split interpretation of the mat building; the volumetric expansion of specified programs of the Smithsons versus the performative landscape urbanism of Allen represents the emerging polarities in the current disorientation of Indian practices as they halfheartedly strive to disembody spiritual traditions from innovations in the built environment in order to "develop." A similar trend was noted by Nita Kumar in Varanasi's primary schools. For an effective schooling, education has to render the local invisible.[59] "Progress" and "modernity" can only thrive when the idea of a "nation" is imaginary and abstract.[60] Yet even "when the child does not go to school, there are two main ways in which she encounters the nation, which are shared by school going children too. One is in the movies and the other is in songs, typically heard over radio, television, or over loudspeakers amplifying their sounds generously in streets and neighborhoods."[61]

Thus, the most powerful sites for the learning of a common habitus are the *mohallas* in the provincial city,[62] as boundaries tend to merge, as encountered by Zeenat, a student of the *Madrasa*[63] *Hamidia Rizvia*. Her family of seven live in a room of the fourth floor of a courtyard house, shared with other Muslim families, where she learns "how to share the bathroom on the landing with the extended family, to cook with her mother, and gradually by herself in the space outside their door, to clean up each time and leave the space unmarked, and otherwise practice a total non-specialization of domestic spaces. All materials were put away after use. No space was called after its function, as the place 'for' some particular activity, including sleeping. The room became, in turn, a bedroom, a dining room, a sitting room, a den, a study, a workplace …"[64]

52 See Aditi Vatsa, "Modi Wants Paris Look for Varanasi, but Residents Say City Identity 'Under Attack from BJP,'" *The Print,* April 30, 2019, available online at: https://theprint.in/politics/modi-wants-paris-look-for-varanasi-but-residents-say-city-identity-under-attack-from-bjp/229079/ (accessed January 13, 2022).

53 Colin Rowe and Fred Koetter, *Collage City* (Basel, 2009), 62.

54 Eck, *City of Light* (see note 23).

55 See Alan Waxman and Simran Singh, "Harvesting the Field: Institutionalizing the Spiritual in the Redevelopment of the Heart of Varanasi," AWED – Alan Waxman Ecosocial Design, 2021, available online at: https://www.awecosocial.com/varanasi (accessed January 13, 2022).

56 Vatsa, "Modi Wants Paris Look For Varanasi" (see note 52).

57 Allen, "Mat Urbanism" (see note 28), 121.

58 See ibid.

59 See Nita Kumar, *The Politics of Gender, Community, and Modernity* (New Delhi, 2007), 247.

60 See ibid., 247.

61 Ibid., 251.

62 See ibid., 239.

63 Institution of higher education in the Islamic sciences.

64 Kumar, *The Politics of Gender* (see note 59), 243–244.

wie sie der Nation begegnet, die sie mit anderen SchülerInnen teilt: Kinofilme und Lieder, die sie typischerweise im Radio, im Fernsehen oder über Lautsprecher hört, welche ihren Klang auf großzügige Weise in den Straßen und Vierteln verstärken".[61]

Die wirkungsvollsten Orte für das Erlernen eines gemeinsamen Habitus sind also die *Mohallas* in der Provinzstadt,[62] wo Grenzen dazu tendieren zu verschmelzen, wie dies Zeenat, einer Studentin an der *Madrasa*[63] *Hamidia Rizvia* widerfuhr. Ihre siebenköpfige Familie lebt in einem Zimmer im vierten Stock eines Hofhauses, das sie mit anderen muslimischen Familien teilt, wo sie lernt, „wie man sich das Badezimmer auf dem Treppenabsatz mit der ausgedehnten Familie teilt, wie sie in dem Raum vor ihrer Tür mit ihrer Mutter und allmählich auch alleine kocht, jedes Mal sauber zu machen und den Ort in makellosem Zustand zu hinterlassen und im Übrigen eine totale Funktionsoffenheit der häuslichen Räume zu praktizieren. Alle Materialien wurden nach dem Gebrauch weggeräumt. Kein Raum wurde nach seiner Funktion benannt, als der Ort ‚für‘ irgendeine bestimmte Tätigkeit, Schlafen inbegriffen. Das Zimmer wurde abwechselnd ein Schlafzimmer, ein Esszimmer, ein Wohnzimmer, ein Hobbyraum, ein Arbeitszimmer, ein Arbeitsplatz".[64]

In einer anderen Variante des Hofhauses, einem mit Räumen auf den drei Seiten, wird eine Erschließung und Kontrolle entlang der diagonalen Axe von der Schwiegermutter im Haus ausgeübt. Von hier aus verwaltet und beobachtet sie ihre Familie, um sich die Freiheit zunutze zu machen, „Zeit mit ihren Kindern in ihren Räumen zu verbringen, sprich denen der Mutter und denen der Kinder, und eine generationsübergreifende Solidarität aufzubauen".[65] Von außen betrachtet, ist dies der romantische Ort der gemeinsamen Erziehung des Kindes, einer gemeinschaftlichen Häuslichkeit zwischen Familien und lebenslangem Lernen. Von innen betrachtet, verbindet man diese Orte mit kulturellen Werten, die zwischenmenschliche Beziehungen, persönliche Identität, Ehre und Scham als Funktionen der häuslichen Umgebung und ihrer Biopolitik ansehen.[66]

Dies löst einen verzerrten Entwicklungsverlauf der Geschichte aus, eine umstrittene Erklärung eines Prinzipienmangels im architektonischen Diagramm. Die Matrix der miteinander verbundenen Räume als primitive Planung zu übersetzen, die geradezu darum bittet, zu etwas Differenzierterem entwickelt zu werden, brachte die moderne Definition von Privatheit hervor.[67] Das Diagramm lies die Anzeichen für Freude an Gesellschaft und nachbarschaftlicher Umgebung als ein Risiko des Selbst in Gegenwart anderer unberücksichtigt und Raumprogramme wurden fortan als etwas extrem Geordnetes katalogisiert, Prinzipien der Architektur und Häuslichkeit darauf aufgebaut.[68]

Dadurch wurden nicht nur Raumprogramme, sondern auch die Strukturen des häuslichen Lebens, auf die die Bauindustrie als sichere Gestaltungsmodelle zurückgreift, radikal umgestaltet: „große Häuser, kleine Häuser, Unterkünfte der Bediensteten, Familienwohnungen, Geschäfts- und Freizeiträume".[69]

Diese Unterscheidungen beherrschen auch die Vision des Council of Architecture. Der Widerstand dagegen, den Austausch von räumlichem Wissen und empirischen Kooperationen staatenübergreifend zu ermöglichen, wird auch durch die Empfehlung gefördert, „dass es für Studierende passender wäre, in ihren eigenen Regionen ausgebildet zu werden, als eine andere weit entfernte und in einem völlig anderen Kontext verwurzelte Institution zu besuchen".[70] Englisch als Unterrichtssprache ist ein weiteres Abschreckungsmittel in einem Land, in dem es 22 offiziell anerkannte Sprachen gibt.[71] Durch die Einschränkung von Vielfalt büßt ein Weber in Varanasi die Gelegenheit ein, seine „Möglichkeiten, ein Feingefühl für textile Oberflächen wiederzugewinnen",[72] in eine körperliche und physische Architekturexistenz zu übersetzen, da er immer „strukturell statt einfach nur formell über die Muster nachdenken muss, die auf der Oberfläche eines Entwurfs erscheinen".[73]

Wenn kultiviert, lässt sich Varanasis kosmisches Feld mit einer „Multiversity" gleichsetzen. Im Unterschied zu dominierenden Formen wie dem akademischen Kloster der Künste oder dem organischen System der Ingenieurschulen, „gibt es hier mehrere ‚Nationen‘ von StudenInnen, Fakultätsmitgliedern, Ehemaligen, TreuhänderInnen, öffentlicher Gruppen. Jede davon hat ihr Territorium, ihre Rechtsprechung, ihre Regierungsform. Es ist eine pluralistische Gesellschaft mit mannigfaltigen Kulturen. Koexistenz ist wahrscheinlicher als Einheit".[74] Ihr insti-

61 Ebd., 251.

62 Vgl. ebd., 239.

63 Islamische Hochschule

64 Kumar: *The Politics of Gender* (wie Anm. 59), 243f.

65 Ebd., 244.

66 Vgl. ebd.

67 Vgl. Robin Evans, *Translations from Drawing to Building and Other Essay*, London, 2011.

68 Vgl. ebd.

69 Ebd., 77.

70 Council of Architecture, „Prospective Plan for Growth" (wie Anm. 2), 24.

71 Vgl. Wikipedia, „Languages of India", online unter: https://en.wikipedia.org/wiki/Languages_of_India (Stand: 13. Oktober 2021).

72 Fer, Briony: „Anni Albers: Weaving Magic", *Tate Etc,* 10. Oktober 2018, online unter: https://www.tate.org.uk/tate-etc/issue-44-autumn-2018/anni-albers-weaving-magic-briony-fer (Stand: 11. Januar 2022).

73 Ebd.

74 Kerr, Clark: *The Uses of The University*, Cambridge 2001, 27.

In another iteration of the courtyard house, with rooms on the three sides, a confinement and a tension of the diagonal is created by the mother-in-law of the house. From here she administers and observes her family, only to take advantage of "the freedom to spend time with her children, in their room, hers and theirs, and build an inter-generational solidarity."[65] For an outsider, this is the romantic location of the communal upbringing of the child, of shared domesticity between families and lifelong learning. On the inside, these sites become associated with values of a culture that regard interpersonal relations, personal identity, honor, and shame as functions of the home environment and its bio-politics.[66]

This triggers a careless and biased trajectory of history, a contentious declaration of a lack of principle in the architectural diagram. To translate the matrix of connected rooms as primitive planning, begging to be evolved into something more differentiated, birthed the modern definition of privacy.[67] The diagram overlooked the indication of a fondness for company and proximity as a risk of the self in the presence of others, and house plans were henceforth catalogued as extremely ordered upon which both architecture and domesticity were to be raised.[68] Not only did it simply rearrange the entire house, but it also radically recast the pattern of domestic life which pervades the industry as distinct models of design: "large houses, small houses, servant quarters, family apartments rooms for business, for leisure."[69]

These distinctions dominate the Council of Architecture's vision, too. The resistance towards enabling the exchange of spatial knowledge and experiential collaborations across states is fostered by the recommendation "that it would be more relevant for students to be trained in their own regions rather than going to another institution located far away and rooted in a completely different context."[70] English as the medium of education is another deterrent for a country with 22 officially recognized languages.[71] By constricting diversity, a weaver of Varanasi loses the opportunity to translate his "ways to regain sensitivity towards textile surfaces"[72] into a bodily and corporeal existence of architecture as he always "has to think structurally rather than simply formally about the patterns that appear on the surface of a design."[73]

If cultivated, Varanasi's field of cosmos can then be likened to a multiversity. Unlike the singular academic cloister of the arts or the research organism of the engineering schools, "here are several 'nations' of students, of faculty, of alumni, of trustees, of public groups. Each has its territory, its jurisdiction, its form of government. It is a pluralistic society with multiple cultures. Coexistence is more likely than unity."[74] Its institutional character cannot be reduced or contained to a settlement of university blocks.[75] From each street, each house, each temple complex branches out an experimental studio of collective dialectical groups, made up of both students and professors whose role constantly evolves upon their spatial orientation. Varanasi is Canella's exploded university, its territory an obvious opposition to the amorphous, incoherent reality of India's architecture schools and the discrete, idyllic new campuses that are proliferating in geographic isolation.[76]

For when education has reformed, so has the architecture of institutions.[77] In an attempt to reread the city, to break from the limitations of its colonial past and religious temporality, Varanasi stands as a latent hotbed of protest against the outdated pedagogies, sterile academic examinations, and discriminatory guidelines of what constitutes an architecture for a new India.[78] A careful rereading focuses our gaze on the "family" as a site of education and social reproduction. To embrace the nature of the modern Indian person, in order to shift our reliance from the European model of history-writing as a singular narrative of subject formation, Varanasi's narrative necessarily embodies the plurality of learning.[79] ∎

65  Ibid., 244.

66  See ibid.

67  See Robin Evans, *Translations from Drawing to Building and Other Essays* (London, 2011).

68  See ibid.

69  Ibid., 77.

70  Council of Architecture, "Prospective Plan for Growth" (see note 2), 11.

71  See Wikipedia, "Languages of India," available online at: https://en.wikipedia.org/wiki/Languages_of_India (accessed 13 October 2021).

72  Briony Fer, "Anni Albers: Weaving Magic," *Tate Etc*, October 10, 2018, available online at: https://www.tate.org.uk/tate-etc/issue-44-autumn-2018/anni-albers-weaving-magic-briony-fer (accessed 11 January, 2022).

73  Ibid.

74  Clark Kerr, *The Uses of The University* (Cambridge, 2001), 27.

75  See ibid.

76  See Francesco Zuddas, "The Idea of the Università," *AA Files* 75 (2017): 119–131.

77  In "The Idea of the Università" Zuddas outlines how the architectures of various universities have transformed with the reform in educational policies: the UK's plate-glass universities, France's banlieues and grand ensembles, the USA's detached, self-sufficient campus, and Germany's industrial scaled complexes.

78  See Zuddas, "The Idea of the Università" (see note 75).

79  See Kumar, *The Politics of Gender* (see note 58).

tutioneller Charakter lässt sich nicht auf eine Ansiedlung von Universitätsgebäuden beschränken oder eingrenzen.[75] Von jeder Straße, jedem Haus, jedem Tempelkomplex aus verzweigt sich ein experimentelles Studio kollektiver dialektischer Gruppen, die sowohl aus StudentInnen als auch aus ProfessorInnen bestehen, deren Rolle sich ständig aus ihrer räumlichen Orientierung weiterentwickelt. Varanasi ist Canellas explodierte Universität, sein Territorium ein offenkundiger Gegensatz zur amorphen, fragmentarischen Realität von Indiens Architekturschulen und den eigenständigen, idyllischen neuen Campussen, die sich in geografischer Isolation immer mehr ausbreiten.[76]

Denn wenn die Ausbildung als reformiert gilt, dann gilt dies auch für die Architektur der Institutionen.[77] In einem Versuch, die Stadt neu zu lesen, sich von den Begrenzungen ihrer kolonialen Vergangenheit und religiösen Zeithaftigkeit zu lösen, verkörpert Varanasi einen latenten Nährboden des Protestes gegen die überholten Pädagogiken, die sterilen akademischen Prüfungen und diskriminierenden Richtlinien bezüglich dessen,

was eine Architektur für ein neues Indien ausmacht.[78] Eine erneute sorgfältige Betrachtung lässt uns das Augenmerk auf die „Familie" als Ort der Ausbildung und gesellschaftlichen Reproduktion richten. Das Narrativ von Varanasi verkörpert zwangsläufig die Pluralität des Lernens, indem es die Natur des modernen indischen Individuums anerkennt und das europäische Modell der Geschichtsschreibung als singuläres, übergeordnetes Narrativ ablöst.[79] ∎

*Übersetzung aus dem Englischen: Nikolaus G. Schneider*

75 Vgl. ebd.

76 Vgl. Zuddas, Francesco: „The Idea of the Università", *AA Files* 75 (2017), 119-131.

77 In „The Idea of the Università" legt Zuddas dar, wie sich die Architekturen verschiedener Universitäten mit der Reform in der Bildungspolitik verwandelt haben: die Flachglas-Universitäten des Vereinigten Königreichs, Frankreichs Banlieus und große Ensembles, die distanzierten, selbstgenügsamen Campusse der U.S.A. und Deutschlands Gebäudekomplexe im Industriemaßstab.

78 Vgl. Zuddas, „The Idea of the Università" (wie Anm. 76).

79 Vgl. Kumar, *The Politics of Gender* (wie Anm. 59).

4 Varanasi fragment plan, reproduced by the author after James Prinsep's map of Banaras, published in 1822 | Plan-Fragment der Stadt Varanasi basierend auf der Stadtkarte von James Prinsep (1822); Reproduktion der Autorin © Simran Singh

# Going beyond the Program
# Das Programm überschreiten

**Anne Lacaton and | und Jean-Philippe Vassal (L&V)
in Conversation with | im Gespräch mit Karine Dana (KD)**

1   Nantes School of Architecture, western façade | Architekturschule in Nantes, Westfassade, Lacaton & Vassal, Nantes, 2009 © Philippe Ruault

Anne Lacaton and Jean-Philippe Vassal designed the Nantes School of Architecture in 2009. In this interview, they look back on this decisive experience during which the concept of "free space" was considerably expanded, opening opportunities for completely new educational exploration.

KD: What are the specifics of an architecture school program, and could you reminisce on the genesis of this project?

L&V: Nowhere is there more knowledge, information, and energy about urban planning than in a school of architecture. More is in circulation there than in an urban planning studio, a city hall, or architects' offices. Sadly, though, there is no sense that these resources are visible, usable, and accessible. It seemed important to us that they should become so.

The thought that the school of architecture should be in the very center of the city of Nantes forced us to go beyond an architecture school program. We had to produce a system for the city. A school of architecture must certainly be part of the city's system. We wanted passers-by to be able to enter it and get into discussions, for students from other schools to be able to come in easily and critique and assess each other. We wanted these debates, these confrontations to happen.

Working on a school of architecture also raises the question of what to give the students by way of space for experimentation. The fact that we worked on the competition while we were involved in the Palais de Tokyo was important here.

In fact we were experimenting in real time with the grand dimension of spaces and the potential of a space in which you could find almost everything you need without the space being closed. On the contrary, the space could remain very porous both inwardly and in relation to the city: a large plane on which you could stay all day, until midnight, doing very different things, without being cut off from either the outside or the inside. We had undergone an experience of wandering that, with

its ambiences, its different heights, its variable lighting and its sequence of spaces of all kinds, took us completely beyond the logic of a building. This learning process infused our thinking on the Nantes School of Architecture. And the idea that what was happening at the Palais de Tokyo could happen in the school also looked interesting. It could be a place where artistic programming or events could create new internal dynamics.

KD: With this point of view, how did you envision the Nantes School of Architecture project and its "overflow" potential?

L&V: One of the main questions we asked ourselves while working on this project was: should we respond strictly to the program, as it is set out, or can we go beyond it?

If one envisages going beyond a program, then that means that some of the built area can become a free space, which is fundamental to the life of a project. And, as we see it, this free space must be generous in order to allow a real transformation: double the size of the surface anticipated from a program. That is always very hard to achieve. The question of going beyond is in fact intimately linked to the questions of the economy and the user's commitment. It crystallizes many fears. In the minds of many project owners it is impossible to stay within a given budget by going beyond a program. Any program would be inseparably defined by the ratio of surface area to construction cost. Today it is very difficult to escape from this economy/budget/programme system which determines standards and prices per square meter, and which always leads to doing the bare minimum or very little more. This fear of going over budget is a real brake on the possibility of overflowing the program.

And if, in the course of competitions, an expectation of expanding the concept is expressed, one senses that the first hint this triggers is a kind of retreat by the applicants, as if fearing they will not be able to extricate themselves. Moreover, giving this additional space, which equates to surfaces whose function cannot be anticipated, puts users in an unusual situation: they

Anne Lacaton und Jean-Philippe Vassal haben 2009 die Architekturschule in Nantes realisiert. Im Rahmen dieses Gesprächs kommen sie heute auf diese entscheidende Erfahrung zurück, in deren Lauf das Konzept der Freiflächen stark erweitert wurde und ganz neue pädagogische Erkundungen möglich gemacht hat.

**KD:** Was ist das Spezifische am Programm für eine Architekturschule, und könntet ihr die Entwicklungsgeschichte des Projekts aufrollen?

**L&V:** Nirgendwo anders kommt ein höheres Maß an Kenntnissen, Informationen und Energie für Stadtplanung zusammen als in einer Architekturschule. Es ist dort mehr davon im Umlauf als in einem Atelier für Stadtplanung, einem Rathaus oder Architekturbüros. Leider hat man nicht das Gefühl, dass diese Ressourcen sichtbar, nutzbar und zugänglich sind. Es schien uns wichtig, dass sie es werden.

Der Gedanke, dass die Architekturschule mitten im Zentrum der Stadt Nantes stehen sollte, zwang uns regelrecht dazu, das Programm im Kern zu überschreiten. Es galt ein System für die Stadt zu schaffen. Denn eine Architekturschule muss zweifellos Teil des urbanen Systems sein. Wir wollten, dass PassantInnen Zutritt zur Schule haben und dort diskutieren können, dass Studierende von anderen Universitäten problemlos zu Besuch kommen und sich gegenseitig kritisieren können. Dass diese Debatten, diese Auseinandersetzungen existieren können.

Eine Architekturschule zu entwerfen, führt auch zu der Frage, was man den Studierenden als Erfahrungs- und Experimentierraum zur Verfügung stellt. Dass wir unseren Beitrag am Wettbewerb entwickelt haben, während wir mit dem Umbau des Palais de Tokyo befasst waren, spielte dabei eine wichtige Rolle.

Denn dort erlebten wir damals in Echtzeit die Größendimension der Räume und das Potenzial eines Volumens, in dem man so gut wie alles Benötigte finden konnte, ohne den Raum abzuschließen. Im Gegenteil, es konnte nach innen wie auch zur Stadt sehr durchlässig bleiben: eine weitläufige Freifläche, auf der man sich den ganzen Tag bis Mitternacht aufhalten konnte und ganz unterschiedliche Dinge tun, ohne von der Außenwelt abgetrennt oder im Inneren beschnitten zu werden. Die dort vorhandenen Stimmungen, Deckenhöhen, variablen Beleuchtungen und Raumsequenzen verschafften uns ein Erlebnis des Umherwandelns, das unsere Denkweise eines Gebäudes erweiterte. Dieser Lernprozess ist in die Entwurfsgedanken der Architekturschule in Nantes eingeflossen. Die Vorstellung, dass das, was wir im Palais de Tokyo erlebten, auch in der Schule stattfinden könnte, schien uns interessant. Es könnte ein Ort sein, an dem künstlerische Projekte oder Veranstaltungen neue innere Dynamiken erzeugen würden.

**KD:** Wie habt ihr mit Blick darauf das Projekt der Architekturschule Nantes in seiner Kraft zur Entgrenzung in Planung genommen?

**L&V:** Eine der Hauptfragen, die wir uns bei der Arbeit an diesem Projekt gestellt haben, war folgende: Muss man sich streng nach dem Programm richten, wie es vorgelegt wurde, oder darf man es überschreiten?

Die Überschreitung eines Programms zu planen, bedeutet, dass ein Teil der gebauten Flächen zum Freiraum werden kann. Und das ist fundamental für das Leben eines Projekts. Dieser Freiraum muss aus unserer Sicht großzügig bemessen sein, um eine echte Veränderung zu bewirken: die von einem Programm erwartete Fläche sollte verdoppelt werden. Was konkret umzusetzen sehr schwierig bleibt. Die Frage der Überschreitung hängt ja eng zusammen mit den wirtschaftlichen Verhältnissen und dem Engagement der NutzerInnen. Da bündeln sich eine Menge Ängste. Nach Auffassung vieler BauherrInnen ist bei Programmänderungen das bewilligte Budget unmöglich einzuhalten. Für sie wird jedes Programm untrennbar vom Verhältnis von Fläche zu Baukosten definiert. Es ist heute sehr schwierig, sich diesem System aus Wirtschaftlichkeit, Budget und Programm zu entziehen, das Standards und Quadratmeterpreise setzt, die immer dazu führen, dass man nur das Mindeste tut – oder doch kaum mehr als das. Diese Angst vor der Budgetüberschreitung bildet für das Überschreiten des Programms einen echten Hemmschuh.

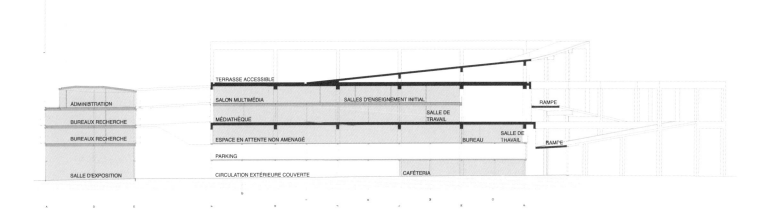

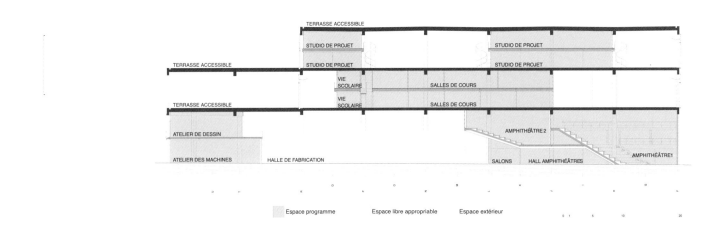

2 Nantes School of Architecture, longitudinal sections | Architekturschule in Nantes, Längsschnitte © Lacaton & Vassal

wonder how they can use the unprogrammed spaces linked to the program overreach. And this raises the question of their commitment to do something with this space.

We were able to experiment with this condition of exceeding the program in realizing the Nantes School of Architecture, and also the Cité Manifeste in Mulhouse and the FRAC Nord-Pas De Calais in Dunkirk—three projects for which we doubled the requested surface areas while remaining within the allocated budget. We were certainly accorded a certain amount of trust, which allowed these projects to succeed, but we had to face this very restrictive logic of cost-per-square-meter together with a fixed program budget, and we had to carry conviction. Many possibilities were suggested at the time of the competition for the school, but there were contradictions between the expectations, or the dream of the director and the teachers, who wanted to give freedom through space, and the program of the

Ministry of Culture, which was more restrictive and had to be adjusted in relation to the surface areas and the budget. We therefore played with surfaces that did not appear in the ratio of habitable surfaces. The roof—a high square in the sky—and the ground floor—a space under stilts with very little planning—were approached in this sense. Highly connected to the city, these two levels are crucial for the general functioning of the school and act entirely as free spaces.

KD: This question of exceeding the program correlates with the question of structural freedom, or how to build structures in which anything can result …

L&V: To make exceeding the program possible, one must work on surfaces of great potential, and hence from a structure that enables them. For the Nantes School of Architecture, the natural ground is the most "capable" surface. We kept it, with its

Bei Wettbewerben kommt zwar oft zum Ausdruck, dass Überschreitung erwartet wird, aber sobald man sich in Richtung Flächenvermehrung bewegt, merkt man, wie die Auftraggeber zurückzucken, als fürchteten sie, in eine Patsche zu geraten. Zusätzlichen Raum bereitzustellen, der Flächen mit unabsehbaren Funktionen erbringt, versetzt die NutzerInnen im Übrigen auch in eine besondere Lage: Sie müssen sich fragen, wie sie die aus der Überschreitung des Programms erwachsenen, nicht-programmierten Räume verwenden wollen. Damit kommt das Engagement der NutzerInnen ins Spiel, etwas aus diesem Raum zu machen.

Die Situation einer Programmüberschreitung haben wir bei der Realisierung der Architekturschule in Nantes erlebt, aber auch bei der Cité Manifeste in Mulhouse und beim FRAC Nord-Pas De Calais in Dünkirchen, drei Projekten, bei denen wir die geforderten Flächen verdoppelt und zugleich das bewilligte Budget eingehalten haben. Sicher hat man uns ein gewisses Vertrauen entgegengebracht, das diese Projekte zum Erfolg führte, dabei waren wir aber mit der sehr restriktiven Logik von Quadratmeterpreis und programmdefiniertem Budget konfrontiert und mussten überzeugen. Beim Wettbewerb für die Architekturschule in Nantes kamen viele Möglichkeiten zur Sprache, doch die Erwartungen widersprachen einander: Rektor und

Lehrende träumten davon, Freiheit durch Raum zu gewähren, während das Kulturministerium mit seinem rigideren Programm Flächen und Budget festschreiben wollte. Deshalb haben wir mit Ausdehnungen gespielt, die nicht unter die Quote der zweckgebundenen Flächen fallen. In diesem Sinn wurde das Dach zu einem Begegnungsort unter freiem Himmel und aus dem Erdgeschoss ein weitgehend unverplanter Raum unter Pfeilern. Diese beiden stark mit der Stadt verknüpften Ebenen sind ausschlaggebend für den allgemeinen Betrieb der Schule und fungieren voll und ganz als Freiflächen.

**KD**: Die Frage der Überschreitung des Programms korreliert mit der Frage der strukturellen Freiheit oder wie man Strukturen baut, in denen alles entstehen kann …

**L&V**: Programmüberschreitungen zu ermöglichen, setzt in der Tat voraus, dass man mit Oberflächen mit großem räumlichem Potenzial arbeitet, also mit einer Struktur, die so etwas erlaubt. Bei der Architekturschule in Nantes war bereits das natürliche Terrain die geeignetste Oberfläche. Wir haben es mit seinen wenigen Mankos und seinen vielen Qualitäten erhalten und eine große Bedachung in 24 Metern Höhe entworfen, dazu eine Außenrampe, die wie ein Verkehrsweg funktioniert und das Erdgeschoss mit dem Terrassendach ebenso verbunden wie mit

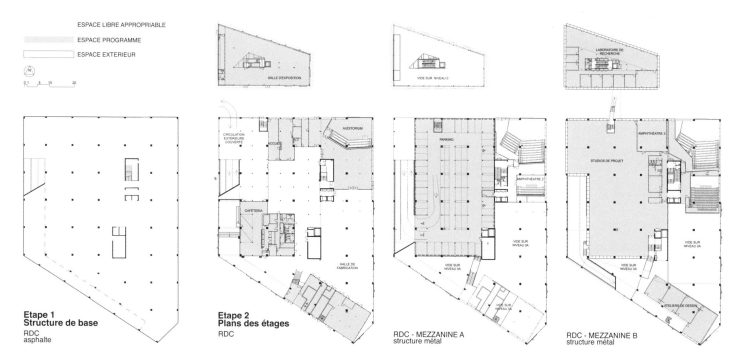

3   Floor plans of levels 0, 0A, 0B (ground floor) | Grundrisse der Ebenen 0, 0A, 0B (Erdgeschoss) © Lacaton & Vassal

allen zwischen Boden und Dach geschaffenen Räumen, die jeweils eigene Klimata aufweisen und Unterrichtssäle, Bibliothek, Studios usw. enthalten.

Unser Konstruktionsverfahren bestand hauptsächlich in einer Primärstruktur aus vorgefertigten Betonpfosten und Hohlraumbodenplatten von großer Belastbarkeit und starker Tragfähigkeit: 1 Tonne pro Quadratmeter. Dieses Potenzial war die notwendige Voraussetzung dafür, dass die Geschossdecken auch als Böden funktionierten. Wir haben ein breites Gerüst geschaffen, damit es möglichst wenig Stützen und Fundamentpunkte erfordert. Durch das Beziehungssysem, das diese Superstruktur enthält, erzeugt sie so etwas wie einen vertikalen Urbanismus, der sehr interessant ist. Hinsichtlich ihrer Tragfähigkeit entlastet sie die darin eingelassene leichte Sekundärstruktur aus Metall, die einfach zu montieren und kostengünstig ist. Indem wir mit den Möglichkeiten von Zwischengeschossen spielten, haben wir sehr viele mehr oder weniger beheizte, offene oder helle Raumvariationen definiert. Sobald das Gerippe mit seinem hohen Fassungsvermögen aufgebaut ist, stellt sich die Frage der Architektur und wie die Räume darin eingegliedert sein sollen. Wie bei der Cité Manifeste in Mulhouse wurden die Nutzräume im Inneren eingeklinkt, nachdem Struktur und Hülle standen.

Bei allen Programmen, mit denen wir uns auseinandersetzen, achten wir darauf, sehr weit gefasste, möglichst zwangfreie und anpassungsfähige Strukturen zu konzipieren, deren Konstruktionselemente – Raster, Fassaden, Trennwände – voneinander unabhängig sind. Die Suche nach struktureller Freiheit, die sich durch alle unsere Projekte hindurchzieht, trifft sich mit der Idee, den Raum als ein Loft aufzufassen: Wie lassen sich die denkbar größten Flächen und Volumen auf die kostengünstigste Weise herstellen?

Diese Absicht impliziert eine Logik der Mehrung, des Zuwachses eines zentralen Raums, dem man mehr Tiefe gibt, als es dem Standard nach normalerweise geschähe. Bei der Architekturschule in Nantes liegen zwischen den Fassaden 60 Meter Tiefe, die wir, statt sie zu aufzubrechen, gefüllt haben. Wenngleich Umriss und Länge der Fassade durch das Terrain vorgegeben sind, entsteht dadurch ein zusätzlicher Innenraum, mit dem sich andere Raumstimmungen herstellen lassen.

Für die Architekturschule in Nantes haben wir an der Idee des freien Grundrisses gearbeitet, aber auch an der des freien Volumens. Zugleich stellt dieses Projekt die Vorstellung einer

Standardhöhe infrage. Wir haben uns überlegt, wie ein in seiner Höhe möglichst flexibler und anpassungsfähiger Raum beschaffen sein sollte und zwischen den Bodenplatten vertikale Abstände von 7 bis 10 Metern vorgesehen. Höhe zu schaffen, bietet sehr interessante Möglichkeiten der Raumunterteilung. In Nantes können die Höhenmaße zwischen den Geschossen durch 2 oder 3 geteilt oder auch in ihrer vollen Spannweite behalten werden. Durch den Ansatz des freien Volumens lassen sich außerdem verschiedenen Funktionen entsprechende Beleuchtungen vorsehen, das heißt, man kann jeweils spezifisch an die Fassade anschließen, aber auch an den zentralen Raum, in den je nach seiner Partitionierung mehr oder weniger viel Licht einfällt.

Von Programmüberschreitung zu sprechen, heißt, auch von Möglichkeiten unterschiedlicher Atmosphären zu sprechen. Es ist ja völlig klar, dass es die Überdimensionierung und der zusätzliche Raum sind, die es erlauben, Raumstimmungen auszuprobieren und zu überprüfen, dass ein Programm gut funktioniert.

Der Freiraum begann also bereits im Entwurfsprozess. Wir haben uns die Freiheit genommen, diese tragfähige Großstruktur zu konzipieren, die eine flexible Sekundärstruktur enthält. Der Überschuss an Tragkraft und Fassungsvermögen bringt viel und hat es uns erlaubt, auf Entwicklungen und Veränderungen einzugehen, die im Lauf der Projektierung, während des Baus und nach der Fertigstellung eingetreten sind. So wurde anstelle einer Parkebene eine zusätzliche Werkstätte von 1.000 Quadratmetern eingezogen, außerdem ein Auditorium und in gemeinsamer Trägerschaft mit der École Centrale eine riesige Maschine zur digitalen Modellherstellung.

KD: Wie haben sich mit Blick auf diese Freiheitsräume die Nutzungen entwickelt?

L&V: Die Architekturschule Nantes ist seit zehn Jahren in Betrieb und was dort zustande kam, ist wirklich weit gespannt. Alles ist möglich. Die Schule zählte bei ihrer Eröffnung drei Vereine und beherbergt heute 17 mit ganz unterschiedlichen Profilen. Sie alle legen enorm viele Projekte vor. Auch das zur Stadt geöffnete Auditorium bietet interessante Austauschmöglichkeiten. Es wird übrigens oft von aushäusigen ReferentInnen genutzt. Im Rückblick sieht man, dass die NutzerInnen der

4   Ramp and terrace on level 2A with stairs leading to the terrace facing West | Rampe und Terrasse auf Ebene 2A mit Treppe auf die zur Westseite ausgerichteten Terrasse, Lacaton & Vassal, Nantes 2009 © Philippe Ruault

few defects and its many qualities, and imagined a large roof 24 meters above it, along with an external ramp functioning as a roadway and connecting ground floor to roof terrace, and all the created spaces between the two, with their specific climates and containing classrooms, library, studios, etc.

Our construction plan involved a primary structure of prefabricated concrete columns and high-capacity, high-resistance alveolar floors: 1 tonne per square meter. This was the necessary precondition for the ceilings to function as floors. We created a wide framework, so as to minimize the number of columns and foundation points needed. The system of relationships this superstructure contains generates a very interesting form of vertical urbanism. In terms of capacity, it supports a light metallic secondary structure that fits inside and is easy to assemble and cost-efficient. Thus, by playing on the possibilities of the mezzanine, we have defined plenty of variations of spaces, heated, open, or lit in different degrees. Once this large-capacity framework is assembled, the question arises of the architecture and the way it integrates this space. Just as at the Cité Manifeste in Mulhouse, the homes were slotted in once the structure and the envelope were in place.

Whatever the programs we tackle, we always aim to design structures that are highly expansive, not too limiting, and adaptable, and whose construction elements—networks, façades, partitions—are uncoupled. This quest for structural freedom, which runs through all our projects, is in line with thinking of space as a loft: how to produce the largest imaginable surfaces and volumes, as economically as possible?

Such an objective implies thinking in terms of increasing, of enlarging a central space and giving it more depth than it would generally be allotted. For the Nantes School of Architecture, 60 meters separates the façades, space that we filled, instead of digging it out. While the perimeter and the alignment of the façade are determined by the ground, we take advantage of any extra interior space to produce other sorts of moods.

For the school of architecture in Nantes, we worked to an open plan concept, but also to one of open volume. This goes on to question the notion of standard height. In adopting inter-story heights of seven to ten meters, we asked ourselves what would be the nature of a space that was as flexible and adaptable as possible in its vertical dimension. Increasing height offers very interesting possibilities for redividing a space. In Nantes, heights between levels are divisible into two or three, or are left in their full amplitude. This free volume approach also allows one to consider differing levels of lighting to accord with different functions, and thus to link in a specific way to the façades, just as to the central interior space, where light will penetrate to a greater or lesser extent according to the way the space is partitioned.

To consider exceeding a program is to consider the possibility of different ambiances. We realize that it is this super-dimension and the extra space that allow us to experiment with ambiances and to verify that a program works well.

So the free space began in the design process. We took the liberty of designing this large, functional structure containing a flexible secondary structure. This excess capacity has a lot of advantages, and it allowed us to adapt to evolutions and modifications that occurred in the course of the project, of the construction itself, and after hand-over. Thus, an extra thousand-square-meter workshop was added at ground-floor level in place of parking space, as also were an amphitheater and a huge digital model-making machine shared with the École Centrale.

KD: How have the uses of these free spaces evolved?

L&V: The Nantes School of Architecture has operated for ten years now, and what has been done there is extremely varied. Everything is possible. The school which encompassed three associations at its opening, today shelters seventeen, of very varied status. All of them have a great deal to offer. The amphitheater, being open to the city, offers interesting possibilities for interaction to it as well. Looking back, one can see that the school's users quickly seized on these additional spaces, something we had already seen in housing spaces we have created, from the Latapie house to the Cité Manifeste, or, later, the 500 housing units of the Grand Parc in Bordeaux.

Schule von den zusätzlichen Räumen ziemlich schnell Besitz ergriffen haben – ein Phänomen, das wir auch bei den von uns realisierten Wohnräumen beobachten konnten, seien es die Maison Latapie oder die Cité Manifeste oder später dann die 500 Wohneinheiten der Cité du Grand Parc in Bordeaux. Das Programm zu überschreiten, erlaubt tatsächlich eine Vervielfachung der Nutzungsvorhaben. So funktionieren in der Schule traditioneller Unterrichtsraum, Projektstudio und Modellwerkstätte nicht voneinander isoliert: Alles ist vernetzt. Die Räume steuern sich gegenseitig und reagieren aufeinander. Deshalb ist es möglich, einen Kurs in einem Studio zu besuchen und gleich nebenan Experimente anzustellen, oder im Studio etwas aufzuführen, auf den freien Flächen Kurse abzuhalten usw. Diese Beschaffenheit regt zu Nutzungserweiterungen, zu Projekten im Projekt an. Andererseits sind diese Freiräume situierte Räume. Sie sind durch unterschiedlichen Lichteinfall und Belüftung lokalisierbar. Diese ambientalen Eigenschaften begünstigen unterschiedliche Aktivitäten.

In die Zirkulationsräume eingebunden, werden diese Räume für nicht festgelegte Nutzungen in ihrer starken Ausdehnung eben viel mehr als das und bleiben doch gleichzeitig auch Zirkulationsräume. Diese Doppeleigenschaft ist sehr interessant. Freiräume sind Zirkulationsräume, die auch zu Nutzungsräumen werden: Räume zum Unterrichten, Aufführen, Experimentieren, Räume der Lehre, die fundamental anders sind. Diese Auslegung ermutigt zur Erfindung. Denn sobald ein Zirkulationsraum überdimensioniert ist, können dort andere Dinge stattfinden, und das lässt die angrenzenden Funktionsräume reagieren. Es handelt sich um einen doppelten Raum, der von einer gewissen Beweglichkeit erfasst wird. Sollte man diesen Raum mit einer häuslichen Funktion vergleichen, könnte man sagen, dass er einem Wohnzimmer vergleichbar ist. Während die Klassen wie „Zimmer" funktionieren, wird der Freiheitsraum zu einem Wohnbereich: einem Raum der Anregung, des Kommentars, des Austauschs. Und gerade da wird es interessant. Im Programm selbst existiert aber dieser Raum nicht. Dort gibt es nur „Zimmer". Niemals wird ein Programm vorgeben, dass Studierende sich irgendwo auf den Boden setzen und diskutieren können … Auch Möglichkeiten zu Aufführungen, Sport, Yoga, Kino oder Tanz waren im Programm nicht vorgesehen. Ein Programm sieht niemals nicht-programmierte Räume vor.

Die Entwicklung der Architekturschule Nantes verläuft im Sinn des Entwurfs, aber die Nutzenden sollten darauf achten, dass der Freiraum nicht ständig ausgefüllt wird. Darin liegt die Schwierigkeit. Die zusätzlichen Räume sind keine Räume, die darauf warten, bespielt zu werden, sondern sie sollten zum Zirkulieren genutzte und belegbare Flächen bleiben, die sich füllen lassen, sich aber auch leeren können, damit das Verhältnis zu den angrenzenden Räumen im Gleichgewicht bleibt. Es bedarf einer besonderen Wachsamkeit, denn wenn alles belegt wird, funktioniert das Projekt nicht mehr. Das bedeutet auch, dass Nutzungen abgesprochen und koordiniert werden müssen.

KD: Welche Faktoren bewirken, dass man sich nicht in einem „Gebäude" fühlt, wenn man sich im Innern dieser Schule bewegt?

L&V: Wie in einem großen Loft hat man in der Architekturschule Nantes keine Angst, irgend etwas kaputtzumachen. Alles ist robust. Alles ist einsatzbereit. Und man ist in ständigem Kontakt zur Außenwelt. Man geht umher, als wäre man an der freien Luft. Man spürt, dass man sich den Raum aneignen kann, denn seine Dimension, seine Höhenmaße verweisen auf nichts. Nie befindet man sich in Kammern. Alle diese Parameter führen dazu, dass man sich nicht in einem Gebäude fühlt, sondern in einer Landschaft. Wenn man vor der Bibliothek steht, meint man nicht, vor einem Ort im Inneren eines Gebäudes zu stehen, sondern draußen. Letztlich kennzeichnen viele Parameter diese – in keiner Weise generischen – Räume, deren Nutzungen und Inneneinrichtungen ambitioniert und sehr ausgeklügelt sind. Das gleiche Gefühl, in einer Landschaft zu gehen, hat man im Palais de Tokyo: ein kontinuierliches Bodensystem, eine Abfolge aufeinander bezogener Räume, die am Begriff der Grenze rütteln und es erlauben, sehr weit zu blicken – bis in die Welt hinaus.

Dieser Umgang mit dem Erdgeschoss und dem Dach, zwischen denen Räume untereinander vernetzt werden, nimmt Bezug auf die Überlegung, die Cedric Price in *The Invisible Sandwich* anstellt. In seinem Text spricht er von der besonderen Beschaffenheit dreigeschossiger Gebäude und zumal von der Beschaffenheit der mittleren Etage. Die Eigenart dieses Raums hängt ihm zufolge mit seiner Möglichkeit des Kontakts zu zwei ganz unterschiedlichen Raumkategorien zusammen, nämlich dem Boden und dem Dach, wo sich Gewächshäuser und Festzelte aufstellen lassen. Die Qualität des Mittelraums besteht in seiner möglichen Doppelbeziehung zur Straße, zur Stadt, zum Himmel. Das ist die ihm eigene Beschaffenheit, und er bietet viel Gelegenheit zu räumlichen Entdeckungen. Dieser Gedanke ist sehr schön. In der Architekturschule in Nantes interagieren die Räume in unterschiedlichen Atmosphären zwischen Boden und Dach miteinander, wie sie dank einer Außenrampe auch gemeinsam in Beziehung zu diesem Boden und Dach stehen. So lassen sich aus dieser Ausgangstopografie von Boden und Dach viele unterschiedliche Situationen gestalten. ∎

*Übersetzung aus dem Französischen: Stefan Barmann*

Going beyond the program allows us to multiply the number of projected uses. Thus, the school's traditional classrooms, the project studio, and the model workshop do not function in isolation. All are interconnected; the spaces control and respond to each other. So it is possible to hold a class in the studio and do experiments right next door, or to put on a performance in the studio while holding classes in the open space, and so on. This state of affairs prompts extensions of use, projects within the project. On the other hand, these free spaces are actual spaces. They are identifiable by their luminosity and their ventilation, more or less necessary. These qualities of atmosphere favor different activities.

While included in the spaces of circulation, these spaces of undefined use, being very expansive, become much more than that while yet remaining spaces of circulation. This double property is very interesting. Free spaces are spaces of circulation morphing into spaces of use, spaces for teaching, for performance, for experimentation: fundamentally different pedagogical spaces. This characteristic encourages invention. From the moment a circulation space is upsized, other things can happen there, and this causes the adjoining functional spaces to react. It is a double space, endowed with a certain mobility. If one had to look for an analogy with daily life, one could compare such a space with a living room. Classrooms monofunction as "rooms," but the free space becomes a living room: a space of incentive, of comment, of interaction. This is what is interesting. But in the program itself such space does not exist; there are only "rooms." A program will never require students to sit on the floor somewhere and talk … Likewise, the possibility of shows, sports, yoga, cinema or dance, was not provided for in the program. A program never envisions unprogrammed spaces.

The evolution of the Nantes School of Architecture in is in line with the project, but the users must be alert and ensure that the free space is not permanently filled. That is the difficulty. These additional spaces are not undifferentiated spaces but must remain in circulation and occupiable, able to be filled but also emptied in order to maintain a relationship of balance and interconnection with adjoining spaces. Particular vigilance is needed over these free spaces because, if all are occupied, the project no longer functions. And this implies that the users need to discuss the sharing of their use.

**KD**: How come one does not feel one is in a "building" when moving around inside this school?

**L&V**: As in a large loft, there is no fear of breaking anything in the Nantes School of Architecture. Everything is solid. Everything is available. And one is in permanent contact with the outside space. You walk as if you were outside. You feel you can appropriate the space, because its size, its height do not refer to anything. We are never in "rooms." All these things together create the feeling that one is not in a building but in a landscape. When we contemplate the library, we do not feel we are faced with a room inside a building but outside. Ultimately there are many factors—not at all generic—that characterize these spaces, whose uses and installations are ambitious and well thought out … We feel this same sensation of walking in a landscape at the Palais de Tokyo: a continuous floor system, successive and related spaces that shake up the notion of limit and that allow us to see a long way, even outside.

This approach, involving ground floor and roof with interconnected spaces in between, refers to a reflection by Cedric Price, "The Invisible Sandwich." In his text, he evokes the particular quality of buildings on three levels, and in particular the quality of the middle floor. For him, the attribute of this space resides in its capacity for contact with two categories of very different spaces: ground and roof, where glasshouses and marquees can be erected. The quality of the space in the middle is to have this possible twofold relationship with the street and city, and with the sky. This, its particular quality, offers plentiful opportunities for spatial discoveries: a very beautiful thought. In the Nantes School of Architecture, spaces, all with very different "feels" interact between ground and roof, both with each other and, thanks to an external ramp, with this ground and this roof. Thus, on the basis of this initial topography of the ground, and the roof, many different situations can be created. ▪

*Translation from French: John Wheelwright*

4  Anne Lacaton & Jean-Philippe Vassal, 2015 © Philippe Ruault

Jean-Louis Violeau

# Reactivating the Loire Front
## An Architecture School in Nantes

# Die Loire-Front reaktivieren
## Eine Architekturschule in Nantes

1   Architekturschule in Nantes, Dachterrasse | Nantes School of Architecture, roof terrace, Lacaton & Vassal, 2009 © Philippe Ruault

Pessimistic forecasts—and there are many—place the entire Île de Nantes below sea level by around 2050. If the oracle speaks the truth, then Anne Lacaton and Jean-Philippe Vassal may have given a visionary twist to their architecture once more, perhaps against their best intentions. The massive concrete pillars, on which simple plateaus rest, can be easily adapted, modeled after a Venetian palace, to the lake landscape soon to arise at this location. This project is in fact incredibly pervious, right down to the selection of bitumen as flooring for the ground level, which, situated along the banks of a moody river, was from the outset designed to be floodable. It is thus that this school of architecture taps into the house in Cap Ferret (1998), which preferred to embrace the tree in its lap than to fell it (just as the school prefers to let in the river rather than to channel it)—but also taps into the dream of an eco-neighborhood, which in Saint-Nazaire (2009) was so successfully and thoroughly innovated that the jury granted it second place. Just imagine, instead of moving into the green, arranging it in such a way that the verdant rises up through 160 housing units positioned on stilts 20 meters above the "natural soil." Lacaton & Vassal harbor utopian inspiration that has never been entirely forsaken.

**A Plan, a Ramp, a Structure: From "Less Is More" to "Cheap Is More."** Concrete prefabricates. The material condenses what words water down an advantage for architects who work concisely. No manifestation of an inspiration without a little idea that forms its base. Structures that "endure" harbor real ideas in their foundation, while those that age poorly generally have feet of clay. The banks of the River Loire in Nantes may be slippery, but Alexandre Chemetoff's urban idea that ended up reclaiming them was solid, and the architectural idea on which the ENSAN (Ecole nationale supérieure d'architecture de Nantes) was founded was already well tried and tested. When the school opened over ten years ago, the architect duo acknowledged this obligation right at the opening: "This project addresses a series of liberties, starting with those arising from urban planning."[1]

The primary structure of prefabricated concrete posts and hollow baseplates is demonstratively oversized? Yes, this strikes the eye: 1 ton per square meter of load-bearing capacity in the base plates,[2] which, by the way, is also one of the requirements for potential flexibility in the building. The spacing between the posts—10.80 meters—is thus wide enough to permit all possible partitioning and dividing-wall solutions. Therefore, the architects were the first to start filling this powerful primary structure with light secondary structures made of metal, which today house various studios for project seminars. At the same time, considering the structures built and the areas available, the cost of materials and the use of resources remain very low. A "poor" architecture that is nonetheless rich in possibility, ultimately meaning that "less is more"?[3] Though the shorthand, like all catchphrases, simplifies it somewhat, it still picks up on certain issues from this era, and certainly the significant ones.

This sequence of found freedoms now leads, at least in my eyes, to the path of the ramp—which, by the way, was exceedingly useful throughout the entire construction period. Complexity under the guise of simplicity: the ramp, in fact, sets beautiful spatial accents each time it transitions into the unconditional regularity of the plateau. Along its route, the wavy surfaces regularly meet the angular, giving rise to highly intimate spaces that amply open up to the city at the same time. Here I am thinking, with the south/southwest still in mind, most especially of the terrace on Level 1A and the small side storage area on Level 2A, where we as stranded colleagues gathered throughout the winter of 2020–21 to eat cold pizza at lunch under social distancing conditions. Then, on the same story, after passing the bend, there is a very lovely terrace facing west—which numerous skateboarders are still enjoying, despite the prohibitions on the part of private security guards hired this year by our building management.

1   "Parole de Lacaton et Vassal," recorded by Karine Dana, *AMC-Le Moniteur architecture* 185 (Februar 2009), 60–61, esp. 61.

2   Instead of the 500 kg/m² stipulated by the program.

3   This is the title selected by the students in my urban planning master's program at Sciences-Po Paris for their brilliant and spirited analysis of the position of the duo Lacaton-Vasall with their three successive projects. "Von less is more zu cheap is more: Ghita Azzouzi, Brunelle Charles, Caterina Dallolio, Juliette Fis, Sonia Kagan, Julie Le Bourhis, Benjamin Robert," *Repartir de l'existant pour bâtir la ville, le travail de Lacaton & Vassal à travers 3 projets* [Maison Latapie, Tour Bois-le-Prêtre, FRAC Nord-Pas-de-Calais], final report of the course "Genèse des Théories Architecturales et Urbaines," Sciences-Po Paris, Spring 2021, 38.

Pessimistische Prognosen, und sie sind zahlreich, sehen die gesamte Île de Nantes zum Horizont 2050 unterhalb des Wasserspiegels. Sollte sich das Orakel bewahrheiten, dürften Anne Lacaton und Jean-Philippe Vassal ihrer Architektur abermals – hier vielleicht gegen ihre Absicht – eine visionäre Wendung gegeben haben. Die mächtigen Betonpfeiler, auf denen schlichte Plateaus ruhen, lassen sich nämlich nach dem Vorbild eines venezianischen Palasts unschwer an die Seenlandschaft anpassen, die man uns nächstens an diesem Ort in Aussicht stellt. Tatsächlich ist dieses Projekt ungeheuer durchlässig, bis hin zur Wahl des Bodenbelags Bitumen für das Erdgeschoss, das, am Ufer eines launischen Flusses, von Beginn an als flutbar gedacht war. Auf diese Weise belehnt diese Architekturschule das Haus in Cap Ferret (1998), das den Baum lieber in seinem Schoß beließ als ihn zu fällen (so wie die Schule den Strom lieber einlässt als ihn zu kanalisieren), aber auch den Traum von einem Ökoquartier, das in Saint-Nazaire (2009) derart gut und gründlich innovierte, dass es, als die Jury ihr Urteil abgab, auf Rang zwei landete. Denken Sie nur, nicht mehr sich ins Grüne verteilen, sondern dieses so einrichten, dass es sich 160 Wohneinheiten hinauf erstreckt, die 20 Meter vom „Naturboden" entfernt auf Stelzen sitzen. Es gibt bei Lacaton & Vassal eine utopische Inspiration, der nie ganz entsagt wurde.

**Ein Plan, eine Rampe, eine Struktur: vom *less is more* zum *cheap is more*.** Beton baut vor. Der Werkstoff verdichtet, was die Wörter verwässern: Vorteil für die ArchitektInnen, die bündig ausführen. Keine Gebäude gewordene Eingebung, der nicht ihre kleine Idee zugrunde läge. Bauwerken, die „Bestand haben", steckt ein richtiger Gedanke im Fundament; solche, die schlecht altern, fußen im Allgemeinen auf einem tönernen. Die Ufer der Loire in Nantes mögen rutschig sein, aber der urbane Gedanke, den Alexandre Chemetoff fasste, der sie zurückeroberte, war solide, und der architektonische Gedanke, der am Ursprung der ENSAN (Ecole nationale supérieure d'architecture de Nantes) stand, war bereits wohl-erprobt. Gleich bei der Eröffnung der Schule vor mehr als zehn Jahren hat das Architektenpaar diese Bringschuld selbst eingeräumt: „Dieses Projekt trägt einer Reihe von Freiheiten Rechnung, angefangen bei denjenigen, die aus der städtebaulichen Planung erwachsen."[1]

Die Primärstruktur aus vorgefertigten Betonpfosten und Hohlraumbodenplatten ist demonstrativ überdimensioniert? Ja, das fällt ins Auge: 1 Tonne pro Quadratmeter Belastbarkeit der Bodenplatten[2], was übrigens auch zu den Voraussetzungen für die potenzielle Flexibilität des Gebäudes zählt. Die Abstände

zwischen den Pfosten – 10,80 Meter – sind demnach weit genug, um alle möglichen Aufteilungen und Zwischenwandlösungen zuzulassen. Daher haben die Architekten als die ersten damit begonnen, diese mächtige Primärstruktur mit leichten Sekundärstrukturen aus Metall zu füllen, die heute zahlreiche Ateliers für den Projektunterricht beherbergen. Dabei bleiben in Anbetracht der gebauten Volumen und gebotenen Flächen der Materialaufwand und Ressourcenverbrauch sehr niedrig. Eine „arme" Architektur, die aber reich an Möglichkeiten ist, im Endeffekt ein *less is more*?[3] Gewiss, die Kurzformel macht es, wie alle Schlagwörter, etwas einfach, greift aber doch bestimmte Anliegen der Epoche auf, und zwar nicht die belanglosesten.

Diese Sequenz von gefundenen Freiheiten führt nun, wenigstens für mich, zum Verlauf der Rampe – die übrigens in der gesamten Baustellenzeit überaus nützlich war. Komplexität unter dem Anschein von Schlichtheit: Tatsächlich setzt die Rampe schöne Raumakzente, jedes Mal, wenn sie mit der unbedingten Regelmäßigkeit der Plateaus in Berührung tritt. In ihrem Verlauf trifft nämlich das Gewellte regelmäßig auf das Eckige, wobei sehr intime Räume entstehen, die sich gleichzeitig weit zur Stadt öffnen. Dabei denke ich insbesondere, immer noch in süd/südwestlicher Ausrichtung, an die Terrasse der Ebene 1A und den kleinen seitlichen Abstellbereich auf Ebene 2A, wo wir uns im gesamten Winter 2020–21 als aufgelaufene KollegInnen scharten, um zu Mittag unter sanitären Einschränkungen kalte Pizzen zu verspeisen. Auf derselben Etage befindet sich dann, sobald man die Biegung passiert hat, eine sehr schöne, genau nach Westen ausgerichtete Terrasse – auf der trotz der Verbote seitens privater Wachleute, die dieses Jahr von unserer Verwaltungsleitung angeheuert wurden, immer noch zahlreiche Skateboarder unterwegs sind.

1  „Parole de Lacaton et Vassal" aufgezeichnet von Karine Dana, *AMC-Le Moniteur architecture* 185 (Februar 2009), 60–61, hier 61.

2  Statt der vom Programm vorgeschriebenen 500 kg pro Quadratmeter.

3  So lautet der Titel, den meine Masterstudierenden in Städtebau an der Sciences-Po Paris für ihre brillante und schwungvolle Analyse zur Position des Duos Lacaton & Vasall und deren drei aufeinander folgende Projekte gewählt haben. *Von less is more zu cheap is more*. Ghita Azzouzi, Brunelle Charles, Caterina Dallolio, Juliette Fis, Sonia Kagan, Julie Le Bourhis, Benjamin Robert, *Repartir de l'existant pour bâtir la ville, le travail de Lacaton & Vassal à travers 3 projets* [Maison Latapie, Tour Bois-le-Prêtre, FRAC Nord-Pas-de-Calais], Abschlussbericht des Kurses „Genèse des Théories Architecturales et Urbaines", Sciences-Po Paris, Frühjahr 2021, 38 Seiten.

2　Nantes School of Architecture, view from the terrace on Level 2A, western façade | Architekturschule in Nantes,
Blick von der Terrasse der Ebene 2A, Westfassade | Lacaton & Vassal, 2009 © Philippe Ruault

The architecture of Lacaton & Vassal makes one fortunate enough to never skip the same floors from one passageway to the next, a bit like one never skips the same passages when re-reading Proust. Sometimes one even misses, for a brief moment, a room or two in this school of 18,000 square meters (26,000 if you count the outside rooms). The program had called for 8,500 m² of usable floor space. After twenty-five years of academic life in the convoluted spaces of the old and distinguished École des Beaux-Arts in Paris (in the ENSA Paris-Malaquais), I intended to quickly analyze the apparently simple geometry of this "new" school. But I needed a year to ascertain, for instance, the entire span and quality of the rooms on Level 2A where scenography is taught. And then, yes, perhaps about two years to make headway on the grand lecture hall for the "marine engineering" elective on Level 2B.

Then there's the parking area situation. Vehicles can still be parked at the center of the school, which is a big advantage be-cause the use of scooters, as one may recall, is only feasible for city residents. So this parking area could have swallowed all of Level 0B, but we were able to "find," as it were, the necessary space to also accommodate a lecture hall with 150 seats. Note-worthy is how — on the story directly above, Level 0C, with a slightly lower ceiling height — room has been made for a plateau primarily used for teaching first-semester classes. As it is aligned due west, the space remains bright throughout the afternoon, and its depth permits all kinds of possible gatherings and group-ings, something that needs to be cultivated due to the uncer-tainty involved in forming teams early on in a study program.

With the exception of several rooms devoted to project work on Level 2A, it should be noted — and this is clearly a stroke of luck — that most of the project studios are situated in the west-ern part of the building and thus make maximum use of the course of the sun in wintertime. In the absence of a central light shaft, the core area of the expansive building remains dark, but

Die Architektur von Lacaton & Vassal verschafft einem das Glück, von einem Durchgang zum nächsten nie dieselben Etagen zu überspringen, ein wenig wie man beim Wiederlesen von Proust nie dieselben Passagen überspringt. Manchmal verpasst man sogar für einen kurzen Moment den einen oder anderen Raum in dieser Schule von 18.000 Quadratmeter (26.000 wenn man die Außenräume einrechnet). Das Programm hatte 8.500 Quadratmeter Nutzfläche verlangt. Nach 25 Jahren akademischen Lebens in den verschachtelten Räumlichkeiten der alten und ruhmreichen Pariser École des Beaux-Arts (in der ENSA Paris-Malaquais) gedachte ich die dem Anschein nach

schlichte Geometrie dieser „neuen" Schule rasch auszuloten. Aber ich brauchte ein Jahr, um beispielsweise die ganze Spannweite und Qualität der Räume auf Ebene 2A zu ermessen, die dem Unterricht in Szenografie dienen. Und dann, ja, vielleicht zwei Jahre, um in den großartigen Hörsaal für das Wahlfach „Schiffstechnik" auf Ebene 2B vorzustoßen.

Dann ist da die Geschichte mit der Parkfläche – das Auto findet noch Abstellmöglichkeiten im Kernbereich der Schule, und das ist ein großer Vorzug, denn die Nutzung von Rollern, daran darf erinnert werden, empfiehlt sich nur für die im Stadtgebiet Ansässigen –, diese Parkfläche also hätte die gesamte Ebene 0B einnehmen können, aber man „fand" sozusagen

3   Ramp leading to the vast terrace on level 2A | Rampe zur großen Terrasse auf Ebene 2A, Lacaton & Vassal, 2009 © Philippe Ruault

4    Studio space on level 2B (upper floor) | Studioräume auf Ebene 2B (Obergeschoss) | Lacaton & Vassal, 2009 © Philippe Ruault

this is really only noticeable on 1A. Starting at the level above, the broad interstitial spaces mitigate this effect, as they are enclosed and protected by large panes of opalescent polycarbonate. And thanks to the generous and freely accessible areas on Level 2A, there is always an option for students who wish to install or present their work in a different way. This has regularly proven especially valuable for the students of Pascal Amphoux, as they roll out their *transects* on "long tables," thus enabling them to effectively show the longitudinal development of their successive project fields.

Once Level 2 has been reached, then most of these rooms offer a direct view of the Loire as well, thus with the advantage of a dual and threefold orientation. The gem of the spacious Plateau 1A—the large, bright library—also faces due west, so toward the sea, at least if you imagine it from Nantes. The picture is tarnished, however, by the fact that it is often difficult to control the atmosphere of light in the spacious exhibition

room, which is situated on the ground floor of the building facing the Loire with ceiling-high glass walls on three sides. The coated floor, in turn, gives rise to occasional surprises with its path here being aligned to the embankment of the Loire.

**In the Beginning, a School Open to the City.** In a recently published book about "air conditions," the architect Emmanuel Doutriaux notes that this school in Nantes is "used as one would use a city."[4] It is not without reason that he titles the long chapter devoted to this building "Thélème-sur-Loire,"[5] being that it is hardly classifiable—although an ordinance of a very petty rule enacted on the occasion of the second lockdown in the fall of 2020 has not allowed the spatial resources of a school that,

4    Emmanuel Doutriaux, *Conditions d'air: Politique des architectures par l'ambiance* (Geneva, 2020).

5    Allusion to the Abbey of Thélème, which François Rabelais felt represented an ideal human community. Motto: "Do as you'd like." (Translator's note, Stefan Barmann.)

den nötigen Raum, um überdies einen Hörsaal mit immerhin 150 Plätzen unterzubringen. Bemerkenswert auf der Ebene genau darüber, der 0C, ist, bei einer allerdings etwas geringen Deckenhöhe, der Raum, der für ein überwiegend zum Unterricht der Anfangssemester dienendes Plateau freigelegt wurde. Dank seiner genau westlichen Ausrichtung bleibt er nämlich den gesamten Nachmittag über hell, und seine Tiefe erlaubt alle möglichen Zusammenkünfte und Gruppenbildungen, was wegen der Ungewissheit der Partnerbildungen zu Beginn des Studiengangs keineswegs zu vernachlässigen ist.

Mit Ausnahme einiger dem Projektunterricht gewidmeter Säle auf Ebene 2A ist festzustellen – und das ist eindeutig ein Glücksfall –, dass die meisten Projektateliers im Westteil des Gebäudes liegen und deshalb im Winter den Lauf der Sonne voll ausschöpfen. Mangels eines zentralen Lichtschachts bleibt der Kernbereich des ausgedehnten Gebäudes zwar dunkel, aber spürbar ist das eigentlich nur auf der 1A. Ab der Ebene darüber mildern die weitgespannten, von großen Schiebeflächen aus opaleszentem Polycarbonat geschützten und umschlossenen Zwischenräume diesen Effekt. Und dank der großzügigen frei verfügbaren Flächen auf Ebene 2A gibt es immer eine Lösung für Studierende, die ihre Arbeiten auf andere Weise anbringen oder präsentieren wollen. Regelmäßig ist das besonders den Studierenden von Pascal Amphoux zugute gekommen, die ihre *Transekte* auf „Langtischen" ausrollen und dadurch die Längserschließungen ihrer aufeinander folgenden Projektgebiete wirkungsvoll vor Augen führen konnten.

Sobald diese Ebene 2 erreicht ist, bieten diese Säle zudem mehrheitlich eine direkte Sicht auf die Loire und haben so den Vorteil doppelter oder dreifacher Ausrichtung. Auch das Schmuckstück des weitläufigen Plateaus 1A, die große helle Bibliothek, ist geradewegs gen Westen gewendet, zum Meer also, zumindest wenn man sich dieses von Nantes aus vorstellt. Getrübt wird das Bild jedoch dadurch, dass der weitläufige, im Erdgeschoss des Gebäudes zur Loire gelegene und dreiseitig auf ganzer Höhe verglaste Ausstellungsraum oft schwer zu bewältigende Lichtambientes aufweist. Der mit einem Belag versehene Boden, der an dieser Stelle der Uferböschung der Loire folgt, sorgt dagegen für manche Überraschungen.

**Am Anfang stand eine zur Stadt durchlässige Schule.** In einem kürzlich erschienenen Buch über „Luftverhältnisse" stellt der Architekt Emmanuel Doutriaux fest, dass man diese Schule in Nantes „nutzt, wie man es mit der Stadt tun würde".[4] „Thélème-sur-Loire"[5] überschreibt er nicht ohne Grund das lange Kapitel, das er diesem letztlich kaum einzuordnenden Gebäude widmet –wenngleich der Erlass eines ausgesprochen kleinlichen Reglements bei Gelegenheit des zweiten Lockdowns im Herbst 2020 es nicht erlaubt hat, die Raumressourcen einer Schule voll auszuschöpfen, die immerhin die bei weitem größte verfügbare Fläche pro StudentIn in Frankreich[6] bietet, nicht zu reden von der „naturgegebenen" Belüftung ihrer Pufferräume.

Dieses Gebäude zeigt, dass sich – von der Fabrik über das Loft zur Schule – das Symbolische verschieben kann. Die Durchlässigkeit der Räume ist hier in der Tat wesentlich, und man darf sich fragen, inwiefern nicht der *Haupt*eingang zum Gebäude in luftiger Höhe liegt, nämlich neun Meter über dem Boden auf der Ebene des (dritten) Plateaus 1A, auch *Place haute* genannt. Polyvalenz bringt diese Schule in Nantes wunderbar zum Ausdruck und widerspricht damit einem Architekturkritiker, der es für angebracht hielt, scheinheilig daran zu erinnern, dass es in einigen der sogenannten „Puffer"-Räume im Winter kalt und im Sommer heiß ist – weil er sich nicht vorstellen konnte, dass die Existenz dieser Räume im Programm schlicht gar nicht vorgesehen waren. Kritik kann (auch) blind sein. Womöglich gewollt?[7] Mit ihrer Fläche von ursprünglich 4.100 Quadratmetern setzen diese (vor Regen) geschützten Zwischenräume in der besonderen Funktionsweise der Schule den Schlussstein.

Die Fertigungshalle im Erdgeschoss ist wieder ebenso weitläufig, eindrucksvoll, hell und gut ausgestattet – der Vergleich mit dem Instrumentarium der Pariser Schulen und zumal Paris-Malaquais, wo ich mich gut auskenne, ist in dieser Hinsicht

4   Emmanuel Doutriaux, *Conditions d'air. Politique des architectures par l'ambiance*, Genève 2020.

5   Anspielung auf die Abtei Thélème, die bei François Rabelais für eine ideale menschliche Gemeinschaft steht. Motto: „Tu, was du möchtest." (A.d.Ü.)

6   Zur Erinnerung: 28,5 Quadratmeter pro StudentIn gegenüber 9,4 Quadratmeter in Val de Seine und 4,20 Quadratmeter in La Villette, der (wie in etlichen anderen Bereichen) am dürftigsten ausgestatteten von allen französischen Schulen. Belleville liegt bei 10,5 Quadratmeter. Nur die neue Schule in Clermont-Ferrand kann mit 23,5 Quadratmeter Nantes das Wasser reichen – dort ist die Gesamtfläche mit 18.000 Quadratmeter (SHON) die größte in Frankreich, für einen angenommenen Bestand von 800 Studierenden. Vgl. Kollektive Untersuchung der Studierenden von Pietro Cremonini, Philippe Dehan und Philippe Lauzanne ihres Studienabschlussprojekts (PFE) „Construire dans le construit" (Im Gebauten bauen), das 2018 den Umzug von der École de Paris-La Villette zur ganz nahe gelegenen „Halle aux cuirs" zum Programm hatte.

7   Valéry Didelon, „Valeur d'usage, valeur d'image: la nouvelle école d'architecture de Nantes", *Criticat* 8 (2011), 6–19.

5  First year student's integration course on the relationship of the human body to space, designed by choreographers and dancers, production hall |
Lehrveranstaltung für Studienanfänger zum Verhältnis von Körper und Raum, gestaltet von ChoreographInnen und TänzerInnen, Fertigungshalle,
Level 1A, Nantes, 2021 © Jean-Louis Violeau

after all, offers by far the largest available space per student in France[6] to be fully exploited, not to mention the "natural" ventilation of its buffer spaces.

This building shows that—from factories to lofts to schools—the symbolic can be shifted. The permeability of these spaces is in fact essential here, and one may well wonder whether the *main* entrance to the building is actually situated at an airy height, that is, nine meters above the ground on the level of (the third) Plateau 1A, also called *Place haute*. Polyvalence is expressed marvelously by this school in Nantes, thus contradicting an architecture critic who, quite sanctimoniously, felt it necessary to remark that some of the so-called "puffer" rooms are cold in the winter and hot in the summer—because he could not imagine that the existence of these rooms had simply not

been foreseen in the original plans. Criticism can (at times) be blind. Possibly deliberately so?[7] Originally having an area of 4,100 square meters, these interstitial spaces, which are protected (against rain), form the keystone of the special functional approach of the school.

6  As a reminder: 28.5 m² per student, as compared to 9.4 m² in Val de Seine and 4.2 m² in La Villette, making it the most poorly equipped of all French schools (which applies to many other areas as well). Belleville has 10.5 m² per student. Only the new school in Clermont-Ferrand, with its 23.5 m², can compete with Nantes—its total area of 18,000 m² (SHON) being the largest in France, catering to an assumed population of 800 students. Source: Collective study by the students of Pietro Cremonini, Philippe Dehan, and Philippe Lauzanne for the final project (PFE) of their degree program called "Construire dans le construit" (Building in the Built), which in 2018 thematically explored the move from the École de Paris-La Villette to the closely situated "Halle aux cuirs."

7  Valéry Didelon, "Valeur d'usage, valeur d'image: la nouvelle école d'architecture de Nantes," *Criticat* 8 (2011): 6–19.

174

gnadenlos. Aber auch hier ist das Virus durchgekommen, und so ist der Hallenboden fortan tapeziert mit grellgelben Lenkungs-und Zebrastreifen, die an einen Autobahnzubringer denken lassen – warum, weiß man nicht, doch offenbar reagiert Covid-19 auf die Farbe Gelb allergisch … Tendenziell ist auch die (verwaltungstechnisch) unkomplizierte Nutzbarkeit der Maschinen mit der Zeit drastisch zurückgegangen. Einige Kollegen, ich denke besonders an Michel Bertreux und Francis Miguet, haben es dennoch geschafft, ihre im Abschlussjahr Studierenden hochgradig davon profitieren zu lassen: Diese erfanden seltsame Weltraummaschinen, die sich vor drei Jahren aufgemacht haben, einen Campingplatz im Nachbar-Departement Morbihan zu erstürmen.

Es besteht jedenfalls durchaus ein Risiko, dass dieses Gebäude, wie schon das Centre Pompidou, seiner eigenen Hyperflexibilität in die Falle geht. Dies war den Architekten sehr wohl klar, zogen sie doch bereits bei der Eröffnung des Bauwerks bewusst eine Parallele zu dem berühmten Vorgänger, der schon „in die Falle seiner Hyperflexibilität" gelaufen sei. Irgendwo im Spannungsfeld zwischen Raum schaffen und Platz lassen habe ich in der Schule dann doch eine Zensurausübung überwiegend administrativer Herkunft beobachtet, allerdings keine oder wenig Selbstzensur seitens der Studierenden oder Lehrenden. „Die Reversibilität [des Centre Pompidou]", fuhren die Architekten fort, „ist nichtsdestoweniger noch immer gegeben. Eine Möglichkeit, der Aufteilung zu entgehen, besteht darin, groß zu sein, sehr viel zu groß. Dann wird es mit dem Aufteilen schwierig!"[8] Optimistisch. Allzu sehr? Nein, wozu sollte es sonst gut sein, Projekte zu schmieden!

Gewiss wurde die Dachterrasse, 2.500 Quadratmeter groß und 24 Meter oberhalb der Straße, nicht nach Maß ihrer Möglichkeiten genutzt. Wie hätte es anders sein sollen in unserer vom Sicherheitsdenken beherrschten Epoche? Vergessen wir nicht, dass es vor dem Virus schon den Antiterrorplan „Vigipirate" gab. Gleichwohl hat die Veranstaltungsreihe *Voyage à Nantes – Reise nach Nantes* dort manchen Sommer Quartier bezogen und auf spektakuläre Weise ein Auto – einen Citroën BX – am Rand des Abgrunds aufgepflanzt, ein temporäres Freilichtkino oder eine Skateboard-Rampe eingerichtet. Doch gibt es ein sehr viel trivialeres und alltäglicheres Risiko: Bei seiner Einweihung 2009 bot die Schule drei (oder sogar mehr) offiziell ins Erdgeschoss eingelassene Eingänge. Seit allzu langem bleibt davon nur noch einer, der zudem im Gefolge mehrerer Lockdowns mit Plexiglas verbarrikadiert und dem Sicherheitsimperativ des obligatorischen Zugangsausweises unterworfen ist. Der Zutritt zur Rampe vom Erdgeschoss aus ist seit 2020 versperrt – wie ja jeder weiß, benutzt das Virus vorzugsweise Rampen … Das Reale ist stärker als du! Es ist wie bei allen Abfallprodukten: Womöglich wird man es nie los. Und das Reale macht sich bemerkbar, wenn man sich stößt, versicherte eines Tages vor seinen mehr oder weniger verblüfften ZuhörerInnen der berühmte Jacques Lacan.[9] ∎

*Übersetzung aus dem Französischen: Stefan Barmann*

8    „Parole de Lacaton et Vassal" (Anm. 1), 61.

9    Im Original: „Il n'y a pas d'autre définition possible du réel que: c'est l'impossible quand quelque chose se trouve caractérisé de l'impossible, c'est là seulement le réel; quand on se cogne, le réel, c'est l'impossible à pénétrer." Jacques Lacan in einem Vortrag am Massachusetts Institute of Technoloogy am 2. Dezember 1975, veröffentlicht in *Scilicet* 6–7 (1976), 53–63.

The production hall on the ground level is again just as spacious, impressive, bright, and well equipped; the comparison with the instruments of the Paris schools, especially Paris-Malaquais, with which I am well familiar, is merciless in this respect. But here, too, the virus has managed to get through, so the floor of the production hall is now decorated with stripes in glaring yellow for guidance and crossing, reminiscent of an autobahn feeder road—why remains a mystery, but apparently Covid-19 cannot abide the color yellow … Also, the (administratively) uncomplicated usability of the machines had tended to decline drastically over time. Some colleagues—I'm thinking of Michel Bertreux and Francis Miguet in particular—have nonetheless managed to have their final-year students benefit strongly from it: the students invented odd outer-space machines that three years ago set out to storm a campsite in the neighboring department of Morbihan.

In any case, there is certainly a risk of this building, as the Centre Pompidou before it, falling into the trap of its own hyperflexibility. The architects were well aware of this, for at the opening they already explicitly drew a parallel to the famous predecessor, noting that it had already walked "into the trap of its hyperflexibility." Somewhere in the field of tension between creating space and leaving space, I observed censorship of predominantly administrative origin being exercised in the school, yet no or little self-censorship on the part of the students and teachers. "The reversibility [of the Centre Pompidou]," the architects add, "is nonetheless still a given. One way to avoid the division is to be big, much too big. Then dividing it up becomes difficult!"[8] Optimistic. Too much so? No! Or else what would be the point of devising projects?

It is true that the roof terrace, which is 2,500 square meters in size and 24 meters above street level, has not been used to its full capacity. How could it have been otherwise in our era dominated by a focus on security? Let's not forget that even before the virus there was the anti-terror plan "Vigipirate." All the same, the event series *Voyage à Nantes – Reise nach Nantes* took up residence there many a summer, spectacularly planting a car—a Citroën BX—at the edge of the precipice or creating a temporary open-air cinema or a skateboard ramp. But there is a much more trivial and commonplace risk: at its inauguration in 2009, the school had three (or even more) official entrances on the ground floor. For a long time now, only one remains, and in the wake of several lockdowns it has been barricaded with plexiglass and subjected to the security imperative of the mandatory access card. Access to the ramp from the ground level has been blocked since 2020—as we all know, the virus much prefers using ramps … The real is stronger than you! It's like all waste products: one may never get rid of it. And, as the famous Jacques Lacan once assured his more or less astounded listeners, the real becomes perceptible upon encounter![9] ∎

*Translation from German: Dawn Michelle d'Atri*

8    "Parole de Lacaton et Vassal" (see note 1), 61.

9    Original quote: "Il n'y a pas d'autre définition possible du réel que: c'est l'impossible quand quelque chose se trouve caractérisé de l'impossible, c'est là seulement le réel; quand on se cogne, le réel, c'est l'impossible à pénétrer." Jacques Lacan at a conference at the Massachusetts Institute of Technology on December 2, 1975, published in *Scilicet* 6–7 (1976): 53–63.

# "Maybe the Corridor Isn't the Best Answer"

# „Vielleicht ist der Korridor nicht die beste Antwort"

**Jeannette Kuo (JK) in Conversation with |
im Gespräch mit Petra Eckhard (GAM)**

1   Rice School of Architecture Extension, multifunctional space | Erweiterungsbau der Rice School of Architecture, Mehrzweckraum,
Karamuk Kuo Architects, Houston, Texas, 2019–2023 © Karamuk Kuo

The work of Zurich-based office Karamuk Kuo, established by Jeannette Kuo and Ünal Karamuk in 2010, focuses on the idea of architecture as the intersection of structures, space, and culture. Currently, Karamuk Kuo are working on an extension to the Rice University School of Architecture in Houston, Texas—a school that is known for its intimate size and the quality of their Bachelor and Master programs focusing on constructive thinking with an integrated curriculum and academic agenda. Petra Eckhard (GAM) met Jeannette Kuo (JK) and talked to her about the nexus of the educational and architectural program, James Stirling's postmodern legacy and the necessity of going beyond traditional academic typologies.

GAM: Jeannette, can you start with telling me a bit about the academic and spatial context out of which the Rice University School extension project evolved?

JK: Rice School of Architecture is one of the few schools where all of the people that teach in the technical fields also teach design or practice design, so there is a very integrated way of working between the different focus fields of architecture. The school is also small, it has about 180 students, which allows them to have a very tight agenda and program, integrating all the technical and theoretical into a holistic design-centered approach.

We were tasked with trying to think about the future of the architectural school, the types of spaces that they would need and what that means to extend onto a kind of existing building that not only has a cultural relevance in terms of the architectural history, but also onto a school that already had a famous extension. James Stirling did his first American project basically as an extension to the original school. So, we are extending an extension (fig. 3). That was already an interesting architectural problematic, but also to think about what are the spaces that would allow the school to develop a kind of pedagogy in

line with their philosophy right now and that would also enable them to do things in the future that they are not yet able to do.

GAM: What exactly is the school's philosophy?

JK: When we were selected for the new project, the school was very clear that they did not want to expand too much the number of students, and that the objective was not so much to provide more classrooms or typical studio spaces, but rather to provide other types of spaces that could rethink the way they work. When we started, we had a very long pre-design phase to develop the program together.

GAM: In the early 1980s Stirling's addition tried to maximize contact between students, professors and visitors through the design of a collective space. This was an architectural gesture towards fostering a strong academic community. In what way does your new extension reflect the current teaching philosophy of the school or enable new forms of pedagogy?

JK: To understand Stirling's contribution, you have to also understand a little bit the context that was there. The existing classroom buildings at Rice back then—and for the most part until now—are quite introverted buildings that are based on a series of long narrow buildings. The campus has beautiful outdoor spaces and old oak trees that makes it a real oasis in Houston. However, the buildings themselves, given their formal typologies of narrow bars, often were simply double-loaded corridors with classrooms or offices on either side. This was also the case at the existing architecture school. Stirling's extension in essence created a very public spine in the building that could be used for school-wide events like reviews, exhibitions, and lectures. It remains one of the few buildings on campus with this larger scale sequence of collective spaces meant to promote

Die Arbeit des in Zürich ansässigen Büros Karamuk Kuo, das 2010 von Jeannette Kuo und Ünal Karamuk gegründet wurde, konzentriert sich auf eine Vorstellung von Architektur als Schnittstelle von Tragwerk, Raum und Kultur. Derzeit arbeiten Karamuk Kuo an einem Erweiterungsbau der Rice University School of Architecture in Houston, Texas, einer Schule, die für ihre überschaubare Größe und die herausragende Qualität ihrer Bachelor- und Master-Studiengänge bekannt ist. Im Zentrum dieser Schule mit ihrem fächerübergreifenden Lehrplan und ihrer integrierten pädagogischen Agenda steht das konstruktive Denken. Petra Eckhard (GAM) traf Jeannette Kuo (JK) und sprach mit ihr über den Zusammenhang zwischen Lehrplan und architektonischem Programm, das postmoderne Vermächtnis James Stirlings und die Notwendigkeit, über traditionelle akademische Typologien hinauszugehen.

GAM: Jeannette, könntest du mir zunächst etwas über den akademischen und räumlichen Kontext erzählen, aus dem heraus sich das Projekt für den Erweiterungsbau der Rice University School entwickelt hat?

JK: Die Rice School of Architecture ist eine der wenigen Schulen, wo alle in den technischen Bereichen Lehrenden auch Entwurf unterrichten oder selbst praktizieren. Es gibt also eine äußerst integrierte Arbeitsweise zwischen den verschiedenen Kernbereichen der Architektur. Außerdem ist die Schule mit ihren etwa 180 StudentInnen relativ klein. Ihre Agenda und ihr Programm sind daher äußerst gestrafft und erlauben es, die gesamte Technik und Theorie in einen ganzheitlichen entwurfszentrierten Ansatz zu integrieren.

Man übertrug uns die Aufgabe, über die Zukunft der Architekturschule nachzudenken, über die Arten von Räumen, die diese benötigt, aber auch darüber, was es heißt, ein vorhandenes Gebäude zu erweitern, das nicht nur in architekturhistorischer Hinsicht kulturell bedeutsam ist, sondern auch als Erweiterung einer Schule, die schon einen berühmten Annex besitzt. James Stirling schuf sein erstes amerikanisches Projekt im Grunde als Erweiterungsbau der ursprünglichen Schule. Wir erweitern also eine Erweiterung (Abb. 3). Das war bereits für sich genommen ein interessantes architektonisches Problem; hinzukam aber noch das Nachdenken darüber, wie die Räume aussehen sollten, die es der Schule ermöglichen würden, eine Form von Pädagogik zu entwickeln, die im Einklang mit ihrer derzeitigen Philosophie steht, die es ihr aber auch ermöglichen würde, Dinge in der Zukunft zu machen, zu denen sie momentan noch nicht imstande ist.

GAM: Was genau ist die Philosophie der Schule?

JK: Als man uns für das neue Projekt auswählte, machte die Schule sehr deutlich, dass sie die Zahl der StudentInnen nicht allzu sehr erhöhen wollte, und dass das Ziel nicht darin bestand, weitere Klassenzimmer oder typische Zeichensäle bereitzustellen, sondern vielmehr andere Arten von Räumen, die ihnen die Möglichkeit geben sollten, ihre Arbeitsweise zu überdenken. Als wir anfingen, gab es vor der eigentlichen Gestaltungsphase einen langen Zeitraum, in dem wir das Programm gemeinsam entwickelten.

GAM: In den frühen 1980ern versuchte Stirlings Annex den Kontakt zwischen den Studierenden, ProfessorInnen und BesucherInnen durch die Gestaltung eines gemeinsamen Raums zu maximieren. Es handelte sich um eine architektonische Geste zur Förderung einer starken akademischen Community. Inwiefern spiegelt euer Erweiterungsbau die aktuelle Lehrphilosophie der Schule wider oder ermöglicht neue pädagogische Spielarten?

JK: Um Stirlings Beitrag zu verstehen, muss man sich auch ein wenig über den damaligen Kontext im Klaren sein. Die vorhandenen Bauten mit Klassenzimmern der Rice University waren damals, und sind bis heute, größtenteils ziemlich introvertierte Gebilde, die auf einer Reihe langer schmaler Gebäude beruhen. Der Campus hat schöne Außenräume und alte Eichen, was ihn in Houston zu einer echten Oase macht. Doch die Gebäude selbst waren aufgrund ihres formalen Erscheinungsbilds – es handelt sich um schmale Riegel –, häufig lediglich zweibündige Klassen- und Bürotrakte. Das war auch bei der existierenden Architekturschule der Fall. Im Kern schuf Stirling mit seinem Erweiterungsbau ein sehr öffentliches Rückgrat, das für die ganze Schule betreffende Veranstaltungen wie Schlusskritiken, Ausstellungen und Vorlesungen genutzt werden konnte. Es ist eines der wenigen Gebäude auf dem Campus mit dieser ein größeres Format aufweisenden Abfolge von Gemeinschaftsräumen, die kollektiv genutzt und dem Austausch dienen sollen. Der übrige Teil seines Erweiterungsbaus aber wiederholte die vorhandene zellenartige Anordnung der Klassenzimmer und Büros, was ihre Flexibilität letztlich einschränkte. Und auch die von ihm eingeführten Gemeinschaftsräume reichen nicht aus, um all die informellen Aktivitäten zu realisieren, die sogenannten Pin-ups (informelle Kritiken) und Kooperationen, die es dort heute gibt.

GAM: Was waren die wichtigsten Entwurfsparameter, die aus der pädagogischen Sicht der Schule berücksichtigt werden mussten?

2   Rice School of Architecture, James Stirling's entrance situation | Eingangsbereich nach dem Entwurf von James Stirling © Jeannette Kuo

student working diligently on their own assigned desk, on their own project. Projects were mainly done with drawings and small models that would fit on those desks. Today, the types of projects have changed both in process and in scale. There is much more group work and also work that happens on a wider spectrum of media and technologies. Even just physical model making today extends from small models to large scale 1:1 prototypes. It also involves a methodology that is not linear or singular but quite fluidly and messily moving between the digital and the physical. Our project therefore proposed not only a large flexible hall for fabrication and events, a gallery to exhibit the work, but also a field of smaller scale but unassigned spaces that would allow for group work, pin-ups and other informal exchanges. Most importantly, these different ways of working should not be separated or siloed. The design therefore really tries to create visual proximity so that students, faculty and visitors could always be aware of the different types of work happening around them.

The project evolved into thinking about what are ways of designing spaces that could be flexibly used over the next 50, 80, maybe even 100 years—what are spaces that allow for things that we may not even be able to predict right now, spaces that are less formalized, with rather informal ways of interaction but still feed into the pedagogical concept of the school.

sharing and exchange. The rest of his extension, however, repeated the existing cellular organization of classroom and office that in the end limited their flexibility. Also, the collective spaces that he introduced is not enough to address all the informal activities, the pin-ups and collaborations that occur today.

**GAM**: What were the most important design parameters that needed to be considered from the school's pedagogical point of view?

**JK**: We had extensive conversations with the school to understand the way they work and to study what was missing with their current space and what they needed. Out of that, we realized that the cellular organization of the classrooms and studios, the highly defined spaces, did not allow them to adapt to their current ways of working. At the time the original building was built, the architectural pedagogy was about each

**GAM**: In what way did Stirling's eclectic approach influence your extension of the extension? Or, put differently, how do the two extensions relate to or differ from each other?

**JK**: Stirling was certainly quite masterful with his play of formal language that created some really iconic moments of composition but also some very awkward moments. For example, at an already tight entrance, he would place a column so that you would have to maneuver around it (fig. 2). It certainly created some forced interaction of people crossing paths as you would have to step aside to let someone through. Perhaps that was his intention. Our play with the architectural elements is maybe not so much along those lines. The main conceptual gesture of the building plays with our collective memory and image of architecture. The new building extends from the upper floor of the existing, taking its gable roof form and turns it

**JK**: Wir hatten ausführliche Gespräche mit der Schule, um zu verstehen, wie sie funktioniert, und zu untersuchen, was bei den derzeitigen Räumen fehlt und was sie benötigten. Daraus ergab sich, dass die zellenförmige Anordnung der Klassenzimmer und Studios, die klare Definition der Räume es unmöglich machte, sie an die aktuelle Arbeitsweise anzupassen. Zum Ent-

stehungszeitpunkt des ursprünglichen Gebäudes sah die architektonische Pädagogik vor, dass alle StudentInnen fleißig an dem ihnen zugewiesenen Schreibtisch an ihrem jeweiligen Projekt arbeiteten. Die Projekte bestanden vor allem aus Zeichnungen und kleinen Modellen, die auf diese Schreibtische passten. Heute haben sich die Projekttypen sowohl in prozessualer als auch in maßstäblicher Hinsicht verändert. Es gibt viel mehr

3   Rice School of Architecture Extension, northern façade | Erweiterungsbau der Rice School of Architecture, Nordfassade, Karamuk Kuo Architects, Houston, Texas, 2019–2023 © Karamuk Kuo/Jeudi Wang

4 Rice School of Architecture Extension, axonometric model | Erweiterungsbau der Rice School of Architecture, axonometrisches Modell, Karamuk Kuo Architects, 2019–2023 © Karamuk Kuo

5 Rice School of Architecture Extension, courtyard | Erweiterungsbau der Rice School of Architecture, Hof, Karamuk Kuo Architects, 2019–2023 © Karamuk Kuo/Jeudi Wang

into a shed. A series of sheds results from this first gesture repeated, producing a sort of industrial sawtooth roof. So, the transition from a very familiar almost domestic scale of the gable roof, which is very present on campus, to the larger-scale image of a shed roof was really key (figs. 4–5).

Programmatically, Stirling's mandate was very different from ours. At the time he did his extension, the school was physically growing. They wanted to have more classroom and studio spaces to accommodate more students. In our case, the school decided to keep the size and intimacy of their program but to enhance it with other ways of working and showing their work. In Stirling's addition there are wonderful double height moments that provoke visual exchange but, for the most part, the studios are off in the wings and closed off from view. As a parti, the school was maybe not so different from what was already there, but simply adding another bar. Many of the more public spaces within the building also could not be used as they were originally intended because of security and acoustical problems.

Our extension is designed to complement what is already available in the school. We looked at the language of the narrow bar and tried to rethink how we can get more out of it and transformed it into a system of bars. We also winked at Stirling's "bridge" moment—a double-height moment where students on the upper floor corridor could look onto the events happening in the collective spaces below. You would find a few moments like that in the new building as well, but in our case systematized into the organization so that the upper floor for quieter work and collaboration and the lower floor for production are visually knitted together (fig. 6).

GAM: What we are currently experiencing is a paradigm shift where the conventional modes of teaching architecture are put into question and require a rethinking of academic structures, but also traditional academic typologies such as lecture halls or seminar rooms require a rethinking. How do you, in both roles as a professor and as a practicing architect experience this shift?

JK: If you look at how educational spaces were designed previously, it was really about closed classroom spaces or formalized

lecture halls that are meant for one function only. There is very little that is informal, there is very little space that is of a certain scale that allows for multiple ways of working. You are always confined to rooms, and you don't see things that are going on. Now the question is, how do you design spaces that inspire people, that allow them to experience things they are not involved in directly but maybe that brings new ideas to what they are doing. So, all of these things essentially force us to re-question certain typologies that we have taken for granted in the educational spaces. Maybe the corridor isn't the best answer, maybe it is, but maybe it is also in connection with something else. We have been looking at what it means when you have spaces that aren't specifically designated for a particular function but that maybe allows them to be used in ways that we can interpret in the future.

GAM: Why are so many architecture schools in Europe still so hesitant to rethink or remodel the existing typologies into something that would fit contemporary modes of teaching and learning? Shouldn't architecture schools in particular offer more progressive spatial approaches to the spaces in which their discipline is taught?

JK: There are some schools that are doing that already. I think it goes a little bit deeper. A lot of the American schools are smaller, they are more agile, because they are often private universities, and because of the way that American universities are structured or the way architecture departments are structured, there usually is more autonomy. For example, when a new director comes in who then rethinks certain things, that can really provoke change. The European model, the one that I know, which is more Central European, so Switzerland or Germany, is a heavy machinery that takes years to enact change because there are traditions and bureaucracies. Also, the model of the professorships is very different. In the American model the professor is in regular and direct contact with the students, so you don't have the kind of umbrella of a chair or institute that weighs that down. A professor might have 12 students in a studio, not 200. The relationship amongst the professors to their colleagues is very direct as well. In the American system, the professors are on each other's studio reviews, interacting quite directly in debates on every student's project. There isn't as strong of a separation into focused groups and disciplines

Gruppenarbeit und Arbeit, die ein breiteres Spektrum von Medien und Technologien betrifft. Selbst die Herstellung physischer Modelle erstreckt sich heute von kleinen Modellen bis zu großformatigen 1:1 Prototypen. Und das methodische Vorgehen ist nicht linear oder singulär, sondern befindet sich im ständigen Fluss und changiert auf ungeordnete Weise zwischen Digitalem und Physischem. Unser Projekt sah daher nicht nur eine große flexible Halle für die Fertigung und für Veranstaltungen vor, eine Galerie für die Präsentation der Werke, sondern auch einen Bereich mit kleineren, aber nutzungsoffenen Räumen für die Gruppenarbeit, Pin-ups und andere informelle Kommunikationsformen. Am wichtigsten aber war, dass diese unterschiedlichen Arbeitsweisen nicht voneinander getrennt oder isoliert werden sollten. Der Entwurf versucht daher wirklich eine visuelle Nähe zu schaffen, sodass die Studierenden, die Lehrkräfte und die BesucherInnen sich immer der unterschiedlichen Arten von Arbeit bewusst sein konnten, die um sie herum stattfand.

Aus dem Projekt entwickelte sich ein Nachdenken darüber, wie sich Räume gestalten lassen, sodass man sie in den nächsten 50, 80, ja vielleicht 100 Jahren flexibel nutzen kann, Räume, die Dinge ermöglichen, die wir derzeit vielleicht noch gar nicht vorhersehen können, Räume, welche weniger stark formalisiert sind, mit eher informellen Interaktionsweisen, die aber dennoch zum pädagogischen Konzept der Schule passen.

GAM: Inwiefern beeinflusste Stirlings eklektizistischer Ansatz eure Erweiterung der Erweiterung? Oder anders gefragt, inwiefern beziehen sich die beiden Erweiterungsbauten auf- und inwiefern unterscheiden sie sich voneinander?

JK: Hinsichtlich seines Spiels mit der formalen Sprache war Stirling sicherlich ein großer Meister, und was die Komposition angeht, schuf er einige wirklich ikonische Momente, aber eben auch einige sehr unbeholfene. So platzierte er etwa an einem ohnehin schon schmalen Eingang eine Säule, sodass man um sie herumgehen muss (Abb. 2). Dadurch kam es zwangsläufig zu Interaktionen zwischen Menschen, die sich dort über den Weg liefen, da man zur Seite treten muss, um jemanden durchzulassen. Aber vielleicht war das ja seine Absicht. Unser Spiel mit den architektonischen Elementen funktioniert ein bisschen anders. Die konzeptionelle Hauptgeste des Gebäudes spielt mit unserem kollektiven Gedächtnis und unserem Bild der Architektur. Das neue Gebäude erstreckt sich von dem Obergeschoss des vorhandenen, greift dessen Giebeldachform auf und verwandelt sie in ein Sheddach. Aus der Wiederholung dieser ersten Geste ergibt sich eine ganze Reihe von Sheds, sodass gewissermaßen ein industrielles Sheddach entsteht. Das Entscheidende war also wirklich der Übergang von einem sehr vertrauten, fast

häuslichen Maßstab des Giebeldaches, das auf dem Campus sehr präsent ist, zum größeren Maßstab eines Sheddachs (Abb. 4–5).

In programmatischer Hinsicht unterschied Stirlings Auftrag sich sehr deutlich von unserem. In der Zeit, als er seinen Erweiterungsbau schuf, erlebte die Schule eine Wachstumsphase. Man benötigte weitere Klassenzimmer und Studioräume, um mehr StudentInnen unterbringen zu können. In unserem Fall beschloss die Schule, an der Größe und Intimität ihres Programms festzuhalten, aber es um andere Arbeitsweisen und Präsentationsweisen ihrer Arbeit zu erweitern. In Stirlings Annex gibt es wunderbare Momente von doppelter Raumhöhe, die einen visuellen Austausch provozieren, doch die Studios befinden sich größtenteils in den Seitenflügeln und sind nicht einsehbar. Als Entwurfsschema unterschied sich die Schule vielleicht nicht so sehr von dem, was bereits da war, sondern fügte ihm einfach einen weiteren Riegel hinzu. Viele der öffentlicheren Räume innerhalb des Gebäudes konnten wegen Sicherheits- und akustischen Problemen ebenfalls nicht so genutzt werden, wie ursprünglich beabsichtigt.

Unser Erweiterungsbau ist als Ergänzung dessen gedacht, was in der Schule bereits zur Verfügung steht. Wir sahen uns die Sprache der schmalen Riegel an, überlegten uns, wie wir da mehr herausholen könnten und machten ein System von Riegeln daraus. Wir würdigten auch Stirlings „Brücken"-Moment, eine Struktur von doppelgeschossigen Räumen, von der aus StudentInnen von dem Korridor im Obergeschoss das Geschehen in den Gemeinschaftsräumen unten verfolgen konnten. In dem neuen Gebäude finden sich ebenfalls einige solche Momente, doch in unserem Fall sind sie systematisch in die Anordnung des Ganzen integriert, sodass das obere Stockwerk für die ruhigere Arbeit und Kooperation und das untere für die Produktion visuell miteinander verknüpft sind (Abb. 6).

GAM: Derzeit erleben wir einen Paradigmenwechsel, wobei die herkömmlichen Formen des Architekturunterrichts infrage gestellt werden und ein Überdenken der akademischen Strukturen erforderlich machen; aber auch traditionelle akademische Typologien wie Vortragssäle oder Seminarräume müssen überdacht werden. Wie erlebst du diesen Wechsel in deiner Doppelrolle als Professorin und praktizierende Architektin?

JK: Wenn man sich ansieht, wie Ausbildungsräume bislang gestaltet wurden, so ging es wirklich um geschlossene Klassenzimmer oder formelle Vortragssäle, die nur eine bestimmte Funktion erfüllen sollen. Es gibt sehr wenig Informelles, sehr

6   Rice School of Architecture Extension, faculty research space | Erweiterungsbau der Rice School of Architecture, Forschungsbereich der ProfessorInnen, Karamuk Kuo Architects, 2019–2023 © Karamuk Kuo

within the architectural field and so it can be more dynamic. There are always advantages and disadvantages to both models. The stability of the European model protects the autonomy of the chair or institute which was supposed to be a way to ensure a freedom from market pressures and therefore the freedom for real independent research that can challenge the norms. If that happens, that's fantastic because the American model often lacks the support for research.

**GAM**: You teach within the American context, at Harvard GSD, with its iconic Gund hall studio space. The structure dates back to the 1970s but still seems to work well as a contemporary learning environment in which new pedagogical formats such as peer-to-peer practices can take place. How do you experience this teaching environment?

**JK**: Half of the experience at Gund Hall is really just the space—the open terraces with all the students under one roof.

You learn so much—not from the professors necessarily—but from the fact that you see everything that is going on. You are always inspired by your colleagues, by people that are even in a different department—because it is not just architecture, it's architecture, landscape, and urban design. That kind of energy in the room, that did half the work for us as professors, we only need to push so much more. This makes a huge difference, but there are still shortcomings to this space, we don't have enough space. We also don't have enough space for informal learning, we are always looking for spaces for pin-ups or good quality spaces for pin-ups. I think that was something at that time not intended for a school of this size, with so many students, but yes, definitely, this idea of what the space could do, and how a space can enable or constrain the way that you work and are inspired to work, that, I think, is a very central architectural question.

**GAM**: Thank you for the interview! ∎

wenig Raum einer gewissen Größe, der verschiedene Arbeitsweisen zulässt. Man ist immer auf einzelne Räume beschränkt und sieht nicht, was darum herum passiert. Die Frage lautet also nun, wie man Räume entwirft, die Menschen inspirieren, indem sie es ihnen ermöglichen, Dinge zu erleben, mit denen sie vielleicht nicht direkt zu tun haben, sie aber vielleicht bei dem, was sie gerade machen, auf neue Ideen bringen. Dies alles zwingt uns also, bestimmte Typologien zu hinterfragen, die wir in den Ausbildungsräumen für selbstverständlich gehalten hatten. Vielleicht ist der Korridor nicht die beste Antwort, vielleicht aber doch, aber vielleicht auch in Verbindung mit etwas anderem. Wir haben uns angesehen, was es bedeutet, Räume zu haben, die nicht eigens im Hinblick auf eine bestimmte Funktion gestaltet sind, sondern die zulassen, dass man sie auf eine Weise nutzt, die erst in der Zukunft festgelegt wird.

**GAM**: Warum zögern so viele Architekturschulen in Europa noch, die vorhandenen Typologien zu überdenken und so umzugestalten, dass sie zeitgenössischen Lehr- und Lerngewohnheiten entsprechen? Sollten nicht gerade Architekturschulen einen fortschrittlicheren räumlichen Umgang mit den Räumen bieten, in denen ihr Fach unterrichtet wird?

**JK**: Einige Schulen tun das ja bereits. Ich glaube aber, dass das Ganze noch etwas tiefer reicht. Viele der amerikanischen Schulen sind kleiner, und agiler, da es sich häufig um private Universitäten handelt, und aufgrund der Art, wie amerikanische Universitäten oder Architekturfakultäten strukturiert sind, gibt es normalerweise größere Autonomie. Wenn es z.B. einen neuen Direktor oder eine neue Direktorin gibt, der oder die bestimmte Dinge überdenkt und anders sieht, kann das tatsächlich zu Veränderungen führen. Das europäische Modell, das ich kenne und das eher zentraleuropäisch ist, wie in der Schweiz oder Deutschland, ist das eines schwerfälligen Betriebs, bei dem es aufgrund der bestehenden Traditionen und Bürokratie Jahre braucht, bis Veränderungen umgesetzt werden. Und die Professuren funktionieren ebenfalls völlig anders. Beim amerikanischen Modell stehen die ProfessorInnen in regelmäßigem und direktem Kontakt mit den Studierenden, es gibt also nicht diesen Überbau eines Lehrstuhls oder Instituts, der alles so schwerfällig macht. Ein Professor oder eine Professorin hat dort 12 Studierende in einem Studio und nicht 200. Auch die Beziehung der ProfessorInnen zu ihren KollegInnen ist sehr direkt. Im amerikanischen System partizipieren die ProfessorInnen in die Schlusskritiken der anderen und interagieren durch die Auseinandersetzung mit den jeweiligen Projekten der Studierenden unmittelbar miteinander. Die Unterteilung in bestimmte Gruppen und Fachrichtungen innerhalb des architektonischen Bereichs ist nicht so stark, sodass er dynamischer sein kann. Beide Modelle haben Vor- und Nachteile. Die Stabilität des europäischen Modells schützt die Unabhängigkeit des Lehrstuhls oder Instituts; damit soll die Freiheit gegenüber dem Druck des Marktes gewährleistet werden und damit die Freiheit zu wirklich unabhängiger Forschung, welche die Normen herausfordern kann. Sofern das geschieht, ist es fantastisch, denn bei dem amerikanischen Modell mangelt es häufig an der Unterstützung der Forschung.

**GAM**: Du unterrichtest im amerikanischen Kontext, an der Harvard GSD mit ihrer ikonischen Gund Hall-Studiohalle. Das Gebäude stammt aus den 1970ern, scheint aber nach wie vor als zeitgenössisches Lern-Environment zu funktionieren, in dem neue pädagogische Formate wie Peer-to-Peer-Praktiken stattfinden können. Wie erlebst du diesen Raum?

**JK**: Die Hälfte des Erlebnisses der Gund Hall ist wirklich einfach nur der Raum – die offenen Terrassen mit all den Studierenden unter einem Dach. Man lernt so viel, nicht unbedingt von den ProfessorInnen, sondern aufgrund der Tatsache, dass man alles mitbekommt, was sich dort abspielt. Man wird immer von den KollegInnen inspiriert, selbst von Leuten aus einem anderen Departement, denn es handelt sich nicht nur um Architektur, sondern um Architektur, Landschaft und Stadtbaukunst. Diese Energie, die da im Raum herrscht, erledigt für uns als ProfessorInnen schon die halbe Arbeit; wir müssen dann nur noch ein paar Anstöße geben. Das ist ein gewaltiger Unterschied, aber auch dieser Raum hat Nachteile, und insgesamt gibt es nicht genug Platz. Wir haben auch nicht genug Platz für informelles Lernen und suchen immer nach Räumen für Kritiken, oder nach qualitätsvollen Räumen für Diskussionen. Die Schule war nicht für so viele Studierende vorgesehen, aber ja, definitiv, diese Vorstellung, was ein Raum leisten könnte und wie ein Raum die eigene Arbeitsweise und Inspiration fördern oder einschränken kann, ist wirklich eine ganz zentrale architektonische Frage.

**GAM**: Danke für das Interview! ∎

*Übersetzung aus dem Englischen: Nikolaus G. Schneider*

# AutorInnen
## Authors

**Karine Dana** ist Architektin und arbeitet als Journalistin und Videofilmerin. Durch diese Doppelkompetenz und ihren architektonischen Blick arbeitet sie regelmäßig mit verschiedenen internationalen Büros (Lacaton & Vassal, 51N4E, AUC, YTAA) an Texten, Wettbewerben, Rechercheprojekten und im Rahmen von Ausstellungen zusammen.
**Karine Dana** is an architect and works as a journalist and videographer. Because of this dual skill and her architectural perspective, she regularly collaborates with international offices such as Lacaton & Vassal, 51N4E, AUC, YTAA in the context of writing, competitions, research projects and exhibitions.

**Sandra Denicke-Polcher** hat 1998 ihr Studium an der Architectural Association School of Architecture in London abgeschlossen. 2013 wurde sie zur stellvertretenden Leiterin des Fachbereichs Architektur der London Metropolitan University ernannt, wo sie seit 2000 das „Live Projects Studio 3" unterrichtet. In ihrer Lehrtätigkeit erforscht sie die Möglichkeiten und Herausforderungen der sogenannten „Live Projects" – ein didaktisches Format, das eine Baupraxis mit realen BauherrInnen als Teil der akademischen Architekturausbildung versteht. Dabei liegt ihr Schwerpunkt auf öffentlichen Projekten, die die komplexen Beziehungen zwischen Architekturausbildung und -praxis aufzeigen. Sie ist außerdem Gründungspartnerin von Studio 3 – Architecture + Urbanism und von public works (www.publicworksgroup.net/) und arbeitete an Projekten im Vereinigten Königreich, Deutschland und dem Iran.

**Sandra Denicke-Polcher** graduated from the Architectural Association School of Architecture in 1998. In 2013 she became Deputy Head of the School of Architecture at London Metropolitan University where she has also been teaching the Live Projects Studio 3 since 2000. Through teaching she explores the opportunities and challenges of engaging with live projects—projects with real clients—as part of the university-based architectural education. With an emphasis on public projects, her work identifies the complex relationships between architectural education and practice. She is also a founding partner of Studio 3 – Architecture + Urbanism and of public works (https://www.publicworksgroup.net/) and has been working on projects in the UK, Germany and Iran.

**Federica Doglio** promovierte 2013 am Politecnico di Torino im Fach Kulturelles Erbe. 2011 war sie Doktorandin an der Graduate School of Architecture, Planning and Preservation (GSAPP) der Columbia University in New York und 2014 Visiting Scholar am Canadian Centre for Architecture (CCA). Ihr Forschungsschwerpunkt liegt auf zeitgenössischer Designtheorie und -kritik zwischen Europa und Amerika. Derzeit unterrichtet sie Theoriekurse und Design Studios an der Nuova Accademia di Belle Arti (NABA) in Mailand und am Politecnico di Torino.
**Federica Doglio** received her PhD degree in Cultural Heritage from Politecnico di Torino in 2013. In 2011 she was a PhD scholar at GSAPP at Columbia University and in 2014 visiting scholar at the Canadian Centre for Architecture in Montreal (CCA). Her research focuses on contemporary design theory and criticism between Europe and America. Currently she teaches both theoretical courses and design studios at the Nuova Accademia di Belle Arti (NABA) in Milan and at the Politecnico di Torino.

**Björn Ehrlemark** ist Architekt und Autor und lebt in Stockholm. Gemeinsam mit Carin Kallenberg leitet er Arkitekturens Grannar/Neighbours of Architecture, ein forschungsbasiertes Büro, das sich der Produktion von Architekturkultur in Form von Ausstellungen, Veranstaltungen, Publikationen, Objekten und anderen Medien widmet. Seine Arbeit wurde kürzlich in Form eines Gastvortrags an der Graduate School of Architecture, Planning and Preservation (GSAPP) der Columbia University in New York sowie auf der Internationalen Biennale für zeitgenössische Kunst in Göteborg gezeigt. Im Sommer 2021 wurde er für das Helsinki Design Residenzprogramm ausgewählt. Von 2013–2016 kuratierte er das öffentliche Programm der KTH School of Architecture. Er ist immer wieder als Dozent und Kritiker an der Schule zu Gast.
**Björn Ehrlemark** is an architect and writer living in Stockholm. With curator Carin Kallenberg, he co-directs Arkitekturens Grannar/Neighbours of Architecture. The research-based practice has recently guest lectured at Columbia GSAPP, taken part in the Gothenburg International Biennial of Contemporary Art, and was selected for the Helsinki Design Residency, hosted by HIAP, Iaspis and Strelka Institute, in the summer of 2021. Between 2013 and 2016 he cu-rated the public program of events and hibitions at the KTH School of Architect Today he is a recurring guest as lec and critic at the school.

**Hélène Frichot** ist Professorin für A tektur und Philosophie und Leiterin des chelor of Design an der Faculty of Arch ture, Building and Planning an der Ur sity of Melbourne, Australien. Zuvor le sie die Forschungsabteilung Critical Stu in Architecture an der KTH Stockholm, dort Professorin für Critical Studies Gender Theory und lehrt dort nach wie als Gastprofessorin. Ihre Forschung ba auf den Disziplinen ihrer Ausbildung, A tektur und Philosophie, und bewegt in einem transdisziplinären Feld, i sie mit feministischen Theorien und tiken experimentiert und sich dabei in sondere auf den Neuen Materialismus, die Post-Humanities stützt. Sie ist die torin von *How to Make Yourself a Fen Design Power Tool* (AADR, 2016), *Dirty ory: Troubling Architecture* (AADR, 2 und Herausgeberin des Doppelba *Architecture in Effect* (Actar, 2019).
**Hélène Frichot** is Professor of Arch ture and Philosophy, and Director o Bachelor of Design at the Faculty of A tecture, Building and Planning, Unive of Melbourne, Australia. Prior to that was the Director of Critical Studies i chitecture, as well as Professor of C Studies and Gender Theory, in the Sc of Architecture at KTH Stockholm, Swe where she still holds a guest-professor Drawing on the two disciplines in v she is trained, architecture and philos

research engages a transdisciplinary
[...] by experimenting with feminist theo-
[...] and practices, specifically drawing on
[...] materialism and the post-humanities.
[...] is the author of *How to Make Yourself a*
*[...]inist Design Power Tool* (AADR, 2016),
*[...]y Theory: Troubling Architecture* (AADR,
[...]9) and editor of the double volume
*[...]hitecture in Effect* (Actar, 2019).

**[...]nnette Kuo** ist Entwurfsprofessorin an
[...] Harvard University Graduate School of
[...]ign und Mitgründerin von Karamuk Kuo
[...]hitekten mit Sitz in Zürich. Das gemein-
[...] mit Ünal Karamuk 2010 gegründe-
[...]üro positioniert seine Arbeiten an der
[...]nittstelle von Raumkonzepten und Bau-
[...]nnologien und versteht Architektur als
[...]erielle sowie soziale Disziplin. Ihre Pro-
[...]e umfassen verschiedene Maßstabs-
[...]nen, von Schulen über Wohnbau bis
[...]omplexen Kulturprojekten und wurden
[...]eits in vielen internationalen Fachzeit-
[...]riften, darunter *Archithese, Werk, Bau +*
*[...]hnen, Metropolis,* und *Casabella* veröf-
[...]licht. Als Lehrende und Gastkritikerin
[...] sie u.a. an der ETH Zürich, der Columbia
[...]versity, dem Pratt Institute oder der
[...]g Kong University beschäftigt. Außer-
[...] war sie Europäische Juryvorsitzen-
[...]für die Holcim Awards for Sustainable
[...]struction, dem weltweit bedeutendsten
[...]ttbewerb für nachhaltiges Bauen.

[...]nnette Kuo is Assistant Professor in
[...]ctice at Harvard Graduate School of De-
[...] and a founding partner of Karamuk Kuo
[...]hitects based in Zurich. Established in
[...]0 with Ünal Karamuk, the work of the
[...]e focuses on the intersection of spa-
[...] concepts and constructive technolo-
[...], recognizing architecture as a social
[...] material discipline. The office works on
[...]ects of a range of scales, from schools
[...] housing to complex cultural projects,
[...] have been published in numerous in-
[...]ational journals including *Archithese,*
*[...]k, Bau + Wohnen, Metropolis,* and
*[...]abella*. She has lectured and been a
[...]st critic at numerous institutions such
[...]TH Zurich, Columbia University, Pratt
[...]tute or Hong Kong University. She reg-
[...]y serves on international competition
[...]s and most recently was European jury
[...]ident for the Holcim Awards for Sus-
[...]able Construction.

**[...]aton & Vassal Architectes** wurde
[...]9 von Anne Lacaton und Jean-Phillip-
[...]assal in Paris gegründet. Seitdem ar-
[...]en sie international an öffentlichen Bau-
[...] Wohnungsbauten und Stadtplanung.
[...] Projekte basieren auf einem Prinzip,
[...] Großzügigkeit und Wirtschaftlichkeit
[...]nt, und verfolgen das Ziel, jenseits von
[...]lierten Standards und mit einem gro-
[...] Engagement für ökologische sowie so-
[...] Nachhaltigkeit zu bauen. Die gestalte-

rische Haltung des Büros drückt sich durch
einen behutsamen Umgang mit dem Klima
und dem Vorhandenen aus, zieht die Umgestaltung und Wiederverwendung dem
Abriss vor. Zu ihren wichtigsten realisierten Arbeiten zählen das Palais de Tokyo in
Paris, die Architekturschule in Nantes, das
FRAC – Öffentliche Sammlung zeitgenössischer Kunst in Dünkirchen (2013) sowie
bedeutende Wohnungsbauprojekte wie das
Einfamilienhaus Latapie in Bordeaux, die
Cité Manifeste in Mulhouse, die Sanierung
von Großwohnanlagen der Spätmoderne in
Paris und Bordeaux sowie ein Wohnturm in
Genf. Das Büro nahm an einer Reihe bedeutender Wettbewerbe teil, vor allem in Europa
und Frankreich.

**Lacaton & Vassal Architectes** was created in 1989 by Anne Lacaton and Jean-
Phillippe Vassal. The international practice
is based in Paris and works on public buildings, housing, and urban planning. All the
projects are based on a principle of generosity and economy, with the aim of changing the standard and a strong commitment
for sustainability and social impact. Working carefully with climate and everything already there, reuse, transformation instead
of demolition, is also a principle of the office's attitude. The main works completed
are the Palais de Tokyo, Paris, the Nantes
School of Architecture, the FRAC – Regional Collection of Contemporary Art in Dunker-
que and significant housing projects: House
Latapie in Bordeaux, "Cité Manifeste," social housing in Mulhouse and Paris, the
transformation of modernist social housing blocks in Paris and Bordeaux, a housing tower block in Geneva. The office did a
number of significant competitions mostly
in Europe and France.

**Christina Linortner** ist Universitätsassistentin am Institut für Grundlagen der Konstruktion und des Entwerfens an der TU
Graz. Sie hat Architektur an der TU Wien
und TU Delft sowie Research Architecture
am Goldsmiths College in London studiert
und in Architekturbüros in Wien, Rotterdam
und London gearbeitet. Seit 2013 ist sie bei
Ausstellungs-, Publikations- und Bauprojek-
ten an der Schnittstelle von Architektur und
künstlerischer Forschung tätig. Sie ist außerdem Vorstandsmitglied der Österreichischen Gesellschaft für Architektur (ÖGFA).
In ihrer Dissertation beschäftigt sie sich mit
alternativen Architekturpädagogiken und
Lernen in nicht-institutionellen Räumen.

Christina Linortner has been a Teaching
Fellow and Research Associate at the Institute for Construction and Design Principles at Graz University of Technology since
2013. She studied architecture at the TU
Vienna and TU Delft as well as Research
Architecture at Goldsmiths College in
London and has worked in architecture offices in Vienna, Rotterdam and London.

Since 2013 she has been involved in exhibitions, publications, and construction projects at the interface of architecture and
artistic research. She is also a board member of the Austrian Society for Architecture
(ÖGFA). In her dissertation she is focusing
on alternative architectural pedagogies and
learning in non-institutional spaces.

**Charlotte Malterre-Barthes** ist Architektin,
Wissenschaftlerin und Assistant Professor
of Urban Design an der Harvard Graduate
School of Design. Sie ist Gründerin des
Stadtplanungsbüros OMNIBUS und leitete
das MAS Urban Design Programm am Lehrstuhl von Marc Angélil von 2014–2019. Sie
promovierte an der ETH Zürich zu den Aus-
wirkungen der politischen Ökonomie von
Lebensmitteln auf die gebaute Umwelt mit
einer Fallstudie zu Ägypten. 2019 war sie
Co-Kuratorin der 12. Architekturbiennale
in Sao Paulo. Sie ist Co-Autorin von *Eileen
Gray: A House Under the Sun* (Nobrow,
2019) und *Some Haunted Spaces in Singapore* (Edition Patrick Frey, 2018) sowie
Mitherausgeberin von *Housing Cairo: The
(Informal) Response* (Ruby Press, 2016).
Sie ist außerdem Gründungsmitglied der
Parity Group und Parity Front, aktivistische
Netzwerke, die sich für die Verbesserung
der Geschlechtergleichstellung und Diversi-
tät in der Architektur einsetzen.

Charlotte Malterre-Barthes is an architect, scholar, and Assistant Professor of
Urban Design at the Harvard Graduate
School of Design. As the principal of the
urban design agency OMNIBUS, she directed the MAS Urban Design at the Chair
of Marc Angélil (2014–2019), and holds a
PhD from ETH Zurich on the effects of the
political economy of food on the built environment, case study Egypt. In 2019, she
was co-curator of the 12th Architecture
Biennale of São Paulo. She co-authored
*Eileen Gray: A House under the Sun* (Nobrow, 2019), *Some Haunted Spaces in
Singapore* (Edition Patrick Frey, 2018) and
co-edited *Housing Cairo: The (Informal)
Response* (Ruby Press, 2016). She is a
founding member of the Parity Group and of
the Parity Front, activist networks dedicated to improving gender equality and diversity in architecture.

**Jane McAllister** ist Akademikerin und Architektin, die an der Architectural Association School of Architecture in London ihren Abschluss gemacht hat. Derzeit leitet
sie das BA Architecture Programm an der
School of Art, Architecture and Design an
der London Metropolitan University und
arbeitet an einer Reihe von Live Commu-
nity-Projekten, an welchen auch internationale Universitäten und NGOs beteiligt
sind. In ihrer Dissertation betreibt sie ent-
wurfsbasierte Forschung und untersucht
das Gemeinwohl als Identität, Erinnerung

und Mythos durch die Bricolage ihrer Praktiken. Sie ist Mitinhaberin eines Designate-
liers, das Interkulturalität, und insbesondere
Themen und Fragen zu Migration und ihren
Auswirkungen auf Besiedelung und Identität erforscht.

**Jane McAllister** is an academic and architect who graduated from the Architectural Association School of Architecture in
London. She is also the BA Architecture
Course Leader for the School of Art, Architecture and Design at London Metropolitan
University and practices on a number
of live community projects at home and
abroad, working with international universities and NGOs. Her design-based PhD
explores community wellbeing as identity,
memory and myth through the bricolage of
their practices. She co-runs a design atelier
which explores 'crossing cultures' and specifically looks at issues around migration
impacting on settlement and identity.

**Nicolas Moucheront** bringt gerade sein
Doktoratsstudium an der Università Iuav di
Venezia und der École des hautes études en
sciences sociales in Paris zum Abschluss.
2018 hielt er im Rahmen der Konferenz „Les
années 1968 et la formation des architectes" einen Vortrag zu Giancarlo De Carlo
und ILAUD, der 2020 im Konferenzband *Architecture 68. Panorama international des
renouveaux pédagogiques* bei MétissPress
veröffentlicht wurde.

Nicolas Moucheront is currently finishing
his PhD at the Università Iuav di Venezia
and the École des hautes études en sciences sociales in Paris. In 2018 he presented
a paper on Giancarlo De Carlo and ILAUD
at the conference "Les années 1968 et la
formation des architectes" which was also
published in the volume *Architecture 68.
Panorama international des renouveaux
pédagogiques* (MétissPress, 2020).

**Lucia Pennati** ist Architektin und Doktorandin am Institut für Geschichte und Theorie der Kunst und Architektur (ISA) an der
Accademia di Architettura di Mendrisio. Ihr
Forschungsinteresse reicht von ungewöhn-
lichen Ritualräumen und ihrer Präsenz im
städtischen Kontext bis zu pädagogischer
Praxis und ihrer Beziehung zur gebauten
Umwelt und zur Entwurfslehre. Ihr Disser-
tationsprojekt handelt von dem Zusammenhang von Raumgestaltung und Pädagogik
im Werk des Schweizer Architekten und
Pädagogen Dolf Schnebli (1928–2009), insbesondere von seiner Idee der Schule, die
in Form seiner Bauten als auch durch seine Unterrichtstätigkeit in Erscheinung trat.
Derzeit ist sie wissenschaftliche Assisten-
tin am Lehrstuhl für Geschichte der Modernen Architektur an der Accademia di
Mendrisio.

Lucia Pennati is an architect and a PhD
candidate at the Institute for the History

and Theory of Art and Architecture (ISA) at the Accademia di Architettura di Mendrisio. Her research interest spans between unconventional ritual spaces and their presence in the urban context to educational practice and its relation with the built environment and design education. Her doctoral project deals with the relationship between spatial design and pedagogy by looking at the specific case of the Swiss architect and educator Dolf Schnebli (1928–2009). She researches Schnebli's idea of school, related to both his buildings and his teaching activity. Currently she is a teaching assistant at the Chair of History of Modern Architecture at the Accademia di Mendrisio.

**Sol Perez-Martinez** ist Architektin, Wissenschaftlerin und Kuratorin in London. Sie hat an der Bartlett School of Architecture (UCL) sowie am Institute of Education zu Colin Wards umweltbasierter Pädagogik und den Bemühungen des Urban Studies Centres (USC) zur Umsetzung von Wards pädagogischem Ansatz promoviert. Zuvor unterrichtete sie in Chile, wo sie auch ein Architekturbüro betrieb und mit ihren Büropartnern öffentliche und private Projekte realisierte. Seit 2013 kuratiert sie gemeinsam mit LehrerInnen, KünstlerInnen und ArchitektInnen Bildungsangebote, Konferenzen und Ausstellungen, um Partizipationsprozesse im Städtebau zu fördern. Derzeit lehrt sie an der Bartlett School of Architecture im Rahmen des MSc Learning Environments-Programms.

Sol Perez-Martinez is an architect, researcher, and curator based in London. She holds a PhD from The Bartlett School of Architecture (UCL) and the Institute of Education on Colin Ward's environment-based education and the efforts of the Urban Studies Centres (USC) to deliver Ward's pedagogical approach. Before researching in the UK, Sol lectured in Chile and ran an architectural practice where she and her firm partners developed public and private projects. Since 2013, Sol has collaborated with teachers, artists, and architects curating educational programs, conferences and exhibitions to widen participation in the construction of cities. She currently is a lecturer at the MSc Learning Environments at The Bartlett.

**Petra Petersson** ist Architektin. Sie hat in Lund, Schweden und an der Mackintosh School of Architecture, Glasgow School of Art in Schottland studiert, wo sie 1991 ihr Diplom erhielt. Seit über 30 Jahren arbeitet sie als Architektin, seit 2003 leitet sie ihr eigenes Architekturbüro REALARCHITEKTUR (www.realarchitektur.de), dessen realisierte Projekte international publiziert, ausgestellt und mit renommierten Architekturpreisen ausgezeichnet wurden. Sie ist Mitglied der Berliner Architektenkammer,

Ziviltechnikerin in Graz und berufenes Mitglied des BDA. Sie wird regelmäßig als Jurymitglied geladen und publiziert, macht Ausstellungen und hält Vorlesungen über ihre Arbeit auf internationaler Ebene. Seit 2013 ist sie Architekturprofessorin an der Technischen Universität in Graz, wo sie das Institut für Grundlagen der Konstruktion und des Entwerfens (www.koen.tugraz.at) leitet. Seit 2018 ist sie Dekanin der Architekturfakultät in Graz.

Petra Petersson is an Architect. She studied architecture in Lund, Sweden and at the Mackintosh School of Architecture, Glasgow School of Art, in Scotland where she received her Diploma of Architecture in 1991. She has 30 years of post-graduate architectural working experience. Since 2003 Petra Petersson owns and runs the architectural practice REALARCHITEKTUR (www.realarchitektur.de) with offices in Berlin and Graz. Several of the projects have been published and exhibited internationally, and have received renowned architectural awards. She is a registered member of the Berlin and Graz Chambers of Architects and an elected member of the BDA. She is regularly invited to be on architectural juries and publishes, exhibits, and lectures about her work internationally. Since 2013 she is a Professor of Architecture at the University of Technology in Graz, Austria, where she is the head of the Institute for Construction and Design Principles (www.koen.tugraz.at). Since 2018 she is the Dean of the Faculty of Architecture in Graz.

**Simran Singh** machte 2019 ihren Abschluss an der Architectural Association School of Architecture in London. Als Architektin und Urbanistin interessiert sie sich für die Rolle der Häuslichkeit bei der Gestaltung von Gemeinschaften und plädierte auf der Healthy City Design Conference 2019 in London und der EURA Conference 2021 für einen stärkeren Einfluss der Interiorität der Architektur auf das städtische Leben. 2009 wurde ihr Beitrag zur Biopolitik des Massenwohnungsbaus unter dem Titel „Power Pursuit of Political Urbanism: Recounting Housing Prototypes & their Domestic Narratives" auf der digitalen Plattform CARTHA veröffentlicht. Derzeit arbeitet sie zu den Auswirkungen der Präfabrikation auf Wohneinheiten im Rahmen virtuellen Docomomo-Konferenz (Israel-Deutschland).

Simran Singh graduated from the Architectural Association School of Architecture in London in 2019. As an architect and urbanist, she is inclined towards the role of domesticity in shaping our communities and has advocated the interiority of architecture to influence the urban life at the Healthy City Design Conference 2019 in London and at the EURA Conference 2021. For the digital magazine CARTHA, she wrote on the biopolitics of mass housing, titled "Power

Pursuit of Political Urbanism: Recounting Housing Prototypes & their Domestic Narratives." Currently she is working on the impact of prefabrication on basic units of habitation for the Docomomo Israel – Germany Online Conference.

**Jean-Louis Violeau** ist Soziologe und Professor an der École Nationale Supérieure d'Architecture de Nantes sowie Lehrbeauftragter an der École Urbaine at Sciences Po in Paris. Er ist Mitglied des Herausgeberbeirats von *Place Publique* und *Urbanisme* und arbeitet regelmäßig mit den Fachzeitschriften *L'Architecture d'Aujourd'hui*, *AMC – Le Moniteur Architecture* und *d'architectures* zusammen. 2018 leitete er das KuratorInnenkollektiv der Ausstellung „Les années 68. L'architecture aussi!" im Pariser Architekturmuseum Cité de l'Architecture et du Patrimoine. 2014 trug er zu der Ausstellung „Radical Pedagogies" sowie zum Katalog des französischen Pavillons an der Architekturbiennale von Venedig bei. 2018 erschien seine Publikation *Les Halles: De la contre-culture aux cultures parallèles (1964–1984)*. Mit Unterstützung von Semiotext(e) und von MIT Press co-editierte und koordinierte er die Übersetzung des Sammelbandes der Fachzeitschrift *Utopie. Text and Projects, 1967–1978*.

Jean-Louis Violeau is a sociologist and professor at the École Nationale Supérieure d'Architecture de Nantes, as well as a lecturer at the École Urbaine at Sciences Po in Paris. He belongs to the editorial board of the journals *Place Publique* and *Urbanisme* and regularly collaborates with the journals *L'Architecture d'Aujourd'hui*, *AMC – Le Moniteur Architecture* and *d'architectures*. In 2018 he led the collective curatorship of the exhibition "Les années 68. L'architecture aussi!" at the Cité de l'Architecture et du Patrimoine in Paris. He contributed to two displays held as part of the Venice Biennale of Architecture in 2014, "Radical Pedagogies" and the French Pavilion catalogue. In 2018 he published *Les Halles: De la contre-culture aux cultures parallèles (1964–1984)*, co-edited and coordinated the translation of *Utopie: Text and Projects, 1967–1978*, supported by Semiotext(e) and MIT Press.

**Marlene Wagner** schloss ihr Architekturstudium an der Technischen Universität Wien mit Auszeichnung ab und war Mitbegründerin des gemeinnützigen Büros buildCollective für Architektur und Entwicklung. Sie realisierte internationale Design Build-Projekte in öffentlichen und privaten Partnerschaften zwischen Europa und Afrika. Sie lehrte u.a. an der Fachhochschule Kärnten, der University of the Witwatersrand Johannesburg und der Universität für Kunst und Design Linz und arbeitete mit Education Africa, der Multidisciplinary

Design & User Research Group und d interuniversitären Zentrum für Technolo und Gesellschaft. Ihre kritische räumli Praxis, Forschung und Lehre zu sozialen chitekturen und transformativen Prozes verbindet Design und Bauen, partizipa Aktion und künstlerische Forschung, tersektionalität und postkoloniale The (www.marlenewagner.online).

Marlene Wagner graduated with hon in architecture at the Vienna University Technology and co-founded the non-pr practice buildCollective for architecture a development, realizing international des build projects within various public and vate partnerships between Europe and rica. She has taught, among others, at University of Applied Sciences Carint the University of the Witwatersrand Joh nesburg and the University of Art and sign Linz and worked with the NGO Edu tion Africa or the Multidisciplinary Des & User Research Group. Her critical spa practice, research and teaching on so architectures and transformative proces connects designing and building, partic tory action and artistic research, inters tionality, post- and decolonial theory praxis (www.marlenewagner.online).

**Adam Wood** hat in Sommercamps, in kulturellen Bildung, als Gymnasialle und als Forscher an Universitäten in en, Australien und London gearbeitet. Hauptinteresse gilt der Frage, wie der sische Raum (von politischen Entsc dungsträgerInnen, ArchitektInnen, Päda gInnen und Studierenden) genutzt wird, Bildungsmöglichkeiten zu definieren.

Adam Wood has worked in sum camps, cultural education, as a high sc teacher and university-based research Italy, Australia, and London. His main i est is how physical space is used (by cymakers, architects, educators, stude to define educational opportunities.

# Faculty News
## Aus der Fakultät

# „Was mich immer interessiert hat, ist der Alltag, das Nicht-Besondere"

**Matthias Castorph (MC) im Gespräch mit Daniel Gethmann (GAM)**

Matthias Castorph ist seit dem 1. September 2021 an der TU Graz Professor für Entwerfen im Bestand und Denkmalpflege. Er hat an der TU München Architektur studiert und wurde an der Universität Kaiserslautern promoviert. Castorph ist in München Partner im Architekturbüro „Lehmann, Tabillion & Castorph Architektur Stadtplanung Gesellschaft mbH".

**GAM:** Als neu berufener Professor an der TU Graz und entwerfender Architekt: Wie würdest du deinen Werdegang vom Studium ins Berufsleben beschreiben?

**MC:** Ich glaube, bis heute eigentlich zweigleisig. Das eine war, dass ich schon im Studium als Studienassistent am Lehrstuhl für Gestaltung und Darstellung den Wunsch hatte, auch zu lehren. Nach dem Diplom hatte ich das Glück, dass Andreas Hild, als er Gastprofessor in Kaiserslautern war, mich von diesem Lehrstuhl an

© GAM.Lab, TU Graz

der TU München bereits kannte und mich als Assiste[nt] mit nach Kaiserslautern genommen hat. Das andere ist, dass es mich immer schon interessiert hat, Dinge zu tun oder zu machen, und nicht nur zu lehren, den[n] man sollte ja auch nur das lehren, was man zumindes[t] ansatzweise schon selbst gemacht hat. So ergab sich parallel zur Universität mein erstes Büro und später bin ich in ein bestehendes Büro als Partner eingestie[gen]. Wenn man in ein Büro reinwächst, das schon ei[ni]ge Jahre weiter ist, kann man zu größeren Projekten beitragen, die man aus dem Stand erstmal nicht errei[chen] kann. Nach dem Intermezzo mit Andreas Hild an der Uni in Kaiserslautern, das mich fast wie ein Postgraduiertenstudium geprägt hat, hatte ich mich noch entschlossen, die Qualifikation als Regierungs[bau]meister anzustreben. Denn wir haben im Studiu[m] viel zu wenig gelernt über die Macht des Faktischen, über die Bedingungen von Bauen oder Architektur.

**GAM:** Worin besteht die Qualifikation eines Regierungsbaumeisters?

**MC:** Es geht formal darum, den Vorbereitungsdienst für den höheren bautechnischen Verwaltungsdienst z[u] machen. Er besteht aus dem Referendariat, der Mitar[beit] in Bauämtern und Behörden, einem Aufbaustud[i]um und Kursen und endet mit der zweiten Staatsprü[fung. Man darf sich dann als Berufsbezeichnung „Re[gierungsbaumeister" nennen. Normalerweise gehen fast 100 Prozent der AbsolventInnen in die staatliche[n] Bauabteilungen und Planungsämter.

**GAM:** Nach diesem Einblick in die Verwaltungsprax[is] der Planung bewegst du dich heute in der Praxis zwi[schen] Gebäudeentwurf und städtebaulichem Kontex[t]. Ist diese Perspektive auch durch die universitäre For[schung geprägt worden oder durch das Büro?

**MC:** Ich glaube durch beides, denn das eine geht für mich nicht ohne das andere. Architektur machen, üb[er] Architektur nachdenken und Architektur lehren, sin[d] verwandt, aber dennoch drei verschiedene Dinge. Nac[h]dem ich meine Dissertation relativ zügig abgeschloss[en] habe, den Ausflug in die Verwaltung hinter mir hatte[,] dachte ich, jetzt will ich wieder zurück an die Uni. Und dann kam der Moment, dass in Deutschland die Juniorprofessuren erfunden wurden. Da war ich eine[r] der ersten, die sich auf eine Stelle bewerben durften und hatte da die Möglichkeit, das allgemeine Thema meiner Dissertation sechs Jahre lang intensiv weiter[zu]entwickeln. Das Lehr- und Forschungsgebiet hieß damals „bauteilorientierte Entwurfsprozesse", und i[ch] habe mich dabei mit unterschiedlichen Fragen besch[äf]tigt: Wie funktioniert eine Bauteillogik im Entwurf? Was bedeutet dies für die Fügung oder auch für Typ[en]

gien? Bei diesen Beschäftigungen stellte sich dann die
age nach dem Kontext, nach dem Verhältnis der Ar-
itektur zur Stadt und das mündete dann letztendlich
eine Vertretungsprofessur für Stadtbaukunst, die
mals zu besetzen war.

AM: Deine Dissertation hast du 1999 abgeschlossen,
trägt den wunderbaren Titel: „Gebäudetypologie als
sis für Qualifizierungssysteme" und handelt unter
derem von Waschbeton und typologischen Fragen.

C: (lacht) Der Untertitel geht noch viel länger. Er
ißt: „Grundlagen einer Theorie zu Gattungen und
pen, entwickelt anhand systematischer Untersu-
ungen von industriell gefertigten Waschbeton-Mini-
l-Baukörpern als Verwahrräume für Entsorgungs-
ter in der Bundesrepublik Deutschland 1998/99".

AM: Deshalb verwendet die Universitätsbibliothek
r TU München für das Buch auch das Schlagwort
ülltonne".

C: Ja, was mich neben der abstrakten Typologiefor-
hung gleichzeitig interessiert hat, ist der Alltag, das
cht-Besondere, das Infraordinäre im Gegensatz zum
traordinären. Meine Hypothese war, dass es mög-
h ist, die meisten typologischen Fragen nach der
nt'schen Unterscheidung zwischen dem Erkennt-
urteil und dem ästhetischen Urteil in den Bereich
s Erkenntnisurteils zu schieben. Dazu gab es dann
Überlegung, einen Modellversuch zu machen. Ähn-
h wie BiologInnen an relativ einfachen Organismen
schen, habe ich Waschbeton-Mülltonnenhäuschen
tersucht und nicht gotische Kathedralen oder fran-
sische Schlösser. Denn das Gute an den Waschbeton-
illtonnenhäuschen ist, dass sie für die Forschung
e abgeschlossene Population bilden, die man nach
n immanenten Kriterien untersuchen konnte. Aber
entlich ging es mir in der Dissertation um den Be-
ff des „fluktuierenden Typus". Dabei werden die
jekte mit ihren Eigenschaften in einer Datenbank
rtfrei gesammelt und der jeweilige Typus entsteht
t im Moment der Abfrage, also nur durch die Ei-
aschaften, die er selbst hat. Ich konnte das damals
Ludger Hovestadt und bei Bernd Meyerspeer
chen und danach waren die sechs Jahre Junior-
ofessur genau das, wo ich auf dieser Basis daran
ter forschen konnte.

AM: Jetzt hast du von deinem eigentlichen Interesse
Infraordinären gesprochen, du verwendest in einer
ren Publikation auch den Begriff „Normalbauten"
r „Normalstadt". Wie unterscheiden sich diese Be-
fe von dem Gewöhnlichen, oder dem, was nicht
fällt und niemandem Fragen zu stellen scheint?

MC: Das Problem ist, dass der Begriff des Normalen,
den ich sehr lange benutzt habe, jetzt mit Corona nicht
mehr funktioniert, mit dem nun inflationär gebrauch-
ten „neuen Normal". Vorher waren die Begriffe „Normalstadt" oder die „Normalsituation" für mich eigentlich wahnsinnig schön, als ich seinerzeit mit dem Soziologen Julian Müller das Büchlein *Veduten der Normalstadt* gemacht habe. Das Prinzip ist vergleichbar der
Denkweise von Philippe Garniers *Über die Lauheit*,
wo er schreibt, dass zwischen den Höhepunkten, also
zwischen heiß und kalt, immer in der Mitte die Lauheit liegt, die eigentlich ideale Temperatur des Lebens.
Was mich daran interessiert, ist dabei nicht der Durch-
schnitt, sondern diese mittlere Amplitude. Das heißt,
die Normalität, oder das Alltägliche, oder wie man es
nennen will, ist das, wie Stadt und Architektur eigentlich stattfinden. Stadt braucht zum Beispiel ebenso die
nicht so guten Orte, wie die ganz phantastischen, genauso wie die Architektur. Auf der einen Seite ist die
Vorstellung, dass man als ArchitektIn eine ideale Welt
herstellen könnte bzw. sollte, einfach illusorisch, weil
die Jagd nach konkreten Idealen eigentlich immer zu
Katastrophen führt. Auf der anderen Seite wurde aus
meiner Sicht sehr selten oder fast nie versucht, sich
für das Nichtideale und in der Folge eben auch für
das Uninteressante zu interessieren, das nahe am Normalen liegt. Und wenn es dann um Stadt geht, wäre
da das „Normalstadtideal", das ich weiter untersuchen möchte.

.

Und wenn man diese Fragen ästhetisch untersucht,
habe ich die Vorstellung, dass, wenn man das Schöne
und das Hässliche nicht polar sieht, also wenn ich mir
die extremen Unterschiede zwischen dem Schönen
und dem Hässlichen als Kreismodell vorstelle – dann
gibt es nur noch eine kleine Lücke zwischen dem ex-
tremst Hässlichen und dem Schönsten und dann könnte man einen Übersprung, eine Verbindung zwischen
den Gegensätzen herstellen, wenn man nicht mehr in
diesen polaren Kategorien denkt. Das ist dann ähnlich
der Erkenntnis, dass die Erde nicht mehr eine Scheibe
ist, sondern eine Kugel. Dann kann man sich auf die
Entdeckung des Seewegs nach Indien machen und
entdeckt in diesem Gap auch ganz andere, unerwartete
Dinge – und das ist dann ein Forschungsmoment, das
mich interessiert.

GAM: Das ist ja eigentlich die Entdeckung des Seewegs in den Alltag, nicht? Wie kann ich den Alltag
tatsächlich als etwas Infraordinäres und gleichzeitig
etwas Spannendes wahrnehmen?

MC: Und wie kann ich mit dem auch arbeiten? Dazu
haben wir dieses Format vor einigen Jahren für die
Studierenden ins Leben gerufen, das ich „Site Repair"

genannt habe. Es ist eine Entwurfsstrategie bei der
man gemeinsam mit Studierenden an realen Fragestellungen, Situationen und Grundstücken arbeitet und
versucht „Reparaturen" vorzunehmen. Auch hier ist es
ein Ansatz, der sich mit dem Scheitern von Idealen im
Alltag beschäftigt. Denn ArchitektInnen formulieren
in ihren Entwürfen zumeist das „Schöne", „Innovative" und „Perfekte" als ideales Ziel und Anspruch und
hoffen so, die Mangelerscheinungen des Alltags heilen
zu können. Jedoch scheinen bei dieser Entwurfsstrategie die realen Orte nicht immer zu gewinnen, da nun
häufig die vorher bereits vorhandenen Unzulänglich-
keiten offensichtlich werden. Im Übertragenen wäre
dies mit der Situation vergleichbar, wenn man z.B. ei-
nem(r) NormalbürgerIn ein „Topmodel" zur Seite
stellen würde.

Bei „Site Repair" wollen wir daher dieses übliche
Entwurfsverfahren überdenken und in Workshops
experimentell untersuchen, ob und wie es möglich
ist, einen „idealen" Eingriff zu formulieren, der eine
reale Situation insgesamt positiv verändert. Es ist ein
Vorgehen, welches das Normale als Ideal beansprucht
und sich – ohne dabei den Anspruch an Qualitäten
aufzugeben – auf den alltäglichen Kontext und seine
Erscheinungen bewusst einlässt. Dabei wird versucht,
aus der Realität des Alltags, die dafür notwendigen
Potenziale zu isolieren, als Referenzen und Analogien
zu benennen und sie im Entwurf zu verwenden und
zu verwandeln. Dazu sollte der Eingriff möglichst
„minimalinvasiv" sein und trotzdem die Substanz so
wandeln, dass ein vorhandenes Defizit, sei es funktional und/oder formal, spannungsfrei behoben wird.

„Site Repair" versteht sich also als architektonischer
Vorgang, bei dem ähnlich einem Zahnarzt oder einem
traditionellen plastischen Chirurgen operiert wird,
wenn z.B. eine Zahnlücke mit einem Implantat geschlossen wird oder durch passende Eingriffe wieder
eine menschliche Erscheinung entsteht – passend zum
„gewachsenen" Kontext.

Ob dabei ein kleines Einzelstück z.B. als „Zahnersatz"
eingefügt wird oder mittels einer Affirmationsstrategie
eine Umwertung der realen Umgebung stattfindet,
bleibt dabei abhängig vom konkreten Ort, der vorge-
fundenen Situation und dem individuellen Ansatz der
Entwerfenden.

GAM: Du bist letztes Jahr an der TU Kaiserslautern
auf die Professur für Stadtbaukunst und Entwerfen be-
rufen worden und jetzt an der TU Graz an das Institut
für Entwerfen im Bestand und Denkmalpflege. Welches werden die Schwerpunkte deiner Arbeit an der
TU Graz sein, im Hinblick auf Entwerfen im Bestand?

MC: Mich interessiert hier – und das gefällt mir an der Benennung des Instituts – das „Entwerfen" im Bestand. Alle reden immer von Bauen im Bestand, aber ich finde, das Bauen kommt erst zum Schluss. Erstmal käme das Nachdenken, dann käme das Entwerfen und dann vielleicht das Bauen. Entwerfen im Bestand heißt für mich aber auch: Entwerfen unter der Macht der Bedingungen. Wenn man sich das wieder als ein Modell vorstellt: Außen liegen die Bedingungen und die sind ökonomisch, ökologisch, gesellschaftlich, historisch, usw., also alles, was auf uns einwirkt, wenn wir entwerfen. Dazu gehört natürlich auch das gebaute Erbe, die gebaute Umwelt. Wenn ich im Rahmen dieser Bedingungen mit den Studierenden entwerfe, habe ich ein starkes Bezugssystem, nämlich den Bestand. Unter dessen Einwirkung entstehen im Entwurf und im Bauen wieder neue Dinge, auf die ich mich dann wieder im Entwurf beziehen kann. Das funktioniert am besten, wenn man erstmal alles vorurteilsfrei anschaut, aufnimmt und dann individuell und rational damit arbeitet. Was wir tun wollen, ist, wenn wir eine Situation vorfinden, sie lesen zu lernen, zu fragen, was erzählt mir der Ort? Das ist der erste Schritt, wie gehe ich mit Geschichte(n) um, und der andere ist, welche Mittel und Werkzeuge habe ich, um dann eine Aussage zu treffen. Denn jeder Entwurf trifft letztendlich eine Aussage, weil er aus einem Entscheidungsprozess besteht. Das macht für mich dieses Entwerfen im Bestand aus und es hat mich sehr fasziniert, dass man das hier anscheinend machen kann und soll – und über die Organisation der Institute auch große wissenschaftliche und didaktische Freiheit hat.

GAM: Welche Rolle spielen die anderen Institute?

MC: Es geht darum, Kooperationen mit den anderen einzugehen, die ihren Input zu den Bedingungen eines Entwurfsprozesses interdisziplinär beitragen können, wie die ForscherInnen aus der Technik oder der Architekturtheorie, der Geschichte, der Soziologie oder auch aus ganz anderen Fachbereichen.

GAM: Wie soll die weitere Lehre am Institut aussehen?

MC: Ich werde unter dem bisherigen Titel „Architekturgeschichte der Moderne und der Gegenwart" Vorlesungen halten. Was ich aber dabei machen möchte, ist eine Entwurfsgeschichte der Gegenwart und eine Entwurfsgeschichte der Vergangenheit zu verknüpfen. Dazu werde ich Objekte aus unterschiedlichen Zeiten zusammennehmen und den Studierenden das, was entwurflich und abstrahiert dahinter liegt, erläutern, sodass deutlich wird, dass z.B. das Parthenon, die Nationalgalerie oder auch das Seagram Building beispielsweise zum Thema des Rasters und der Eckproblematik

erstaunlich nah beieinanderliegen. Bestenfalls wird dann klar, warum es Sinn macht, sich mit Begeisterung auch alte Sachen anzuschauen und den Hintergründen nachzuspüren. Meine Hoffnung ist, dass man so die Architekturgeschichte weniger als eine Personengeschichte betrachtet und vielmehr einen Kanon an Gebäuden oder Entwürfen vorstellt, an denen man bestimmte Fragestellungen sieht, die immer wieder beim Entwerfen aufkommen und darin erkennen kann, dass es offensichtlich zeitlose Möglichkeiten, Werkzeuge und Entwurfstechniken gibt, um sich diesen Fragen zu stellen.

GAM: Du hast einmal darüber gesprochen, dass du dieses Zurückschauen auf die Entwurfs- und Planungsgeschichte auch für forschungsrelevant hältst und du der Meinung bist, dass es durchaus Sinn macht, Werke neu zu editieren. Du hast ja Cornelius Gurlitts *Handbuch des Städtebaus* herausgegeben, du arbeitest gegenwärtig zu Theodor Fischer, Karl Henrici hast du ebenfalls neu herausgegeben; das sind Architekten der Zeit Ende des 19., Anfang des 20. Jahrhunderts, die für dich eine gewisse Aussagequalität besitzen. Sind das laufende Vorhaben, die du nach Graz mitbringst?

MC: Ich glaube, man bringt ja immer Dinge mit, die man hat, ob man will oder nicht. Aber es ist schon so, dass es auch darum geht, ein paar Dinge abzuschließen, was uns hoffentlich im nächsten Frühjahr mit einem Symposium an der TU Graz über Theodor Fischer und der Veröffentlichung einer wissenschaftlichen Ausgabe der 6 *Vorträge zur Stadtbaukunst* einen Schritt weiterbringen wird. Das Großartige bei Fischer ist, dass man in seinen 6 *Vorträgen zur Stadtbaukunst* auf ca. 90 Seiten, zu fast allen Themen der Stadtbaukunst, also wie Stadtbau und Baukunst zusammengehören, einen extrem klugen Einstieg bekommen kann.

Und zu dieser Beschäftigung zählen dann auch Camillo Sitte und Karl Henrici, die mit Fischer eine Reihe bilden, auch wenn die beiden letzteren etwas in Vergessenheit geraten waren. Uns interessieren ihre zeitlosen Entwurfswerkzeuge und Entwurfsregler und ein paar Aspekte mehr, die man einmal wieder zur Diskussion stellen sollte. Bei Gurlitt ist das Interessante, dass er um kurz vor 1920 versuchte, auch bedingt durch das Wissen, dass er von der Moderne überrollt würde, nochmal das gesamte Wissen des 19. Jahrhunderts zur Stadtbaukunst zusammenfasste, weil er wohl vermutete, dass bald danach keiner mehr darüber sprechen würde. Was ich beobachtet habe, ist ja der Verlust eines architektonischen Grundlagenwissens im 20. Jahrhundert, verursacht auch von Architekten wie Gropius oder Le Corbusier, die behaupteten, dass man es nicht

mehr bräuchte, obwohl sie es selbst noch exzessiv gelernt hatten.

Im eigenen Büro habe ich festgestellt, dass mich beim Entwurf zeitgenössischer Architekturen dieses „alte" Wissen sehr inspiriert. Und ich glaube, dass man beim Blick nach vorne unbedingt auch zurückblicken sollt[e]. Das klingt heute vielleicht paradox und für andere absurd, weil ich mich auch mit den vergessenen Erkenntnissen der Jahrhundertwende für moderne Entwürfe beschäftige.

GAM: Das klingt gar nicht absurd, ganz und gar nicht. Noch einmal zurück zu deiner Beschäftigung mit dem Alltag oder der Normalität in der Architektur. Geht daraus auch ein Forschungsthema hervor?

MC: Wenn ich mich mit Bestand auseinandersetze, finde ich Themen wie den Stadtrand, die Shoppingcity und so weiter genauso interessant wie das Weltkulturerbe Altstadt. Und ich möchte auch gerne zu Bestandsgebäuden des 20. Jahrhunderts arbeiten, die es jetzt schon nicht mehr gibt oder die es demnächst nicht mehr geben wird. Da geht es dann auch darum, dass man Alltagsgebäude und Typen anschaut wie z.B. die Videothek, das Internetcafé, den Sex-Shop, [d]as Bahnhofskino, die sind ja schon weg, oder vermutlich auch demnächst die Tankstelle in ihrer heutigen For[m]. Ganz viele dieser Alltagstypen verschwinden und sin[d] meist nur sehr schlank dokumentiert. Das ist auch ei[n] Problem des Denkmalschutzes, denn schließlich wir[d] dann nur noch das letzte, was noch vorhanden ist, unter Denkmalschutz gestellt, aber nicht, weil es das Beste ist, sondern weil es noch da ist. Deswegen wür[de] ich hier dringend für eine pro-aktive Vorgehensweis[e] plädieren.

GAM: Danke für das Gespräch. ∎

# "What Has always Inte[r]ested Me Is the Everyday-Life, the Mundane and Non-Special"

## Matthias Castorph (MC) in Conversation with Daniel Gethmann (GAM)

Matthias Castorph is Professor of Design in Consisti[ng]
Structure and Architectural Heritage Protection at G[raz]
University of Technology since September 1, 2021.

...e studied architecture at the Technical University ...Munich and was awarded his doctorate from ...[K]aiserslautern. Castorph is also associate partner ...Lehmann, Tabillion & Castorph Architektur Stadt-...[pl]anung Gesellschaft mbH in Munich.

...AM: As a newly appointed professor at the TU Graz ...[bu]t also as a practicing architect and designer: how ...[w]ould you describe your career path, from studying ...leading a professional working life?

...C: I think it is actually two-pronged to this day. One ...[th]ing is that as a student assistant to the Chair of Ar-...[ch]itectural Design and Conception, I wanted to teach ...[to]o. After graduating, I was lucky that Andreas Hild, ...[wh]o already knew me from this chair at TU Munich ...[an]d who was at the time a visiting professor at TU ...[K]aiserlautern, took me with him to Kaiserlautern as ...assistant. The other thing is that I have always been ...[ke]en on really doing or making things, and not just ...[te]aching, because one should only teach what one has ...least partly already done himself. That is how it ...[ca]me about that I started my first office in parallel to ...[un]iversity teaching and later on, joined an existing of-...[fic]e as partner. When you start working for an office ...[th]at is a few years ahead of you, you can contribute to ...[lar]ger projects, that you could not have achieved all ...yourself from scratch just like that. After working ...[wi]th Andreas Hild at the University in Kaiserlautern, ...[wh]ich shaped me just as much as a postgraduate course ...[do]es, I decided to pursue the title of a *Regierungsbau-*...*[me]ister*. The reason behind this was that we learned far ...[to]o little about the significance of real-life situations ...[du]ring our studies; and also about the conditions of ...[bu]ilding or of architecture even.

...AM: What is the qualification of a *Regierungsbau-*...*[me]ister*?

...C: It is a formality which involves doing the prepa-...[ra]tory services for the higher civil engineering admin-...[ist]ration. The requirements consist of professional ...[tra]ining, working for building authorities, postgradu-...[ate] studies and courses and finally passing the second ...[sta]te examination. You can then call yourself *Regie-*...*[ru]ngsbaumeister*. Usually almost 100 percent of the ...[gr]aduates end up working for in-state building depart-...[me]nts and planning authorities.

GAM: So after gaining insight into the administrative practice of planning, you find yourself today juggling between designing buildings and urban planning. Was this perspective shaped by your university research or by your office experience?

MC: I believe both, because to me, you cannot have one without the other. Making architecture, thinking about architecture and teaching architecture are re-lated, but nonetheless are three different things. After I had finished my dissertation quite quickly and the excursion into administration was all done, I thought to myself, now I would like to go back to university. And that is when junior professorships were invented in Germany. I was amongst the first to apply for a po-sition and had the opportunity to develop the general topic of my dissertation intensively for six years. The field of teaching and research back then was called *bauteilorientierte Entwurfsprozesse* (component-ori-ented design processes), and I dealt with different questions: How does component-logic work in de-sign? What does this mean for cohesion or also for ty-pologies? With these issues in mind, the question arose about context, and about the relationship between ar-chitecture and the city; and this ultimately led me to a deputy professorship for the Chair of Urban Art, which was to be filled at the time.

GAM: You completed your dissertation in 1999, with the wonderful title *Gebäudetypologie als Basis für Qua-lifizierungssysteme* (Building Typology as a Basis for Qualification Systems). It deals with exposed aggregate concrete and typological issues, amongst other things.

MC: (laughs) The subtitle is much longer! It goes: *Grundlagen einer Theorie zu Gattungen und Typen, entwickelt anhand systematischer Untersuchungen von industriell gefertigten Waschbeton-Minimal-Baukör-pern als Verwahrräume für Entsorgungsgüter in der Bundesrepublik Deutschland 1998/99* (Basics of a Theory on Genres and Types, developed on the Basis of Systematic Investigations of Industrially Manufac-tured Exposed Aggregate Concrete in Minimal Struc-tures as Storage Rooms for Disposal Goods in the Federal Republic of Germany 1998/99).

GAM: Right, which is why the university library of the Technical University of Munich also uses the keyword "garbage can" for the book!

MC: Yes, well, in addition to abstract typology re-search, what has always interested me is the everyday-life … the mundane and non-special; the infra-ordinary as opposed to the extraordinary. My hypothesis was that it is possible to consider most of the typological questions, in reference to Kant's distinction between the cognitive judgement and the aesthetic judgement, a matter of cognitive judgement. Then there was the idea of doing a model test. Similar to the way biologists research relatively simple organisms, I examined ex-posed aggregate concrete garbage cans, and not Gothic cathedrals or French castles. You see, the good thing about exposed aggregate concrete garbage can storage rooms is that they form a self-contained population for research that could be examined according to all immanent criteria. But actually, my dissertation was rather about the term "fluctuating type." The objects with their properties are collected, unbiased, in a data-base and the respective types only arise at the moment of inquiry; in other words, only through the properties that it itself has. At the time, I was able to do this re-search with Ludger Hovestadt and Bernd Meyerspeer. After that, the six-year junior professorship was exact-ly what I needed, to do further research on this basis.

GAM: Now, you have spoken about your real interest in the infra-ordinary. In another publication you also use the term "normal buildings" or "normal city." How do these terms differ from the ordinary, or from what goes unnoticed and doesn't seem to raise any questions?

MC: The problem is that the concept of the normal, which I have used for a very long time now, no longer works with Corona, due to the inflationary use of the phrase "new normal." Before, the terms "normal city" or "normal situation" were actually incredibly beauti-ful to me, back then when I was working on the book-let *Veduten der Normalstadt* (Imaginary Views of the Normal City), together with the sociologist Julian Müller. The approach is comparable to the way of thinking of Philippe Garnier's *Über die Lauheit* (About Lukewarmness), where he writes that between the high points, as in between hot and cold, the lukewarmness is always in the middle, which is actually the ideal temperature for life. What interests me in this concept is not the average, but this central amplitude. In other words, normality, the ordinary, or the everyday-life, or whatever you want to call it, is how the city and architecture actually exist. A city, for example, needs the not-so-good areas just as much as it needs the fantastic ones; the same applies for architecture. On the one hand, there is this idea that an architect could or even should create an ideal world, which is simply illusory, because the hunt for precise ideals always leads to disappointment. On the other hand, in terms of my point of view, hardly any attempts were made in finding interest in the non-ideal and, as a result, in the non-interesting, which is the closest to "normal." When it comes to cities, there is what I call the "normal city ideal," that I would like to further explore.

When you examine these questions aesthetically, I find that if you do not see the beautiful and the ugly as polar; in other words, when I see the extreme differences between the beautiful and the ugly in a circular model—then there is only a tiny gap between the extremely ugly and the most beautiful—and then you could actually take a leap and create a connection between these opposites, given you no longer think in polar categories. This is very similar to the realization that the earth is no longer a disk, but a sphere. Then you can set out on the discovery of the sea route to India and discover completely different and unexpected things in this gap—and this is the kind of research that interests me.

GAM: In other words, the discovery of the sea route in the everyday-life, isn't it? But how can I really perceive everyday-life as something infra-ordinary and something exciting at the same time?

MC: Right, and how can I work with all this too? To that end, we launched a format for students a few years ago, which I called "Site Repair." It is a design strategy in which you work with students on real issues, situations, and properties and try to make "amends." And here again, it is an approach that deals with the failure of ideals in everyday-life. Because architects in their designs, usually formulate the "beautiful," "innovative" and "perfect" as ideal goals and aspirations, and hope to be able to cure the deficiencies of everyday-life. However, the real site locations do not seem to always win with this design strategy, as the previously existing inadequacies often become apparent. In a figurative sense, this would be comparable to the situation, say if we were to place a "top model" next to a normal citizen, for example.

Therefore, with "Site Repair" we want to rethink this common design process and conduct experimental workshops to investigate whether and how it is possible to formulate an "ideal" intervention that alters a real situation in a positive way. It is a procedure that claims the normal as an ideal and—without giving up the claim to quality—consciously gets involved in the everyday context and its appearances. Attempts are made to isolate the necessary potentials from everyday reality, to name them as references and analogies, and to use and transform them in the design. For this purpose, the intervention should be as "minimally invasive" as possible and nevertheless transform the substance in such a way that an existing deficit, be it a matter of function and/or form, is eliminated without tension.

To sum it up, "Site Repair" is an architectural process in which an operation is carried out, similar to a dentist or a traditional plastic surgeon, if for example a tooth gap is closed with an implant, or a human appearance is recreated through appropriate intervention—matching the "evolved" context. Whether a small single-piece is inserted, as a "denture" for example, or whether the real environment is reassessed using an affirmation-strategy, all depends on the specific location, the situation found there and the individual approach of the designer.

GAM: Last year you were appointed to the professorship for the Chair of Urban Art and Design at TU Kaiserslautern and now at TU Graz at the Institute of Design in Consisting Structure and Architectural Heritage Protection. What will the focus of your work at TU Graz be, with regard to "Design in Consisting Structure?"

MC: What interests me here in Graz—and that is what I like about the name of the institute—is "designing" in consisting structure. Everyone is always talking about building on consisting structures, but according to me, building only comes towards the end. First comes thinking, then designing and then maybe building. To me, designing in consisting structures also means: designing under the influence of conditions. Again, if you think of it as a model: the conditions are on the outside and they can be economical, ecological, social, historical, etc., so everything that affects us, when we design. This of course also includes the built heritage

and the built environment. When I design with the students within this framework, I have a very strong frame of reference, namely the consisting structure. Under its influence, new things arise in the design and construction that I can then refer to again in the design. This works best, if you first look at everything without prejudice, note it down, protocol it and then work with it individually and rationally. What we want to do when we come across a situation, is to learn to read it and to ask ourselves: what is this place telling me? This is the first step in how I deal with stories; and then the next thing is to ask: which means and tools do I have to then make a statement? Because ultimately, every design makes a statement because it consists of decision-making process. To me, that is what defines "Design in Consisting Structure" and I was very fascinated by the fact that you could and should actually do it here in Graz—and that you have great scientific and didactic freedom throughout the organization of the institutes.

GAM: Which role do the other institutes play?

MC: It is about collaborating with others, who can contribute their input under the conditions of a design process in an interdisciplinary manner, such as technology researchers, or researchers of architectural theory, history, sociology or even of completely different disciplines.

GAM: How will all this apply to the teaching at the institute then?

MC: I will be giving lectures under the title Eine Architekturgeschichte der Moderne und der Gegenwart (A History of Contemporary Architecture). What I would like to do, however, is to link design history of the present with a design history of the past. For this purpose, I will bring objects from different times together and explain to the students how to read them in terms of design and abstraction, so that it becomes clear to them that, for example, the Parthenon, the National Gallery in Berlin or the Seagram Building, are astonishingly close to one another, in regard to the grid and the corner problem, for example. At best, it will become very clear, why it makes sense to look at old things with enthusiasm and to trace the background behind them.

hope that this way, the history of architecture will be viewed less as a history of persons but rather as a canon of buildings or designs that show certain issues that arise again and again during design, and that there are clearly timeless possibilities, tools, and design techniques available to deal with these issues.

**AM**: You once mentioned that you consider looking back at the history of design and planning to be relevant for research, and that according to you it is absolutely worthwhile to re-edit pieces of work. You are the editor of Cornelius Gurlitt's *Handbuch des Städtebaus* (Handbook of Urban Development), and currently you are working on Theodor Fischer; and you have also re-edited Karl Henrici. These are architects from the late 19th and early 20th centuries, who to you have a certain message. Are these ongoing projects perhaps something that you are bringing to Graz as well?

**MC**: Well, I think you always end up bringing things with you, whether you want to or not. But in any case, it is also about finishing a few things one started, which will hopefully bring one a step further. For example, this spring at the TU Graz, there will be a symposium on Theodor Fischer and the publication of a scientific edition of the *Sechs Vorträge zur Stadtbaukunst* (Six Lectures on Urban Design). The great thing about Fischer is that in his *Sechs Vorträge zur Stadtbaukunst* on approximately 90 pages, one gets an extremely smart introduction to almost all urban planning topics, for example how urban planning and architecture go hand in hand.

Other great thinkers include Camillo Sitte and Karl Henrici, who are just as important as Fischer, even though the latter two were somewhat forgotten. We are interested in their timeless design tools, design controls, and a few more aspects that should be revised. The interesting thing about Gurlitt is that shortly before 1920, also due to his knowledge that he would be overwhelmed by the modern age, he tried to summarize all of the 19th century knowledge of urban architecture one more time, because he probably suspected that soon enough nobody would want to talk about it. What I have observed is the loss of basic architectural knowledge in the 20th century, also caused by architects such as Gropius or Le Corbusier, who claimed that it was no longer needed, even though they had learned it extensively themselves.

In my own office, I noticed that I was quite inspired by this "old" knowledge when designing contemporary architecture. And I believe that when you look ahead, you should definitely look back too. That may sound paradoxical today and for others even absurd, because I also deal with the forgotten insights of the turn of the century for modern designs.

**GAM**: That doesn't sound absurd at all. I would like to go back to your pursuit of everyday-life or normality in architecture. Might this also become a research topic?

**MC**: When I deal with consisting structure, I find topics such as the outskirts, the shopping malls and so on, just as interesting as the old town, as a world cultural heritage site. And I would also like to work on consisting structures from the 20th century that no longer exist or that will no longer exist in the near future. It is also about looking at everyday-buildings and types, such as the video store, the internet café, the sex-shop, the train station cinema—they are all gone. Probably the petrol station in its current form will also soon be gone. Many of these everyday-types are disappearing and are usually hardly documented. This is also the problem with monument protection, because ultimately only the last piece standing is placed under monument protection; but not because it is the best of its kind, but because it is still here. That is why I would urgently argue for a proactive approach.

**DG**: Thank you for the interview. ▪

# Welten I–IV.
# Ein Zwischenbericht

Vier Semester lang dürfen wir – Anne Femmer, Florian Summa und Alexander Barina – die Professur Integral Architecture betreuen. Drei Semester davon sind schon vergangen. Im Folgenden einige unsortierte, ungeordnete und unvollständigen Erkenntnisse:

**(1) Uns werden unerwartet viele Türen geöffnet.** Von Grazer Institutionen, Einrichtungen und Privatleuten. Sie alle lassen die Studierenden bei sich vor Ort arbeiten, ermöglichen 1:1-Interventionen an ihren Gebäuden oder auf ihren Grundstücken. Vom Theatercafé, über das Bad Straßgang bis hin zum Elisabethhochhaus. Zu jedem ihrer Entwürfe haben die Studierenden einen Ausschnitt im Originalmaßstab gebaut und vor Ort mit der real existierenden Architektur verschmolzen. Durch das präzise Fotografieren wurden so „Welten" festgehalten, die auf eigenartige Weise beides sind: Realität und Fiktion, Original und Modell, Bestand und Entwurf.

**(2) Geld ist genügend da.** Das Bauen der großen Modelle ist nur möglich, weil unser Studio die Mittel dazu hat. Das Geld versuchen wir möglichst strategisch für die Lehre einzusetzen: Statt teuren Bürotischen etwa, haben wir einfache Klappböcke gekauft, statt drei Laptops nur einen. Dafür kaufen wir Baumaterial für die Studierenden, mit dem sie ihre großen 1:1-Entwürfe realisieren. Oder wir bezahlen Miettransporter, mit denen wir gebrauchte Holzmöbel abholen, um daraus neue Dinge entstehen zu lassen.

**(3) Es gibt großzügige UnterstützerInnen.** Manchmal brauchen wir ganz viel Material auf einmal. Zum Beispiel 3.500 weiße Fliesen im Format 10×10, womit die Studierenden eine ganze Wand bei uns im Studio gefliest haben. Agrob Buchtal hat sie sofort spendiert. Oder 90 Liter Lack für das Anpinseln von Möbeln im Rahmen eines W3-Workshops – geschenkt von Akzo Nobel Coatings, gemixt und geliefert von der Firma Mautner. Im aktuellen Semester wollen wir probieren, solche Mittel (aber auch die Arbeitsleistung von den Studierenden und uns) noch stärker für die Allgemeinheit einzusetzen: 20 Studierende werden eine Woche lang Gebäude von gemeinnützigen Institutionen pflegen, unterhalten und reparieren.

**(4) Unsere Dachterrasse ist unbezahlbar.** Direkt am Studio angeschlossen wird hier gesägt, gemalert, geschliffen, gegessen, geredet, geraucht … Wir hoffen mit unserem Staub und Lärm den NachbarInnen nicht allzu sehr auf die Nerven zu gehen.

**(5) Es geht nicht ohne physische Präsenz.** Eben weil wir so viel Freude haben am Sägen, Malern und Schleifen. Und weil wir denken, dass das unmittelbare Anpacken und Machen auch beim Entwerfen hilft. Dazu müssen Lehrende und Lernende physisch zusammenkommen. In den warmen Monaten hat dies bei uns immer gut geklappt. Im Winter war es oft zäh – für uns, aber vor allem für die Studierenden.

**(6) Das Internet im Zug ist stabil.** Das ist wichtig, denn wir fahren während dem Semester jede Woche mit dem Zug von Leipzig nach Graz und wieder zurück. Mit gutem Internet sind Graz und Leipzig eigentlich gar nicht so weit voneinander entfernt. Mit schlechtem Internet – alle paar Wochen – fragen wir uns manchmal schon, was das alles eigentlich für eine Schnapsidee war. ▪

*Anne Femmer/Florian Summa*

# Worlds I-IV. An Interim Progress Report

For four semesters, we—Anne Femmer, Florian Summa and Alexander Barina—are selected to hold the professorship Integral Architecture. Three

Projektübung | Integral Design Studio „Welten III"
© Integral Architecture, TU Graz

semesters have already passed. Here are some unsorted, unorganized, and incomplete thoughts:

**(1) Unexpectedly, many doors have opened to us:** such as Graz institutions, facilities and private individuals. They all allow students to work on site, enabling one-to-one interventions on their buildings or on their properties, such as the legendary Theater Café, the natural pool Bad Straßgang and the high-rise building Elisabethhochhaus. For each of their designs, the students built a fragment in the original scale and merged it with the existing architecture on site. Thus, the precise photography captured "worlds" that are strangely both reality and fiction, original and model, actual structure and draft version.

**(2) There is enough money.** Building the big models is only possible because our studio has the financial means to do this. We try to use the money as strategically as possible for teaching, instead of expensive office desks, for example, we bought simple folding trestles and only one instead of three laptops. With the saved money in return, we buy building materials for the students, which they use to create their large 1:1 designs, or we pay for rental vans with which we pick up used wooden furniture in order to create new things from it.

**(3) There are generous supporters.** Sometimes we need a lot of material at once. For example, 3,500 white tiles in 10×10 size, with which the students tiled an entire wall in our studio. Agrob Buchtal donated it immediately. We also received 90 liters of paint for painting furniture as part of a W3 workshop, donated by Akzo Nobel Coatings, and was mixed and supplied by Mautner. In the current semester, we want to try and use such funds (but also the labor of the students and ours) even more for the general public: 20 students will spend a week looking after, maintaining and repairing buildings of non-profit institutions.

**(4) Our roof terrace is priceless.** Directly connected to the studio, we saw, paint, sand, eat, talk, and smoke there … We hope that our dust and noise does not bother the neighbors too much.

**(5) It does not work without physical presence.** Precisely because we enjoy sawing, painting, and sanding so much. And because we think that getting to grips with things and doing things together directly also helps

when designing. To do this, teachers and learners must come together physically. In the warm months, this has always worked well for us. In winter it was tough—for us, but especially for the students.

**(6) The internet on the train is stable.** That's important because we take the train from Leipzig to Graz and back every week during the semester. With good internet, Graz and Leipzig are actually not that far apart. With poor internet every few weeks we sometimes wonder what kind of crazy idea we got ourselves into! ▪

**Professur Integral Architecture Team 2020–2022 ▸**
**Professorship of Integral Architecture Team 2020–2022:**
Anne Femmer, Florian Summa, Alexander Barina

# Gastprofessur
# Martin Knight

Im Wintersemester 2021 war Martin Knight erneut Gastprofessor am Institut für Tragwerksentwurf und leitete die Lehrveranstaltung „Big Scale: Hohe und weitgespannte Tragwerke" sowie, gemeinsam mit Stefan Peters und Andreas Trummer, die Projektübung „Highway Bridge", die sich mit Entwurfslösungen für eine neue Flussquerung über die Mur am südlichen Stadtrand von Graz auseinandersetzte. In einem integrativen Designprozess, der im Dialog mit BauherrenvertreterInnen der ASFINAG und des Landes Steiermark sowie ExpertInnen für Verkehrsplanung und Nachhaltiges Bauen entwickelt wurde, untersuchten die Studierenden Brückentyplogien, statische Verhältnisse sowie ökologische und energetische Aspekte einer Autobahn- und Radwegebrücke.

Martin Knight ist Architekt mit Sitz in London, England. Seit 2006 entwirft er außergewöhnliche Brückenprojekte und Infrastrukturbauwerke, die durch den Einklang von architektonischer Perfektion und gestalterischer Kreativität bereits mehrfach preisgekrönt wurden. Seine Entwurfsphilosophie setzt auf die praktische Umsetzung künstlerischer Prinzipien, die in unterschiedlichsten Dimensionen – von einer kleinen Fußgängerbrücke bis zu mächtigen Autobahnbrücken – zur Anwendung kommen. Er ist Mitglied des Royal Institute of British Architects (RIBA) und der Institution of Civil Engineers (ICE) und wurde zum Ehrenmitglied der Institution of Structural Engineers (IStructE) ernannt. ▪

*Andreas Trummer*

Martin Knight © Jenny Kaye/Knight Architects

# Visiting Professor
# Martin Knight

In the winter semester of 2021, Martin Knight was once again a visiting professor at the Institute of Structural Design and taught the course "Big Scale: Hohe und weitgespannte Tragwerke" (High and Wide-Span Structures) as well as the Integral Design Studio "Highway Bridge," together with Stefan Peters and Andreas Trummer. The Integral Design Studio dealt with design solutions for a new river crossing above the Mur in the southern outskirts of Graz. In an integrative design process, which was developed in dialogue with client representatives from ASFINAG and the State of Styria as well as experts in traffic planning and sustainable construction, the students examined bridge typologies, static conditions, and ecological and energy-related aspects of a motorway and cycle path bridge.

Martin Knight is an architect based in London. Since 2006 he has been designing extraordinary bridge projects and infrastructure constructions, that have already won several awards for the harmony of architectural perfection and design creativity. His design philosophy relies on the practical implementation of artistic principles that are used in a wide variety of dimensions—from a small pedestrian bridge to mighty motorway bridges. He is a Fellow of the Royal Institute of British Architects (RIBA) and the Institution of Civil Engineers (ICE), and an Honorary Fellow of the Institution of Structural Engineers (IStructE). ▪

River Thames Footbridge © Knight Architects

# Österreichisches Doktorand_innensymposium der Architektur

Das bereits zum vierten Mal organisierte „Österreichische Doktorand_innensymposium der Architektur", das von allen sechs österreichischen Universitäten, die ein Architekturstudium anbieten, als gemeinsames Anliegen betrieben wird, fand von 21. bis 22. Oktober 2021 an der Fakultät für Architektur der Universität Innsbruck statt. Die zweitägige Veranstaltung, die in Anselm Wagners Eröffnungsrede als „einziges fakultätsübergreifendes Zusammentreffen aller österreichischen Architekturhochschulen" vorgestellt wurde, gab 16 DissertantInnen die Möglichkeit, ihre Arbeiten einem Fachpublikum in den vier Kategorien „Geschichte/Theorie", „Raumwahrnehmung/Raumerfahrung", „Stadt/Urbanismus/Landschaft" und „Entwurf/Medien/ Technologie" zu präsentieren. Unter den Vortragenden befanden sich mit Birgit Androschin („Josef Lackner – Architekt und Hochschullehrer"), Christina Linortner („Alternative Pedagogies in Architecture") und Tobias Gruber („Die Kleinwohnung – Ein Entwurf") drei VertreterInnen der Architekturfakultät der TU Graz, die in jeweils zwanzigminütigen Vorträgen ihre Dissertationsprojekte zur Diskussion stellten.

© Universität Innsbruck

Neben RepräsentantInnen der Österreichischen Architekturfakultäten, ProfessorInnen und den OrganisatorInnen waren mit Jane Rendell, Bernd Nicolai, Lara Schrijver, Sonja Hnilica und Benjamin Dillenburger namhafte VertreterInnen internationaler Hochschulen geladen, denen die Rolle als RespondentInnen der einzelnen Themenpanels zukam. ▪

*Tobias Gruber*

# Austrian Symposium for Doctoral Students of Architecture

The "Austrian Symposium for Doctoral Students of Architecture" that has been organized for the fourth time as an issue of common interest for all six Austrian universities that offer architecture study programs, took place from October 21 to October 22, 2021 at the Faculty of Architecture of the University of Innsbruck. The two-day event, which was described in Anselm Wagner's opening speech as "the only cross-faculty meeting of all Austrian architecture schools," gave 16 doctoral students the opportunity to present their work to a specialist audience in the four categories "History/Theory," "Spatial Perception/Spatial Experience," "City/Urbanism/Landscape" and "Design/Media/Technology." Among the speakers and representatives of the Faculty of Architecture at TU Graz were Birgit Androschin ("Josef Lackner – Architect und University Professor"), Christina Linortner ("Alternative Pedagogies in Architecture") and Tobias Gruber ("The Small Apartment – A Design"), who each put up their dissertation projects for discussion after a twenty-minute presentation.

In addition to representatives of Austrian architecture faculties, professors and organizers, well-known representatives of international universities such as Jane Rendell, Bernd Nicolai, Lara Schrijver, Sonja Hnilica und Benjamin Dillenburger took part in the event, acting as respondents for the individual topic panels. ▪

# Zu Gast im Club Hybrid

Der für das Kulturjahr 2020 von Heidi Pretterhofer und Michael Rieper initiierte Demonstrativbau Club Hybrid in der Grazer Herrgottwiesgasse 161 diente der Fakultät für Architektur im Sommersemester 202 als Außenstelle für die Abhaltung diverser Lehrveranstaltungen. Das offene Konzept der temporären, proaktiven Installation, das die Hybridität von Nutzungen sowie die Diversität von Diskursen in sein Zentrum stellt, lud unterschiedliche Institute der Architekturfakultät ein, den Raum zu bespielen: So entstand i Oktober 2021 am Gelände des Club Hybrid eine aus Holzlatten errichtete temporäre Siedlung im Maßstab 1:1, die im Rahmen des „Beginners Workshop" (KOEN von 180 StudienanfängerInnen und 13 Lehrbeauftragten konzipiert und realisiert wurde. Im November nutzten Studierende und Lehrende des Instituts für Zeitgenössische Kunst (IZK) den Club im Zuge des Seminars „Artistic Practice II", das unter der Leitung von Milica Tomić, Rose-Anne Gush und Philipp Sattler performative Antworten auf Linda Nochlins Essay „Why Have There Been No Great Women

"Artistic Practice II" © IZK, TU Graz

rtists?" entwickelte und zur Diskussion stellte. Auch
ßerhalb der Lehre fanden sich Architekturstudie-
nde und Fakultätsangehörige wie Dekanin Petra
etersson oder Leiterin des Instituts für Städtebau
glaée Degros regelmäßig im Club Hybrid ein, um
n vielfältigen Programm wie beispielsweise der
iskussionsreihe „Talking Heads" teilzunehmen.

er Demonstrativbau wird ab März 2022 unter
m Titel „Werkstatt für Stadtstücke" weitergeführt
d lädt zur Abhaltung weiterer wissenschaftlicher,
instlerischer und aktivistischer Formate ein, die
bane Teilhabe, Stadtentwicklung und Hybridität
proben und baukulturelle Fragen unserer Zeit
skutieren. Mehr zum Programm unter:
ww.clubhybrid.at. ▪

ristine Rossegger

# isiting Club Hybrid

itiated by Heidi Pretterhofer and Michael Rieper as
rt of the *Kulturjahr 2020*, the Club Hybrid—a

KOEN's "Beginners Workshop" © Club Hybrid

demonstration building located at Herrgottwiesgasse 161 in Graz served the Faculty of Architecture as
a field site for holding various courses in the summer
semester of 2021. The club's identity as a temporary,
proactive installation, which encourages the hybridity
of uses and the diversity of discourses, invited various
institutes of the Faculty of Architecture to use the
space: In October 2021, a temporary 1:1 settlement
made of wooden slats was created on the Club Hybrid
site, designed and implemented by 180 first-year students and 13 lecturers as part of the "Beginners Workshop" (KOEN). In November, students and teachers
of the Institute of Contemporary Art (IZK) used the
Club during the seminar "Artistic Practice II," led by
Milica Tomić, Rose-Anne Gush, and Philipp Sattler,
which provided performative responses to Linda
Nochlin's Essay "Why Have There Been No Great
Women Artists?" and put them up for discussion.
Outside of teaching, both architecture students and
faculty members such as Dean Petra Petersson, or the
head of the Institute of Urbanism Aglaée Degros,
regularly took part in the Club's diverse program, such
as the discussion series "Talking Heads."

The demonstration building will continue its program
in March 2022 under the title "Workshop for City-

Pieces" and calls for other scientific, artistic, and
activist formats, that test urban participation, urban
development, and hybridity, in addition to discussing
building culture issues of our time. More about the
program at: www.clubhybrid.at. ▪

# Gender Taskforce – Geschlechter-gerechtigkeit in der Architekturlehre

Die Gender Taskforce, bestehend aus Dekanin **Petra Petersson**, **Ena Kukić**, **Anna Sachsenhofer** und **Budour Khalil**, versteht sich als eine Arbeitsgruppe am Institut für Grundlagen der Konstruktion und des Entwerfens (KOEN), die sich seit Januar 2021 für Geschlechter-gleichstellung und -gerechtigkeit in der Architektur-ausbildung stark macht. Nach neun Monaten inten-siver Vorbereitungszeit lud die Taskforce zu einem fakultätsweiten Vernetzungstreffen, bei dem gemein-sam mit VertreterInnen der einzelnen Institute und den zugeschalteten Gästen Charlotte Malterre-Barthes (Harvard GSDS/Parity Front ETH Zürich) und Bernadette Krejs (TU Wien/Claiming Spaces Kollek-tiv) Strategien zur gendersensiblen Lehre erarbeitet wurden. Zu den vielfältigen Tasks, die bereits umge-setzt wurden zählt beispielsweise eine breit angelegte Analyse von Lehrmaterialen in Hinblick auf Referenz-projekte von Architektinnen, die ergeben hat, dass nur 4,2 Prozent der in der Lehre referenzierten Beispiele von Frauen stammen – und das bei einem Studen-tinnenanteil von über 50 Prozent. Aktuell setzt die Gender Taskforce ihre Strategie zur Aktualisierung der Lehrmaterialien um. Auch der Vortrag von Ena Kukić und Armin Stocker im Rahmen der TU Graz Ringvorlesung „Vielfalt im Zentrum der Forschung" mit dem Titel „Haben Sie gewusst, dass Architek-tur … angeblich männlich ist?", machte deutlich, wel-chen maßgeblichen Anteil Frauen an der Gestaltung von gebauter Umwelt und Forschungslandschaft, so-wie an der Weiterentwicklung der Disziplin geleistet haben und nach wie vor leisten.

Die Initiative der Gender Taskforce wurde am 4. November 2021 mit dem TU Graz Mind the Gap – Diversity Award ausgezeichnet. Der von Vizerektor Stefan Vorbach überreichte Preis wird einmal jährlich an die fünf besten Einreichungen von Studierenden und Mitarbeitenden der TU Graz ver-geben, die sich im Rahmen von wissenschaftlichen Arbeiten, Initiativen oder Publikationen mit dem Faktor Mensch und seiner Diversität in Technik und Naturwissenschaften auseinandersetzen. Die Jury betonte die „bemerkenswerte Perspektivenvielfalt und den partizipativen Ansatz" der Initiative. ▪

*Christine Rossegger*

Gender Taskforce Team: Petra Petersson, Ena Kukić, Budour Khalil, Anna Sachsenhofer © KOEN, TU Graz

# Gender Taskforce – Gender Equality in Architectural Education

The Gender Taskforce, consisting of Dean **Petra Petersson**, **Ena Kukić**, **Anna Sachsenhofer** and **Budour Khalil**, sees itself as a working group at the Institute of Construction and Design Principles (KOEN), which has been campaigning for and made remarkable efforts to promote gender equality in architectural edu-cation since January 2021. After nine months of inten-sive preparation, the task force arranged a faculty-wide network meeting to discuss strategies developed for gender-sensitive education together with the represen-tatives of the individual institutes, as well as with the guests Charlotte Malterre-Barthes (Harvard GSD/Parity Front ETH Zurich) and Bernadette Krejs (TU Wien/Claiming Spaces collective), who joined the meeting online. The diverse tasks that have already been im-plemented include, for example, a broad analysis of teaching materials with regard to reference projects by female architects, which showed that only 4.2 percent of the examples referenced in teaching materials come from women—this while the proportion of female students is over 50 percent. Currently, the Gender Taskforce is implementing its strategy for updating the teaching materials. Also the lecture by Ena Kukić und Armin Stocker as part of the TU Graz Lecture Series "Vielfalt im Zentrum der Forschung" titled "Haben Sie gewusst, dass Architektur … angeblich männlich ist?" made very clear, what significant role women have played and still play in the design of built envi-ronment and the research landscape, as well as in the further development of the discipline.

On November 4, 2021 the Initiative Gender Task-force received the TU Graz Mind the Gap – Diversity Award. The prize, presented by Vice Rector Stefan Vorbach, is awarded once a year to the five best submis-sions by students and employees of Graz University of Technology that deal with the human factor and in diversity in technology and the natural sciences carried out within the parameters of scientific work, initiatives or publications. The jury emphasized the "remarkable diversity of perspectives as well as the participatory approach" of the initiative. ▪

206

## GAD Awards 2021

Zum 19. Mal wurden am 14. Oktober 2021 die Grazer Architekturdiplompreise verliehen. Die internationale Jury, darunter **Jeannette Kuo** (Harvard GSD/Karamuk Kuo, Zürich), **Vera Bühlmann** (TU Wien) und **Irmgard Frank** (Wien) versammelte sich an der TU Graz, um aus insgesamt 40 nominierten Masterarbeiten sechs DiplomandInnen aufgrund ihrer hervorragenden Leistung auszuwählen und zu prämieren. Der 1. Preis, gestiftet von der Steiermärkischen Landesregierung, Abteilung 16 Verkehr und Landeshochbau – Fachteam

Baukultur, wurde an **Bruno Raškaj** für sein Projekt „**Reliquiae Reliquiarum**" vergeben. Das von **Petra Petersson** am Institut für Grundlagen der Konstruktion und des Entwerfens (KOEN) betreute Projekt thematisiert das verborgene Potenzial einer ehemaligen Seidenfabrik in Zagreb und entwickelt im städtischen Kontext des Viertels Trešnjevka ein Revitalisierungskonzept. Raškajs rückwirkendes Programm stellt die Tragstruktur des Hauptgebäudes und des umliegenden Ruinenparks, die zuvor unabhängig voneinander waren, in den gestalterischen Mittelpunkt und schafft somit eine poetische Verbindung zwischen Innen und Außen. Das Projekt überzeugte die Jury aufgrund der sorgfältigen und pointierten Recherche industrieller Architektur, der klar formulierten These sowie seiner

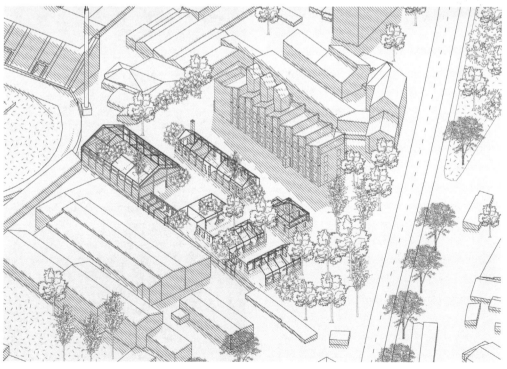

1. Preis „Reliquiae Reliquiarum", Bruno Raškaj

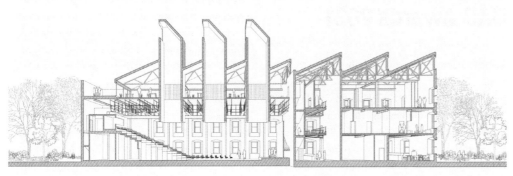

1. Preis „Reliquiae Reliquiarum", Bruno Raškaj

Relevanz hinsichtlich sozialer und ökologischer Nachhaltigkeit. Dabei betonte die Jury die genaue und einfühlsame Ausarbeitung des Projekts auf unterschiedlichen Maßstabsebenen sowie die gelungene architektonische Umsetzung des Dialogs von Alt und Neu.

# GAD Awards 2021

On October 14, 2021 the Grazer Architekturdiplompreise (Graz Architecture Diploma Awards) were awarded for the 19th time. The international jury, including **Jeannette Kuo** (Harvard GSD/Karamuk Kuo, Zurich), **Vera Bühlmann** (TU Wien) und **Irmgard Frank** (Vienna), met at the Graz University of Technology to select and award six diploma students out of a total of 40 nominated master's theses, for outstanding performance. The 1st prize, donated by the State Government of Styria, Department 16 for Transport and Building Construction, was awarded to **Bruno Raškaj** for his project "**Reliquiae Reliquiarum.**" The project, supervised by **Petra Petersson** (Institute of Construction and Design Principles) addresses the hidden potential of an abandoned silk factory in Zagreb and develops a renewal concept in the urban context of the Trešnjevka district. The project convinced the jury due to the thorough research on industrial architecture, the clearly formulated proposal and its relevance with regard to social and ecological sustainability. The jury highlighted in their statements the sensitive development of the project on different scales, as well as the successful architectural implementation of dialogue between the old and the new.

**Laura Nefeli Chromecek** erhielt für ihre Masterarbeit „**Loutra – Eine meteorologische Landschaft**" den 2. Preis der GAD Awards. Betreut von **Klaus K. Loenhart** (Institut für Architektur und Landschaft), erweitert das Projekt den Raumbegriff durch die Dimension der Atmosphäre und erklärt sie zur eigentlichen Aufgabe der Architektur. Dies wird am Beispiel eines Thermalbads auf der griechischen Vulkaninsel Nisyros veranschaulicht, indem Räume als „Atmosphären-Behälter" konzipiert und physikalisch greifbar gemacht werden. Die Jury würdigte das originelle und gut informierte Entwurfskonzept, das einen wichtigen Theoriediskurs anstößt – nämlich Klima und Wetter physikalisch zu denken – und diesen mit den Mitteln der Architektur auf ehrgeizige Weise ausdrückt.

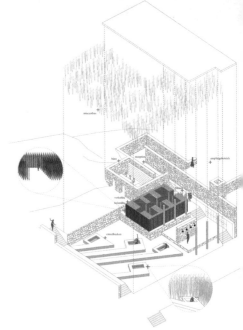

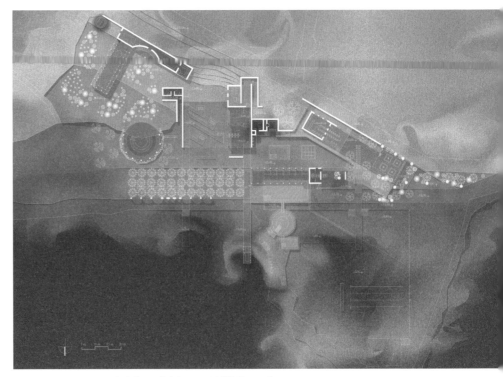

2. Preis „Loutra – Eine meteorologische Landschaft", Laura Nefeli Chromecek

Preis „Loutra – Eine meteorologische Landschaft",
ura Nefeli Chromecek

ura Nefeli Chromecek was awarded the 2nd prize
 her diploma project "Loutra – Eine meteorologi-
 e Landschaft." The project, supervised by Klaus K.
 enhart (Institute of Architecture and Landscape),
 pands the concept of space through atmosphere and
 clares it to be the real task of architecture. This idea
 llustrated through an example of a thermal bath on
 e Greek volcanic island Nisyros, in which rooms are
 signed as "atmosphere-containers" and are made
 ysically tangible. The jury praised the original and
 ll-informed design concept that initiates an impor-
 t theoretical discourse, namely to think physically
 out climate and weather and to express these in an
 bitious way through architecture.

 r 3. Preis ging an das Projekt von Katharina
 hnwarter und Michael Hafner mit dem Titel
 Douro e as Águas do Moledo. Eine topologische
 näherung", das sich mit der Struktur eines ehema-
 en Grand Hotels im Douro-Tal beschäftigt. Die
 n Uli Tischler am Institut für Gebäudelehre (IGL)
 creute Masterarbeit überzeugte die Jury durch die

solide Analyse der spezifischen Landschaft und Topografie, aus der sich ein linearer Entwurf ableitet. Die
Uminterpretation des einst elitären Thermenhotels in
einen öffentlich zugänglichen Pavillon, der von einem
Thermalpark durchdrungen wird und schließlich ein
„Straßendorf" entlang des Flusses bildet, überzeugte
die Jury u.a. auch durch die poetische Ausarbeitung
der Pläne und zwei ausdrucksstarke Modelle in unterschiedlichen Maßstäben.

The 3rd prize went to the project titled "O Douro e as
Águas do Moledo. Eine topologische Annäherung" by
Katharina Hohenwarter and Michael Hafner. The
project, supervised by Uli Tischler (Institute of Design
and Building Typology), deals with the structure of a
former Grand Hotel in the Douro Valley. The master's
thesis convinced the jury with its robust analysis of the
specific landscape and topography, out of which a

3. Preis „O Douro e as Aguas do Moledo", Katharina Hohenwarter & Michael Hafner

209

linear design was derived. The reinterpretation of the once elite Grand Hotel with hot springs into a publicly accessible pavilion, permeated by a hot springs park, that ultimately transforms into a "street village" along the river, convinced the jury; in addition to the poetic elaboration of the plans and the two expressive models in different scales.

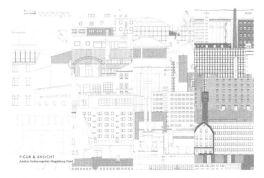

Hollomey Reisepreis „Grammatik einer Industrielandschaft", Maike Gold

Der diesjährige Hollomey Reisepreis wurde **Maike Gold** für ihre Abschlussarbeit **„Grammatik einer Industrielandschaft. Spekulatives Magdeburg in Figur und Struktur"** überreicht. Das laut Jury gut durchdachte Projekt positioniert sich an der Schnittstelle zwischen Theorie und Praxis und entwirft aufbauend auf semiotischen Analysen einen sprachlichen Ausdruck für Industrie- und Infrastrukturelemente aus der lokalen Situation Magdeburgs und versucht in Analogie zur Vorstellung eines Sprachspiels eine Grammatik zu erfinden. Betreut wurde das Projekt von **Andreas Lechner** (Institut für Gebäudelehre).

This year's Hollomey Travel Award went to **Maike Gold** for her thesis **"Grammatik einer Industrielandschaft. Spekulatives Magdeburg in Figur und Struktur."** According to the jury, the well thought-out project positions itself at the interface between theory and practice. Based on semiotic analysis, the project "designs" a linguistic expression for industrial and infrastructure elements from the local situation in Magdeburg and attempts to invent a grammar, analogous to the idea of a language game. The project was supervised by **Andreas Lechner** (Institute of Design and Building Typology).

**Amila Smajlović** erhielt mit ihrer Diplomarbeit **„Äquilibrium. Über Distanz und Nähe in der Stadt"**, betreut von **Armin Stocker** (KOEN), den Tschom Wohnbaupreis. Das Projekt setzt sich mit flexibler Wohnraumerweiterung auseinander und überzeugte durch die Entwicklung eines modularen Systems in Grundriss, Schnitt und Ansicht, die eine Staffelung der privaten und gemeinschaftlichen Bereiche erlaubt, und dennoch keinem Schematismus verfällt.

Amila Smajlović received the Tschom Housing Award for her diploma thesis **"Äquilibrium. Über Distanz und Nähe in der Stadt,"** supervised by **Armin Stocker** (Institute of Construction and Design Principles). The project deals with flexible living space expansion and impressed the jury with the development of a modular system applied to the floor plan, section and elevation. The system allows for the private and commercial areas to be staggered, without lapsing into schematism.

Anerkennung für ressourcensschonende und klimagerechte Architektur „BENUTZEN", David Ortner

Die Anerkennung für ressourcenschonende und klimagerechte Architektur, die seit 2019 von der ZiviltechnikerInnenkammer für Steiermark und Kärnten gestiftet wird, ging in diesem Jahr an **David Ortner** für seine Masterarbeit **„BENUTZEN. Obsolete Strukturen als Ressource – Konversion des Krankenhaus Oberwart"** betreut von **Hans Gangoly** (IGL). Das Projekt überzeugte durch die präzisen und punktuellen Interventionen, die basierend auf einer strengen Ökonomie der Mittel und dem Ziel des Erhalts von bestehender Bausubstanz, ein ehemaliges Krankenhaus in ein Altenpflegewohnquartier der fünften Generation und einen Ort des aktiven Gesundbleibens überführt.

The "Recognition for Resource and Climate Friendly Architecture," which has been kindly donated by the Chamber of Civil Engineers of Styria and Carinthia since 2019, went to **David Ortner** for his diploma project **"BENUTZEN. Obsolete Strukturen als Ressource – Konversion des Krankenhaus Oberwart,"** supervised by **Hans Gangoly** (Institute of Design and Building Typology). With the intention of saving resources paired with the goal of preserving the existing buildings, the project converts a former hospital into a fifth-generation residential home for the elderly, transforming it into a place for actively staying healthy. It was the precise and punctual intervention that convinced the jury.

Tschom Wohnbaupreis, „Äquilibrium", Amila Smajlović

# Herbert Eichholzer Förderungspreis 2021

Magdalena Zoller, Sarah Höllisch © KOEN, TU Graz

Das diesjährige Wettbewerbsthema des Herbert Eichholzer Förderungspreises lautete „Studentisches Leben in St. Leonhard" und stellte Studierende der Fakultät für Architektur vor die Herausforderung, ein Studierendenwohnhaus in der Leonhardstraße 61, auf einem zwischen zwei Universitäten gelegenem Grundstück, zu entwerfen. Das Gewinnprojekt von **Sarah Höllisch** und **Magdalena Zoller** überzeugte durch einen klaren Entwurf, der die studentischen Wohneinheiten durch geschickt platzierte Schwellenräume ergänzt und dabei vielfältige individuelle als auch ge-

meinschaftliche Nutzungsoptionen ermöglicht. Als größter gemeinschaftlich nutzbarer Aufenthaltsbereich fungiert das Erdgeschoss, in dem sich ein Laden mit Café, sowie ein öffentlich zugänglicher Garten befindet, der ebenso als Anbaufläche als auch für Veranstaltungen genutzt werden kann.

Die diesjährige Anerkennung ging an **Stefanie Obermayer** und **Sebastian Stubenrauch**, die mit ihrem Projekt „Hommage Orange", den ehemaligen Treppenturm des Studentenwohnheims am Hafnerriegel (Werkgruppe Graz) in ihrem Entwurfskonzept referenzierten. Das Raumprogramm gestaltet sich durch verschiebbare Schlafboxen flexibel und reagiert damit auf unterschiedliche Wohnbedürfnisse.

Vergeben wurden die von der Stadt Graz und der Fakultät für Architektur ausgeschriebenen Preise im Rahmen einer digitalen Preisverleihung am 24. November 2021, an der Dekanin und KOEN-Institutsleiterin Petra Petersson, Universitätsassistentin Lisa Obermayer (KOEN) sowie Stadtrat Günter Riegler (Stadt Graz) mitwirkten. Mit dem Herbert Eichholzer Förderungspreis, der seit 1992 zweijährlich vergeben wird, bringen die Stadt Graz und die Technische Universität Graz ihre tiefe Verbundenheit mit Herbert Eichholzer und seinem Wirken als wichtiger Vertreter der Architekturmoderne der Zwischenkriegszeit und des Widerstands gegen den Nationalsozialismus zum Ausdruck. Ausgerichtet und organisiert wurde die Preisverleihung in diesem Jahr vom Institut für Grundlagen der Konstruktion und des Entwerfens (KOEN).

e prämierten Arbeiten wurden von 15. bis 22. Oktor 2021 im Foyer der Alten Technik ausgestellt und 1 8. November 2021 von den GewinnerInnen in urzvorträgen im HDA – Haus der Architektur Graz rgestellt. Alle nominierten Projekte sowie die Jurytements sind auf der Homepage der GAD Awards ww.gad-awards.tugraz.at) zugänglich. ▪

*ra Eckhard*

e award-winning projects were displayed in the yer of the Alte Technik from October 15 to Octor 22, 2021. The winners presented their projects a wider audience on November 8, 2021 in the DA – Haus der Architektur Graz. All nominated projts as well as the jury statements can be found on the AD Awards homepage: www.gad-awards.tugraz.at. ▪

Gewinnerprojekt Herbert Eichholzer Förderungspreis 2021, Magdalena Zoller, Sarah Höllisch © KOEN, TU Graz

Der diesjährigen Jury gehörten an: **Vanessa Bauer** (Stadtplanungsamt Graz), **Alex Lehnerer** (Institut für Raumgestaltung), **Petra Petersson** (Dekanin der Fakultät für Architektur, KOEN), **Antje Senarclens de Grancy** (Institut für Architekturtheorie, Kunst- und Kulturwissenschaften) und **Florian Summa** (Integral Architecture). ▪

*Christine Rossegger*

# Herbert Eichholzer Award 2021

The central theme of this year's Herbert Eichholzer Award was titled "Student Life in St. Leonhard" and challenged students from the Faculty of Architecture to design an ideal student habitat on the building site Leonhardsraße 61 in Graz, selected because of its central location between two universities. The winning project by **Sarah Höllisch** and **Magdalena Zoller** stood out with its clear design that complements the student housing units with well-placed threshold-level spaces, thereby enabling a wide range of individual and communal functions. The ground floor serves as the main lounge area, in which there is a shop with a café and a publicly accessible garden, that can also be used for cultivation and events.

Sebastian Stubenrauch, Stefanie Obermayer © KOEN, TU Graz

This year's Recognition Award went to **Stefanie Obermayer** and **Sebastian Stubenrauch**, who in their project "Hommage Orange" referenced the former "Treppenturm" (stair tower) of the student dormitory on Hafnerriegel (Werkgruppe Graz). The room arrangement is flexible thanks to moveable sleeping boxes, thus responding to different living needs.

Anerkennung „Hommage Orange", Sebastian Stubenrauch, Stefanie Obermayer © KOEN, TU Graz

The prizes announced by the City of Graz and the Faculty of Architecture were awarded at a virtual award ceremony on November 24, 2021, hosted by the Institute of Construction and Design Principles, represented by Petra Petersson and Lisa Obermayer, and City of Graz representative Günter Riegler. The Herbert Eichholzer Award, held every two years, symbolizes the unity of the City of Graz and the Graz University of Technology, with Herbert Eichholzer and his work as an important representative of modern architecture in the interwar period and in his resistance to National Socialism. This year's jury included **Vanessa Bauer** (Graz Department of Urban Planning), **Alex Lehnerer** (Institute of Spatial Design), **Petra Petersson** (Dean of the Faculty of Architecture, KOEN), **Antje Senarclens de Grancy** (Institute of Architectural Theory, Art History and Cultural Studies) and Florian Summa (Integral Architecture). ▪

# „WAUXI"-Wandkonstruktion erhält 3. Preis beim IASS Symposium

Das Projekt „WAUXI – Wall Auxetic Structure Installation", das am Institut für Tragwerksentwurf im Rahmen der Lehrveranstaltung „Tragwerke im Entwurf" (WS20/21) unter der Leitung von Christoph Holzinger und David Gierlinger initiiert und von einem Studierendenteam selbstständig weiterentwickelt wurde, überzeugte die Jury beim diesjährigen Online Symposium der International Association for Shell and Spatial Structures (IASS). Die von den Studierenden **Simon Winter**, **Kilian Hoffmann** und **Hanna Gletthofer** entworfene zweischalige Wandkonstruktion besteht aus Y-förmigen Sperrholzelementen und dreieckigen flexiblen Teilen und verformt sich durch einen Seilzugmechanismus zu einem Pavillon. Dieses Entwurfskonzept basiert auf sogenannten „Auxetic Structures", die es ermöglichen, dass Leichtbaukonstruktionen eben angeliefert werden können und erst vor Ort ihre finale Größe und Krümmung durch Krafteinwirkung entfalten, ohne verzerrt zu werden. ▪

*Christine Rossegger*

## "WAUXI"-Wall Structure Awarded 3rd Prize at the IASS Symposium

The project "WAUXI – Wall Auxetic Structure Installation" was developed as part of the course "Supporting Structures in Design" in the winter semester 2020/21 at the Institute of Structural Design under the direction of Christoph Holzinger and David Gierlinger and was further developed independently by a student team. The project captivated the jury at this year's online symposium of the International Association for Shell and Spatial Structures (IASS). The double-shell wall construction, designed by the students **Simon Winter**, **Kilian Hoffmann** and **Hanna Gletthofer**, is made of Y-shaped plywood elements and triangular flexible parts, and deforms into a pavilion by means of a pulley mechanism. This design is based on the concept of "auxetic structures," that allows lightweight constructions to be delivered flat so that they can develop their final size and curvature on-site. By using simple application of force, these constructions unfold without distortion. ▪

„WAUXI"-Studierendenteam

# Digital Teaching

## Platform(x) unterstützt Online-Lehre

Das Institut für Architektur und Medien (IAM) verwendet für seine Lehrveranstaltungen seit vielen Jahren eine eigene Software, welche den Austausch der Studierenden untereinander und das Lernen voneinander unterstützt. Die sogenannte Platform(x) geht auf eine Entwicklung an der ETH Zürich zurück und wurde an der Harvard Graduate School of Design weiterentwickelt. IAM-Institutsleiter Urs Hirschberg ist einer der Entwickler von Platform(x). Er hat sie seit seiner Berufung an die TU Graz mit seinem Team kontinuierlich in der Lehre eingesetzt und jeweils an neue Bedürfnisse angepasst. Das Programm ermöglicht es, Abgaben von Studierenden in beliebigen Formaten zu verwalten, archivieren und visualisieren und, dem Open Source-Gedanken folgend, für alle zugänglich zu machen. Mit Platform(x) können komplexe Projekte, an denen NutzerInnen parallel arbeiten ebenso durchgeführt werden, wie einfache Übungen oder Seminare

für große Studierendengruppen, wie sie im Bachelorstudium an der Fakultät üblich sind. Die Studierende können ihre Abgaben gegenseitig kommentieren und besonders gelungene Arbeiten einander empfehlen. Während der Pandemie, als die Lehre fast ausschließlich online stattfand, hat sich Platform(x) besonders bewährt. Voneinander angeregt und inspiriert zu werden, andere Ideen und Herangehensweisen kennenzulernen, das sind wichtige Teile des universitären Lernens, gerade in der Architektur. Mit Platform(x) konn diese Vielfalt und dieser Austausch wenigstens zum Teil auch aus der Isolation des Homeoffice erlebt werden.

Im Jahr 2020 konnte die Software im Rahmen der vo Rektorat der TU Graz initiierten Förderung TELma ketplace (Technology Enhanced Learning Marketplac überarbeitet und niederschwelliger gestaltet werden. Die neue Version von Plattform(x) ist seit dem Winte semester 2021 bereits in sämtlichen IAM-Kursen in V wendung. Wer Interesse hat, Platform(x) in der Lehr einzusetzen, kann sich an das Institut für Architektu und Medien (iam.tugraz.at) wenden. ∎

*Urs Hirschberg/Stefan Zedlacher*

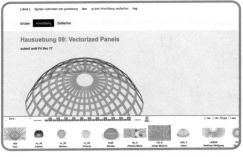

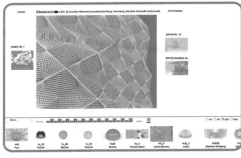

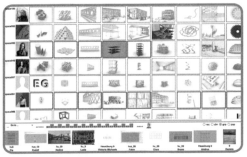

Web-Interface, Platform(x) © IAM, TU Graz

## Platform(x) Supports Online-Education

The Institute of Architecture and Media has long use a special software in its courses which supports students' easy exchange of information and peer-to-pee learning. Platform(x) goes back to a development at ETH Zurich and was subsequently developed furthe at the Harvard Graduate School of Design. Urs Hirschberg, head of IAM, is one of the developers Since his appointment at TU Graz, he and his team have continuously used Platform(x) in their teaching adjusting it to new needs as necessary. The software makes it easy to manage submissions of students in kinds of formats, to archive and visualize them and, following an open source spirit, to give everyone access to them. Complex projects with multiple authors contributing in parallel can be hosted on Platform(x) just as well as standard courses and sem nars with large numbers of participants, as common the Bachelor studies at our faculty. Students can che out and comment on each other's submissions and recommend outstanding works to one another.

uring the pandemic, when teaching happened almost
clusively online, Platform(x) proved to be especially
luable. To be inspired by the works of others, to get
 know other people's approaches and ideas, these are
nportant aspects of academic learning, particularly in
chitecture. Thanks to Platform(x) at least some of this
nportant experience of diversity and exchange could
ke place even from the isolation of the home office.

 2020 the software could be developed further and
ade easier to use as part of a grant provided by TU
raz' TELmarketplace (Technology Enhanced Learn-
g Marketplace) initiative. The new version of Plat-
rm(x) has been in use in all IAM courses since the
nter semester of 2021. If you are interested to use
atform(x) in your teaching, please get in touch with
e Institute of Architecture and Media (iam.tugraz.at). ▪

*anslation: Urs Hirschberg/Stefan Zedlacher*

## On/Offline: Architektur-
lehre am KOEN

Am KOEN wurden seit 2020 diverse Lehrveranstaltungen der ersten beiden Semester teils rein digital,
teils im Blended Learning Format abgehalten. Die
Gruppengrößen reichten von 15 Studierenden (Seminare, Exkursionen) bis 180 Studierenden (Vorlesungen), wobei der didaktische Fokus der modifizierten
Aufgabenstellungen auf Kommunikation, Kollaborati-
on und zeitgemäße Wissensvermittlung durch den un-
terstützenden Einsatz digitaler Medien sowie auf dem
Erlangen analoger als auch digitaler Kompetenzen lag.
Pandemiebedingt wurde im März 2020 die Präsenz-
lehre vorerst auf rein digitale Lehrformate umgestellt.
Innerhalb kürzester Zeit wurde die analoge Kleingrup-
peneinteilung auf die Online-Plattform Webex übertragen, wodurch ein unterbrechungsfreier Seminarbe-
trieb gewährleistet wurde. Lehrende zeichneten ihre
Vorlesungen zunächst im Homeoffice auf, um sie auf
TUGRAZonline zur Verfügung zu stellen. Flexibilität
und Kreativität waren im Modellbau gefordert, da es
während des Lockdowns zu einem Engpass an Modell-
baumaterialien kam, der viele Studierende vor die Herausforderung stellte, mit im eigenen Haushalt verfügbaren Materialien Modelle zu bauen. Außerdem konnten
die Studierenden ihren Pandemie-Alltag dokumentieren
und bei einem Kurzfilm-Videowettbewerb einreichen.

Seit Sommer 2020 wird am KOEN ein Broadcasting
Studio betrieben, das durch den „Projektfonds Lehre"

des Vizerektorats für Lehre an der TU Graz ermöglicht wurde. Im Studio finden unterschiedliche Lehr-
und Veranstaltungsformate ihre Umsetzung: Aufzeich-
nungen oder Live-Streamings von Lehrveranstaltungen, Greenscreens (Flipped-Classroom-Konzept),
oder Gastvorträge wie beispielsweise im Rahmen der
Vortragsreihe „Am KOEN zu Gast" oder der fakul-
tätsübergreifenden Vortragsreihe „Graz Architecture
Lectures" ermöglichen den fachlichen Austausch zwischen Studierenden, Lehrenden und internationalen
Gästen. Parallellaufende, moderierte Chats bilden hier-
für eine besondere Möglichkeit der Interaktion. Der
Einsatz des Broadcasting Studios und die Verwendung
von Webex und digitalen Whiteboards ermöglichen
auch weiterhin eine zeitgemäße Kommunikation mit
den Studierenden. Abgabensammlungen in der Cloud
dienen der gruppenübergreifenden Vernetzung sowie
als Pool für gesammeltes Know-how mit Überblick
über Wissensstand und Fortschritt. Unter Berücksichtigung verschiedener didaktischer Taxonomiestufen
und der Kombination von synchroner und asynchro-
ner Lehre können damit zeitgemäße Blended Learning
Methoden optimal umgesetzt werden. ▪

*Lisa Obermayer*

## On/Offline: Architecture
Education at the KOEN

Since 2020, various courses in the first two semesters
have been held at KOEN, some purely online and

KOEN Studio © KOEN, TU Graz

KOEN Studio © KOEN, TU Graz

some in "blended learning" format. The group sizes ranged from 15 students (seminars, excursions) to 180 students (lectures), whereby the didactic focus of the modified tasks was on communication, collaboration, and contemporary knowledge transfer via digital media, as well as on the acquisition of analogue and digital skills. Due to the pandemic, classroom teaching was initially switched to purely digital teaching formats in March 2020. Within a very short time, the analogous small group allocation was transferred to the online platform Webex, which ensured uninterrupted seminar classes. Lecturers at first recorded their lectures in their home offices in order to make them available to TUGRAZonline. Flexibility and creativity were required when constructing models, as there was a shortage of modelling materials during the lockdown, which led to many students faced with the challenge of building models with materials available in their own homes. In addition, students were able to document their everyday life during the pandemic and submit it to a short film video competition.

Since summer 2020, a broadcasting network and studio has been operated at KOEN, which was enabled by the "Project Fund Teaching" of the Vice Rectorate for Academic Affairs of Graz University of Technology. Various teaching and event formats have been implemented: recordings or live streaming of courses, green screens (flipped classroom concept), or guest lectures, for example as part of the lecture series "Am KOEN zu Gast" or the faculty's lecture series "Graz Architecture Lectures," has enabled thematic exchange between students, lecturers, and international guests. Moderated chats running in parallel provided a special way of interacting. The use of the broadcasting studio and network as well as the use of Webex and digital whiteboards continue to facilitate up-to-date communication with the students. The collection of student work in the cloud plays a role in cross-group networking and serves as a pool of collected expertise with an overview of the state of knowledge and progress. By taking different didactic taxonomy levels into account plus the combination of synchronous and asynchronous teaching, modern blended learning methods can be implemented optimally. ∎

# Thinking Design. Blueprint for an Architecture of Typology

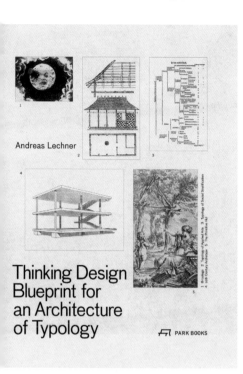

Andreas Lechner
[Zü]rich | Zurich: Park Books, 2021
[En]glisch, 460 Seiten, kartoniert |
[En]glish, 460 pages, paperback
[IS]BN 978-3-03860-246-0
[EU]R 58,00 | EUR 58.00

[An]dreas Lechners Atlas formaler und funktionaler bau[ty]pologischer Referenzen, der 2018 erstmals bei Park [Bo]oks veröffentlicht wurde, ist jetzt auch in englisch[sp]rachiger Erstauflage erschienen. Das Entwerfen von [Ge]bäuden basiert immer auf einem Wissen über Typo[lo]gien. In drei Grundlagentexten unter den themati[sch]en Überschriften „Tektonik", „Typus" und „Topos" [ha]t Andreas Lechner sein eigenes profundes typologi[sch]es Wissen zusammengetragen. In jedem der drei [Ka]pitel betrachtet er vier der insgesamt zwölf Typolo[gie]n Theater, Museum, Bibliothek, Staat, Büro, Freizeit, [Re]ligion, Einzelhandel, Fabrik, Bildung, Kontrolle [un]d Krankenhaus. Die insgesamt 144 ausgewählten [Be]ispiele aus einer Vielzahl klassischer Entwürfe und [Ba]uten erläutern die Grundlagen kollektiven Wissens [üb]er Architektur, mit dem sich in den transformativen Prozessen der Entwurfsarbeit stets neue Verbindungslinien ziehen lassen. 2018 erstmals erschienen, wurde das Buch nun in einer umfassend überarbeiteten Neuauflage in englischer Sprache veröffentlicht. Es offeriert eine Gebäudelehre, die mit der Komposition als ästhetischer Festlegung der architektonischen Form einen Entwurfsaspekt betont, der – vor Fragen nach Funktion, Zweck und Atmosphäre – Zeiten und Nutzungszyklen überdauern kann. Es versammelt herausragende Referenzen für die kulturelle Dimension des Bauens und ist damit weit mehr als eine reine Planungshilfe. Alle Beispiele sind mit Ansichten, Schnitten und Grundrissen illustriert, die für optimale Vergleichbarkeit neu gezeichnet wurden. Ein beigelegtes Heft (32 Seiten, 19,5 × 28 cm, 58 SW-Abbildungen) präsentiert Diplomarbeiten von zwölf Studierenden der Technischen Universität Graz, die Andreas Lechners Lehr- und Entwurfsansatz zusätzlich verdeutlichen. Die erste Auflage in deutscher Fassung wurde als eines der Schönsten Bücher Österreichs 2018 und 2020 mit der Goldmedaille im Wettbewerb der schönsten Bücher aus aller Welt ausgezeichnet. Grafische Gestaltung: CH Studio. ∎

**Andreas Lechner** lehrt als assoziierter Professor am Institut für Gebäudelehre an der TU Graz und führt sein eigenes Architekturbüro in Graz.

A clearly distilled architectural atlas based on 144 major designs from ancient times to the twenty-first century, showcasing the cultural dimension of building. However disparate the style or ethos, beneath architecture's pluralism lies a number of categorical typologies. In *Thinking Design*, Austrian architect Andreas Lechner has condensed his profound typological understanding into a single book. Divided into three chapters—Tectonics, Type, and Topos—Lechner's book reflects upon twelve fundamental typologies: theater, museum, library, state, office, recreation, religion, retail, factory, education, surveillance, and hospital. Encompassing a total of 144 carefully selected examples of classic designs and buildings, ranging across an epic sweep from antiquity to the present, the book not only explains the fundamentals of collective architectural knowledge but traces the interconnected reiterations that lie at the heart of architecture's transformative power. As such, *Thinking Design* outlines a new building theory rooted in the act of composition as an aesthetic determinant of architectural form. This emphasis on composition in the design process over the more commonplace aspects of function, purpose, or atmosphere makes it more than a mere planning manual. It reveals also the cultural dimension of architecture that gives it the ability to transcend not only use cycles but entire epochs. Each example is meticulously illustrated with a newly drawn elevation or axonometric projection, floor plan, and section, not only invigorating the underlying ideas but also making the book an ideal comparative compendium. An enclosed booklet (32 pages, 19.5 × 28 cm, 58 b/w illustrations) features theses by twelve students of Graz University of Technology that further illustrate Andreas Lechner's approach in teaching and design. The first edition of the German version was awarded the Most Beautiful Books of Austria Award 2018 and in 2020 received the gold medal in the competition of the most beautiful books from all over the world. Graphic design: CH Studio. ∎

**Andreas Lechner** teaches as an associate professor at the Institute of Design and Building Typology at TU Graz and runs his own architecture and research practice in Graz.

*Translation: Park Books*

# Basics of Urbanism. 12 Begriffe der territorialen Transformation

Aglaée Degros/Anna Maria Bagarić/Sabine Bauer/
Radostina Radulova-Stahmer/Mario Stefan/
Eva Schwab (Hg. | eds.)
Zürich | Zurich: Park Books, 2021
Deutsch und Englisch, 320 Seiten, kartoniert |
German and English, 320 pages, paperback
ISBN: 978-3-03860-260-6
EUR 38,00 | EUR 38.00

Zwölf für die Umsetzung städtebaulicher Projekte grundlegende Begriffe werden in diesem Buch besprochen und ihre praktische Anwendung anhand internationaler Beispiele veranschaulicht. Dabei wird der zentrale Ansatz verfolgt, dass es der Raum zwischen den Gebäuden ist, dem im Sinne einer zukunftsorientierten urbanen Entwicklung höchste Relevanz zukommt – ein Zugang, der die Interaktion von BewohnerInnen und Umgebung, die Berücksichtigung ökologischer und sozialer Komponenten sowie das Miteinbeziehen vorhandener Ressourcen beinhaltet. Zusätzlich beleuchten Essays von Aglaée Degros, Marcel Smets, Markus Bogensberger und Eva Schwab verschiedene Aspekte der städtebaulichen Disziplin. ∎

**Aglaée Degros** ist Architektin und Stadtplanerin sowie Gründerin des Büros Artgineering in Brüssel. Seit 2016 ist sie Professorin am Institut für Städtebau der

TU Graz, das sie auch leitet. **Anna Maria Bagarić** und **Sabine Bauer** sind als Universtitätsassistentinnen am Institut für Städtebau der TU Graz tätig. **Radostina Radulova-Stahmer** ist Architektin und Universtitätsassistentin am Institut für Städtebau der TU Graz. **Mario Stefan** ist Architekt. Während seines Studiums war er als studentischer Mitarbeiter am Institut für Städtebau der TU Graz tätig. **Eva Schwab** ist Landschaftsarchitektin und stellvertretende Leiterin des Instituts für Städtebau der TU Graz.

The publication *Basics of Urbanism – 12 Notions of Territorial Transformation* discusses twelve fundamental notions relevant for the implementation of urbanistic projects, demonstrating their practical implementation with international examples. The focus lies on the significance of the space between buildings for sustainable urban development—an approach that takes into account the interaction between inhabitants and environment, ecological and social components, as well as the integration of existing resources. Essays by Aglaée Degros, Marcel Smets, Markus Bogensberger, and Eva Schwab also critically examine various aspects of urbanism as a discipline. ∎

**Aglaée Degros** is an architect, urban designer and founding principal of Artgineering, a design firm based in Brussels. She is also a professor and head of the Institute of Urbanism, TU Graz. **Anna Maria Bagarić** and **Sabine Bauer** are university assistants at the Institute of Urbanism, TU Graz. **Radostina Radulova-Stahmer** is an architect and university assistant at the Institute of Urbanism, TU Graz. **Mario Stefan** is an architect and former student assistant at the Institute of Urbanism, TU Graz. **Eva Schwab** is a landscape designer and deputy director of the Institute of Urbanism, TU Graz.

*Translation: Park Books*

# The Ancient Monastic Complexes of Tholing, Nyarma, and Tabo

Holger Neuwirth/Carmen Auer (Hg. | eds.)
Graz: Verlag der TU Graz | Publishing Company of Graz University of Technology, 2021
Englisch, 413 Seiten, kartoniert | English,
413 pages, paperback
ISBN: 978-3-85125-774-8
ISBN: 978-3-85125-775-5 (E-Book)
EUR 98,00 | EUR 98.00

Das Gebiet des Westlichen Himalayas umfasst heute Teile von China (Autonome Region Tibet/Ngari), Nordindien (Himachal Pradesh, Jammu und Kaschmir Pakistan (Baltistan) und Nordwest-Nepal (Dolpo und Mustang). Diese ausgedehnte Region hat im Laufe der Geschichte unterschiedliche Wellen der kulturellen Konfrontation und des Wandels erlebt. Die politische Dominanz hat sich von einer Region zur anderen verschoben, aber die wirtschaftlichen Verflechtungen und die ethnischen und religiösen Beziehungen haben im Laufe der Jahrhunderte zu einer sich ständig verändernden kulturellen Dialektik beigetragen. Mit der zweiten Verbreitung des Buddhismus in Tibet im spät 10. und 11. Jahrhundert verlagerte sich die politische Macht an die westlichen Grenzen der tibetischen Kulturwelt, wobei sich die Hauptstadt zunächst in Pura

nd dann in Tholing und Tsaparang befand. Obwohl
eses Königreich auf dem Höhepunkt seiner Macht
ur 100 Jahre bestand, entstand in dieser Zeit eine un-
rwechselbare Kultur, die aus einer Verschmelzung
on tibetischen, nordindischen (Groß-Kaschmir),
hinesischen, zentralasiatischen und lokalen Elemen-
n bestand und deren Einfluss über die Grenzen des
önigreichs hinaus für viele Jahrhunderte bestimmend
ieb. Der dritte Band der Reihe „Buddhistische Archi-
ktur des Westlichen Himalaya" stellt die Bauwerke
r Klöster in Tholing, Nyarma und Tabo vor. Diese
ei Klöster wurden an der Wende vom 10. zum 11. Jahr-
undert gegründet und sind ein entscheidendes Zeug-
s für die frühe Entwicklung des Königreichs Guge.
ährend in Nyarma heute nur noch ein beeindrucken-
es Ruinenfeld an die ehemalige Klosteranlage erinnert
nd einige Tempel in Tholing während der Kulturre-
olution der Zerstörung ausgesetzt wurden, ist Tabo
as einzige der drei Klöster, das bis heute ununterbro-
en religiös und rituell genutzt wird. Da die Verfüg-
arkeit von schriftlichen oder bildlichen Quellen über
e Architektur in diesem Zusammenhang generell
ärlich ist, sind die Gebäude selbst die wichtigste In-
rmationsquelle für die Bauforschung. Dementspre-
end ist die Feldforschung unverzichtbar, denn sie
ldet die Grundlage für die Dokumentation, Analyse
nd nachhaltige Restaurierung der Klosteranlagen. ∎

olger Neuwirth ist Architekt und Lehrbeauftragter
n Institut für Architekturtheorie, Kunst- und Kultur-
issenschaften an der TU Graz. **Carmen Auer** war als
ojektassistentin und Lehrbeauftragte am Institut für
rchitekturtheorie, Kunst- und Kulturwissenschaften
der TU Graz tätig.

he area defined as the Western Himalayas currently
mprises parts of China (Tibet Autonomous Region/
gari), Northern India (Himachal Pradesh, Jammu and
ashmir), Pakistan (Baltistan) and Northwest Nepal
Dolpo and Mustang). This extended region has wit-
essed different waves of cultural confrontation and
ange throughout history. Political dominance has
ifted from one region to another, but economic inter-
pendence and ethnic and religious relationships have,
er the centuries, contributed to an ever-changing cul-
ral dialectic. With the Second Diffusion of Buddhism
Tibet in the late 10th and 11th century, political power
ifted toward the western borders of the Tibetan cul-
ral world, with the capital first being located in
arang and then in Tholing and Tsaparang. Although
is kingdom lasted only 100 years at the height of its
wers, a fusion of Tibetan, North Indian (Greater

Kashmir), Chinese Central-Asian and local elements
created a distinctive culture during that time, the impact
of which was felt beyond the kingdom's borders for
many centuries. The third volume of the series entitled
"Buddhist Architecture of the Western Himalayas"
presents the monuments of the monasteries in Tholing,
Nyarma and Tabo. These three monasteries were
founded from the turn of the 10th to the 11th century
and are a decisive testimony to the early development
of the Kingdom of Guge. While only an impressive
field of ruins reminds visitors of Nyarma's former
monastery complex, and some monuments in Tholing
broke down during the Cultural Revolution, Tabo is
the only one of these three monasteries to have been
used without interruption to this day. Since the availability of textual or pictorial sources of information
about the architecture in this context is generally scarce,
the buildings themselves serve as the most reliable
sources of information. Accordingly, field research is
essential in that it forms the basis for documentation,
analysis and sustainable restoration of the monastery
complexes. ∎

**Holger Neuwirth** is an architect and lecturer at the
Institute of Architectural Theory, Art History and
Cultural Studies at TU Graz. **Carmen Auer** was
project assistant and lecturer at the Institute of
Architectural Theory, Art History and Cultural
Studies at TU Graz.

*Translation: Publishing Company of Graz
University of Technology*

# Breathe – Erkundungen unserer atmosphärisch verflochtenen Zukunft

Klaus K. Loenhart (Hg. | ed.)
Basel: Birkhäuser, 2021
Deutsch/Englisch, 290 Seiten, kartoniert |
German/English, 290 pages, paperback
ISBN: 978-3-0356-1209-7
ISBN: 978-3-0356-1210-3
EUR 45,00 | EUR 45.00

Das Buch erkundet das Atmen und die Atmosphäre
als Leitmotive für die Gestaltung einer inklusiven Zukunft in einem neuen Klimaregime. Dabei werden
die atmosphärischen Verknüpfungen künftiger gesellschaftlicher Aktivitäten aufgespürt. Mit diesem
verflochtenen Bewusstsein rücken die performativen
Eigenschaften von Luft, Atmosphäre und Klima in
den Vordergrund, um sie als maßgebende Akteure für
die Konzeption und Gestaltung unseres planetaren
Daseins neu zu entdecken. Das sorgfältig editierte
Buch versammelt namhafte AutorInnen verschiedener
Disziplinen, die mit ihren Ideen, Beobachtungen und
Beispielen dazu anregen, unser gesellschaftliches
Handeln und Gestalten neu zu denken. Mit Beiträgen
von: Gernot Böhme, Heather Davis, Rosetta Sarah

Elkin, Eva Horn, Bruno Latour, Klaus K. Loenhart, David Life, Tomás Saraceno, Matthias Schuler, Anja Thierfelder, Wolfgang Kessling, Peter Sloterdijk, Bronislaw Szerszynski und Jean-Paul Thibaud. ▪

**Klaus K. Loenhart** ist Universitätsprofessor und leitet das Institut für Architektur und Landschaft an der TU Graz.

The book explores breathing and the atmosphere as leitmotifs for the design of an inclusive future in a new climate regime, uncovering intertwinements of societal activities with the air and the atmosphere. With this awareness of entanglement, the deeply performative characteristics of the air, atmosphere, and climate are foregrounded and can be discovered as central agents in the conception and design of our planetary existence. This carefully edited collection brings together renowned authors from various disciplines, and their ideas, observations, and examples inspire us to rethink our forms of social action and design. With contributions by Gernot Böhme, Heather Davis, Rosetta Sarah Elkin, Eva Horn, Bruno Latour, David Life, Klaus K. Loenhart, Tomás Saraceno, Matthias Schuler, Anja Thierfelder, Wolfgang Kessling, Peter Sloterdijk, Bronislaw Szerszynski and Jean-Paul Thibaud. ▪

**Klaus K. Loenhart** is a university professor and head of the Institute of Architecture and Landscape at TU Graz.

*Translation: Birkhäuser*

# SOS Grazer Schule

Anselm Wagner/Sophia Walk (Hg. | eds.)
Graz: Verlag der TU Graz | Publishing Company of Graz University of Technology, 2021
Deutsch, 40 Seiten | German, 40 pages,
Open Access E-Book
ISBN: 978-3-85125-840-0
ISBN: 978-3-85125-841-7 (E-Book)
EUR 12,00 | EUR 12.00

Wertvolle Bauten der jüngeren Vergangenheit fallen immer öfter der Spitzhacke zum Opfer, weil der Denkmalschutz der Architektur nach 1945 nur sehr zögerlich begegnet. *SOS Grazer Schule* dokumentiert in Text und Bild 125 Grazer Bauwerke aus der zweiten Hälfte des 20. Jahrhunderts, die (noch) nicht unter Denkmalschutz stehen, sich außerhalb der Altstadt-Schutzzonen befinden und die es wert sind, als wichtige Elemente des Stadtbildes und bedeutende Dokumente der Baukunst erhalten zu werden. Die Publikation in Form einer Zeitung geht aus dem Masterstudio „gut/achten – Grazer Architektur 1945–2000" im Wintersemester 2020/21 am Institut für Architekturtheorie, Kunst- und Kulturwissenschaften der TU Graz hervor. ▪

**Anselm Wagner** ist Universitätsprofessor und Leiter des Instituts für Architekturtheorie, Kunst- und Kultur-

wissenschaften an der TU Graz. **Sophia Walk** ist Universitätsassistentin am Institut für Architekturtheorie, Kunst- und Kulturwissenschaften an der TU Graz.

Valuable buildings from the recent past are increasingly falling victim to the pickaxe, because the protection of historical monuments has been very reluctant to address architecture after 1945. *SOS Grazer Schule* documents 125 Graz buildings from the second half of the 20th century, which are not (yet) listed, are located outside the old town protection zones and which are worthwhile as important elements of the Cityscape and significant architectural documents to be preserved. The publication in the form of a newspaper results from the Integral Design Studio "gut/achten – Grazer Architektur 1945–2000" in the winter semester 2020/21 at the Institute of Architectural Theory, Art History and Cultural Studies at Graz University of Technology. ▪

**Anselm Wagner** is university professor and head of the Institute of Architectural Theory, Art History and Cultural Studies at TU Graz. **Sophia Walk** is a university assistant at the Institute of Architectural Theory, Art History and Cultural Studies at TU Graz.

*Translation: Publishing Company of Graz University of Technology*

# Kunst (Haus (Graz

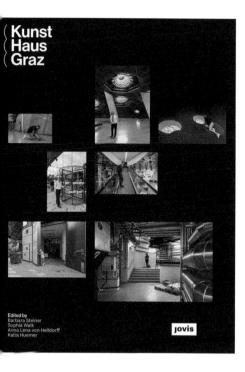

rbara Steiner/Sophia Walk/Anna Lena von Helldorff/
tia Huemer (Hg. | eds.)

rlin: Jovis, 2021

utsch/Englisch, 368 Seiten | German/English,

8 pages, flexocover

BN 978-3-86859-679-3

BN: 978-3-86859-680-9

R 29,00 | EUR 29.00

s Kunsthaus Graz ist heute fester Bestandteil
r städtebaulichen Identität der zweitgrößten Stadt
terreichs. Auch wenn dieser 2003 gelandete „Friend-
Alien" der Architekten Peter Cook und Colin
urnier inzwischen zu einem vertrauten Objekt ge-
rden ist, sind die Perspektiven auf das Gebäude
n Wandel der Zeit unterworfen. Das Buch schaut
rück auf fast 20 Jahre seit seiner Entstehung, ent-
et einen kaleidoskopischen Blick und fokussiert vor
m die Nutzung des Kunsthauses. In lokaler sowie
baler Hinsicht wird das Kunsthaus Graz context-
isiert und zu seinen NutzerInnen in Beziehung
etzt. Mit Textbeiträgen von Barbara Steiner, Sophia
lk, Pablo von Frankenberg, Anselm Wagner, Katia
emer, Niels Jonkhans, Elisabeth Schlögl, Peter Cook
d Colin Fournier und fotografischen Beiträgen von
hur Zalewski und Martin Grabner. ∎

---

**Sophia Walk** ist Universitätsassistentin am Institut für
Architekturtheorie, Kunst- und Kulturwissenschaften
an der TU Graz.

Today, the Kunsthaus Graz is integral to the urban
identity of Austria's second-largest city. The "Friendly
Alien" designed by architects Peter Cook and Colin
Fournier has become a familiar object in the city since
landing in 2003. But views on the building have changed
with the times. Looking back at nearly twenty years of
history since the building's creation, the book opens
up a kaleidoscopic perspective with a primary focus
on how the Kunsthaus is used. It contextualizes the
Kunsthaus Graz both locally and globally while exploring its relation to those who use it. With written contributions by Barbara Steiner, Sophia Walk, Pablo von
Frankenberg, Anselm Wagner, Katia Huemer, Niels
Jonkhans, Elisabeth Schlögl, Peter Cook, and Colin
Fournier, and photographic contributions by Arthur
Zalewski and Martin Grabner. ∎

**Sophia Walk** is a university assistant at the Institute of
Architectural Theory, Art History and Cultural Studies
at TU Graz.

*Translation: Jovis*

---

# Institut für Gebäudelehre. Jahrbuch 19/20

Hans Gangoly (Hg. | ed.)
Graz: Verlag der TU Graz | Publishing Company of
Graz University of Technology, 2021
Deutsch, 416 Seiten, kartoniert | German,
416 pages, paperback
ISBN: 978-3-85125-784-7
ISBN: 978-3-85125-785-4 (E-Book)
EUR 28,00 | EUR 28.00

Das *Jahrbuch 19/20*, die zweite Ausgabe der Jahrbuch-
Reihe des Instituts für Gebäudelehre, versammelt ausgewählte Arbeitsergebnisse der Entwurfslehre, die
während des Studienjahres 2019/20 entwickelt wurden.
Das in den Lehrveranstaltungen „Entwerfen 2", „Entwerfen 4" und „Projektübung" behandelte Themen-
spektrum reichte von der Reaktivierung ländlicher Gebiete am Exempel Goričko in Slowenien, bis hin zu
einer architektonischen Auseinandersetzung mit kollektiver Erinnerung, die anhand des Dokumentations-
archivs des österreichischen Widerstands in Wien ex-
emplifiziert wurde. Neben den Beiträgen zur Entwurfslehre und Berichten über die Zusammenarbeit
mit internationalen GastprofessorInnen, enthält das

Buch auch eine Auswahl über die am Institut verfassten Masterarbeiten. ▪

**Hans Gangoly** ist Architekt, Universitätsprofessor für Gebäudelehre und leitet das gleichnamige Institut an der TU Graz.

The publication, *Jahrbuch 19/20* (Yearbook 19/20), is the second edition of the yearbook series put together by the Institute of Design and Building Typology. It includes a selection of contributions based on design theory from the academic year of 2019/20. The topics covered in the courses Design 2, Design 4 and the Integral Design Studio span a wide spectrum; from the reactivation of rural areas, illustrated using the example of Goričko in Slovenia, to an architectural examination of collective memory at the Documentation Centre of Austrian Resistance in Vienna. In addition to contributions based on design theory and reports regarding the cooperation with international visiting professors, the book also contains a selection of master's theses written at the institute. ▪

**Hans Gangoly** is an architect, university professor, and head of the Institute of Design and Building Typology at TU Graz.

*Translation: Katie Louise Gough*

# TU Graz Nachhaltigkeitsbericht 2020

Harald Kainz/Alexander Passer (Hg. | eds.)
Graz: Verlag der TU Graz | Publishing Company of Graz University of Technology, 2021
ISBN: 978-3-85125-822-6
ISBN: 978-3-85125-823-3 (E-book)

Der Nachhaltigkeitsbeirat ist die zentrale Stelle für Agenden der Nachhaltigkeit an der TU Graz. Neben der Beratung der Universitätsleitung in Fragen der Nachhaltigkeit entwickelt der Beirat im Auftrag des Rektorats die Nachhaltigkeitsstrategie weiter, bündelt Aktivitäten und initiiert neue Vorhaben und Projekte. Das Thema Nachhaltigkeit soll durch die Tätigkeiten des Beirates auf allen Ebenen der Universität verankert werden. So soll der Nachhaltigkeitsbeirat beispielsweise die Technikfolgenabschätzung in Forschung und Lehre integrieren, das Energie- und Mobilitätsmanagement der TU Graz optimieren, Maßnahmen zur Erreichung der UN Sustainable Development Goals erarbeiten, (Forschungs-)Projekte im Bereich der Nachhaltigkeit initiieren und regelmäßig einen Nachhaltigkeitsbericht erstellen. Bedienstete und Studierende werden dabei

aktiv eingebunden. Für die Berichtsperiode 2016–201 wurde ein umfassender Nachhaltigkeitsbericht erstell an dem auch das Institut für Städtebau in Form von Studien, Prozessanalysen und Vorschlägen zum Then Mobilität beteiligt war. So soll der Leitspruch „Stay grounded, but keep connected" zu weniger Dienst- reisen bzw. mehr Zugreisen führen. Aber auch lokale Maßnahmen für mehr aktive Mobilität sind ein Bau- stein für eine Reduktion der Emissionen im Mobilität sektor. ▪

**Alexander Passer** ist Stiftungsprofessor für Nachhal ges Bauen am Institut für Tragwerksentwurf, TU Gra

*Markus Monsberger*

The Sustainability Advisory Board is the key institu tion for sustainability agendas at Graz University of Technology. In addition to advising the university management on sustainability issues, the advisory board further develops the sustainability strategy on behalf of the Rectorate, bundles activities and initiate new plans and projects. The topic of sustainability is to be established at all levels of the university throug the activities of the advisory board. For example, the Sustainability Advisory Board ensures to integrate technological impact assessment into research and teaching, optimize the energy and mobility manage- ment of the TU Graz, develop measures to achieve t UN Sustainable Development Goals, initiate (resear projects in the field of sustainability and regularly pr pare a sustainability report. Staff and students are ac tively involved in this process. For the reporting peri 2016–2018, a detailed sustainability report was prepar also including studies, process analyses, and proposa on the topic of mobility contributed by the Institute Urbanism. Thus, the motto "Stay grounded, but kee connected" is intended to lead to fewer business trip and more train journeys. But also, local measures fo an increase in active mobility are an element for a po sible reduction of emissions in the mobility sector. ▪

**Alexander Passer** holds the Endowed Professorship Sustainable Construction at the Institute of Structur Design, TU Graz.

*Translation: Markus Monsberger*

## The Incomputable

### Institut für Zeitgenössische Kunst

Das von Antonia Majaca geleitete Forschungsprojekt untersucht, wie unerwartete Formen kollektiver Intelligenz vor dem Hintergrund des epistemischen Regimes von Datenpositivismus, algorithmischer Klassifizierung und Vorhersage entstehen. Das Projekt geht von der Forderung aus, die Spezifität von und die Beziehungen zwischen Begriffen wie Intelligenz, Technologie, Plantarität und allgemeinem Wissen neu zu überdenken und gleichzeitig zu überlegen, welche einzigartigen kognitiven und politischen Fähigkeiten benötigt werden, um sich mit der Verbindung zwischen dem Zusammenbruch der Erdsysteme und der Verbreitung digitaler Technologien in einem globalen Maßstab auseinanderzusetzen. Die These des Sammelbandes *Incomputable Earth: Digital Technologies and the Anthropocene*, der demnächst bei Bloomsbury erscheint, geht davon aus, dass das neue geologischen Zeitalter als „Anthropozän" bezeichnet wird und impliziert, dass die Erde durch den Einfluss des Menschen künstlich geworden ist. Daher ist es essenziell, den Fokus speziell auf das Verständnis dieses Prozesses zu konzentrieren. In diesem Buch wird untersucht, wie sich die kapitalistische Gestaltung dieser „künstlichen Erde" in den letzten Jahrzehnten parallel zur

Ausbreitung digitaler technologischer Systeme beschleunigt hat. Ein zentraler Punkt ist die künstliche Intelligenz, die selbst eine Extraktionstechnologie ist – von den Bodenschätzen bis hin zur Arbeit von NiedriglohnempfängerInnen des Informationsgewerbes. Das Buch fordert daher einen radikalen Bruch mit einer Konzeption von Intelligenz und Wert, die auf Instrumentalisierung und Ressourcengewinnung beruht. Dies fordert einen radikalen epistemischen Wandel, der auf der Abschaffung der patriarchalen Vergeschlechtlichung von Technologie und Natur beruht und beinhaltet eine vielschichtige, aber grundlegend materialistische Kritik an den aktuellen theoretischen Trends wie dem digitalen Vitalismus und der Hegemonie technologisch-positivistischer Paradigmen, welche die Zentralität digitaler Systeme der wirtschaftlichen Optimierung und sozialen Kontrolle widerspiegeln. Die zeitlichen und räumlichen Dimensionen, mit denen wir konfrontiert sind, stellen uns vor neue Herausforderungen für zukünftige Entwicklungen. Die Rechenleistung macht zwar den Klimazusammenbruch sichtbar, jedoch die komplexen Verflechtungen dahinter nicht denkbar. Vielmehr schließt die rechnergestützte Modellierung unsere Fähigkeit aus, die Verflechtung der technischen Systeme mit dem Zusammenbruch der Erdsysteme zu erfassen. ∎

© Hanns-Martin Wagner

# The Incomputable

## Institute of Contemporary Art

The research project led by Antonia Majaca investigates how unexpected forms of collective intelligence emerge against the backdrop of the epistemic regime of data positivism, algorithmic classification and prediction. The project starts from a demand to rethink the specificity of and relations among notions such as intelligence, technology, planetarity and general intellect, while considering what unique cognitive and political capacities are needed to grapple with the link between the breakdown of earth systems and the proliferation of planetary-scale digital technologies. The thesis of the forthcoming edited volume, *Incomputable Earth: Digital Technologies and the Anthropocene*, due to be published by Bloomsbury, supposes that calling the new geological era "Anthropocene" implies that the Earth has been rendered artificial by the impact of humanity. Thus, a specific focus on understanding this process is needed. This book looks at how the capitalist engineering of this "artificial earth" has accelerated over recent decades, in parallel with the expansion of digital technological systems. A central focus is artificial intelligence, itself a technology of extraction—from the earth minerals to the labor of low-wage information workers. Thus, the book calls for a radical break with a conception of intelligence and value based on instrumentality and extraction. This entails a radical epistemic shift based on abolishing the patriarchal gendering of both technology and nature and involves a multifaceted but fundamentally materialist critique of the current theoretical trends such as digital vitalism, and the hegemony of techno-positivist paradigms which echo the centrality of digital systems of economic optimization and social control. The temporal and spatial scales we are confronting pose new challenges to envision a future. Although computational power now makes visible the climate breakdown it does not make the complex entanglements behind it more thinkable. Rather, computational modeling actually forecloses our ability to grasp the imbrication of technical systems in the collapse of earth systems. ∎

**Projektdauer | Project duration:**
2016–2022

**Finanzierung | Funding:**
Fonds zur Förderung der wissenschaftlichen Forschung Österreichs (FWF – PEEK) | Austrian Science Fund
Land Steiermark | State Government of Styria
Bundesministerium für Kunst, Kultur, öffentlicher Dienst und Sport | Federal Ministry Republic of Austria Arts, Culture, Civil Service and Sport

**Projektteam | Project team:**
Institut für Zeitgenössische Kunst | Institute of Contemporary Art: Antonia Majaca (Projektleitung | Project leader), Lola Pfeiffer, Dejan Marković

**ProjektpartnerInnen | Project partners:**
Staatliche Hochschule für Gestaltung Karlsruhe | Karlsruhe University of Arts and Design
Dipartimento di Scienze Umane e Sociali, Università di Napoli | Department of Human and Social Sciences, University of Naples
Institut für Medien und Kommunikation | Department of Media and Communications, Goldsmiths College, University of London

# Digitizing the Design of Masonry Structures (DDMaS)

## Institut für Tragwerksentwurf

Ziegel aus gebranntem Ton gehören zu den ältesten Bauelementen und beweisen ihre Zukunftsfähigkeit durch die kontinuierliche Weiterentwicklung zu einem hochmodernen Baumaterial. Um das volle Potenzial dieser Bauweise ausschöpfen zu können, gilt es, zeitgemäße Berechnungs- und Nachweiskonzepte zu entwickeln und so den Anforderungen einer digitalen 3D-Planung, auch im Zusammenhang von Building Information Modeling (BIM) zu genügen. Das interdisziplinäre Team rund um das kooperative Forschungsprojekt DDMaS begann 2018 mit der Entwicklung einer realitätsnahen digitalen Modellierung von Mauerwerksstrukturen in einer branchenüblichen Softwareumgebung. Die ProjektpartnerInnen aus Wissenschaft und Wirtschaft brachten ihre Expertise bei der Gestaltung des Entstehungsprozesses der softwaretechnischen Lösung ein und profitierten dadurch analog von einer Erweiterung ihrer eigenen Wissensbasis in Bezug auf einen bewährten Werkstoff. Durch das im Projekt entwickelte Materialmodell können Mauerwerksbau

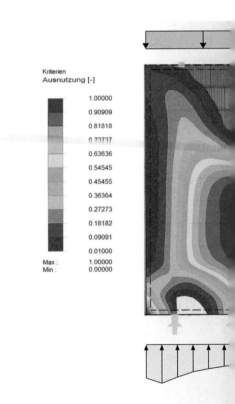

FE-Software © Stefan Leitner/ITE, TU Graz

n nahe an den Eurocodes mittels nichtlinearer Finite-
Elemente (FE) Berechnung untersucht und nachgewiesen werden. Dieses Verfahren ermöglicht es auch,
zusammenhängende Strukturen oder ganze Gebäude
zu untersuchen.

Im Rahmen des Forschungsprojektes wurde die Im-
plementierung des Materialgesetzes abgeschlossen und
Verifikationsbeispiele erstellt. Um die Akzeptanz des
Modells in der Fachwelt zu fördern, wurden beglei-
tend Stellungnahmen zu Abweichungen bzw. Modifi-
zierungen von Eurocode 6 erstellt, welche auch in die
Diskussion um die Neuauflage des Nationalen Anwen-
dungsdokumentes eingebracht werden. Im März 2022
fand eine erste, von der ZT: Akademie organisierte
Schulung in Form eines Webinars statt. ▪

# DDMaS. Digitizing the Design of Masonry Structures

## Institute of Structural Design

Bricks made of fired clay are among the oldest building elements and prove their future viability through

continuous further development into a highly modern
building material. In order to be able to use the full
potential of this construction method, it is also necessary to develop contemporary calculation and verification concepts for the building material and thus meet
the requirements of digital 3D planning, also in the
context of Building Information Modeling (BIM). In
2018, the interdisciplinary team within the cooperative
research project "DDMaS. Digitizing the Design of
Masonry Structures," started researching the development of a realistic digital modeling of masonry structures in an industry-standard software environment.
By contributing their expertise, the project partners
directly shape the development process of the software
solution and at the same time benefit from the expansion of their own knowledge base. The material model
developed in the project allows masonry structures
to be analyzed and verified close to Eurocode using
nonlinear Finite Element Analysis (FEA). This method
also makes it possible to investigate interconnected
structures or entire buildings.

As part of the research project, the material model was
implemented in the software and verification examples
were created. In order to promote the acceptance of
the model among experts, accompanying statements
on deviations or modifications from Eurocode 6 were
prepared, and are also included in the discussion about
the new edition of the national application document.
In March 2022, the first training course took place,
organized by the ZT: Academy as a webinar series. ▪

**Projektdauer | Project duration**:
2018–2021
**Finanzierung | Funding**:
Österreichische Forschungsförderungsgesellschaft (FFG) |
Austria Research Promotion Agency
Initiative Ziegel
**Projektteam | Project team**:
Institut für Tragwerksentwurf | Institute of Structural
Design (Projektleitung | Project leader): Stefan Leitner,
Stefan Peters
**ProjektpartnerInnen | Project partners**:
Initiative Ziegel
Dlubal Software GmbH
Dr. PECH Ziviltechniker GmbH
Kammer der Architekten und Ingenieurkonsulenten
Wienerberger AG

# Urban MoVe

## Institut für Städtebau

Das Forschungsprojekt Urban MoVe geht der Frage
nach, inwiefern sich privatrechtliche Verträge (z.B.
Mobilitätsverträge, -fonds, städtebauliche Verträge)
als kommunale Planungs- und Steuerungsinstrumen-
te für Mobilität an Wohnstandorten eignen. Im Zuge
dessen wurden erste Praxisbeispiele in Graz mit dem
Wiener Mobilitätsfond, einem internationalen städtebaulichen Vertrag, verglichen und analysiert. Neben
dem Schwerpunkt auf energieeffiziente Gebäude in
Hinblick auf nachhaltigen städtischen Wohnbau und
Klimaschutz, war das Thema der postfossilen Mobilität an Wohnstandorten ein wesentlicher Baustein des
Projekts. Gebäude sind nicht isoliert oder autonom,
sondern müssen in ein größeres Netzwerk eingebunden sein, um ihr entscheidendes $CO_2$- und Energie-
Einsparungspotenzial zu entfalten und die ambitionierten (verkehrspolitischen) Zielsetzungen zu erreichen,
die u.a. auf die Verbesserung der Fortbewegung ohne
den Privatbesitz eines Pkws setzen. So ist es unum-
gänglich, vielfältige Mobilitätsbelange und innovative
Mobilitätslösungen schon in einer frühen Planungs-
phase zu berücksichtigen und zu planen. Wichtig ist
ein genereller Zugang zu Mobilität: Anschluss und Er-
reichbarkeit mit dem Fahrrad sowie öffentlichem Verkehr oder den Sharing-Angeboten. Gleichzeitig sind
aber auch qualitative Kriterien im Zuge der Planung für
den Neubau von Wohnungen zu berücksichtigen – be-
ginnend mit verkehrssparender Raumordnung – „Stadt
der kurzen Wege" lautet hier die Devise. In den letzten
Jahren wurde bereits versucht, viele neue Ideen und
Maßnahmen für die Steuerung dieser Mobilitätskonzepte durch privatrechtliche Vereinbarungen bei Neubauten umzusetzen. Beispielsweise erlauben Mobilitätsverträge, die im Zuge der Bebauungsplanung verhandelt werden, von der vorgeschriebenen Pkw-Stell-
platzanzahl abzuweichen – regeln aber im Gegenzug
die Investition des eingesparten Geldes in ein nachhaltiges Mobilitätsangebot für das Wohngebäude. Das
Projekt zeigt, dass durch Maßnahmen wie Vertrags-
regelungen zwischen Städten bzw. Gemeinden und
BauprojektwerberInnen sowie prozessuale Neu- und
Weiterentwicklungen die Mobilitätswende an Wohnstandorten hin zu multimodalen Mobilitätsangeboten
und einem aktivierendem, qualitativen Wohnumfeld
vorangetrieben werden kann. ▪

Green City © Markus Monsberger/stdb, TU Graz

# Urban MoVe

## Institute of Urbanism

The research project Urban MoVe investigates the extent to which private-law provisions (e.g. mobility contracts, mobility funds, urban development contracts) qualify as municipal planning and management tools for mobility in residential areas. To this end, the project analyzed and evaluated the first practical examples in Graz, comparing it with the *Wiener Mobilitätsfond*, an international urban development contract. In addition to the focus on energy-efficient buildings with regard to sustainable urban housing and climate protection, the topic of post-fossil mobility in residential areas was an essential component of the project. Buildings are not isolated nor autonomous, but must be integrated into a larger network in order to unfold their significant $CO_2$ and energy reduction potential and to achieve the ambitious (transport political) goals, which include improving mobility without owning a private car, among other things. Thus, it is essential to consider and plan for a wide range of mobility concerns and innovative solutions already at an early planning stage.

General access to mobility is key: connection and accessibility by bicycle, public transport, and sharing proposals. At the same time, however, qualitative criteria must also be taken into account in the course of planning and new development of residential housing—starting with traffic-saving spatial planning—"City of Short Distances" is the motto here! Over the past years, attempts have already been made to implement many new ideas and measures for controlling these mobility concepts through private-law agreements in new buildings. For example, mobility contracts that are negotiated during the course of development planning allow deviations from the prescribed number of car parking spaces—but in return regulate the investment of the money saved in a sustainable mobility proposal for the residential building. The project demonstrates that measures such as contractual regulations between cities or municipalities and construction project applicants as well as routine and further developments can steer the mobility turnaround at residential locations towards multimodal mobility proposals and an activating, qualitative residential environment. ▪

**Projektdauer | Project duration**:
2018–2021
**Finanzierung | Funding**:
Österreichische Forschungsförderungsgesellschaft (FFG)
The Austrian Research Promotion Agency (Stadt der Zukunft | City of Tomorrow)
**Projektteam | Project team**:
Institut für Städtebau | Institute of Urbanism: Aglaée Degros (Projektleitung | Project leader), Markus Monsberger, Michael Malderle
**ProjektpartnerInnen | Project partners**:
yverkehrsplanung GmbH, Technischen Universität Wien/ Forschungsbereich Bodenpolitik und Bodenmanagement TU Wien/Research Unit Land Policy and Land Management, Grazer Energieagentur GesmbH, UIV Urban Innovation Vienna GmbH

# Buddhistische Architektur im westlichen Himalaya

## Institut für Architekturtheorie, Kunst-, und Kulturwissenschaften

Die umfangreiche Sammlung von Forschungsmaterial zur buddhistischen Architektur im westlichen Himalaya, die in den letzten zwei Jahrzehnten an der TU Graz im Rahmen von FWF-geförderten Projekten zusammengestellt werden konnte, konzentriert sich auf die Erforschung religiöser Monumente, die im Kontext der zweiten Diffusion des Buddhismus im zehnten und elften Jahrhundert stehen, als sich die politische Macht an die westlichen Grenzen des tibetischen Kulturraumes nach Nordindien und Westtibet verschob.

Der Fokus des im März 2021 abgeschlossenen Forschungsprojekts liegt auf Sakralbauten der Grenzregion des westlichen Himalayas, im Speziellen auf den Tempelbauten der kulturell tibetisch geprägten Region Dolpo in Westnepal, die einer ausführlichen Untersuchung unterzogen wurden, um eine vergleichende Analyse zu den bereits dokumentierten Bauwerken der buddhistischen Architektur dieses Gebiets zu ermöglichen.

Als Ergebnis des Forschungsprojekts stehen erstmals Bestandsaufnahmen und detaillierte architektonische und technische Bauwerksdokumentationen in Form von Siedlungs- und Lageplänen, Grundrissen, Deckenplänen, Schnitten und Ansichten in unterschiedlichen Maßstäben zur Verfügung, welche die Grundlage für künftige Bauforschung und notwendige Restaurierungsmaßnahmen bilden. Einen weiteren Schwerpunkt des Forschungsprojekts bildete die Fertigstellung des Vergleichsmaterials zu den drei frühen Klosteranlagen in Tholing (Tibet), Nyarma und Tabo (Nordindien). Die Ergebnisse wurden sowohl auf der Website des Forschungsprojektes (www.archresearch.tugraz.at) als auch im dritten Band der Publikationsreihe „Buddhist Architecture in the Western Himalaya" unter dem Titel *The Ancient Monastic Complexes of Tholing, Tabo und Nyarma*, herausgegeben von Holger Neuwirth und Carmen Auer, veröffentlicht. Darüber hinaus wurde die Architekturdokumentation der Tempelanlage von Alchi/Ladakh überarbeitet und ergänzt, die Ergebnisse werden als Beitrag in der Publikation *ALCHI – Ladakh's Hidden Buddhist Sanctuary*, herausgegeben von Christian Luczanits (SOAS University of London), veröffentlicht. ∎

© Carmen Auer

# Buddhist Architecture in the Western Himalayas

## Institute of Architectural Theory, Art History and Cultural Studies

The extensive collection of research material on Buddhist Architecture in the Western Himalayas compiled at Graz University of Technology over the last two decades as part of FWF-funded projects, focuses on the survey and documentation of religious monuments which are related to the Second Diffusion of Buddhism in the 10th and 11th centuries, when political power shifted toward the western borders of the Tibetan cultural world to Northern India and Western Tibet. The research project completed in March 2021 focused on sacred buildings in the border region of the Western Himalayas, in particular on temple architecture in the culturally Tibetan region of Dolpo in Western Nepal. To expand the existing research material, these buildings were subject to an in-depth comparative analysis which resulted in an inventory and a detailed building documentation—including settlement and site plans, floor plans, ceiling plans, sections and views in different scales—serving as the basis for future research and restoration measures. Another essential part of the project involved the completion of the comparative material concerning the three early monastic complexes in Tholing (Tibet), Nyarma and Tabo (Northern India).

The results have been published both on the research project website (www.archresearch.tugraz.at) and in the third volume of the publication series *Buddhist Architecture in the Western Himalaya: The Ancient Monastic Complexes of Tholing, Tabo and Nyarma*, edited by Holger Neuwirth and Carmen Auer. In addition, the architectural documentation of the temple complex of Alchi/Ladakh was revised and supplemented, and the results have been published as a contribution to the book *ALCHI – Ladakh's Hidden Buddhist Sanctuary*, edited by Christian Luczanits (SOAS London). ∎

**Projektdauer | Project duration**:
2018–2021
**Finanzierung | Funding**:
Fonds zur Förderung der wissenschaftlichen Forschung Österreichs (FWF) | Austrian Science Fund
**Projektteam | Project team**:
Institut für Architekturtheorie, Kunst- und Kulturwissenschaften | Institute of Architectural Theory, Art History and Cultural Studies: Anselm Wagner (Projektleitung | project leader), Carmen Auer, Birgit Androschin, Dieter Bauer, Holger Neuwirth

# Architektur im Klassenzimmer

## Institut für Gebäudelehre

Workshop „Farbe" © Tobias Gruber/IGL, TU Graz

Die Vermittlung baukultureller Themen und das Bestreben, einem möglichst jungen Publikum die Bedeutung einer nachhaltig und qualitätsvoll gestalteten Umwelt näher zu bringen, ist eine zentrale Aufgabe des Vereins BauKultur Steiermark. Um die bisherigen Aktivitäten und Bemühungen zu intensivieren und zugleich auf eine breitere Basis zu stellen, hat das Institut für Gebäudelehre der TU Graz im Auftrag des Vereins mehrere unterschiedliche pädagogische Übungen entwickelt, welche auf den Erfahrungen mit jungen Studierenden in der Architekturlehre basieren und für SchülerInnen unterschiedlicher Altersstufen adaptiert wurden. Im Vordergrund dieser fortlaufenden Kooperation stehen das bewusste Wahrnehmen von räumlichen und gestalterischen Bedingungen und Zusammenhängen sowie deren Auswirkungen auf die gebaute Umwelt. Dabei wird vermittelt, dass die Orte, an denen wir uns bewegen und die unser unmittelbares Lebensumfeld darstellen, keine Selbstverständlichkeit und auch keine vorgegebene Tatsache sind, sondern das Ergebnis eines kulturellen und politischen Zustands unserer Gesellschaft. Das Ziel der Kooperation ist es, durch das Wahrnehmen und Sehen zu vermitteln, dass alle Menschen für ihre (gebaute) Umwelt Verantwortung tragen.

Am einfachsten lässt sich dies anhand der Übung „Fotografie" erläutern. Hier werden vier thematisch ausgewählte Bilder von GerambRose-PreisträgerInnen von den SchülerInnen mithilfe einer eigenen Kamera oder dem eigenen Handy anhand eines selbst ausgewählten gebauten Objekts im näheren Lebensumfeld nachgestellt und analysiert. Im ersten Bild geht es um die Einfügung in den jeweiligen Kontext und damit um seine Verträglichkeit mit dem Umfeld. Das zweite Bild fokussiert auf den Eingang und gibt Auskunft über Orientierung und Bedeutung. Im dritten Bild soll der räumlich spannendste Bereich dargestellt und seine Wahl begründet werden. Zuletzt wird der Blick nach draußen zur Methode, um das Verhältnis zwischen Innen- und Außenraum zu veranschaulichen. Die SchülerInnen werden im Rahmen dieser Übung aber auch mit den konkreten grundlegenden Begrifflichkeiten konfrontiert, welche notwendig sind, um über Architektur zu sprechen. Die Übungen selbst – Fotografie, Farbe, Collage und Material – verfeinern nicht nur die eigene Wahrnehmung, sondern dienen auch in der Gemeinschaft der SchülerInnen als Anstoß zur Diskussion sowohl untereinander als auch mit Lehrenden. ∎

# Architecture in the Classroom

## Institute of Design and Building Typology

Communicating *Baukultur* (cultural knowledge)—hence also the ambition to bring the significance of a sustainable and high-quality designed environment closer to a young audience—is a central task of the BauKultur Steiermark association. In an aim to reinforce the previous activities and efforts, and at the same time to place them on a broader base, the Institute of Design and Building Typology at TU Graz has developed several various pedagogical exercises on behalf of the association. These are based on experiences with young students of architecture and have been adapted for schoolchildren of different ages. The focus of this ongoing cooperation is the conscious perception of spatial and design conditions and interrelations, as well as their effects on the built environment. The conveyed message, is that the places where we move and which represent our immediate living environment are neither a matter of course nor a given fact, but the result of a cultural and political situation in our society. The aim of this cooperation is to covey this message through perception and observation, and to conclude that all people are responsible for their built environment.

The easiest way to explain this is through a "photography" exercise, in which four thematically selected pictures of GerambRose award winners are reproduced and analyzed by schoolchildren. To do this, they use their own camera or mobile phone and a built object in their immediate living environment, that they select themselves. The first picture is about the insertion or incorporation into the respective context, and thus about its compatibility with the environment. The second image focuses on the entrance to the space and provides information about orientation and meaning. In the third image, the spatially most exciting area is to be shown and its selection justified. Finally, in the fourth image, looking outside becomes a method to illustrate the relationship between interior and exterior space. In the course of this exercise, the schoolchildren are confronted with the specific basic concepts that are necessary to talk about in architecture. The exercises themselves—photography, color, collage and material—not only refines their own perception, but also serve as an impetus for discussion in the community of schoolchildren, both among themselves and with their teachers. ∎

**Projektdauer | Project duration**:
2020 laufend | ongoing
**Finanzierung | Funding**:
Verein BauKultur Steiermark
Land Steiermark A16 Fachteam Baukultur | State Government of Styria, Department A16
**Projektteam | Project team**:
Institut für Gebäudelehre | Institute of Design and Building Typology: Hans Gangoly (Projektleitung | Project leader), Eva Sollgruber, Tobias Gruber, Alexander Barina, Emilian Hinteregger, Georg Dornhofer, Lukas Boß, Juliane Geldner, Beatrice Koch, Dina Sauer, Theresa Schleinitz, Maximilian Schlichtinger, Fabian Steinberger, Lea Zinnbauer
**ProjektpartnerInnen | Project partners**:
Schulen steiermarkweit | Schools throughout Styria

# Dissertationen
# Dissertations

Andrej Žižek (2021), „Evaluation of Public Squares Based
Geospatial and Social Media Activity Data"
Institut für Städtebau | Institute of Urbanism
Gutachter | 1st reviewer: Grigor Doytchinov
Gutachter | 2nd reviewer: Danijel Rebolj

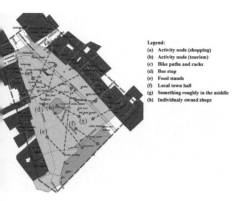

Andrej Žižek

ährend sich zeitgenössische Städte unter dem Ein-
ss der neuen IKT-angetriebenen Technologien
iterentwickeln, werden auch neue Datenquellen ver-
gbar, die eine unterliegende Logik der Stadtstruktur
d der städtischen Dynamik beschreiben. In der Ar-
it werden zwei Forschungsmethoden zur Bewertung
r Komplexität der Konfiguration und zur Bewertung
r räumlich-zeitlichen Dynamik am Beispiel öffent-
her Plätze in Graz und Maribor vorgestellt. ▪

contemporary cities develop under the influence of
e new ICT-driven technologies, new sources of data
the underlying logic of urban structure and urban
namics emerge. This study introduces two research
thodologies for the evaluation of configurational
mplexity and for the evaluation of spatiotemporal
namics, exemplified by public squares in Graz and
aribor. ▪

▪ ▪ ▪

a Sollgruber (2020), „Die Idee der Großform. Eine neue
nt auf das Werk des Architekten Oswald Mathias Ungers
d die Frage nach einem möglichen Entwurfswerkzeug"
titut für Gebäudelehre | Institute of Design and
ilding Typology
Gutachter | 1st reviewer: Hans Gangoly
Gutachterin | 2nd reviewer: Sonja Hnilica

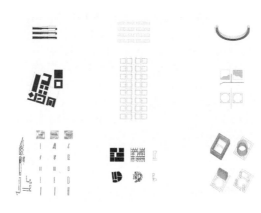

© Eva Sollgruber

In dieser Arbeit werden Texte und Projekte des Architekten Oswald Mathias Ungers hinsichtlich seines
Konzepts der Großform untersucht und eine neue
Interpretation seines Werks formuliert, wie auch eine
spezifische Entwurfsmethode dargestellt. Dem geht
eine begriffsgeschichtliche Untersuchung des „Großen"
in der Architektur voraus. Das Ergebnis ist zum einen
eine Präzession des Begriffs, zum anderen eine Formulierung von Entwurfsinstrumenten, die ein architektonisches Entwerfen anleiten können. ▪

In this research, texts and projects by the architect
Oswald Mathias Ungers are examined and analyzed
with regard to his concept of "Grossform," thus formu-
lating a new interpretation of his work and also illustrating a specific design method. This is preceded by a historical investigation of the notion of "greatness" in
architecture showing the complexity of the concept.
The result of this research is, on the one hand, a pre-
cession of the term itself and, on the other hand, an
illustration of design instruments which can inform
an architectural design process. ▪

▪ ▪ ▪

Wolfgang List (2020), „Entwerfen mit Modellen.
Untersuchung zur Relevanz analoger Modelle für
die Entwurfslehre"
Institut für Grundlagen der Konstruktion und des
Entwerfens | Institute of Construction and Design
Principles
1. Gutachterin | 1st reviewer: Petra Petersson
2. Gutachter | 2nd reviewer: Andreas Lechner
3. Gutachterin | 3rd reviewer: Margitta Buchert

Diese Untersuchung stellt die einzigartige Bedeutung
des analogen Modells für die Entwurfslehre im Architekturstudium dar. Das analoge Modell ist nicht nur
ein Entwurfsmedium, das die Entwerfenden bei der

Generierung von Entwurfsvarianten unterstützt, sondern auch ein Erkenntnisinstrument, das beim Erlernen des Erkennens der vielversprechendsten Entwurfsvarianten und des optimalen Zeitpunkts für deren Reduktion und deren Weiterentwicklung helfen kann.
Die Forschung wird von Fallstudien basierend auf dem
Lehrmaterial des Instituts für Grundlagen der Konstruktion und des Entwerfens begleitet. ▪

© KOEN, TU Graz

This research is about the unique influence of analogue
models on the process of teaching design in architectural education. The handmade study model is not
just a design tool, that assists in testing architectural
thoughts and ideas, but also a cognitive tool, to recognize the most promising design solutions and the optimal moment for their reduction and further development. The research is accompanied by case studies
taken from the teaching material at the Institute of
Construction and Design Principles at Graz University
of Technology. ▪

▪ ▪ ▪

Andrea Redi (2020), „Regeneratives Urbanes Wohnen"
Institut für Wohnbau | Institute of Housing
1. Gutachter | 1st reviewer: Hansjörg Tschom
2. Gutachter | 2nd reviewer: Mark Blaschitz

Die Stadt ist ein von Menschen erzeugtes komplexes
System. Komplexe Systeme, die sich selbst immer
wieder erneuern, finden sich auch in der Natur. Aus

einer genaueren Auseinandersetzung mit biologischen Systemen und dem Vergleich mit von Menschen gemachten Systemen werden in der Arbeit Prinzipien abgeleitet, die – angewendet auf die Entwicklung und Umsetzung von Wohnstrukturen – zu regenerativen urbanen Umgebungen führen. ▪

Bosco Verticale, Stefano Boeri Architetti © AFP/Getty Images

The city is a complex system created by humans. Complex systems that renew themselves over and over again are also found in nature. From a closer examination of biological systems and the comparison with man-made systems, principles are derived that can be applied to the development and implementation of residential structures, leading to regenerative urban environments. ▪

▪ ▪ ▪

**Matthias Raudaschl** (2019), „Klettbeton – Analyse und Herstellung verbindungsfähiger Betonstrukturen am Vorbild der Klettverbindung"
**Institut für Architekturtechnologie | Institute of Architecture Technology**
**1. Gutachter | 1st reviewer**: Roger Riewe
**2. Gutachter | 2nd reviewer**: Harald Kloft

© Matthias Raudaschl

Die Klettverbindung ermöglicht einen einfach zu trennenden und wiederherzustellenden Verbund von kurzlebigen und langlebigen sowie materiell heterogenen Bauteilen und eröffnet damit anpassungsfähige und rückbaufähige Gebäude entsprechend einer Kreislaufwirtschaft. In diesem Kontext und unter dem Aspekt der vielfältigen Formbarkeit des Rohbaustoffes Beton, untersucht die Arbeit die Herstellung von Beton-Klettkomponenten unter Anwendung der Wachsschalungstechnologie. ▪

The application of the hook-and-loop fastener enables a composite of easily detachable and reconnectable, short-lasting and long-lasting, as well as materially heterogeneous components. Therefore, this opens up great potential for adaptable and deconstructable buildings, in accordance with circular economy. In this context and with regard to the versatile mouldability of concrete as a building material, the research objective is the basic investigation and manufacturing of a concrete-hook-and-loop component, based on the application of Wax-Formwork technology. ▪

# Graz Architecture Lectures 2021: Korrekturen

Eine Veranstaltung der **Fakultät für Architektur** vom **Institut für Architekturtheorie, Kunst- und Kulturwissenschaften**, **Institut für Raumgestaltung** und der **Professur Integral Architecture**.

Die Korrektur schließt das vorher und nachher mit ein. Sie ist ein evolutionärer Akt. Ein bewusster Akt. Wie oft kommt es vor, dass ich denke: Eigentlich müsste ich es anders machen? Nicht von vorne anfangen, wohl aber etwas ändern. Manchmal ist es zu spät, oft aber zu früh, weil sich die Sicht auf die Dinge noch nicht gänzlich geändert hat. Woher kommt dieses plötzliche Verlangen — nicht einen unbewusst gemachten Fehler zu korrigieren, sondern eine vormals bewusste Entscheidung über den Haufen zu werfen?

Mit den Gästen der Graz Architecture Lectures 2021 wurde nicht über ihre Werke, sondern über die Korrekturen in ihren Werken gesprochen. Wann und warum wurde etwas korrigiert? Und was passiert, wenn eine Korrektur nötig wird, nicht um etwas zu verbessern, sondern weil sich die eigene Einstellung zu den Dingen geändert hat? Oder einfach, weil sie sein muss? Es diskutierten Reem Almannai (München), Alessandra Cianchetta (New York), Aita Flury (Zürich), Beate Hølmebakk (Oslo), Christian Inderbitzin (Zürich), Sam Jacob (London), Bart Lootsma (Innsbruck), Dinko Peračić und Miranda Veljačić (Split), Paul Preissner (Chicago), Oda Pälmke (Berlin), Philippe Rahm (Paris), Hugh Strange (London) und Jeremy Till (London). Das Symposium fand an zwei Nachmittagen im April 2021 online statt und wurde von den ProfessorInnen Anne Femmer, Alex Lehnerer, Florian Summa und Anselm Wagner moderiert. ∎

*Alex Lehnerer*

# Graz Architecture Lectures 2021: Korrekturen

An Event of the **Faculty of Architecture** from the **Institute of Architectural Theory, Art History and Cultural Studies**, **Institute of Spatial Design**, and the **Professorship of Integral Architecture**.

A "Korrektur" (correction) includes the before and after. It is an evolutionary act. A conscious act. How often do I think to myself: actually, should I do it differently? Not necessarily starting from scratch, but change something. Sometimes it is too late, but often too early, because the point of view has not completely changed. Where does this sudden desire come from—not to correct an unconscious mistake, but to discard a previously conscious decision. The guests of the Graz Architecture Lectures 2021 did not talk about their works, but about the corrections in their works. When and why was something corrected? And what happens, when a correction becomes necessary, not to improve something, but because one's attitude towards things has changed? Or simply because it must be done?

Participants in the discussion: Reem Almannai (Munich), Alessandra Cianchetta (New York), Aita Flury (Zurich), Beate Hølmebakk (Oslo), Christian Inderbitzin (Zurich), Sam Jacob (London), Bart Lootsma (Innsbruck), Dinko Peračić und Miranda Veljačić (Split), Paul Preissner (Chicago), Oda Pälmke (Berlin), Philippe Rahm (Paris), Hugh Strange (London) und Jeremy Till (London). The symposium took place online on two afternoons in April 2021 and was moderated by professors Anne Femmer, Alex Lehnerer, Florian Summa and Anselm Wagner. ∎

Florian Summa, Anselm Wagner, Anne Femmer, Alex Lehnerer © GAM.Lab, TU Graz

# „Annenstrasse 53,"

Ein ehemaliges Geschäftslokal wurde zu „Annenstrasse 53," einem unabhängigen Ausstellungsraum der vom Verein Das Gesellschaftliche Ding. Kunst, Architektur und Öffentlichkeit kuratiert und betrieben wird und seit 2020 eng mit dem Institut für Zeitgenössische Kunst (IZK) zusammenarbeitet. Durch die Verlagerung von universitärer Lehre, Forschung, Diskursen und Untersuchungen in das Grazer Bahnhofsviertel, vollzieht diese Zusammenarbeit aktiv eine Praxis, die Normen infrage stellt und einen Prozess des „Verlernens" innerhalb der Lehre, Forschung, künstlerischen Produktion und Ausstellung umfasst. Vor diesem Hintergrund wird angestrebt, das Ausstellen als einen kontinuierlichen, offenen Prozess zu begreifen und zu praktizieren, und zwar als bewusste Verweigerung der zeitlichen Schließung. Durch das langsame Hinzufügen und Wegnehmen von Objekten, Publikationen, künstlerischen Arbeiten und Gesprächen im Ausstellungsraum sollen fließende Diskurse etabliert werden, die Themen und Positionen in Bezug auf Lehre und studentische Arbeit verbinden. Forschung wird dabei als ein untersuchender, transformativer Prozess für alle Beteiligten verstanden. Die Konfrontation mit einem Ausstellungsraum, der zwischen Produktion

© IZK, TU Graz

und Repräsentation oszilliert, macht auch eine Auseinandersetzung und Präsentation der Möglichkeiten und Spannungen zwischen virtueller und physischer Präsenz notwendig.

Als entscheidender Schritt zur Etablierung und Artikulation dieser Praxis fand am 16. Dezember 2020 ei[ne] Eröffnungserklärung mit einem Screening und einer öffentlichen Diskussion zwischen den Gästen Ariella Aïsha Azoulay und Wayne Modest statt. Die Diskussion konzentrierte sich auf Azoulays Buch *Potential History: Unlearning Imperialism* (2019) in Verbindu[ng] mit ihrem jüngsten Film „Un-documented: Unlearni[ng] Imperial Plunder", der zeitgleich in der „Annenstras[se] 53," und online gezeigt wurde. Darauf folgten divers[e] Vorträge, Ausstellungen, Filmvorführungen, Lesunge[n] und Diskussionsrunden von internationalen Gästen und Studierenden des IZK: Nina Valerie Kolowratni[k] „The Language of Secret Proof" (Vortrag und Ausste[l]lung); David Frohnapfel: „Alleviative Objects: Solida[ri]ty & Conflict in the Art World of Port-au-Prince" (V[or]trag); Myung Mi Kim, Momtaza Mehri und Christin[e] Chalmers: „Poetics of Unlearning" (Vorlesung und Diskussion im Rahmen der IZK-Lehre in Zusamme[n]arbeit mit der Halle für Kunst Steiermark); Marcell Mars: „Distributed Resources versus Distributed Tech" (Vortrag); „Flowers (Not) Worthy of Paradise[" ](Ausstellung des IZK Master Studios); „Semmering – Land, Besitz und Commons" (studentische Arbeite[n] in Zusammenarbeit mit Hedwig Saxenhuber und Kunst im Öffentlichen Raum Niederösterreich); „Fil[m] for a Free Palestine" (Filmvorführungsreihe als Teil des Parallelprogramms des steirischer herbst'21); Nou[r] Shantout: „Map of Military Influence in Syria" (Aus[]stellung); Dejan Marković mit Abdelrahman Elbashi[r]

„Free Cinema" © IZK, TU Graz

Books: Arbeiterwille and the Sudanese Workers
Movement" (Ausstellung); „REPAIR" (Gastvorträge
nd Ausstellung im Rahmen des Workshops „REPAIR"
n IZK unter der Leitung von Ameli Klein); Jacob
ard-Rosenberg: „The writing on the wall destroyed"
Vortrag); „Free Cinema" (Filmvorführungen und
orträge von Pavle Levi (Stanford University) und
ikolaus Perneczky); in der folgenden Reihe wird es,
nter anderem, Vorträge und Workshops mit Saidiya
artman, Brenna Bhandar und Ruth Wilson Gilmore
eben. ▪

*bersetzung. Petra Eckhard*

„Slow Burn" © Amel Bešlagić

# 'Annenstrasse 53,"

vacant shop unit has been transformed into "Annen-
rasse 53," an independent exhibiting space curated
d run by the society Das Gesellschaftliche Ding.
unst, Architektur und Öffentlichkeit, collaborating
d closely working with the Institute of Contempo-
ry Art (IZK) since 2020. By dislocating academic
aching, research, discourse and investigations into
e district around Graz main station, the collabora-
on actively works towards a praxis that questions
rms and encompasses a process of "unlearning"
ithin teaching, research, artistic production, and ex-
biting. In this context, exhibiting is conceptualized
d practiced as a continuous, open-ended process, as
e deliberate refusal of temporal closure. By slowly
ding and subtracting objects, publications, artistic
orks and conversations within the exhibiting space,
is possible to establish discourses in flux, connecting
pics and positions, in relation with teaching and stu-
nt work. Within this flux, research is positioned as
investigative, transformative process, transformative
r everyone involved. Confronted with an exhibition
ace caught between production and representation,
is highly relevant to investigate and simultaneously
esent the possibilities and tensions between virtual
d physical presence.

pivotal step to establish and articulate this praxis as
ublic matter was the Opening Statement on Decem-
r 16, 2020, during which Ariella Aïsha Azoulay in-
oduced and discussed her book *Potential History:
nlearning Imperialism* (2019) with scholar and author
ayne Modest. Within this event, Azoulay's recent

film, "Un-documented: Unlearning Imperial Plunder"
was shown and installed in the space and online. The
program that followed the opening included lectures,
exhibitions, screenings, readings and discussion sessions
by international guests, as well as IZK students, for example: Nina Valerie Kolowratnik: "The Language of
Secret Proof" (lecture/exhibition); David Frohnapfel:
"Alleviative Objects: Solidarity & Conflict in the Art
World of Port-au-Prince" (lecture); Myung Mi Kim,
Momtaza Mehri and Christina Chalmers: "Poetics
of Unlearning" (lecture and discussion as part of
IZK teaching in collaboration with Halle für Kunst
Steiermark); Marcell Mars: "Distributed Resources
versus Distributed Tech" (lecture); "Flowers (Not)
Worthy of Paradise" (exhibition of the master studio
work); "Semmering – Land, Property and Commons"
(work by students in collaboration with Hedwig
Saxenhuber and Lower Austrian Culture Art in Public
Space); "Films for a Free Palestine" (film screening as
part of the steirischer herbst'21 parallel program); Nour
Shantout: "Map of Military Influence in Syria" (exhi-
bition); Dejan Marković with Abdelrahman Elbashir:
"Books: Arbeiterwille and the Sudanese Workers
Movement" (exhibition); "REPAIR" (guest lectures
and exhibition as part of the IZK "REPAIR" work-
shop held by Ameli Klein); Jacob Bard-Rosenberg:
"The writing on the wall destroyed" (lecture); "Free
Cinema" (film screenings and lectures by Pavle Levi

(Stanford University) and Nikolaus Perneczky); in the
following sequence talks and workshops will be given
by Saidiya Hartman, Brenna Bhandar and Ruth Wilson
Gilmore, among others. ▪

*Philipp Sattler/Anna Schoissengeyer*

# „Where City and Territory Meet …"

Unter dem Titel „Where City and Territory Meet …" fand am 16. und 17. September 2021 ein vom Institut für Städtebau initiiertes Online-Symposium statt, das Mitglieder der Fakultät und internationale Gäste versammelte. Aglaée Degros (Leiterin des Instituts für Städtebau, TU Graz), Marcel Smets (ehem. KU Leuven), Eva Schwab (Institut für Städtebau, TU Graz) und Markus Bogensberger (Land Steiermark, Abteilung 16 Verkehr und Landeshochbau) trugen die Keynotes zu dem umfangreichen Programm bei, das Paper Sessions, Video-Präsentationen und ein Abschlussplenum mit Ehrengast Han Meyer (ehem. TU Delft) umfasste. Ausgehend von aktuellen und historischen, städtischen als auch ländlichen Projekten wurden theoretische, praktische, methodische und empirische Beiträge aus einer Vielzahl von Disziplinen diskutiert, die sich mit der Frage beschäftigen, wie sich der aktuelle gesellschaftliche Diskurs im Raum manifestiert. Die vorgestellten Projekte und Beiträge lieferten neue Erkenntnisse zur Neupositionierung des Städtebaus aus ökologischer, ökonomischer, kultureller, sozialer oder politischer Sicht. Die Ergebnisse und ausführliches Material zu den präsentierten Papers sind auf der Homepage des Instituts für Städtebau frei zugänglich. ▪

*Sabine Bauer*

# "Where City and Territory Meet …"

Initiated by the Institute of Urbanism, the online symposium entitled "Where City and Territory Meet …," held on September 16 and 17, 2021 brought together members of the faculty and international guests. The keynote speakers were Aglaée Degros (Head of the Institute of Urbanism, TU Graz), Marcel Smets (formerly KU Leuven), Eva Schwab (Institute of Urbanism, TU Graz) and Markus Bogensberger (State Government of Styria, Department 16 Transport and Building Construction). The symposium's extensive program included paper presentation sessions, video presentations and a closing plenary panel with the honorary guest speaker Han Meyer (formerly TU Delft). Taking current and historic urban and rural projects as a base to move beyond a reconsideration of the profession's fundamental goals and means, theoretical, practical, methodological and empirical contributions from a variety of disciplines were discussed, that look at how the ongoing public discourse manifests itself in space. The projects and contributions provided new insights and possibilities on how influences — be they of ecological, economic, cultural, social or political nature — can reposition urban design as part of the territorial project. The results and detailed material of the presented papers are freely accessible on the institute's homepage. ▪

# Green Sofa Interviews

Das Institut für Städtebau hat mit den Green Sofa-Inteviews ein Format geschaffen, das internationale Positionen zum Städtebau versammelt, dokumentiert und

© stdb, TU Graz

kommuniziert. Die Gäste, die bislang auf dem Sofa Platz nahmen – darunter nationale und internationale HochschuldozentInnen, ArchitektInnen, PlanerInnen und StädtebauerInnen, oder VertreterInnen aus Verwaltung und Politik – wurden eingeladen, spontan auf für festgelegte Fragen rund um die Disziplin des Städtebaus zu antworten. Aus ihren Positionen und spontanen Reaktionen entsteht ein dichtes Gefüge an Fragestellungen und Vorschlägen für mögliche Transformationsprozesse und Zukunftsvisionen. Werden die Inhalte relational aufeinander bezogen, können Schnittstellen aber auch fehlende Verbindungen zum Vorschein kommen, die Ansatzpunkte für eine weitere Beschäftigung mit den einzelnen Themen eröffnen. Das Green Sofa bietet dem Institut neben einem regen Austausch und sachlichen Diskurs auch eine Möglichkeit, die Lebendigkeit und die Interdisziplinarität des Diskurses über die Disziplin zum Ausdruck zu bringen. Die Gespräche folgen der Logik einer Kunstserie und sind als ein kollektives und zusammenhängendes Werk zu verstehen, bei dem sich aus vielschichtigen Perspektiven Haltungen und unterschiedlichen Tätigkeitsbereichen eine Art Gedankenkörper zu aktuellen Entwicklungen im Städtebau formiert. ▪

*Jennifer Fauster*

Eva Schwab, Markus Bogensberger, Aglaée Degros © stdb, TU Graz

# Green Sofa Interviews

With the Green Sofa Interviews, the Institute of Urbanism has created a format that collects, documents, and communicates international positions on urban design. The guests who have sat on the sofa so far—in-

cluding national and international university lecturers, architects, planners and urbanists, or representatives from administration and politics—were invited to spontaneously answer five fixed questions relating to the discipline of urbanism. From their positions and spontaneous reactions, a dense structure of issues and suggestions for possible transformation processes and future visions has emerged. While referring contents to each other in a relational manner, not only intersections but also missing connections appear, opening up other starting points for further dealing with the individual topics. In addition to the lively exchange and objective debate, the Green Sofa also offers the institute an opportunity to express the vitality and interdisciplinary nature of the discourse about the discipline. The conversations follow the logic of an art series and are to be understood as a collective and coherent work in which a kind of body of thought on current developments in urbanism is formed from complex perspectives, approaches, and various fields of expertise. ∎

# Velux Daylight Talk mit Hemma Fasch

Im Rahmen der Daylight Talks präsentierte die Architektin und Professorin Hemma Fasch (TU Wien) am 29. April 2021 Projekte aus dem Portfolio von fasch&fuchs.architekten, die für ihre lichtdurchfluteten Raumstimmungen und den gezielten Einsatz von Tageslicht als Gestaltungskriterium bekannt sind. Neben der Grazer Auster, einem Sport- und Wellnessbad, stand vor allem der Schulcampus Neustift im Stubaital in Tirol im Fokus der Betrachtungen. Der für den Mies van der Rohe Preis 2022 nominierte Schulcampus beherbergt mehrere Schulen und Schultypen sowie ein Internat und liegt wie ein grüner Teppich am Hang in der Tiroler Gemeinde. Zwischen einem straßenbegleitenden Baukörper am oberen Ende des Grundstücks sowie dem städtebaulichen Abschluss durch den punktartigen Baukörper des Internats, ist ein Großteil der Funktionen in einem lichtdurchfluteten, von Aus-, Ein- und Durchblicken durchdrungenen Raumkontinuum untergebracht. Durch seine Einbettung in die Topografie des Grundstücks wurden die Grenzen zwischen Innen und Außen nahezu aufgehoben und die Lern- und Lebensbereiche der SchülerInnen mit Tageslicht versorgt. Durch die Integration der Gebäudestruktur in die Nachbarschaft und die gelungene Einbettung des Volumens in die Landschaft ist es den ArchitektInnen gelungen, den Schulcampus mit dem Ort zu vernetzen und den EinwohnerInnen zusätzlichen, qualitätsvollen Außenraum zur Nutzung auch außerhalb des Schulbetriebs anzubieten.

Der Daylight Talk fand in der Halle des Instituts für Grundlagen der Konstruktion und des Entwerfens live statt. Moderiert wurde die Veranstaltung von KOEN-Institutsleiterin und Dekanin Petra Petersson und Armin Stocker (KOEN). Die Daylight Talks sind eine Initiative des international tätigen Dachflächenfensterproduzenten Velux, um den Fokus von ArchitektInnen und Studierenden auf die Bedeutung von Tageslicht für die Gestaltung von architektonischem Raum aufzuzeigen und aktuelle, innovative Lösungen zur Diskussion zu stellen. ∎

*Armin Stocker*

# Velux Daylight Talk with Hemma Fasch

As part of the Daylight Talks, on April 29, 2021, the architect and professor Hemma Fasch (TU Wien) presented projects from the portfolio of fasch&fuchs. architekten, which are known for their light-flooded room atmospheres and the targeted use of daylight as a design criterion. In addition to the Grazer Auster, a water sports and wellness facility, the School Campus Neustift in Stubaital in Tyrol was the focus of the considerations. The school campus nominated for the Mies van der Rohe Award 2022 houses several schools and school types as well as a boarding school and blends into the hillside of the Tyrolean municipality like a green carpet. Between a building alongside the street at the upper end of the property and the urban

Velux Daylight Talk

fasch&fuchs

Thursday, 29th of April 2020 at 16:00 CET
Online via WebEx Meetings

hosted by TU Graz | KOEN

© Hertha Hurnaus

planning conclusion through the point-like building of the boarding school a spatial continuum unfolds, which is permeated by views to the outside, inside and through, and in which a large part of the functions are accommodated. By embedding it in the topography of the property, the boundaries between inside and outside are almost abolished and the learning and living areas of the students are supplied with daylight. By integrating the building structure into the neighborhood and successfully embedding the volume into the landscape, the architects have succeeded in connecting the school campus with the location and offering the residents additional, high-quality outdoor space for use outside of school hours.

The Daylight Talk took place in the hall of the Institute of Construction and Design Principles. The event was moderated by KOEN institute head Petra Petersson and Armin Stocker (KOEN). The Daylight Talks are an initiative of the international operating roof-window manufacturing company Velux, to draw the attention of architects and students to the importance of daylight for the design of architectural space, and to put current and innovative solutions up for discussion. ▪

# Exhibitions

## Semmering – Land, Property and Commons

Eine von **Hedwig Saxenhuber** kuratierte **Ausstellung**, die unter Mitwirkung von **Milica Tomić**, **Anastasiia Kutsova** und **Abdelrahman Elbashir** vom **25. Juli bis 17. Oktober 2021** in der Umgebung des **Kurhauses Semmering** stattfand

Die Ausstellung thematisierte die Transformation der Natur, insbesondere die Bilder und Wahrnehmung des Semmerings, wobei kritisch untersucht wurde, wie dieser Ort als eine durch den Tourismus und die globale Erwärmung veränderte Landschaft erscheint. Zu Beginn des Sommers leitete Milica Tomić (IZK) die Projektübung „Flowers (Not) Worthy of Paradise", in welcher sich die Studierenden mit verschiedenen Formen von Eigentum, Boden und der Kultivierung als Diskurs, der die Geschichte mit der Gegenwart verbindet auseinandersetzten. Milica Tomić erklärt: „Der Semmering ist mehr als nur eine Kulisse. Wenn wir die Landschaft betrachten, sehen wir sich überschneidende Motive. Die Natur, die den Semmering umgibt, ist erhaben, geschichtsträchtig und gleicht einer Postkarte. So wurde das Verhältnis zwischen denen, die kamen,

„Flowers (Not) Worthy of Paradise" © Simon Oberhofer/IZK

nd denen, die gingen untersucht und die Fragen ge-
ellt: Wer wurde gezwungen zu gehen, und wessen
and wurde besetzt?

ie gleichnamige Installation von Milica Tomić thema-
siert den Garten als eine Form des Widerstands gegen
oloniale Barbarei und erzwungene Akkulturation.
nastasiia Kutsovas Projekt „Flowers are (Not)" befasst
ch mit dem Phänomen der kommunalen Gärten in den
ohnbaukomplexen in den ehemaligen Sowjetländern –
er sogenannten ZhKh-art (ЖКХ-арт) – die von ihren
ewohnerInnen erschaffen wurden, um der Tristesse
rer Umgebung entgegenzuwirken und damit Kon-
olle über die Umgebung zu erlangen. Abdelrahman
bashir performte „Planting a Stone" indem er einen
renzstein in einer Wiese vergrub. Damit entschlüssel t
die materialisierte Entstehung des Politischen aus der
grarlandschaft im zeitgenössischen Sudan im Kontext
r britischen Besatzungsherrschaft. Die am Semmering
urchgeführte Performance referenziert den britischen
okumentarfilm „They Planted a Stone" von 1953 – ge-
uer gesagt, die Darstellung der Ankunft des ersten
ropäischen Mannes im Anglo-Ägyptischen Sudan,
n die Bevölkerung jemals einen Grenzstein setzen
h – und markiert eine neue Epoche, die die Gezira
ene im Zentralsudan radikal verändern sollte. ∎

*bersetzung: Christine Rossegger*

# Semmering – Land, Property and Commons

An **Exhibition** Curated by **Hedwig Saxenhuber**
in Cooperation with **Milica Tomić**, **Anastasiia
Kutsova** and **Abdelrahman Elbashir** Held from
**July 25 to October 17, 2021** in the Surroundings
of **Kurhaus Semmering**.

The exhibition dealt with the transformation of nature, particularly with the images and perception of
Semmering, critically examining how this place appears
as a landscape transformed by tourism and global warming. Earlier in the summer of 2021, Milica Tomić held
the Integral Design Studio entitled "Flowers (Not)
Worthy of Paradise" at the IZK in which students
dealt with the different forms of property, soil, and
cultivation as a conversation connecting history to the
present. Milica Tomić explains: "Semmering is more
than a backdrop. Looking at the landscape, we see
overlapping motifs. The nature surrounding Semmering is sublime, rich in history, resembling a postcard."
The concept of the installation explored the relationship between those who came and those who left and
revolves around gardens as a form of resistance against
colonial barbarism and enforced acculturation.

Anastasiia Kutsova's "Flowers are (Not)" deals with
the phenomenon of communal garden and housing
art—so called ZhKh-art (ЖКХ-арт)—created by residents of panel houses in countries of the former Soviet
Union as a response to the dullness of their environment
and to feel control over their environment. Abdelrahman
Elbashir performed "Planting a Stone," burying a
boundary stone in a meadow. His research unpacks the
materialized emergence of the political from the agricultural landscape in contemporary Sudan in the context of British occupational rule. The act performed
at Semmering references the 1953 British film "They
Planted a Stone"—in particular the depiction of the
arrival of the first European man in Anglo-Egyptian
Sudan who plants a marker stone—thus marking a
new epoch that would radically transform the plain
of the Gezira in central Sudan. ∎

*Abdelrahman Elbashir*

# Models

Eine **Ausstellung** von **Diskursiv – Verein zur
Architekturforschung** in Kooperation mit dem
**Institut für Raumgestaltung** im **Forum Stadtpark**,
Graz von **23. September bis 2. Oktober 2021**.

Modellbausituation © Simon Oberhofer

Als Aufruf zur Entschleunigung im Entwurfsprozess
der Architektur widmete sich die Ausstellung „Models" dem Entwerfen am Modell, den handwerklichen
Fähigkeiten und der physischen Auseinandersetzung
mit Materialien. Fünfundachtzig internationale Architekturbüros wurden gebeten, ihre Modellbauprozesse
einzureichen und ihr bevorzugtes Material, Maßstäbe,
Werkzeuge und Modelle zu nennen. Das gesammelte
Material wurde in Form einer Videoinstallation präsentiert, die zeigte, wie Architekturschaffende das Modell als Entwurfswerkzeug in ihrem Alltag einsetzen.
Darüber hinaus waren im Raum verteilte Modellbau-
situationen zu sehen. Beispielsweise haben die Studierenden der Lehrveranstaltung „Entwerfen 4" des
Instituts für Raumgestaltung durch die Zerlegung von
Alltagsgegenständen eine Vielzahl von architektonischen Elementen gefunden. Ihre Arbeit machte deutlich, welche Möglichkeiten EntwerferInnen haben,
wenn sie sich achtsam ihrer Umgebung widmen. Die
Arbeit des Wiener Architekten Leonhard Panzenböck
zeigte die zentrale Halle einer Villa mit einem gärtne-
rischen Eingriff und stellte die Bedeutung des 1:1-Mo-
dell zur Diskussion. In seiner Arbeit „Garten am

Brand" beschäftigte er sich mit der Darstellung von Modellen und thematisierte die Simultanität von Modell und Garten. Als weiteres Exponat wurde Johannes Scherffig's Styrocutter 3 präsentiert, der mit seinem langjährigen Betrieb die Entwicklung des Modellbaus maßgeblich beeinflusst hat. Die Videoinstallation von Ellena Ehrl und Tibor Bielicky (EHRL BIELICKY architects) zeigte eine Gegenüberstellung des Atlantis-Gebäudes von Arquitectonica im Modell des Künstlers Alexander Schöpfel, gemischt mit Realaufnahmen aus Miami und Bildern aus ikonischen Serien, welche die Stimmung zur Zeit der Errichtung des Gebäudes widerspiegeln. ▪

*Übersetzung: Christine Rossegger*

# Models

**Exhibition** by **Diskursiv – Verein zur Architekturforschung** in Cooperation with the **Institute of Spatial Design** at **Forum Stadtpark, September 23 to October 2, 2021**.

As a call to slow down the design process of architecture, the exhibition "Models" was devoted to model making, craftsmanship skills and the physical examination of materials. Eighty-five international architecture offices were asked to submit model-making situations and to name their favorite material, scale, tool and model. The gathered material was presented in the form of a video installation which showed how architects use the model as a design tool in their everyday practice. In addition, model building situations were put to display throughout the room. For example, the work of students of the course "Design 4" at the Institute of Spatial Design showcased the rich architectural elements that surface when taking apart everyday objects and highlighted the possibilities designers have when they carefully observe their surroundings. The work by Vienna based architect Leonhard Panzenböck depicted the central hall of a villa with a horticultural intervention and questions the significance of the 1:1 model. In his work "Garten am Brand," he focused on the representational dimension of models, illustrating the simultaneity of model and garden. Among the exhibits was also Johannes Scherffig's Styrocutter 3, a tool that has had a significant influence on the development of model making. The video installation by

the architects Ellena Ehrl and Tibor Bielicky (EHRL BIELICKY architects) showcased Alexander Schöpfel's model of Arquitectonica's Atlantis building and added real footage from Miami together with images from iconic series that reflect the mood at the time the building was constructed. It is an overlay of different media that generates a mixture of image, mood, and myth. ▪

*Julian Brües*

Mit Arbeiten von | With works by:
**Jasmin Monschein, Marry-Ann Lackner, Leonhard Panzenböck, Irene Zluwa, Marie Lambropoulos, Katarina Hollan, Wolfgang Bohusch, Ellena Ehrl, Tibor Bielicky**
Mitwirkende | Contributors:
**Alex Lehnerer, Julian Brües, Philipp Sternath, Stephan Damm, Simon Steinberger, Simon Schindele**

# „Steiermark Schau"

Die **Ausstellung des Landes** zeigte im **Volkskundemuseum, Kunsthaus Graz** und im **Museum für Geschichte** Ergebnisse aus Forschung und Lehre der **Architekturfakultät**, von **10. April bis 31. Oktober 2021**.

Unter dem Titel „Was wäre wenn?" wurden im Gartensaal des Volkskundemuseums die Entwurfsergebnisse der unter der Leitung von Petra Simon und Elemer Ploder abgehaltenen Projektübung des Instituts für Entwerfen im Bestand und Denkmalpflege ausgestellt. Die Entwürfe der Studierenden, die sich dem Umbau des Volkskundemuseums und der Neugestaltung des angrenzenden Grünraums widmeten, wurden in Kooperation mit dem Bundesdenkmalamt und dem Volkskundemuseum entwickelt.

Das Institut für Tragwerksentwurf bespielte im Rahmen der Ausstellung des Landes das Kunsthaus Graz mit dem innovativen Konstruktionsentwurf einer gewichtsreduzierten Stahlbetondecke, der aufbauend auf den Forschungsergebnissen des Projekts „COEBRO – Additive Fabrication of Concrete Elements by Robots" (Additive Herstellung von Betonbauteilen mittels 3D Druckverfahren) entworfen und im Labor für Konstruktiven Ingenieurbau mittels 3D-Druckverfahren hergestellt wurde.

Ebenfalls im Kunsthaus Graz wurde ein neuer, am Institut für Architektur und Medien entwickelter Kompositwerkstoff präsentiert. „MyCera" besteht aus 3D-gedruckten ziegelähnlichen Modulen aus Ton, deren Hohlkammern und Öffnungen aus einem Gemisch aus Zellstoff und Myzelium – dem vegetativen Teil von Pilzen – befüllt ist und dazu beiträgt, dass Ziegelelemente zusammenwachsen, wodurch auf zementbasierte Bindemittel verzichtet werden kann. Außerdem zu sehen: Ein 3D-gedrucktes Lehmgerüst mit Myzeliumstruktur, die für ein gesundes mikrobielles Klima sorgt, das Honigbienen zugute kommt und in weiterer Folge auch Teil menschlicher Lebensräume werden könnte. Die Struktur ist das Ergebnis der experimentellen Architekturstudie „The Living Arch. Study Model for a Novel Wellbeing Architecture for Honeybees" von Asya Ilgün, Dissertantin am IAM.

Inwiefern sich das analoge Konzept der Architekturausbildung in die sozialen, gebauten und digitalen Räume übersetzen lässt, zeigte das KOEN in seinem Videobeitrag zum „Architecture Broadcasting Net-

ork", das in Kooperation mit der TU Berlin und der
H Erfurt entwickelt wurde. So ermöglicht das Archi-
cture Broadcasting Network Einblick in Strategien
r eine chancengerechtere Lehre im sogenannten
Blended Learning" und erweiterte damit die Erarbei-
ng und Reflexion von Wissen um die Schnittstelle
zwischen digitaler und gelebter Welt. Diese Installatio-
n wurde ebenfalls im Kunsthaus zur Schau gestellt. ▪

*hristine Rossegger*

# "Steiermark Schau"

**he Exhibition** Presented Results of Research
nd Teaching of the **Faculty of Architecture**
the **Volkskundemuseum**, the **Kunsthaus Graz**
d the **Museum für Geschichte**,
**pril 10 to October 31, 2021**.

ntitled "Was wäre wenn?" (What if?), the results of
e Integral Design Studio at the Institute of Design in
onsisting Structure and Architectural Heritage Pro-
ction, led by Petra Simon and Elemer Ploder, were
t on display at Volkskundemuseum's Gartensaal.
e designs of the students, which developed a con-

version of the Volkskundemuseum and a redesign of
the adjacent green space, were developed in cooperation with the Federal Monuments Authority Austria
and the Volkskundemuseum.

As part of the "Steiermark Schau," the Institute of
Structural Design presented the innovative structural
design of a lightweight reinforced concrete ceiling at
the Kunsthaus Graz, which was based on the results
of the research project "COEBRO – Additive Fabrication of Concrete Elements by Robots" and produced in the Laboratory for Structural Engineering
using 3D printing.

Also presented at the Kunsthaus Graz was a new
composite material developed at the Institute of Architecture and Media (IAM). "MyCera" consists of
3D printed brick-like modules made of clay. Its hollow chambers and openings are filled with a mixture
of cellulose and mycelium—the vegetative part of
fungi—helping brick elements to grow together,
therefore eliminating the need for cement-based
binders. Additionally on display: A 3D printed clay
framework with a mycelium structure that provides a
healthy microbial climate that benefits honeybees and
could subsequently become part of human habitats.

The structure is the result of the experimental architectural study "The Living Arch: A Study Model for
a Novel Wellbeing Architecture for Honeybees" by
Asya Ilgün, PhD student at the IAM.

The extent to which the analogue concept of architectural education can be translated into social, built, and
digital spaces was shown by KOEN in a video contribution to the "Architecture Broadcasting Network,"
which was developed in cooperation with the Technical University of Berlin and the University of Applied
Sciences Erfurt. The Architecture Broadcasting Network gives an insight into strategies for more opportu-
nity-oriented teaching methods in so-called "blended
learning," and expanded the development and reflection of knowledge around the interface between the
digital and the real world. These installations were also
displayed at the Kunsthaus. ▪

*Translation: Katie Louise Gough*

GAM.Lab, TU Graz

# „Transforming City Regions"

Eine **Ausstellung** von Architekturstudierenden der **Stiftungsprofessur Holzbau** und des **Instituts für Städtebau** im **Rathaus** in **Sindelfingen** von **5. bis 25. Juli 2021**.

Im Wintersemester 20/21 erarbeiteten Studierende im Rahmen der Projektübung „Transforming City Regions – IBA'27 Konversion Klinikumsareal Sindelfingen" die gruppenübergreifend von der Stiftungsprofessur für Holzbau unter der Leitung von Tom Kaden und Aglaée Degros (Institut für Städtebau) abgehalten wurde, Entwürfe für die Internationale Bauausstellung 2027 StadtRegion Stuttgart (IBA'27). Dafür wurden Nachnutzungskonzepte auf bzw. um das Krankenhausareal Sindelfingen entwickelt. Diese sollten nicht nur die Wünsche künftiger BewohnerInnen miteinbeziehen, sondern auch die ansässigen StadtbewohnerInnen zum Verweilen einladen. Die Studierenden erstellten ein städtebaulich, für den Ort verträgliches Gesamtkonzept, um ein soziales, nachhaltiges und produktives Quartier zu schaffen. Die Gebäudeentwürfe der Zu-, Auf- und Neubauten wurden in Holz-Hybridbauweise entwickelt. Auch der Rückbau und die prinzipielle energetische Bestandsoptimierung waren relevante Entwurfsparameter. Aus der interdisziplinären Zusammenarbeit der beiden Institute entstanden Synergien und Entwürfe in unterschiedliche Maßstabsebenen – vom Territorium bis zum Gebäudedetail. Die Projektübung fand ihren Abschluss bei der Präsentation der Ergebnisse in der gleichnamigen Ausstellung. ∎

*Sabine Bauer*

# "Transforming City Regions"

An **Exhibition** by Architecture Students from the **Endowed Chair of Architecture and Timber Construction** and the **Institute of Urbanism** in the **Town Hall** in **Sindelfingen** from **July 5 to 25, 2021**.

In the winter semester 2020/21, as part of the Integral Design Studio "Transforming City Regions – IBA'27 Konversion Klinikumsareal Sindelfingen," which was held across groups by the Endowed Chair of Architecture and Timber Construction under the direction of Tom Kaden and Aglaée Degros (Institute of Urbanism), students developed designs for the International Building Exhibition 2027 StadtRegion Stuttgart (IBA'27). To this end, concepts for subsequent use were developed in and around the Sindelfingen hospital area. These should not only include the wishes of the future residents, but also invite the local city dwellers to participate. The students created an overall urban planning concept that was compatible with the location, in order to create a social, sustainable, and productive district. The designs of the extensions, superstructures and new buildings were developed in a hybrid timber construction. In addition, the dismantling and the optimization of the energy systems of the existing properties were also relevant design parameters in the Integral Design Studio. The interdisciplinary cooperation between the two institutes resulted in synergies and designs on different scales—from the territory to the building detail. The Integral Design Studio ended with the presentation of the results in an exhibition of the same name.

© Dettenmeyer

# Reviews

# Reviews

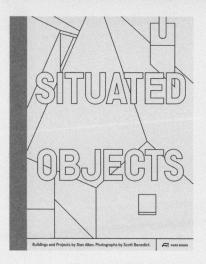

**Situated Objects: Buildings
and Projects by Stan Allen**
Stan Allen
Mit Beiträgen von Helen Thomas
und Jesús Vassallo sowie
Fotografien von Scott Benedict |
With contributions by Helen Thomas
and Jesús Vassallo, as well as
photographs by Scott Benedict
Zürich | Zurich: Park Books, 2020
Englisch, 256 Seiten, 110 Abbildungen Farbe and 118 Zeich-
nungen, Hardcover | English,
256 pages, 110 duotone illustrations
and 118 drawings, hardback
ISBN 978-3-03860-204-0
EUR 48,00 | EUR 48.00

# Abstraktion und Realismus

Cameron McEwan

*Situated Objects* dokumentiert Zeichnungen, Gebäude und Projekte, die Stan Allen seit
2012 realisiert hat. Das Buch konzentriert sich
auf acht kleine Gebäude in ländlichen Gegenden,
darunter Häuser, Studios und temporäre Konstruktionen. Es ist in drei Abschnitte unterteilt,
die sich mit „Außengebäuden", „Materiellen
Historien" und „Neuen Naturen" befassen. Jeder
Abschnitt beginnt mit prägnanten Überlegungen
Allens zum jeweiligen Thema und stellt die dazugehörigen Bauten vor. Essays von Allen, Jesús
Vassalla und Helen Thomas kontextualisieren
das Werk. Die Texte und Allens Zeichnungen
halten Zwiesprache mit einer das gesamte Buch
durchziehenden Fotofolge Scott Benedicts. Das
Buch ist handwerklich schön gemacht und besteht aus exklusiven Strichzeichnungen und
monochromen Fotografien.

In den Bereichen Architektur und kritischer Diskurs ist Allen eine fesselnde Gestalt.
Sein Werk befasst sich mit Architektur und Urbanismus - in der Praxis, Theorie und Ausbildung. Nachdem er in den 1980ern für Richard
Meier und Rafael Moneo gearbeitet hatte, gründete Allen 1991 Stan Allen Architects und war
bis 2000 und dem Erscheinen des letzten Hefts
Redakteur der wichtigen Zeitschrift *Assemblage*.
Von 2002 bis 2012 war Allen Dekan der Princeton School of Architecture und ist dort weiterhin als Professor tätig. Am bekanntesten ist er
vielleicht für den Essay „Field Conditions" [Feld-
bedingungen], in dem er über das veränderte
Verständnis von Architektur und Stadt nach-
dachte – weg von einem einheitlichen, dichten
und punktuellen Objekt, hin zu einer Architektur als Teil eines verstreuten und dynamischen
Feldes materieller und immaterieller Kräfte.[1] Der
Aufsatz war Teil eines umfassenderen Projekts,
das sich mit Ideen befasste, die um kritische Praxis, Landschaftsurbanismus und Stadttheorie
kreisen.

In *Situated Objects* weitet sich Allens Interesse an der Kontingenz der Kräfte aus, die bei
der Architektur auf dem Spiel stehen. Allen ver-

tritt die These, Architektur operiere mittels einer
Reihe von Paradoxa, die er in der Einleitung unter dem Begriff „situierte Objekte" beschreibt.
Allen schreibt: „Gebäude sind ‚situierte Objekte': objektartig insofern sie feste Grenzen haben
und frei stehen; situiert insofern Gebäude stets
in einer komplizierten Beziehung zu einem größeren Kontext stehen" (S. 13). Für Allen sind
Gebäude, Landschaften und Städte „in der Welt
situiert und an einen Ort gebunden" (S. 9); doch
der Architekt bzw. die Architektin arbeitet normalerweise weit entfernt von der Baustelle und
bedient sich „abstrakter Werkzeuge" wie Zeichnungen, Schaubilder und Computermodelle. Allen denkt über die parallele disziplinäre Debatte
zwischen Architektur als konstruierter Realität
und Architektur als abstraktem Repräsentations-
system nach. Doch Architektur kann ihren Ausdruck in der Gestalt eines Gebäudes finden oder
nicht. Architektur ist eine diskursive Praxis, bei
der Fragen der Repräsentation immer schon in
die Geschichte der Disziplin eingebettet waren;
und heute ist Architektur Teil der Imageindust-
rie des Kapitalismus. Allen meint, das „Zeichnen
erlaubt es dem Architekten, effektiv zwischen
dem Abstrakten und dem Realen zu operieren"
(S. 10). Folgerichtig behandelt *Situated Objects*
Ideen aus den Themenbereichen Abstraktion
und Realismus, Tektonik und Repräsentation,
Natur und ortstypisches bzw. anonymes Bauen,
Architektur als kulturelle Praxis und die Wirklichkeit des Bauens vor Ort. Allen zeigt, dass
Architektur „objektartig", aber immer auch im
Feld sozialer Beziehungen angesiedelt ist, ob es
sich dabei um lokale Geschichten oder globalen
Urbanismus, kulturelle Normen und verschie-
dene ideologische Faktoren handelt, darunter
das eigene auktoriale Streben des Architekten.

Der Essay „Design Rules" eröffnet den
Abschnitt über Außengebäude und stellt eine
Folge von drei Gebäuden vor: M/M House &
Studio, E/V House & Studio und L/B Studio.

1   Allen, Stan: „From Object to Field: Field Conditions in
    Architecture and Urbanism" [1996], in *Practice: Architecture,
    Technique and Representation*, London, New York 2009,
    216–243. Der Essay erschien ursprünglich als „Field
    Conditions in Architecture and Urbanism", in *The Berlage
    Papers* 17 (1996), und wurde in der Folge mehrmals
    überarbeitet. Siehe auch Allen, Stan: *Points+Lines:
    Diagrams and Projects for the City* [1999], New York 2012.

Obwohl Allen die Designstrategien speziell in Bezug auf diese Gebäude diskutiert, schwingen die „Regeln" ganz allgemein in den im Buch geschilderten Projekten mit. Allen definiert drei Designstrategien. Die erste ist eine formale Sprache, die auf gewöhnlichen Materialen basiert. Allen vertritt die Auffassung, das Bauen heute befasse sich größtenteils mit der Montage vorgefertigter standardisierter Elemente vor Ort. Die meisten Projekte in dem Buch folgen einfachen, leicht zugänglichen Technologien: leichte Holzrahmen, Schiebewände aus Holz, blechgedeckte Dächer, Standardfenster und -türen. Das führt eher zu einer Sprache kompakter und vertrauter Objekte als zu komplizierten Assemblagen. Die zweite Strategie ist das figürliche Dach. Alle Projekte außer einem, dem kubischen J/S House, arbeiten mit Variationen an einem Satteldach. Es gibt das Falt- und das Spanndach (M/M House, W/H House), das falsch ausgerichtete Dach (E/V Studio), das doppelte Satteldach (L/B Studio, Ghost Shed) und den wiederholten oder extrudierten Giebel (Lyceum, Olana Orchard Studio). Die dritte Strategie betrifft die Arbeit in Serien. Allen entfernt sich von Vorstellungen wie Neuartigkeit und Einzigartigkeit zugunsten von Kohärenz, serieller Wiederholung und kritischer Transformation. Das Ergebnis dieser Designregeln ist sowohl ein situiertes Objekt als auch ein „unheimliches Objekt" (S. 120), irgendwo zwischen Abstraktion und Realismus im Register des „seltsam Vertrauten".

Vassallos Essay „Der Wert des Da-Seins" situiert Allens Arbeit vor einer konzisen Genealogie der amerikanischen einheimischen Abstraktion. Vassallo denkt über Venturis und Rauchs Trubeck- und Wislocki-Häuser nach (1972) und zeichnet eine Abstammungslinie zu Steven Holls Studien ländlicher und städtischer Haustypen in *Pamphlet Architecture* (1983) und Vincent Scullys Reflexionen in *The Shingle Style Today* (1974) bis hin zu den Fotografien Charles Sheelers, der in den 1910er- und 20er-Jahren die Landschaft und ärmlichen Gebäude von Bucks County im ländlichen Philadelphia dokumentierte. Vasallo

vertritt die These, Allens kritische Architekturpraxis oszilliere „zwischen den Polen der Avantgarde und des Traditionellen, zwischen dem Konzeptionellen und dem Improvisatorischen" (S. 104). Thomas' Essay „Ein Schritt entfernt" denkt über Allens Zeichnungen nach und konzentriert sich dabei auf seine „Collageverfahren". Thomas interessiert sich dafür, dass Zeichnungen bereits „einen Schritt von der Wirklichkeit eines Gebäudes entfernt sind, eine intellektuelle Beschäftigung, der man in weiter Entfernung von der Baustelle nachgeht" (S. 171). Ein Beispiel ist die höchst verführerische Zeichnung des Olana Orchard Studios – eine Hommage an Stanley Tigermans Hot Dog House – auf der die Bäume am Waldrand in der Ebene gezeichnet und mit einem Grauton überzogen sind; das Gebäude ist in einer 90°-axonometrischen Ansicht gezeichnet, die Oberfläche schwarz getönt; und ein Raster identischer Bäume, die den Obstgarten darstellen, sind im Aufriss gegeben. Ebene, Axonometrie und Aufriss überlagern einander. Eine Reflexion über den Ort, das Programm und die Geschichte der Avantgarde wird präsentiert. Die Zeichnung stellt einen Untersuchungsort dar.

*Situated Objects* schließt mit Allens Essay, der den Titel „Erklären durch Zeichnen: Auf Axonometrisch" trägt. Er erweitert Allens Reflexionen über Zeichnen und Repräsentation, die er in seiner Einleitung entwickelt hat. Allen denkt darin über sein Studium an der Cooper Union in Manhattan unter John Hejduk nach, den viele für den Urheber der 90°-Axonometrie halten, wo der Plan rechtwinklig zur Projektionsebene ist. Allen interessiert an dieser Art von Zeichnung, dass sie die Messbarkeit der orthografischen Projektion – Plan und Aufriss sind unverzerrt – mit einer pikturalen Form der Repräsentation verbindet. Für Allen „lenkt es die Aufmerksamkeit auf die Zeichnung als Kunstgriff" (S. 240). Jedes der in diesem Buch versammelten Projekte beginnt mit einer 90°-axonometrischen Zeichnung, gefolgt von Plänen, Schnitten, Aufrissen, nur mit Strichlinien gezeichneten Perspektiven und Variationen über die Axono-

metrie. Es handelt sich um eine rhythmische Struktur und bringt eine Reihe von Wiederholungen mit kleineren Modifikationen hervor. Allen gelangt zu dem Schluss, dass die axonometrischen Studien Teil eines Designprozesses sind – eine Serie – als „ein außerordentlich erhellendes Werkzeug und als unabhängige Artefakte" (S. 244).

Allgemeiner gesagt gewinnen die axonometrische Zeichnung und das pikturalere gegenständlichere Element der Architekturzeichnung heute wieder die Oberhand gegenüber dem „gerenderten" für Marketingzwecke produzierten Bild. In einer Zeit, in der wir von einer Bildkultur durchtränkt sind und wo Wünsche nach Selbstausdruck in der Architektur weiter reichlich vorhanden sind, ist es Allens Überzeugung, dass der Architekt bzw. die Architektin am „Horizont der Vorstellungskraft" arbeitet, um neue Subjektivitäten und Daseinsweisen in der Welt zu konstruieren, eine willkommene kritische Einstellung, die von den hier versammelten Zeichnungen, Schriften und Fotografien veranschaulicht wird. ∎

*Cameron McEwan (Übersetzung: Nikolaus G. Schneider)*

# Abstraction and Realism

*Situated Objects* documents drawings, buildings, and projects realized by Stan Allen since 2012. The book focuses on eight small buildings in landscape settings, incorporating houses, studios, and temporary constructions. It is organised into three sections dealing with "Outbuildings," "Material Histories," and "New Natures." Each section opens with concise reflections by Allen on the respective theme and introduces the buildings under that theme. A series of essays by Allen, Jesús Vassallo, and Helen Thomas contextualise the work. The texts and Allen's drawings are in dialogue with a suite of photographs by Scott Benedict, which are threaded throughout. The book is beautifully crafted; exclusively made up of line drawings and monochrome photographs.

Allen is a compelling figure in architecture and critical discourse. His work operates across architecture and urbanism; practice, theory, and education. Having worked for Richard Meier and Rafael Moneo in the 1980s, Allen set up Stan Allen Architects in 1991 and was projects editor at the important journal *Assemblage* until its final issue in 2000. Allen was Dean of Princeton School of Architecture from 2002 to 2012 and continues to serve as a professor. He is perhaps best known for the essay "Field Conditions," which reflected on the shift in understanding architecture and the city as a unified, dense, and punctual object; towards architecture as part of a dispersed and dynamic field of material and immaterial forces.[1] It was part of a wider project that engaged ideas around critical practice, landscape urbanism, and urban theory.

In *Situated Objects* Allen's interest in the contingency of forces at stake in architecture is extended. Allen argues that architecture operates under a series of paradoxes, which he describes in the introduction under the term "situated objects." As Allen writes: "Buildings are 'situated' objects: object-like, in that they have fixed limits and stand free; situated, in that buildings always exist in an intricate relationship with a larger context" (p. 13). For Allen, buildings, landscapes, and cities are "situated in the world and bound to a place" (p. 9); yet the architect usually works at a distance from the building site using "abstract working tools" such as drawings, diagrams, and computer models. Allen reflects on the parallel disciplinary debate between architecture as constructed reality and architecture as abstract representational system. Yet architecture may or may not have its expression in the form of a building. Architecture is a discursive practice where issues of representation have always been embedded in the history of the discipline; and today architecture is part of the image industry of capitalism. Allen argues that "drawing allows the architect to operate effectively between the abstract and the real" (p. 10). Consequently, *Situated Objects* addresses ideas about abstraction and realism, tectonics and representation, nature and the vernacular, architecture as cultural practice and the reality of building on site. Allen shows how architecture is "object-like" but always situated in the field of social relations, whether local histories or global urbanism, cultural norms, and varying ideological forces including the architects own authorial pursuit.

The essay "Design Rules" opens the section on outbuildings and introduces a suite of three buildings: M/M House & Studio, E/V House & Studio, and L/B Studio. Although Allen discusses the design strategies specifically in relation to these buildings, the "rules" reverberate across the projects in the book more generally. Allen defines three design strategies. The first is a formal language based on ordinary materials. Allen argues that building today is largely concerned with assembling pre-made standardised elements on site. Most projects in the book follow simple readily available technologies: lightweight timber frame, timber or cement panel siding, metal roofs, standard windows and doors. It leads to a language of compact and taught objects rather than complicated assemblages. The second strategy is the figural roof. All but one project—the cubic J/S House—work with variations on a pitched roof. There is the folded and stretched roof (M/M House, W/H House), the misaligned roof (E/V Studio), the double pitched roof (L/B Studio, Ghost Shed), and the repeated or extruded gable (Lyceum, Olana Orchard Studio). The third strategy concerns working in series. Allen moves away from

1   Stan Allen, "From Object to Field: Field Conditions in Architecture and Urbanism" [1996], in *Practice: Architecture, Technique and Representation* (London; New York: Routledge, 2009), 216–43. The essay was originally published as "Field Conditions in Architecture and Urbanism" in *The Berlage Papers* No. 17, January 1996, and was subsequently reworked several times. Also see Stan Allen, *Points+Lines: Diagrams and Projects for the City* [1999] (New York, 2012).

notions of novelty and uniqueness towards co-herence, serial repetition, and critical transfor-mation. The result of these design rules is both a situated object and also an "uncanny object" (p. 120), somewhere between abstraction and realism in the register of the "strangely familiar."

Vassallo's essay, "The Value of Being There," situates Allen's work against a concise genealogy of American vernacular abstraction. Vassallo reflects on Venturi and Rauch's Trubeck and Wislocki Houses (1972) and draws a lineage to Steven Holl's studies of rural and urban house types in *Pamphlet Architecture* (1983) and Vincent Scully's reflections in *The Shingle Style Today* (1974), to the photography of Charles Sheeler who in the 1910s and 20s documented the landscape and humble buildings of Bucks County in rural Philadelphia. Vassallo argues that Allen's critical architectural practice oscil-lates "between the poles of the avant-garde and the vernacular, between the conceptual and the improvisatory" (p. 104). Thomas' essay, "One Step Removed," reflects on Allen's drawings and focuses on his "collaged techniques." Thomas is interested in the way that drawings are already "one step away from the reality of a building, an intellectual pursuit carried out remotely from the site of construction" (p. 171). One example is the highly seductive drawing of Olana Orchard Studio—an homage to Stanley Tigerman's Hot Dog House—in which the trees at the forest edge are drawn in plan and overlaid with a grey tone; the building is drawn in 90-degree axonometric, its surface toned in black; and a grid of identical trees constituting the orchard are drawn in eleva-tion. Plan, axonometric, and elevation are super-imposed. A reflection on the site, the programme, and the history of the avant-garde is presented. The drawing constitutes a site of inquiry.

*Situated Objects* concludes with Allen's essay entitled "Explaining by Drawing: In Axo-nometric." It extends Allen's reflections on draw-ing and representation put forward in his intro-duction. Allen reflects on his studies at Cooper Union in Manhattan under John Hejduk, who many consider as the originator of the 90-degree axonometric, where the plan is square to the plane of projection. What interests Allen in this type of drawing is that it combines the measur-ability of orthographic projection—plan and ele-vation are undistorted—with a pictorial form of representation. For Allen: "it calls attention to the drawing as artifice" (p. 240). Each project compiled in this book opens with a 90-degree axonometric drawing, followed by plans, sec-tions, elevations, line drawn perspectives, and variations on the axonometric. It is a rhythmic structure and produces a series of repetitions with minor modifications. Allen concludes that the axonometric studies are part of a design pro-cess—a series—as "a powerful explanatory tool, and as independent artifacts" (p. 244).

In more general terms, the axonometric drawing and the more pictorial representational element of architectural drawing is today regain-ing a critical purchase against the "rendered" im-age produced for marketing purposes. At a time when we are saturated by an image culture and where desires for self-expression continue to abound in architecture, Allen's conviction that the architect works on the "horizon of imagina-tion" to construct new subjectivities and ways of being in the world, is a welcome critical attitude; exemplified by the drawings, writings, and pho-tographs collected here. ▪

*Cameron McEwan*

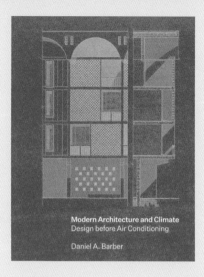

**Modern Architecture and Climate: Design Before Air Conditioning**

Daniel A. Barber
Princeton/Oxford: Princeton
University Press, 2020
Englisch, 336 Seiten, 272 teilw.
farbige Abbildungen und
Grundrisse, gebunden |
English, 336 pages, 272 some
color illustrations and floor plans,
hardcover
ISBN 978-0-69117-003-9
EUR 48,00 | EUR 48.00

# „Here, Climate Control began with a Tree"

Ingrid Böck

Wie lösten Architekten der Moderne Fragen des Wohnkomforts in klimatisch stark unterschiedlichen Regionen, bevor Klimaanlagen und die mit ihnen verbundene Nutzung fossiler Brennstoffe weit verbreitet waren? Dieses wiederkehrende Thema durchzieht Daniel A. Barbers Forschung zur optimalen Klimatisierung und wie diese überwiegend mit architektonischen statt haustechnischen Mitteln bewerkstelligt wurde – z.B. mit komplexen Beschattungssystemen, mit geeigneter Materialwahl oder mit topografischer Orientierung.

Barber formuliert im vorliegenden Band nicht nur einen theoretischen Rahmen für aktuelle Debatten des Klimawandels, sondern sieht die globale Krise als weiteren Schritt in der historischen Entwicklung des klimagerechten, modernen Bauens. In seinen detailreichen Analysen zeichnet er den Übergang in der Geschichtsschreibung nach, die die Entstehung der Moderne nicht mehr als progressives Narrativ aus der Industrialisierung und ihren Auswirkungen versteht, sondern als Bildung von und Beziehung zur Umwelt: Klimawirkung und Umweltbewusstsein als Bausteine der Moderne.[1]

Im ersten Teil „The Globalization of the International Style", der sich mit dem Zeitraum zwischen 1920 bis in die 1940er-Jahren befasst, widmet sich Barber den frühen Experimenten mit Solarhäusern (S. 24). Die Planer sahen, angespornt durch die Rohstoffknappheit der Zwischenkriegszeit, im passiven Solarhausprinzip eine ökonomische Möglichkeit, Ressourcen- und Komfortfragen mit zeitgenössischen Entwürfen zu lösen. Als Modell für diese These dient Barber Le Corbusiers 1931 entworfener Apartmentblock in Barcelona, dessen Fassade als Medium einer Kulturtechnik gelesen wird, die den Übergang von Innen nach Außen bewusst artikuliert und wahrnehmbar gestaltet (S. 2ff). Als weiteres Beispiel folgen Richard Neutras Projekte für den Wiederaufbau, die sogenannten „Planetary Tests" (1935), die in Puerto Rico oder dem Mittleren Ostens Freiluftlaboratorien konzipieren, in denen der Unterricht in halboffenen, natürlich beschatteten Räumen stattfindet (S. 115). Antonin Raymond fasst die universellen Prinzipien eines klimagerechten Entwerfens in seinem schlichten, 1947 entworfenen Diagramm einer Wohnung als querdurchlüftete Box zusammen (S. 132): „1 humidity, 2 temperature, 3 radiation, 4 air movement".

Barber widmet sich in zahlreichen Fallbeispielen auch der unterschiedlichen Anwendung des *Brise Soleil*, der mit den festmontierten, horizontalen Lamellen als „Sonnenbrecher" wirkt und gleichzeitig einen plastischen und funktionalen Überschwang des Entwurfs spiegelt. In Josep Lluis Serts US Botschaften in Bagdad (1955–61) und New Delhi (1957) werden *Brise Soleil* in einer Kombination mit baulichen Strategien für eine natürliche Klimatisierung eingesetzt: Die expressive Fassadengestaltung und das freischwebende Dach schirmen wie eine zweite Hülle die Innenräume und den Dachgarten ab (S. 144ff).

Im zweiten Teil widmet sich Barber dem Diskurs über solare Haustechnik im Amerika der Nachkriegszeit, in der die Klimaanlage als omnipräsentes Steuerungsinstrument von Gebäuden eingesetzt wurde. Er dokumentiert ausführlich die 1949 vom Magazin *House Beautiful* gestartete Artikelserie „Climate Control Project", die neue Formen der Visualisierung gezielt einsetzt, um erneuerbare Energiekonzepte und Klimafragen einer breiteren Öffentlichkeit anschaulich zu vermitteln (S. 181ff). Mit diesen Beiträgen wird die Eigeninitiative der Bewohner moderner Einfamilienhäuser und deren Abenteuergeist geweckt, damit sie sich den Herausforderungen einer bedrohlichen Umwelt gewachsen fühlen („Face up to the worst things in your climate – and *master them*", S. 189; „Here, Climate Control began with a Tree", S. 193).

Um die enge Beziehung zwischen architektonischer Form und spezifischem Mikroklima abzubilden, kommen in Barbers Band auch Meteorologen und Physiker zu Wort, die mit vielfältigem Bildmaterial ihre fachspezifischen

1 Foucault, Michel: *Security, Territory, Population: Lectures at the College de France, 1977–1978*, New York 2007.

Perspektiven darlegen und zum großen Abbildungsreichtum des Bandes mit Archivalien, Entwurfsplänen, Fotografien und Diagrammen beitragen.

Barber lehrt als Professor an der Universität von Pennsylvania, erwarb seinen PhD an der Columbia Universität und war Visiting Lecturer bzw. Visiting Fellow unter anderem an der Yale Universität, der Princeton Universität und dem Max-Planck-Institut in Berlin. Bereits in früheren Aufsätzen betonte Barber, wie stark die Erforschung der scheinbar endlosen Möglichkeiten der Sonnenenergienutzung mit einer Veränderung der geopolitischen Dynamik verbunden ist, da eine effiziente Solartechnik eine Umverteilung der Ressourcen hin zu sonnenreichen Gebieten bedeuten würde.[2] Zwar könnte man durch technische Fortschritte die Abhängigkeit von fossilen Brennstoffen verringern, doch würde mit dieser Entwicklung gleichzeitig weltwirtschaftlich und politisch ein neues, nie da gewesenes Ungleichgewicht entstehen.

Barber gelingt es, die epistemischen Folgen von Klimaveränderungen und weiterer Naturkatastrophen nicht nur als Diskurs der letzten Jahrzehnte zu verstehen, sondern als zentrales Leitmotiv in der Entwicklung der modernen Architektur, die er als eine Geschichte der „environmentalisation" bezeichnet.[3] Der Schritt zur Globalisierung des Umweltdiskurses seit den 1950er-Jahren sei jedoch erst mit der „rainforest community" möglich geworden, wie er hervorhebt: Erst durch die explizite Formulierung der Bedeutung der „Tropen" als Projektionsfläche für den anthropogenen Klimawandels wurden aus einzelnen Natur- und Umweltveränderungen die Darstellung einer globalen Krise möglich.[4] ▪

2   Barber, Daniel A.: „The World Solar Energy Project, ca. 1954", *Grey Room* 51 (2013), 64–93.

3   Barber, Daniel A.: „Environmentalisation and Environmentality: Re-Conceiving the History of 20th Century Architecture", *Design Philosophy Papers* 7, 3 (2009), 145–160, online unter: http://www.desphilosophy.com/dpp/dpp_journal/journal.html.

4   Ebd., 148.

# "Here, Climate Control Began with a Tree"

How did the architects of modernism resolve issues related to housing comfort in regions strongly differing in terms of climate, before air conditioning was invented and the related use of fossil fuels was widespread? This recurring theme pervades Daniel A. Barber's research on optimal climate control, and on how it has been achieved primarily through architectural means rather than building technology—for example, using complex shading systems, an appropriate selection of materials, or topographical orientation.

In the volume *Modern Architecture and Climate*, Barber not only outlines a theoretical framework for current discourse on climate change; he also sees the global crisis as yet another step in the historical development of climate-friendly modern construction. In his detailed analyses, he traces the shift that took place in historiography when the emergence of modernism was no longer viewed as a progressive narrative based on industrialization and its effects, but rather as the development of and relationship to the environment: climate impact and environmental awareness as building blocks of modernism.[1]

In the first section of the book, "The Globalization of the International Style," which deals with a time period starting in 1920 and spanning into the 1940s, Barber explores early experimentation with solar housing (p. 24). Prompted by the shortage of raw materials during the interwar period, planners saw the passive solar house principle as an economical way of addressing issues related to resources and comfort with con

temporary designs. Serving Barber as a model for this thesis is Le Corbusier's 1931 design for an apartment complex in Barcelona, its façade being read as a medium of cultural technology that purposefully articulates and perceptually designs the transition between inside and outside (pp. 2ff.). Richard Neutra's reconstruction projects, the so-called "planetary tests" (1935), are another example cited; they conceived open-air laboratories in Puerto Rico or the Middle East, where classes could be held in semi-open, naturally shaded spaces (p. 115). Antonin Raymond, in turn, consolidated the universal principles of climate-friendly design in his simple 1947 diagram of a housing unit drafted as a cross-ventilated box (p. 132): "1 humidity, 2 temperature, 3 radiation, 4 air movement."

Barber also focuses his attention, citing numerous case studies, on the various applications of *brise-soleil*, which uses fixed horizontal slats as a "sunbreaker" and at the same time signifies sculptural and functional enthusiasm in the design. In Josep Lluís Sert's US embassies in Baghdad (1955–61) and New Delhi (1957), *brise-soleil* were integrated in combination with structural strategies to achieve natural climate control: the expressive façade design and the free-floating roof shield the interior spaces and the roof garden like a second shell (pp. 144ff.).

In the second section of the book, Barber examines discourse solar house technology in the United States during the postwar period, where the air conditioner was employed as an omnipresent instrument for controlling buildings. He extensively documents the series of articles called

"Climate Control Project," initiated in 1949 by the magazine *House Beautiful*, which specifically earmarked new forms of visualization in order to communicate renewable energy concepts and climate issues to a broader public in a clear way (pp. 181ff.). These contributions served to awaken the initiative of the inhabitants of modern single-family homes and their spirit of adventure, enabling them to feel up to the challenges posed by a menacing environment ("Face up to the worst things in your climate—and *master them*," p. 189; "Here, Climate Control Began with a Tree," p. 193).

In order to portray the close relationship between architectural form and specific microclimates, Barber's volume makes room for the voices of meteorologists and physicists. These specialists present their discipline-specific perspectives through diverse visual material and contribute to the volume's extensive wealth of imagery with their archival documents, design proposals, photographs, and diagrams.

Barber is a professor at the University of Pennsylvania. He earned his PhD from Columbia University and has been a visiting lecturer or visiting fellow at various educational institutions, including Yale University, Princeton University, and the Max Planck Institute in Berlin. In previous essays, Barber has already emphasized how strongly the exploration of the seemingly endless possibilities of solar energy use is associated with a shift in geopolitical dynamics, since efficient solar technology would imply a redistribution of resources to sunny areas.[2] Although technological advances could reduce reliance on fossil fuels, this development would simultaneously give rise to a new, unprecedented imbalance in terms of global economics and politics.

Barber succeeds in understanding the epistemic ramifications of climate change and other natural disasters not only as a discourse covering the last few decades, but as a central leitmotif in the development of modern architecture, which he calls the history of "environmentalisation."[3] He emphasizes, however, that the step toward globalizing environmental discourse, which started in the 1950s, initially became possible due to the "rainforest connection": it was the explicit formulation of the meaning of "tropics" as a projection surface for anthropogenic climate change that first made it possible to render a global crisis from individual changes in nature and the environment.[4] ∎

*Ingrid Böck (Translation: Dawn Michelle d'Atri)*

1   Michel Foucault, *Security, Territory, Population: Lectures at the College de France, 1977–1978* (New York, 2007).

2   Daniel A. Barber, "The World Solar Energy Project, ca. 1954," *Grey Room* 51 (Spring 2013): 64–93.

3   Daniel A. Barber, "Environmentalisation and Environmentality: Re-Conceiving the History of 20th Century Architecture," *Design Philosophy Papers* 7, no. 3 (2009): 145–60, http://www.desphilosophy.com/dpp/dpp_journal/journal.html.

4   Ibid., 148.

Ideas of Ambiente: History
and Bourgeois Ethics in
the Construction of Modern
Milan 1881–1969
Angelo Lunati
Zürich | Zurich: Park Books, 2020
English, 312 Seiten, 41 farbige und
91 SW-Abbildungen, broschiert |
English, 375 pages, ca. 150 b/w
and color illustrations, paperback
ISBN 978-3-03860-153-1
EUR 38,00 | EUR 38.00

## Mailand als *Ambiente*: eine behutsame Historie

Katie Filek

Das Buch *Ideas of Ambiente: History and Bourgeois Ethics in the Construction of Modern Milan 1881-1969* von Angelo Raffaele Lunati ist ein Geschenk für jede/n an der Stadt Mailand Interessierte/n. Im weiteren Sinne ist es aber auch für all diejenigen beachtenswert, die sich mit der Frage befassen, wie man eine Geschichte der gebauten Umwelt schreibt. Im Verlauf der dreihundert, sorgfältig komponierten Seiten präsentiert Lunati den LeserInnen ein behutsam gewebtes, gründlich recherchiertes Narrativ der Stadt- und Architekturgeschichte, das auf den Forschungen zu seiner an der ETH Zürich entstandenen Doktorarbeit beruht. Das Ergebnis ist sowohl eine Untersuchung der politischen, wirtschaftlichen und sozialen Bedingungen, die über einen Zeitraum von fast einem Jahrhundert zur Entstehung von Mailands Stadtgefüge beitrugen, als auch eine Untersuchung der Idee des *Ambiente*. Dieser italienische Begriff lässt sich nicht leicht übersetzen, hat mit der Zeit einen Bedeutungswandel erfahren und hatte im Diskurs und der Praxis der Architektur in Mailands Nachkriegszeit eine Schlüsselposition inne. *Ideas of Ambiente*, das elegant aufgebaut und mit Archivmaterial sowie mit einer Reihe neuer Fotografien Daniele Marzoratis illustriert ist, ist deshalb bemerkenswert, weil es sich durch Maßstäbe, Gebiete und Akteure hindurchbewegt und so die komplexen, der Bauweise einer Stadt zugrunde liegenden Schichten offenlegt. Und auch wenn es von einem praktizierenden Architekt verfasst wurde und für sich betrachtet durchaus ein sanftes Manifest ist, das auf dezente Weise einem zeitgenössischen Ansatz das Wort redet, ist es dank Lunatis architektonischer Analysen in Verbindung mit einer präzisen Auswahl von Akteuren und Fallstudien ein wichtiger Beitrag zur Architekturgeschichte. Möglicherweise ist es ein Geschichtsbuch, das von einem Architekten geschrieben werden musste.

Die Verbindung des Autors zu der Stadt, um die es hier geht, ist persönlicher Natur: Lunati selbst ist Mailänder, das Politecnico di Milano ist seine Alma mater, und er ist Mitbegründer des Mailänder Architekturbüros Onsitestudio (welches er seit 2006 zusammen mit Giancarlo Floridi leitet). Diese enge Beziehung dürfte den umfassenden Untersuchungsgegenstand und die sachkundige Auswahl der Fallstudien erklären; gleichwohl ist das Buch für ein breites Publikum geschrieben. Insgesamt ist der Aufbau schnörkellos: nach einem Vorwort Adam Carusos, dem Betreuer von Lunatis Dissertationsvorhaben an der ETH, sowie einigen dem Begriff Ambiente gewidmeten Seiten, ist der Inhalt in vier chronologisch aufeinanderfolgende Abschnitte unterteilt. Jeder Abschnitt konzentriert sich auf eine chronologische Phase aus Mailands Geschichte der Jahre 1881 bis 1969. Wie der Autor selbst erklärt, handelt es sich bei zwei der Kapitel (dem ersten und dem vierten) um als Rahmen fungierende, Hintergründe und Theorie behandelnde Lesezeichen, während der Kern des Arguments sich in den mittleren beiden Kapiteln findet, die jeweils ebenfalls einen historischen Moment umrahmen, aber auch tief in spezifisch urbane, architektonische Fallstudien eintauchen.

Lunatis Erzählung beginnt mit dem Kapitel „Die romantischen Wurzeln des *Ambiente* im neunzehnten Jahrhundert" und konzentriert sich auf die Phase nach der Einigung Italiens. Wie auch alle folgenden schildert dieses Kapitel sowohl die wichtigen Figuren und Themen im Architekturdiskurs im Mailand jener Zeit als auch die wirtschaftlichen, politischen und sozialen Bedingungen, welche die Stadt damals prägten. Die wichtigsten Protagonisten sind hier der Mailänder Architekt und Pädagoge Camillo Boito sowie das aufstrebende Bürgertum aus Self-made-Industriellen, die in Mailands sanftem Übergang von einer ländlichen zu einer industriellen, urbanen Wirtschaft und in Boitos Vorstellungen von einer ökologischen Einheit beim Umgang mit der historischen Stadt Kontur gewinnen. Außerdem widmet Lunati sich dem ersten Entwicklungsplan (von 1889) und Mailänder Theorien der Denkmalerneuerung in derselben Zeit und schafft so die Rahmenstruktur für die weitere Entwicklung der Stadt. Das zweite Kapitel des Buches, „Novecento und *Ambiente*", thematisiert Mailands architektonisches Milieu während der beiden Jahrzehnte der faschistischen Herrschaft in Italien von 1920 bis 1943. Dieses Kapitel führt die LeserInnen durch den nationalen Wettbewerb für einen neuen Stadtplan und stellt die Architekten Piero Partaluppi und Giovanni Muzia neben der von Muzio geleiteten Kooperative *Club degli Architetti Urbanisti* als Schlüsselfiguren vor. Außerdem zeichnet Lunati wieder ein umfassendes Bild, indem er von einer Auseinandersetzung der privaten Interessen, Persönlichkeiten und politischen Kräfte hinter Mailands städtischen und architektonischen Projekten in der Zwischenkriegszeit zu den Einzelheiten mehrerer Fallstudien übergeht, darunter Projekte von Portaluppi wie Muzio in der Gegend um das Kloster Sant' Ambroglio. Letztere werden aufgrund ihrer ökologischen Qualität sehr gründlich analysiert, von ihrer Stellung in der Stadt über die architektonische Gestalt bis hin zu ihren materiellen Eigenschaften und der Anordnung der Fenster, und werden dabei von historischen Grundrissen, Fotografien und baulichen Details begleitet. Auch Bramantes Einfluss wird erwähnt, sein Weg kurz nachgezeichnet; das Ganze ergibt ein rundes Bild.

Kapitel Drei („Was fehlt?") präsentiert Ernesto Nathan Rogers vom Studio BBPR als führende Figur in der Debatte um das *Ambiente* in der dem Wiederaufbau gewidmeten Mailänder Nachkriegszeit. Lunati zeichnet den Weg von Boito zu Rogers nach und erläutert die philosophischen Grundlagen von Rogers historischem Ansatz, wobei er die Bedeutung seiner Verbindungen zu den Philosophen Antonio Banfi, Benedetto Croce und vor allem Enzo Paci für die Entwicklung eines Verständnisses von Permanenz und Emergenz, sprich der Beziehung von Dauer und Erneuerung, Altem und Neuem, betont. Neben einer Auseinandersetzung mit wichtigen Publikationen jener Zeit und zwei Projekten von BBPR wird hier die Gegend um San Nazaro (und BBPRs Torre Velasca) einer näheren Analyse unterzogen. Lunati analysiert Projekte von Asnago Vender und Luigi Caccia Dominioni, um die Gestaltung der Gegend als „eine Konstellation moderner Gebäude in der historischen Stadt" (218) zu illustrieren. Das vierte und letzte Kapitel, „Was ist nur mit dem *Ambiente* geschehen?", befasst sich mit den politischen Veränderungen seit den späten 1960ern.

Lunati skizziert hier, wie ein zunehmend ideologischer Umgang mit der Geschichte Rogers' Vorstellung von *Ambiente* nicht mehr unterstützte, während Veränderungen in der lokalen und nationalen Politik zu einer Verschiebung innerhalb der Machtstrukturen und der Wirtschaft sowie im Verhältnis zwischen Architekten und Kunden führte. Aldo Rossi mit seiner Kritik des *Ambiente* als ein von der sich rasch ausbreitenden Stadt abgekoppelter „Illusionismus", ist der Protagonist dieses Kapitels. (Lunati widerspricht dieser aus den späten 1960ern stammenden Kritik mit dem Hinweis darauf, dass sie auf einen Bedeutungswandel des Begriffs selbst zurückzuführen sei und nicht auf die Ideen, die ihn ursprünglich prägten. *Ambiente* ist nach wie vor okay.)

Zweierlei ergibt sich aus dieser ausgedehnten Übersetzung eines Begriffs: Erstens handelt es sich um eine nuancierte Darstellung der komplexen Schichten hinter der Struktur einer Stadt, die Industrielle, Politiker, Aristokraten, Philosophen und Architekten (nebst Plänen, Fotografien, Detailzeichnungen) zusammenbringt, um ein geschlossenes Narrativ des urbanen Raums zu entwerfen. Auch wenn die Geschichte in diesem Fall naturgemäß spezifisch für Mailand ist (für die Besonderheit seiner bürgerlichen Entwicklung und der Anti-Monumentalität als Grundierung für das *Ambiente*), lässt sich dieser Ansatz auch gut immer wieder bei der Untersuchung einer gebauten Umwelt übernehmen, umsetzen und anwenden. Es ist ein Experiment hinsichtlich der Erforschung und Beschreibung eines Narrativs des Ortes. Zweitens, und noch subtiler, lässt sich *Ideas of Ambiente* als das Manifest eines Architekten lesen, der dafür plädiert, im Einklang mit der Geschichte zu arbeiten, sprich als ein sanftes Manifest dafür, wie man zeitgenössisch sein und zugleich auf die Tradition und das bereits vorhandene Bemühen um die harmonische Koexistenz von Alt und Neu achten und auf sie zurückgreifen kann. Für eine Architektur der Kontinuität statt für eine des Bruchs. Indem er hervorhebt, wie das in Mailand erreicht wurde, und einem zeitgenössischen Publikum die Ideen Boitos, Portaluppis, Muzios und Rogers' übermittelt, legt Lunati das Fundament für einen ähnlichen Ansatz heute und hinterfragt zugleich, wie dieser aussehen könnte. Doch wie immer

man *Ideas of Ambiente* liest: Es ist ein schöner Beitrag zur Forschung und Praxis gleichermaßen. ∎

*(Übersetzung: Nikolaus G. Schneider)*

## Milan as *Ambiente*: A Gentle History

The book *Ideas of Ambiente: History and Bourgeois Ethics in the Construction of Modern Milan 1881–1969* by Angelo Raffaele Lunati is an offering to those interested in the city of Milan. More widely, it is also of note for those considering how to write a history of the built environment. Over the course of the book's three hundred thoughtfully crafted pages, Lunati presents readers with a carefully woven, deeply researched narrative of urban and architectural history informed by his doctoral research at the ETH in Zurich. The result is both an investigation of the political, economic, and social conditions that contributed to producing Milan's urban fabric over a period of nearly a century and an investigation of the notion of *ambiente*—an Italian term that eludes easy translation, that has shifted in its meaning over time, and that held a key position in architectural discourse and practice in Milan's post-war period. Elegantly composed and illustrated with both archival material and a new set of photographs taken by Daniele Marzorati, *Ideas of Ambiente* is notable for moving across scales, fields, and actors to reveal the complex layers behind a city's construction. And while it is written by a practicing architect—and may well be a gentle manifesto in its own right, in quiet support of a contemporary approach—Lunati's architectural analyses combined with a precise selection of actors and case studies make it an important contribution to architectural history. It is a history book, perhaps, that needed to be written by an architect.

The author's connection to the city in question is personal: Lunati himself is Milanese, the Politecnico di Milano is his alma mater, and he is co-founder of the Milanese architecture office Onsitestudio (which he has been leading together with Giancarlo Floridi since 2006). This close relationship may inform the broad topic of investigation and the informed selection of case studies; the book, however, is written for a wide audience. Overall, its composition is straightforward: following a foreword by Adam Caruso—the supervisor of Lunati's doctoral research at the ETH—and several pages dedicated to the term *ambiente*, the content is divided into four chronologically sequential sections. Each section focuses on one chronological period in Milan's history from the years 1881 to 1969. As the author himself explains, two chapters form framing bookmarks of background and theory (the first and the fourth) while the core of the argument can be found in the central two chapters, each which equally frames a historical moment but also goes deeply into specific urban, architectural case studies.

Lunati's narrative begins with the chapter "The nineteenth century Romantic roots of *ambiente*," focusing on the period following Italy's unification. This chapter, as each that will follow, lays out both the important figures and topics in architectural discourse in Milan at the time and the economic, political, and social conditions shaping the city during the period in question. Here the protagonists are the Milanese architect-educator Camillo Boito and the emerging bourgeoisie of self-made industrialists, outlined in Milan's gentle shift from a rural to industrial, urban economy and Boito's notions of environmental unity in approaching the historic city. Lunati also gives space to the city's first master plan (in 1889) and Milanese theories of monument restoration in the same period, thus laying the framework for the city's subsequent development. The book's second chapter "Novecento and *ambiente*" addresses Milan's architectural milieu during Italy's two decades of fascist rule,

from 1920-1943. This chapter takes the reader through the national competition for a new urban plan and introduces architects Piero Portaluppi and Giovanni Muzio as key figures, along with the Muzio-led collaborative *Club degli Architetti Urbanisti*. Again, Lunati is comprehensive as he moves from a discussion of the private interests, personalities, and political drivers of Milan's urban and architectural projects in the interwar period to the specifics of several case studies, including projects by both Portaluppi and Muzio in the area surrounding the Sant'Ambrogio convent. The latter are each analyzed in depth for their environmental quality, from urban position to architectural form to materiality and fenestration, and accompanied by historic floor plans, photographs, and construction details. Bramante's influence is also noted, his path briefly traced; the picture is full.

Chapter Three ("What is missing?") features Ernesto Nathan Rogers of the studio BBPR as the leading figure in the debate on *ambiente* in the period of Milan's post-war reconstruction. Lunati traces the path from Boito to Rogers and explains the philosophical grounding of Rogers' approach to history, noting his connections to philosophers Antonio Banfi, Benedetto Croce, and in particular Enzo Paci in forming an understanding of permanence and emergence—that is, of the relationship between duration and renewal, the old and the new. In addition to a discussion of important publications at the time and two projects by BBPR, here the area around San Nazaro (and BBPR's Torre Velasca) is selected for analysis. Lunati analyses projects by both Asnago Vender and Luigi Caccia Dominioni to illustrate the area's composition as "a constellation of modern buildings in the historic city" (218). The fourth and final chapter, titled "Whatever happened to *ambiente*?" addresses the political shift that occurred starting in the late 1960s. Lunati outlines how an increasingly ideological approach to history no longer supported Rogers'

notion of *ambiente*, while changes in local and national politics shifted power structures and economies—and, in relation, architect-client relationships. Aldo Rossi enters as this chapter's protagonist in his criticism of *ambiente* as "illusionism," as disconnected from a rapidly expanding city. (Lunati counters this late 1960s criticism by pointing out that it derived from a change in meaning of the term itself, and not from the ideas that had once defined it. *Ambiente* is still ok.)

What arises from this extended translation of a term is twofold: first, it is a nuanced exposition of the complex layers behind a city's construction, bringing together industrialists, politicians, aristocrats, philosophers, and architects (along with plans, photographs, detail drawings) to outline a cohesive narrative of urban space. While in this case the story is of course specific to Milan—to the particularity of its bourgeois development and anti-monumentality as primers for *ambiente*—this is an approach which might well be taken, transposed, applied again and again in investigating the history of a built environment. It is an experiment in researching and writing a narrative of place. Secondly, and more subtly, *Ideas of Ambiente* can be read as an architect's manifesto for working in harmony with history. That is, as a gentle manifesto for how to be contemporary while paying attention to—and drawing on—tradition and the pre-existing, striving for the harmonious co-existence of old and new. For an architecture of continuity versus rupture. In highlighting how that was once achieved in Milan and in transmitting the ideas of Boito, Portaluppi, Muzio, and Rogers to a contemporary audience, Lunati both lays the foundation for a similar approach today and questions how that might be possible. Yet however *Ideas of Ambiente* is read: it is a beautiful contribution to scholarship and practice alike. ▪

*Katie Filek*

**Knowledge Worlds. Media,
Materiality, and the Making
of the Modern University**
Reinhold Martin
New York: Columbia University
Press, 2021
Englisch, 384 Seiten, ca.
90 SW-Abbildungen, broschiert |
English, 384 pages, ca. 90 b/w
illustrations, softcover
ISBN: 978-0-2311-8983-5
EUR 33,85 | EUR 33.85

## Architekturen des Wissens

Stefan Fink

Mit *Knowledge Worlds*, erschienen 2021
bei Columbia University Press, legt Reinhold
Martin, Architekturhistoriker und einer der
Gründungsherausgeber der Zeitschrift *Grey
Room*, die Ergebnisse einer intensiven Auseinandersetzung mit der Geschichte und Entwicklung
der US-amerikanischen Universitäten und Colleges von 1890 bis 1975 vor. Martin, bis 2008
Partner des New Yorker Architekturbüros
Martin/Baxi Architects und derzeit Professor
für Architektur an der Graduate School of Architecture, Planning, and Preservation der Columbia
University, erhebt trotz dieser räumlichen Ein-
grenzung schon mit dem Titelzusatz „Media,
Materiality, and the Making of the Modern University" den Anspruch, das Phänomen der modernen Universität in seiner Gesamtheit zu erfassen, basierend auf der Arbeitshypothese, dass
sich im untersuchten US-amerikanischen Mikrokosmos der Makrokosmos globaler Wissenswelten widerspiegelt. „Universität" wird dabei begriffen als Medienkomplex mit besonderem Augenmerk auf Materialität und Herstellung im
Sinne einer vielschichtigen Konstruktion, errichtet und kontinuierlich umgebaut von verschiedenen Akteuren, die ihrerseits wiederum in unterschiedlicher Weise von Universitäten und Colleges „gemacht" wurden.

Diese Metaphorik verweist auf das im Titel
ungenannte, aber den Text bestimmende Thema:
Architektur. Martin versteht unter „Architektur"
auf der einen Seite alle Ausprägungen der materiellen Struktur einer akademischen Institution,
vom Campusgelände über die Universitätsgebäude bis hin zu den Möbeln in diesen Gebäuden. Auf der anderen Seite kann „Architektur"
auch eine abstrakte Ordnungsstruktur bedeuten,
die ihrerseits die materiellen Architekturen zu-
sammenhält und ihnen erst Bedeutung verleiht
(vgl. S. 16). In einer weiteren Interpretation beschreibt Martin Architektur im Kontext der
Auseinandersetzung mit der modernen Universität folgendermaßen: „As a science of walls,
lines, and foundations, architecture rests both

inside and outside the university, drawing distinctions and inserting doors, windows, and
gates" (S. 6). Und tatsächlich hält *Knowledge
Worlds* durchgehend das in der Einleitung ge-
gebene Versprechen: „[A]rchitecture is everywhere in the book" (S. XI).

Die „Architektur" des Textes selbst ist klar
und streng symmetrisch: Martin gruppiert acht
Hauptkapitel jeweils in Paaren zu vier Haupttei-
len, flankiert von einem Prolog und einem Epilog und in der Mitte um ein „Zwischenspiel" an-
gereichert. Jedes dieser Kapitel funktioniert auch
für sich alleinstehend und bietet jeweils eine spe-
zielle Perspektive auf verschiedene „Wissenswelten":

Der Prolog führt in die Zeit um 1800 und
fokussiert das gesellschaftliche und geistige Leben rund um Thomas Jefferson auf dessen Land-
gut Monticello bei Charlottesville in Virginia.
Als wichtiger Akteur wird dabei der Speiseauf-
zug – „dumbwaiter" – herausgearbeitet, der es
der Herrschaft erlaubt, sich ungestört von der
Dienerschaft der Gelehrsamkeit hinzugeben. Die
ersten beiden Hauptkapitel widmen sich hier-
nach unter dem gemeinsamen Motto „Figures"
der Etablierung der Hochschule als juristische
Person, von Beginn an konfrontiert mit überaus
starken Emotionen seitens der sich parallel dazu
formierenden Studentenschaft, sowie der Entwicklung der Lehre der Geometrie und auch
Architektur an amerikanischen Colleges und
Universitäten.

Kapitel 3 und 4 – zusammengefasst zum
zweiten Hauptteil „Temporalities" – stellen zeit-
liche Aspekte in den Mittelpunkt: Die schrittweise Öffnung der Hochschulausbildung gegen
Ende des neunzehnten Jahrhundert für Frauen
und AfroamerikanerInnen korreliert mit der Etablierung eines fixen Lehrplans sowie einer vorgegebenen Tagesroutine für Studierende sowie
mit der Entstehung der typischen neugotischen
Hochschularchitektur in Nordamerika – architektonischer Ausdruck für das Streben nach
Höherem, für Wachstum und Entwicklung
(vgl. S. 101). Ebenfalls Ende des neunzehnten
Jahrhunderts rückt auch die Landwirtschaft in
den Blick akademischen Interesses, und Kultivierung wird in den USA zur Wissenschaft. Umgekehrt bedarf auch die zunehmende Flut wissen-

schaftlicher Publikationen einer Kultivierung und so zieht Martin Parallelen zwischen agrikultureller Forschung und der Entwicklung der Dezimalklassifikation von Melville Dewey, die auch heute noch vor allem die amerikanische Bibliothekslandschaft prägt.

Im Zwischenspiel „c. 1900" verknüpft Martin die Frontierthese von Frederick Jackson Turner mit der Gestaltung des zentralen Gebäudeensembles der Chicagoer Weltausstellung von 1893, der von Daniel Burnham entworfenen „White City": Das Ende des „Wilden Westens" erzeugt den Bedarf an neuen Symbolen für „[d]as rechnende Wesen der Neuzeit".[1]

Der dritte Hauptteil – die Kapitel fünf und sechs umfassend – widmet sich den Stimmen („Voices") in Wissenswelten: Bibliotheksbauten bilden den architektonischen Rahmen für stilles Lernen – also die Abwesenheit von Stimmen –, der durch eine ausgeklügelte diffuse Beleuchtung entsprechend inszeniert werden kann, wie in der von Charles F. McKim entworfenen Low Memorial Library der Columbia University in New York, wo zeitweise eine riesige, dem Mond nachempfundene runde Leuchte den Lesesaal ins richtige Licht rückte. Andere Räume in Hochschulbauten sollen umgekehrt gerade die einzelne Stimme verstärken – wie die Rockefeller Memorial Chapel der University of Chicago. Dem gegenüber stellt Martin das akademische Forschungsseminar, das gerade von der Vielstimmigkeit lebt, ausgehend von der Intimität einer um einen gemeinsamen Tisch versammelten und sich austauschenden Kleingruppe.

Die letzten beiden Kapitel thematisieren schließlich „Symbole" von Wissenswelten im zwanzigsten Jahrhundert: Im Fall der Anlage des Campus der University of Berkeley, dessen früheste Planungen auf Frederick Law Olmsted zurückgehen, attestiert Martin – im Rückgriff auf das Zwischenspiel – einen starken Bezug zum Mythos des Wilden Westens als symbolische Form. Zwei von Eero Saarinen für das MIT in Boston entworfene Gebäude – die MIT Chapel und das Kresge Auditorium – sind wiederum Ausdruck für die Betonung einer spirituellen und sozialen Dimension von Wissenschaft und Forschung, korrespondierend mit der Etablierung von geisteswissenschaftlichen Fakultäten

an naturwissenschaftlich-technisch ausgerichteten Universitäten. Der abschließende kurze Epilog lässt noch einmal einige der zahlreichen Highlights des Textes Revue passieren und knüpft an die Gegenwart an, deren Wissenswelten zunehmend virtuell sind.

Reinhold Martin gelingt mit *Knowledge Worlds* die Konstruktion eines faszinierenden und dichten Netzwerks akribisch recherchierter historischer Fakten und fundierter theoretischer Analysen und belegt dabei eindrucksvoll die Bedeutung von Architektur für die untersuchten Wissenswelten. Ob als gebaute Umwelt, Metapher, gestalterische Praxis oder akademische Diszilpin: „[A]rchitecture puts knowledge in the world" (S. 6). ▪

1    Simmel, Georg: *Die Philosophie des Geldes*, München/Leipzig 1907, XIII.

# Architectures of Knowledge

Reinhold Martin, an architectural historian and cofounding editor of the journal *Grey Room*, is presenting the results of an intensive study of the history and development of US colleges and universities from 1890 to 1975 in his new book *Knowledge Worlds*, released in 2021 by Columbia University Press. Currently a professor of architecture in the Graduate School of Architecture, Planning, and Preservation at Columbia University and previously (until 2008) a partner at the New York architectural firm Martin/Baxi Architects, Martin claims to capture, despite this spatial delimitation, the phenomenon of the modern university in its entirety, as the book's subtitle already indicates: *Media, Materiality, and the Making of the Modern University*. His approach is based on the working hypothesis that the macrocosm of global knowledge worlds is mirrored by the US microcosm he is studying. Here, "university" is taken as a media complex with special attention paid to materiality and production in the sense of multilayered construction, erected and continually converted by various protagonists, who in turn were "made" by colleges and universities in various ways.

This use of metaphor references the topic informing the text, though it remains unmentioned in the title: architecture. Martin takes "architecture" to mean, on the one hand, all manifestations of material structure at an academic institution, from the campus to the university buildings to the furniture in these buildings. On the other hand, "architecture" can also imply an abstract structural order, which for its part binds together the material architectures and gives them meaning in the first place (see p. 16). In another interpretation, Martin describes how architecture engages in the context of the modern university as follows: "As a science of walls, lines, and foundations, architecture rests both inside and outside the university, drawing distinctions and inserting doors, windows, and gates" (p. 6). And *Knowledge Worlds* truly does keep the promise it makes in the introduction: "[A]rchitecture is everywhere in the book" (p. XI).

The "architecture" of the textual material itself is clear and stringently symmetrical: Martin groups eight main chapters in pairs to create four principal sections, flanked by a prologue and an epilogue, and fortified by an "interlude" in the middle. The chapters work in a stand-alone way as well, each offering a special perspective on various "knowledge worlds."

The prologue introduces the reader to the period around 1800, focusing on the social and intellectual life of Thomas Jefferson and his circle at his estate Monticello near Charlottesville, Virginia. Identified as a significant protagonist here is the "dumbwaiter," allowing the home's master to devote himself to scholarship without being disturbed by servants. The first two chapters are respectively devoted, under the joint motto "Figures," to the establishment of institutions of higher education as corporate persons, which from the very outset were confronted with strong emotions on the part of the student body forming in parallel, and to the development of the teaching of geometry and also architecture at American colleges and universities.

Chapters 3 and 4, subsumed under the second principal section "Temporalities," place temporal aspects center stage. The gradual opening of higher education to women and African-Americans in the late nineteenth century correlates with the establishment of a steady curriculum and a specified daily routine for students; it also cor-

relates with the emergence of typical neo-Gothic university architecture in North America—expressing through architecture a striving for the higher things, for growth and development (see p. 101). Also at the end of the nineteenth century, academic interest came to be focused on agriculture, and cultivation became a science in the United States. Conversely, the rising tide of scholarly publications also required cultivation; Martin draws parallels between architectural research and the development of Melville Dewey's decimal system, which still today influences classification, particularly in American libraries.

In the interlude "c. 1900," Martin links the frontier thesis of Frederick Jackson Turner with the design of the central building ensemble at Chicago's world's fair of 1893, the "White City" designed by Daniel Burnham. The end of the "Wild West" created a need for new symbols reflecting the "calculating character of modern times."[1]

The third main section, comprising Chapters 5 and 6, is dedicated to "Voices" in knowledge worlds. Here, library buildings form an architectural framework for quiet learning—for the absence of voices—which can be staged accordingly by clever, diffuse lighting. An example of this is Low Memorial Library at Columbia University in New York, designed by Charles F. McKim, where a giant round lamp modeled after the moon shed felicitous light on the reading room from time to time. Other rooms in university buildings, by contrast, were meant to emphasize the individual voice in particular—such as Rockefeller Memorial Chapel at the University of Chicago. Martin contrasts this with academic research seminars that thrive on this very polyphony, based on the intimacy of a small

group gathered around a common table to exchange ideas.

Finally, the last two chapters thematize "Symbols" of knowledge worlds in the twentieth century. In the case of the University of Berkeley campus, its earliest plans going back to Frederick Law Olmsted, Martin asserts—taking recourse to the interlude—a strong connection to the myth of the Wild West as a symbolic form. Two buildings designed by Eero Saarinen for the Massachusetts Institute of Technology—the MIT Chapel and the Kresge Auditorium—are in turn an expression of the emphasis placed on a spiritual and social dimension of science and research, corresponding to the establishment of humanities departments at universities that are oriented to science and technology. The short concluding epilogue reviews some of the many highlights of the book, bringing them into the present, with the knowledge worlds becoming increasingly virtual.

With *Knowledge Worlds*, Reinhold Martin succeeds in weaving a dense, fascinating web of meticulously researched historical facts and well-founded theoretical analyses. In the process, he impressively substantiates the meaning of architecture for the knowledge worlds examined. Whether as built environment, metaphor, design practice, or academic discipline: "[A]rchitecture puts knowledge in the world" (p. 6). ∎

*Stefan Fink (Translation: Dawn Michelle d'Atri)*

1  Georg Simmel, *The Philosophy of Money*, ed. David Frisby, trans. Tom Bottomore and David Frisby (London and New York, 2005), x.

**Manor Lessons**
Commons Revisited

laba EPFL
Teaching and Research in Architecture

**Manor Lessons.**
**Commons Revisited**

Harry Gugger/Sarah Barth/
Augustin Clément et al. (Hg. | eds.)
Basel: Birkhäuser, 2021
Englisch, 200 Seiten, 248 Farb- und
110 SW-Abbildungen, broschiert |
English, 200 pages, 248 color and
110 b/w illustrations, paperback
ISBN 978-3-03860-196-8
EUR 48,00 | EUR 48.00

# Englische Lektionen zu
# Gemein- und Landgütern

Maike Gold

Mit *Manor Lessons. Commons Revisited* findet die *Teaching and Research in Architecture*-Serie des „Laboratory Basel" (laba) ihren Abschluss, die von der École Polytechnique Fédérale de Lausanne (EPFL) 2011 bis 2021 in Basel als Studioexpositur für Architektur und Urban Design unter der Leitung des bekannten Architekten Harry Gugger abgehalten wurden. Iaba widmete sich in seinen Untersuchungen der Frage, wie räumliche Gestaltung an der Schnittstelle von urbanen Prozessen und architektonischen Objekten analytisch und produktiv gedacht werden kann. Mit der Überzeugung, dass sich die ideellen und materiellen Faktoren menschlicher Gestaltungskraft auf allen Maßstabsebenen finden und anwenden lassen, gingen die „Labore" jeweils von konkreten Orten aus, deren territorialen Grundlagen sie mit historischen, städtebaulich-typologischen und architektonischen Phänomenen zu einer dynamischen Umwelt verknüpften, um so „Design" als Vermittler zwischen diesen Maßstäben herauszuarbeiten. Gestaltung fungiert als Medium und die produktive Rolle der Gestaltungsdisziplin Architektur ist kontextuell, d.h. auf unterschiedliche Maßstäbe des Kontexts Bezug nehmend, bestimmt. Nach der Barentssee, der Schweiz, Island, Israel, Portugal und dem marokkanischen Fez widmet sich das diese Reihe beschließende Buch nun der ländlichen Region Südwestenglands, in der beispielhaft Fragen nach der Verteilung, dem Eigentum und der Nutzung von gemeinsamen ländlich-landschaftlichen Ressourcen und ihrer zukünftigen Entwicklung durchgespielt werden.

*Manor Lessons. Commons Revistited* blickt dabei sowohl auf die lange Tradition der Privatisierung aufgrund von Landeinschließungen, als auch auf das klassische englische Herrenhaus – dem „Manor" – und bietet damit die Möglichkeit, die vielfältigen Beziehungen zur Landschaft neu zu bewerten, d.h. Land als gemeinschaftlichen Boden und nicht als Privateigentum zu denken. Fernab der urbanen Zentren sind die einstigen Herrensitze in Englands *countryside* weitläufige Güter, in denen die Beziehungen zwischen Objekten und umgebender Landschaft weit über den vermeintlich einfachen baulich-typologischen Dualismus von Stadt und Land hinausgehen.

Die Publikation ist in drei Teile gegliedert, die auch den Ablauf des Studios widerspiegeln. Das erste Kapitel „Territory" beschreibt mit geschichtlichen und geografischen Informationen die Region Wessex und bietet eine Übersicht über die Gebiete Avon Green Belt, Dorset Coast, South Hams und Taw & Exe Valley, die mit Fotos und Kartierungen zu Topografie, urbanen Räumen, Klimadiagrammen und Infrastrukturen unterlegt werden. In Unterkapiteln werden diese geografischen Informationen um politische, landwirtschaftliche und verwaltungstechnische Informationen erweitert, um so eine grundlegende Bestandsaufnahme zu bilden. Der zweite Teil „Field" entspricht der Studioexkursion und beschreibt als Fotostrecke den Reiz und die landschaftlichen Besonderheiten Südwestenglands. Das abschließende Kapitel „Architecture" vertieft die eigentliche Thematik des Buches in Form von konkreten Entwürfen. Die Studierenden des laba entwickeln dabei zukunftsorientierte Nutzungskonzepte, indem sie sowohl im regionalen als auch im architektonischen Maßstab detaillierte Projekte ausarbeiten, die sie an elf Standorten als strategischen Umbau von bestehenden „Manors" konkretisieren. Diese elf Entwürfe liefern Visionen zur Entwicklung regional-kommunaler oder landschaftlich-urbaner Nutzungsstrategien, die sich von alternativen Wohnformen, Besucherzentren, Bildungsstätten oder Landschaftseingriffen zur Attraktivitätssteigerung der Umgebung bis hin zu Ideen zur Wiederbelebung von landwirtschaftlichen Produktionsformen erstrecken.

Aus den elf Projekten sei hier exemplarisch das Projekt „Mendip Quarries Visitor Center" von Raphaël Vouillouz (S. 136–141) erläutert: Das im frühen 15. Jahrhundert errichtete Manor Southill House im Avon Green Belt, Cranmore Somerset liegt weit außerhalb des Kerngebiets Bristol-Bath. Durch die Reaktivierung des noch vorhandenen gebietsübergreifenden Eisenbahnsystems (*Beeching Cuts* von 1965) soll auch auf infrastruktureller Ebene die Revitalisierung der Region eingeläutet werden, die mit dem Southill House ein neues Besucherzentrum für dieses großräumlich gedachte Resort erhalten soll. Das bestehende Gebäude wird mithilfe von Freiraumgestaltung um einen neuen Hof und das „Museum of Mendip Quarries" erweitert, das über den zentral im Projekt verwendeten Baustoff und zugleich den in regionalen Steinbrüchen abgebauten Kalkstein, informiert. Dieser wird für die geplanten Anbauten genutzt und illustriert damit die grundsätzlichste Form des materiellen Zusammenhangs von Bau und Landschaft. Das Projekt wird gleich wie die zehn anderen Entwürfe dargestellt: In monochromen zehn bis fünfzehn Darstellungen wird auf jeweils vier Doppelseiten die Geschichte und Vision der Intervention am und um das Manor erzählt. Eine Bestandsaufnahme erfolgt hier mithilfe von vereinfachten Axonometrien und Fotografien und wird in Folge durch das klassische Spektrum der Architekturdarstellung – Lageplan mit Intervention, Axonometrien, Grundrisse, Ansichten, Schnitte, Detailschnitte und Visualisierungen – ergänzt. Dabei werden die verändernden Eingriffe in Rot, der Bestand durchgängig schwarz dargestellt. Kurztexte erläutern dabei die Bestandsbauten und die Interventionen.

Mit *Manor Lessons. Commons Revisited* gelingt eine anschauliche und ansprechende Dokumentation des letzten laba Studios, das vor allem das grundsätzlich transdisziplinäre Herangehen architektonischer Lehre und Forschung an einen spezifischen Themenkreis hochinformativ illustriert. Das Buch ist weit mehr als bloße Dokumentation von Entwurfsstudios mit einer Auswahl der ansprechendsten Ergebnisse, sondern zollt der einzigartigen Offenheit und Kreativität der architektonischen Disziplin Tribut, indem es dessen Schärfe in der Wahrnehmung und Stärke im Konzeptuellen demonstriert. Mit den gegenwärtig herausforderndsten Regionalfragen konfrontiert, verstehen sich die Projekte sowohl als Teil natürlicher wie auch gesellschaftlicher Kreisläufe. Dass Architekturentwürfe auf regionaler Ebene über typischerweise eingesetzte Materialien und Konstruktionen identitätssichernd verankern, ist natürlich keine grundlegend neue Herangehensweise, wird aber mit den elf Manors

des Studios in angewandter Form auf interessante, neue und hochaktuelle Punkte gebracht, die den regionalen Kontext zu einem ganz konkreten Teilaspekt der Architekturentwürfe und ihrer jeweiligen Vision macht. Diese deutlich reflektierte und reflektierende Arbeit entspricht einer Entwurfsmethodik, die zwischen Forschung und Lehre keine Unterscheidung einziehen muss. Da sie ebenso präzise analytisch wie synthetisch vorgeht, ohne dabei aber auf die sinnige und

sinnliche Überzeugungskraft einer zukünftigen baulichen Veränderung zu verzichten. Diese Architekturauffassung kann sich auch den Krisen der Gegenwart stellen und mit vielfältigen Lösungen bestehende Grenzen und Barrieren hinterfragen. Das Buch zeigt dabei eindrücklich, wie ein solches Architekturverständnis ebenso optimistisch wie eindringlich mit visionären Beispielen vorangehen kann. ∎

## English Lessons on Commons and Manors

*Manor Lessons: Commons Revisited* marks the conclusion of the *Teaching and Research in Architecture* series of the Laboratory Basel (laba). The series ran from 2011 to 2021 at the École Polytechnique Fédérale de Lausanne (EPFL) in Basel as a studio branch for architecture and urban design under the direction of the well-known architect Harry Gugger. Iaba devoted its investigations to the question of how spatial design can be analytically and productively conceived at the interface between urban processes and architectural objects. Starting from the conviction that ideational and material factors of human design power can be found and applied at all levels of scale, the "laboratories" each took concrete sites as their point of departure. The territorial foundations of these sites were then linked to historical, urban-typological, and architectural phenomena to create a dynamic environment meant to establish "design" as a mediator between these scales. Design functions as a medium, and the productive role of the design discipline of architecture is contextually determined, that is, it refers to different scales of context. After focusing on the Barents Sea, Switzerland, Iceland, Israel, Portugal, and Fez, Morocco, the series is now devoting its last book to the rural area of southwest England. Explored here are paradigmatic questions about the distribution, ownership, and use of shared landscape resources in a rural setting and their future development.

*Manor Lessons: Commons Revistited* looks at the long-standing tradition of privatization due to land enclosures, but also at the classic English manor house. It thus presents an opportunity to reassess the multiple and varied relationships to landscape, seeing land as a territorial commons rather than as private property. Situated far away from urban centers, the former manors of England's countryside are sprawling estates where relations between objects and the surrounding landscape extend far beyond the purportedly simple structural-typological dualism of town and country.

The publication is divided into three parts, reflecting the operations of the architectural studio. The first chapter "Territory" describes the region of Wessex, including information about its history and geography, and offers an overview of the areas of Avon Green Belt, Dorset Coast, South Hams, Taw Valley, and Exe Valley, all underscored by photographs and maps related to topography, urban spaces, climate diagrams, and infrastructures. In subchapters, this geographic data is supplemented by political, agricultural, and administrative information to arrive at a basic survey of the region. The second chapter, "Field," relates to the studio excursion and, through a series of photographs, describes the appeal and scenic characteristics of southwest England. The concluding chapter, "Architecture," delves into the actual subject matter of the book by citing concrete designs. Here, the laba students developed future-oriented utilization concepts by planning detailed projects on both a regional and an architectural scale; they fleshed out these projects at eleven sites as the strategic conversion of existing manors. The eleven designs deliver visions of how utilization strategies for regions and communities or landscapes and cities could be developed, including, among other things, alternative forms of housing, visitor centers, educational institutions, or landscape interventions meant to enhance the attractiveness of the surrounding area and also ideas for revitalizing agricultural methods of production.

Of the eleven projects, "Mendip Quarries Visitor Center" by Raphaël Vouilloz (pp. 136–41) is taken as an example in this review and explored in more detail. Built in the early fifteenth century, the manor Southill House in the Avon Green Belt, Cranmore, Somerset, is situated well outside the core area of Bristol-Bath. The reactivation of the still-existing, cross-territorial rail system (the Beeching cuts of 1965) is meant to herald the revitalization of the region on an infrastructural level, with Southill House providing a new visitor center for this resort envisioned on a large scale. The idea is to expand the present building with the help of open space design to include a new courtyard and the Museum of Mendip Quarries, which is meant to provide

information about the main building material used in the project and also the limestone extracted from regional quarries. Limestone is used for the planned extensions, thus illustrating the most fundamental form of the material connection between building and landscape. The project is presented in the same way as the ten other designs: ten to fifteen monochrome representations across four double-page spreads tell the story and convey the vision of the intervention at and around the manor. A survey is conducted here, aided by simplified axonometric depictions and photographs; it is then supplemented by the classic spectrum of architectural renderings: site plan with interventions, axonometry, floor plans, views, sections, detailed sections, and visualizations. The interventions effecting changes are shown in red throughout, the existing buildings in black, with short texts describing both.

*Manor Lessons: Commons Revisited* is a vivid and appealing documentation of the last laba studio, successfully illustrating above all the fundamentally transdisciplinary approach taken by architectural teaching and research in addressing a specific range of topics in a highly informative way. The book goes well beyond merely documenting design studios with a selection of the most appealing results. Instead, it pays tribute to the unique openness and creativity of the architectural discipline by demonstrating its sharpness in perception

and strength in the conceptual. Confronted by the most challenging issues of the present, the projects are meant to be viewed as part of both natural and societal cycles. That architectural designs anchor identity in a regional context through typically employed materials and construction methods is of course not a fundamentally new approach. However, it is brought to interesting, new, and very topical heights in the applied analysis of the eleven manors examined by the studios, making the regional context a very concrete partial aspect of the architectural designs and their respective vision. This clearly reflected and reflecting work corresponds to a design methodology that need not make a distinction between research and teaching, for it proceeds with both analytical and synthetic precision, yet without sacrificing the appropriate and sensory persuasiveness of future architectural change. This take on architecture is capable of dealing with present-day crises and of challenging existing boundaries and barriers through a wide range of solutions. In the process, the book impressively shows how such an understanding of architecture can lead the way with equally optimistic and striking examples. ▪

*Maike Gold (Translation: Dawn Michelle d'Atri)*

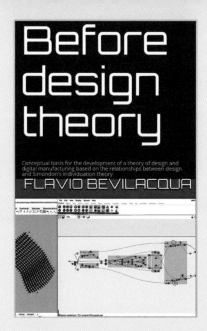

**Before Design Theory:**
**Conceptual Basis for the**
**Development of a Theory**
**of Design and Digital**
**Manufacturing Based on**
**the Relationships between**
**Design and Simondon's**
**Individuation Theory**

Flavio Bevilacqua

Neuquén: Flavio Bevilacqua, 2019

Englisch, 227 Seiten, broschiert |
English, 227 pages, softcover
Taschenbuch, E-Book |
Softcover, e-book

ISBN 978-9878624075

EUR 18,89 | EUR 18.89

# Gilbert Simondons Technikphilosophie im Kontext von Digital Design Theory

Gert Hasenhütl

Flavio Bevilacqua – argentinischer Architekt und Theoretiker – übersetzt in *Before Design Theory* Teile von Gilbert Simondons Technikphilosophie in die Architekturtheorie und Designforschung. Diese Arbeit kann damit als erste längere Übertragung des theoretischen Ansatzes von Simondon in diese Bereiche gesehen werden. Das Werk des französischen Technikphilosophen Gilbert Simondon (1924–1989) wurde aufgrund seines anspruchsvollen philosophisch-hermeneutischen Charakters bisher eher in der Technikphilosophie und Wissenschaftstheorie rezipiert. Eine konkrete Entwurfstheorie in der Technikphilosophie von Simondon zu lokalisieren ist allerdings schwierig, weil er hauptsächlich an technischen Individuationsprozessen interessiert ist, die mit einem diffizilen Spezialvokabular als komplexes Zusammenspiel von Subjekt, technischen Objekten und deren operativen Milieus einhergehen. Bemerkungen zum technischen Entwurf, zu Entwurfshandlungen oder Entwurfsoperationen in der Technik können zu Ableitungen komplizierter Formulierungen des „Unbestimmtheitsgrades" werden, wobei das Augenmerk immer eher auf der Genese, auf Objektreihen, oder auf der Aktivität von Objekten während ihrer Individuation liegt.[1]

Das Buch hat zwei Teile: Einen historischen, der der Bestimmung von Technik und Natur nachgeht und einen entwurfstheoretischen, der versucht „design operations" mit dem Vokabular und der Theorie von Simondon zu bestimmen. Anhand der Positionen von u.a. Ernst Kapp, Martin Heidegger, Lewis Mumford, José Ortega y Gasset, Sigfried Giedion, Jacques Ellul, Jacques Lafitte, Bernard Stiegler, Michel Serres oder Bruno Latour werden Spuren des „Werdens" von Technik nachgezeichnet. Dieses „Werden" von technischen Objekten wird stark angelehnt an den Simondon'schen Prozess der Konkretisation, der grob vereinfacht als Verwachsung einzelner Funktionselemente über die Zeit gesehen werden kann. „What defines a technical object as such is its concretization" (S. 166). Was über technische Objekte gesagt wird, führt der Autor über in seine Betrachtung von Entwurfstätigkeiten im digitalen Design: Wenn ein technisches Objekt mit einer Evolution und Genesis verknüpft werden kann, dann ist es doch auch möglich Entwurfshandlungen oder -tätigkeiten – die vom Abstrakten zum Konkreten verlaufen – unter dem Aspekt der Individuation zu betrachten. Und damit sind sie auch technische Objekte. Was ein technisches Objekt, und damit eine entwerferische Operation im Wesentlichen ausmacht ist deren Genese und weniger deren Funktion. Diese Genese lässt sich wiederum als Individuation fassen. So kommt der Autor z.B. zu folgender Definition der Entwurfstätigkeit: „The design operation appears as a place characterized by the existence of precarious metastable equilibria that threaten to break, exposed to failure. […] The design operation is an invisible, unaffordable phenomenon that can be captured at the time it is being carried out or through the task of observing and registering products of this operation (drawings, CAD files, models)" (S. 169, 176).

Entwurfstheoretisch spannend ist die Abgrenzung von Simondon zur Aristotelischen Trennung von Stoff (*hyle*) und Form (*morphe*), welche unser okzidentales Denken prägt und sogar unsere Auffassung des Mentalen oder Sozialen beeinflusst.[2] In diesem sogenannten „hylemorphischen" Schema kommt ein „passiver" Stoff (*hyle*) mit einer „aktiven" Form (*morphe*) zusammen.[3] Dieses Paradigma wird zum zentralen Anknüpfungspunkt des Autors, der in digitalen Entwurfsprozessen eine Loslösung von diesem eher linear verlaufenden Prozess sieht.

1 Vgl. Simondon, Gilbert: *Die Existenzweise technischer Objekte*, Zürich 2012, 126, und Del Fabbro, Olivier: *Philosophieren mit Objekten. Gilbert Simondons prozessuale Individuationsontologie*, Frankfurt am Main 2021, 66.

2 Vgl. Delitz, Heike: „Gilbert Simondons Theorie der sozialen ‚Form'", in: Moebius, Stephan/Prinz, Sophia (Hg.): *Das Design der Gesellschaft. Zur Kultursoziologie des Designs*, Bielefeld 2012, 109–130, hier 110.

3 Simondon, Gilbert: *Individuation in Light of Notions of Form and Information* (orig: L'individuation à la lumière des notions de forme et d'information, Grenoble 2005), übers. Taylor Adkins, Minneapolis 2020, 36.

Die zentrale These des Buches lautet entsprechend: Im digitalen Design gibt es so etwas wie eine nicht-hylemorphische Formwerdung (S. 15). Zunächst werden dazu die Kategorien Stoff und Form näher für die Bereiche Architektur und Design bestimmt (S. 19). Simondon folgend versucht der Autor dann Entwurfsprozesse in Architektur und Design als Prozesse der Konkretisierung während einer Individuation zu verstehen. Das führt auch zu einer neuen Sichtweise von Entwerfen: „The designer acts […] by provoking and sustaining processes in order to design" (S. 143). Entwerfende werden in digitalen Designprozessen zunehmend zu Zeugen innerhalb informationsverarbeitender Prozesse, auf die aber noch punktuell Einfluss genommen werden kann.

Der Autor stellt sich die nicht-lineare Koppelung von Form, Material und Information als etwas synergetisches vor: hier ergeben unterschiedliche „Heterogenitäten" Entwurfszustände, die anders ausfallen als im linearen – d.h. im hylemorphischen – Modell. Aufgrund der zumeist nur schwach strukturierten Design-Probleme, schließt der Autor auch auf eine Co-Evolution von Design-Problem und deren Lösung (S. 142) und beschreibt diese enaktiv verlaufende Design-Operation als quasi blinden Fleck im Entwurfsprozess. Jegliche Entwurfsschritte („design moves") stellen sich von selbst ein: „The operation of design is, we could say, self-maintaining. It has achieved a certain operational autonomy, because the potentials of the heterogeneities have been intertwined in such a way that they regulate the transfer of information between them" (S. 192f). Im Sinne von Simondon werden dann verschiedene Materialien und Medien als „energetische Felder" aufgefasst. 3D Modell, Materialien, 3D Drucker, Software, etc. befinden sich systemisch gesehen in einem Status der Ungleichheit („disparity"): „When the synergy began, the disparity rolled over into an emergent continuity, but the differentials between all those heterogeneities (among which it is possible to consider the designer) are still there" (S. 193).

Das Buch zeigt, wie schwierig es ist, Simondons Technikphilosophie in die Entwurfstheorie zu übertragen, weil man mit seinem Vokabular häufig auf einer beschreibenden Ebene verbleibt, und nur schwer zu einer prozessorientieren Entwurfstheorie gelangt. Die Frage ist: Braucht man die Theorie von Simondon um, wie etwa Mario Carpo, zu erkennen, dass Autorschaft, Intuition oder autografische Darstellungen im digitalen Entwurf eine immer geringere Rolle spielen? Parametrisches Entwerfen oder BIM relativieren die Rolle menschlicher und technischer Individuen so stark, dass deren Konsequenzen aktuell noch nicht absehbar sind. Das Simondon'sche Schema ist aktuell nicht das einzige, dass mit dem hylemorphischen Schema bricht. „Heterogeneous Engineering", „Material Driven Design", „Active Matter"-Ansätze oder Teile feministischer Wissenschaftsforschung hinterfragen ebenso allzu intentionalistische Theorien zum Entwurf kritisch. Auch die Co-Evolution von Design-Problem und Lösung ist in der Entwurfsforschung ein zentrales Thema.[4] Nichtsdestotrotz steckt das Buch einen theoretischen Rahmen ab, der die Eignung des Simondon'schen Vokabulars zur Bildung einer Entwurfstheorie testet und damit eine „Vorgeschichte" mit Adaptierungen zur Diskussion stellt, an denen es sich lohnt weiterzudenken. ∎

4  Vgl. Kees, Dorst/Cross, Nigel: „Creativity in the Design Process: Co-Evolution of Problem–Solution", *Design Studies* 22 (2001), 425–437.

# Gilbert Simondon's Philosophy of Technology in the Context of Digital Design Theory

In *Before Design Theory*, the Argentinean architect and theoretician Flavio Bevilacqua applies segments of Gilbert Simondon's philosophy of technology to architectural theory and design research. Hence, this book may be seen as the first more extensive transfer of Simondon's theoretical approach to these fields. Previously, the work of the French philosopher of technology Gilbert Simondon (1924–1989) had been applied more to the areas of technology and science philosophy due to its demanding philosophical, hermeneutic character. It is, however, difficult to localize a concrete theory of design in Simondon's philosophy of technology, because he is mainly concerned with processes of individuation that involve intricate specialist vocabulary as a complex interplay of subject, technical objects, and their operative environments. Observations on technical design, design actions, or design operations in a technology context can become derivations of complicated formulations of the "degree of indeterminacy," with attention always rather placed on the genesis, on object series, or on object activity during their process of individuation.[1]

The book has two parts: one focused on history, tracing the determination of technology and nature, and one on design theory, attempting to define "design operations" using Simondon's vocabulary and theory. Paths of technology's state of "becoming" are pursued based on positions by various individuals, including Ernst Kapp, Martin Heidegger, Lewis Mumford, José Ortega y Gasset, Sigfried Giedion, Jacques Ellul, Jacques Lafitte, Bernard Stiegler, Michel Serres, and Bruno Latour. This "becoming" of technical objects is strongly informed by the Simondonian process of concretization, which can be broadly simplified as the coalescence of individual functional elements over time. "What defines a technical object as such is its concretization" (p. 166). The author moves from what is said about technical objects to his views on design activity in the digital realm: if a technical object can be linked to an instance of evolution or genesis, then it is surely also possible to view design actions or activities, running from abstract to concrete, under the aspect of individuation. And this also makes them technical objects. What essentially constitutes a technical object, and thus also a design-related operation, is its genesis rather than its function. This genesis in turn can be considered individuation. The author thus arrives at the following definition of design activity: "The design operation appears as a place characterized by the existence of precarious metastable equilibria that threaten to break, exposed to failure. … The design operation is an invisible, unaffordable phenomenon that can be captured at the time it is being carried out or through the task of observing and registering products of this operation (drawings, CAD files, models)" (pp. 169, 176).

What is exciting in terms of design theory is the distinction between Simondon and the Aristotelian separation of matter (*hyle*) and form (*morphe*), which informs our Occidental thought and even influences our understanding of mental and social issues.[2] In this so-called "hylomorphic" model, "passive" matter (*hyle*) unites with "active" form (*morphe*).[3] This paradigm becomes the author's main connecting point, for it is in digital design processes that he sees a way of detaching from this more linear process. The central argument of this book is made accordingly: in digital design, there is such a thing as non-hylomorphic morphogenesis (p. 15). First, the categories of matter and

form are defined for the fields of architecture and design in more detail (p. 19). Following Simondon, the author then attempts to understand design processes in architecture and design in terms of concretization during individuation. This also leads to a new perspective on design: "The designer acts … by provoking and sustaining processes in order to design" (p. 143). In digital design situations, designers are increasingly becoming witnesses within information-processing processes which, however, can still be influenced selectively.

The author imagines the nonlinear coupling of form, material, and information as something synergetic: here, different "heterogeneities" result in design states that differ from the linear—that is, the hylomorphic—model. Owing to design problems that are usually only weakly structured, the author extrapolates a co-evolution of the design problem and its solution as well (p. 142) and describes this enactive design operation as a blind spot in the design process, as it were. All "design moves" play out on their own: "The operation of design is, we could say, self-maintaining. It has achieved a certain operational autonomy, because the potentials of the heterogeneities have been intertwined in such a way that they regulate the transfer of information between them" (pp. 192f.). According to Simondon, various materials and media are then comprehended as "energetic fields." Systemically speaking, 3D models, materials, 3D printers, software, et cetera, are all in a state of "disparity": "When the synergy began, the disparity rolled over into an emergent continuity, but the differentials between all those heterogeneities (among which it is possible to consider the designer) are still there" (p. 193).

This book shows that it is very difficult to translate Simondon's philosophy of technology, because our vocabulary often remains on a descriptive level, making it hard to arrive at a process-oriented design theory. The question is: Do we need Simondon's theory to recognize, like Mario Carpo, that authorship, intuition, and autographic representation play an ever more minor role in digital design? Parametric design and BIM relativize the role of human and technical individuals to such a strong extent that their consequences are not yet foreseeable. The Simondonian model is not the only one currently departing from the hylomorphic model. Approaches like "heterogeneous engineering," "material-driven design," and "active matter" or aspects of feminist theory of science likewise critically challenge theories about design that are particularly intentionalist in nature. The co-evolution of design problems and solutions is also a pivotal topic in research on design.[4] In any case, the book stakes out a theoretical framework that tests how well Simondon's vocabulary can be applied to the formation of design theory, thus putting up for discussion an adapted "prehistory" worth further consideration. ■

*Gert Hasenhütl (Translation: Dawn Michelle d'Atri)*

1   See Gilbert Simondon, *Die Existenzweise technischer Objekte* (Zurich, 2012), 126, and Olivier Del Fabbro, *Philosophieren mit Objekten: Gilbert Simondons prozessuale Individuationsontologie* (Frankfurt am Main, 2021), 66.

2   See Heike Delitz, "Gilbert Simondons Theorie der sozialen 'Form,'" in *Das Design der Gesellschaft: Zur Kultursoziologie des Designs*, ed. Stephan Moebius and Sophia Prinz (Bielefeld, 2012), 109–30, esp. 110.

3   Gilbert Simondon, *Individuation in Light of Notions of Form and Information*, trans. Taylor Adkins (Minneapolis, 2020), 36. Originally published as: L'individuation à la lumière des notions de forme et d'information (Grenoble, 2005).

4   See Dorst Kees and Nigel Cross, "Creativity in the Design Process: Co-Evolution of Problem–Solution," *Design Studies* 22 (2001): 425–37.

Histoire naturelle de
l'architecture: Comment
le climat, les épidémies et
l'énergie ont façonné la ville
et les bâtiments
Philippe Rahm
Paris: Éditions du Pavillon de
l'Arsenal, 2020
Französisch, 312 Seiten,
zahlr. Farbabbildungen |
French, 312 pages, numerous
color illustrations
ISBN 978-2-35487-058-4
EUR 24,00 | EUR 24.00

## Form Follows Climate.
## Eine Neubetrachtung
## der Architekturgeschichte

Johannes Bernsteiner

*Histoire naturelle de l'architecture* (dt. Naturgeschichte der Architektur) basiert auf der Dissertation des Schweizer Architekten Philippe Rahm, die unter der Leitung von Philippe Potié und Antoine Picon verfasst und vor einer Jury rund um Bruno Latour im Dezember 2019 verteidigt wurde. Die Publikation wird begleitet von der gleichnamigen Ausstellung im Pariser Pavillon de l'Arsenal, welche vom 24. Oktober 2020 bis (coronabedingt verlängert) 19. September 2021 stattgefunden hat.

Philippe Rahm argumentiert in seinem Werk, dass die Geschichtsschreibung der Architektur die physikalischen, biologischen und kli-, matischen Beweggründe aufgrund des medizinischen Fortschrittes (Entwicklung von Impfstoffen und Antibiotika) und des Zugangs zu fossiler Energie im 20. Jahrhundert weitestgehend ausklammert. Vor dem Hintergrund der aktuellen ökologischen Herausforderungen (Pandemien, Ressourcenknappheit, Klimakrise) schlägt der Autor mit *Histoire naturelle de l'architecture* daher eine umfassende Neubetrachtung der Geschichte der Architektur unter diesen Gesichtspunkten vor.

Für Philippe Rahm entsteht Architektur aus der Notwendigkeit unsere Körpertemperatur bei 37°C zu halten. Architektonische Elemente wie Dächer und Wände erzeugen ein künstliches Klima und schützen uns vor Witterungseinflüssen, damit der Körper nicht durch Konvektion (Wind) und Konduktion (Regen) abkühlt oder durch Radiation (Sonne) aufheizt. Architektur ist somit die Kunst, das natürliche Klima so zu verändern, dass es für den Menschen bewohnbar wird und das geschieht, ähnlich wie bei der Kleidung, durch einen mehr oder weniger dicken Luftfilm mit einer idealen Temperatur von 20° bis 28°C.

Einleitend erläutert der Autor den Zusammenhang zwischen Ernährung und Architektur. Nach dem Untergang des römischen Reiches entstand in Folge von Hungersnöten eine vereinfachte Architektur, die ohne großen Energieaufwand umgesetzt werden konnte. Erst der Anbau von proteinreichen Hülsenfrüchten am Beginn der Jahrtausendwende lieferte die erforderliche Muskelkraft zum Bau der großen Kathedralen. Die Erfindung der Dampfmaschine am Beginn der industriellen Revolution vervielfachte die zur Verfügung stehende Energie für die Errichtung von Gebäuden in nie zuvor gesehenen Dimensionen.

Im antiken Rom und später in der Renaissance schaffte die Basilika mit ihren hohen überdachten Räumen und ihren dicken Mauern einen Ort der Abkühlung in der Stadt. Parallel dazu war die mittelalterliche Kneipe und das Café im Zeitalter der Aufklärung ein Ort der Wärme und Geselligkeit. Klimatische Funktionen übernahmen aber auch vermeintlich bloß dekorative Architekturelemente wie Tapeten, Holzverkleidungen und Wandteppiche, die durch den Einsatz fossiler Brennstoffe im 20. Jahrhundert aus der Formensprache puristisch getilgt werden konnten.

Des Weiteren argumentiert Philippe Rahm, dass die Villa Rotonda von Palladio allen voran nach klimatischen Anforderungen entworfen wurde. Die symmetrische Anordnung der Fenster erlaubt eine großzügige Querlüftung, während der hohe überkuppelte Zentralraum durch die peripheren Räume vor Sonneneinstrahlung geschützt wird, die wiederum nach ihrer jahreszeitlichen Nutzung ausgerichtet sind. Kuppelbauten fanden vor allem im 18. Jahrhundert in Krankenhäusern und öffentlichen Gebäuden Anwendung. Auch hier verweist der Autor auf die klimatische und hygienische Funktion anstelle der oftmals interpretierten symbolischen Bedeutung.

Der griechische Arzt Hippokrates stellte in der Antike die These auf, dass schlechte Luft die Ursache für Krankheiten sei. Im 18. Jahrhundert beobachtete der englische Chemiker Joseph Priestley, dass Mäuse unter einer Glocke mit einem Minzezweig länger überleben und schlussfolgerte daraus die Fähigkeit von Pflanzen, die Luft zu „reinigen". Diese Erkenntnis wurde auf die Stadtplanung übertragen, allen voran mit der Errichtung von großflächigen öffentlichen Parks (z.B. Victoria Park in East London, Central Park in Manhattan).

Im Jahr 1832 kam es zur Cholera-Epidemie in Europa, welche auf den Ausbruch des Vulkans Tambora in Indonesien zurückzuführen ist. Da man den Krankheitserreger fälschlicherweise in abgestandener Luft vermutete (anstatt in kontaminierten Abwässern), leiteten Metropolen wie London und Paris große städtebauliche Transformationen ein, um insbesondere durch die Gestaltung von breiten Boulevards die freie Zirkulation von Frischluft zu ermöglichen. Hier widerlegt Philippe Rahm die weit verbreitete Annahme, dass die Umgestaltung von Paris durch Napoleon III und Hausmann primär zur strategischen Bekämpfung von Aufständen diente.

Im 20. Jahrhundert erkannte man schließlich, dass $CO_2$ nicht giftig ist (sondern der Mangel an Sauerstoff) und dass Vegetation in der Stadt nur sehr marginal zur Luftverbesserung beiträgt. Zudem zeigt Rahm, dass Bäume zwar Schatten spenden, jedoch nicht in der Lage sind das städtische Klima abzukühlen. Städtische Parks verloren somit ihre Legitimation und wurden fortan als rein kulturelles und soziales Konstrukt betrachtet (z.B. Parc de la Villette in Paris). Heute spielen Grünflächen vor allem aufgrund der zunehmenden Bodenversiegelung und der daraus resultierenden Überschwemmungsgefahr sowie zur Erhaltung der Artenvielfalt eine wichtige Rolle. Parallel dazu rückt die Klimakrise den Ausstoß von $CO_2$ und die damit verbundene Erderwärmung zurück in den Fokus der Stadtplanung.

In weiterer Folge argumentiert Philippe Rahm, dass die Bauten der klassischen Moderne aus hygienischen Gründen mit weißer Farbe gestrichen wurden, da Kalkfarbe seit dem 19. Jahrhundert als starkes Antiseptikum galt und Weiß die Sonnenstrahlen reflektiert, von denen man annahm, dass sie keimtötend wirken. Zur Behandlung von Tuberkulose wurden (trotz minimaler Heilungserfolge) Sanatorien in den Bergen errichtet, mit großen nach Süden ausgerichteten Fenstern, Balkonen und Terrassen, die es den PatientInnen ermöglichten, in Sonne und Frischluft zu „baden". Heute erlebt die weiße Farbe aufgrund von zunehmenden Hitzeperioden in Städten ein Revival. Helle Dächer reflektieren die Sonneneinstrahlung und sind dem Autor zufolge wirksamer als Dachbegrünungen in der Reduktion von sogenannten Hitzeinseln.

Antibiotika und Impfstoffe befreiten schließlich die Architektur und den Städtebau von gesundheitlichen Bedenken, die sie seit jeher umtrieben. Die durchschnittliche Lebenserwartung von 40 Jahren im Jahr 1900 liegt mittlerweile bei über 80 Jahren. Die Moderne wurde von der Postmoderne abgelöst, welche ab den 1970er-Jahren für die Wiederentdeckung der traditionellen Stadt plädierte. Die Architektur konzentrierte sich von nun an auf den symbolischen, sozialen und kulturellen Wert von Gebäuden. Dank Antibiotika mussten sich Architekten nicht mehr mit den medizinischen, biologischen und chemischen Wissenschaften befassen, sondern konnten sich den Humanwissenschaften zuwenden.

Der Gebäudesektor macht heute 39 Prozent der für die globale Erderwärmung verantwortlichen $CO_2$-Emissionen aus, hauptsächlich durch Heizen und Kühlen. Die Architektur steht somit an vorderster Front im Kampf gegen die Klimakrise, was sich in der Einführung von Wärmeschutzvorschriften, neuen Normen und Empfehlungen niederschlägt, die in erster Linie auf die Begrenzung des Energieverbrauchs abzielen. Als Antwort auf die klimatischen, energetischen und gesundheitlichen Herausforderungen des 21. Jahrhundert plädiert Philippe Rahm abschließend für einen neuen architektonischen Stil, in dem die meteorologischen Parameter wieder zu einem zentralem Gestaltungsaspekt in Architektur und Städtebau werden. *Histoire naturelle de l'architecture* analysiert dazu in objektiver und nachvollziehbarer Weise die Hintergründe von Materialien, Formen und Konzepten und eignet sich daher als grundlegende französische Lektüre zur klimatologischen Entwicklung der Architektur und Stadtplanung – von der Urgeschichte bis zur Gegenwart und abseits der traditionellen Geschichtsschreibung. ∎

# Form Follows Climate: A New Angle on the History of Architecture

*Histoire naturelle de l'architecture* (Natural History of Architecture) is based on the dissertation by the Swiss architect Philippe Rahm. It was written under the direction of Philippe Potié and Antoine Picon and then defended in front of a jury led by Bruno Latour in December 2019. The publication was accompanied by an eponymous exhibition at the Pavillon de l'Arsenal in Paris, which ran from October 24, 2020, to September 19, 2021 (prolonged due to the coronavirus pandemic).

In his work, Philippe Rahm argues that the historiography of architecture largely excludes the physical, biological, and climatic motivations associated with medical advancement (development of vaccines and antibiotics) and with access to fossil fuels in the twentieth century. Against the backdrop of current ecological challenges (pandemics, scarcity of resources, the climate crisis), the author, with his *Histoire naturelle de l'architecture*, thus proposes that the history of architecture be thoroughly reevaluated with these aspects in mind.

For Philipp Rahm, architecture arises from the necessity to keep our body temperature at 37 degrees centigrade. Architectural elements like roofs and walls engender an artificial climate and protect us against weather conditions, so that our bodies do not cool down due to convection (wind) and conduction (rain) or heat up through radiation (sun). Thus, architecture is the art of changing the natural climate in such a way that it becomes habitable for humans; and this happens, similar to clothing, thanks to a more or less thick layer of air at an ideal temperature of 20 to 28 degrees centigrade.

In his introduction, the author analyzes the connection between nutrition and architecture. After the fall of the Roman empire, famine caused simplified architecture to be created that could be built without much expenditure of energy. It was not until protein-rich legumes were cultivated at the turn of the millennium that the muscle power needed to build the great cathedrals was ensured. The invention of the steam engine at the beginning of the Industrial Revolution then multiplied the energy available for the construction of buildings to previously unseen dimensions.

In ancient Rome and later in the Renaissance, the basilica, with its high canopied spaces and thick walls, provided a place to cool off in the city. Similarly, the pub in medieval times and the café in the Age of Enlightenment were places of warmth and conviviality. However, architectural elements that supposedly served merely decorative purposes, such as wallpaper, wood paneling, and tapestries, also took on climatic functions. Through the use of fossil fuels starting in the twentieth century, these elements could be puristically eradicated from the architectural language of form.

Philippe Rahm further argues that Andrea Palladio's Villa Rotonda was designed first and foremost according to climatic requirements. The symmetrical arrangement of the windows permits generous cross-ventilation, while the lofty, domed central space is protected from solar radiation by the peripheral rooms, which in turn are positioned according to their seasonal use. Domed buildings were mainly used in the eighteenth century, in hospitals and public buildings. Here, too, the author refers to climatic and hygienic functions instead of the symbolic meaning found in most interpretations.

In ancient times, the Greek physician Hippocrates postulated that poor air was the cause of disease. In the eighteenth century, the English chemist Joseph Priestley noticed that mice survived longer under a bell with a sprig of mint and thus concluded that plants must be able to "purify" air. This finding was then applied to urban planning, resulting especially in

the creation of large-scale public parks (such as Victoria Park in East London or Central Park in Manhattan).

In 1832, there was a major cholera epidemic in Europe, which can be traced back to the eruption of the Tambora volcano in Indonesia. Because the pathogen was mistakenly thought to be found in stale air (rather than in contaminated wastewater), large cities such as London and Paris initiated major urban transformation projects to facilitate the free circulation of fresh air, particularly through the design of wide boulevards. Here, Philippe Rahm refutes the widely held assumption that Paris was restructured by Napoleon III and Haussmann with the primary aim of strategically countering insurgency.

Finally, in the twentieth century, it became known that a lack of oxygen is toxic rather than $CO_2$ itself, and that vegetation in an urban setting only very marginally contributes to improving the quality of air. It also became known, as Rahm notes, that while trees do provide shade, they are not in a position to lower the climate of cities. Urban parks thus lost their legitimacy and were henceforth regarded as a purely cultural and social construct (such as Parc de la Villette in Paris). Today, green spaces play an important role, mainly due to increasing soil sealing and the resulting risk of flooding, but also in maintaining biodiversity. In parallel, the climate crisis is bringing $CO_2$ emissions and related global warming back into the focus of urban planning.

Furthermore, Philippe Rahm argues that classical modernist buildings were painted white for hygienic reasons. Since the nineteenth century, lime paint had been considered a strong antiseptic and white also reflects the sun's rays, which were thought to have a germicidal effect. Sanitoriums were erected in the mountains to treat tuberculosis (despite little chance of success in healing the disease), featuring large south-facing windows, balconies, and patios that enabled the patients to "bathe" in the sun and fresh air.

Today, white paint is experiencing a revival due to longer periods of heat in cities. Light-colored roofs reflect solar radiation and, according to the author, are more effective than landscaped roofs in reducing so-called heat islands.

Antibiotics and vaccines ultimately liberated architecture and urban design from the health-related concerns that had long caused worry. While in 1900 the average life expectancy was forty years, today it is twice that at over eighty years. Modernism was superseded by postmodernism, which in the 1970s advocated the rediscovery of the traditional city. From that point on, architecture concentrated on the symbolic, social, and cultural value of buildings. Thanks to antibiotics, architects no longer needed to focus on the medical, biological, and chemical sciences but could turn to the humanities instead.

Today, the building sector accounts for about 39 percent of the $CO_2$ emissions responsible for global warming, mainly due to heating and cooling activity. Architecture is thus at the very forefront of the fight against the climate crisis, which plays out through the introduction of thermal insulation regulations as well as new norms and recommendations, all of which are primarily aimed at limiting energy consumption. As a response to the climate, energy, and health challenges of the twenty-first century, Philippe Rahm concludes by arguing for a new architectural style in which meteorological parameters once again become a central design aspect in architecture and urban planning. To this end, *Histoire naturelle de l'architecture* takes an objective and transparent approach to analyzing the original contexts of materials, forms and concepts. This makes it suitable as a foundational French book on the climatological development of architecture and urban planning—ranging from prehistory to the present, yet deviating from traditional historiography. ▪

*Johannes Bernsteiner (Translation: Dawn Michelle d'Atri)*

**Sorge um den Bestand.**
**Zehn Strategien für**
**die Architektur**
Olaf Bahner/Matthias Böttger/
Laura Holzberg (Hg. | eds.)
Berlin: Jovis, 2020
Deutsch, 208 Seiten, zahlreiche
farbige Abbildungen, Schweizer
Broschur | German, 208 pages,
numerous color illustrations,
Swiss brochure
ISBN 978-3-86859-659-5
EUR 28,00 | EUR 28.00

# Bekenntnis zum Bestehenden

Armin Stocker

Das Wesen des Bestands ist das Vorhandensein, das Existieren und das Wirken aus der Vergangenheit in die Gegenwart. Erst wenn etwas existiert, – materiell oder immateriell – können wir von Bestehendem sprechen und sobald wir darüber sprechen können, ist es uns auch möglich, zur Handlung überzugehen und dadurch Zukünftiges zu gestalten. Dieses im Heute beginnende Sprechen und Handeln stellt die ersten Schritte zur aktiven Fürsorge dar; für ein tätiges Bemühen um den Gebäudebestand als gesamtgesellschaftliche Struktur sowie dessen Fortbestand und Weiterentwicklung.

*Sorge um den Bestand. Zehn Strategien für die Architektur* bespricht im Rahmen einer Wanderausstellung und der vorliegenden, die Ausstellung begleitenden Publikation, das Sorgetragen um den Gebäudebestand und die damit verbundenen, gesellschaftlichen und ökonomischen Rahmenbedingungen. Die Frage nach dem Umgang mit gewachsenen sozialen Strukturen wird dabei genauso verhandelt, wie der Wert verbauter Ressourcen und die Zukunftsfähigkeit des baulich Vorhandenen konkretisiert wird. Über die Pflege des Gebauten als Weiterbauen, als Verdichtung oder als Um- und Weiternutzung nachzudenken, ist nicht nur eine Frage ökologischer Notwendigkeit in Zeiten des Klimawandels und schwindender Ressourcen, sondern auch eine kulturelle und wirtschaftliche Herausforderung. Wie ein solches Weiterdenken des baulichen Bestands für neue Wohn-, Lebens- und Arbeitsformen aussehen kann, wird von den ArchitektInnen und UrbanistInnen der Ausstellung und Publikation in zehn engagierte Strategien gegossen. Die von Olaf Bahner, Matthias Böttger und Laura Holzberg für den Bund Deutscher Architektinnen und Architekten herausgegebene Publikation stellt gesellschaftliche Denk- und Handlungsansätze für ein kreatives Unterlassen vor, das nicht automatisch Verzicht bedeuten muss.

Den ersten Teil des handbuchartigen, hochwertig ausgestatteten Paperbacks bilden Essays, die zu den zehn Strategien hinführen und diese einleiten, ohne die Ansätze der Strategien aber vorwegzunehmen. Hier werden Fragen des Heutigen und des Zukünftigen eigenständig ins Visier genommen, werden Gebautes und Soziales kontextualisiert und das Bestehende als aktives Zusammenspiel vielfältiger Handlungen herausgearbeitet. Susanne Wartzeck, Präsidentin des BDA, leitet mit der Aufforderung „Erhalte das Bestehende!" in das Thema ein, Anne Katrin Bohle weist auf die Dringlichkeit und Aktualität der Thematik hin, um gleichzeitig wichtige Fragen zur Herangehensweise zu formulieren („Sorge um den Bestand" ab S. 11). „Das Problem mit der Zukunft" thematisiert Amica Dall (ab S. 37), indem sie einerseits feststellt, dass die eigentliche Kunst darin besteht, sowohl das Bestehende als auch das Mögliche zu sehen und beides genau, klar und mit Sorgfalt zu betrachten, denn: Was zählt, ist, was wir heute tun (S. 39). Damit eröffnet Dall eine Sichtweise auf Vergangenheit, Gegenwart und Zukunft, die die Zukunft als fiktives Land, als etwas, das nicht gesichert ist und lediglich einen Möglichkeitsraum darstellt, postuliert. Die sieben einleitenden Beiträge verdeutlichen die Dringlichkeit, sich des Bestandes als gesellschaftliche wie bauliche Ressource anzunehmen, den Diskurs darüber zu vertiefen und zur aktiven Handlung überzugehen. Gemeinsam mit den realisierten Projekten am Ende des Buches bilden diese Essays die Klammer für die zehn titelgebenden Strategien.

Katja Fischer und Jan Kampshoffs „Aufbruch ins Bestehende" (ab S. 61) manifestiert die These: „Die Welt ist gebaut!". Die beiden Architekturschaffenden sprechen in ihrer Strategie nicht über ein generelles Neubauverbot, sondern fordern eine neue Verbindlichkeit gegenüber dem Vorhandenen sowie einen Perspektivenwechsel hin zu einer ganzheitlichen Fürsorge für anstehende Transformationen. Inspiriert von Max Frischs thematischen Fragebögen arbeiten Fischer und Kampshoff gemeinsam mit der Architekturhistorikerin Turit Fröbe „Fragen an die Architektinnen und Architekten" aus, die sie in Berufung, Ethos, Verantwortung und Bestand unterteilen. Dieser Fragenkatalog soll als Richtschnur und indirekte Handlungsanweisung fungieren, wenn er Architekturschaffende, AuftraggeberInnen und BewohnerInnen beim gemeinsamen Aufbruch ins Bestehende begleitet und die Architektur als sorgetragende Disziplin neu verankert.

Wie ein gemeinsamer Aufbruch funktionieren kann, verdeutlicht auch Eike Roswag-Klinge in seinem Gespräch mit Nanni Grau und Frank Schönert vom Berliner Architekturbüro Hütten und Paläste („Einfach umbauen – einfach transformieren" ab S. 123). Das mit Projektbeispielen hinterlegte Gespräch über maßvolle Transformation, die bezahlbar bleibt, sowie auf Reduktion, Teilhabe und Partizipation basiert, zeigt, dass interdisziplinäre Wertegemeinschaften, Möglichkeitsräume für Zukünftiges schaffen können, wenn das Ideelle im Vordergrund steht und in der Programmierung der Architektur bewusst Felder offengelassen werden. Der Bogen über das Bestehende wird so weit gespannt, wie unsere Welt davon erfüllt ist. Die Strategien reichen vom kleinen Kiosk mit Vorplatz in der Nähe des Alexanderplatzes, der als Ausgangspunkt für partizipativen Städtebau in der Großstadt dient („Schön, dass ihr da seid!" ab S. 89) über Michael Obrists Strategie einer „Urban Blockchain" (ab S. 135) und der Zwischenstadt als einem neuen Ort der Vielfalt („Verteilung auf das Vorhandene in der Zwischenstadt" ab S. 143) bis hin zur Strategie von Donuts, die zu Krapfen werden müssen, als Paraphrase für die Wiederbelebung von verlassenen, ländlichen Ortskernen (ab S. 155), um sich letztendlich dem Vorhandenen als Material, als Rohstofflager für Zukünftiges zu widmen („100% Ressource; Bauten als Rohstofflager" ab S. 165).

*Sorge um den Bestand.* Zwei Lesarten des Titels sind offensichtlich: Wir sind besorgt um den Bestand, wir machen uns also Sorgen, haben Bedenken, ob das so alles richtig ist, wie wir mit dem Bestehenden in und auf unserer Welt umgehen. Haben wir erkannt, dass wir als Individuen und als Gesellschaft in unserem Umgang mit dem Vorhandenen, dem Sozialen wie dem Gebauten, Änderungen vornehmen und ein neues Bewusstsein ausbilden müssen, können wir uns um den Bestand sorgen, ihn pflegen, also zur Handlung übergehen, wie es die Strategie „Bestand als Handlung" von Tabea Michaelis und Ben Pohl („Bestand als Handlung" ab S. 109) sowie diese empfehlenswerte und aktuelle Publikation in ihrer Gesamtheit vermitteln.

Mit der *Sorge um den Bestand. Zehn Strategien für die Architektur* legt der Bund Deutscher Architektinnen und Architekten ein zeitgemäßes Buch vor, das nicht moralisieren will, aber mit den versammelten Beiträgen verdeutlicht, dass unsere gegenwärtigen Handlungen auf dem baulich wie sozial Vorhandenen basieren, und die Zukunft prädestinieren, auch wenn diese ein fiktives Land ist und bleiben wird. Diese Forderung, die zeitlichen Ebenen unserer gebauten wie sozialen Umwelt zu lesen, sie weiterzuverfolgen und weiterzubauen anstatt auf Neubau und Ressourcenverbrauch zu setzen, ist nicht nur als lohnenswerte Lektüre und Einstieg in das hochaktuelle Thema zu empfehlen, sondern dient auch als Impuls zur individuellen Auseinandersetzung mit der gleichnamigen Ausstellung.[1] ∎

1   Vgl. die virtuelle Ausstellung unter https://heinze.spherovision.de/DAZ/index.htm (Stand: 12. September 2021).

## Committing to the Existing

The essence of building stock lies in the presence, existence, and effects that start in the past and move into the present. Only once something subsists—materially or immaterially—can we speak of the existing; and as soon as we can talk about it, then we are able to transition to action and thus to the designing of something for the future. This speaking and acting, which begins today, represents the first steps of active caring—in terms of operative efforts to maintain building stock as a macrosocial structure and to promote their continued existence and further development.

In the context of a traveling exhibition, the accompanying publication *Sorge um den Bestand: Zehn Strategien für die Architektur* (Concern about Building Stock: Ten Strategies for Architecture) discusses caring for building stock and the related social and economic framework conditions. The question of how to deal with evolved social structures is negotiated here, as the value of built resources and the future sustainability of existing structures are examined in concrete terms. Reflecting on the care of built structures as continued building, as densification, or as conversion and reuse is not only a question of ecological necessity in times of climate change and dwindling resources; it is also a cultural and economic challenge. The architects and urbanists involved in the exhibition and the publication present ten dedicated strategies, so as to illustrate how one might conceptually expand on building stock to create new forms of housing, living, and working. This publication, edited by Olaf Bahner, Matthias Böttger, and Laura Holzberg for the Association of German Architects (BDA), introduces approaches to social thought and action for creative restraint, which does not necessarily have to imply sacrifice.

The first section of this high-quality paperback, which resembles a manual of sorts, contains essays that lead up to and introduce the ten strategies, but without anticipating the strategies' approaches. Here, questions of the present and the future are addressed independently, the built and the social are contextualized, and existing building stock is presented as an active synergy of various actions. Susanne Wartzeck, President of the BDA, introduces the topic with a call to preserve existing structures, while Anne Katrin Bohle in "Sorge um den Bestand" (Concern about Building Stock) points out the urgency and topicality of the issue, at the same time posing important questions about the approach taken (pp. 11ff.). Amica Dall in turn explores "Das Problem mit der Zukunft" (The Problem with the Future) (pp. 37ff.), stating on the one hand that the real art lies in seeing both what exists and what is possible, and in considering both precisely, clearly, and with care, because: what we do today counts (p. 39). In so doing, Dall opens up a view of past, present, and future that renders the future as a fictional terrain, as something that is not certain but is merely a space of potentiality. The seven introductory contributions highlight the urgency of embracing the existing as a social and structural resource, deepening the related discourse and transitioning to hands-on activity. Together with the realized projects presented at the end of the book, these essays bracket the ten strategies mentioned in the book's title.

Katja Fischer and Jan Kampshoff's "Aufbruch ins Bestehende" (Into the Existing) (pp. 61ff.) manifests the thesis "The world is built!" Addressing their strategy, the two architects do not discuss a general ban on new construction; instead, they call for a fresh sense of commitment to already existing buildings and for a shift in perspective allowing more holistic attention to be paid to forthcoming transformations. Inspired by Max Frisch's thematic questionnaires, Fischer and Kampshoff worked to-

gether with the architectural historian Turit Fröbe to draft "Questions for Architects" divided into the categories of vocation, ethos, responsibility, and building stock. This list of questions is meant to serve as a guideline and step to action, accompanying architects, clients, and residents in their joint exploration of existing buildings and newly anchoring architecture as a care-focused discipline.

Eike Roswag-Klinge's conversation with Nanni Grau and Frank Schönert from the Berlin-based architectural firm Hütten und Paläste ("Einfach umbauen – einfach transformieren" or Simply Convert – Simply Transform) illustrates how well a collaborative approach can work (p. 123ff.). The talk, during which case projects are cited, involves discussion about moderate, affordable transformation based on reduction, participation, and sharing. It shows how interdisciplinary value communities can give rise to avenues of possibility for the future if the ideal remains in the foreground and fields are deliberately left open in terms of architectural programming. A bridge is forged over existing structures so far as to fill our entire world with it. The range of strategies is broad: a small kiosk with a forecourt near Alexanderplatz in Berlin, which serves as a point of departure for participatory urban planning in a metropolis ("Schön, dass ihr da seid!" or Glad you're here!) (pp. 89ff.); Michael Obrist's strategy of an "Urban Blockchain" (pp. 135ff.); the *Zwischenstadt* as a new place of diversity ("Verteilung auf das Vorhandene in der Zwischenstadt" or Distribution of the Existing in the Intermediary City) (pp. 143ff.); the strategy of donuts that have to become fritters as a way of paraphrasing the revival of abandoned town centers in rural areas (pp. 155ff.); and finally devotion to the existing as material, as raw material storage for the future ("100% Ressource: Bauten als Rohstofflager" or 100% Resources: Buildings as Raw Material Storage) (pp. 165ff.).

*Concern about Building Stock*. In German there are two ways to read the title. To be concerned about building stock means both to actively take care of and to worry and have misgivings about whether we are dealing with the existing buildings in our world in the right way. Once we have recognized that we as individuals and as a society need to make changes in how we deal with existing structures, both social and built, and to form a new consciousness toward them, then we can care for the building stock, nurture it, and start taking action, as conveyed by the strategy "Bestand als Handlung" (Stock as Action) by Tabea Michaelis and Ben Pohl (pp. 109ff.) and by this highly recommendable and topical publication as a whole.

In the case of *Sorge um den Bestand: Zehn Strategien für die Architektur*, the Association of German Architects has presented an up-to-date book that eschews a moralizing tone and instead illustrates through the compiled contributions how our current actions are based on both architectural and social existing structures, and how our actions determine the future, even if it is and will remain a fictitious terrain. This call to interpret the temporal levels of our built and social environment, to pursue and build on them instead of relying on new construction and resource consumption, is not only recommended as worthwhile reading and a point of entry to the highly topical subject; it also inspires one to individually explore the eponymous exhibition.[1] ▪

*Armin Stocker (Translation: Dawn Michelle d'Atri)*

1 See the virtual exhibition at: https://heinze.spherovision.de/DAZ/index.htm (accessed September 12, 2021).